STREET

Dorset

Bournemouth and Poole

Christchurch, Dorchester, Weymouth

www.philips-maps.co.uk
First published in 2002 by Philip's
a division of Octopus Publishing Group Ltd
www.octopusbooks.co.uk
Endeavour House, 189 Shaftesbury Avenue
London WC2H 8JY
An Hachette UK Company
www.hachette.co.uk

Third edition 2010
First impression 2010
DORCA

ISBN 978-1-84907-096-6 (pocket)

© Philip's 2010

o|s Ordnance Survey®

This product includes mapping data licensed from
Ordnance Survey® with the permission of the
Controller of Her Majesty's Stationery Office.
© Crown copyright 2010. All rights reserved.
Licence number 100011710.

Contents

II	Mobile safety cameras
III	**Key to map symbols**
IV	**Key to map pages**
VI	**Route planning**
X	Major administrative and Postcode boundaries
1	**Street maps** at 2⅔ inches to 1 mile
188	**Street maps** of at 1⅓ inches to 1 mile
212	**Street map** at 2⅔ inches to 1 mile
213	**Index** of towns, villages, streets, hospitals, industrial estates, railway stations, schools, shopping centres, universities and places of interest

Digital Data

The exceptionally high-quality mapping found in this atlas is available as digital data in TIFF format, which is easily convertible to other bitmapped (raster) image formats.

The index is also available in digital form as a standard database table. It contains all the details found in the printed index together with the National Grid reference for the map square in which each entry is named.

For further information and to discuss your requirements, please contact philips@mapsinternational.co.uk

II

Mobile safety cameras

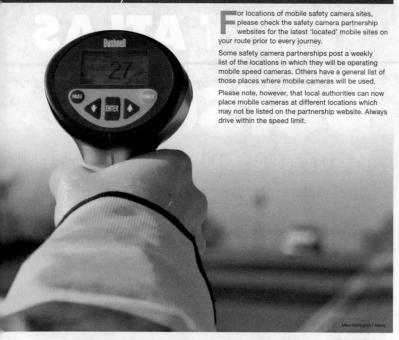

Mike Harrington / Alamy

For locations of mobile safety camera sites, please check the safety camera partnership websites for the latest 'located' mobile sites on your route prior to every journey.

Some safety camera partnerships post a weekly list of the locations in which they will be operating mobile speed cameras. Others have a general list of those places where mobile cameras will be used.

Please note, however, that local authorities can now place mobile cameras at different locations which may not be listed on the partnership website. Always drive within the speed limit.

Useful websites

Dorset Safety Camera Partnership
www.dorsetsafetycameras.org.uk

Devon and Cornwall Safety Camera Partnership
www.dcsafetycameras.org

Hampshire and Isle of Wight Safer Roads Partnership
www.saferroadspartnership.co.uk

Safecam
www.safecam.org.uk

Somerset Road Safety Partnership
www.roadsafetysomerset.org.uk

Wiltshire and Swindon Safety Camera Partnership
www.safetycameraswiltshire.co.uk

Further information
www.dvla.gov.uk
www.thinkroadsafety.gov.uk
www.dft.gov.uk
www.road-safe.org

Key to map symbols

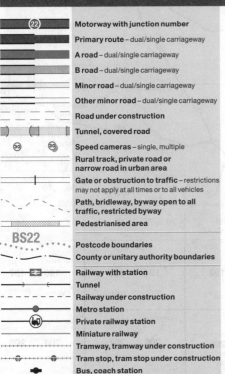

(22)	Motorway with junction number
	Primary route – dual/single carriageway
	A road – dual/single carriageway
	B road – dual/single carriageway
	Minor road – dual/single carriageway
	Other minor road – dual/single carriageway
	Road under construction
	Tunnel, covered road
(30) (30)	Speed cameras – single, multiple
	Rural track, private road or narrow road in urban area
	Gate or obstruction to traffic – restrictions may not apply at all times or to all vehicles
	Path, bridleway, byway open to all traffic, restricted byway
	Pedestrianised area
BS22	Postcode boundaries
	County or unitary authority boundaries
	Railway with station
	Tunnel
	Railway under construction
	Metro station
	Private railway station
	Miniature railway
	Tramway, tramway under construction
	Tram stop, tram stop under construction
	Bus, coach station

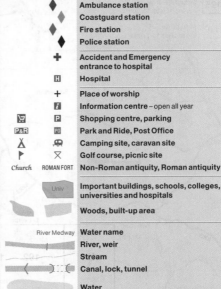

◆	Ambulance station
◆	Coastguard station
◆	Fire station
◆	Police station
✚	Accident and Emergency entrance to hospital
H	Hospital
+	Place of worship
i	Information centre – open all year
	Shopping centre, parking
P&R PO	Park and Ride, Post Office
Ă	Camping site, caravan site
► ✕	Golf course, picnic site
Church ROMAN FORT	Non-Roman antiquity, Roman antiquity
Univ	Important buildings, schools, colleges, universities and hospitals
	Woods, built-up area
River Medway	Water name
	River, weir
	Stream
	Canal, lock, tunnel
	Water
	Tidal water

Adjoining page indicators and overlap bands – the colour of the arrow and band indicates the scale of the adjoining or overlapping page (see scales below)

The dark grey border on the inside edge of some pages indicates that the mapping does not continue onto the adjacent page

The small numbers around the edges of the maps identify the 1-kilometre National Grid lines

Abbreviations

Acad	Academy	Meml	Memorial
Allot Gdns	Allotments	Mon	Monument
Cemy	Cemetery	Mus	Museum
C Ctr	Civic centre	Obsy	Observatory
CH	Club house	Pal	Royal palace
Coll	College	PH	Public house
Crem	Crematorium	Recn Gd	Recreation ground
Ent	Enterprise	Resr	Reservoir
Ex H	Exhibition hall	Ret Pk	Retail park
Ind Est	Industrial Estate	Sch	School
IRB Sta	Inshore rescue boat station	Sh Ctr	Shopping centre
Inst	Institute	TH	Town hall / house
Ct	Law court	Trad Est	Trading estate
L Ctr	Leisure centre	Univ	University
LC	Level crossing	W Twr	Water tower
Liby	Library	Wks	Works
Mkt	Market	YH	Youth hostel

The map scale on the pages numbered in blue is 2⅔ inches to 1 mile
4.2 cm to 1 km • 1:23 210

0	¼ mile	½ mile	¾ mile	1 mile

0	250m	500m	750m	1km

The map scale on the pages numbered in green is 1⅓ inches to 1 mile
2.1 cm to 1 km • 1:47 620

0	½ mile	1 mile	1½ miles	2 miles

0	500m	1 km	1½km	2km

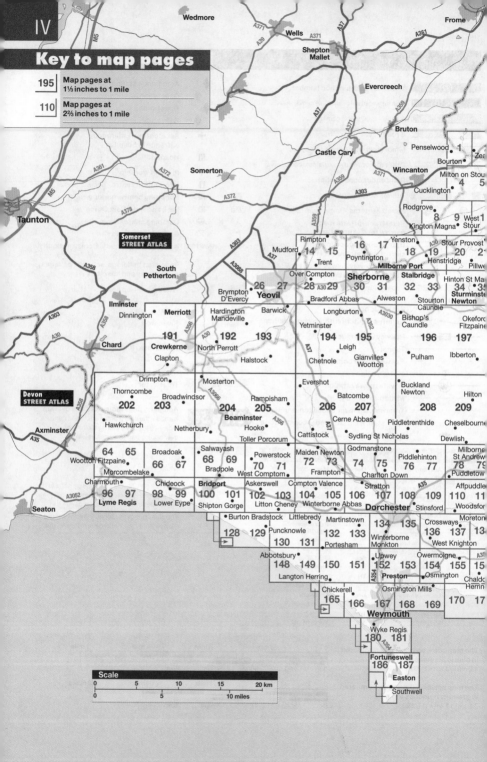

IV

Key to map pages

| 195 | Map pages at 1⅛ inches to 1 mile |
| 110 | Map pages at 2⅔ inches to 1 mile |

Wedmore

Frome

A371

A37

Wells

A371

A339

Shepton Mallet

A361

Evercreech

Bruton

Penselwood 1

Bourton Zea

Castle Cary

Wincanton

Milton on Stou

Somerton

A372

Cucklington

5

A359

A371

A303

Rodgrove

Taunton

A372

Kington Magna

West 1 Stour

A361

M5

A378

A303

Somerset
STREET ATLAS

South Petherton

A3088

A37

Rimpton

Yenston

Mudford 14 15

16 17

18 19 Stour Provost

20 2

Trent

Poyntington

Henstridge

Pillwe

Over Compton

Milborne Port

Hinton St Ma

Brympton D'Evercy 26 27

28 A30 29

Sherborne

Stalbridge

30 31

32 33

34 3

Yeovil

Bradford Abbas

Alweston

Stourton Caundle

Sturminster Newton

Ilminster

Dinnington

Merriott

Hardington Mandeville

Barwick

Longburton

A3030

Bishop's Caundle

Okeford Fitzpaine

191 192 193

194 195

196 197

Chard

Crewkerne

North Perrott

Yetminster

Leigh

Pulham

Ibberton

Clapton

Halstock

Chetnole

Glanvilles Wootton

Drimpton

Mosterton

Evershot

Buckland Newton

Hilton

Devon
STREET ATLAS

Thorncombe

Broadwindsor

A3066

Rampisham

Batcombe

202 203

204 205

206 207

208 209

Beaminster

Cerne Abbas

Piddletrenthide

Cheselbourne

Hawkchurch

Netherbury

Hooke

A356

Cattistock

Sydling St Nicholas

Dewlish

Axminster

Toller Porcorum

A35

Godmanstone

Milborne St Andrew

64 65

Broadoak

Salwayash

68 69

Powerstock

Maiden Newton

72 73

74 75

Piddlehinton

76 77

78 7

Wootton Fitzpaine

66 67

Bradpole

70 71

Frampton

Charlton Down

Puddletow

Morcombelake

West Compton

Affpuddle

Charmouth

Chideock

Bridport

Askerswell

Compton Valence

104 105

Stratton

A35

108 109

110 11

96 97

98 99

100 101

102 103

106 107

Woodsfor

Lyme Regis

Lower Eype

Shipton Gorge

Litton Cheney

Winterborne Abbas

Dorchester

Stinsford

Seaton

A3052

Burton Bradstock

Littlebredy

Martinstown

134 135

Crossways

Moretor

128 129

Puncknowle

132 133

136 137

13

130 131

Portesham

Winterborne Monkton

West Knighton

Abbotsbury

Upwey

Owermoigne

A35

148 149

150 151

152 153

154 155

15

Langton Herring

Preston

Osmington

Chickerell

Osmington Mills

A354

Chaldc
Herrin

165

166 167

168 169

170 17

Weymouth

Wyke Regis

180 181

A354

Fortuneswell

186 187

Easton

Southwell

Scale

| 0 | 5 | 10 | 15 | 20 km |
| 0 | | 5 | | 10 miles |

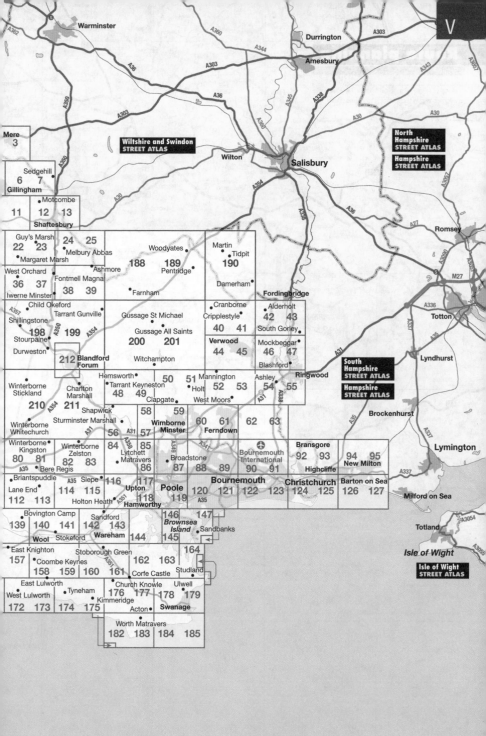

Warminster

Durrington

A303

A344

Amesbury

A303

A36

A360

A362

A303

A36

A350

A338

A345

A338

A30

A343

A303

A36

Wiltshire and Swindon
STREET ATLAS

A350

A303

Wilton

A354

Salisbury

North
Hampshire
STREET ATLAS

Hampshire
STREET ATLAS

A30

A338

A36

Romsey

M27

A336

Totton

A35

Lyndhurst

Mere
3

Sedgehill
6   7
Gillingham

Motcombe
11   12   13
Shaftesbury

Guy's Marsh
22   23   24   25
Melbury Abbas
Margaret Marsh

West Orchard
36   37   38   39
Iwerne Minster
Fontmell Magna

Woodyates
188   189
Pentridge

Ashmore

Farnham

Martin   Tidpit
190
Damerham

Fordingbridge

Child Okeford
Shillingstone
198   199
Stourpaine
Durweston

Tarrant Gunville

Gussage St Michael
200   201
Gussage All Saints
Witchampton

Cranborne
Cripplestyle
40   41

Alderholt
42   43
South Gorley

Verwood
44   45

Mockbeggar
46   47
Blashford

South Hampshire
STREET ATLAS

Hampshire
STREET ATLAS

212   Blandford
Forum

Hemsworth
Tarrant Keyneston
48   49
Shapwick

50   51
Clapgate

Mannington
Holt
52   53
West Moors

Ashley
54   55

Ringwood

Winterborne
Stickland
210

Charlton
Marshall
211
Sturminster Marshall

58   59

Brockenhurst

Lymington

Winterborne
Whitchurch

56   57

Wimborne
Minster

60   61   62   63
Ferndown

Winterborne
Kingston
80   81
Bere Regis

Winterborne
Zelston
82   83

84   85
Lytchett
Matravers
86

Broadstone
87   88   89

Bournemouth
International
90   91

Bransgore
92   93

94   95
New Milton
Highcliffe

A337

Milford on Sea

Briantspuddle
Lane End
112   113

Slepe
114   115   116
Holton Heath

117
Upton
118   119
Hamworthy

Poole
120   121

Bournemouth

122   123
Christchurch

124   125
Barton on Sea
126   127

Totland

Isle of Wight

Isle of Wight
STREET ATLAS

A3054

Bovington Camp
139   140   141
Wool   Stokeford

Sandford
142   143
Wareham
144

146   147
Brownsea
Island
145
Sandbanks

A3055

East Knighton
157   158   159
Coombe Keynes

Stoborough Green
160   161
Corfe Castle

162   163
Studland

164

East Lulworth
West Lulworth
172   173
Tyneham

174   175
Kimmeridge
Acton

Church Knowle
176   177

Ulwell
178   179
Swanage

182   183   184   185
Worth Matravers

Route planning

Scale

0 — 5 — 10 km

0 1 2 3 4 5 6 miles

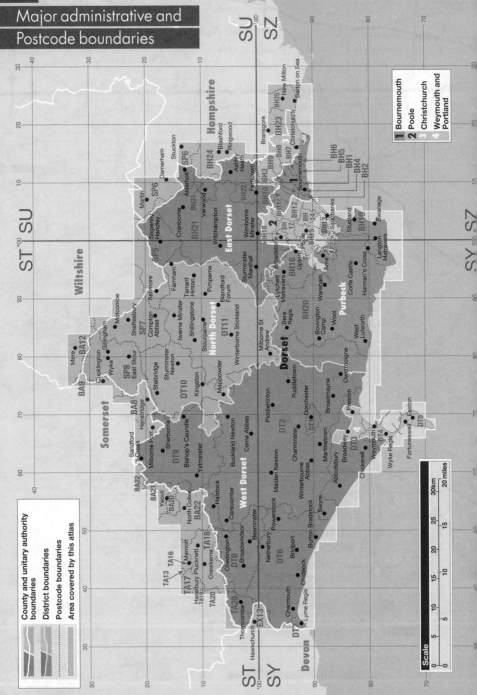

Legend:
1 Bournemouth
2 Poole
3 Christchurch
4 Weymouth and Portland

County and unitary authority boundaries
District boundaries
Postcode boundaries
Area covered by this atlas

Scale
0   5   10   15   20   25   30km
0   5   10   15   20 miles

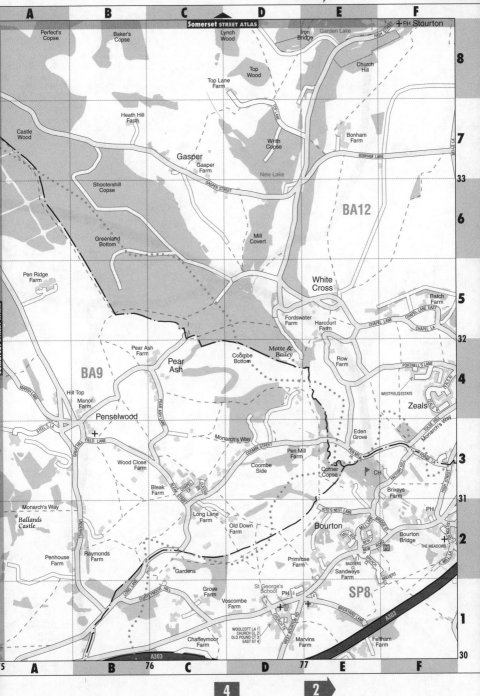

Somerset STREET ATLAS

A **B** **C** **D** **E** **F**

8

Perfect's Copse

Baker's Copse

Lynch Wood

Iron Bridge

Garden Lake

PH Stourton

Top Wood

Church Hill

Top Lane Farm

Heath Hill Farm

Bonham Farm

7

Castle Wood

Gasper

Gasper Farm

Writh Copse

Bonham Lane

33

Shootershill Copse

New Lake

GASPER STREET

BA12

6

Greenland Bottom

Mill Covert

Pen Ridge Farm

White Cross

5

Fordswater Farm

Harcourt Farm

Batch Farm

CHAPEL LANE

CHAPEL LANE EAST

CHAPEL LA

32

Pear Ash Farm

Pear Ash

Coombe Bottom

Motte & Bailey

Row Farm

PORTNELL'S LANE

BA9

WESTFIELD ESTATE

4

Hill Top Manor Farm

Zeals

Penselwood

Monarch's Way

Eden Grove

Monarch's Way

FIELD LANE

STEELS LA

Wood Close Farm

COOMBE STREET

Pen Mill Farm

TONGE LA

3

Coombe Side

Corner Copse

CH

Brixeys Farm

HIGH STREET

Bleak Farm

PH

31

Monarch's Way

Long Lane Farm

Old Down Farm

KITE'S NEST LANE

Bourton

Bourton Bridge

THE MEADOWS

Ballands Castle

2

Penhouse Farm

Raymonds Farm

Gardens

Primrose Farm

BADGERS CL

Sandways Farm

PO

MILLERS CL

SP8

St George's School

PH

A303

1

CHAFFEYMOOR HILL

Grove Farm

Voscombe Farm

Marvins Farm

Feltham Farm

Chaffeymoor Farm

WOOLCOTT LA 1
CHURCH CL 2
OLD POUND CT 3
EAST ST 4

A303

30

A **B** **C** **D** **E** **F**

5   76   77

A   B   C   D   E   F

8   Cross Dykes
Wood Farm
Mid Wilts Way

7   Zeals Knoll
33

6   Nor Wood   A303   MERE BY-PASS
BA12   Mere Cast (site of)
Tumuli   Recn G
Long Hill
CADDY LA   UNDERHILL
LONG PL   SHAWFIELD
Quarry Fields Industrial Estate   DALEY
PROSPECT PL

5   Quarry Cottages   HILLSIDE CL   B3092   B3095   CASTLE STREET
Long Cross   TOWER END

32   Lower Zeals   Greenhouses
Manor Farm   Zeals House
St Martin Farm   Whitesheets Prim Sch

4   + PO   PH   Castle Ground Farm
PRETNELLS LA   ZEALS GREEN DR
Zeals   South Lodge
TUSE HILL LA   NEW ROAD   Wolverton   Monarch's Way

3   Zeals Fish Farm
NEW RD   Queen Oak
31   PARTEY LANE

2   Bagmore Wood   Mapperton Hill Farm
A303   Silton Wood
MAPPERTON HILL

1   SP8   Redmoor Farm   B3092
Fitz Farm   Ridge Hill Farm
PARTEY LANE   SLODBROOK LANE
CHURCH ROAD

30   Bagmore Farm   SPRINGFIELD
78   A   B   79   C   D   80   E   F

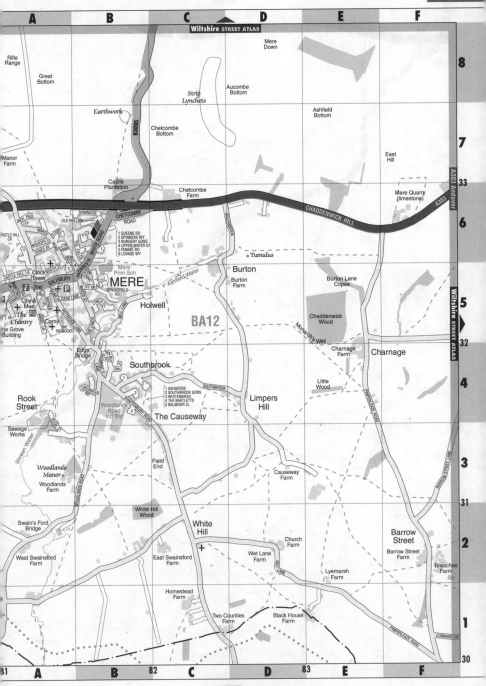

Wiltshire STREET ATLAS

Mere
Down

Rifle
Range

Great
Bottom

Strip
Lynchets

Aucombe
Bottom

Earthwork

Chetcombe
Bottom

Ashfield
Bottom

Manor
Farm

East
Hill

Castle
Plantation

Chetcombe
Farm

Mere Quarry
(limestone)

CHADDENWICK HILL

B3095

A303 Andover

JACK PAUL
CL
DOWNSIDE CL
OLD HOLLOW
CHETCOMBE
ROAD

1 QUEENS RD
2 SPINNERS WY
3 NURSERY GDNS
4 UPPER WATER ST
5 FENNEL RD
6 LOVAGE WY

Burton

Burton
Farm

Burton Lane
Copse

NORTH
ST

WHITE ROAD

Mere
Prim Sch
SPRINGFIELD
RD

Ashfield Water

Tumulus

Chaddenwick
Wood

Monarch's Way

Charnage
Farm

Charnage

Clock
Tower
SALISBURY

THE
SQ
P
DARK LANE
IVY MEAD

MERE

Liby &
Mus
The
Chantry
ne Grove
Building

MILL LANE

LYNCH LA

Holwell

BA12

Southbrook

SOUTHBROOK

Little
Wood

Edge
Bridge

1 ASHGROVE
2 SOUTHBROOK GDNS
3 WHITEMARSH
4 THE BARTLETTS
5 BALMOOR CL

Limpers
Hill

LONGMEAD RD

The Causeway

Rook
Street

WOODLANDS ROAD

SHAFTESBURY ROAD

BARROW STREET LANE

Wiltshire STREET ATLAS

Sewage
Works

Field
End

Causeway
Farm

Barrow
Street

Shreen Water

Woodlands
Manor

Woodlands
Farm

White Hill
Wood

Barrow Street
Farm

Swain's Ford
Bridge

White
Hill

Church
Farm

Breaches
Farm

West Swainsford
Farm

East Swainsford
Farm

Wet Lane
Farm

WET LANE

Lyemarsh
Farm

Homestead
Farm

PIMPERLEAZE ROAD

Two Counties
Farm

Black House
Farm

CUNNAGE LA

8

7

33

6

5

32

4

31

3

2

1

30

A | B | C | D | E | F

81 | 82 | 83

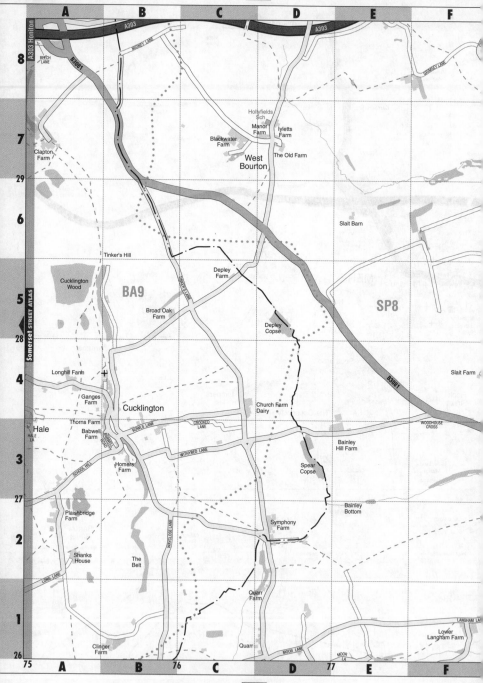

A303 Honiton

BEECH LANE

B3081

A303

MIDNEY LANE

A303

GRIMSEY LANE

Clapton Farm

Hollyfields Sch

Manor Farm

Iyletts Farm

Blackwater Farm

West Bourton

The Old Farm

Slait Barn

Tinker's Hill

Cucklington Wood

BA9

TINKER'S LANE

Depley Farm

Broad Oak Farm

Depley Copse

SP8

Longhill Farm

Ganges Farm

Cucklington

ROWLS LANE

CROOKED LANE

Church Farm Dairy

B3081

Slait Farm

Hale

HALE LA

Thorns Farm

Babwell Farm

B3081 ROAD

WITHYBED LANE

WOODHOUSE CROSS

Bainley Hill Farm

SCHOOL HILL

Homers Farm

Spear Copse

Plaishbridge Farm

HAYCLOSE LANE

Bainley Bottom

Symphony Farm

Shanks House

The Belt

LONG LANE

Quarr Farm

Clinger Farm

Quarr

MOOR LANE

MOOR LA

LANGHAM LA

Lower Langham Farm

Somerset STREET ATLAS

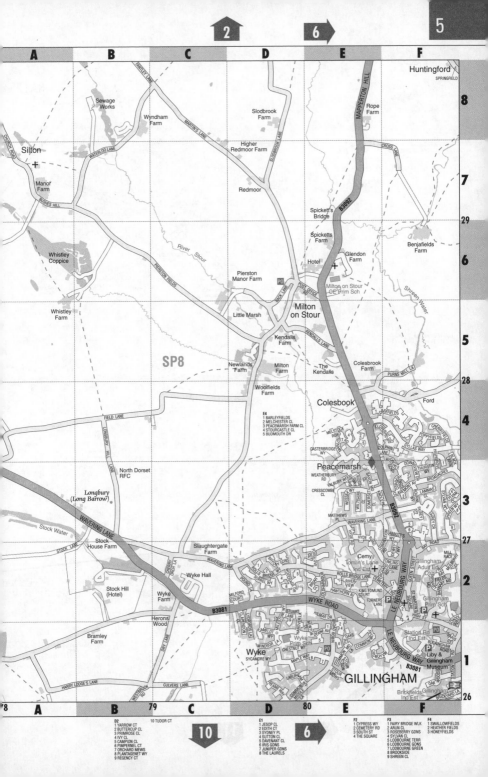

Huntingford
SPRINGFIELD

A B C D E F

8

Sewage
Works

Wyndham
Farm

Slodbrook
Farm

Rope
Farm

Silton

Manor
Farm

Higher
Redmoor Farm

7

29

Redmoor

Spickett's
Bridge

B3092

Whistley
Coppice

River Stour

PIERSTON FIELDS

Pierston
Manor Farm

Spicketts
Farm

Hotel

Glendon
Farm

Benjafields
Farm

6

Whistley
Farm

Little Marsh

Milton
on Stour

Milton on Stour
CE Prim Sch

Shreen Water

SP8

Newlands
Farm

Kendalls
Farm

Milton
Farm

The
Kendalls

KENDALLS LANE

Colesbrook
Farm

PURNS MILL LA

5

28

Woolfields
Farm

Colesbrook

Ford

E4
1 BARLEYFIELDS
2 MELCHESTER CL
3 PEACEMARSH FARM CL
4 STOURCASTLE CL
5 BUDMOUTH DR

4

FIELD LANE

North Dorset
RFC

Peacemarsh

WEATHERBURY
RD

CRESSCOMBE
CL

B3092

3

27

Longbury
(Long Barrow)

Stock Water

WAVERING LANE

Stock
House Farm

Slaughtergate
Farm

WAVERING LANE

MATTHEWS

WAVERING LANE

Cemy

Tomlin's Lane
Ind Est

Gillingham
Adult Ed

MILL
RACE

Wyke Hall

Wyke
Farm

MILFORD
COURT

ROLLS BRIDGE LANE

RIVER
VIEW

KING EDMUND
COURT

TURNERS
LANE

P

LE NEUBOURG WAY

Gillingham
Prim Sch

2

Stock Hill
(Hotel)

B3081

Herons
Wood

Wyke

WYKE ROAD

Wyke
Prim Sch

Station Rd
Ind Est

P

Libry &
Gillingham
Museum

Bramley
Farm

Wyke
SYCAMORE WY

CHESTNUT WY

GILLINGHAM

B3081

Brickfields
Ind Est

Gillingham

BACKYARD LA

1

26

HARRY LODGE'S LANE

CULVERS LANE

8 A B 79 C D E 80 F

D2
1 YARROW CT
2 BUTTERCUP CL
3 PRIMROSE CL
4 IVY CL
5 CAMPION CL
6 PIMPERNEL CT
7 ORCHARD MEWS
8 PLANTAGENET WY
9 REGENCY CT

10 TUDOR CT

E1
1 JESOP CL
2 EDITH CT
3 SYDNEY PL
4 SUTTON CL
5 DAVENANT CL
6 IRIS GDNS
7 JUNIPER GDNS
8 THE LAURELS

F2
1 CYPRESS WY
2 CEMETERY RD
3 SOUTH ST
4 THE SQUARE

F3
1 FAIRY BRIDGE WLK
2 ARUN CL
3 ROSEBERRY GDNS
4 SYLVAN CL
5 LODBOURNE TERR
6 LODBOURNE GDNS
7 LODBOURNE GREEN
8 BROOKSIDE
9 SHREEN CL

F4
1 SWALLOWFIELDS
2 HEATHER FIELDS
3 HONEYFIELDS

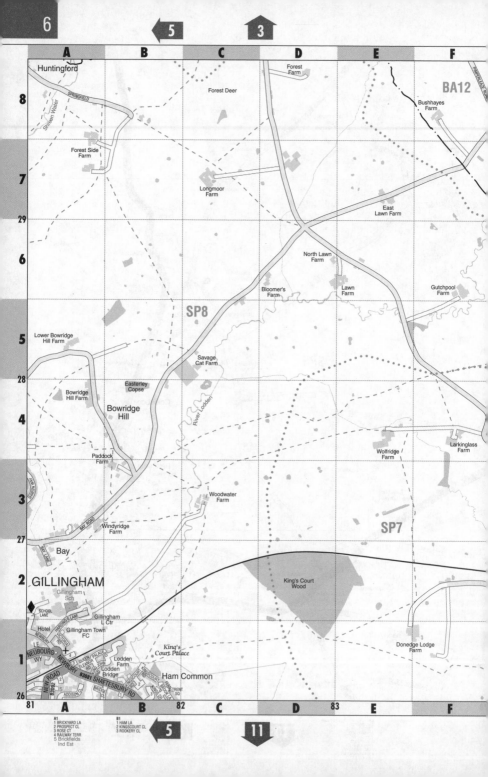

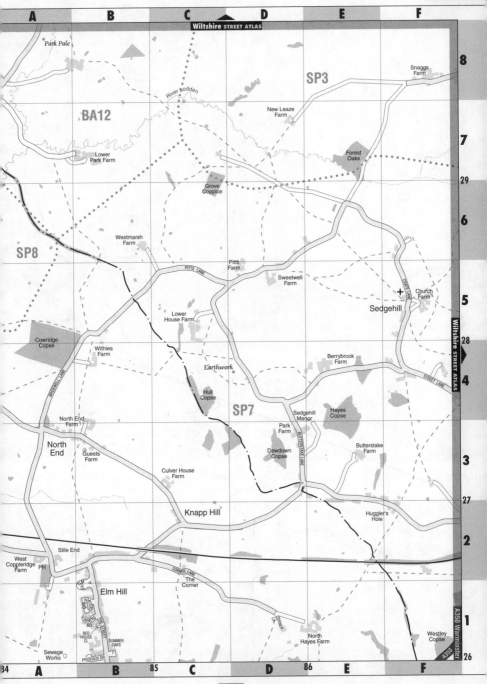

A B C D E F

8

Park Pale

SP3

Snaggs Farm

River Sodden

BA12

New Leaze Farm

7

Lower Park Farm

Forest Oaks

29

Grove Coppice

6

SP8

Westmarsh Farm

Pitts Farm

PITTS LANE

Sweetwell Farm

Church Farm

5

Sedgehill

Lower House Farm

Cowridge Copse

Withies Farm

Earthwork

Berrybrook Farm

28

STREET LANE

4

Hull Copse

SP7

Sedgehill Manor

Hayes Copse

Park Farm

North End Farm

Butterstake Farm

North End

Guests Farm

Dewdown Copse

BUTTERSTAKE LANE

3

Culver House Farm

Knapp Hill

Huggler's Hole

27

Stile End

2

West Coppleridge Farm

PH

CORNER LANE

The Corner

Elm Hill

THE STREET

RED HOUSE CL

SUMMER OAKS

North Hayes Farm

Westley Copse

1

Sewage Works

PRIDEAUX DR

26

84 A B 85 C D 86 E F

12

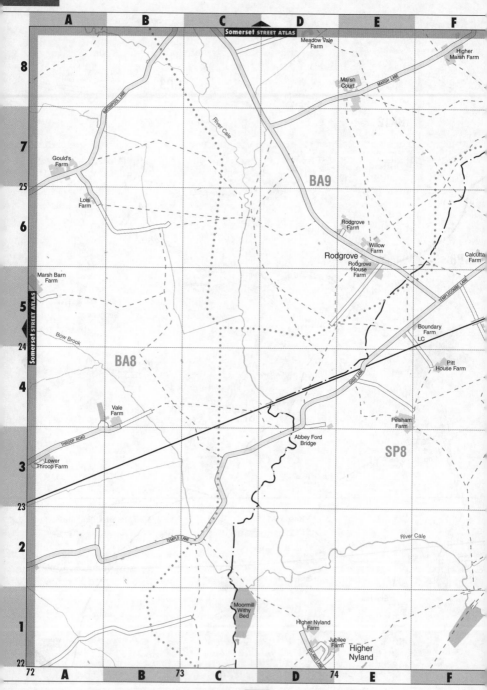

A B C D E F

8

7

25

6

5

24

4

23

3

2

1

22

72 A B 73 C D 74 E F

Somerset STREET ATLAS

Meadow Vale Farm

Higher Marsh Farm

Marsh Court

MARSH LANE

BA9

River Cale

MONKTON LANE

Gould's Farm

Lois Farm

Rodgrove Farm

Willow Farm

Rodgrove

Rodgrove House Farm

Calcutta Farm

Marsh Barn Farm

TEMPLECOMBE LANE

Boundary Farm LC

Bow Brook

BA8

DIKE LANE

Pitt House Farm

Vale Farm

THROOP ROAD

Pelsham Farm

SP8

Abbey Ford Bridge

Lower Throop Farm

TEMPLE LANE

Moormill Withy Bed

River Cale

Higher Nyland Farm

Jubilee Farm

Higher Nyland

NYLAND LANE

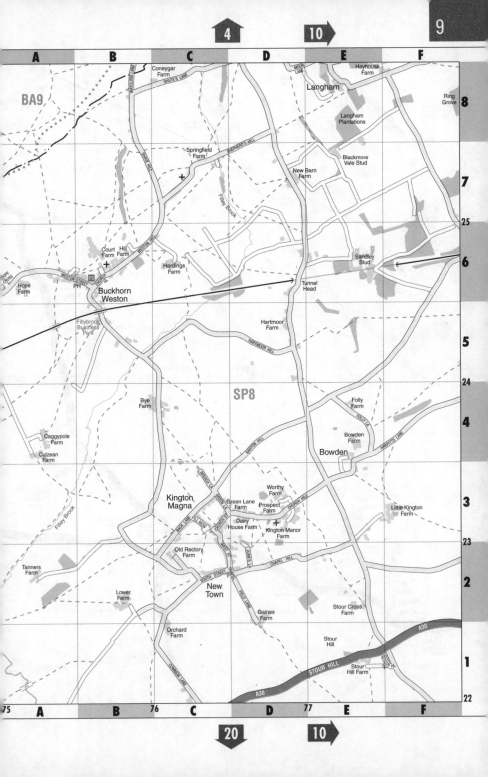

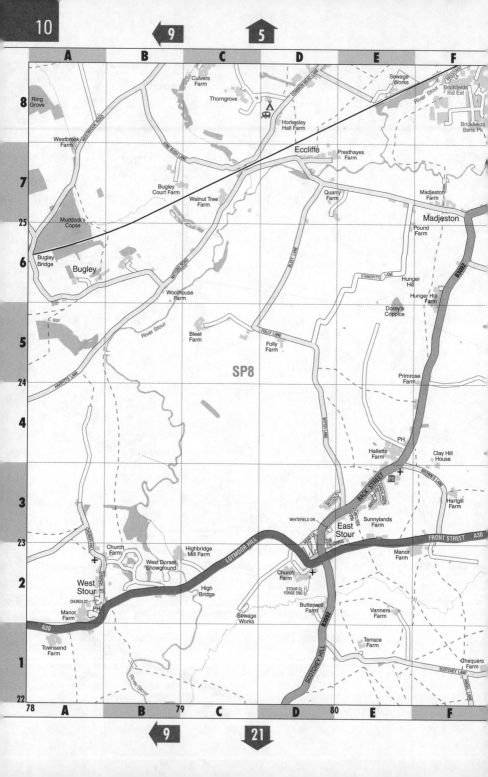

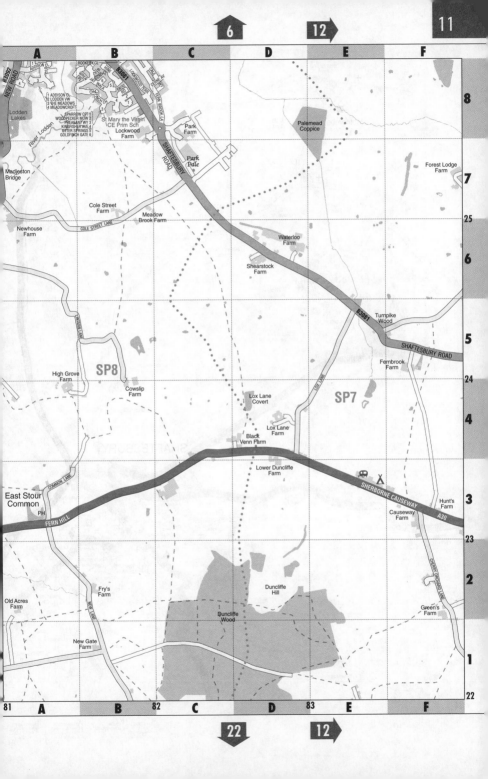

Lyefield's Copse

Oysters Coppice

Oysters Farm

Harthill Farm

Benett's Copse

Froud's Copse

Stib Acre Copse

Westwood Farm

Gutch Common

Clift Farm

Knipes Farm

Hilldown Copse

Donhead Clift

Hatts Farm

Crates Wood

Tittle Path Hill

Aldermoor Copse

Castle Rings

Semley Hill

Lodge Wood

Bungalow Castle Farm

Lower Wincombe Farm

Nadder Head

Wincombe Business Park

Morgan's Copse

Wincombe Park

Ramshill Farm

Mullins' Copse

Great Hanging

Step Cross Copse

Higher Wincombe Farm

WINDWHISTLE CORNER

Ivy Cross

Shaftesbury CE Prim Sch

SP7

Eastleaze Farm

BURTON

Langdale Farm

Mampits Farm

Dockham Bottom

St Marys Sch

Cemy

Long Bottom

Ten Acre Copse

Landsley Farm

Cave Copse

Coombe

Hotel

Long Copse

Knights Barn Farm

PH

White Close Farm

Mayo Farm

NEW LANE

A30 Salisbury

Boyne Hollow

Hillside Farm

SALISBURY ROAD

CHARLTON LANE

87   A   B   88   C   D   89   E   F

8
7
25
6
5
24
4
3
23
2
22

A1
1 BUTTS MD
2 LWR BLANDFORD RD
3 BRINSCOMBE LA

A4
1 HAWTHORN CL
2 SPRINGFIELD CL
3 GREAT GROUND

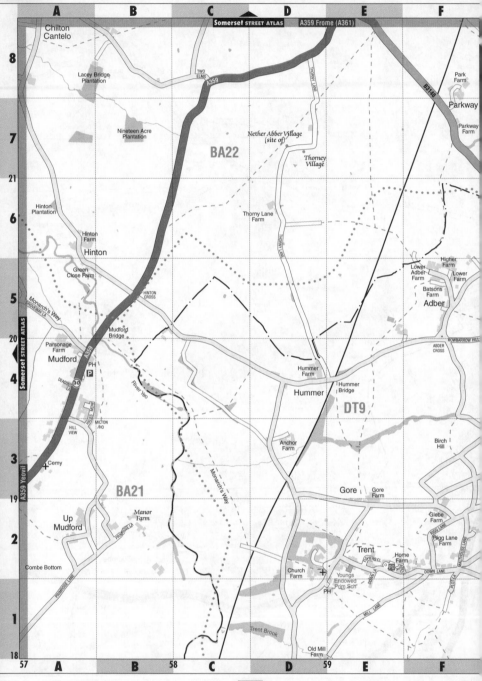

A359 Frome (A361)

8

7

21

6

5

20

4

3

19

2

1

18

A B 58 C D 59 E F

57

Chilton Cantelo

Lacey Bridge Plantation

TWO ELMS

A359

Nineteen Acre Plantation

BA22

Nether Abber Village (site of)

Thorney Village

THORNY LANE

B3148

Parkway

Park Farm

Parkway Farm

Hinton Plantation

Hinton Farm

Hinton

Green Close Farm

Thorny Lane Farm

THORNY LANE

HINTON CROSS

Lower Adber Farm

Higher Farm

Lower Farm

Batsons Farm

Adber

Monarch's Way

GROVE WAY LA

Mudford Bridge

ROWBARROW HILL

ABDER CROSS

Parsonage Farm

Mudford

A359

PH

P

30

BEACONS LA

River Yeo

MUDFORD BRIDGE

Hummer Farm

Hummer

Hummer Bridge

DT9

HILL VIEW

MILTON HO

Anchor Farm

Birch Hill

A359 Yeovil

✝ Cemy

BA21

Monarch's Way

Gore

Gore Farm

Glebe Farm

Up Mudford

Manor Farm

PRIMROSE LA

Rigg Lane Farm

RIGG LANE

MALTHOUSE LANE

Combe Bottom

PRIMROSE LANE

Trent

CHERIS CL

Home Farm

DOWN LANE

A3027

Church Farm

✝ PH

Youngs Endowed Prim Sch

MILL LANE

Trent Brook

Old Mill Farm

Somerset STREET ATLAS

Somerset STREET ATLAS

A B C D E F

8

7

21

6

5

20

4

3

19

2

1

18

Home Farm
Park Farm
Lower Farm
Weathergrove Farm
HOME FARM LA
MIDDLE ST
Barton Farm
CHURCH LA
PIRK KNOLL HOLLOW
Macmillan Way
Higher Farm
Windmill Hill
Staffords Green Farm
Rimpton
BA22
Heaven's Door
Manor Farm
Sandford Orcas Manor
PITHELD DRV
SLADE LANE
Smithy Farm
DARK LANE
PARK LANE
SHILLER'S LANE
WHITE LANE
Hanging Covert
PENMORE RD
Cottage Farm
Sandford Orcas
White Post
Haile's End
PH
PH
Crossways Farm
GREAT PIT LANE
PENMORE ROAD
MIDDLE FIELD LANE
Higher Sandford
SPRING
ROWBARROW HL
Rowbarrow Farm
MOORWAY LANE
Higher Sandford Farm
SANDFORD ORCAS RD
20
Trent Wood
DT9
Benchy Hill
Rosedown Farm
Monarch's Way
Patson Hill
CLATCOMBE LANE
Ambrose Hill
SANDFORD ORCAS ROAD
Macmillan Way
Patson Hill Farm
HAM LANE
PATSON HILL LANE
Ryland Plantation
Marlpits
Trent Barrow
COOMBE LA
Charlock Hill
Coombe Farm
Monarch's Way
Monarch's Way
MARSTON RD
B3148
B3148

15

15

30

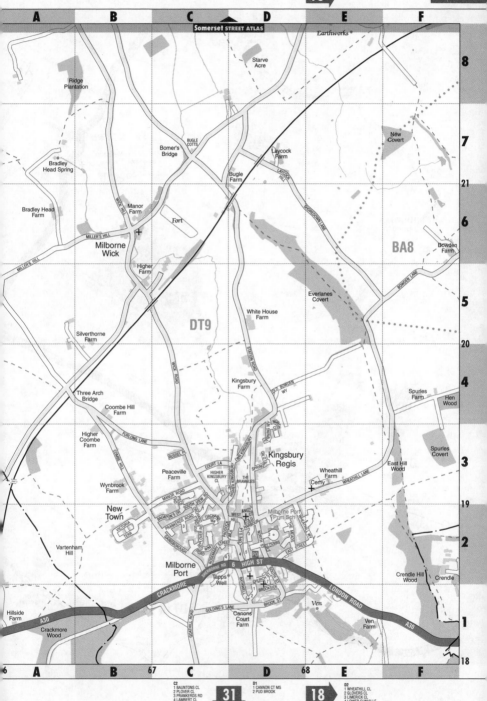

Somerset STREET ATLAS

Earthworks

	A	B	C	D	E	F	

Ridge Plantation

Starve Acre

8

New Covert

7

Bomer's Bridge

BUGLE COTTS

Laycock Farm

Bradley Head Spring

Bugle Farm

21

Bradley Head Farm

WICK HILL

Manor Farm

Fort

SHERBORNE LANE

6

BA8

MILLER'S HILL

Milborne Wick

Bowden Farm

Higher Farm

MILLER'S HILL

BOWDEN LANE

Silverthorne Farm

Everlanes Covert

DT9

White House Farm

5

20

Three Arch Bridge

WICK ROAD

Kingsbury Farm

STATION ROAD

Spurles Farm

Hen Wood

4

Coombe Hill Farm

MILL BOWDEN WY

Higher Coombe Farm

FURLONG LANE

Spurles Covert

COOMBE HILL

Peaceville Farm

RUSSEL PL

COURT LA

HIGHER KINGSBURY CL

Kingsbury Regis

Wheathill Farm
Cemy

East Hill Wood

3

Wynbrook Farm

MANOR ROAD

THE BRAMBLES

WHEATHILL LANE

New Town

SOUTH FEN LA

SPRINGFIELD

19

Vartenham Hill

VICTORIA TERR

BALLAM'S OR

PRANKERDS ROAD

GAINSBOROUGH ROAD

ROSEMARY STREET

ORCHARD

WEST HILL

ANGEL

Milborne Port Prim Sch

THE MEADS

Milborne Port

HIGH ST

GLOVERS

EAST STREET

Crendle Hill Wood

Crendle

2

CRACKMORE

Tapps Well

MELMOUTH RD

BATH WELL

PO

CHURCH ST

BROOKSIDE

Ven

LONDON ROAD

A30

Hillside Farm

A30

GOATHILL ROAD

GOLDING'S LANE

Canons Court Farm

BROOK ST

Ven Farm

1

Crackmore Wood

18

	A	B	C	D	E	F	

C2
1 BAUNTONS CL
2 PLOVER CL
3 PRANKERDS RD
4 LAMBERT CL

D1
1 CANNON CT MS
2 PUD BROOK

D2
1 WHEATHILL CL
2 GLOVERS CL
3 LIMERICK CL
4 LOWER GUNVILLE
5 HIGHER GUNVILLE
6 SANSOME'S HL
7 CHAPEL LA

17

Somerset STREET ATLAS

A357 Wincanton

Elm Farm

Common Lane Farm

Cantrall Light Railway

West Wood

Coombe Farm

WEST ST

OVERCOMBE

COMBE HILL

YENSTON HL

COMMON LANE

Newleaze Farm

BOWDEN RD

Burnt House Farm

Martin's Copse

Windmill Hill

Manor Farm

Yenston

Perhams Farm

Home Farm

SALLY LOVELL'S LA

Redhouse Farm

Sedgemoor Farm

Fir Tree Farm

Sewage Works

HIGH ST

21

BOWDEN ROAD

Henstridge Bowden

CHAPEL LANE

Manor Farm

Inwood

BA8

Cox Far

BOWDEN LANE

A357

20

SHERBORNE ROAD

PH

Summerleaze Copse

Yarn Copse

Quarry Farm

Higher Spurles Covert

Toomer Hill

DT9

Broadsill Copse

Toomer Farm

19

Gospel Ash Farm

THE OLD ROAD

SHERBORNE ROAD

LANGSHIRE LA

Furge Plantation

DT10

Caundle Brake

Copse Farm

A30 LONDON ROAD

18

69

70

71

17

32

A B C D E F

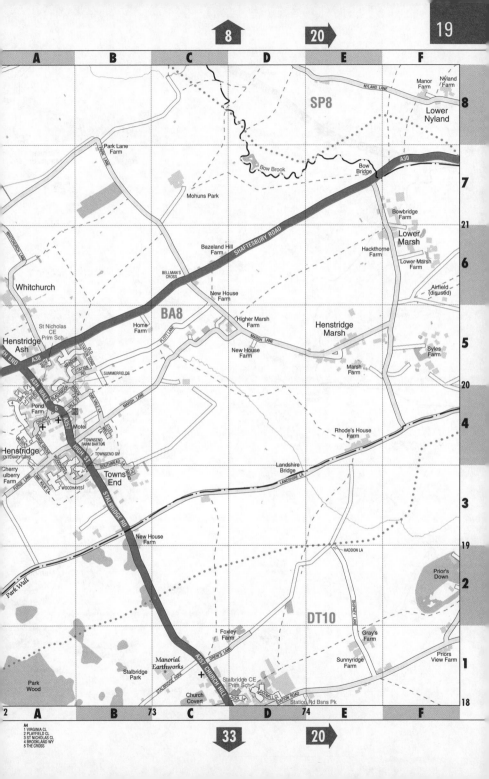

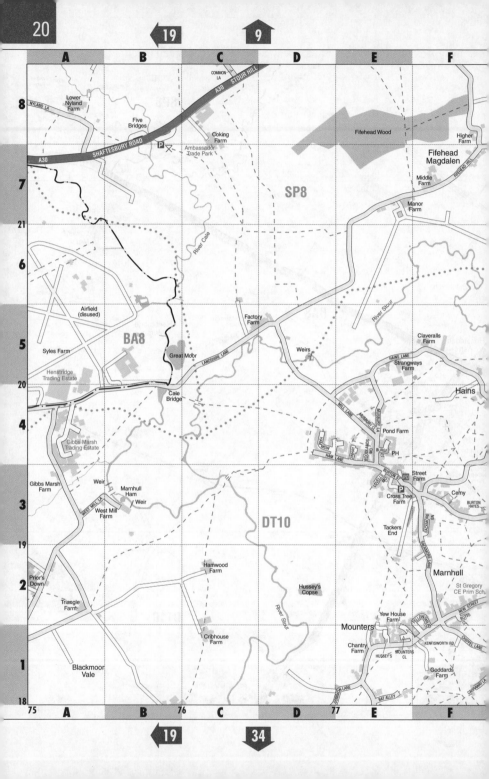

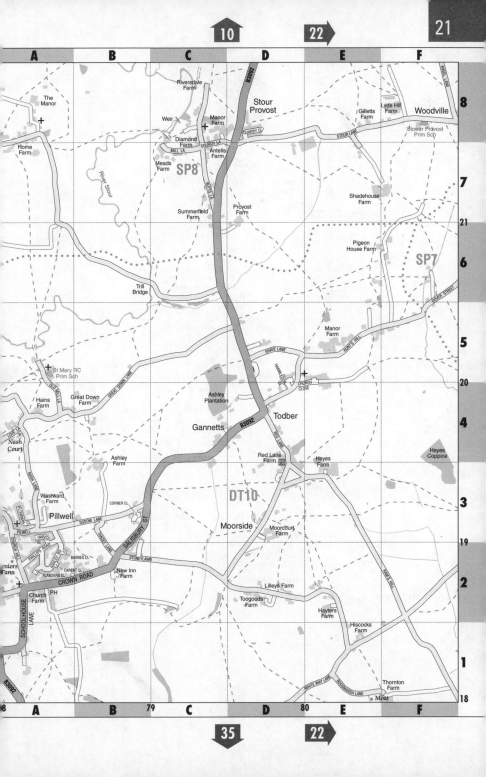

	A	B	C	D	E	F

8

SP8

Hawkers Farm

Duncliffe Wood

Jolliffes Farm

Thomas's Farm

Blynfield Farm

Blakes Farm

HAWKERS LA

STOUR LANE

Hill Farm

7

Duncliffe Home Farm

Stour Row

Yew Tree Farm

Paynthouse Farm

DOVER STREET

CHURCH CL

21

Yeatmans Farm

COLLEGE ARMS CT

Woodville Farm

Froghole Farm

6

Good's Farm

Great House Farm

Hunts Farm

Gore Farm

Sweets Farm

5

Tile House Farm

Doncliffe Hall Farm

SP7

Gupple's Copse

60

GREEN LANE

4

Wadmill Farm

Marsh Common

Jopps Farm

3

Lymburghs Farm

Elm Farm

Jolliffes Farm

Green Farm

Venns Farm

Black Ven Farm

Blackven Common

19

Marsh Farm

Lower Farm

Cherry Grove

2

DT10

Margaret Marsh

CHURCH LA

New House Farm

Lower Hartgrove Farm

Blackberry Farm

Church Farm

Cowgrove Farm

1

BLEAX CL

Bleax Hill

Hartgrove

B3091

CHURCH LA

18

RAM'S HL

81	A	B	82	C	D	83	E	F

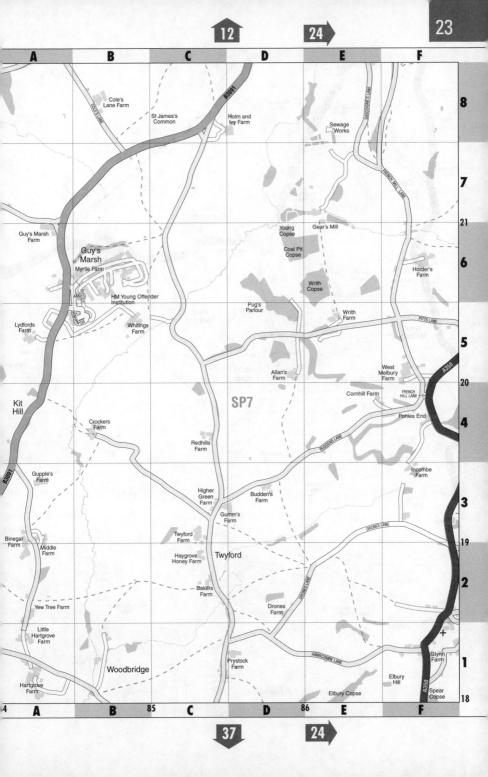

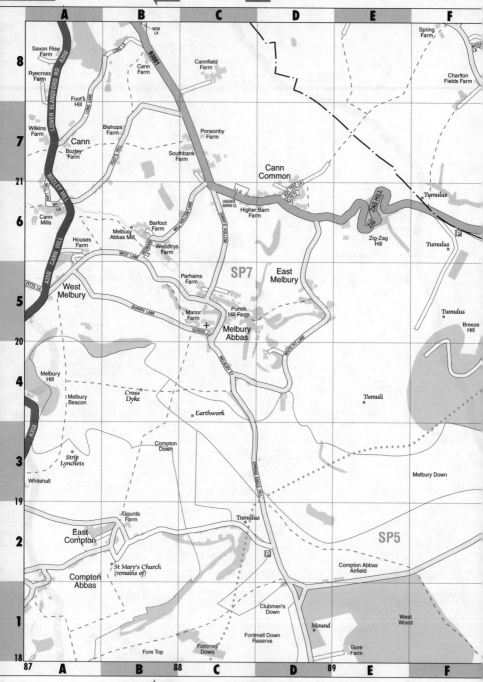

Wiltshire STREET ATLAS

Home Farm

Manor Farm

BARTERS LANE

CHARLTON LANE

Wessex Ridgeway

SP7

Higher Berrycourt Farm

Beech Clump

Elliott's Shed

TOWERED HOLLOW

Charlton Down

Tumulus

B3081

Tumulus

Hawcombe Copse

Charlton Down

Cross Dyke

Win Green

P

Melbury Wood

Win Green Plantation

Long Barrow

Wessex Ridgeway

Quarry Bottom

Melbury Down

SP5

Ashmore Down

POSSESSIONS CORNER

Abbot's Copse

Hatts Copse

Hatts Barn

Cross Dyke

NORTH ROAD

Ashgrove Farm

Boyne Bottom

South's Farm

Woodley Down

Wessex Ridgeway

B3081

Somerset STREET ATLAS

Thorne Coffin

Manor Farm

Shrewsbury Rd

Mast

Oak Farm

Lufton Coll of FE

Lufton Trading Estate

Huish Park (Yeovil Town FC)

BA21

Manor Farm

Lufton

Artillery Road

Yeovil Small Bsns Ctr
Yeovil Coll

Houndstone

BA22

Clarks Close

High Leaze Farm

Superstore

Tithe Barn

Preston Sch

Stratford

Houndstone Close

Alvington

Crem

Preston Plucknett

A3088 Ilminster (A303)

A3088

New Road

New Road

Lower Odcombe

Bank Farm

Home Farm

Brympton D'Evercy

Brympton House

Alvington Farm

Bunford Lane

Playing Field

Lynx West Trading Estate

BA20

Lynx Trading Estate

Lysander Road

Sampson's Wood

Ash Copse

Pye Corner

Leaze Cottages

Camp Hill

Broadleaze Farm

Dry Copse

Camp Road

Feebarrow

WEST COKER RD

A30

Nash Farm

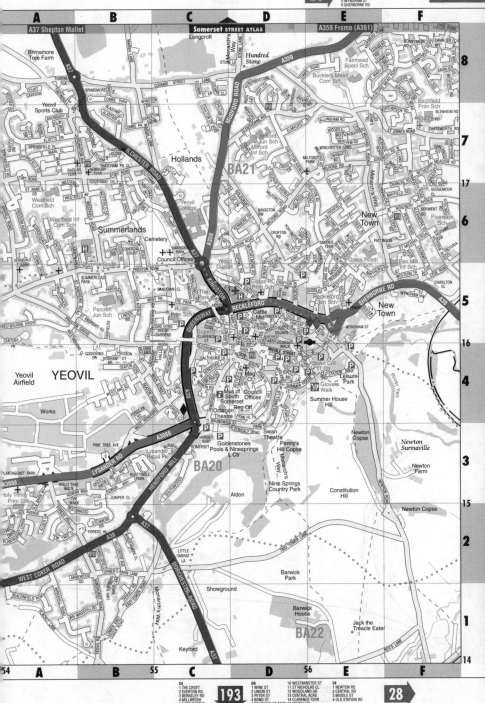

28

E5
1 ST THOMAS CROSS
2 DAMPIER PL
3 DAMPIER ST
4 HILLSIDE TERR
5 WYNDHAM ST
6 SHERBORNE RD

Somerset STREET ATLAS

A37 Shepton Mallet

A359 Frome (A361)

BA21

YEOVIL

Yeovil
Airfield

BA20

BA22

28

C4
1 THE CROFT
2 EVERTON RD
3 BERKELEY RD
4 MILLBROOK
5 YARN BARTON

D4
1 WINE ST
2 UNION ST
3 PETER ST
4 BOND ST
5 ST NICHOLAS PARK
6 HENDFORD
7 PARK ST
8 TAUNSSTEIN WAY
9 WOODLAND TERR

10 WESTMINSTER ST
11 ST NICHOLAS CL
12 WOODLAND GR
13 CENTRAL ACRE
14 CLARENCE TERR
15 MIDDLE ST
16 GLOVERS WALK

E4
1 NEWTON RD
2 CENTRAL RD
3 MIDDLE ST
4 OLD STATION RD

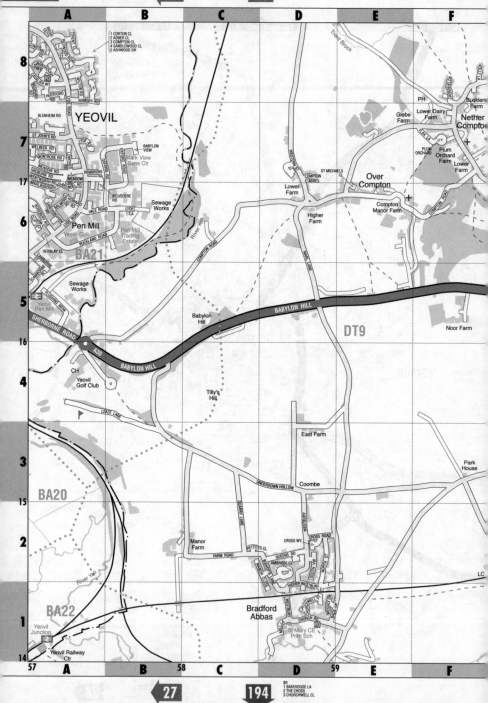

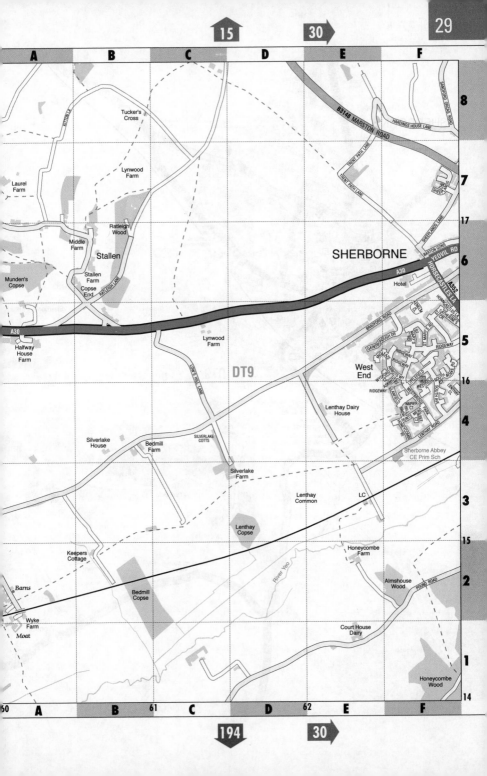

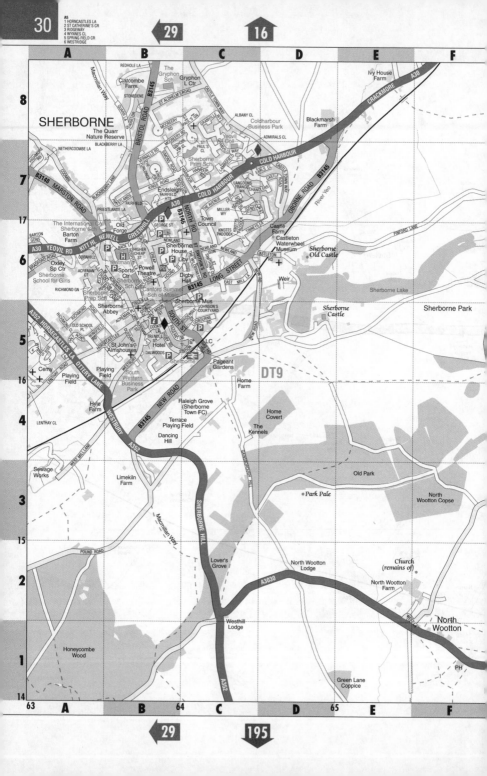

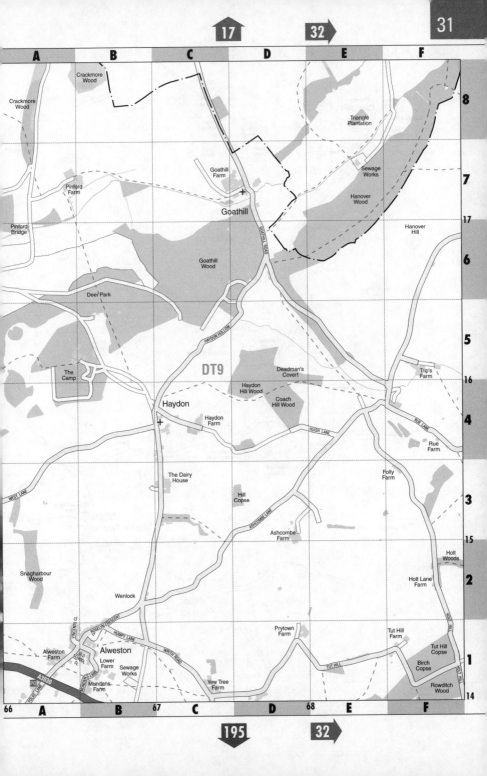

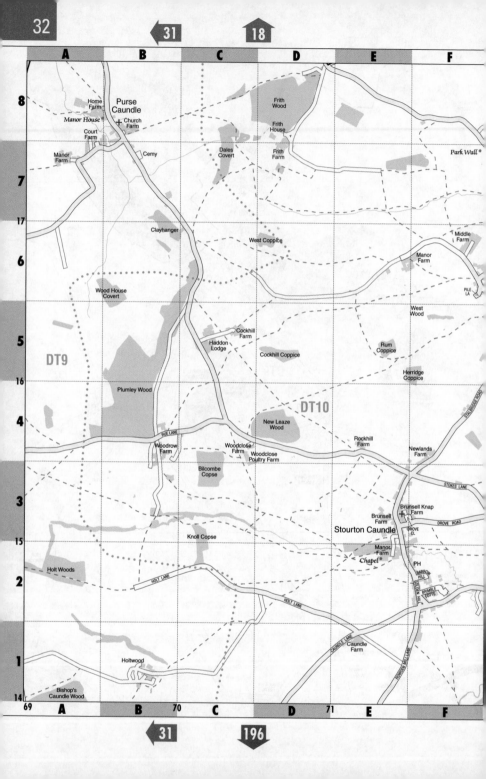

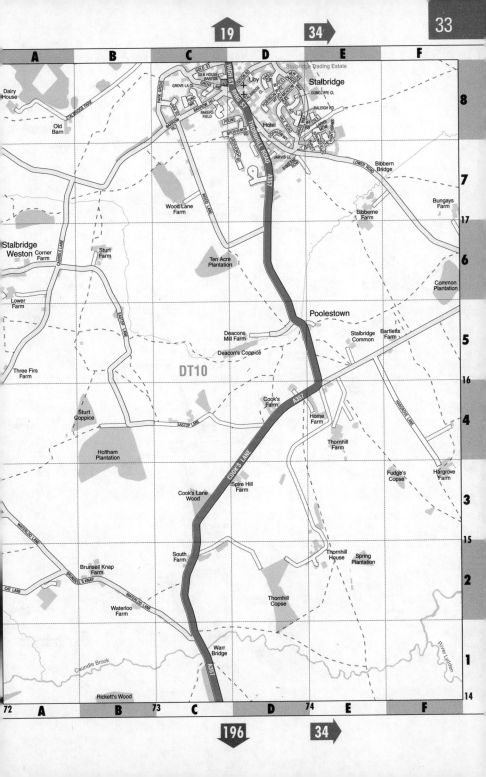

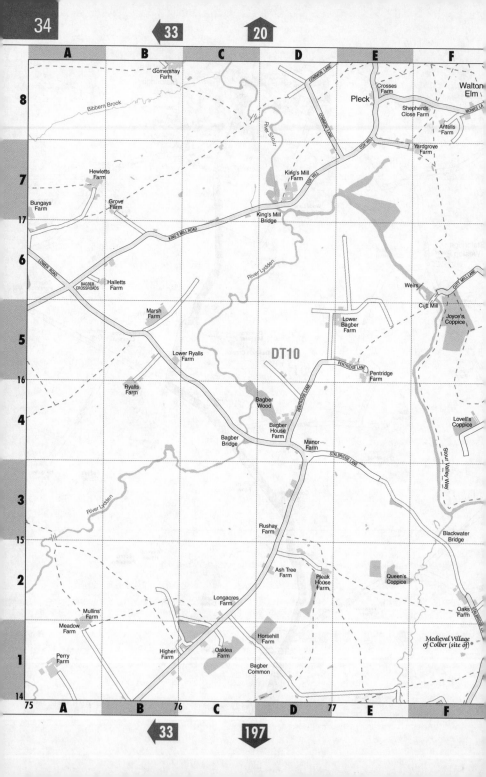

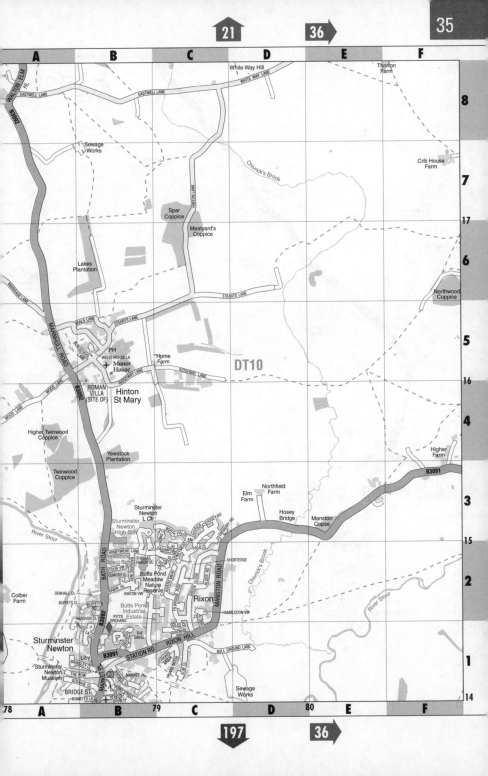

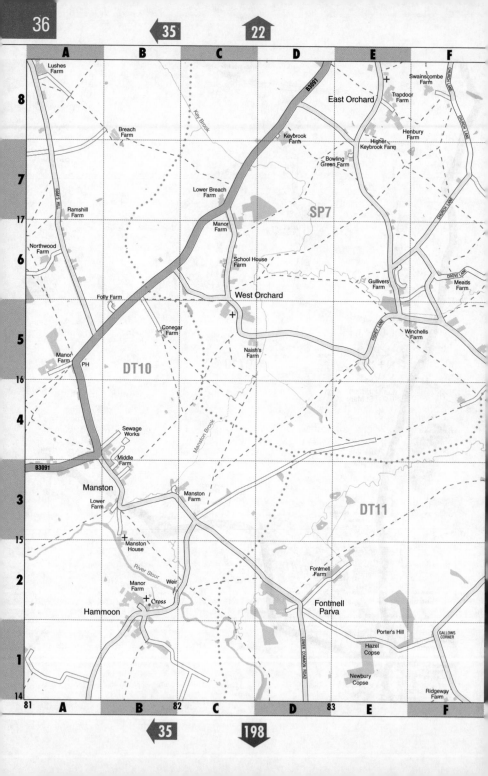

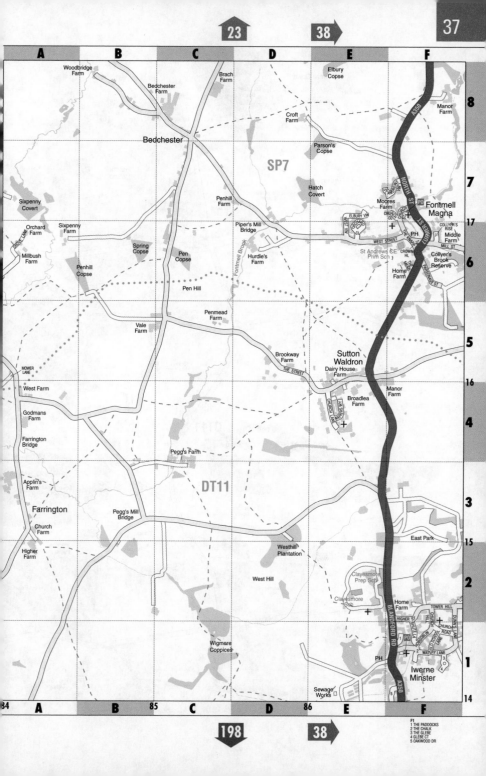

Fontmell Down

Fore Top

National Trust

Longcombe
Bottom

West
Wood

SP5

Cross
Dyke

Shepherd's
Bottom

SP7

Littlecombe
Bottom

Fontmell
Wood

Springhead
Farm

MILL STREET

Fontmell Hill
House

Washers
Pit

Strip
Lynchets

Balfour's Wood

Washers
Pit Coppice

STUBHAMPTON BOTTOM

Stubhamton
Bottom

Enclosure

Combe Bottom

Sutton
Hill Farm

West Lodge

STUBHAMPTON BOTTOM

Sutton Hill

DT11

Folly
Barrow

Spinney Pits Coppice

Higher Barn
Plantation

Freak's
Coppice

Lower Freaks
Coppice

Higher Barn
Plantation

Bareden
Down

Tumuli

Tumuli

Payne
Coppice

Wales
Wood

Bareden
Wood

Common
Bushes

Great Peakey
Coppice

TOWER HILL

MILES
FIELD

Iwerne
Hill

TOWER HILL

Hill Farm

BOWE'S LANE

Brookman's
Valley

Heron Grove
Coppice

Rolf's Wood

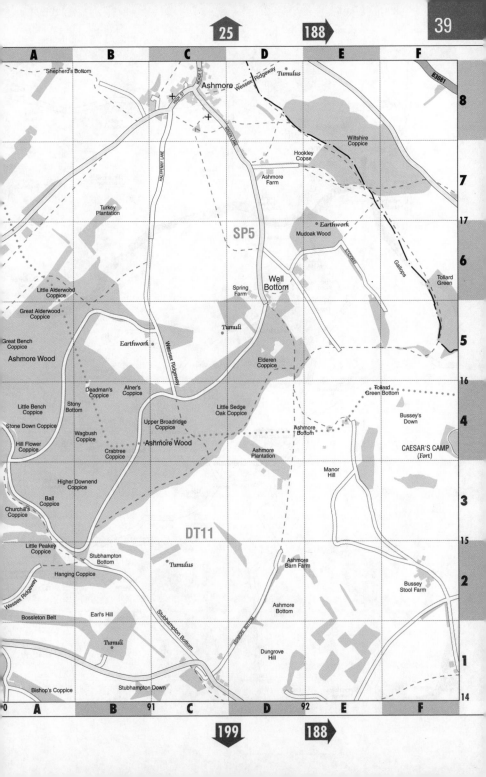

A   B   C   D   E   F

Shepherd's Bottom

B3081

8

Ashmore

Wessex Ridgeway   Tumulus

HIGH ST

ADDER ST

Wiltshire
Coppice

Hookley
Copse

7

Ashmore
Farm

GUSSAGE LANE

HALFPENNY LANE

Turkey
Plantation

SP5

Earthwork   17

Mudoak Wood

Gallops   6

Well
Bottom

Spring
Farm

Little Alderwood
Coppice

Tollard
Green

Great Alderwood
Coppice

Great Bench
Coppice

Tumuli

Ashmore Wood

Earthwork

Wessex Ridgeway

Elderen
Coppice

5

16

Deadman's
Coppice

Alner's
Coppice

Tollard
Green Bottom

Little Bench
Coppice

Stony
Bottom

Little Sedge
Oak Coppice

Bussey's
Down

4

Stone Down Coppice

Upper Broadridge
Coppice

Ashmore
Bottom

Wagbush
Coppice

Hill Flower
Coppice

Ashmore Wood

Crabtree
Coppice

Ashmore
Plantation

CAESAR'S CAMP
(Fort)

Higher Downend
Coppice

Manor
Hill

Ball
Coppice

3

Churchill's
Coppice

DT11

15

Little Peakey
Coppice

Stubhampton
Bottom

Tumulus

Ashmore
Barn Farm

Bussey
Stool Farm

2

Hanging Coppice

Wessex Ridgeway

Stubhampton Bottom

Ashmore
Bottom

ASHMORE BOTTOM

Bossleton Belt

Earl's Hill

Tumuli

Dungrove
Hill

1

Bishop's Coppice

Stubhampton Down

14

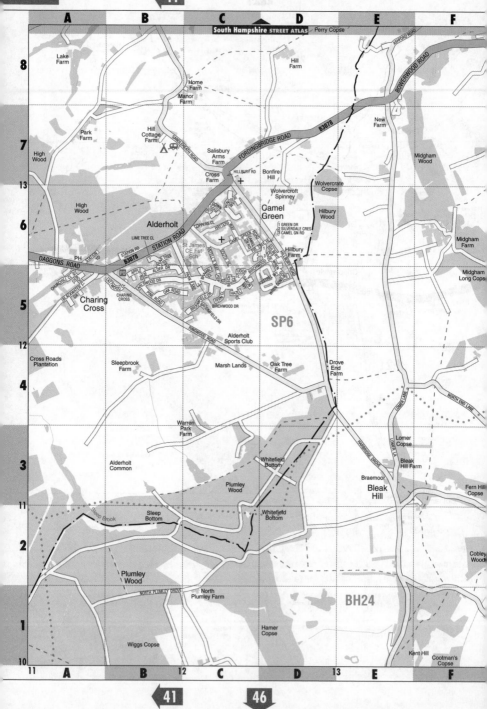

South Hampshire STREET ATLAS

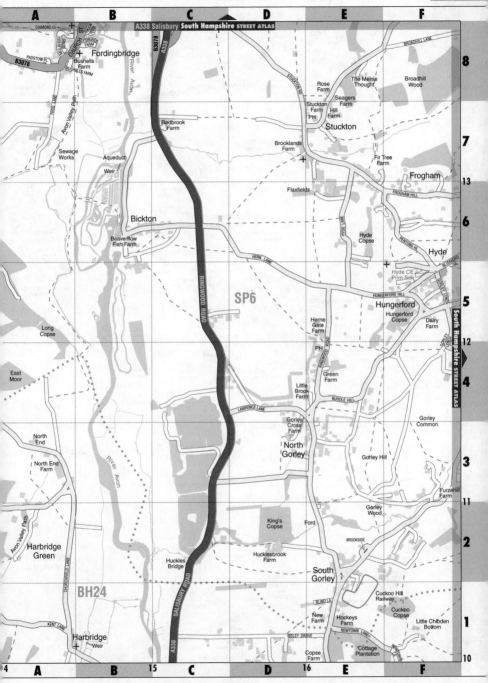

A B C D E F

8

7

13

6

5

12

4

3

11

2

1

10

Fordingbridge

DIAMOND CL
PADSTOW PL
B3078
SALISBURY
CHURCH ST
CHURCH FARM
Bushells Farm
BUSHELLS FARM
FROG LANE
CHURCH LANE
River Avon
Avon Valley Path

Sewage Works
Aqueduct
Weir

Redbrook Farm
Stuckton Rd
Brooklands Farm
Flaxfields

Rose Farm
The Merrie Thought
Broadhill Wood
Seagers Farm
Stuckton Farm
Hill Farm
Stuckton
PH

BROADHILL LANE

Fir Tree Farm
Frogham
FROGHAM HILL
Hyde Copse
Hyde
Bickton
Beaverflow Fish Farm
HERN LANE
HYDE LANE
FENTONS HL
Hyde CE Prim Sch
Hungerford Hill
Hungerford
BLISSFORD RD
GORLEY TRACK

RINGWOOD ROAD
SP6

Long Copse
East Moor

Herne Gate Farm
PH

Hungerford Copse
Dairy Farm
GORLEY RD

Green Farm
Little Brook Farm
BUDDLE HILL
Gorley Common

North End
North End Farm
River Avon

LAWRENCE LANE
Gorley Cross Farm
North Gorley
Gorley Hill
Gorley Wood
Furzehill Farm

South Hampshire STREET ATLAS

Harbridge Green
CHURCHFIELD LANE

King's Copse
Ford
BROOKSIDE

Huckles Bridge
Hucklesbrook Farm
South Gorley
Cuckoo Hill Railway
Cuckoo Copse
Little Chibden Bottom

BH24
Avon Valley Path
KENT LANE
Harbridge
Weir

SALISBURY ROAD
A338

BLIND LA
New Farm
Hockeys Farm
NEWTOWN LANE
Cottage Plantation

IBSLEY DRIVE
Copse Farm

A

15

C

16

E

F

45
42

A **B** **C** **D** **E** **F**

8

Plumley
Wood

Wiggs
Copse

Hamer
Copse

Cootman's
Copse

Kent Hill
Plantation

Harbridge
Farm

Ford

Turmer

7

Harefield Plantation

Plumley
Farm

Lower
Turmer

09

SHEPHERDS LA

6

Home
Farm

Reservoir
Cottage

CHESTNUT AVENUE

SHEPHERDS HILL

Home
Wood

Dog Kennel
Wood

ELLINGHAM DRIVE

5

FERWOOD ROAD

Ringwood
Forest

Nursery
Cottages

NEA DRIVE

Somerley
Park

Somerley

New
Bridge

08

BH24

4

Bluehaze

Park
Cottage

ELLINGHAM DR

B3081

3

BH31

Sunderton
Wood

Withybed
Copse

07

DUNCOMBE DRIVE

Tumulus

2

Tumuli

Sunderton
Wood

ASHLEY DRIVE

Ashley
Heath

Duncombe
Lodge

VERWOOD ROAD

1

Moors Valley
Country Park

Ashley
Farm

B3081

Baker's
Hanging

06

VERWOOD ROAD

11 **A** **B** 12 **C** **D** 13 **E** **F**

45
54

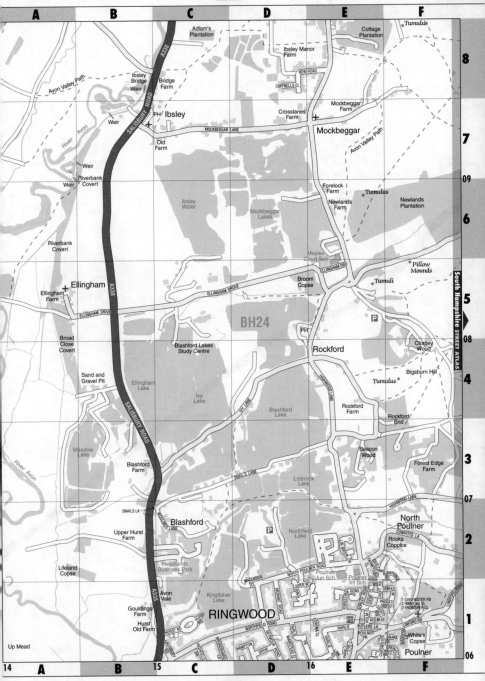

A **B** **C** **D** **E** **F**

Tumulus

Adlam's Plantation

Cottage Plantation

8

Ibsley Manor Farm

NEW ROAD

Ibsley Bridge Weir

Bridge Farm

CUFFNELLS CL

Avon Valley Path

Ibsley

Crosslanes Farm

Mockbeggar Farm

SALISBURY ROAD

A338

PH

Weir

MOCKBEGGAR LANE

Mockbeggar

7

River Avon

Old Farm

Avon Valley Path

09

Weir

Riverbank Covert

Forelock Farm

Ibsley Water

Tumulus

Weir

Newlands Farm

Newlands Plantation

6

Mockbeggar Lakes

Riverbank Covert

Moyles Court Sch

Pillow Mounds

A338

Ellingham

Broom Copse

ELLINGHAM RD

Tumuli

5

Ellingham Farm

ELLINGHAM DRIVE

South Hampshire STREET ATLAS

BH24

P

08

Broad Close Covert

Blashford Lakes Study Centre

PH

Rockford

Chatley Wood

SALISBURY ROAD

Sand and Gravel Pit

Ellingham Lake

Bigsburn Hill

4

Ivy Lake

Tumulus

HIGHWOOD LANE

IVY LANE

Blashford Lake

Rockford Farm

Rockford Bnd

Meadow Lake

SNAILS LANE

Beacon Wood

3

Blashford Farm

Linbrook Lake

Forest Edge Farm

River Avon

07

SNAILS LA

North Poulner

MOCKBEGGAR LANE

Blashford

Northfield Lake

Rooks Coppice

LOWPITTS LA

2

Upper Hurst Farm

P

Lifeland Copse

Headlands Business Park

Poulner Jun Sch

Poulner Inf Sch

1 CHICHESTER RD
2 HAWLING CL
3 FROBISHER CL

A338

Avon Vale

Kingfisher Lake

WATERSIDE CL

NORTH POULNER ROAD

LINFORD RD

1

Gouldings Farm

RINGWOOD

NORTHFIELD ROAD

White's Copse

Hurst Old Farm

HURST RD

HAMPTON DRIVE

WINSTER CL

BUTLERS LA

POULNER

Poulner

Up Mead

06

A 14 **B** 15 **C** **D** 16 **E** **F**

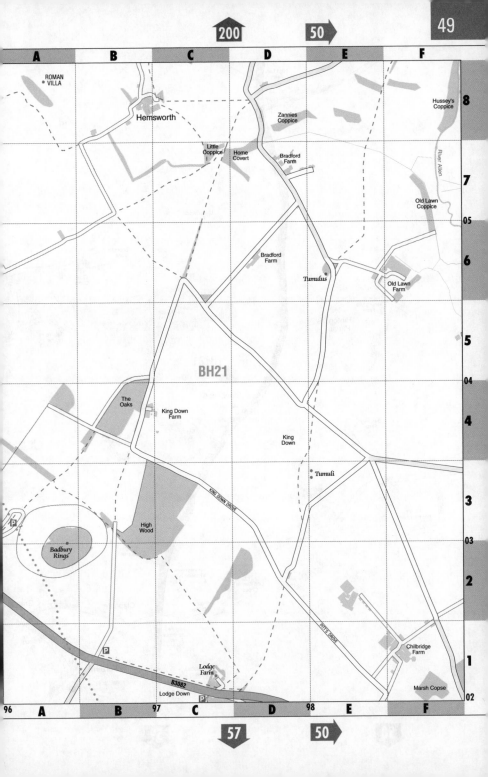

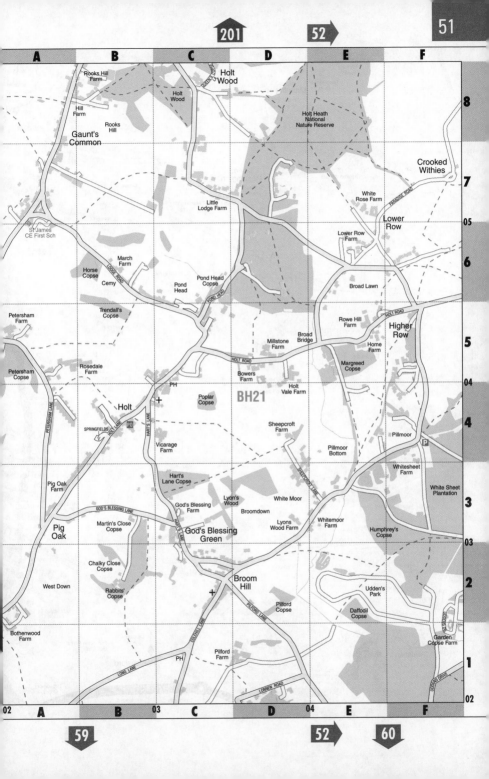

A B C D E F

8

ERIDGE ROAD

ALBANY DR
FRYERS RD
BRACKENDALE ST
HORTON ROAD
Earlys
Farm
Brooklands
Farm
Mannington
Skies
Farm

30
RINGWOOD RD
HOLT ROAD

7

Crooked Withies
Farm

Bulbarrow
Poultry Farm
Lower
Mannington
Jubilee
Farm
Mannington
Copse
Mannington
Farm
The
Copse
Haddons
Farm

05

Bull
Barrow
Barewood Copse

6

PH

Holt
Heath
Summerlug Hill

Sturts
Farm

5

Enclosure

BH21

Newman's
Farm
Meadows
Farm
NEWMAN'S LANE

WEST MOORS ROAD

04

Holt Heath
National
Nature Reserve

Gulliver's
Farm

4

BH22

WOODSI
RD
DENEWOO
RINGWOOD RD
B3072
POND AV

3

White Sheet Plantation

Hatchard's
Copse
St Marys CE
Fleet Sch
30
HESTON WY
RITCHIE
PL

KNIGHTSTONE
GR
Iby

NEWMAN'S LANE

03

Clayford
Farm
Ferndown Stour and Forest Trail
INVERDALE ROAD
KNIGHTSTONE
GR

2

Park
Copse
Uddens Water
UDDENS
DRIVE
PENNINGTON RD
Pennington's
Copse

1

UDDENS
DRIVE
Red
Bridge
Ferndown   Forest
CH
Dolman's
Farm
Ameysford
Ferndown Forest
Golf Club
Broadmoor
Coppice

02

05 A B 06 C D 07 E F

FOREST LINKS ROAD
AMEYSFORD RD
A31
COBHAM ROAD
AMEYSFORD RD

B7
1 THE SWEEP
2 STAR LA
3 FURLONG MEWS
4 PEDDLARS WK
5 COTTAGE MEWS
6 EBENEZER LA

7 GOOSEBERRY LA
8 DEWEYS LA

B8
1 LINDEN GDNS
2 MANOR GDNS
3 ORCHARD MD

C6
1 HARRY BARROW CL
2 CHARING CL
3 WATERLOO WY
4 SOUTHFIELD MS

D6
1 CROW ARCH LA
2 JOYCE DICKSON CL

D8
1 BEECHCROFT LA
2 BEECHCROFT MS
3 WANSTEAD CL
4 Lumby Dr
  Mobile Home Pk

E6
1 OLD STACKS GDNS
2 THE CLOISTERS
3 SANDERLINGS

E8
1 WHITEHART FIELDS
2 PIPERS ASH
3 RALEIGH CL
4 CUNNINGHAM CL
5 MERRYWEATHER EST

F6
1 HOLMWOOD GARTH
2 ASHBURN GARTH
3 FOREST HILLS CT

47

55

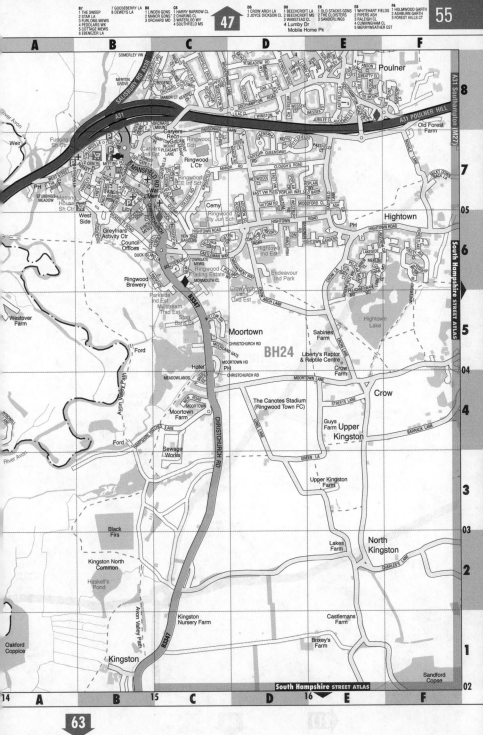

A **B** **C** **D** **E** **F**

8

Bishops Court Farm
Hyde Farm
Shapwick

WEST STREET PH
P CHURCH ST

Tumulus

Kings Farm

HIGH STREET
PICCADILLY LANE
STEWARD'S LANE

Park Lane

DT11

New Barn Farm

7

A350

River Stour

Stour Valley Way

MILL LANE

THE BURROW

01

Moorcourt Farm

White Mill Farm
P

White Mill

6

GREEN LANE

White Mill Bridge

Cross
Church Farm
PH

5

Millmoor Farm

Walnut Tree Field Nature Reserve

MOOR LANE
FIRST LA
CRUSOE ST

BH21

Black Horse Farm

KING'S STREET
BELL LANE
JEWES DR
HIGH
CL

Sturminster Marshall

CHURCHILL CLOSE
CHURCHILL
HIGH ST

CH

4

Newton Peveril

Newton Peveril Farm

PH NEWTON ROAD

A350

Springfield Farm

RAILWAY DRIVE
MAY DRIVE
TOWNSEND

CHURCHILL CL

MOOR LA

Sturminster Marshall Prlst Sch

00

PO
STATION RD

BRIDGE ST
MIDDLE ST
DUGDELL CL

Bailie Gate Ind Est

MOOR LANE

Gravel Pit

3

A31

LAMBS LANE

NURSERY GDNS

Bailie House

POOLE ROAD

99

DULLAR LANE

Bailie House

2

DT11

Lion Lodge

Lion Lodge Wood

POOLE ROAD

Henbury Stud Farm

A31

1

Ash Grove

Charborough Park

Wareham's Plantation

Dullar Farm

Henbury Barrow

POOLE ROAD
A350

Henbury

Little Henbury Farm

Henbury Hall

98

BH16

Dullar Wood

93 **A** **B** 94 **C** **D** 95 **E** **F**

B4
1 CHARBOROUGH WY
2 HAYCOCK WY
3 PARKELEA
4 TATTERSHALL GDNS
5 SHERIDEN WY

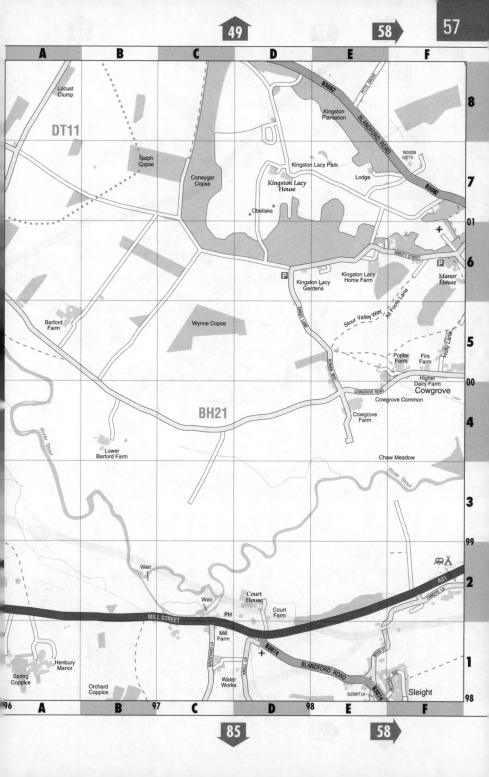

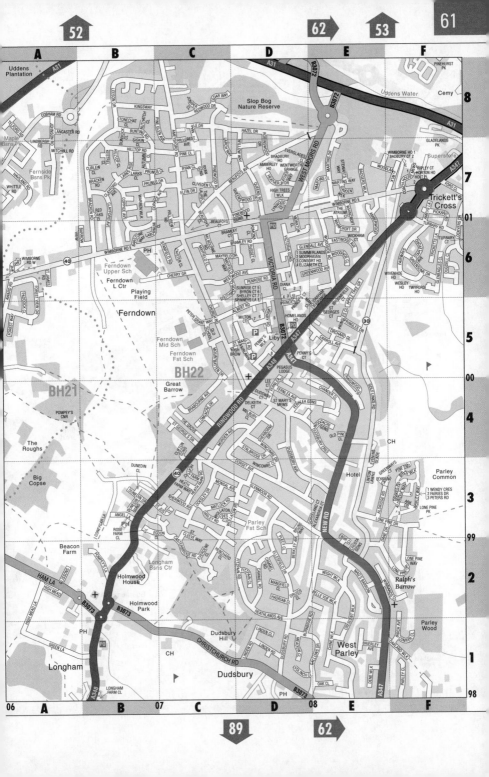

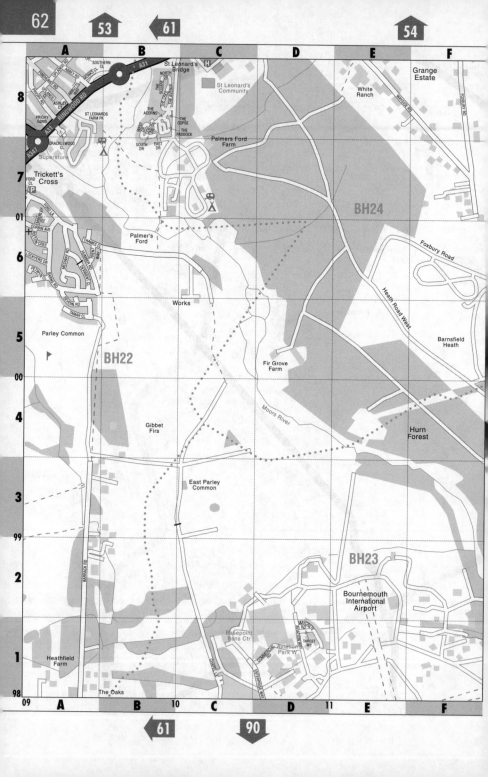

202

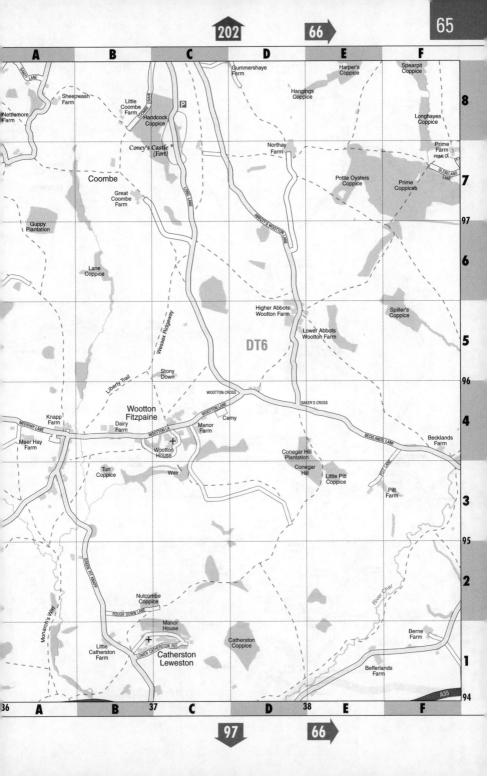

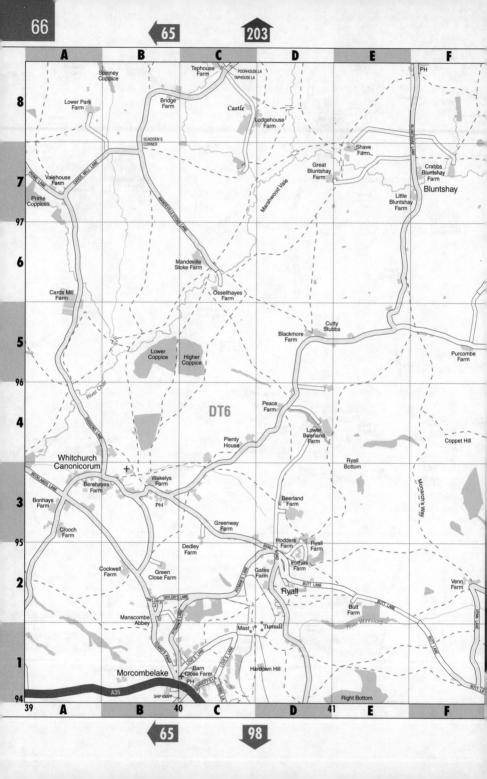

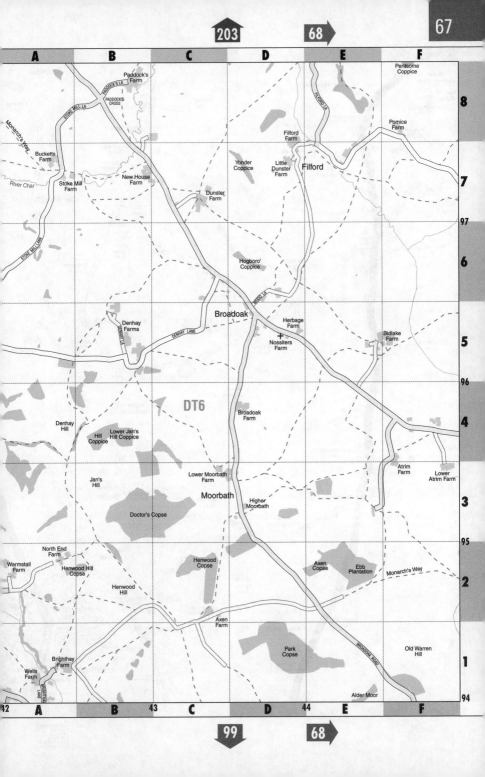

A B C D E F

8

Higher
Kingsland Farm

Kershay
Farms

Nurserymead
Coppice

Long Bottom
Coppice

Salway Ash CE
Prim Sch

Shatcombe
Coppice

Kingsland

B3162

WHITHAY LA

Higher Kershay
Farm

Perhay
Farm

PH

Myrtle
Farm

Waytown

White House
Farm

Way Farm

Oxbridge

Oxbridge
Farm

7

STRONGATE LA

Strongate
Farm

Lower
Kershay Farm

Marlis
Farm

Camesworth

97

Church
Grounds

Brinsham
Farm

Ash
Farm

WHITHAY LANE

Elwell
Lodge

6

Hill
Farm

PH

GALWAY DR
BYGROVE

Pineapple
Bsns Pk

Pineapple
Farm

Salwayash

Higher Ford
Farm

PINEAPPLE LANE

Elwell
Farms

Higher
Elwell
Farm

Snailscroft
Farm

Foxmoor
Coppice

River Brit

5

Broadenham
Farm

Ash Lane
Farm

ASH LANE

Lambrook

Lambrook
Farm

Bingham's
Farm

96

Limbury

Ashleigh
Farm

Ash

Higher
Ash Farm

Seaview
Farm

DT6

Higher
Wooth Farm

4

Atrim

Sewage
Works

3

Colly Farm

Dottery

Higher
Pymore Farm

PYMORE LANE

Lower Ash
Farm

Wooth Old
Farm

Wooth
Farm

Wooth

95

Bilshay
Farm

BILSHAY LANE

WATFORD LANE

Watford
Farm

A3066

2

Monarch's Way

DOTTERY ROAD

Middle
Pymore
Farm

PYMORE ROAD

MORDENS
GROVE
THREAD MILL LA

Factory

PH

THREAD
MILL
LA

Gore Cross
Business Park

GORE
CROSS

GORE LANE

LONGSENG WY

BLIND LANE CR

B3162

1

River Simene

New Close
Farm

Washingpool
Farm

Seymour
Farm

Lower
Pymore
Farm

Pymore

CORBIN WAY

QUEENWELL

RIDGEWAY

The Sir John
Colfox Sch

ST ANDREW'S
ROAD

KNIGHTSTONE RI

River Brit

DODHAM'S LANE

BEAMINSTER ROAD

HILLVIEW

KINGS
WILLIAMS

BANTON
SHARD

VILLAGE

94

45 A **B** 46 **C** **D** 47 **E** **F**

F1
1 FISHWEIR FIELDS
2 ACER AVE
3 WHITE CL
4 SPRING CL
5 GORE CROSS WY
6 BATH ORCHARD

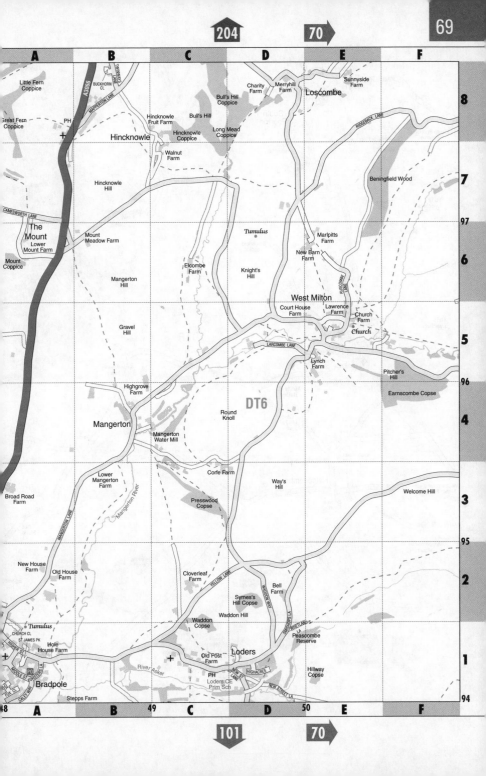

| | A | B | C | D | E | F |

8

RIDGEBACK LANE
South Poorton Farm
Spring Hill Farm
Leggland Farm
Bottom Farm
South Poorton
Lower Long Hay Coppice
Strap's Coppice
Regent's Coppice

South Poorton Reserve
Elmside Coppice
Poorton Hill Farm
Hungry Hill
Caseley's Coppice

7

LIME HILL
Poorton Hill
Strip Lynchets
Swyre Hill
Wytherston Wood

97

Swyre Bottom
Swyre Coppice
Broadfield Coppice
Wytherston Farm

Quarry
Strip Lynchets
Powerstock Common Reserve

6

DUGBERRY HILL

5

Lower Townsend Farm
Townsend Farm
DT6
Whetley
Strip Lynchets
Manor Farm
Glebe Farm
+ Powerstock
Whetley Farm

Powerstock CE Prim Sch
PH
Eastwater Farm
KING'S LANE

96

Merriott
Motte & Bailey
King's Farm

4

PH
Castle Mill Farm

Southmead Farm
THE SQUARE

3

Mappercombe Manor Farm
Browns Farm
Nettlecombe
Marsh Farm
KING'S LANE
Bell Stone

95

Mappercombe Manor
Ridge Copse
Belstone Covert
Warren Plantation

2

Sweed's Copse
Marsh Copse
Chaffins Coppice
Eggardo Hill

Whinhill Copse
Knowle Hill
Knowle Copse
Knowle Plantation

1

Shedbush Copse
DT2
North Eggardon Farm

94

| 51 | A | B | 52 | C | D | 53 | E | F |

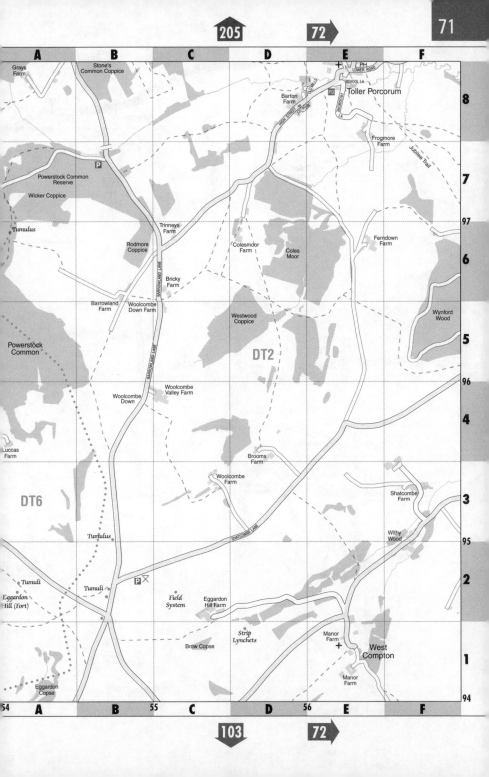

A B C D E F

Grays
Farm

Stone's
Common Coppice

8

+
PH
LOWER ROAD
SCHOOL LA
Toller Porcorum

Barton
Farm

P

Frogmore
Farm

Jubilee Trail

P

7

Powerstock Common
Reserve

Wicker Coppice

97

Tumulus

Trinneys
Farm

Colesmoor
Farm

Coles
Moor

Ferndown
Farm

Rodmore
Coppice

6

Bricky
Farm

BARROWLAND LANE

Barrowland
Farm

Woolcombe
Down Farm

Westwood
Coppice

Wynford
Wood

5

Powerstock
Common

DT2

96

Woolcombe
Down

Woolcombe
Valley Farm

BARROWLAND LANE

4

Luccas
Farm

Brooms
Farm

Shatcombe
Farm

3

DT6

Woolcombe
Farm

SHATCOMBE LANE

Withy
Wood

Tumulus

95

Tumuli

P

Tumuli

Eggardon
Hill (Fort)

Field
System

Eggardon
Hill Farm

Strip
Lynchets

Manor
Farm

2

Brow Copse

+
West
Compton

1

Eggardon
Copse

Manor
Farm

94

71
206

A   B   C   D   E   F

8

7

97

6

5

96

4

95

3

2

1

94

TOLLER LA

River Hooke

Toller Fratrum Farm

Toller Fratrum

A356

Station Road Ind Est

MANOR FARM CL

STATION RD

Greenford CE Prim Sch

CHILFROME LANE

GREENFORD LANE

CHAPEL LANE

Cem

Tollerford

PH

WHITEHORSE MWS

BACK LANE

FROME LANE

KINGSLEY PADDOCK

Beacon Farm

Blanchard's Plantation

Frome Vauchurch

Frome Vauchurch Farm

Chammen's Hill

Jubilee Trail

Wynford Wood

Fore Hill Plantation

Thistle Farm

DT2

Manor Farm

Wynford Eagle

GREENFORD LANE

Tumulus

Brookside Farm

Wynford House

Round Hill Plantations

Greenford Farm

Winholes Coppice

Winholes Plantation

Jubilee Trail

Notton Hill Barn

Soapers Hill Plantation

Macmillan Way

71
104

Maiden Newton

Maiden
Newton

Fore
Hill

Maiden
Newton
Coppice

Parson's
Coppice

Hog Cliff
National
Nature Reserve

Park
Coppice

Strip
Lynchets

Langcombe
Bottom

Sewage
Works

Hogcliff
Farm

South
Field Hill

River
Frome

Macmillan Way

DORCHESTER ROAD

SKILLING LANE

Hog Cliff National
Nature Reserve

Hog Cliff
Bottom

Hog Cliff
Hill

Tumulus

Hog Cliff
National
Nature Reserve

South
Field Down

A37

LONG ASH LANE

Cruxton

Chalkhams
Plantation

DT2

Hyde Crook
House

A356

Crockway
Farm

LC

Notton
Farm

Notton

Notton
Valley
Farm

Notton
Bottom

Nunnery Mead
Reserve

Throop Dairy
House

Hyde
Farm

DORCHESTER ROAD

Coler's
Plantation

CHURCH LANE

Frampton

NORTH
SHERIDAN CL
BARNES
P.

Gayden
Coppice

River Frome

A356

Notton
Down

Southover
Farm

Blind Walk
Plantation

Southover

Lanchards
Plantation

West
End

Frampton
House

Southover
Bottom

Southover
Bottom

Lambert's
Plantation

P

Metland's Wood

Littlewood
Farm

Longlands
Farm

Steppes Farm

8
7
97
6
5
96
4
3
95
2
1
94

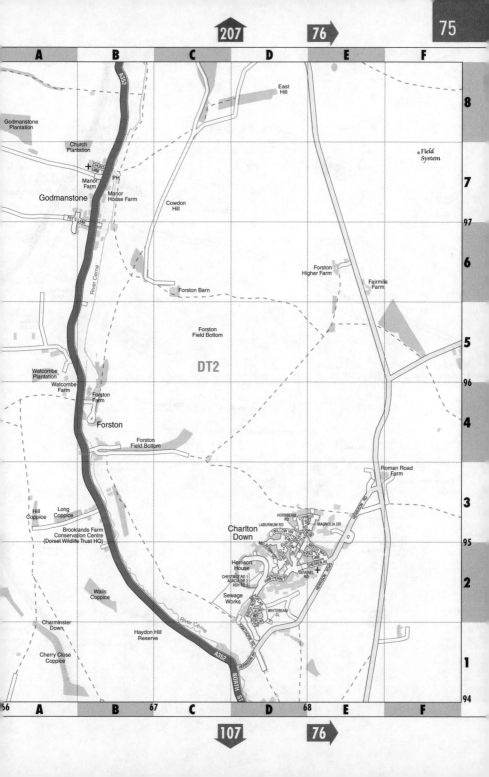

Godmanstone Plantation

Church Plantation

CHURCH LANE

Manor Farm

PH

Godmanstone

Manor House Farm

FRY'S LANE

River Cerne

East Hill

Field System

Cowdon Hill

Forston Barn

Forston Higher Farm

Fairmile Farm

Forston Field Bottom

DT2

Watcombe Plantation

Watcombe Farm

Forston Farm

Forston

Forston Field Bottom

Roman Road Farm

Hill Coppice

Long Coppice

Brooklands Farm Conservation Centre (Dorset Wildlife Trust HQ)

Charlton Down

HORNBEAM RD
CYPRESS RD
LABURNUM RD
MAGNOLIA DR
WILLOW VW
BEECH WAY
SHERREN AV

Herrison House

CHESTNUT RD 1
ACACIA DR 2
ASH RD 3

HAWTHORN RD

DEVEREL RD

Walls Coppice

Sewage Works

WHITEBEAM CL

POPLAR DR

Charminster Down

Cherry Close Coppice

Haydon Hill Reserve

River Cerne

A352

NORTH ST

HERRISON ROAD

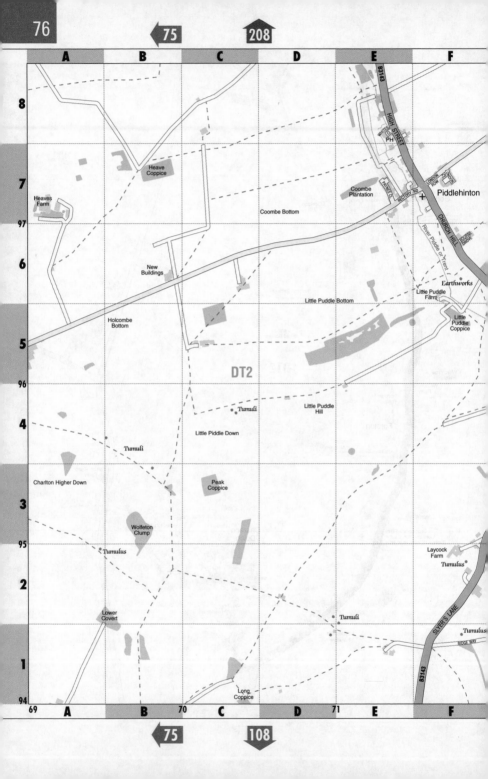

A B C D E F

8

7

Heaves Farm

Heave Coppice

97

Coombe Bottom

Coombe Plantation

HIGH STREET

B3143

WHITECROSS

PH

PANNERS LN

RECTORY RD

Piddlehinton

LONDON ROW

CHURCH HILL

6

New Buildings

River Piddle or Trent

BOURNE DROVE

Earthworks

Little Puddle Farm

Holcombe Bottom

Little Puddle Bottom

Little Puddle Coppice

5

DT2

96

Tumuli

Little Puddle Hill

4

Little Piddle Down

Tumuli

Charlton Higher Down

Peak Coppice

3

Wolfeton Clump

95

Tumulus

Laycock Farm

Tumulus

2

SILVER'S LANE

Lower Covert

Tumuli

Tumulus

RIDGE WAY

1

B3143

Long Coppice

94

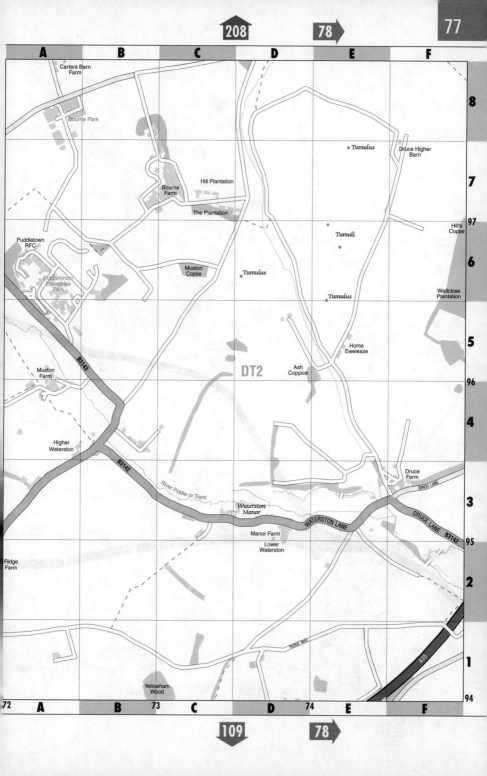

← 77
209

A **B** **C** **D** **E** **F**

8

Tumuli

Hazel
Copse

Shailes
Copse

Park Hill

Dewlish House

7
Puddletown
Down

97

Hill's
Copse

Warren
Plantation

Lower
Farm

JOCK'S HILL

Crawthorne
Farm

Devil's Brook

6

WARREN ROAD

WARREN HILL

Warren Hill
Farm

Wreden
Plantation

DT2

Basan
Plantation

Basan Hill

Fryer's
Bridge

Tumuli

5

96

BASAN HILL

Burleston
Down

4

BIRCH LANE

LONG LANE

WARREN ROAD

ATHELHAMPTON ROAD

Bardolf
Manor

Burleston
Plantation

3

A354

B3142

Druce Lane
Northbrook

Stafford
Park Farm

Hill Top

Home
Farm

A35

95

2

A35

DRUCE LANE

Bardolfeston
Village

BURLESTON DROVE

River Piddle or Trent

THOMPSON

1

Puddletown

Puddletown CE
First Sch

St Mary's CE
Middle Sch

Libr

Ilsington House

MILOM LANE

Little Knoll
Copse

Henroost
Wood

Athelhampton
House & Gardens

Athelhampton

ATHELHAMPTON ROAD

West
End

Burleston

94

75 **A** **76** **B** **C** **77** **D** **E** **F**

← 77
110 ↓

B1
1 BELLBURY CL
2 ASH TREE CL
3 WILLOUGHBY CL
4 BRYMER RD
5 WHITE HILL
6 CHAPEL VIEW

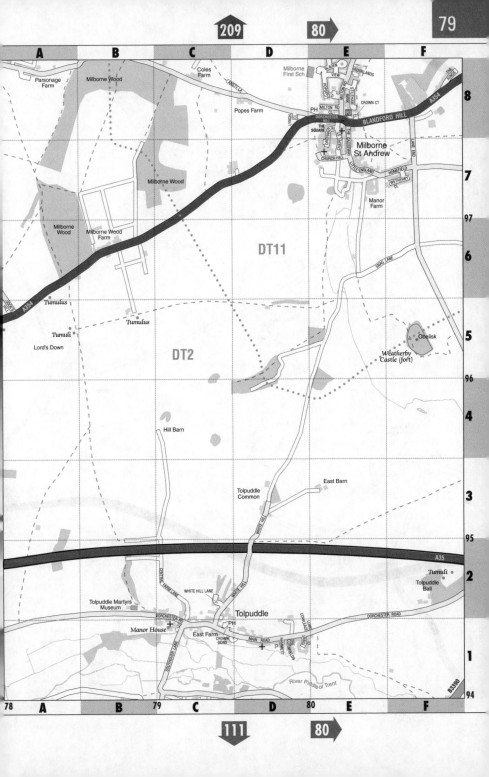

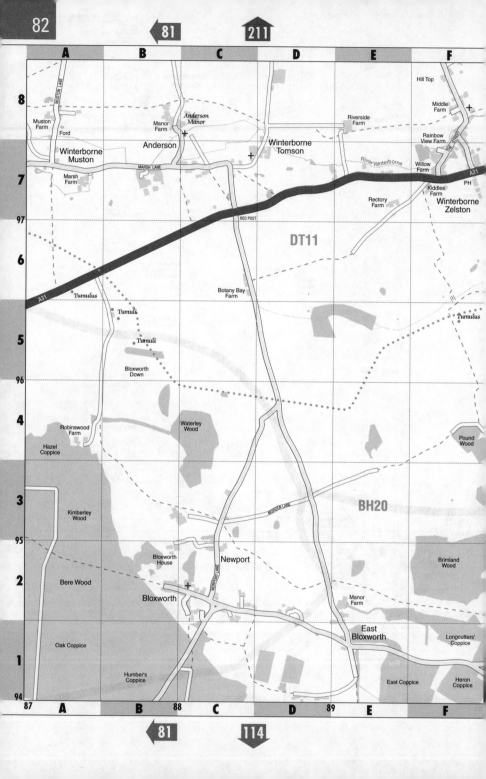

Charborough Park

High Wood

Windmill Barrow Farm

Dullar Wood

West Wood

West Wood

Fox Holes Wood

Limekiln Coppice

Heron Grove

Windmill Barrow

BH21

Combe Almer

POOLE ROAD

A350

Higher Coombe Farm

Notting Hill

OLD MARKET RD

Brock Hill

Loop Farm

Village Earthworks

Sandpits Farm

Bokers Farm

DULLAR LANE

Winter's Coppice

Castle Hill

Warmwell Farm

CASTLE FARM ROAD

FLOWERS DROVE

A350

White Heather

CRUMBLERS CL

COLEHILL ROAD

Goat House Farm

BH16

Barrow Hill

Lytchett House

Garden Wood

Dyett's Coppice

Phillips's Coppice

Allots

Sunnyside Farm

Dowdens Farm

WIMBORNE ROAD

Bridge End

PEATONS LANE

HIGH STREET

HOOMANS

Lytchett Matravers

North House Farm

Elder Moor

Peatons Farm

JENNYS LANE

PH

Ash Farm

Druce Farm

Eddy Green Farm

Libby

HIGH STREET

ABBOTTS MEADOW

PH

HUNTICK ROAD

Redbridge Farm

OLD POUND CLOSE

Vineyard Cl

Recn Gd

HUNTICK ESTATE

Foxhills Farm

GYPSY LA

Bartom's Hill

MIDDLE ROAD

PALMERS DR

Lytchett Matravers Prim Sch

1 FOSTERS SPRING
2 PRYORS WK
3 LANDERS REACH

Huntick Farm

Holly Farm

BARTOM'S LANE

DEANS DROVE

Race Farm

DOLMANS HILL

Quarr Farm

QUARR LA

Quarr Hill Farm

GLEBE ROAD

FOXHILLS ROAD

H Bulbury Farm

BILBURY LA

HALLS DNR

HALLS ROAD

CASTLE DW DR

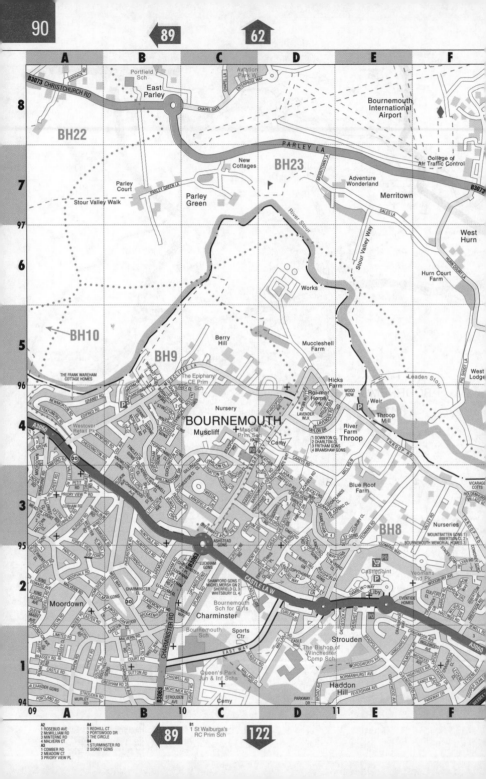

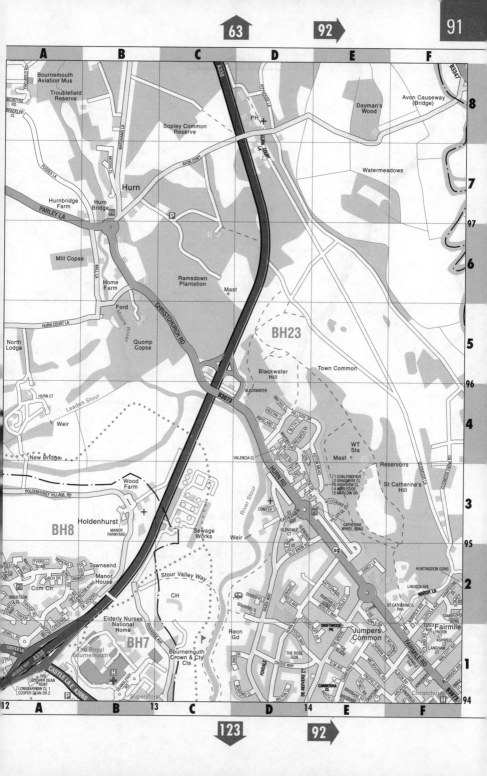

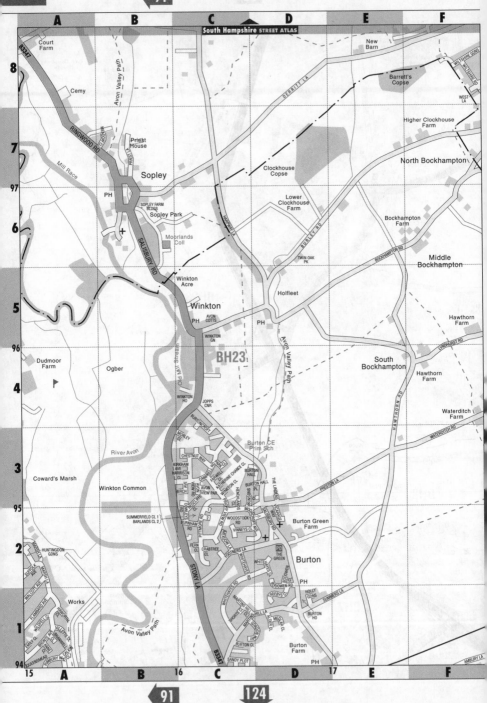

South Hampshire STREET ATLAS

A B C D E F

Court Farm

New Barn

WILTSHIRE GDNS

WILTSHIRE

Barrett's Copse

8

Cemy

WEST LA

Higher Clockhouse Farm

Avon Valley Path

RINGWOOD RD

Mill Race

7

Priest House

Sopley

North Bockhampton

Clockhouse Copse

SALISBURY RD

PH

97

SOPLEY FARM BLDGS

Sopley Park

Lower Clockhouse Farm

Bockhampton Farm

6

Moorlands Coll

BURLEY RD

BOCKHAMPTON RD

Middle Bockhampton

Winkton Acre

TWIN OAK PK

Holfleet

5

Winkton

PH

AVON GOTTS

PH

Hawthorn Farm

Old Mill Stream

96

WINKTON GN

BH23

Avon Valley Path

LYNDHURST RD

Dudmoor Farm

Ogber

South Bockhampton

Hawthorn Farm

HAWTHORN RD

4

WINKTON HO

JOPPS CNR

Waterditch Farm

WATERDITCH RD

BURTON RD

River Avon

MERLEY CL

Burton CE Prim Sch

3

Coward's Marsh

CHESTNUT BSH

KIRKHAM AVE

HARRISON CL

CARNELL RD

HEYWEL L

CATHERINE CHARKE CL

WINKTON CL

BINGHAM RD

Burton Hall

Burton Hall

PRESTON LA

THE LINDENS

Winkton Common

AVE BIRCH

AVON VIEW PK

HENGIST GDNS

ACACIA CL

95

SUMMERFIELD CL 1

BARLANDS CL 2

BURNHAM RD

LITTLE CL

WOODSTOCK RD

VINNEYS CL

Burton Green Farm

2

Huntingdon Gdns

SURREY AVE

MARSH LA

LAMBROOK RD

FERN CL

CRABTREE CL

JOYNERS LA

WHITTLES WAY

WHITE CL

DOWER CL

THE GREEN

Burton

PH

Works

HOLLY GDNS

SUMMERS LA

Burton Ho

1

Avon Valley Path

STONY LA

WHITEORCHARD RD

MARTINS HILL LA

SHORT CL

SHELLEY CL

MEAD CL

Burton Farm

PH

B3347

BURTON CL

SANDY PLOT

94

AMBURY LA

15 A B 16 C D 17 E F

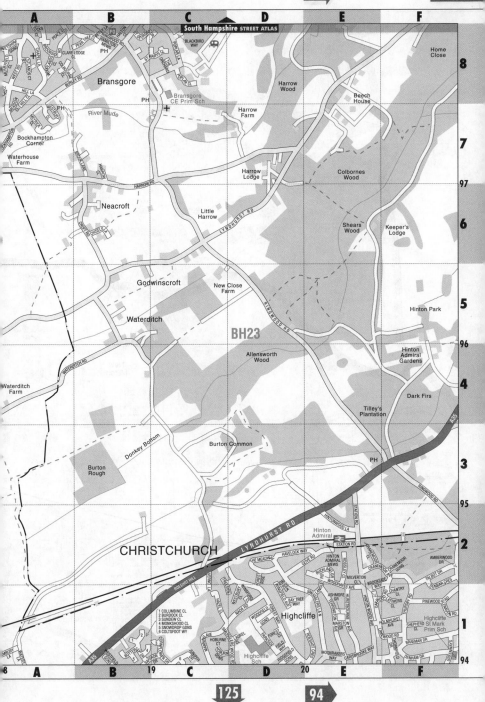

South Hampshire STREET ATLAS

127

A1		A3	B1	B2	B3	F3
1 KEATS HO	9 SHELLEY CL	1 HEATHER LO	1 HAZEL CT	1 SPENCER CT	1 TANGLEWOOD CT	1 WOODLANDS
2 SHENSTONE CT	10 BYRON HO	2 VINCENT CL	2 ST DENYS	2 ORCHARD LEIGH	2 ALVANO GDNS	2 KINGS BROOK
3 CLIFTON CT	A2	3 CHARLOTTE CT	3 DUDLEY PL	3 CORNERWAYS CT	3 ASHTON CT	
4 WINSTON CT	1 VINCENT RD	4 BURSLEDON HO	4 CHERRY TREE CT	4 JACMAR CT	4 MORANT CT	
5 SOLENT LO	2 VINCENT CL	5 ELM CT	5 YEW TREE CT	5 ASHLEY ARNEWOOD CT	5 TREVONE	
6 WINSTON PAR	3 CHARLOTTE CT	6 CASSELLES CT	6 GREENWOODS	6 YEOMANS LODGE	6 FREMINGTON CT	
7 BOUVERIE CL	4 BURSLEDON HO	7 HOMEFIELD HO		7 WESTCROFT PAR	7 YORK PL	
8 EDMUNDS CL	5 ELM CT	8 MALLARD BLDGS		8 ELIZABETH CT	8 FAIRCOURT	
9 BARTON COURT AVE	6 CASSELLES CT			9 WAVERLEY HO	9 MERLEWOOD CT	
10 SPINDLEWOOD CL	7 HOMEFIELD HO				B3	
	8 ELIOT HO				10 CONWAY CT	
	9 PEGASUS CT				11 STIRLING CT	
	10 BEAU CT				12 BLUEBELL GDNS	

Devon Street Atlas

LYME REGIS

Lyme   Bay

Poker's Pool

DT7

DT6

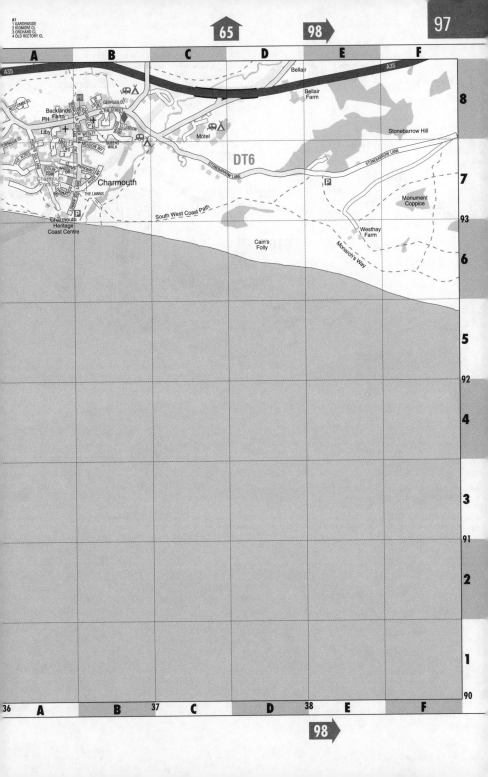

97
66

97

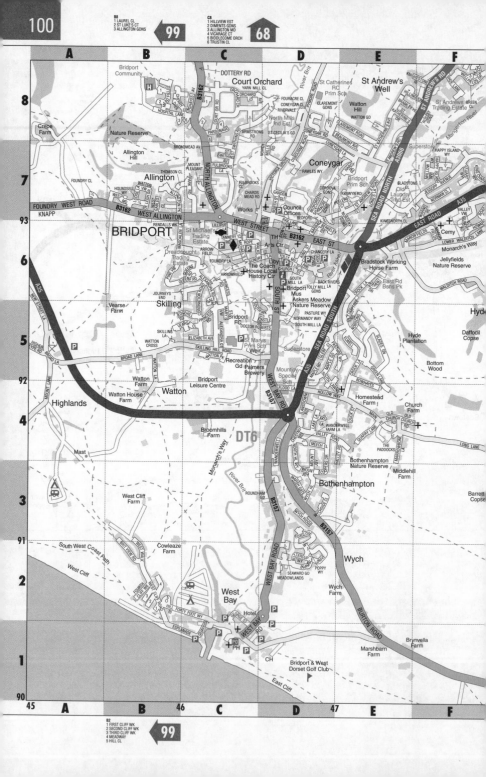

101
70

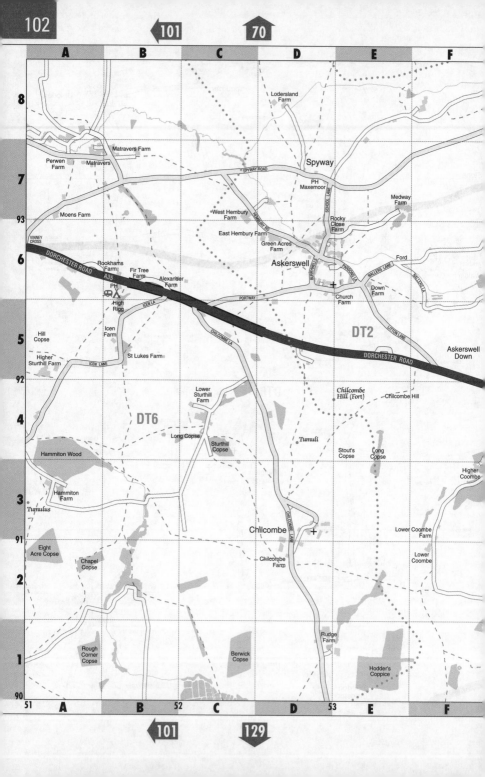

101
129

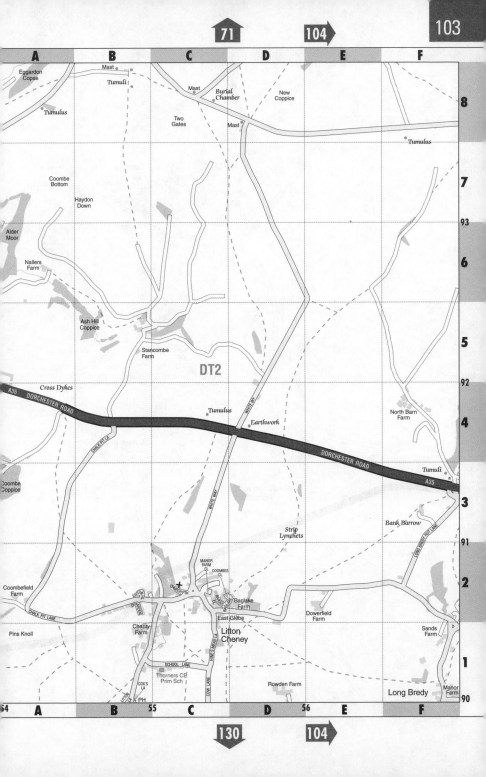

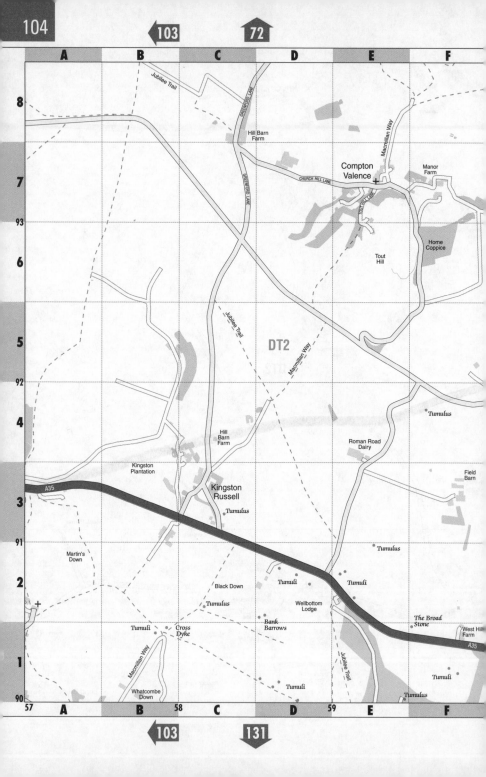

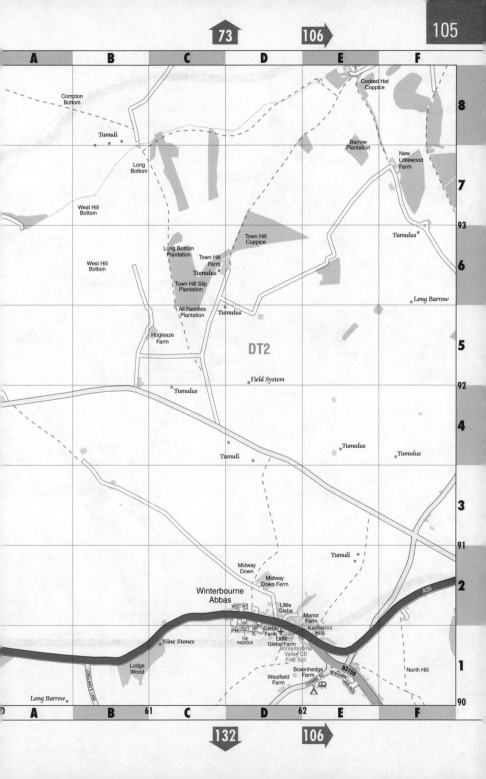

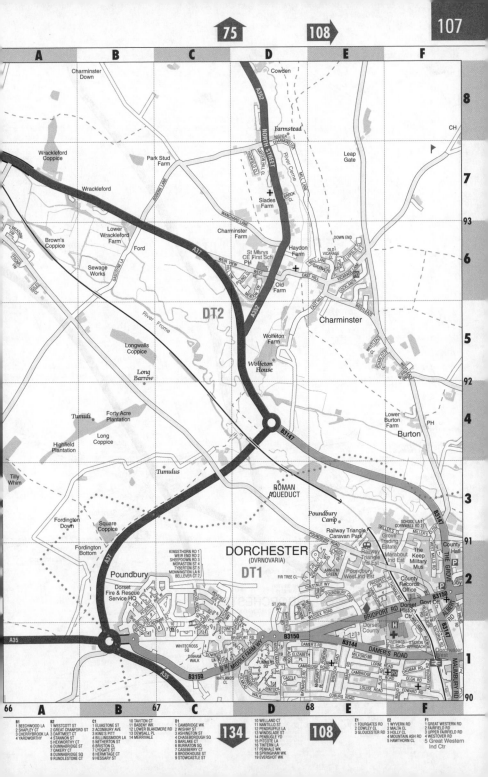

Charminster Down

Charminster

Wrackleford Coppice

Wrackleford

Brown's Coppice

Lower Wrackleford Farm

Park Stud Farm

Farmstead

Cowden

Leap Gate

CH

Ford

Sewage Works

MEADOW VW

Slades Farm

Charminster Farm

St Marys CE First Sch PH

Haydon Farm

Old Vicarage

Down End

DT2

River Frome

Longwalls Coppice

Long Barrow

Old Farm

Wolfeton Farm

Charminster

Wolfeton House

Lower Burton Farm

PH

Burton

Tumuli

Forty Acre Plantation

Highfield Plantation

Long Coppice

Tumulus

B3147

Tilly Whim

Fordington Down

Square Coppice

Fordington Bottom

ROMAN AQUEDUCT

Poundbury Camp

Railway Triangle Caravan Park

School La 1 Cornwall Rd 2

Grove Trading Estate

Marabout Ind Est

The Keep Military Mus

County Hall

A35

Poundbury

Dorset Fire & Rescue Service HQ

KINGSTHORN RD 1
WEIR END RD 2
SHEEPDOWN RD 3
MORASTON ST 4
TYBERTON ST 5
MONNINGTON LA 6
BELLEVER CT 7

DORCHESTER
(DVRNOVARIA)

DT1

Railway Triangle Ind Est

Poundbury West Ind Est

Dorset County

County Records Office

Dorset History Ctr

Govt Off

B3150

Whitecross SQ

Dinham Walk

Haylands

B3150

Middle Farm Wy

Bridport Rd

Summers

Damers Rd

B3144

Damers First Sch

Station Approach

Dorchester West

Damer's Road

A35

B3150

Cambridge Road

Coburg Road

Louise Road

Maud Road

Edward Rd

Dagmar Rd

Olga Rd

Maumbury Rd

66   A   67   B   C   68   D   E   F   90

A1
1 WEST WALKS RD
2 NEW ST
3 CROMWELL RD
4 FAIRFIELD RD
5 UPPER FAIRFIELD RD

A2
1 NORTHERNHAY
2 NORTH SQ
3 THE BOW
4 ALINGTON ST
5 CHURCH ST
6 ACLAND RD
7 ANTELOPE WK
8 ALEXANDRA TERR

9 The Tutankhamun Exhibition & The Mummies Exhibition

107

B1
1 EARL CL
2 ATHELSTAN RD
3 FORDINGTON GDNS
4 SYDENHAM WAY
5 BARNES WAY
6 CULLIFORD RD NTH

135

B2
1 LONDON CL
2 POUND LANE
3 CHURCH ACRE
4 CHANNONS CT
5 FORDINGTON GN
6 ALINGTON TERR

C1
1 ALINGTON AVE
2 SANDRINGHAM CT
3 Jonson Trad Pk

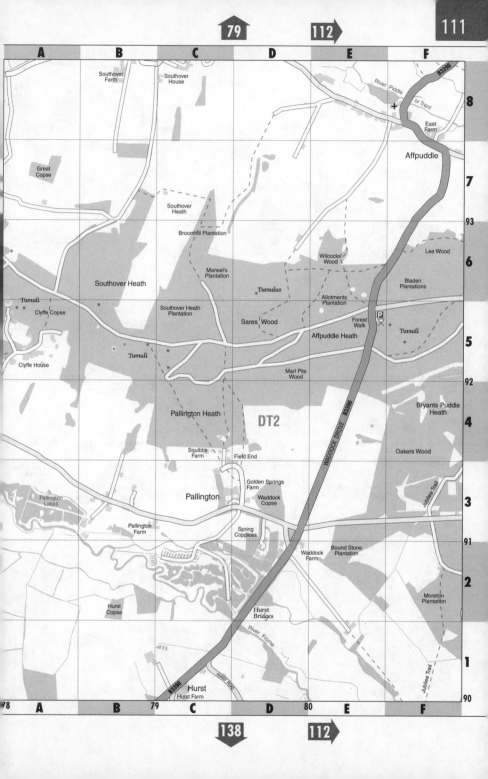

111
80

A B C D E F

8
7
93
6
5
92
4
3
91
2
1
90

81 82 83

Spring Garden Coppice
Tumulus
Sand and Gravel Pits
Damerhill Coppice
Turners Puddle
Jubilee Trail
Turnerspuddle Farm
River Puddle or Trent
Throop
Throop Farm
Landshare Coppice
Cecily Bridge
Brockhill Coppice
Brockhill Fish Farm
Briantspuddle
Jubilee Trail
Bladen Plantations
Battle Farm
Eweleaze Coppice
Bladen Valley
Bryants Puddle Allotments Plantation
Smokeham Bottom
DT2
THE HOLLOW
THROOP HOLLOW
Cull Peppers Dish
Tumuli
Longcroft Coppice
Tumulus
Tumulus
Bryants Puddle Heath
Rimsmoor Pond
Oakers Wood
Jubilee Trail
Throop Heath
Tumulus
Tumulus
Millicent's Plantation
DANGER AREA
BH20
Okers Wood House
Moreton Plantation
Tonerspuddle Heath
Chamberlayne's Heath
East Plantation
Round Barrow
91
IVERTON DR
Clouds Hill (Lawrence of Arabia's Cottage)
Moreton Plantation
Tank Training Area
90

111
139

A35

A **B** **C** **D** **E** **F**

Little Wood
Sand and
Gravel Pits

Rye Hill
Farm

Spear's
Coppice

Lower
Hove Wood

Hundred
Barrow

Hollow
Oak

Mate's
Coppice

Lower
Woodbury
Farm

8

DT2

Hundred
Barrow Farm

Dodding's
Farm
Ford

Bedlam

SUGAR HILL

Yearlings
Bottom

7

Heath
View

End
Barrow

Jenkins
Farm

Lockyer's Hill

93

Yearlings
Poultry
Farm

Snatford
Bridge

Don Barrow

Little
Coppice

+

Bere
Heath

Bere Heath

6

Lane End
Farm

Lane End

Bere Heath
Farm

Chamberlayne's
Farm

Culeaze
Farm

Culeaze
House

Tanpits
Coppice

Tumulus

BH20

Philliols
Heath

5

Culeaze
Coppice

Pickard's
Coppice

92

Warren
Farm

Lower Stockley
Farm

4

Warren Heath

Warren

Philliols Farm

3

Tumulus

Tumulus

Philliols
Coppice

91

Gallows
Hill

Hyde Woods

Woodlands

Hanging
Covert

Hyde
Farm

2

Bere Heath

Skinner's
Coppice

Weir

Dorset
Gliding
Club

Higher Hyde Heath
Reserve

Heather
Lodge

1

PUDDLETOWN ROAD

90

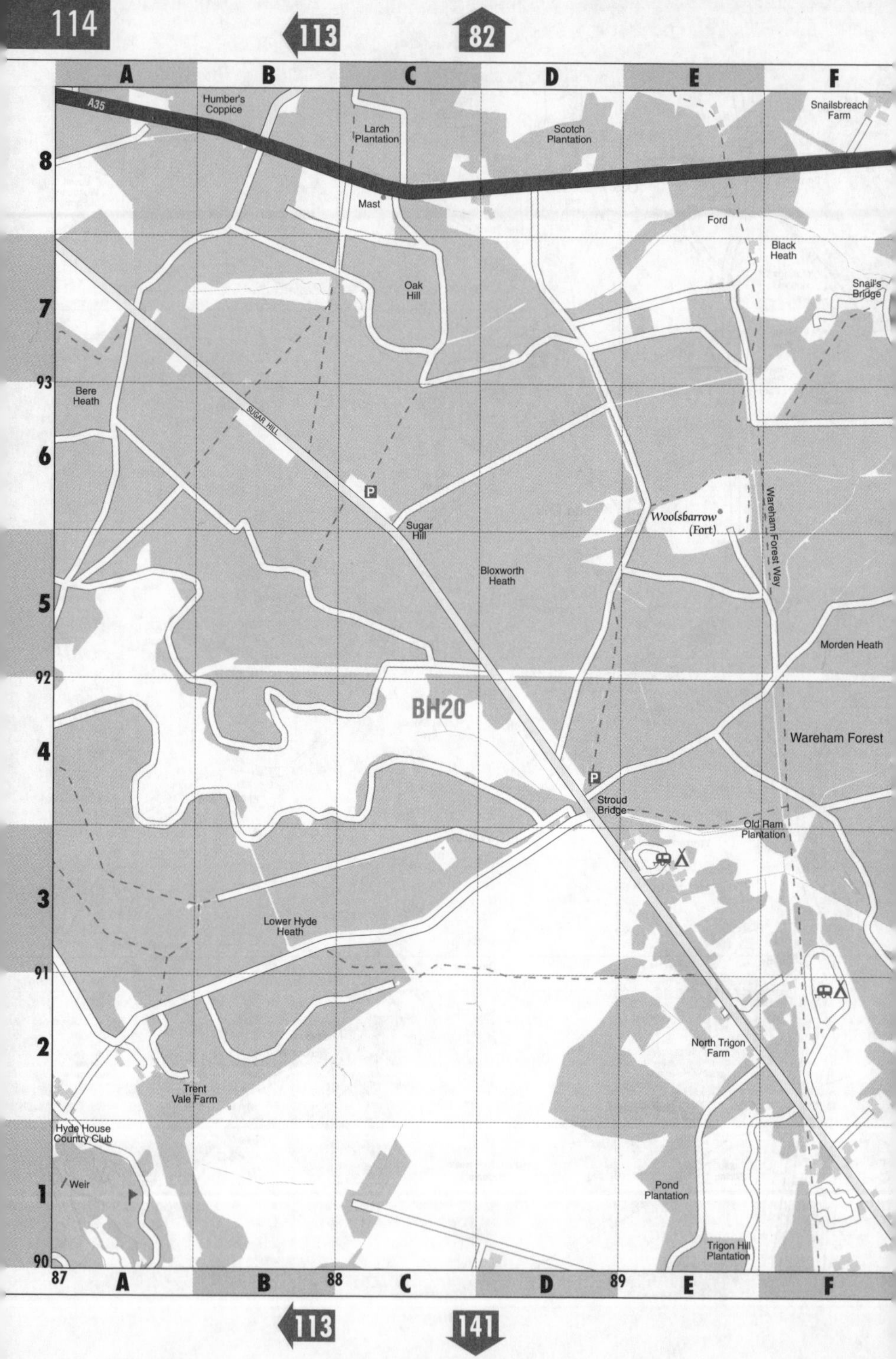

113
82

A B C D E F

A35
Humber's Coppice
Snailsbreach Farm
Larch Plantation
Scotch Plantation
8
Mast
Ford
Black Heath
Snail's Bridge
7
Oak Hill
93
Bere Heath
SUGAR HILL
6
P
Sugar Hill
Woolsbarrow (Fort)
Wareham Forest Way
Bloxworth Heath
5
Morden Heath
92
BH20
Wareham Forest
4
P
Stroud Bridge
Old Ram Plantation
3
Lower Hyde Heath
91
North Trigon Farm
2
Trent Vale Farm
Hyde House Country Club
/ Weir
1
Pond Plantation
Trigon Hill Plantation
90
87 A B 88 C D 89 E F

115

84

A B C D E F

8

Shot Lake Wood

Hill Wood

Post Green Farm

Lytchett Minster Sch

Bere Farm

7

A35

Newton Farm

Post Green

Post Green Road

New Road

93

Pike's Farm

French's Coppice

Cuzenage Coppice

Hill Farm

Lytchett Minster

OLD FORGE CL

ORCHARD CL

B3067

6

Charity Farm

PH

Organford

Farmer Palmer's Farm Park

King's Bridge

A35

Higher Wood

King's Bridge Coppice

5

Lower Wood

Organford Bridge

Sherford River

BH16

A351

92

Youngs Farm

Heatherdene

Holton Heath

4

Gore Heath

WAREHAM ROAD

Pear Tree Farm

Heath View

FIR AVE

PH

Holton Heath National Nature Reserve

3

Holton Heath

CHESTNUT AVE

MEADOW

OAK AVE

ASH AVE

ELM AVE

SYCAMORE PARK DRIVE

BIRCH

BEECH AVE

LARCH AVE

BLACKHILL ROAD

St Martin's Hill

BLACKHILL ROAD

HOLTON RD

91

Rustlings Farm

Black Hill

Sandford House

SANDFORD DRIVE

Holton Heath Industrial Estate

2

BH20

SANDFORD ROAD

STATION RD

HOLTON ROAD

Holton Heath

A351

1

Sandford Middle Sch

STATION ROAD

LC Holton Heath

90

A351

93 A 94 B C 94 D 95 E F

A1
1 LABURNUM CL
2 HOLLY CL
3 ALDER CL

115

143

85 118 144 118

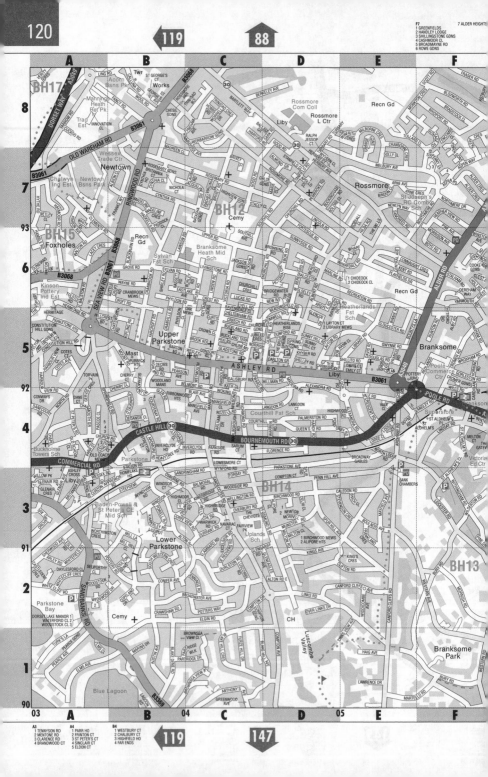

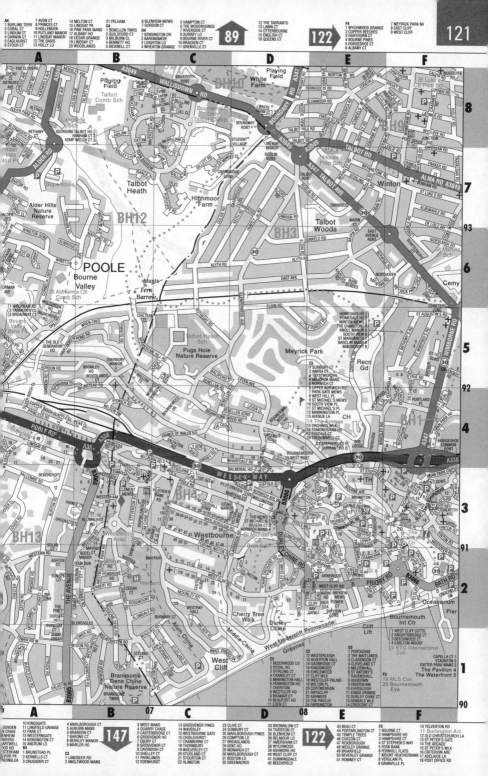

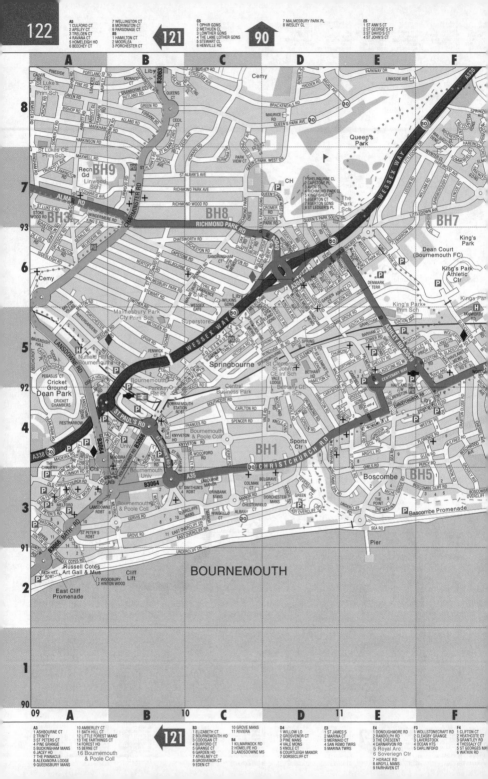

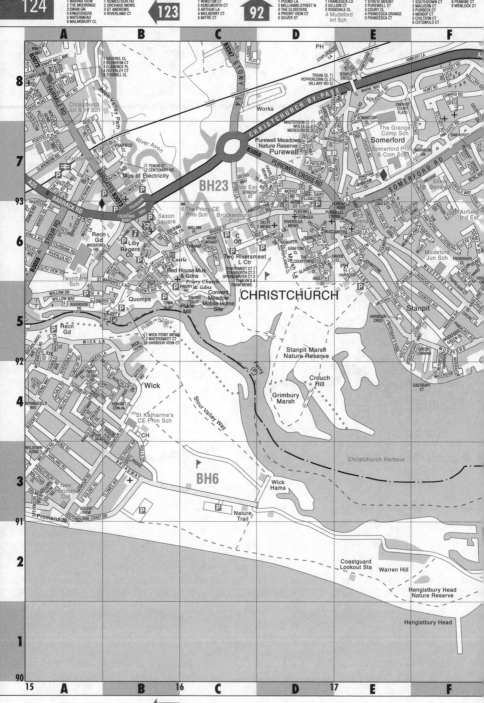

123

92

A5
1 MARINA VIEW
2 THE MOORINGS
3 SWAN GN
4 KINGFISHERS
5 WATERMEAD
6 MALMSBURY CL

A6
1 HOMESTOUR HO
2 ORCHARD MEWS
3 ST ANDREWS
4 RIVERLAND CT

A7
1 WINSTON CT
2 KENILWORTH CT
3 ARTHUR LA
4 MULBERRY CT
5 MITRE CT

B6
1 POUND LA
2 MILLHAMS STREET N
3 THE CLOISTERS
4 PRIORY VIEW CT
5 SILVER ST

E6
1 FRANCESCA LO
2 GILLION CT
3 ROSEDALE CL
4 Mudeford Inf Sch

E7
1 STRETE MOUNT
2 PUREWELL CT
3 COURT CL
4 FRANCESCA GRANGE
5 FRANCESCA CT

F6
1 SOUTHDOWN CT
2 MALVERN CT
3 PURBECK CT
4 MENDIP CT
5 CHILTERN CT
6 COTSWOLD CT

F7
1 QUANTOCK CT
2 PENNINE CT
3 WENLOCK CT

Groynes

A7
1 BUCKINGHAM CT
2 CASTLE CT
3 WINDSOR CT
4 HURST CT
5 BERMUDA CT
6 CLAIRE CT
7 DIANA CT
8 TRACEY CT

B7
1 CARISBROOKE CT
2 MERTON CT
3 BALMORAL CT
4 PEMBROKE CT
5 EXETER CT
6 HERTFORD CT
7 FRANCES CT
8 ROSEMARY CT
9 KENNETH CT
10 ALAN CT
11 WILLIAM CT
12 PENELOPE CT
13 STELLA CT

Barton on Sea

8

7

93

6

92

5

4

3

91

2

1

90

A   B   C   D   E   F

Barton Common

BH25

CH

1 LYNRIC CL
2 WHITE KNIGHTS
3 HIGH MARRYATS
4 DOLPHIN PL
5 ALDBURY CT
6 GROVE GDNS
7 MARINERS REACH
8 SECOND MARINE AVE
9 GAINSBOROUGH HO

Barton
Common

Barton Cliff

Becton Bunny

MILFORD RD

Angel
Cottage

ANGEL LA

HOME
FARM

Ashley
Clinton
House

Ashley
Bridge

A337 LYMINGTON RD

CHRISTCHURCH RD   A337 Lymington

PH

Downton

SO41

Hordle
Bridge

Taddiford
Farm

Dales Stream

Hordle Manor
Farm

B3058   CLIFF RD

WHATELY
RD

Christchurch Bay

Durlston Court
Sch

South Hampshire STREET ATLAS

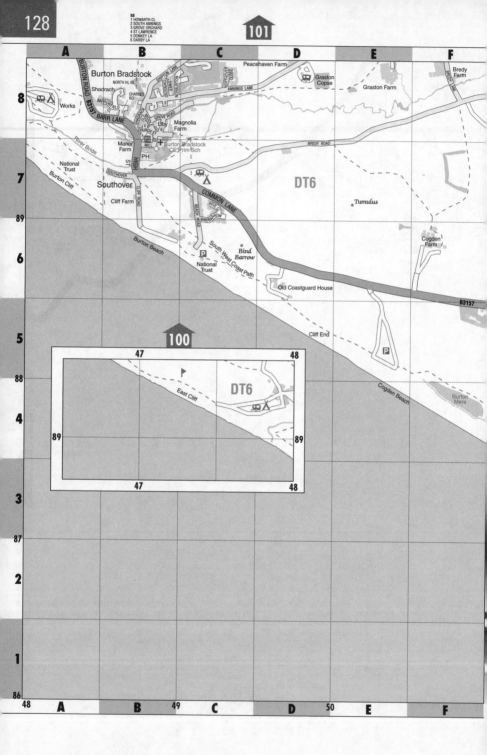

101

B8
1 HOWARTH CL
2 SOUTH ANNINGS
3 GROVE ORCHARD
4 ST LAWRENCE
5 DONKEY LA
6 DARBY LA

Burton Bradstock

Peacehaven Farm

Graston Copse

Graston Farm

Bredy Farm

Works

Shadrach

NORTH HL DR

CHARLES RD

Libby

Magnolia Farm

BREDY ROAD

DT6

Manor Farm

PH

Burton Bradstock CE Prim Sch

National Trust

Southover

Cliff Farm

Tumulus

Cogden Farm

Burton Cliff

Burton Beach

COMMON LANE

BEACH ROAD

Bind Barrow

South West Coast Path

National Trust

Old Coastguard House

Cliff End

B3157

100

47

48

East Cliff

DT6

89

89

Cogden Beach

Burton Mere

47

48

48

49

50

86

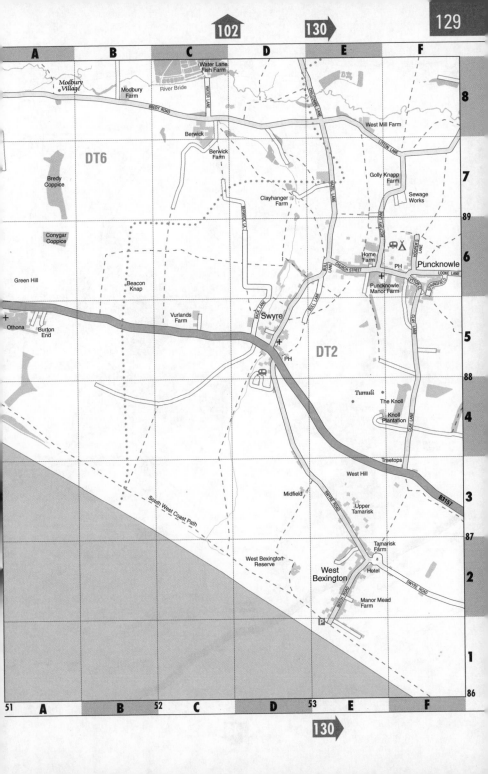

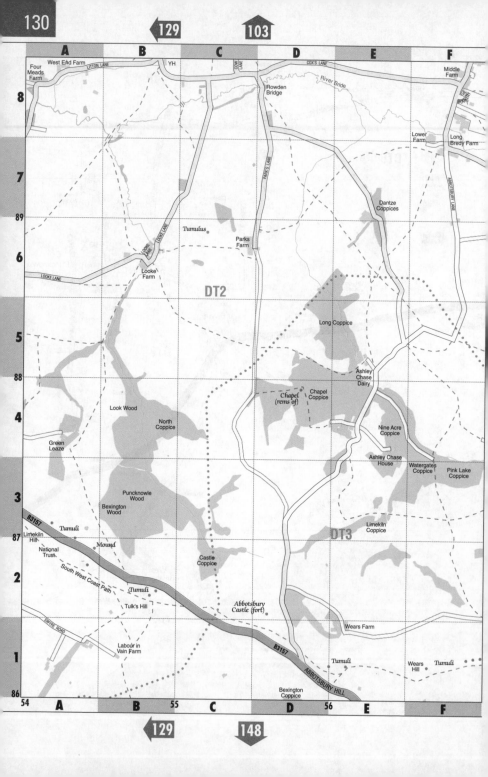

129
103

Four
Meads
Farm
West End Farm
LITTON LANE
YH
COW LANE
COX'S LANE
River Bride
Middle
Farm
Rowden
Bridge
Lower
Farm
Long
Bredy Farm
PARKS LANE
ABBOTSBURY LANE

8

7

89

Tumulus
Parks
Farm
Dantze
Coppices

6

LOOKE LANE
Looke
Farm
LOOKE LANE

DT2

Long Coppice

5

88

Ashley
Chase
Dairy

4

Look Wood
North
Coppice
Chapel
(rems of)
Chapel
Coppice
Nine Acre
Coppice

Green
Leaze
Ashley Chase
House
Watergates
Coppice
Pink Lake
Coppice

3

Puncknowle
Wood
Bexington
Wood
Limekiln
Coppice

B3157
Tumuli
DT3

87

Limekiln
Hill
National
Trust
Mound

2

South West Coast Path
Tumuli
Castle
Coppice

Tulk's Hill
Abbotsbury
Castle (fort)
Wears Farm

SWYRE ROAD
B3157

1

Labour in
Vain Farm
ABBOTSBURY HILL
Tumuli
Wears
Hill
Tumuli

86

Bexington
Coppice

54
55
56

129
148

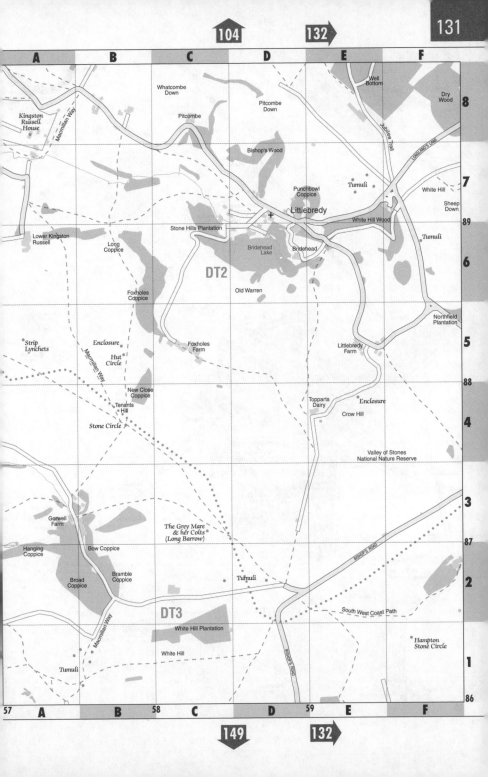

A B C D E F

8

Well Bottom

Dry Wood

Whatcombe Down

Pitcombe

Pitcombe Down

Kingston Russell House

Macmillan Way

Bishop's Wood

Jubilee Trail

LONGLANDS LANE

7

Punchbowl Coppice

Tumuli

White Hill

Littlebredy

Sheep Down

89

Lower Kingston Russell

Stone Hills Plantation

White Hill Wood

Tumuli

Long Coppice

Bridehead Lake

Bridehead

6

DT2

Foxholes Coppice

Old Warren

Northfield Plantation

Strip Lynchets

Enclosure

Foxholes Farm

Littlebredy Farm

5

Macmillan Way

Hut Circle

88

New Close Coppice

Topparts Dairy

Enclosure

Tenants Hill

Crow Hill

Stone Circle

4

Valley of Stones National Nature Reserve

Gorwell Farm

3

The Grey Mare & her Colts (Long Barrow)

87

Hanging Coppice

Bow Coppice

BISHOP'S ROAD

Broad Coppice

Bramble Coppice

Tumuli

2

DT3

South West Coast Path

White Hill Plantation

Hampton Stone Circle

Macmillan Way

White Hill

BISHOP'S ROAD

1

Tumuli

86

A B C D E F

	A	B	C	D	E	F

Longlands

Tumuli

Dry Wood

8

LONGLAND'S LANE

Big Wood

Tumulus

Coombe Farm

COOMBE ROAD

Strip Lynchets

Steepleton Farm

Greater Whitway Farm

B3159

Manor Farm

Winterbourne Steepleton

Loscombe Plantation

Jubilee Trail

7

Loscombe Farm

Loscombe Down

Tumulus

Dairy

Mast

89

Sheep Down

COOMBE ROAD

Loscombe Wood

Tumulus

6

Tumuli

DT2

Tumulus

Ballarat Farm

Long Barrow

Conygar Meadow Coppice

East Rew Farm

5

Enclosure

Jubilee Trail

Tumulus

88

Tumuli

Goldcombe Farm

4

Black Down

Tumuli

South West Coast Path

P Hardy Monument

Black Down Plantation

Tumuli

Tumulus

BISHOP'S ROAD

Hardy Coppice

Tumuli

Bronkham Hill

3

Portesham Hill

Benecke Wood

Tumuli

87

South West Coast Path

Hell Stone (Long Barrow)

Wig Plantation

Jubilee Trail

Tumuli

2

Tumuli

DT3

Hell Bottom Quarry (disused)

Bench

Hell Bottom

1

HAMPTON
FRONT ST
BACK
PORTESHAM HILL
HELSTON

Portesham

Portesham Farm

86

60

61

62

A	B	C	D	E	F

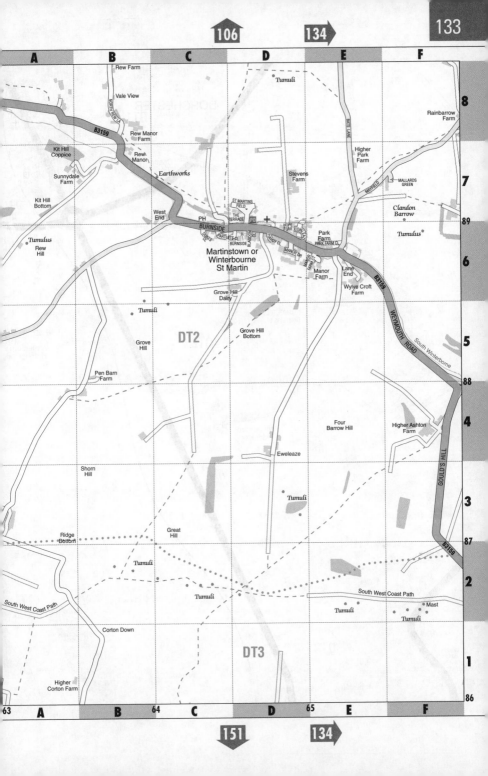

108
136

B8
1 GABRIEL GN
2 EVERDENE RD
3 NONESUCH CL
4 DIGGORY CRES
5 HIGHGROVE CL
6 MOYNTON RD

7 YORK TERR
8 BATHSHEBA TERR
9 ST DAVIDS CL
10 LORNTON WLK
11 CULLIFORD RD S
12 KNAPWATER WLK
13 BUCKBURY MEWS

14 MARSHWOOD RD
15 MIXEN LA
16 STANDFAST WLK
17 TALBOTHAYS RD

C8
1 SANDRINGHAM CT
2 FRIARS CL
3 SMOKEY HOLE LA
4 CAERNARVON CL
5 OSBORNE CL
6 GATCOMBE CL

7 CONWAY WLK
8 KENSINGTON WLK

St Marys RC Fst Sch
Conquer Barrow
Henge
Tumulus

Maumbury Rings

South County Avenue

St Osmunds Com Sp Ctr

St Osmunds CE Mid Sch
Park CE First Sch
Manor

DT1

Renfrew Cl
Carrick Cl
Max Gate

Weatherbury Way

A35

Frome Hill

North Plantation

Tumuli

North Plantation

Well Plantation

Bunker's Hill Plantation

Conygar Hill

Tumulus

South Winterborne

Came Park

Cole Hill Wood

Jubilee Trail

Winterbourne Faringdon Village

Winterborne Came

Came House

Whitcombe

Home Wood

DT2

Cole Hill Wood

Whitcombe Manor

Tumuli

Brick Hill Plantation

Jubilee Trail

Tumulus

Higher Came Farm

South Plantation

Tumuli

Down Wood

Tumuli

Cripton Wood

Cripton Cottage

Whitcombe Barn Plantation

Tumuli

Whitcombe Down

Tumulus

Gallop

Tumuli

South Drove Farm

Tumulus

Cripton Spinney

Whitcombe Barn

Tumuli

Warren Barn

SOUTH DROVE

153
136

139
113

8

7

89

6

5

88

4

3

87

2

1

86

139
158

A B C D E F

84 85 86

Stoke
Heath

Grants
Farm

CH

Tumuli

Longthorns
Farm

Sand and
Gravel Pit

Woolbridge
Heath

Lower Long
Bottom

Birch Wood

Great
Plantation

DUNCAN CRES
COLCOME ROAD

Monkey
World Ape
Rescue
Centre

Battery
Bank

Sand and
Gravel Pits

Bovington
Middle Sch

Eight Acre Wood
Nature Reserve

Hethfelton

BH20

BOVINGTON LA
COLE RD

LYTCHETT LANE

LYTCHETT LANE

TOUT HILL

Tout
Hill

Stokeford Common

Holly Wood

PH

Stokeford

Wool
Bridge

A352

River Frome

Stony
Weir

Hethfelton
Farm

LC

Wool

EAST BURTON ROAD

DORCHESTER ROAD

PH
St Marys RC
First Sch

HYDE
RD

STATION RD

HIGH ST

P

Manor
Farm

1 JEREMY CL
2 BINDON WY
3 THE CROSS

Bindon Abbey
(rems)

Church

Manor
Farm

Liby

COLLIER'S LANE

HIGH ST CL

Wool

East Stoke Fen
Reserve

East
Stoke

FOLLY LA

KNOWLE HILL

DUCK LANE

B3071

Braytown

Wool CE
First Sch

BINDON LANE

LAWRY HILLSIDE RD

LULWORTH ROAD

Quarr
Hill

Cole
Wood

Inglewood
Farm

E3
1 HEMSBACH CT
2 CHURCH GN
3 THE QUAY
4 ABBOTS QUAY
5 TANNER'S LA
6 ST MICHAEL'S RD
7 HILLARD CT
8 REMPSTONE SHOPPING ARCADE
9 MORETON'S LA

E4
1 ST MARTIN'S CL
2 COOPER'S CL
3 DOLLIN'S LA
4 CARRION LA
5 KENNINGTON SQ
6 CONCHES CT

A   B   C   D   E   F

8

BH16

Birch
Wood

7

Jubilee
Wood

Willow
Wood

Keysworth
Point

Poole
Harbour

Keysworth
Farm

89

Sewage
Works

West Field
Coppice

6

Buck's Cove
Saltmarsh

Wareham Channel

5

BH20

88

Swineham
Farm

Swineham
Point

Gigger's
Island

Arne
Heath

4

River Frome

Arne Reedbeds
National Nature
Reserve

3

Ridge
Wharf

The Moors

87

Redclyffe
Yacht Club

Salterns
Copse

The
Moors

2

Redcliffe
Farm

BARNDALE
DR

Ridge
Farm

Mound

Slepe
Copse

Ridge

ARNE ROAD

Slepe Heath

Broad
Marsh

1

Slepe
Heath

Stoborough Heath
National Nature
Reserve

SOLDIERS ROAD

86

93   A   B   94   C   D   95   E   F

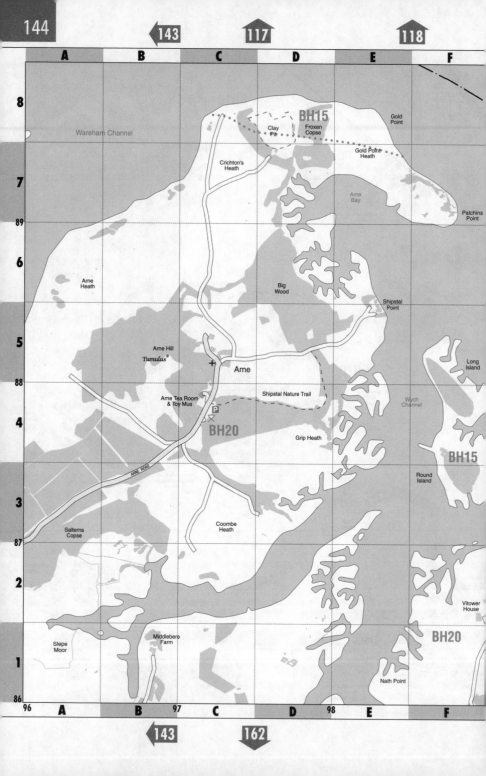

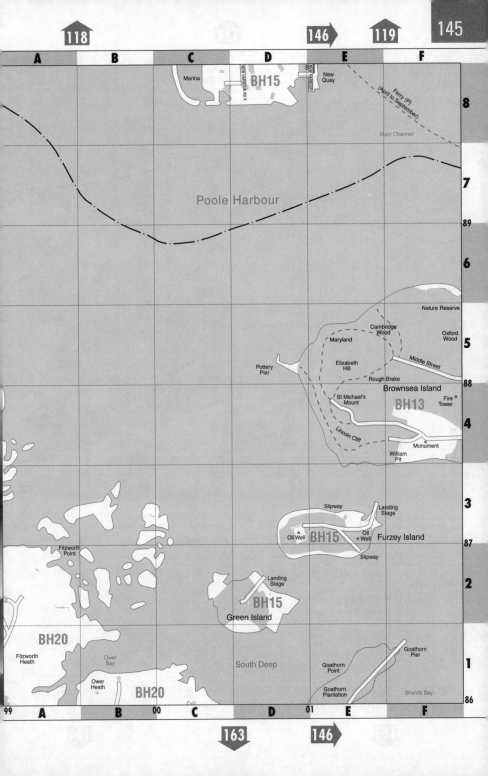

A   B   C   D   E   F

8

Marina   NEW HARBOUR RD S   BH15   NEW HARBOUR RD   New Quay   Ferry (P) (April to September)

Main Channel

7

Poole Harbour

89

6

Nature Reserve

Cambridge Wood   Oxford Wood   5

Maryland

Pottery Pier   Elizabeth Hill   Middle Street

Rough Brake   88

Brownsea Island

St Michael's Mount   BH13   Fire Tower   4

Lincoln Cliff   Monument

William Pit

3

Slipway   Landing Stage

Oil Well   BH15   Oil Well   Furzey Island

87

Slipway

Landing Stage   2

BH15

Green Island

BH20

Goathorn Pier   1

Fitzworth Point

Fitzworth Heath   Ower Bay   Goathorn Point

Ower Heath   BH20   South Deep   Goathorn Plantation   Brands Bay   86

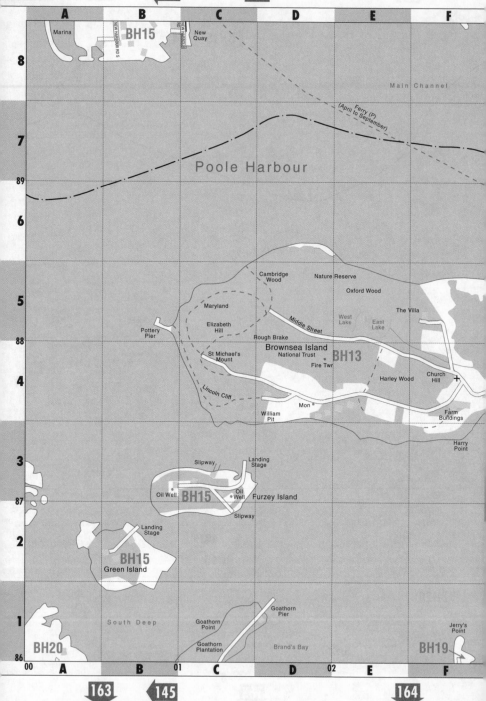

F8
1 KENILWORTH CT
2 BRACKENS WAY
3 STONELEIGH
4 BRANKSOME CT
5 MARTELLO HO

147

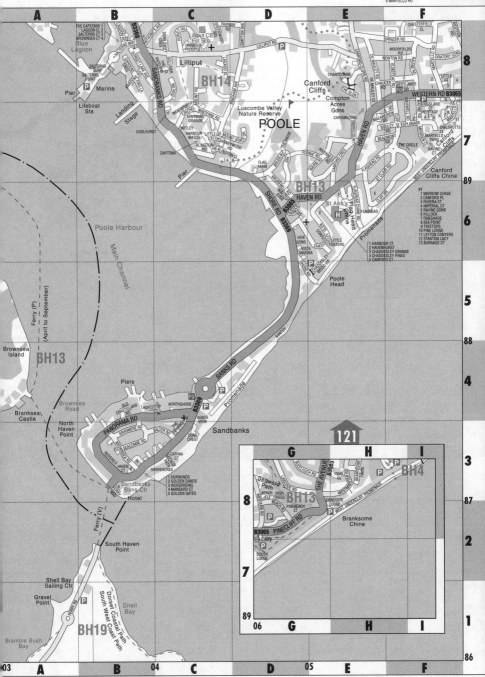

120

164

121

Poole Harbour

Main Channel

Brownsea
Island

BH13

Branksea
Castle

North
Haven
Point

Brownsea
Road

Ferry (P)
(April to September)

Blue
Lagoon

Pier

Marina

Lifeboat
Sta

Landing
Stage

COOLHURST

DAYTONA

Lilliput

BH14

THE CAPSTANS 1
LAGOON CL 2
SALTERNS CT 3
BROWNSEA CT 4

SALTERNS
QUAY

SALTERNS
POINT

SANDBANKS RD

B3369

Luscombe Valley
Nature Reserve

POOLE

Canford
Cliffs

Compton
Acres
Gdns

CARISBROOKE

Lilliput CE
1st Sch

FAIRWAY
RD

LILLIPUT RD

CHARTCOMBE

THE GLEN

CHESTERFIELD
CL

SPENCER RD

MOORFIELDS
RD

NEWTON RD

WESTLANDS

ORATORY GDNS

LITTLE
CLOSE

HERITAGE

KINGSLAND

OWLSHOTTS

Canford
Cliffs

THE CIRCLE

MARTELLO
TWRS

RAVINE
RD

Canford
Cliffs Chine

WEST UNDERCLIFF PROMENADE

WESTERN RD B3065

HAVEN RD

BH13

St Ann's
H
Flag Head
Chine

LITTLE
FOSTERS

Flag
Farm

Pier

HAVEN RD

B3369

SHORE RD

B3369

HIVE
GDNS

VISTA
MARINA

FLAGHEAD

Promenade

Poole
Head

89

8

7

6

5

88

4

F7
1 MERROW CHASE
2 CANFORD PL
3 RIVIERA CT
4 IMPERIAL CT
5 RAVINE GDNS
6 KILLOCK
7 FINESHADE
8 SEA POINT
9 TREETOPS
10 PINE LODGE
11 LEYTON CONYERS
12 STANTON LACY
13 BURNAGE CT

1 HARBOUR CT
2 HAVENHURST
3 CHADDESLEY GRANGE
4 CHADDESLEY PINES
5 CANFORD CT

Piers

OLD
COASTGUARD
RD

HORSESHOE

PANORAMA RD

GRASMERE RD

SEACOMBE RD

HAVEN
CT

Sandbanks
Bsns Ctr

Hotel

Northshore

SALTER RD

CARINA
CT

DUNE
CREST

SHOREACRES

BANKS RD

B3369

BEACH
VIEW

Promenade

Sandbanks

SANTOV

1 FAIRWINDS
2 GOLDEN SANDS
3 WOODRISING
4 MANSARD CT
5 GOLDEN GATES

3

87

2

Ferry (V)

South Haven
Point

Shell Bay
Sailing Ctr

Gravel
Point

BH19

Dorset Coastal Path
South West Coast Path

Shell
Bay

Bramble Bush
Bay

BH19

03

A

04

B

05

C

D

E

F

86

Inset map 121:

G

H

I

BH4

Seaward
Path

BH13

BEACH HIGH
CL TREES

PINEBEACH
CT

DENECOTE
LODGE

Branksome
Chine

THE AVENUE

BICCLEUGH RD

TEAK RD

WEST UNDERCLIFF PROMENADE

B3065

PINECLIFF RD

Lbry

SOUTH
LODGE

8

7

89

06

G

H

I

1

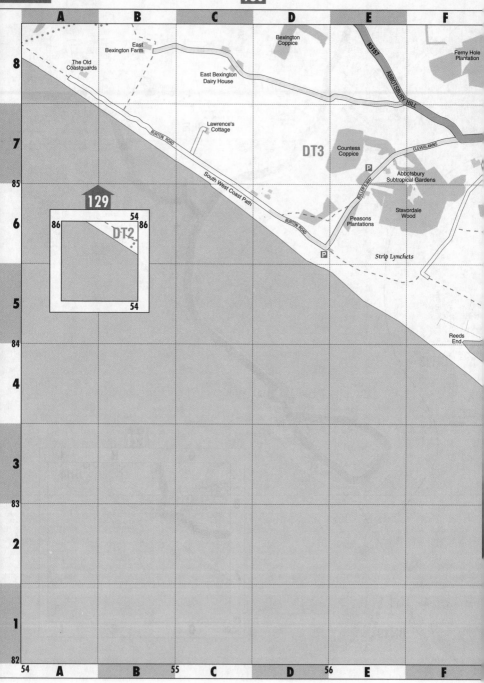

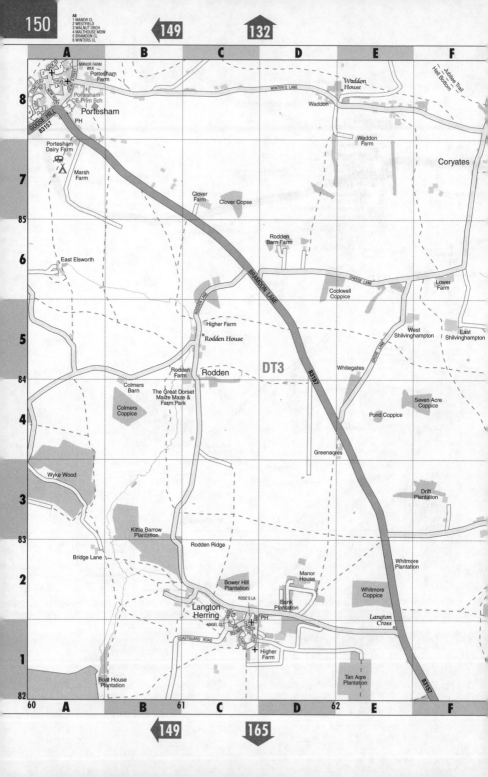

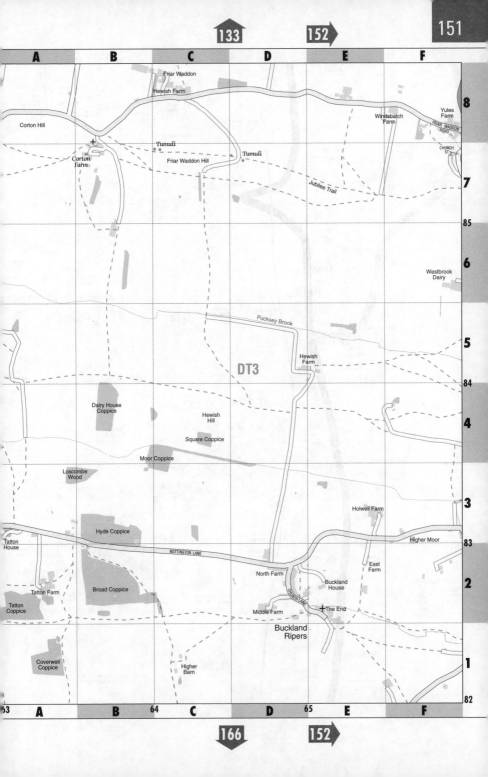

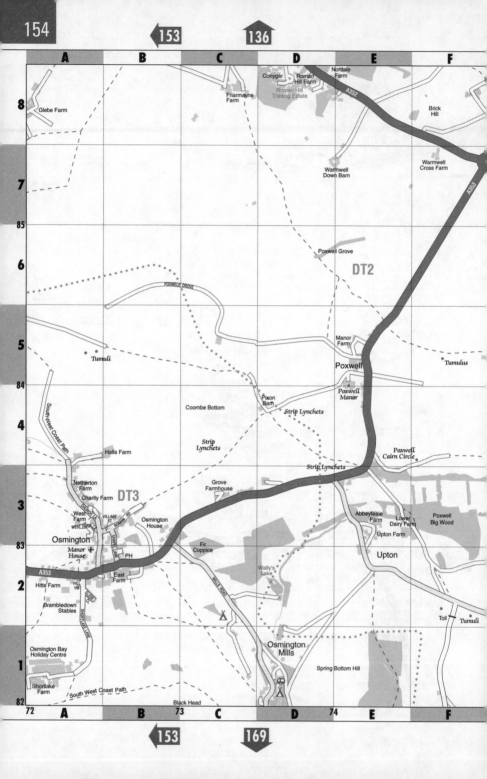

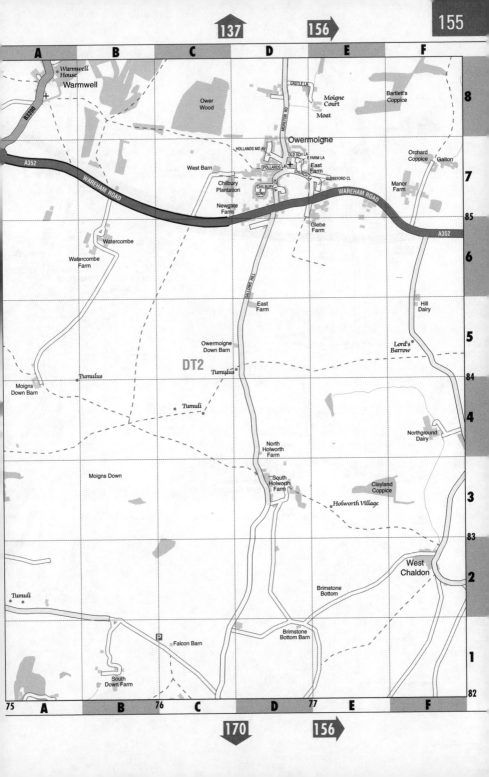

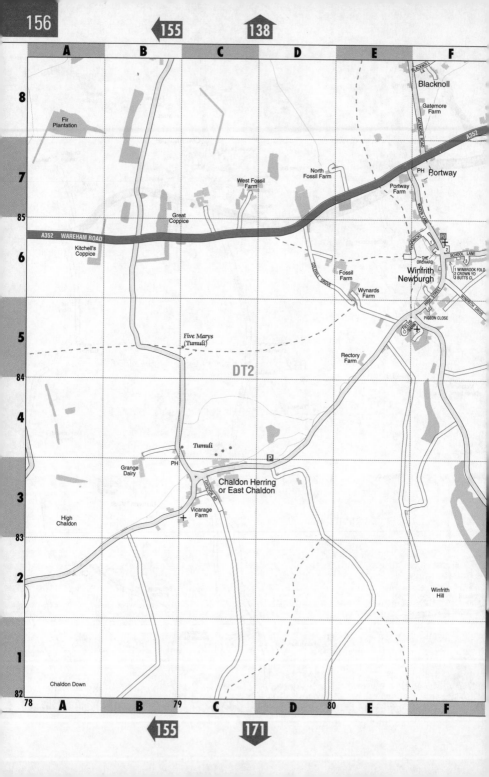

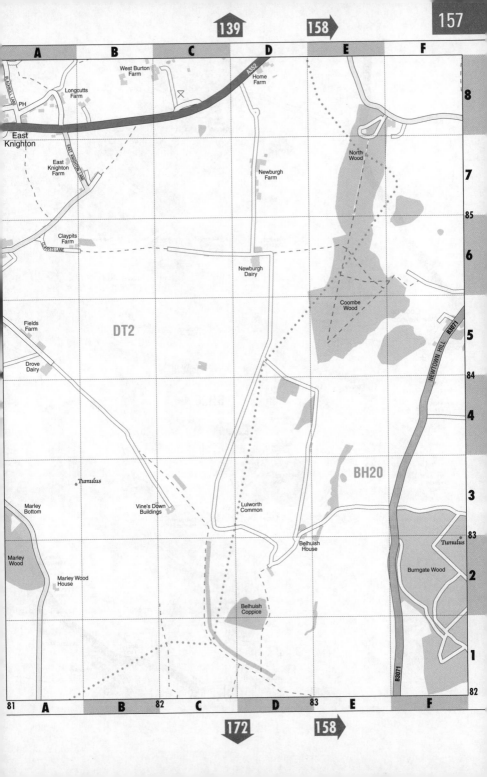

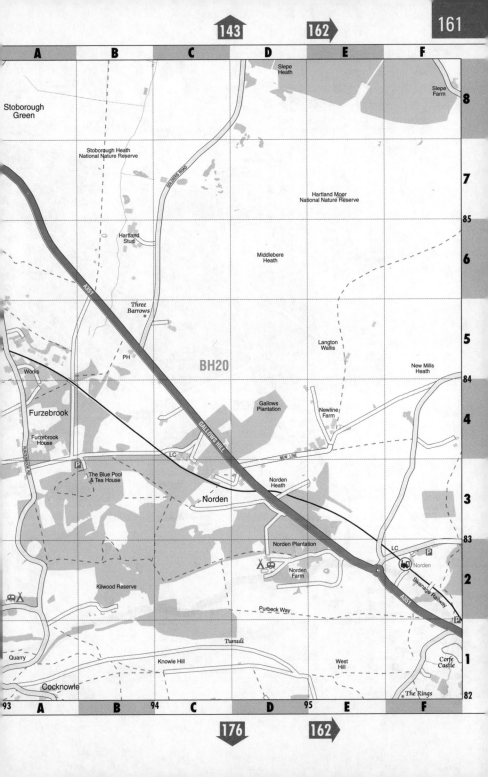

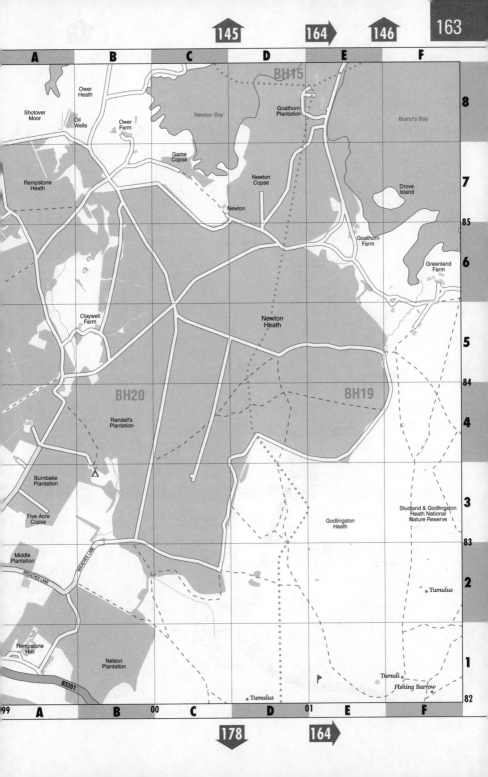

A   B   C   D   E   F

8

Ower Heath

Shotover Moor

Oil Wells

Ower Farm

BH15

Newton Bay

Goathorn Plantation

Brand's Bay

Game Copse

Rempstone Heath

7

Newton Copse

Drove Island

85

Newton

Goathorn Farm

6

Greenland Farm

Claywell Farm

Newton Heath

5

BH20

84

BH19

Randall's Plantation

4

Burnbake Plantation

Studland & Godlingston Heath National Nature Reserve

3

Five Acre Copse

Godlingston Heath

83

Middle Plantation

BREACHES LANE

Tumulus

2

Rempstone Hall

Nelson Plantation

Tumuli

Fishing Barrow

1

B3351

Tumulus

82

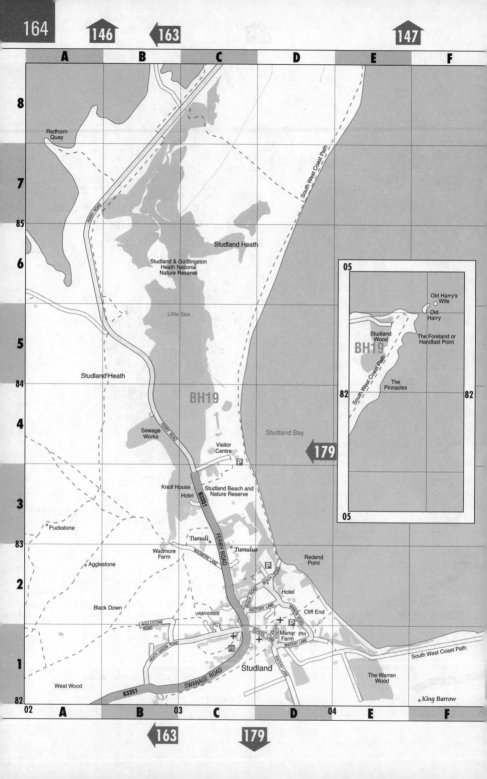

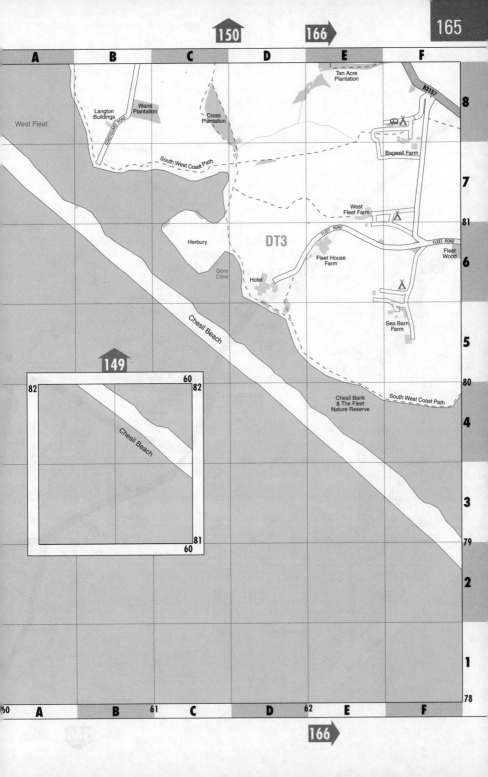

165
151

165
180

B8
1 MOORCOMBE DR
2 CHALBURY LODGE
3 HAZEL DR
4 WINGREEN CL
5 MAPLE CL
6 DEANSLEIGH CL

A   B   C   D   E   F

St Andrews
CE Prim Sch

ALLBERRY
GDNS

LITTLEMOOR ROAD

PRESTON ROAD

Preston

FELFORD
ROAD

FISHE
ROAD

TALLIDGE
CL

HOLCOMBE CL

Osmington Hill

8

CHALBURY

A353

YEW TREE
CL

1 HALSTOCK CL
2 BROOKSIDE CL
3 HORYFORD CL

ROMAN VILLA

Wyke Oliver
Farm

WYKE OLIVER ROAD

TORHILL
CLOSE

River Jordan

Overcombe

7

DALBURY DRIVE

SUNNINGDALE RD

JORDAN HILL
ROMAN
TEMPLE

DT3

KINGSMERE

82

BODKIN

SOUTHDOWN AV

PINGSTED DR OVERCOMBE RD

BOWLEAZE COVEWAY

South West Coast Path

New
Barn

P

Hotel

6

HERON CL

1 BRACKENDOWN AV
2 EASTDOWN AV
3 EASTDOWN GDNS

PH

Furzy Cliff

Bowleaze
Cove

Redcliff
Point

5

PRESTON ROAD

Weymouth Bay

81

A353

4

80

3

2

1

79

69   A   B   70   C   D   71   E   F

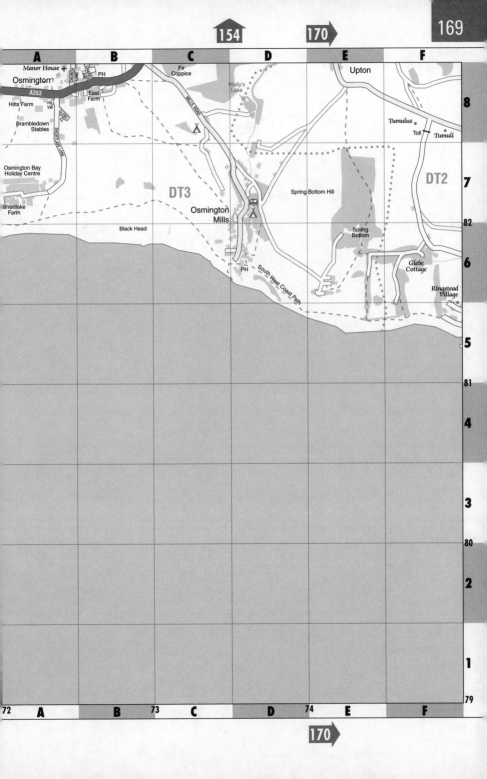

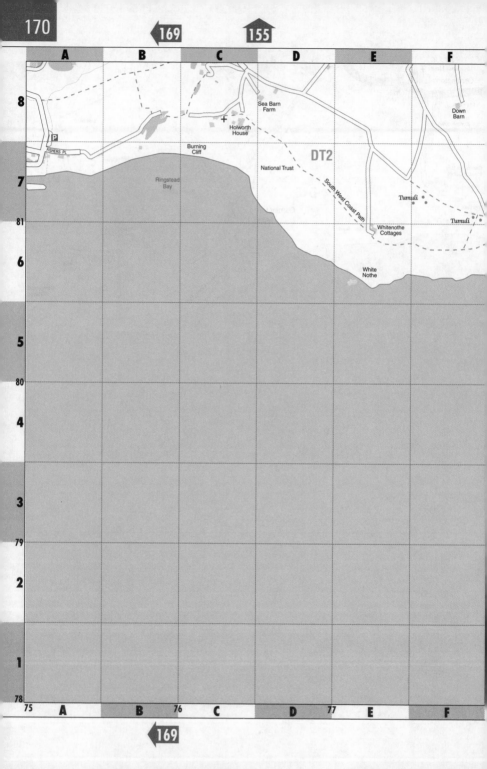

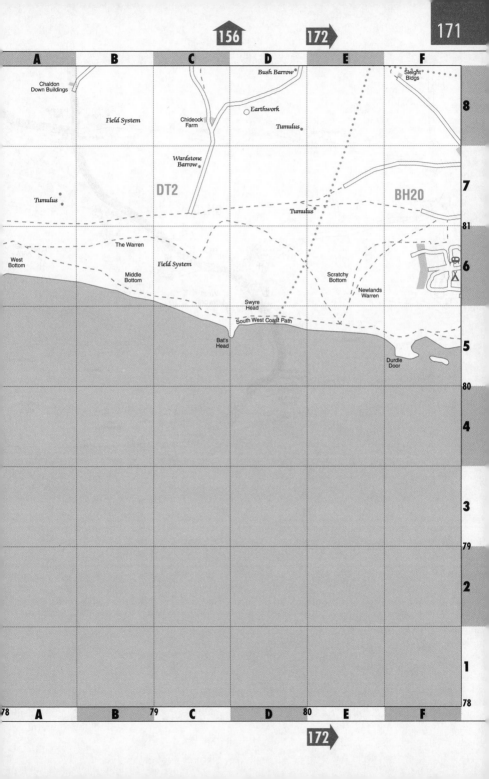

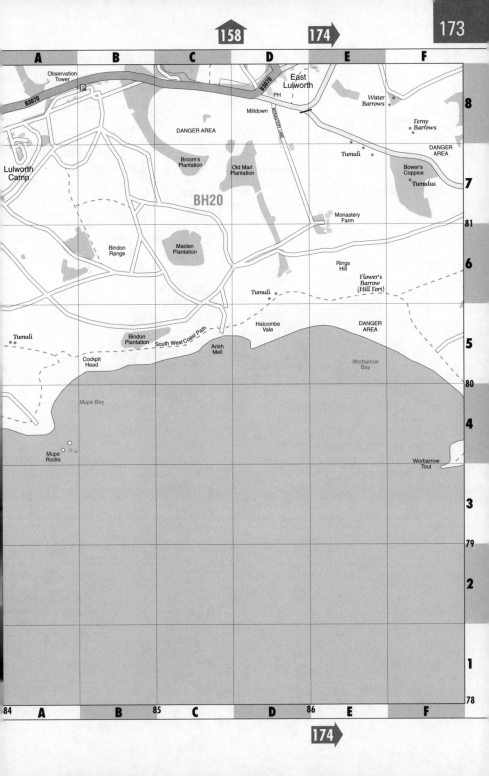

A   B   C   D   E   F

Observation
Tower
P

B3070

DANGER AREA

Milldown

MONASTERY LANE

B3070

East
Lulworth

PH

Water
Barrows

8

Ferny
Barrows

Broom's
Plantation

Old Marl
Plantation

Tumuli

DANGER
AREA

Lulworth
Camp

BH20

Bower's
Coppice

Tumulus

7

81

Bindon
Range

Maiden
Plantation

Monastery
Farm

Rings
Hill

6

Flower's
Barrow
(Hill Fort)

Tumuli

Tumuli

Halcombe
Vale

DANGER
AREA

Bindon
Plantation

South West Coast Path

Arish
Mell

Worbarrow
Bay

5

Cockpit
Head

80

Mupe Bay

4

Mupe
Rocks

Worbarrow
Tout

3

79

2

1

78

84   A   B   85   C   D   86   E   F

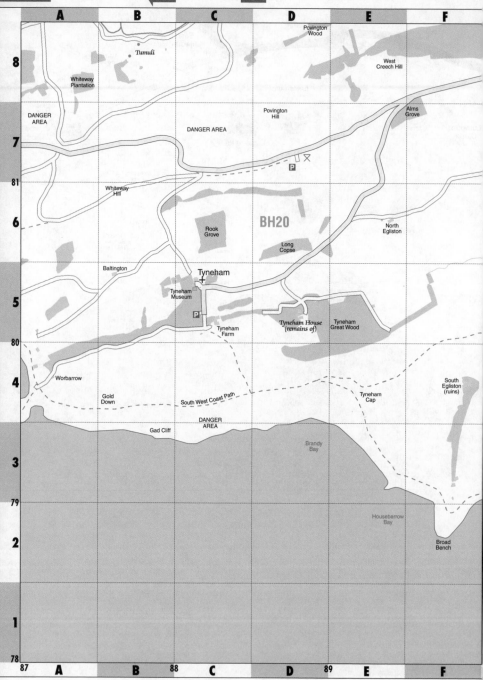

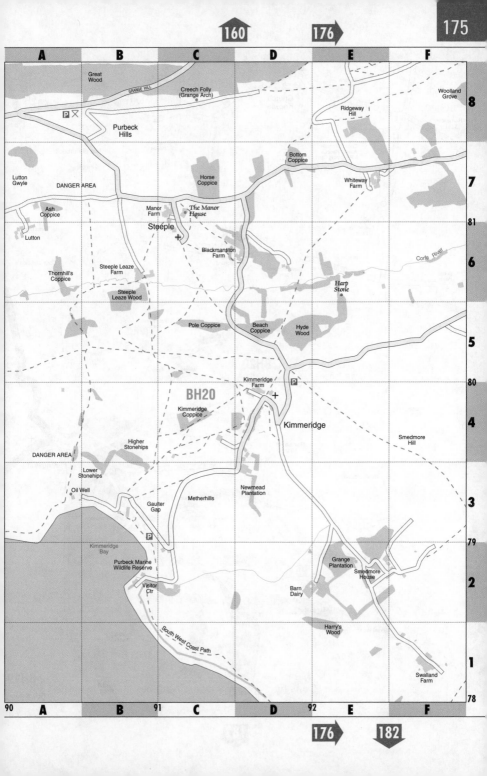

A B C D E F

8

Barneston
Manor

Heath View

PH

Church
Farm

Church
Knowle

Glebe
Farm

Cemy

HOLLANDS
CLOSE

WEBBER
CL

WEBBER CL

Church Knowle
Animal Rescue
& Rehoming Ctr

Bucknowle
House

Isle of Purbeck

7

West Bucknowle
House

81

Puddlemill
Farm

Tumuli

6

Bridle
Farm

West Orchard
Farm

East
Orchard

Corfe Common

5

Chettle Wood

Blashenwell
Farm

West
Lynch

Lynch
Farm

BH20

Willwood Plantation

80

Bradle
Barn

4

Orchard Hill
Farm

KINGSTON HILL

WEST ST

WEST STREET

LYTRE LANE

PH

B3069

Kingston

3

Newfoundland

Quarry Wood

The Plantation

SOUTH STREET

79

Polar Wood

John Strange
Wood

2

Long Wood

Encombe
House

Swyre Wood

Broadley
Wood

Westhill
Farm

1

Tumulus

Swyre Head

BH19

78

Big Wood

Westhill
Wood

Field Systems

93 A B 94 C D 95 E F

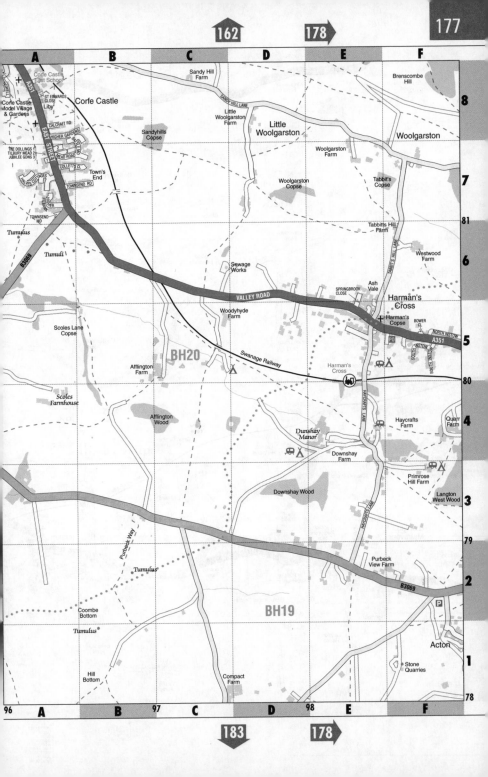

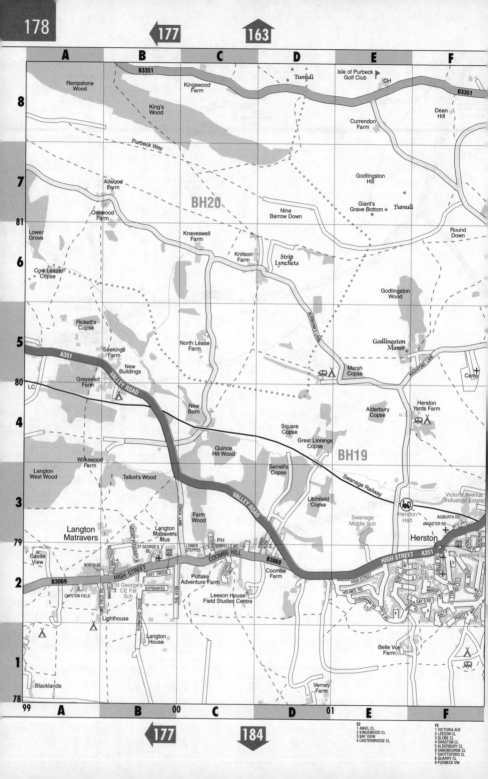

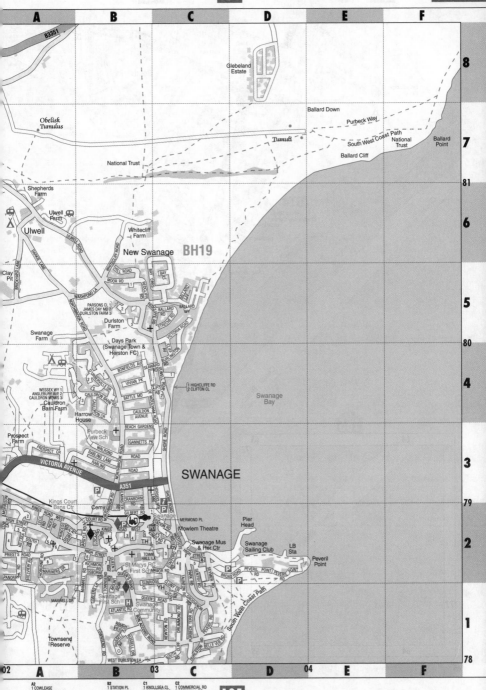

Glebeland Estate

Obelisk Tumulus

Ballard Down

Purbeck Way

Tumuli

National Trust

South West Coast Path

National Trust

Ballard Point

Ballard Cliff

Shepherds Farm

Ulwell Farm

Ulwell

Whitecliff Farm

New Swanage

BH19

Clay Pit

Moor Rd

BAY CL

PARSONS CL 1
JAMES DAY MD 2
DURLSTON FARM 3

BALLARD RD

BALLARD WY

STRECHE RD

Swanage Farm

Durlston Farm

Days Park
(Swanage Town & Herston FC)

VICTORIA ROAD

BONFIELDS AVE

1 HIGHCLIFFE RD
2 CLIFTON CL

Swanage Bay

SEAWARD

VIVIAN PK

WESSEX WY 1
ANGLEBURY AVE 2
CAULDRON MDWS 3

Cauldron Barn Farm

BATTLE MD

CAULDRON AVENUE

Harrow House

BEACH GARDENS

Purbeck View Sch

GANNETTS PK

Prospect Farm

PROSPECT CR

WALDING

RABLING LANE

ROAD

VICTORIA AVENUE

A351

SWANAGE

CRANBORNE RD

Kings Court Bsns Ctr

Cemy

GILBERT RD

Swanage

MERMOND PL

Pier Head

Mowlem Theatre

Swanage Mus & Her Ctr

Swanage Sailing Club

LB Sta

Peveril Point

PEVERIL POINT

TOWN HALL RD

St Marys Rd First Sch

MANOR RD

QUEEN'S ROAD

BROAD ROAD

PEVERIL RD

Swanage First Sch

Swanage Community

ATLANTIC RD

South West Coast Path

Townsend Reserve

WEST DURLSTON LA

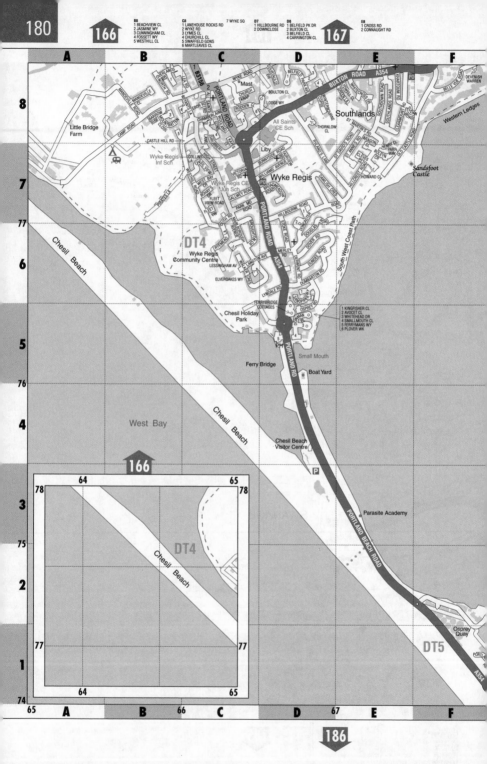

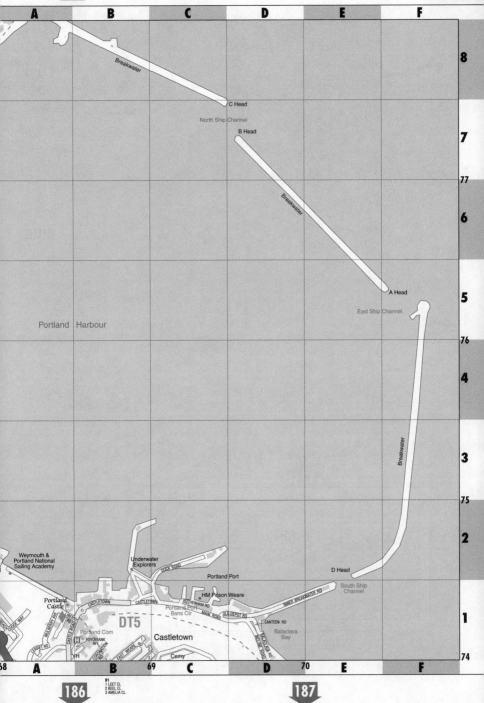

A B C D E F

8

Breakwater

C Head

North Ship Channel

7

B Head

77

6

Breakwater

A Head

5

East Ship Channel

Portland Harbour

76

4

Breakwater

3

75

2

Weymouth &
Portland National
Sailing Academy

Underwater
Explorers

ROCK ROAD

Portland Port

D Head

South Ship
Channel

Portland Port
Bsns Ctr

HM Prison Weare

INNER BREAKWATER RD

Portland
Castle

CASTLETOWN   CASTLETOWN

ROTHERHAM RD

MAIN ROAD   OLD DEPOT RD

CANTEEN RD

Balaclava
Bay

1

Portland Com

DT5

FOYLEBANK WY

Castletown

EAST WEARE RD

Cemy

74

B1
1 LEET CL
2 BEEL CL
3 AMELIA CL

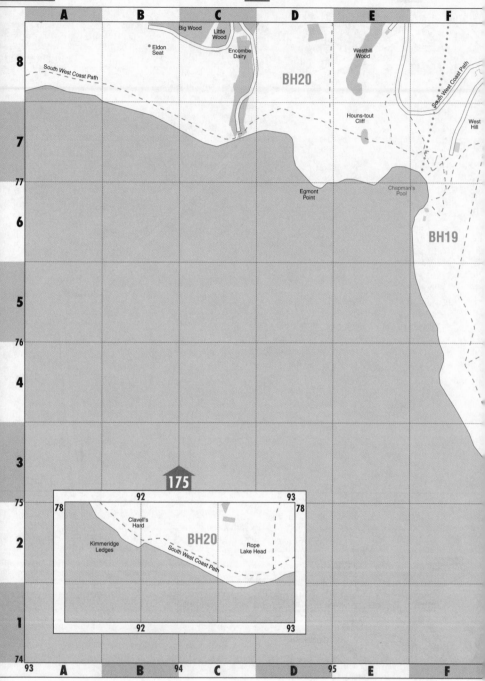

South West Coast Path

Big Wood

Little
Wood

Eldon
Seat

Encombe
Dairy

BH20

Westhill
Wood

South West Coast Path

Houns-tout
Cliff

West
Hill

Egmont
Point

Chapman's
Pool

BH19

South West Coast Path

92

93

78

78

Clavell's
Hard

Kimmeridge
Ledges

BH20

South West Coast Path

Rope
Lake Head

92

93

74

93   A   B   94   C   D   95   E   F

8

77

7

6

5

76

4

3

75

2

1

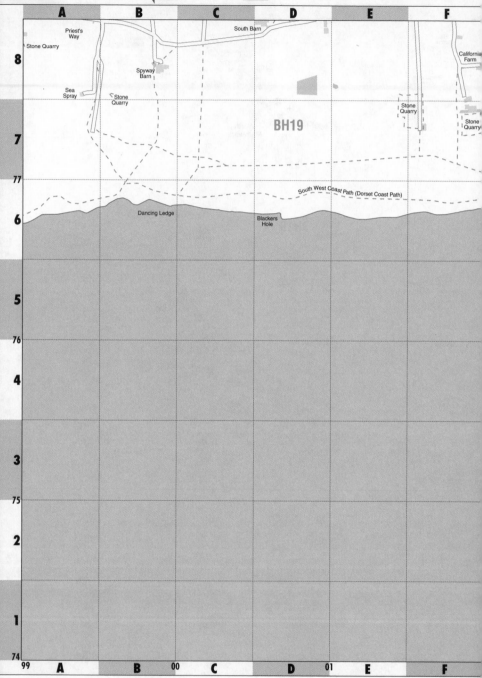

183
178
183

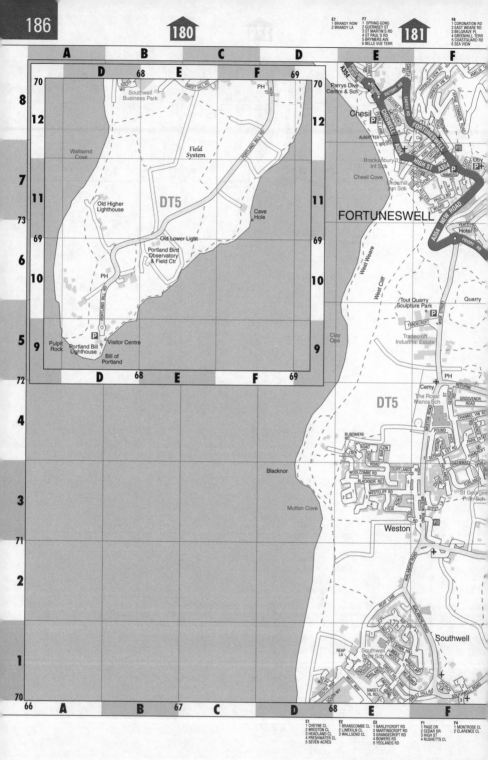

180

181

Parrys Dive
Centre & Sch

Chesil

Southwell
Business Park

Field
System

Wallsend
Cove

DT5

Old Higher
Lighthouse

Cave
Hole

Old Lower Light

Portland Bird
Observatory
& Field Ctr

PH

Pulpit
Rock

Portland Bill
Lighthouse

Visitor Centre

Bill of
Portland

Albert Terr

Brackenbury Inf Sch

Chesil Cove

Underhill
Jun Sch

FORTUNESWELL

Hotel

West Weare

West Cliff

Tout Quarry
Sculpture Park

Quarry

Tradecroft

Tradecroft
Industrial Estate

Clay
Ope

PH

Cemy

The Royal
Manor Sch

DT5

GROSVENOR
ROAD

BLINDMERE
RD

Blacknor

Mutton Cove

St George
Prim Sch

WOOLCOMBE RD

COURTLANDS

BLACKNOR RD

WESTCLIFF RD

Weston

Southwell
Prim Sch

Southwell

REAP
LA

	A	B	C	D	E	F	

Cemy

H.M. Prison

The Verne

8

King's Pier

Masts

INCLINE ROAD

7

73

East Weare

King Barrow Quarries Reserve

erne eates

Admiralty Quarries

PORTLAND

6

Grove

Grove Inf Sch

Portland United Football Club

INCLINE RD

AUGUSTA CL

HM Young Offender Institution

WITHIES CFT

VICTORIA RD

SHEPHERDS CFT

Mast

5

SHEPHERDS CROFT

CROWN FARM TERR

DT5

72

LONG ACRE

NEW CHURCH CL

Easton

Quarry

Durdle Pier

STRAITS

MOORFIELD RD

4

Liby

Easton

Grove Cliff

Works

BUMPERS LA

Bottom Coombe Quarries

3

Portland Mus

Church (rems of)

Rufus Castle

71

Hotel

Church Ope Cove

WESTON STREET

2

SOUTHWELL ROAD

1

Freshwater Bay

70

	A	B	C	D	E	F	

69   70   71

A4
1 REFORNE CL
2 STATION RD
3 LADYMD CL
4 EASTON SQ
5 SILKLAKE MEWS
6 LOVELLS CFT

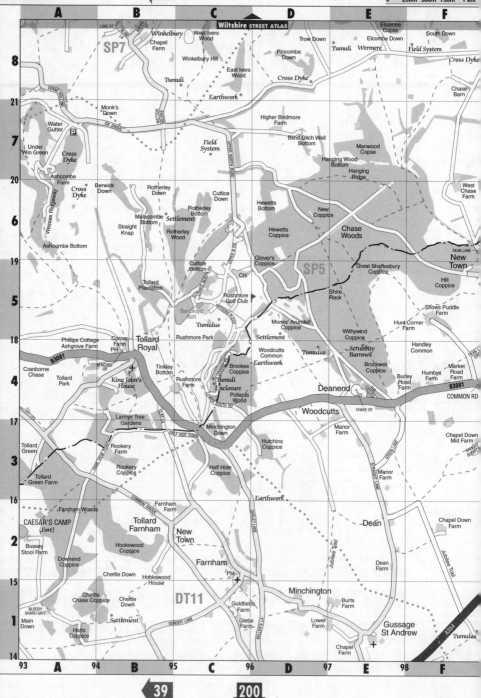

Scale: 1½ inches to 1 mil

0   ¼   ½ mile
0   250m 500m 750m 1 km

Wiltshire STREET ATLAS

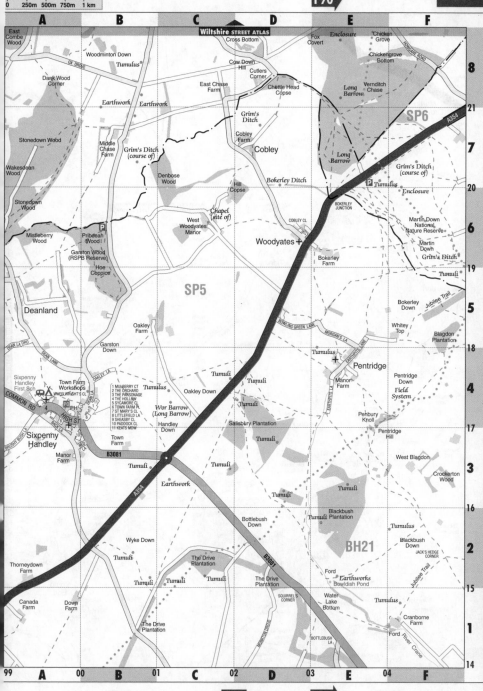

Scale: 1⅓ inches to 1 mile

0 ¼ ½ mile
0 250m 500m 750m 1 km

190

Wiltshire STREET ATLAS

East Combe Wood
Woodminton Down
Tumulus
Dank Wood Corner
Earthwork Earthwork
Stonedown Wood
Middle Chase Farm
Grim's Ditch (course of)
Wakesdean Wood
Denbose Wood
Stonedown Wood
Mistleberry Wood
Pribdean Wood
Garston Wood (RSPB Reserve)
Hoe Coppice
Deanland
Oakley Farm
Garston Down

Cross Bottom
Cow Down Hill
Cutlers Corner
East Chase Farm
Chettle Head Copse
Grim's Ditch
Cobley Farm
Hill Copse
Cobley
Bokerley Ditch
Chapel (site of)
West Woodyates Manor
Woodyates
Cobley Cl
Bokerley Farm

Fox Covert
Enclosure
Chicken Grove
Chickengrove Bottom
Verndlitch Chase
Long Barrow
SP6
Long Barrow
Grim's Ditch (course of)
Tumulus
Enclosure
Bokerley Junction
Martin Down National Nature Reserve
Martin Down
Grim's Ditch
Tumuli

SP5

Bokerley Down
Whitey Top
Jubilee Trail
Blagdon Plantation

Bowling Green Lane
Morgan's La
Tumulus
Pentridge
Manor Farm
Earthen's Lane
Pentridge Down
Field System

1 MULBERRY CT
2 THE ORCHARD
3 THE PARSONAGE
4 THE HOLLOW
5 SYCAMORE CL
6 TOWN FARM PL
7 ST MARY'S CL
8 LITTLEFIELD LA
9 SHEASBY CL
10 PADDOCK CL
11 KEATS MDW

Tumuli
Oakley Down
Wor Barrow (Long Barrow)
Handley Down
Salisbury Plantation
Tumuli
Penbury Knoll
Pentridge Hill
West Blagdon
Crockerton Wood

Sixpenny Handley First Sch
Town Farm Workshops
WHEELWRIGHT'S CL
COMMON RD
HIGH ST
Sixpenny Handley
Manor Farm
B3081
Tumuli
Earthwork
Town Farm
Tumuli
Tumuli

Blackbush Plantation
Tumuli
Tumulus
Blackbush Down
JACK'S HEDGE CORNER

Thorneydown Farm
Wyke Down
Tumuli
The Drive Plantation
Bottlebush Down
Tumuli
The Drive Plantation
Ford
Earthworks
Bowldish Pond
BH21
Jubilee Trail

Canada Farm
Down Farm
Tumuli Tumuli
The Drive Plantation
SQUIRREL'S CORNER
Water Lake Bottom
Tumulus
Cranborne Farm
Ford River Crane
BOTTLEBUSH LA

99 A 00 B 01 C 02 D 03 E 04 F

201 190

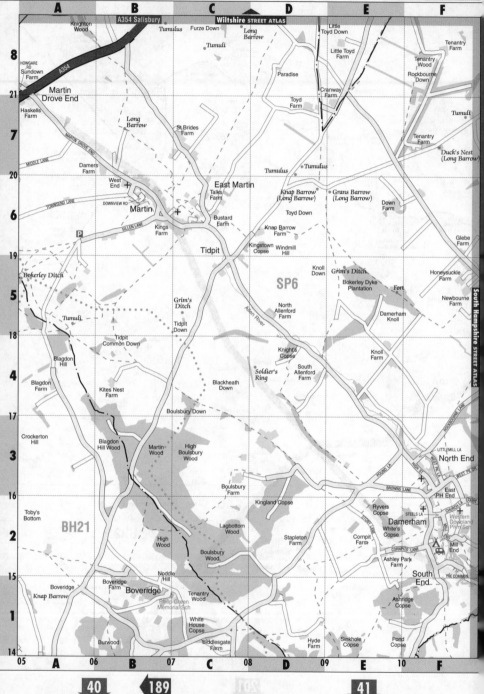

Scale: 1½ inches to 1 mile

0 ¼ ½ mile
0 250m 500m 750m 1 km

A354 Salisbury

Wiltshire STREET ATLAS

South Hampshire STREET ATLAS

Knighton Wood
Tumulus
Furze Down
Long Barrow
Little Toyd Down
Little Toyd Farm
Tenantry Farm

8

HOWGARE RD
Sundown Farm
Paradise
Tenantry Wood
Rockbourne Down

21
Martin Drove End
Toyd Farm
Cranway Farm
Tumuli

Haskells Farm
Long Barrow
St Brides Farm
Tenantry Farm

7
MARTIN DROVE END
Duck's Nest (Long Barrow)

20
MIDDLE LANE
Damers Farm
Tumulus
Tumulus

TOWNSEND LANE
West End
East Martin
Knap Barrow (Long Barrow)
Grans Barrow (Long Barrow)
Down Farm

6
DOWNVIEW RD
Martin
Talks Farm
Toyd Down
Glebe Farm

SILLEN LANE
Kings Farm
Bustard Farm
Knap Barrow
Tidpit
Kingstown Copse
Windmill Hill

19
P
Knoll Down
Grim's Ditch
Honeysuckle Farm

Bokerley Ditch
Grim's Ditch
SP6
Bokerley Dyke Plantation
Fort
Newbourne Farm

5
Tumuli
Tidpit Down
North Allenford Farm
Allen River
Damerham Knoll

18
Tidpit Common Down
Knight's Copse
Knoll Farm

Blagdon Hill
Blackheath Down
Soldier's Ring
South Allenford Farm

4
Blagdon Farm
Kites Nest Farm
Boulsbury Down

Crockerton Hill
Blagdon Hill Wood
Martin Wood
High Boulsbury Wood

3
LITTLEMILL LA
North End
BROCKHOUSE LANE

17
Boulsbury Farm
POUND LA
HIGH ST
East End
PH
WEST PK DR

16
Toby's Bottom
BH21
Kingland Copse
BROWNS LANE
Ryvers Copse
CHURCH LA
STEELS LA
Western Downland Phry Sen
COURT HL

2
High Wood
Lagbottom Wood
Stapleton Farm
Cornpit Farm
White's Copse
Damerham
Mill End

Noddle Hill
Boulsbury Wood
CORNPIT LANE
Ashley Park Farm
THE COMMON

15
Boveridge Farm
Tenantry Farm
South End
Ashridge Copse

1
Boveridge
Philip Green Memorial Sch
White House Copse
Hyde Farm
Sinkhole Copse
Pond Copse

Knap Barrow
Burwood
Biddlesgate Farm

14

A 05 B 06 C 07 D 08 09 E 10 F

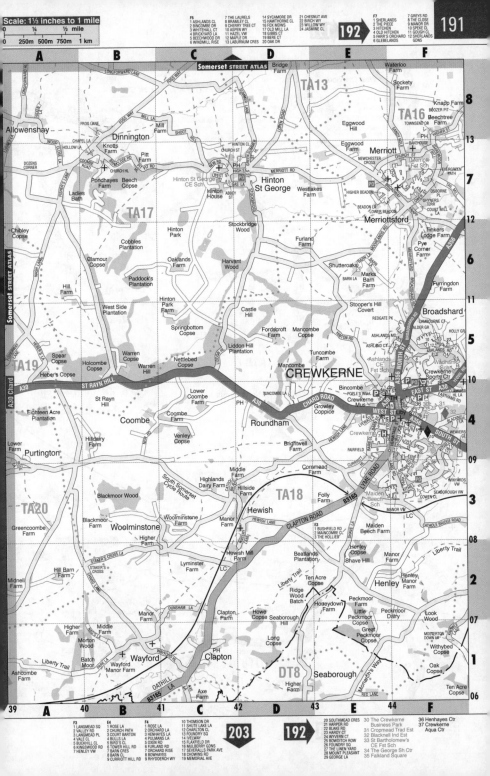

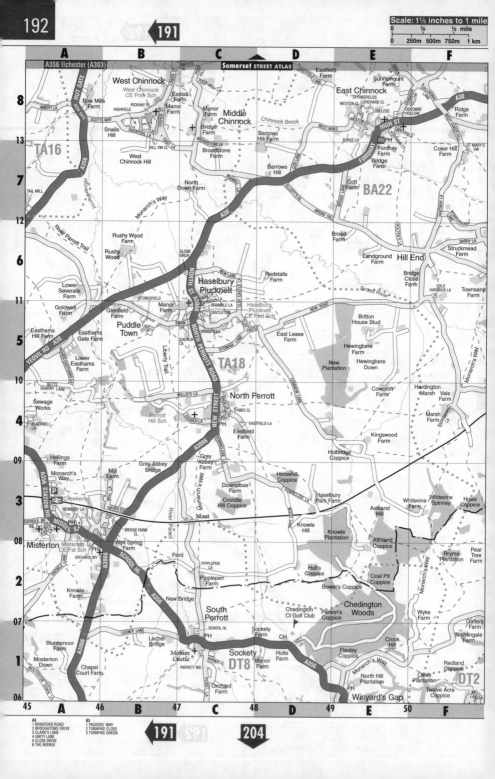

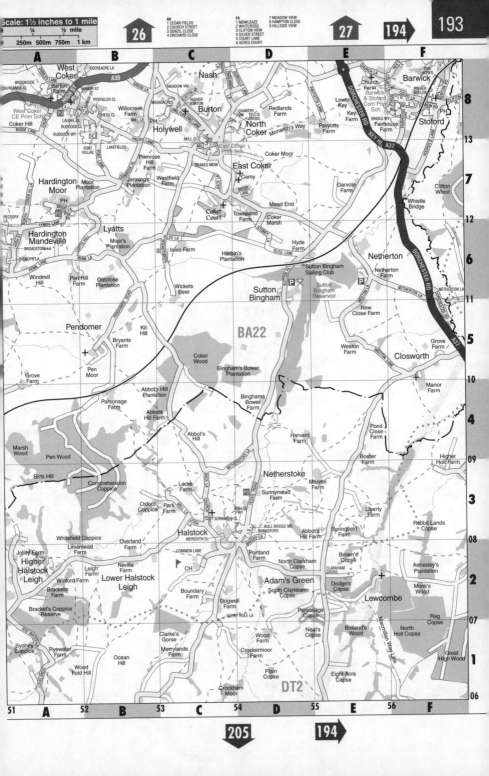

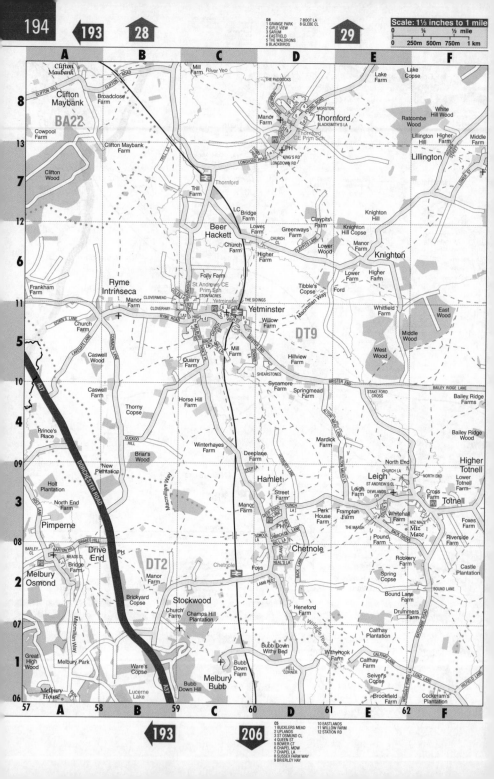

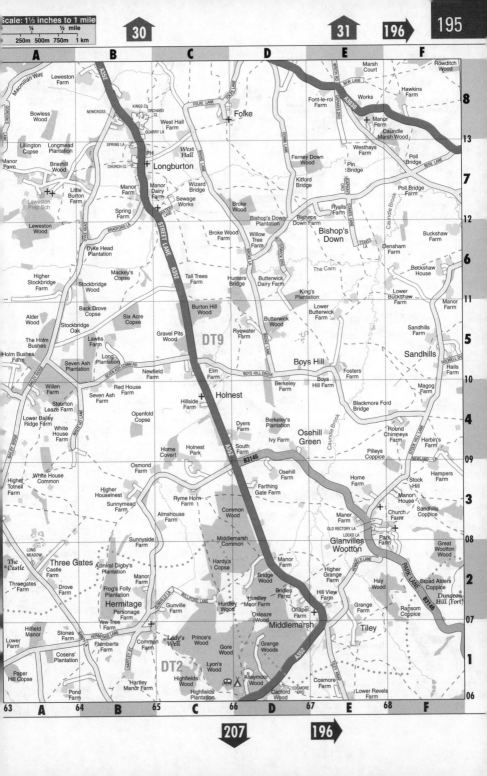

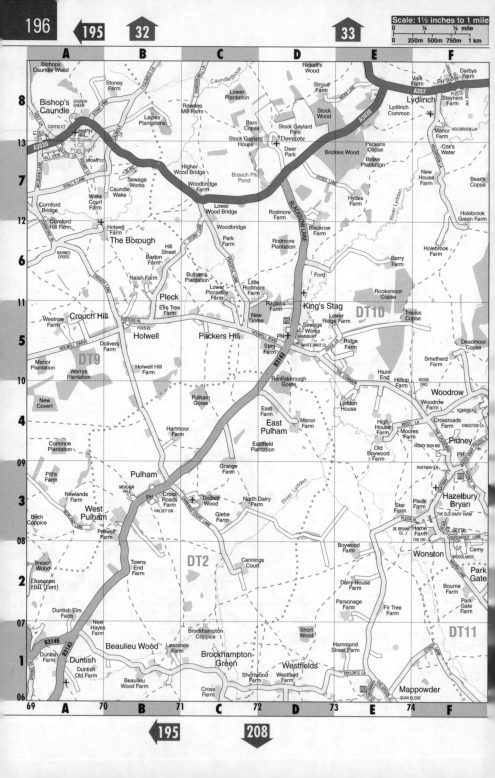

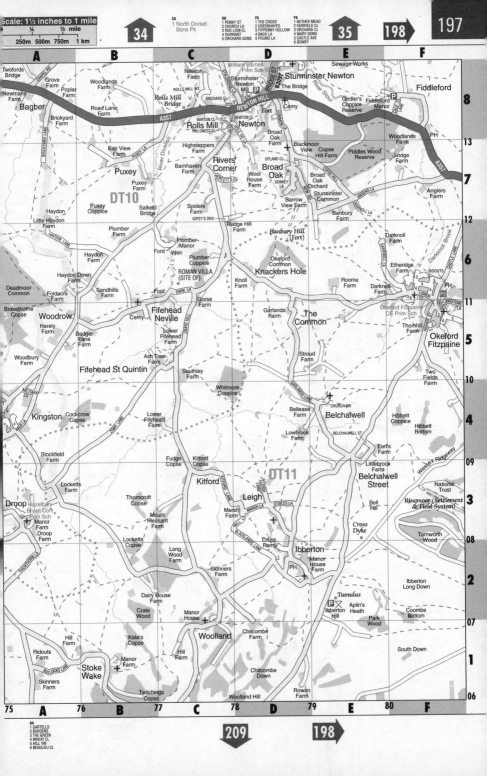

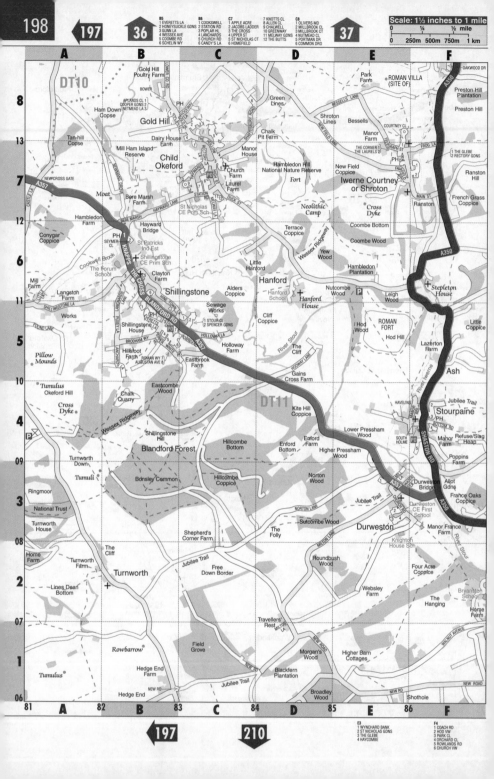

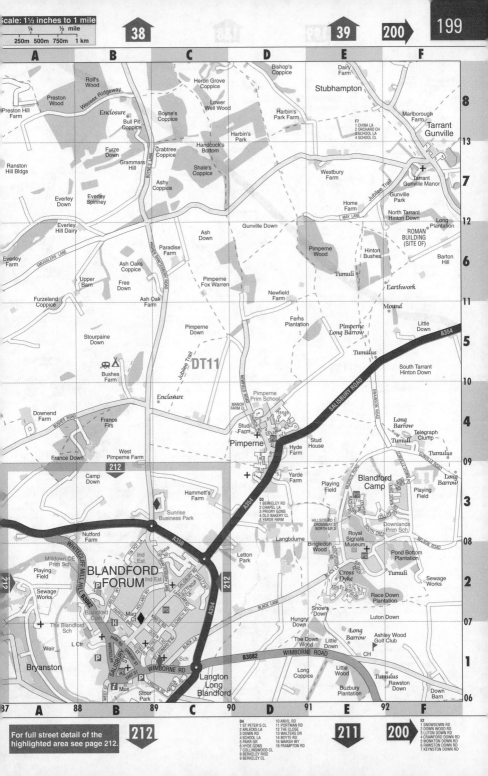

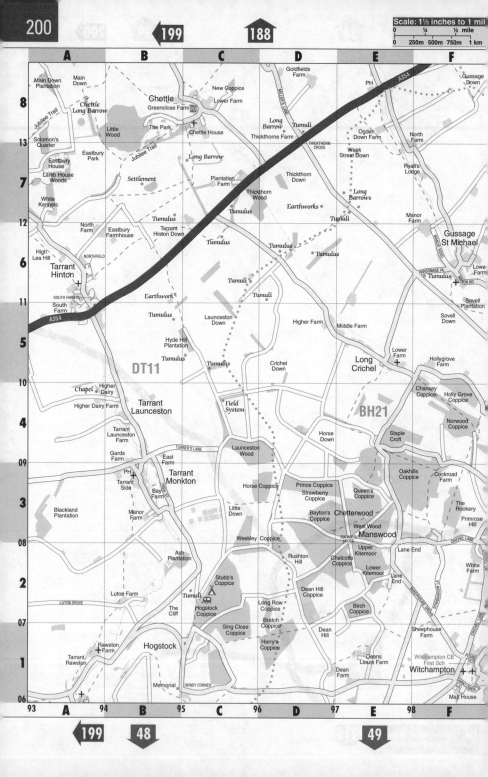

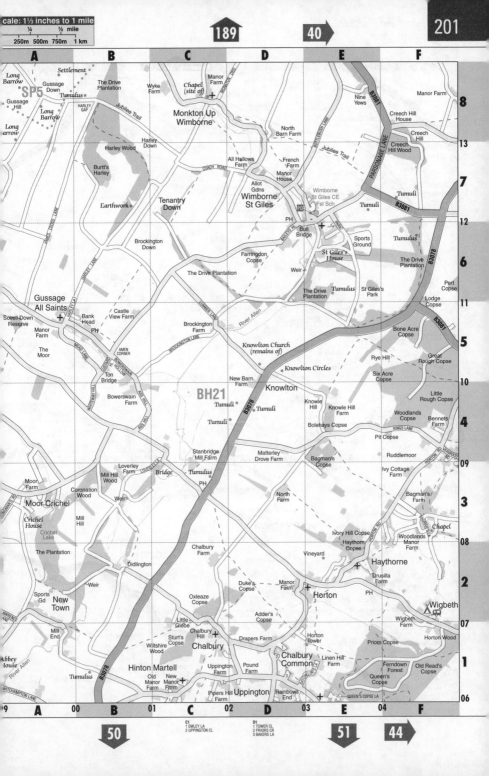

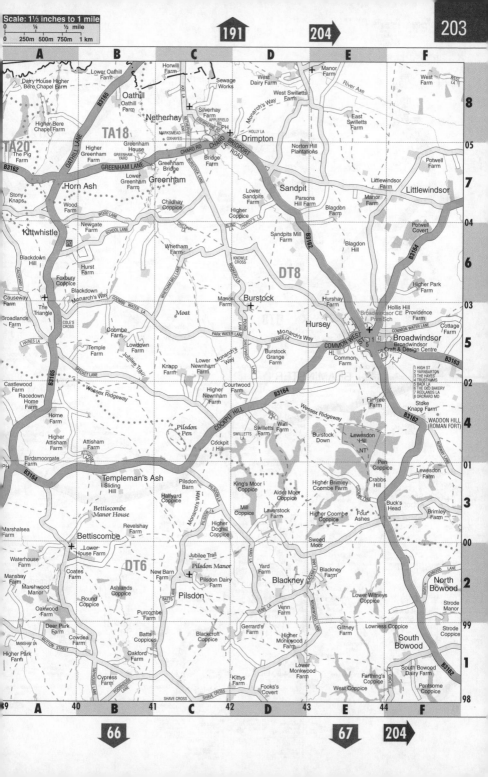

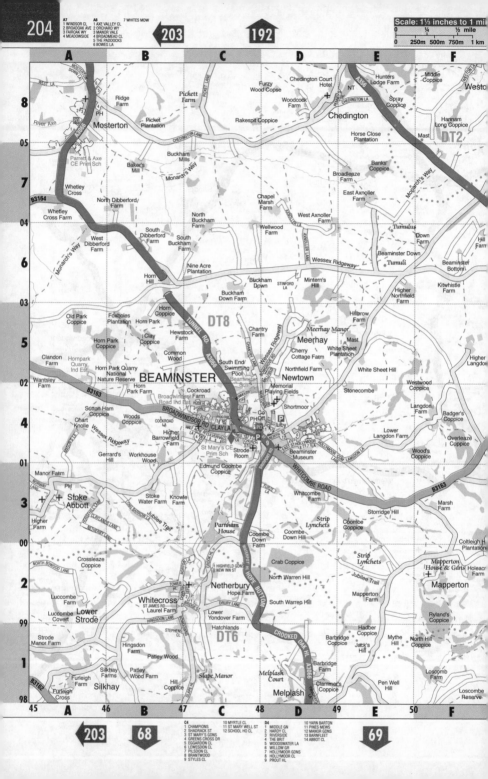

A7
1 WINDSOR CL
2 BROADOAK AVE
3 FAIROAK WY
4 MEADOWSIDE

A8
1 AXE VALLEY CL
2 ORCHARD WY
3 MANOR VALE
4 BROADMEAD CL
5 THE PADDOCKS
6 BOWES LA

7 WHITES MDW

203
192

Scale: 1½ inches to 1 mile

West
DT2

DT8

BEAMINSTER

Mosterton

Chedington

Meerhay

Newtown

Stoke Abbott

Whitecross

Netherbury

Lower Strode

Silkhay

Melplash

Mapperton

DT6

203
68
69

C4
1 CHAMPIONS
2 SHADRACK ST
3 ST MARY'S GDNS
4 GREENS CROSS DR
5 EGGARDON CL
6 LEWESDON CL
7 PILSDON CL
8 BRANTWOOD
9 STYLES CL

10 MYRTLE CL
11 ST MARY WELL ST
12 SCHOOL HO CL

D4
1 MIDDLE GN
2 HARDY CL
3 RIVERSIDE
4 THE BRIT
5 WOODSWATER LA
6 WILLOW GR
7 HOLLYMOOR GDNS
8 HOLLYMOOR CL
9 PROUT HL

10 YARN BARTON
11 PINES MEWS
12 MANOR GDNS
13 BARNFLEET
14 ABBOT CL

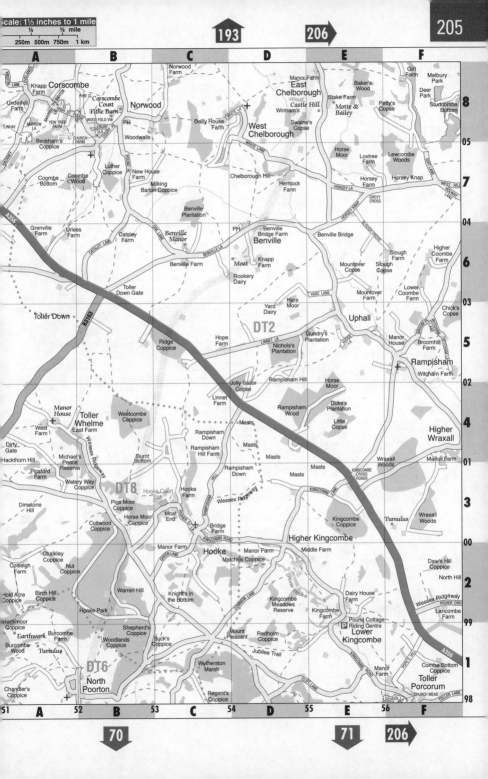

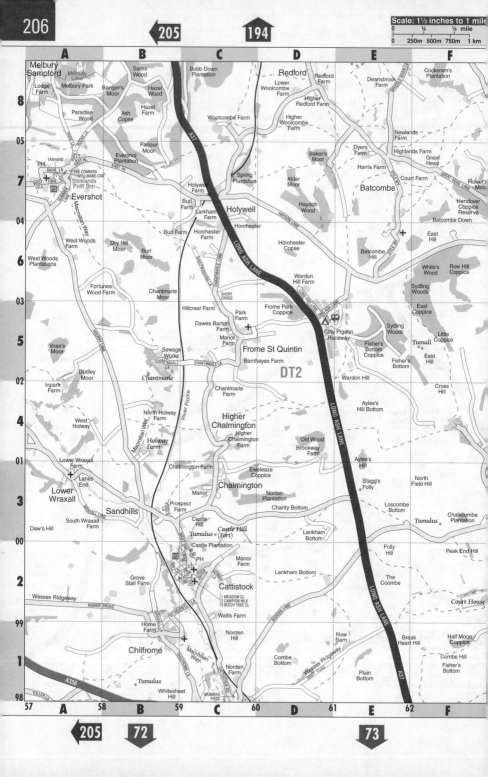

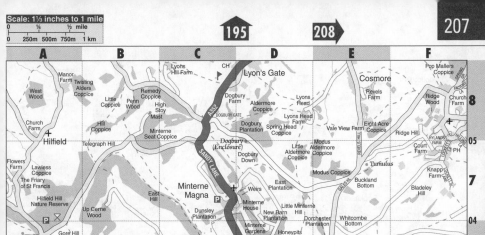
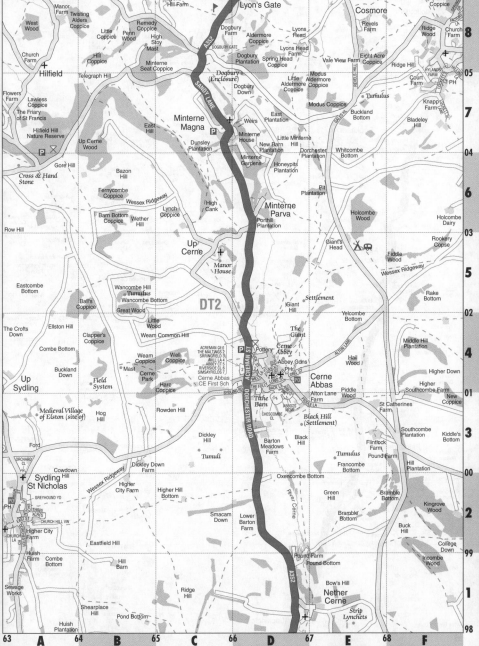

Pop Mallers Coppice

Manor Farm

West Wood

Twisting Alders Coppice

Lyons Hill Farm

CH

Lyon's Gate

Cosmore

Ridge Wood

Church Farm

Little Coppice

Remedy Coppice

Penn Wood

High Stoy Mast

Dogbury Farm

Aldermore Coppice

Lyons Head

Lyons Head Farm

Revels Farm

Church Farm

PH

Church Farm

Hill Coppice

Minterne Seat Coppice

DOGBURY GATE

Dogbury Plantation

Spring Head Coppice

Vale View Farm

Eight Acre Coppice

Ridge Hill

HYLANDS FARM

Court Farm

05

Hilfield

Telegraph Hill

A352

SANDY LANE

Dogbury (Enclosure)

Dogbury Down

Little Aldermore Coppice

Modus Aldermore Coppice

Modus Coppice

Tumulus

Knapp Farm

Bladeley Hill

7

Flowers Farm

Lawless Coppice

The Friary of St Francis

East Hill

Up Cerne Wood

Dunsley Plantation

Minterne Magna

P

Minterne House

Weirs

East Plantation

Little Minterne Hill

New Barn Plantation

Dorchester Plantation

Whitcombe Bottom

04

Hilfield Hill Nature Reserve

P

Minterne Gardens

Minterne Parva

Honeypits Plantation

Cross & Hand Stone

Gore Hill

Bazon Hill

High Cank

Porthill Plantation

Pit Plantation

Holcombe Wood

Holcombe Dairy

Row Hill

Fernycombe Coppice

Wessex Ridgeway

Lynch Coppice

Minterne Parva

Giant's Head

03

Rookery Copse

Eastcombe Bottom

Barn Bottom Coppice

Wether Hill

Up Cerne

Fiddle Wood

Wessex Ridgeway

Ball's Coppice

Manor House

Wancombe Hill

Tumulus

Wancombe Bottom

Great Wood

Settlement

Giant Hill

Yelcombe Bottom

Rake Bottom

02

The Crofts Down

Ellston Hill

Clapper's Coppice

Little Wood

Weam Common Hill

DT2

The Giant

Middle Hill Plantation

Combe Bottom

Buckland Down

Weam Coppice

Well Coppice

Mast

Cerne Park

Hare Coppice

ACREMAN Ct

THE MALTINGS

SPRINGFIELD

MILL LA

ABBEY Ct

RIVERSIDE

SIMSAYFIELDS

P

Pottery

Cerne Abbey

Abbey Gdns

Higher Southcombe Farm

Higher Down

Up Sydling

Field System

Cerne Abbas CE First Sch

Tithe Barn

PH

Cerne Abbas

Hail Wood

Piddle Wood

St Catherines Farm

Southcombe Plantation

New Coppice

01

Medieval Village of Elston (site of)

Hog Hill

Rowden Hill

CHESCOMBE CL

ABBOTS MDW

Black Hill (Settlement)

Alton Lane Farm

Kiddle's Bottom

Ford

Dickley Hill

Barton Meadows Farm

Black Hill

Tumulus

Flintlock Farm

Pound Farm

Hill Plantation

00

Sydling St Nicholas

GREYHOUND YD

Cowdown Hill

Higher City Farm

Higher Hill Bottom

Dickley Down Farm

Tumuli

Francombe Bottom

Green Hill

Bramble Bottom

Bramble Bottom

Kingrove Wood

2

PH

THREE ACRES

CHURCH HILL VW

Wessex Ridgeway

Smacam Down

Oxencombe Bottom

River Cerne

Buck Hill

Higher City Farm

Huish Farm

Combe Bottom

Eastfield Hill

Hill Barn

Lower Barton Farm

College Down

99

Sewage Works

Shearplace Hill

Pond Bottom

Ridge Hill

Pound Farm

A352

Pound Bottom

Bow's Hill

Nether Cerne

Incombe Wood

Strip Lynchets

1

Huish Plantation

98

63 64 65 66 67 68

74 75 208

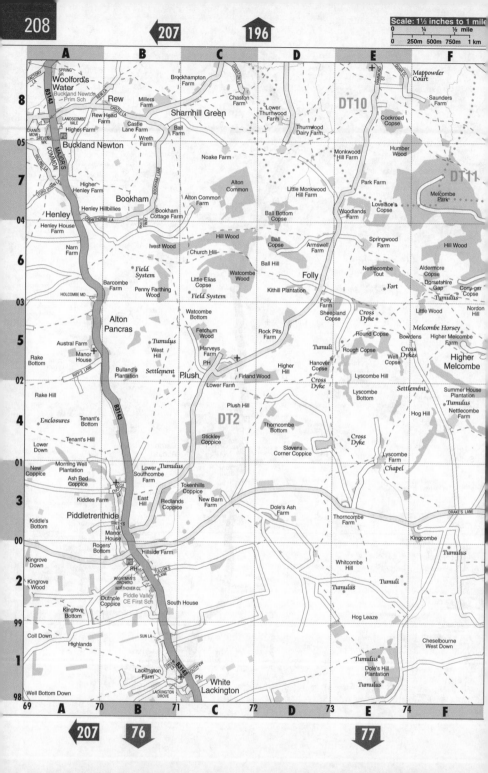

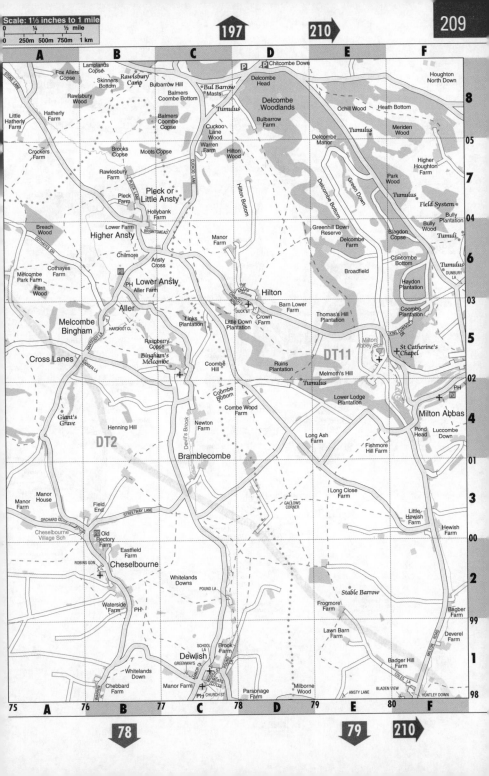

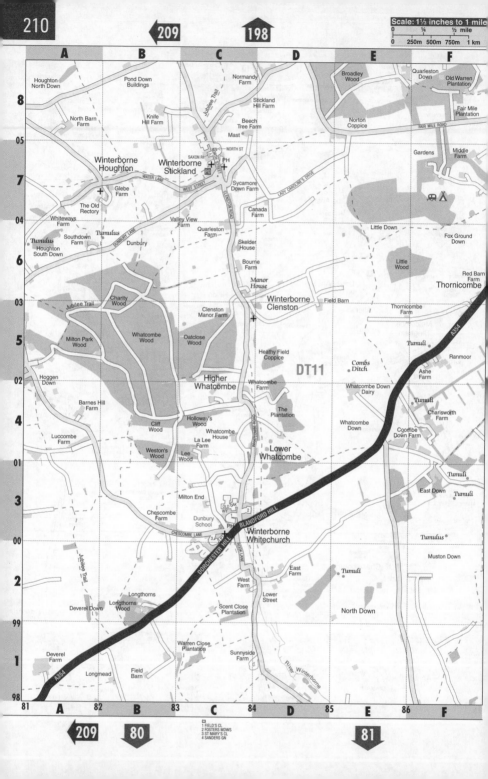

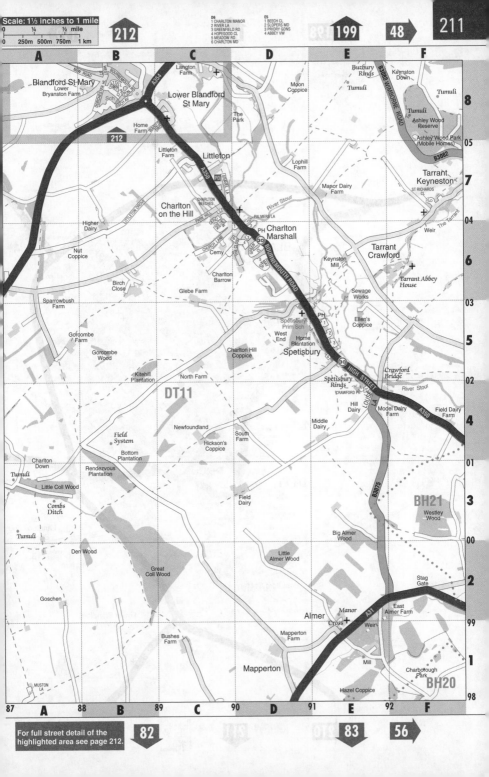

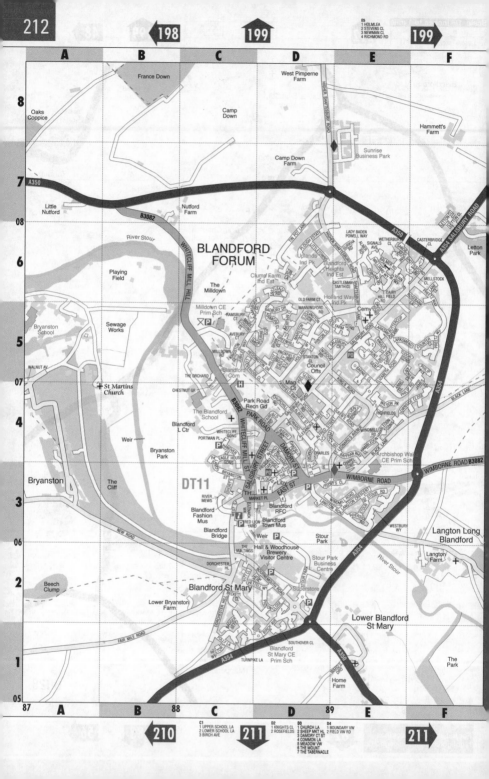

Index

Place name May be abbreviated on the map

Location number Present when a number indicates the place's position in a crowded area of mapping

Locality, town or village Shown when more than one place has the same name

Postcode district District for the indexed place

Page and grid square Page number and grid reference for the standard mapping

Church Rd **6** Beckenham BR2.........**53** C6

Cities, towns and villages are listed in CAPITAL LETTERS

Public and commercial buildings are highlighted in magenta **Places of interest** are highlighted in blue with a star ★

Abbreviations used in the index

Acad	**Academy**	Comm	**Common**	Gd	**Ground**	L	**Leisure**	Prom	**Promenade**
App	**Approach**	Cott	**Cottage**	Gdn	**Garden**	La	**Lane**	Rd	**Road**
Arc	**Arcade**	Cres	**Crescent**	Gn	**Green**	Liby	**Library**	Recn	**Recreation**
Ave	**Avenue**	Cswy	**Causeway**	Gr	**Grove**	Mdw	**Meadow**	Ret	**Retail**
Bglw	**Bungalow**	Ct	**Court**	H	**Hall**	Meml	**Memorial**	Sh	**Shopping**
Bldg	**Building**	Ctr	**Centre**	Ho	**House**	Mkt	**Market**	Sq	**Square**
Bsns, Bus	**Business**	Ctry	**Country**	Hospl	**Hospital**	Mus	**Museum**	St	**Street**
Bvd	**Boulevard**	Cty	**County**	HQ	**Headquarters**	Orch	**Orchard**	Sta	**Station**
Cath	**Cathedral**	Dr	**Drive**	Hts	**Heights**	Pal	**Palace**	Terr	**Terrace**
Cir	**Circus**	Dro	**Drove**	Ind	**Industrial**	Par	**Parade**	TH	**Town Hall**
Cl	**Close**	Ed	**Education**	Inst	**Institute**	Pas	**Passage**	Univ	**University**
Cnr	**Corner**	Emb	**Embankment**	Int	**International**	Pk	**Park**	Wk, Wlk	**Walk**
Coll	**College**	Est	**Estate**	Intc	**Interchange**	Pl	**Place**	Wr	**Water**
Com	**Community**	Ex	**Exhibition**	Junc	**Junction**	Prec	**Precinct**	Yd	**Yard**

Index of towns, villages, streets, hospitals, industrial estates, railway stations, schools, shopping centres, universities and places of interest

A

Aaron Cl BH17 .... 119 F7
Abbey Cl
  Sherborne DT9 .... 30 B5
  9 Tatworth TA20 ..... 202 A8
Abbey Ct DT2............ 207 D4
Abbey Gdns * DT2 ..... 207 D4
Abbey Gdns BH21........ 60 D5
Abbey Mews **2** TA20 ... 202 A8
Abbey Prim Sch SP7 .... 12 D1
Abbey Rd
  Sherborne DT9 .... 30 B6
  West Moors BH22 ...... 62 A8
  Yeovil BA21 .... 26 F6
Abbey St
  Cerne Abbas DT2 ..... 207 D4
  Crewkerne TA18 ...... 191 E4
  Hinton St George TA17 . 191 C7
Abbey Trading Est BA21 . 26 E6
Abbey View **4** DT11 ... 211 E5
Abbey Wlk SP7 .... 12 E2
Abbot Cl **10** DT8 ..... 204 D4
ABBOTSBURY DT3 ..... 149 B8
Abbotsbury Abbey (ruin)★
  DT3..................... 149 B7
Abbotsbury Castle (Hill
  Fort)★ DT3........... 130 D2
**Abbotsbury Children's
  Farm**★ DT3.......... 149 B7
Abbotsbury Hill DT3... 130 F7
Abbotsbury La DT2..... 130 F7
Abbotsbury Rd
  Bournemouth BH9 .... 122 B8
  6 Dorchester DT1 . 108 A2
Abbotsbury Subtropical
  Gdns★ DT3........... 148 E7
Abbotsbury Swannery★
  DT3..................... 149 B3
Abbots Cl DT3.......... 125 F7
Abbots Mdw DT2....... 207 D3
Abbots Meade BA21.... 26 F5
Abbots Quay **4** BH20 . 142 C6
Abbots Way
  Sherborne DT9 .... 29 F5
  Yeovil BA21 .... 207 D4
Abbots Wlk DT2 .... 207 D4
Abbott Cl BH9.......... 122 A8
Abbott La TA16 .... 192 A8
Abbott Rd BH9......... 122 A8
Abbotts Mdw BH16..... 84 D3
Abbott St BH21......... 57 F6

Abbotts Way BH22 ...... 62 A8
Abbott's Way SP8........ 5 F3
Abbott's Wootton La
  Marshwood DT6 ...... 202 E1
  Whitechurch Canonicorum
    DT6................... 65 D7
Abber Cross DT9........ 14 F4
Abels La DT9 .... 14 E2
Aberdare Rd BH10 ..... 89 E3
Abingdon Dr BH23 .... 126 C8
Abingdon Rd BH17 ... 119 D8
Abinger Rd BH7........ 123 B6
Abney Rd BH10 .... 89 D3
Acacia Ave BH31....... 45 E4
Acacia Cl DT4........... 167 B6
Acacia Dr DT2 .... 75 D2
Acacia Rd SO41........ 95 F3
Acer Ave **2** DT6 ..... 68 F1
Acer Dr BA21 .... 26 E7
Ackerman Rd DT1..... 108 C1
Acland Rd
  Bournemouth BH9 .... 122 B8
  6 Dorchester DT1 . 108 A2
Aconbury Ave **2** DT1 . 107 C1
Acorn Ave BH15........ 119 D2
Acorn Bsns Pk BH2 ... 120 B8
Acorn Cl
  Christchurch BH23.... 123 F8
  New Milton BH25...... 95 C4
  St Leonards BH24 ..... 54 A3
Acorns The
  West Moors BH24 ..... 62 B8
  Wimborne Minster BH21. 60 A4
Acorn Way BH25........ 95 C6
Acreman Cl DT2 ...... 207 D4
Acreman Ct DT9 .... 30 A6
Acreman Pl DT9 .... 30 B5
Acreman St
  Cerne Abbas DT2..... 207 D4
  Sherborne DT9 .... 30 B6
Acres Ct **5** BA22 .... 193 F8
Acres Rd BH11.......... 89 B2
ACTON BH19 .... 177 F1
Acton Rd BH10......... 89 B1
Adamsfield Gdns BH10.. 89 C2
ADAM'S GREEN BA22... 193 D2
Adastral Rd BH17 ..... 119 F8
Adastral Sq BH17 ..... 119 C5
Ad Astro Fst Sch BH17 .. 87 F1
ADBER DT9 .... 14 F5
Adber Rd BA21 .... 28 A8
Addington Pl BH23..... 124 D6
Addiscombe Rd BH23 .. 124 A7

Addison Cl SP8 .... 6 A1
Addison Sq BH24 ...... 55 D7
Addlewell La BA20..... 27 D4
Adelaide Cl BH23 ..... 123 F8
Adelaide Cres DT4 ... 167 B3
Adelaide La **17** BH1 ... 121 F3
Adeline Rd BH1, BH5.. 122 E4
Admirals Cl DT9 ...... 30 D8
Admirals Way BH20 .. 142 E6
Admirals Wlk **13** BH2.. 121 D2
Airfield Rd BH23 ..... 123 F3
Adventure Wonderland★
  BH23.................... 90 E7
Aerial Pk BH21........ 60 E6
Aggis Farm Rd BH11... 45 A6
Agglestone Rd BH19 . 164 B1
Aigburth Rd BH19..... 178 F3
Airetons Cl BH18...... 87 C3
Airfield Cl DT2......... 137 D5
Airfield Rd BH23 ..... 124 F6
Airfield Way BH23 ... 124 F7
Airspeed Rd BH23.... 125 B7
Akeman Ct **13** BA22 .. 26 F7
Akeshill Cl BH25....... 95 B5
Alamanda Rd BH3..... 152 E2
Alamein Rd BH20 ..... 139 F6
Alan Ct **11** BH23.... 126 B7
Alastair Cl BH21 ...... 27 B7
Alastair Dr BA21 ...... 27 B7
Albany
  Old Milton BH25 ...... 94 F1
  Sherborne DT9 .... 30 C8
Albany Ct **6** BH2..... 121 F4
Albany Dr BH21 .... 45 A1
Albany Gdns BH15 ... 118 F2
Albany Ho 7 BH13.... 121 A4
Albany Pk BH17 ...... 119 B8
Albany Rd DT4......... 166 E4
Albemarle Rd BH3 ... 121 F7
Albert Cl BA21 .... 27 A7
Albert Rd
  Bournemouth BH1 ... 121 F3
  Dorchester DT1....... 107 F1
  Ferndown BH22....... 61 D5
  New Milton BH25..... 94 F2
  Poole BH12 .... 120 D6
  Poole BH21 .... 85 E5
Albert St
  Blandford Forum DT11.. 212 D4
  5 Radipole DT4...... 167 D4

Albert Terr DT5......... 186 E8
Albion Cl BH12........ 120 B7
Albion Rd BH23 .... 91 F1
Albion Way BH31 ...... 44 F6
Alby Rd BH12........... 120 F5
ALCESTER SP7 .... 12 D2
Alder Ct BH12 .... 120 D6
Aldabrand Cl DT3..... 166 D4
Aldbury Ct BH25 ..... 127 A7
Alderbury Cl **5** BH19.. 178 F2
Alder Cl
  Burton BH23 .... 92 D1
  3 Sandford BH20... 116 A1
  Sturminster Newton DT10.. 35 C2
Alder Cres BH12 ...... 120 F7
Alder Dr SP6 .... 42 B5
Alder Gr
  Crewkerne TA18...... 191 F5
  Yeovil BA20 .... 27 A2
Alder Hills BH12 ...... 121 A7
Alder Hills Ind Pk BH12 . 121 A7
Alder Hills Nature Reserve★
  BH12.................... 121 A7
Alderholt Sports Club
  SP6....................... 42 C5
Alder Hts BH12 .... 121 A7
Alderley Rd BH10 ..... 89 D4
ALDERNEY 88 C1
Alderney Ave BH12.... 88 D1
Alderney Hospl BH12.. 88 C2
Alderney Rdbt BH12.. 88 D2
Alder Rd
  Poole BH12 .... 120 F6
  Sturminster Newton DT10.. 35 C2
Aldis Gdns BH15 ..... 118 E2
Aldondale Gdns BA20 . 27 C3
Aldridge Rd
  Bournemouth BH10 .. 89 C5
  Ferndown BH22....... 62 B6
Aldridge Way BH22 ... 61 F3
Alexander Cl
  Christchurch BH23.... 124 E6
  New Milton BH25..... 95 A3
Alexander Gdns **6** BH9.. 90 A1
Alexandra Lodge **8** BH1 122 A3
Alexandra Rd
  Bournemouth BH6 ... 123 C5
  Bridport DT6 .... 100 C6
  Dorchester DT1....... 107 F1
  Poole BH14 .... 120 D5
  Radipole DT4.......... 167 D5

Aar–Alm

Alexandra Rd continued
  Weymouth DT4 .... 166 E3
  Yeovil BA21 .... 27 F6
Alexandra St DT11 ... 212 D4
Alexandra Terr **9** DT1.. 108 A2
Alexandria Cl BH22 .... 61 E3
Alford Rd BH3 .... 121 D7
Alfred Pl DT1 .... 108 A1
Alfred St DT11......... 212 D4
Alice Rd DT1 .... 107 E1
Alington **22** BH4 ..... 121 C3
Alington Cl **1** DT1 ... 108 C1
Alington Cl BH14...... 147 C7
Alington Ho BH14..... 147 C7
Alington Rd
  Bournemouth BH3 ... 122 A6
  Dorchester DT1....... 108 B1
  Poole BH14 .... 147 C7
Alington St **4** DT1 ... 108 A2
Alington Terr **6** DT1.. 108 B2
Alipore Cl BH14....... 120 D3
Alipore Hts BH14..... 120 D3
Alisons The DT3 ...... 139 E2
Allberry Gdns DT3 ... 168 A8
Allenbourn Mid Sch BH21 59 C5
Allenby Cl BH17....... 87 B2
Allenby Rd BH17 ...... 87 B2
Allen Cl **6** DT11 ..... 198 C7
Allen Cl BH17.......... 59 C5
Allen Rd BH21 .... 59 C4
Allens La BH16......... 117 F5
Allens Rd BH16 .... 117 F6
Allenview Rd BH21 ... 59 C5
ALLER DT2............. 209 B5
Allingham Rd BA21... 27 E7
Allington Cl BH18..... 87 F3
Allington Gdns **3** DT6 . 100 B8
Allington Mead **3** DT6 . 100 C8
Allington Pk DT6..... 100 B7
ALLOWENSHAY TA17... 191 A8
All Saints CE Prim Sch
  DT9.................... 196 A7
All Saints CE Sch DT4.. 180 D8
All Saints' Rd
  Dorchester DT1....... 108 B2
  Weymouth DT4 .... 180 C8
Alma Rd
  Bournemouth BH9 ... 122 A7
  Weymouth DT4 .... 167 C3

ALMER DT11 . . . . 211 E2
Almer Rd BH15 . . . . 118 E3
Almond Gr
  Poole BH12 . . . . 120 D7
  Radipole DT4 . . . . 167 B6
Almshouses BH10 . . . . 89 C1
Alner Rd DT11 . . . . 212 E6
Alpha Ctr The BH17 . . . . . . 119 B7
Alpine Rd BH24 . . . . 54 E2
Alton La DT2 . . . . 207 E4
Alton Mead La DT2 . . . . . . 194 E4
ALTON PANCRAS DT2 . . . . 208 B5
Alton Rd
  Bournemouth BH10 . . . . . 89 B1
  Poole BH14 . . . . 120 C3
Alton Road E BH14 . . . . . . 120 D2
Alum Chine Rd BH4 . . . . . . 121 B3
Alumdale Rd BH4 . . . . 121 B2
Alumhurst Rd BH4 . . . . 121 B2
Alvandi Gdns [2] BH25 . . . . 95 B3
Alverton Ave BH15 . . . . . . 119 F3
Alverton Hall [3] BH4 . . . . 121 C2
ALVINGTON BA22 . . . . 26 C4
Alvington La BA22 . . . . 26 C4
ALWESTON DT9 . . . . 31 B1
Alyth Rd BH3 . . . . 121 D6
Ambassador Cl BH23 . . . . . 125 A6
Ambassador Ind Est
  BH23 . . . . 125 A6
Ambassador Trade Pk
  SP8 . . . . 20 C7
Amberley Cl BH23 . . . . 125 F8
Amberley Ct [10] BH1 . . . . 122 A3
Amberley Ho BH22 . . . . 61 D7
Amelia Cl DT5 . . . . 186 F8
Amberwood BH22 . . . . 61 E7
Amberwood Dr BH23 . . . . . . 93 F2
Amberwood Gdns BH23 . . . . 94 A2
Amberwood Ho BH23 . . . . . . 94 A2
Ambleside
  Christchurch BH23 . . . . . . 91 E3
  Radipole DT4 . . . . 167 B7
Ambleside Cl BH18 . . . . 87 C2
Ambury La BH23 . . . . 124 F8
Amelia Cl DT5 . . . . 186 F8
Amen Cnr BH21 . . . . 201 B5
Amersham Ct [5] BH4 . . . . 121 C3
Amesbury BH6 . . . . 123 C6
Amethyst Rd BH23 . . . . 124 F7
AMEYSFORD BH22 . . . . 52 E1
Ameysford Rd
  Ferndown BH22 . . . . 52 E1
  Ferndown BH22 . . . . 61 C7
Ameys La BH22 . . . . 61 F7
Amiens Rd BH20 . . . . 139 E2
Amira Ct [2] BH2 . . . . 121 E3
AMMERHAM TA20 . . . . 202 D8
Ammerham La TA20 . . . . . 202 D8
Ampfield Rd BH8 . . . . 90 D3
Amsterdam Sq BH23 . . . . . 124 D6
Ancaster Rd BH19 . . . . 178 F3
Anchor Cl
  Bournemouth BH11 . . . . . . 88 F6
  Christchurch BH23 . . . . . 125 A5
Anchor Rd BH11 . . . . 88 F5
Ancrum Lo [15] BH4 . . . . . 121 B3
Andbourne Ct BH6 . . . . 123 F3
ANDERSON DT11 . . . . 82 B7
Andover Cl BH23 . . . . 124 A2
Andover Gn BH20 . . . . 139 C6
Andre Cl BH23 . . . . 126 B8
Andrew Cl DT11 . . . . 212 E5
Andrews Cl BH11 . . . . 89 A3
Angel Cl DT3 . . . . 150 C1
Angel Ct DT9 . . . . 17 D2
Angeline Cl BH23 . . . . 125 F8
Angel La
  Barton on Sea BH25 . . . . 127 D8
  Ferndown BH22 . . . . 61 B3
  Langton Herring DT3 . . . . 150 C2
  Mere BA12 . . . . 3 A5
  Shaftesbury SP7 . . . . 12 E3
  Stour Provost SP8 . . . . . . 10 F1
Angel Mews BH15 . . . . 119 B2
Angel Sq SP7 . . . . 12 E3
Angers Ct DT1 . . . . 197 F2
Anglebury Ave BH9 . . . . . . 179 B4
Anglebury Bsns Pk BH20 . . 142 E3
Anglewood Mans [2]
  BH4 . . . . 121 C3
Anglo-European Coll of
  Chiropractic [8] BH5 . . . 123 A4
Angus Cl DT11 . . . . 212 E5
Anjou Cl BH11 . . . . 88 D5
Annandale Ct BH16 . . . . . . 123 D4
Anncott Cl BH16 . . . . 84 D3
Anne Cl
  Blandford Forum DT11 . . 212 E4
  Christchurch BH23 . . . . . . 92 A1
Annerley Rd BH1 . . . . 122 C4
Annet Cl BH15 . . . . 118 E2
Anning Rd DT7 . . . . 96 C6
Annings La DT6 . . . . 101 E1
Anson Cl
  Christchurch BH23 . . . . . 124 F6
  Ringwood BH24 . . . . 55 E8
Anstey Cl BH11 . . . . 89 A6
Anstey Rd BH11 . . . . 89 A6
Ansty La DT11 . . . . 79 C8
Antell's Way BH24 . . . . 42 C6
Antelope Wlk [7] DT1 . . . . 108 A2
Anthony's Ave BH14 . . . . . 120 C1
Antler Dr BH25 . . . . 94 E4

Anvil Cl [1] BH19 . . . . 178 E2
Anvil Cres BH18 . . . . 86 F5
Anvil Rd [10] DT11 . . . . . . 199 D4
Aplands Cl DT11 . . . . 198 B8
Apollo Cl
  Dorchester DT1 . . . . 134 F8
  Poole BH12 . . . . 120 D7
Apple Acre [8] DT11 . . . . . 198 C7
Applebee Way [2] DT1 . . . . 96 C6
Apple Cl BH13 . . . . 121 A4
Applefield Rd DT8 . . . . 203 C8
Apple Gr BH23 . . . . 91 E2
Appleslade Way BH25 . . . . . 95 B5
Appletree Cl
  Bournemouth BH6 . . . . . 123 C5
  New Milton BH25 . . . . . . 95 A1
  Radipole DT4 . . . . 167 C8
Apple Tree Gr BH22 . . . . . . 61 E6
Apple Tree Rd SP6 . . . . 42 B5
Apple Trees La DT6 . . . . 99 A6
Approach Rd BH14 . . . . . . 120 B3
April Cl BH11 . . . . 89 A4
Apsley Cres BH17 . . . . 87 C1
Apsley Ct [9] BH8 . . . . 122 A5
Aragon Cl DT4 . . . . 180 E8
Aragon Way BH9 . . . . 90 B4
Arbutus Cl DT1 . . . . 108 A1
Arcade BH4 . . . . 121 B3
Arcade The [14] BH1 . . . . . 121 F3
Arcadia Ave BH8 . . . . 122 B7
Arcadia Rd BH23 . . . . 91 F1
Archbishop Wake CE Prim
  Sch DT11 . . . . 212 E4
Archdale Cl BH10 . . . . 89 D2
Archway Rd BH14 . . . . 120 C4
Arden Rd BH9 . . . . 89 F3
Arden Wlk BH25 . . . . 95 B2
Ardmore Rd BH14 . . . . 120 B4
Argyle Rd
  Christchurch BH23 . . . . . 124 C5
  Radipole DT4 . . . . 167 D6
  Swanage BH19 . . . . 179 B2
Argyll Mans [8] BH1 . . . . . 122 E4
Argyll Rd
  Bournemouth BH5 . . . . . 122 E4
  Poole BH12 . . . . 120 D6
Ariel Cl BH6 . . . . 124 B4
Ariel Dr BH6 . . . . 124 B4
Ark Dr BH22 . . . . 61 F3
Arlecks La [2] DT11 . . . . . 199 D4
Arley Rd BH14 . . . . 120 A2
Arlington Cl BA21 . . . . 26 E7
Arlington Ct BH25 . . . . 127 B8
Armoury Rd BA22 . . . . 26 C6
Armoury Yd SP7 . . . . 12 E3
Armstrong Rd DT6 . . . . 100 C8
ARNE BH20 . . . . 144 C5
Arne Ave BH12 . . . . 120 E7
Arne Cres BH12 . . . . 120 F7
Arne Rd BH20 . . . . 143 D1
Arne Reedbeds National
  Nature Reserve*
  BH20 . . . . 143 D3
Arne Tea Room & Toy Mus*
  BH20 . . . . 144 C4
Arnewood Ct BH21 . . . . . . 121 E2
Arnewood Gdns BA20 . . . . . 27 B2
Arnewood Rd BH6 . . . . 123 D5
Arnewood Sch The BH25 . . 94 F2
Arnold Cl BH22 . . . . 53 A3
Arnold Rd BH22 . . . . 53 A3
Arnolds Cl BH23 . . . . 126 F8
Arran Way BH23 . . . . 94 B1
Arras Cres BH20 . . . . 139 D7
Arras Rd BH20 . . . . 139 D7
Arrowfield DT6 . . . . 100 C6
Arrow Field DT6 . . . . 100 C6
Arrowsmith Ct BH18 . . . . . . 87 A4
Arrowsmith La BH21 . . . . . . 87 E7
Arrowsmith Rd BH21 . . . . . . 87 E7
Arthur Cl BH2 . . . . 121 F5
Arthur La [3] BH24 . . . . . . 124 A7
Arthur Rd BH23 . . . . 124 A7
Arthurs Pleck SP5 . . . . 188 C5
Artillery Rd BA22 . . . . 26 C6
Artist Row DT5 . . . . 186 F7
Arun Cl [2] SP8 . . . . 5 F3
Arundel Cl BH25 . . . . 94 E3
Arundel Rd BA21 . . . . 28 A6
Arundel Way BH23 . . . . 125 F7
Ascham Rd BH8 . . . . 122 B5
Ascot Rd BH18 . . . . 87 A4
ASH
  Blandford Forum DT11 . . 198 F5
  Bridport DT6 . . . . 68 C5
Ash Ave
  Dorchester DT1 . . . . 139 C2
  Holton Heath BH16 . . . . 114 A6
Ashbourne Cl BH1 . . . . 122 A3
Ashbourne Rd BH5 . . . . . . 122 E2
Ashbrook Wlk BH16 . . . . . 117 A6
Ashburn Garth [2] BH24 . . 55 F6
Ashburton Gdns BH10 . . . . . 89 D1
Ash Cl
  Alderholt SP6 . . . . 42 C5
  Sandford BH20 . . . . 143 A8
  Shaftesbury SP7 . . . . 13 A4
  Swanage BH19 . . . . 178 F2
  Upton BH16 . . . . 118 B4
Ashcombe La DT9 . . . . 31 D3
Ashdene Cl BH21 . . . . 59 D5
Ashdown [8] BH21 . . . . 121 D2
Ashdown Cl BH17 . . . . 87 F1
Ashdown L Ctr BH17 . . . . . 87 E1
Ashdown Tech Coll BH17 . . 87 E1

Ashdown Wlk BH25 . . . . 95 C2
Ash End BA8 . . . . 19 A5
Ash Gdns BH15 . . . . 118 E3
Ashford Rd
  Bournemouth BH6 . . . . . 123 D7
  Fordingbridge SP6 . . . . . . 42 E8
Ash Gdns BH15 . . . . 118 E3
Ash Gr BH24 . . . . 55 E7
Ashgrove BA12 . . . . 3 A4
Ash Hill DT2 . . . . 106 F8
ASHINGTON 59 A1
Ashington Gdns BH21 . . . . . 86 F8
Ashington La BH21 . . . . 59 A1
Ashington Pk BH25 . . . . 95 B1
Ashington St [3] DT1 . . . . 107 D1
Ashlake La DT4 . . . . 116 E5
Ashland CE Fst Sch
  TA18 . . . . 191 E5
Ashlands CE Fst Sch
  TA18 . . . . 191 F5
Ashlands Mdw TA18 . . . . . 191 F5
Ashlands Rd TA18 . . . . 191 F5
Ashleet Gdns BH25 . . . . 95 D4
ASHLEY
  New Milton 95 D3
  Ringwood BH24 . . . . 54 F5
Ashley Arnewood Ct [5]
  BH25 . . . . 95 B2
Ashley Cl
  Bournemouth BH1 . . . . . 122 C6
  Ringwood BH24 . . . . 54 F5
Ashley Common Rd BH25 . . 95 C4
Ashley Cross BH14 . . . . . . 120 A4
Ashley Cres BH15 . . . . 118 F1
Ashley Dr BH24 . . . . 46 E2
Ashley Drive N BH24 . . . . . 54 B5
Ashley Drive S BH24 . . . . . 54 B5
Ashley Drive W BH24 . . . . . 54 B5
ASHLEY HEATH BH24 . . . . . 54 C6
Ashley Heath Ind Est
  BH21 . . . . 53 D7
Ashley Inf Sch BH25 . . . . . . 95 D3
Ashley Jun Sch BH25 . . . . . 95 C3
Ashley La BH25, SO41 . . . . 95 E4
Ashley Meads BH25 . . . . . . 95 D4
Ashley Pk BH24 . . . . 54 C6
Ashley Rd
  Bournemouth BH1 . . . . . 122 E5
  Dorchester DT1 . . . . 135 A8
  Marnhull DT10 . . . . 21 A2
  New Milton BH25 . . . . . . 95 C3
  Poole BH14 . . . . 120 C5
Ashley Wood Park DT11 . . 211 F8
Ashley Wood Rd DT11 . . . . 199 E2
Ashley Wood Reserve*
  DT11 . . . . 211 F8
Ashling Cl BH8 . . . . 122 C8
Ashling Cres BH8 . . . . 122 B8
Ashmead
  [22] Bournemouth BH4 . . 121 C2
  Yeovil BA20 . . . . 26 E2
Ashmeads Cl BH21 . . . . 60 A6
Ashmeads Way BH21 . . . . . 60 A6
ASHMORE SP5 . . . . 59 C8
Ashmore Ave
  Barton on Sea BH25 . . . . 127 B8
  Hamworthy BH15 . . . . . 118 F1
Ashmore Bottom DT11 . . . . 39 D1
Ashmore Cres BH15 . . . . . 118 F1
Ashmore Dr BH23 . . . . 93 E1
Ashmore Ho [50] BH4 . . . . 121 C3
Ash Rd DT2 . . . . 75 D2
Ashridge Ave [1] BH10 . . . . 89 D5
Ashridge Gdns BH10 . . . . . . 89 D5
Ashridge Par [2] BH10 . . . . 89 D5
Ashstead Gdns BH8 . . . . 90 C3
Ashton Cl
  [3] New Milton BH25 . . . . 95 B3
  Poole BH13 . . . . 121 A2
Ashton Rd
  Bournemouth BH9 . . . . . . 89 F2
  [1] Weymouth DT4 . . . . . 167 C2
Ashtree Cl BH25 . . . . 95 D2
Ash Tree La SP7 . . . . 24 D6
Ashurst Rd
  Bournemouth BH8 . . . . . . 90 D3
  Ferndown BH22 . . . . 53 A3
Ashwell Ct BH23 . . . . 91 F1
Ash Wlk BA8 . . . . 19 A5
Ashwood Dr
  Broadstone BH18 . . . . . . 87 C4
  Yeovil without BA21 . . . . . 28 A8
Asker Gdns DT6 . . . . 100 D6
Asker's Mdw Nature
  Reserve* BH16 . . . . 100 D6
ASKERSWELL DT2 . . . . 102 D6
Askwith Cl DT11 . . . . 29 F5
Aspen Cl BH31 . . . . 45 D6
Aspen Gdns BH12 . . . . 120 F7
Aspen Pl BH25 . . . . 95 B1
Aspen Rd
  Charminster DT2 . . . . 75 D3
  Poole BH12 . . . . 120 F7
Aspen Way
  [10] Crewkerne TA18 . . . 191 F5
  Poole BH12 . . . . 120 F7
Asquith Cl BH23 . . . . 124 D6
Ass Hill BH21 . . . . 201 B4
Astbury Ave BH12 . . . . 121 A8
Aston Mead BH23 . . . . 91 E4
Astrid Way DT4 . . . . 167 E4
ATHELHAMPTON DT2 . . . . . 78 E1

Athelhampton House &
  Gdns* DT2 . . . . 78 E1
Athelhampton Rd
  Poole BH17 . . . . 78 E1
  Puddletown DT2 . . . . 78 D3
Athelney Ct [7] BH11 . . . . 122 B3
Athelney Way BA21 . . . . 26 F6
Athelstan Rd
  Bournemouth BH6 . . . . . 123 E5
  [2] Dorchester DT1 . . . . 108 B1
Atkinson Cl BH25 . . . . 127 B8
Atlantic Rd BH19 . . . . 179 B1
ATRIM DT6 . . . . 68 A4
Atrium The BH21 . . . . 61 E7
Attisham La DT6 . . . . 203 D8
Attwood Cl SP6 . . . . 42 B5
Auburn Mans [8] BH13 . . . 121 B4
Auckland Rd BH23 . . . . 125 C7
Audemer Ct BH24 . . . . 55 E8
Audrayton Ct [6] BH6 . . . . 123 E3
Augusta Cl DT5 . . . . 187 B5
Augusta Cl [1] DT11 . . . . . 134 F7
Augustan Ave SP8 . . . . 5 D2
Augustan Cl [1] DT1 . . . . . 108 B1
Austen Ave BH10 . . . . 89 E6
Auster Cl BH23 . . . . 125 B1
Austin Ave BH14 . . . . 120 B1
Austin Cl BH1 . . . . 122 D5
Australia Rd DT3 . . . . 166 D3
Autumn Cl BH22 . . . . 61 B7
Autumn Copse BH25 . . . . . . 95 D2
Autumn Rd BH11 . . . . 88 D3
Avalanche Rd DT5 . . . . 186 E2
Avalon BH14 . . . . 147 C8
Avebury Ave BH10 . . . . 89 E6
Avebury Ct DT11 . . . . 212 D5
Avenel Way BH15 . . . . 119 D2
Avenue Cl BH13 . . . . 121 B3
Avenue La [18] BH2 . . . . . . 121 E3
Avenue Rd
  Bournemouth BH2 . . . . . 121 E3
  Christchurch BH23 . . . . . 123 F7
  Lyme Regis DT7 . . . . 96 B5
  New Milton BH25 . . . . 95 A1
  Radipole DT4 . . . . 167 D4
  Walkford BH23 . . . . 94 C2
  Wimborne Minster BH21 . . 59 D4
Avenue The
  Bournemouth BH9 . . . . . . 89 F3
  [6] Crewkerne TA18 . . . . 192 A3
  Ferndown BH22 . . . . 53 A3
  Poole BH13 . . . . 121 A3
  Sherborne DT9 . . . . 30 C7
  West Moors BH22 . . . . . . 62 B8
  Yeovil BA21 . . . . 27 D6
Aviation Park W
  East Parley BH23 . . . . 90 D1
  Hurn BH23 . . . . 62 D1
Aviation Way BH23 . . . . 62 D1
Avocet Cl
  Chickerell DT3 . . . . 166 D5
  Weymouth DT4 . . . . 180 D6
AVON 63 F2
Avon Ave BH24 . . . . 54 F3
Avon Bldgs BH23 . . . . 124 B7
Avonbourne Girls Sch
  BH7 . . . . 123 A4
Avon Cl
  Bournemouth BH8 . . . . . 122 D6
  Weymouth DT4 . . . . 166 E4
  Yeovil BA21 . . . . 27 F6
Avoncliffe Rd BH6 . . . . 123 E3
Avon Cotts BH23 . . . . 92 C5
Avon Cswy BH23 . . . . 91 C7
Avon Ct
  Christchurch BH23 . . . . . 124 C6
  [7] Poole BH13 . . . . 121 A4
Avondale Gdns SP8 . . . . 5 F3
Avon Dr BH20 . . . . 142 E5
Avon Farm Cotts BH23 . . . . 63 E3
Avon Heath Ctry Pk
  (Matchams View)*
  BH24 . . . . 54 E1
Avon Heath Ctry Pk (North
  Pk)* BH24 . . . . 54 D3
Avon Heath Ctry Pk (South
  Pk)* BH24 . . . . 63 B8
Avon Ho [1] BH22 . . . . 121 E2
Avon Mews BH8 . . . . 122 C6
Avon Pk BH24 . . . . 54 F6
Avon Rd
  Bournemouth BH8 . . . . . 122 C6
  Ferndown BH22 . . . . 53 A3
  Avon Road E BH23 . . . . . 124 A8
  Avon Road W BH23 . . . . 123 F8
  Avon Run Cl BH23 . . . . . 125 B5
  Avon Run Rd BH23 . . . . . 125 B5
Avonsands BH23 . . . . 125 A5
Avon View Par BH23 . . . . . . 92 C3
Avon View Rd BH23 . . . . 92 C3
Avon Wharf BH23 . . . . 124 C5
Award Rd
  Ferndown BH21 . . . . 60 F5
  Wimborne Minster BH21 . . 61 A6
Axeford TA20 . . . . 202 B8
Axe La
  Broadwindsor DT8 . . . . . 203 C8
  West Crewkerne TA18 . . . 191 C1
Axe Valley CE Sch [1] DT8 . 204 A8
Axford Cl DT11 . . . . 29 F5
Axminster Rd DT6 . . . . 96 F8
Axnoller La DT8 . . . . 204 D6
Aylesbury Rd BH1 . . . . 122 E4
Aynsley Cl DT4 . . . . 167 C4
Aysha Cl BH25 . . . . 95 B1

Azalea Cl BH24 . . . . 54 C5
Aztec Ctr BH17 . . . . 119 D8
Azura Cl BH21 . . . . 53 D6

B

Babeny Wlk [11] BH11 . . . 107 C1
Babwell Rd BA9 . . . . 4 B3
Babylon Hill DT9 . . . . 28 D5
Babylon View BA21 . . . . 28 B7
Babys Dro BH23 . . . . 194 E3
Back La
  Bradford Abbas DT9 . . . . . 28 D3
  Broadwindsor DT8 . . . . . 203 E5
  Cerne Abbas DT2 . . . . . . 207 D4
  Chetnole DT9 . . . . 194 D3
  East Coker BA22 . . . . 193 C7
  Evershot DT2 . . . . 206 A7
  Frome Vauchurch DT2 . . . 72 F7
  Gillingham SP8 . . . . 5 D5
  Halstock BA22 . . . . 193 C3
  Hazelbury Bryan DT10 . . 197 A4
  Kington Magna SP8 . . . . . . 9 C3
  North Perrott TA18 . . . . . 192 C4
  [4] Okeford Fitzpaine DT11 197 F5
  Rimpton BA22 . . . . 15 B8
  Sherborne DT9 . . . . 30 B6
  Sixpenny Handley SP5 . . . 189 A4
  Sturminster Marshall BH21 . 56 D5
  Swyre DT2 . . . . 129 D5
  Sydling St Nicholas DT2 . . 207 A2
  Wareham BH20 . . . . 139 F1
Back Rivers La DT6 . . . . . . 100 D6
Back St
  Abbotsbury DT3 . . . . 149 B7
  East Stour SP8 . . . . 10 E3
  Portesham DT3 . . . . 132 A1
Backwater DT7 . . . . 78 B2
Badbury Cl BH18 . . . . 87 C2
Badbury Ct BH22 . . . . 61 F7
Badbury Dr DT11 . . . . 212 D1
Badbury Rings (Hill Fort)*
  DT11 . . . . 49 A2
Badbury View BH21 . . . . 59 D5
Badbury View Rd [2] BH23 . 85 F8
Baden Cl BH21 . . . . 95 B1
Baden–Powell & St Peter's
  CE Mid Sch BH14 . . . . . 120 B3
Bader Rd BH17 . . . . 119 E8
Badger Hts BA22 . . . . 26 D5
Badger La BH22 . . . . 209 A5
Badgers Cl
  Gillingham SP8 . . . . 1 E2
  St Leonards BH24 . . . . . . 54 B5
Badgers Copse BH25 . . . . . . 95 C6
Badger Sett DT11 . . . . 212 C2
Badgers Way DT10 . . . . 35 B2
Badger Way BH31 . . . . 45 B5
BAGBER DT10 . . . . 197 A8
Baglake DT2 . . . . 103 C2
Bagwood Rd [9] BH11 . . . . 81 E8
Bailey Cl BH25 . . . . 95 D4
Bailey Cres BH15 . . . . 119 C7
Bailey Dr BH23 . . . . 123 F7
Bailey Hall BH23 . . . . 123 F7
Bailey Ridge DT9 . . . . 195 A4
Bailey Ridge La BH19 . . . . 194 F4
Bailey's Dro BH23 . . . . 139 F2
Baileys Hill BH21 . . . . 201 D6
Baillie Gate Ind Est BH21 . . 56 E3
Baiter Gdns BH15 . . . . 119 C1
Bakehouse La BH21 . . . . . . 198 F1
Bakehouse La [1] DT9 . . . . 28 F7
Baker Rd BH11 . . . . 89 A5
Baker's Cross DT6 . . . . 65 D4
Bakers Farm Rd BH31 . . . . . 45 A7
Bakers Field DT10 . . . . 33 C8
Bakers La BA21 . . . . 201 D1
Bakers Paddock DT2 . . . . . 136 C2
Bakers View BH21 . . . . 85 F5
Balaclava Rd
  Bovington Camp BH20 . . 139 F2
  Fortuneswell DT5 . . . . . . 181 D1
Balcombe Rd BH13 . . . . . . 121 A4
Baldwin Cl BH23 . . . . 124 D6
Balena Cl BH17 . . . . 119 A8
Balfour Cl BH23 . . . . 125 D8
Balfour Rd BH9 . . . . 89 F1
Ballam Cl BH14 . . . . 117 E7
Ballam Gr BH12 . . . . 120 D8
Ballard Cl
  Lytchett Matravers BH16 . . 84 D4
  New Milton BH25 . . . . 95 B4
  Poole BH15 . . . . 119 D1
Ballard Coll BH25 . . . . 95 A4
Ballard Lee BH19 . . . . 179 C5
Ballard Rd
  Poole BH15 . . . . 119 D1
  Swanage BH19 . . . . 179 C5
Ballard Sch BH25 . . . . 95 A4
Ballard Way BH19 . . . . 179 C5
Ball's Hill BA22 . . . . 194 A7
Ball's La DT6 . . . . 56 D5
Balmer Rd DT11 . . . . 212 E6
Balmoral Ave BH8 . . . . 90 E1
Balmoral Cl BH21 . . . . 135 C8
Balmoral Cres [3] BH23 . . 126 B7
Balmoral Ho BH21 . . . . 121 D7
Balmoral Rd
  Poole BH14 . . . . 120 C3
  Yeovil BA21 . . . . 28 A6
Balmoral Wlk BH25 . . . . 94 F3
Balston Rd BH14 . . . . 120 A6
Balston Terr BH15 . . . . 119 B2
Banbury Rd BH17 . . . . 119 C7

Bancroft Ct **1** BH15 . . . . . 119 E4
Bank Chambers BH14 . . . . 120 E3
Bank Cl BH23 . . . . 124 B6
Bankes Sch The BH17 . . . . 118 E8
Bankside Rd BH9 . . . . 90 A3
Banks Rd BH13 . . . . 147 C4
Banstead Rd BH18 . . . . 87 A5
Banton Shard DT6 . . . . 68 F1
Barberry Way BH11 . . . . . . 45 E5
Barbers Gate **8** BH15 . . . 119 B1
Barbers Piles **1** BH15 . . . 119 B1
Barbers Wharf **8** BH15 . . 119 B1
Barclay Mans BH2 . . . . 121 F5
Barclay Rd DT4 . . . . 167 C3
Bardolfeston Village★
    DT2 . . . . 78 D2
Bargates BH21 . . . . 124 B7
Barges Cl DT2 . . . . 103 C2
Barham Cl BH11 . . . . 122 E5
Baring Rd BH6 . . . . 124 A3
Barlake Ct **5** DT1 . . . . . . 107 D1
Barlands Cl
    Burton BH23 . . . . 92 C2
    Portland DT5 . . . . 186 E1
Barley Cl DT2 . . . . 194 A2
Barleycroft Rd DT5 . . . . . . 186 E3
Barleyfields **1** SP8 . . . . . 5 F2
Barley Way DT4 . . . . 167 E1
Barlynch Ct **1** BA21 . . . . 26 F6
Barnaby Mead SP8 . . . . . . 5 F2
Barnack Wlk DT11 . . . . . . 212 C3
Barn Cl
    8 Crewkerne TA18 . . . 191 E4
    Upton BH16 . . . . 117 C7
Barn Cres **7** TA18 . . . . . 191 E4
Barndale Dr BH20 . . . . . . 143 A1
Barnes Cl
    Blandford Forum DT11 . . 212 E5
    Bournemouth BH10 . . . . 89 D3
    Marnhull DT10 . . . . 21 A2
    Sturminster Newton DT10 . . 35 B1
Barnes Cres
    Bournemouth BH3 . . . . . 89 D3
    Wimborne Minster BH21 . 59 E4
Barnes Rd **1** BA12 . . . . . 3 A5
Barnes Rd
    Bournemouth BH10 . . . . 89 D3
    Wareham Town BH20 . . . 142 D2
Barnes Wallis Cl DT3 . . . . 166 E3
Barnes Way **5** DT1 . . . . . 108 B1
Barnet BA21 . . . . 27 A7
Barney's Cl DT5 . . . . 97 B8
Barnfield BH23 . . . . 125 D8
Barnfleet **18** BH18 . . . . . 204 D4
Barnhaven Cl DT4 . . . . 167 B1
Barnhill Rd BH20 . . . . 143 A1
Barn La TA18 . . . . 191 E6
Barn Rd BH18 . . . . 87 B3
Barnsfield Rd BH24 . . . . . . 54 C4
Barnsley Dro BH21 . . . . . . 50 A3
Barns Rd BH22 . . . . 62 A6
Barn St TA18 . . . . 191 E4
Barons Ct **2** BH12 . . . . . 121 D4
Barosmede **2** BH2 . . . . . 121 D4
Barons Rd BH11 . . . . 88 D6
Barrack La BH24 . . . . 55 F4
Barr La
    Burton Bradstock DT6 . . 128 A8
    Shipton Gorge DT6 . . . . 101 D4
Barrow Cl DT1 . . . . 134 E7
Barrow Dr BH8 . . . . 90 F2
Barrowfield Cl DT6 . . . . . . 128 A8
Barrow Rd BH8 . . . . 90 D3
Barrowgate Way BH8 . . . . 90 D3
BARROW HILL BH16 . . . . . 84 F4
Barrow Hill
    Bere Regis BH20 . . . . . . 81 B3
    Stalbridge DT10 . . . . . . 33 C8
    Stourton Caundle DT10 . . 32 F2
Barrowland La DT2 . . . . . . 71 E5
Barrow Rise DT4 . . . . 180 B8
BARROW STREET BA12 . . . 3 F2
Barrow Street La BA12 . . . . 3 F3
Barrow View BH22 . . . . . . 61 B6
Barrow Way BH6 . . . . 90 F2
Barrs Ave BH25 . . . . 95 B4
Barr's La DT6 . . . . 97 A8
Barrs Wood Dr BH25 . . . . . 95 B4
Barrs Wood Rd BH25 . . . . . 95 B4
Barry Gdns BH18 . . . . 86 F5
Barstone Way BH22 . . . . . . 61 B6
Barter Rd BH12 . . . . 121 A7
Barters La
    Broadstone BH18 . . . . . 86 F3
    Donhead St Mary SP7 . . 25 B8
Bartlets Cl DT2 . . . . 133 C6
Bartlett Dr BH7 . . . . 123 D8
Bartletts Pl BA21 . . . . 26 F5
Bartletts The BA12 . . . . . . 3 B4
Bartlett Way BH11 . . . . . . 122 A7
Bartley Ct **2** BH21 . . . . . 59 B5
Bartom's La BH16 . . . . 84 B2
Barton Chase BH25 . . . . . 126 F7
Barton Cl
    Sturminster Newton
      DT10 . . . . 197 C8
    Toller Porcorum DT2 . . . 71 D8
West Stafford DT2 . . . . . 136 B8

Barton Common La
    BH25 . . . . 127 B8
Barton Common Rd
    BH25 . . . . 127 B7
Barton Court Rd BH25 . . . 127 A8
Barton Court Rd BH25 . . . . 95 A1
Barton Croft BH25 . . . . . . 127 A7
Barton Dr
    Barton on Sea BH25 . . . 126 F8
    Overcombe/Preston DT3 . 153 B3
Barton Gdns BH25 . . . . . . 29 F6
Barton Grn BH25 . . . . 127 B6
Barton Hill
    Kington Magna SP8 . . . . 9 D4
    Melbury Osmond DT2 . . 194 A2
    Shaftesbury SP7 . . . . . . 12 E3
Barton Ho BH25 . . . . 126 E7
Barton La
    Barton on Sea BH25 . . . 126 E8
    Mere BA12 . . . . 3 A5
Barton on Sea BH25 . . . . . 126 F8
Barton Way BH25 . . . . . . 126 F8
Barton Wood Rd BH25 . . . 126 C7
BARWICK BA22 . . . . 193 F8
Barwick & Stoford Com Prim
    Sch BA22 . . . . 193 F8
Basan Hill DT2 . . . . 78 D5
Bascott Cl BH11 . . . . 89 A1
Bascott Rd BH11 . . . . 89 A1
Bashley Common Rd
    BH25 . . . . 95 A8
Bashley Cross Rd BH25 . . . 94 E5
Bashley Dr BH25 . . . . 95 B6
Bashley Rd BH25 . . . . 95 A6
Bassett Rd BH12 . . . . 120 B6
Bat Alley DT10 . . . . 19 B1
Batchelor Cres BH11 . . . . . 88 F3
Batchelor Rd BH11 . . . . . . 89 A3
Batchelor's La BH21 . . . . . 201 D1
Batchpool La BA8 . . . . 8 A7
BATCOMBE DT2 . . . . 206 E2
Batcombe Cl BH11 . . . . . . 88 E3
Batcombe Rd DT9 . . . . . . 194 F1
Bath Cl BH31 . . . . 45 D4
Bath Hill Ct **10** BH1 . . . . 122 F2
Bath Hill Rdbt BH1 . . . . . 122 A2
Bath Orch **6** DT6 . . . . . . 68 F1
Bath Rd
    Bournemouth BH1 . . . . . 122 A3
    Sturminster Newton DT10 . 35 B2
Bathsheba Terr **8** DT1 . . 135 B8
Bath St DT4 . . . . 167 D3
Bathwell La DT9 . . . . 17 C7
Bats La DT2 . . . . 106 E1
Batten Cl BH23 . . . . 124 D7
Batterley Dro BH21 . . . . . 41 B4
Battle Hill
    Corfe Castle BH20 . . . . 177 A8
    Swanage BH19 . . . . . . 179 B4
Batts La DT6 . . . . 203 C2
Bauntons Cl **1** DT9 . . . . . 17 C2
Baunton's Orch DT9 . . . . . 17 C2
Baverstock Rd BH12 . . . . . 121 B8
Bay Cl
    Bournemouth BH2 . . . . . 121 E2
    3 Swanage BH19 . . . 178 E2
Bayard Rd DT3 . . . . 152 E2
Bay Cl
    Swanage BH19 . . . . . . 179 C5
    Three Legged Cross BH21 . 53 A8
    Upton BH16 . . . . 117 D6
Baycliffe Rd DT4 . . . . 167 B2
Bay Cres BH19 . . . . 179 B5
Baydon Cl BH21 . . . . 153 B3
Bay Fields SP8 . . . . 5 F2
Bayfran Way DT11 . . . . . . 212 E4
Bay Hog La BH15 . . . . 119 B2
Bay La SP8 . . . . 6 A2
Baynard's Rd BH21 . . . . . 107 D1
Bay Rd SP8 . . . . 5 F2
Bay Tree Way BH23 . . . . . 93 D1
Bay View
    Swanage BH19 . . . . . . 179 C5
    3 Swanage BH19 . . . 178 E2
Bayview Gdns BH21 . . . . . 121 E2
Bayview Mews BH21 . . . . 121 E2
Bayview Rd DT7 . . . . 96 B6
Beach Ave BH25 . . . . 126 F7
Beach Cl BH13 . . . . 147 G8
Beachcroft BH13 . . . . 121 A3
Beach Gdns BH19 . . . . . . 179 B3
Beach Rd
    Burton Bradstock DT6 . . 128 C7
    Poole BH13 . . . . 147 G8
    Studland BH19 . . . . . . 164 C8
    Upton BH16 . . . . 117 C6
Beach View BH13 . . . . . . 147 C4
Beachview Cl **1** DT4 . . . 180 B8
Beacon Ct BH23 . . . . 125 F7
Beacon Dr BH25 . . . . 127 F7
Beaconfield Rd BA20 . . . . . 27 A1
Beacon Gdns BH18 . . . . . . 86 E3
BEACON HILL BH16 . . . . . . 85 C2
Beacon Hill La BH21 . . . . . 85 D3
Beacon Park Cres BH18 . . 118 A8
Beacon Park Rd BH18 . . . 118 B7
Beacon Rd
    Bournemouth BH2 . . . . . 121 F2
    Corfe Mullen BH18 . . . . . 85 F3
    1 Upton BH16 . . . . . 117 D7
Beaconsfield Rd
    Christchurch BH23 . . . . 124 B7
    Poole BH12 . . . . 120 D6
Beacon Way BH18 . . . . . . 86 E3
Beacon La TA16 . . . . 191 E7
BEAMINSTER DT8 . . . . . . 204 B5
Beaminster Mus★ DT8 . . 204 D4

Beaminster Rd DT6 . . . . . . 68 F1
Beaminster Sch DT8 . . . . 204 C5
Beamish Rd BH17 . . . . . . 119 F8
BEAR CROSS 88 F5
Bear Cross Ave BH11 . . . . . 88 F6
Bear Cross Rdbt BH11 . . . . 88 F6
BEARWOOD 88 F4
Bearwood Cty Prim Sch
    BH11 . . . . 88 C6
Beatty Cl BH24 . . . . 55 E8
Beatty Rd BH9 . . . . 90 B1
Beauchamp Pl BH23 . . . . 124 C6
Beauchamps Gdns BH7 . . 123 A8
Beaucroft Foundation Sch
    BH21 . . . . 59 E6
Beaucroft La BH21 . . . . . . 59 E5
Beaucroft Rd BH21 . . . . . . 59 E6
Beau Ct
    43 Bournemouth BH4 . 121 C3
    9 New Milton BH25 . . 95 A3
Beaufort Cl BH23 . . . . 125 B7
Beaufort Dr BH21 . . . . 59 C5
Beaufort Rd **10** BH4 . . . 121 C7
Beaufort Mews BH21 . . . . . 59 C6
Beaufort Rd BH6 . . . . 123 D6
Beaufoy Cl SP7 . . . . 13 A3
Beaufoys Ave BH22 . . . . . . 61 D7
Beaufoys Cl BH22 . . . . 61 C6
Beaulieu Ave
    Bournemouth BH4 . . . . . 121 B1
    Christchurch BH23 . . . . 123 B1
BEAULIEU WOOD DT2 . . . 196 B1
Beaumont Ave
    Bridport DT6 . . . . 100 D8
    Radipole DT4 . . . . 167 D6
Beaumont Rd BH24 . . . . . 147 F4
Beaver Ind Est BH23 . . . . 125 A7
Beccles Cl BH15 . . . . 118 F2
Becher Rd BH14 . . . . 120 E4
Beckett Cl DT11 . . . . 212 C2
Beckhampton Rd BH15 . . 118 E3
Becklands La DT6 . . . . 65 E4
BECKLEY 94 C5
Beckley Copse BH23 . . . . . 94 A2
Becton La BH25 . . . . 127 B7
Becton Mead BH25 . . . . . . 95 B1
Bedale Way BH15 . . . . . . 119 F5
BEDCHESTER SP7 . . . . 37 C7
Bedford Cres BH7 . . . . . . 123 C7
Bedford Pl DT6 . . . . 100 D7
Bedford Rd
    Weymouth DT4 . . . . . . 167 A3
    Yeovil BA21 . . . . 27 F8
Bedford Road N BH12 . . . . 88 C2
Bedford Road S BH12 . . . . 88 C2
Bedford Terr 100 D8
Beech Ave
    Bournemouth BH6 . . . . . 123 C4
    Christchurch BH23 . . . . 123 D8
    Holton Heath BH16 . . . . 116 B3
Beechbank Ave BH17 . . . . . 86 F1
Beech Cl
    Alderholt SP6 . . . . 42 C5
    Broadmayne DT2 . . . . . 136 B1
    Broadstone BH18 . . . . . 86 E4
    1 Spetisbury DT11 . . 211 E5
    West Lulworth BH20 . . . 172 D6
Beechcroft BH1 . . . . 122 A5
Beechcroft La BH24 . . . . . 55 D8
Beechcroft Mews **2**
    BH24 . . . . 55 D8
Beech Ct BH21 . . . . 123 A8
    1 Shaftesbury SP7 . . 12 E3
Beeches The
    Bournemouth BH7 . . . . . 123 A8
    1 Shaftesbury SP7 . . 12 E3
    Wareham St Martin BH20 . 143 A8
Beechey Ct **6** BH8 . . . . 122 A5
Beechey Rd BH8 . . . . 122 A5
Beechfield **42** BH4 . . . . . 121 C3
Beech La
    Hawkchurch EX13 . . . . 202 B1
    St Leonards BH24 . . . . . 54 A2
    Wincanton BA9 . . . . 4 A8
Beech Rd
    Puddletown DT2 . . . . . . 78 B1
    Puncknowle DT2 . . . . . 129 E2
    Radipole DT4 . . . . 152 B4
    Beer Tree Ct DT2 . . . . . 206 C2
Beechwood Ave
    Bournemouth BH5 . . . . . 123 A4
    New Milton BH25 . . . . . . 94 F4
Beech Wood Ct BH18 . . . . . 87 A3
Beechwood Ct BH21 . . . . 121 E2
Beechwood Dr **5** TA18 . 191 F5
Beechwood Gdns BH5 . . . 123 A4
Beechwood La **1** BH24 . . 107 B1
Beechwood Rd **1** BH24 . 121 C3
Beechwood Rd DT5 . . . . . . 53 B1
Beel Cl **2** DT5 . . . . 181 H1
BEER HACKETT DT9 . . . . . 194 C6
Beer St BA20 . . . . 27 B4
Belben Cl BH12 . . . . 88 D2
Belben Rd BH12 . . . . 88 D2
BELCHALWELL DT11 . . . . . 197 E4
BELCHALWELL ST DT11 . . 197 E4
BELCHALWELL STREET
    DT11 . . . . 197 E3
Belfield Cl **3** DT4 . . . . . 180 D8
Belfield Park Ave DT4 . . . 167 B1

Belfield Park Rd **1** DT4 . 180 D8
Belfield Rd BH6 . . . . 124 A4
Belgrave DT4 . . . . 167 B6
Belgrave Ct BH1 . . . . 122 D3
Belgrave Pl **3** DT5 . . . . . 186 F8
Belgrave Rd BH13 . . . . . . 121 A2
Belbury Cl **1** BH17 . . . . . 88 B8
Bell Chase BA20 . . . . 26 F5
Bellever Ct DT1 . . . . 107 C2
Belle Vue Cl BH6 . . . . 123 D4
Belle Vue Cl BH6 . . . . 123 D4
Belle Vue Gdns **2** BH6 . 123 F4
Belle Vue Gr BH22 . . . . . . 53 B2
Belle Vue Mans BH6 . . . . 123 E3
Belle Vue Rd
    Bournemouth BH6 . . . . . 123 E3
    Poole BH14 . . . . 120 C3
    Swanage BH19 . . . . . . 179 C1
    Weymouth DT4 . . . . . . 167 D1
Belle Vue Terr **5** DT5 . . 186 F7
Belle Vue Wlk BH22 . . . . . 53 B2
Bell Heather Cl **5** BH14 . 117 D8
Bellman's Cross BA8 . . . . . 19 C6
Bellows Cross BH21 . . . . . . 40 D8
Bells Ho BH21 . . . . 59 D6
Bells La BA21 . . . . 2 A6
Bell's Orch La BH20 . . . . . 142 E4
Bell St
    Shaftesbury SP7 . . . . . . 12 E3
    Swanage BH19 . . . . . . 178 F2
Belmont Ave BH8 . . . . 90 C2
Belmont Cl
    Shaftesbury SP7 . . . . . . 12 F2
    Verwood BH31 . . . . 45 C5
Belmont Rd
    New Milton BH25 . . . . . . 95 C4
    Poole BH14 . . . . 120 C5
Belmour La **10** BH4 . . . . 121 C3
Belvedere Rd
    Bournemouth BH3 . . . . 122 A6
    Christchurch BH23 . . . . 124 A7
    3 Swanage BH19 . . . 179 C1
    Yeovil BA21 . . . . 28 B6
Belvoir Pk **8** BH13 . . . . 121 B3
Bembury La DT9 . . . . 194 D8
Bemister Rd BH9 . . . . 122 B8
Benbow Cres BH12 . . . . . . 88 E1
Benbridge Ave BH11 . . . . . 88 F5
Benches La SP5 . . . . 188 B4
Bendigo Rd BH23 . . . . . . 123 E8
Benellen Ave BH4 . . . . . . 121 C4
Benellen Gdns BH4 . . . . . 121 D4
Benellen Rd BH4 . . . . 121 D4
Benellen Twrs **1** BH4 . . 121 C4
Bengal Rd **1** BH9 . . . . . 121 E8
Beningfield Wood★ DT6 . . . 69 F7
Benjamin Ct BH23 . . . . . . 123 F7
Benjamin Rd **6** BH15 . . 117 F2
Benlease Way BH19 . . . . . 178 E2
Benmoor Rd BH17 . . . . . . 119 A8
Benmore Cl BH25 . . . . 94 F3
Benmore Rd BH9 . . . . 90 A1
Bennett Ho **4** BH4 . . . . 121 C4
Bennett Rd BH8 . . . . 122 C6
Bennetts Rd Cl **1** DT6 . . 100 C2
Bennetts Water Gdns★
    DT3 . . . . 166 C4
Ben Nevis Rd DT4 . . . . . . 167 C1
Bennion Rd BH10 . . . . 81 A2
Benridge Bsns Pk BH17 . . 87 B3
Benson Rd BH17 . . . . 119 D7
Bentley Rd BH9 . . . . 89 F3
BENVILLE DT2 . . . . 205 D6
Benville La DT2 . . . . 205 C6
Bere Cl BH17 . . . . 87 D2
Bere Down La BH20 . . . . . 80 F5
Bere Marsh DT11 . . . . . . 198 B2
Bere Rd
    Northport BH20 . . . . . . 142 D5
    Winterborne Kingston DT11 . 81 B2
    Bere Regis Bsns Pk BH20 . 81 B2
    Bere Regis Fst Sch BH20 . 81 B1
Bere Regis Sports Club
    BH20 . . . . 81 C3
Beresford Cl BH12 . . . . . . 120 D6
Beresford Gdns BH23 . . . . 124 E6
Beresford Rd
    Bournemouth BH5 . . . . . 123 B4
    Poole BH12 . . . . 120 D6
Berkeley Ave BH12 . . . . . 120 D8
Berkeley Cl
    9 Pimperne DT11 . . . 199 D4
    1 Yetminster DT9 . . . 45 A7
Berkeley Ct DT6 . . . . 100 D6
Berkeley Rd
    Bournemouth BH3 . . . . 121 E7
    1 Pimperne DT11 . . . 199 D3
    3 Yeovil BA20 . . . . . 27 C4
Berkeley Rise **8** DT11 . . 199 D4
Berkley Manor **8** BH13 . 121 B4
Berkley Rd BH22 . . . . 61 D2
Bermuda **5** BH23 . . . . . 126 A7
Bernards Cl BH23 . . . . . . 123 E8
Berne Ct **18** BH1 . . . . . 122 A3
Berne Rd BH23 . . . . 119 E4
Berrans Ave BH11 . . . . 89 B6
Berrans Ct BH11 . . . . 89 A6
Berry La EX13 . . . . 202 D3
Bertram Rd BH23 . . . . 95 C4
Berwick Cl DT6 . . . . 129 D6
Berwick Rd BH3 . . . . 121 E6

Bessells La DT11 . . . . 198 D8
Bessemer Cl BH31 . . . . 45 E4
Bestwall Cres BH20 . . . . . 142 F3
Bestwall Rd BH20 . . . . . . 142 F3
Beswick Ave BH10 . . . . 89 D2
Bethany CE Jun Sch
    BH1 . . . . 122 D5
Bethany Cl BH12 . . . . 121 A7
Bethany Ho BH1 . . . . 122 D5
Bethia Cl BH8 . . . . 122 D6
Bethia Rd BH8 . . . . 122 D6
BETTISCOMBE DT6 . . . . . 203 B3
Bettiscombe Cl BH17 . . . . . 87 E2
Beulieu Cl **6** BH10 . . . . . 197 A4
Beverley Gdns BH10 . . . . . 89 D3
Beverley Grange **50** BH4 . 121 C3
Beverley Rd DT3 . . . . 152 D3
Bexington Cl BH11 . . . . 88 E3
Bibberne Row DT10 . . . . . . 33 D7
Bickerley Gdns BH24 . . . . . 55 B6
Bickerley Rd BH24 . . . . 55 B6
Bicknell Ct **5** BH4 . . . . . 121 C4
Bicknell Gdns BA21 . . . . . . 27 D8
Bicknell Specl Sch BH7 . . 123 A4
BICKTON 43 B6
Bicton Rd BH11 . . . . 89 B3
Biddlecome Orch **5**
    DT6 . . . . 100 C8
Biddlesden Rd **2** 26 E7
Big Ope DT5 . . . . 186 E7
Billingsmoor La **4** DT11 . 107 C1
Bilshay La DT6 . . . . 68 A2
Bimport SP7 . . . . 12 D2
Bincleaves Rd DT4 . . . . . . 167 E1
BINCOMBE DT3 . . . . 152 E6
Bincombe Dr **2** TA18 . . . 191 F5
Bincombe Rise DT3 . . . . . 152 E3
Bindbarrow Rd DT6 . . . . . 128 C6
Bindells The DT3 . . . . 166 D5
Bindon Abbey (rems of)★
    BH20 . . . . 140 D2
Bindon Cl
    Poole BH12 . . . . 120 E7
    West Lulworth BH20 . . . 172 E7
Bindon Rd BH20 . . . . 140 D1
Bindon Rd BH20 . . . . 172 C5
Bindon Way BH20 . . . . . . 140 B2
Bingham Ave BH14 . . . . . 147 D8
Bingham Cl
    Christchurch BH23 . . . . 124 E7
    Verwood BH31 . . . . 45 D4
Bingham Dr BH31 . . . . 45 C4
Bingham Rd
    Bournemouth BH9 . . . . 122 A7
    Christchurch BH23 . . . . 124 E7
    Verwood BH31 . . . . 45 C4
Bingham's Melcombe
    (House)★ DT2 . . . . 209 B5
Binghams Rd DT12 . . . . . 137 D6
BINNEGAR BH20 . . . . 141 B3
Binnegar La BH20 . . . . . . 141 C3
Binnie Rd BH12 . . . . 120 E5
Birch Ave
    Beckley BH25 . . . . 94 D5
    3 Blandford St Mary
      DT11 . . . . 212 C1
    Burton BH23 . . . . 92 C3
    Ferndown BH22 . . . . 61 F1
    Holton Heath BH16 . . . . 116 B3
Birch Cl
    Poole BH14 . . . . 120 E3
    Poole BH21 . . . . 85 F6
    St Leonards BH24 . . . . . 53 F3
Birch Copse BH17 . . . . . . 119 A8
Birchdale **6** BA20 . . . . . . 26 F2
Birchdale Rd BH21 . . . . . . 59 C5
Birch Dr BH8 . . . . 91 A2
Birchfield Prim Sch BA21 . 27 F8
Birchfield Rd BA21 . . . . . . 27 F7
Birch Gr
    Ferndown BH22 . . . . 52 F2
    Old Milton BH25 . . . . . . 95 A1
Birch La
    Puddletown DT2 . . . . . . 77 F3
    Yetminster DT9 . . . . . . 194 C5
Birch Rd BH24 . . . . 54 D4
Birch Way
    2 Crewkerne TA18 . . 191 F5
    Dorchester DT2 . . . . 75 D2
Birch Wlk BH22 . . . . 61 F3
Birchwood Cl BH23 . . . . . 125 E8
Birchwood Dr SP6 . . . . 42 C5
Birchwood Mews BH14 . . 120 D3
Birchwood Rd
    Poole BH14 . . . . 120 D3
    Upton BH16 . . . . 117 D6
Bird's Cl **5** TA18 . . . . . . 191 E4
Birds Hill Gdns **1** BH15 . 119 E3
Bird's Hill Rd BH15 . . . . . . 91 A2
Birkdale Cl BH18 . . . . 87 A5
Birkdale Rd BH18 . . . . 87 A5
Bishop Cl BH12 . . . . 121 C7
Bishop Rd BH9 . . . . 122 A4
Bishop Down DT9 . . . . 55 C7
Bishop of Winchester Comp
    Sch The BH8 . . . . 90 D1
Bishop Rd BH9 . . . . 122 A8
BISHOP'S CAUNDLE DT9 . 196 A8
Bishops Cl
    Shaftesbury DT3 . . . . . 149 B7
    Wimborne BH7 . . . . . . 122 F7
    Mere BA12 . . . . 3 A6
Bishops Ct DT8 . . . . 87 A3
BISHOP'S DOWN DT9 . . . 195 E6 C6
Bishops La BA22 . . . . 193 A6
Bishop's La DT9 . . . . 28 D2

Bishop's Rd
Abbotsbury DT3 . . . . 149 C8
Portesham DT2 . . . . 131 D1
Bishops Row 5 BH19 . . . 179 A2
BISTERNE 63 F6
Bitchams Mead BH20 . . . . 81 A2
Bitterne Way BH31 . . . . . . 45 C5
BITTLES GREEN SP7 . . . . . . 12 D7
Blackberry La
Christchurch BH23 . . . . . . 124 F6
Radipole DT3 . . . . 152 C2
Sherborne DT9 . . . . 30 A7
Blackbird Cl BH17 . . . . . . 118 E8
Blackbirds 6 DT9 . . . . . . 194 D8
Blackbird Way BH12 . . . . 93 C8
Blackburn Rd BH12 . . . . . 120 B6
Blackers Hole (Cave)★
BH19 . . . . 184 D6
Blackfield La BH22 . . . . . . 53 A3
Blackfield Rd BH6 . . . . 90 D3
Black Hill BH31 . . . . 45 C6
Blackhill Rd BH16 . . . . . . 116 D3
Black Road W BH16 . . . . 116 D2
Black La DT11 . . . . 212 E4
Blacklands La DT11 . . . . . 197 D3
Black Mere BA22 . . . . 26 C5
Blackmoor La BA8 . . . . . . 19 A4
Black Moor Rd BH31 . . . . 45 E4
Blackmore Rd
Shaftesbury SP7 . . . . 13 A4
Stalbridge DT10 . . . . 33 D8
Blacknell Ind Est 32
TA18 . . . . 191 F4
Blacknell La TA18 . . . . . . 191 F4
BLACKNEY DT6 . . . . 203 D2
Blackney La DT6 . . . . 203 E2
Blacknoll La DT2 . . . . 138 F1
Blacknor Rd DT5 . . . . 186 E3
Blackpool Cnr DT6 . . . . . . 202 B1
Blackrow La DT10 . . . . . . 196 D7
Blacksands Cl BH21 . . . . . 85 F5
Blacksmith's La DT9 . . . . 194 D8
Blacksmith's Piece DT2 . 105 E1
Blackthorn Way
New Milton BH25 . . . . 95 C4
Verwood BH31 . . . . 45 D5
BLACKWATER 91 D4
Blackwater BH23 . . . . 91 D4
Blackwater Dr BH21 . . . . . 87 F7
Blackwater Gr SP6 . . . . . . 42 A5
Blackwater La EX13 . . . . 202 C3
Bladen Valley DT2 . . . . . 112 A7
Bladen View DT11 . . . . . . 79 E8
Blagdon Cl DT2 . . . . 133 D6
Blagdon Rd DT1 . . . . 107 D1
Blair Ave BH14 . . . . 120 C4
Blair Cl BH25 . . . . 95 C3
Blake Dene Rd BH14 . . . 120 B1
Blake Hill Ave BH14 . . . 120 D1
Blake Hill Cres BH14 . . . 120 C1
Blake Rd 22 TA18 . . . . . 191 F4
BLANDFORD CAMP
DT11 . . . . 199 E3
Blandford Cl BH15 . . . . . . 118 F2
Blandford Com Hospl
DT11 . . . . 212 C5
Blandford Fashion Mus The★
DT11 . . . . 212 C6
BLANDFORD FORUM
DT11 . . . . 212 C6
Blandford Hill
Milborne St Andrew DT11 . . 79 E8
Winterborne Whitechurch
DT11 . . . . 210 C3
Blandford Hts Ind Est
DT11 . . . . 212 E4
Blandford L Ctr★ DT11 . 212 C4
Blandford Rd N
Lytchett Minster & Upton
BH16 . . . . 85 B2
Upton BH16 . . . . 118 B7
BLANDFORD ST MARY
DT11 . . . . 212 D1
Blandford St Mary CE Prim
Sch DT11 . . . . 212 D1
Blandford Sch The DT11 212 C4
Blandford Town Mus★
DT11 . . . . 212 D3
Blaney Way BH21 . . . . . . 59 C4
BLASHFORD BH24 . . . . 47 C2
Blashford Lakes Study Ctr★
BH24 . . . . 47 C4
BLEAK HILL BH24 . . . . 42 E3
Bleak St BA9 . . . . 1 C3
Bleax Cl SP7 . . . . 22 E1
Bleet La SP8 . . . . 10 D6
Bleke St SP7 . . . . 12 E2
Blemheim Rd DT3 . . . . . . 152 B1
Blenheim 5 BH3 . . . . 121 B3
Blenheim Cres SO41 . . . . 95 F4
Blenheim Ct
35 Bournemouth BH4 . . . 121 C3
Christchurch BH23 . . . . . . 124 A8
Blenheim Dr BH23 . . . . . . 125 B6

Blenheim Mews 6 BH4 . 121 C4
Blenheim Rd BA21 . . . . . . 27 F7
Blind La
Beaminster DT8 . . . . 203 C6
Berwick St John SP7 . . . . 188 B8
Ringwood SP6 . . . . 43 E1
Sherborne DT9 . . . . 196 B7
Thorncombe TA20 . . . . . . 202 E6
Wimborne Minster BH21 . . 59 B5
Blind Lane Cl DT6 . . . . . . 68 F2
Blindmere Rd DT5 . . . . . 186 E4
Blind St BH20 . . . . 81 B2
Blissford Hill SP6 . . . . . . 43 F5
Bloody Shard Gate DT11 . 188 A1
Bloomfield Ave BH9 . . . . . 89 F2
Bloomfield Pl BH9 . . . . 89 F2
BLOXWORTH BH20 . . . . 82 B2
Bloxworth Rd BH12 . . . . 120 F8
Bluebell Cl BH23 . . . . . . 125 B8
Bluebell Gdns 12 BH25 . 95 B3
Bluebell La BH17 . . . . 86 F1
Bluebell Rd BH22 . . . . . . 26 D5
Blue Pool & Tea House The★
BH20 . . . . 161 A3
Bluff The BH10 . . . . 89 F4
BLUNTSHAY DT6 . . . . 66 F7
Bluntshay La DT6 . . . . . . 66 E8
Blyth Cl BH23 . . . . 91 D4
Blythe Rd BH21 . . . . 85 F6
Blythswood Ct BH25 . . . . 126 F7
Boar St BA12 . . . . 3 A5
Bob Hann Cl BH12 . . . . . 120 D5
Bockhampton Cross
DT2 . . . . 109 A3
Bockhampton La DT2 . . . 109 A3
Bockhampton Rd BH23 . . 92 E6
Bodkin La DT3 . . . . 168 A6
Bodley Rd BH13 . . . . 147 F7
Bodorgan Rd BH2 . . . . . . 121 F4
Bodowen Cl BH23 . . . . . . 92 D2
Bodowen Rd BH23 . . . . . . 92 D1
Bodsmarsh La DT10 . . . . 21 E1
Bognor Rd BH18 . . . . 86 F4
Bohay's Dr DT4 . . . . 180 C7
Bokerley Ditch★ SP6 . . . . 190 A5
Bokerley Junc SP25 . . . . 189 E6
Boldre Cl
Barton on Sea BH25 . . . . 126 D8
Poole BH12 . . . . 120 D7
Boleyn Cres
Bournemouth BH9 . . . . . . 90 C4
Weymouth DT4 . . . . 180 E7
Bolton Cl BH6 . . . . 123 E3
Bolton Cres BH22 . . . . . . 62 A6
Bolton Ct 8 BH6 . . . . . . 123 E3
Bolton Rd BH6 . . . . 123 E3
Bon Accord Rd BH19 . . . 179 B1
Bond Ave BH22 . . . . 52 F4
Bond Rd BH15 . . . . 119 F5
Bond St
Radipole DT4 . . . . 167 D3
4 Yeovil BA20 . . . . 27 C4
Yeovil BA22 . . . . 26 C5
Boney Rd BH20 . . . . 139 E8
Bonfields Ave BH19 . . . . 179 B4
Bonham La BA12 . . . . 1 E7
Bonham Rd BH9 . . . . 121 F7
Bonhole La DT6 . . . . 101 E4
Bonington Cl BH23 . . . . . 124 E8
Bonnett's La BH20 . . . . . 142 E4
Bonscombe La DT6 . . . . 101 C5
Bonvils Rd BH19 . . . . . . 183 B7
BOOKHAM DT2 . . . . 208 B7
Bookham La DT2 . . . . . . 208 B7
Boot La 7 DT9 . . . . 194 D8
Boozer Pit TA16 . . . . 191 F8
Border Dr BH16 . . . . 117 E5
Border Rd BH16 . . . . 117 E5
Boreham Rd BH6 . . . . . . 123 D5
BOROUGH THE DT9 . . . . . 196 B6
Borthwick Rd BH1 . . . . . 122 E5
BOSCOMBE 122 E3
Boscombe Cliff Rd BH5 . 122 F3
Boscombe Grove Rd
BH1 . . . . 122 E3
Boscombe Overcliff Dr
BH5 . . . . 123 A3
Boscombe Spa Rd BH5 . 122 D3
Bosley Cl BH23 . . . . 91 E2
Bosley Way BH23 . . . . . . 91 E2
Boston Lo 31 BH4 . . . . . 121 C3
Boswell's Cl BH20 . . . . . . 81 B3
Bosworth Mews BH9 . . . 90 B4
Bothen Dr DT6 . . . . 100 E6
BOTHENHAMPTON DT6 . . 100 E3
Bothenhampton Nature
Reserve★ DT6 . . . . 100 E4
Bottlebush La BH21 . . . . 189 E1
Bottom Rd DT11 . . . . . . 198 F4
Boulnois Ave BH14 . . . . 120 E3
Boulton Cl DT4 . . . . 180 D8
Boundary Ave BA22 . . . . 26 D7
Boundary Cl
Swanage BH19 . . . . 185 C8
Yeovil BA21 . . . . 27 A7
Boundary Dr BH21 . . . . . 59 D6
Boundary La BH21 . . . . . 53 F1
Boundary Rd
Bournemouth BH10 . . . . . 89 E1
Yeovil BA22 . . . . 26 C5
Boundary Rdbt BH3,
BH10 . . . . 121 D8
Boundary View 1 BH21 . 212 D4
Boundary Way BA22 . . . . 26 C7
Bound La DT9 . . . . 194 F2
Bountys La BH12 . . . . . . 120 E5
Bourne Ave BH2 . . . . . . 121 E3
Bourne Cl BH21 . . . . 121 D3

Bourne Ct
1 Bournemouth BH2 . . . 121 F3
Wimborne Minster BH21 . . 59 D5
Bourne Dr BH20 . . . . 142 C6
Bourne Dro DT2 . . . . 76 F6
BOURNEMOUTH 122 A2
Bournemouth Aviation Mus★
BH23 . . . . 91 A8
Bournemouth Collegiate Coll
BH5 . . . . 123 A4
Bournemouth Eye★ 20
BH1 . . . . 121 F3
Bournemouth Ho 2
BH1 . . . . 122 B3
Bournemouth Int Ctr★
BH2 . . . . 121 F2
Bournemouth International
Airport BH23 . . . . 90 E8
Bournemouth Learning
Support Centre PACS
BH10 . . . . 90 D1
Bournemouth Memorial
Homes BH8 . . . . 90 C2
Bournemouth Nuffield Hospl
(Private) BH8 . . . . 122 A5
Bournemouth & Poole Coll
(Constitution Hill Ctr)
BH14 . . . . 119 F5
Bournemouth & Poole Coll
(Lansdowne Ctr) BH1 . 122 B3
Bournemouth & Poole Coll
(Lansdowne Enterprise Ctr)
22 BH1 . . . . 122 A3
Bournemouth & Poole Coll
(North Road Ctr) BH14 . 119 F4
Bournemouth & Poole Coll
(Redlands Ctr) BH1 . . . 122 C4
Bournemouth Rd
Blandford Forum DT11 . . 212 D2
Charlton Marshall DT11 . . 211 D6
Poole BH14 . . . . 120 D4
Bournemouth Sch BH8 . . . 90 C1
Bournemouth Sch for Girls
BH8 . . . . 90 C2
Bournemouth Sta BH8 . . 122 B4
Bournemouth Station Rdbt
BH8 . . . . 122 B4
Bournemouth Univ
(Lansdowne Campus)
BH1 . . . . 122 B3
Bournemouth Univ (Talbot
Campus) BH12 . . . . 121 C8
Bournemouth West Rdbt
BH2 . . . . 121 D3
Bourne Pines 4 BH2 . . . 121 F4
Bourne Rd DT9 . . . . 77 B8
Bourne River Cl 3 BH4 . 121 D4
BOURNE VALLEY 121 B6
Bourne Valley Bsns Pk
BH12 . . . . 121 B6
Bourne Valley Nature
Reserve★ BH12 . . . . 88 E1
Bourne Valley Rd BH12 . 121 A5
Bourne Way SP8 . . . . 5 F3
Bournewood Dr BH4 . . . . 121 C4
BOURTON SP8 . . . . 1 E2
Bourton Gdns BH7 . . . . . 123 B7
Bouverie Cl 7 BH25 . . . . 95 A1
BOVERIDGE BH21 . . . . . . 190 B1
Boveridge Gdns BH9 . . . 90 B4
BOVINGTON CAMP
BH20 . . . . 139 D6
Bovington Cl BH17 . . . . . 87 D1
Bovington Fst Sch BH20 . 139 D6
Bovington La BH20 . . . . 139 E5
Bovington Mid Sch
BH20 . . . . 140 A3
BOWDEN SP8 . . . . .9 E4
Bowden La
Henstridge BA8 . . . . 18 C5
Milborne Port BA8 . . . . . . 17 F5
Bowden Rd
Abbas & Templecombe
BA8 . . . . 18 B8
Poole BH12 . . . . 120 F5
Bowditch Row 25 TA18 . 191 F4
Bowdowns DT6 . . . . 204 B2
Bower Cl BH19 . . . . 177 F5
Bower Ct 5 DT9 . . . . . . 194 C5
Bower Rd BH8 . . . . 122 D8
Bowers Rd DT5 . . . . 186 E4
Bowerswain Hollow
BH21 . . . . 201 B5
Bowerwood Rd SP6 . . . . . 42 E8
Bowes Gdns DT10 . . . . . 204 A8
Bowey 13 DT11 . . . . . . 197 F6
Bow Gate TA18 . . . . 192 A8
Bowgrove Rd DT8 . . . . . 204 D5
Bowhayes
Bridport DT6 . . . . 100 E5
8 Crewkerne TA18 . . . . 191 F4
Bowland Rise BH25 . . . . . 95 C2
Bowleaze Coveway DT3 . 168 B6
Bowling Green La SP5 . . 189 D5
Bown Hill DT5 . . . . 186 E1
BOWRIDGE HILL SP8 . . . . . 6 A4
Bow The 3 DT1 . . . . 108 A2
Box Cl BH17 . . . . 119 B7
Boyd Rd BH12 . . . . 120 F6
Boyle Cl DT10 . . . . 33 D8
Boyne's La DT11 . . . . 33 D1
BOYS HILL DT9 . . . . 195 E5
Boys Hill Dro DT9 . . . . . 195 D5
Boyte Rd 14 DT11 . . . . 199 D4
Bozley Hill SP7 . . . . 24 A7
Brabazon Dr BH23 . . . . . 125 B7

Brabazon Rd BH21 . . . . . 59 F1
Brabourne Ave BH22 . . . . 61 C4
Brackenbury Inf Sch
DT5 . . . . 186 E2
Bracken Cl BH24 . . . . 53 F4
Bracken Ct 10 BH4 . . . . 121 D4
Brackendale Cl BH21 . . . . 52 F8
Brackendale Rd BH21 . . 128 C8
Brackendown Ave DT3 . . 167 F8
Bracken Glen BH15 . . . . . 119 E5
Brackenhill BH13 . . . . . . 121 A1
Brackenhill Rd BH21 . . . . 60 A7
Bracken Lodge 3 BH6 . . 123 F4
Bracken Rd
Bournemouth BH6 . . . . . 123 C4
Ferndown BH22 . . . . 61 B7
Brackens Way 2 BH23 . . 147 F8
Bracken Way BH23 . . . . . 94 B1
Bracket's Coppice Reserve★
BA22 . . . . 193 A2
Bracklesham Pl BH25 . . 126 F7
Brackley Cl BH23 . . . . 91 A8
Bradbourne Rd BH2 . . . . 121 E3
Bradbury Ho BH22 . . . . . . 61 B7
BRADFORD ABBAS DT9 . . . 28 D1
Bradford La DT9 . . . . . . 195 B6
BRADFORD PEVERELL
DT2 . . . . 106 F6
Bradford Rd
Bournemouth BH9 . . . . . . 90 C4
1 Crewkerne TA18 . . . . 192 A3
Sherborne DT9 . . . . 29 E5
Weymouth DT4 . . . . 167 B2
BRADPOLE DT6 . . . . 69 A1
Bradpole Rd BH8 . . . . 90 E1
Bradstock Cl BH12 . . . . . 120 F8
Braemar Ave BH6 . . . . . . 124 A4
Braemar Cl BH6 . . . . 124 A4
Braemar Dr BH23 . . . . 93 F1
Braemar Rd BH13 . . . . . . 135 C8
Braeside Bsns Pk BH15 . . 119 B8
Braeside Rd
Ferndown BH22 . . . . 53 B3
St Leonards BH24 . . . . . . 54 A4
Braidley Rd BH2 . . . . 121 E4
Brailswood Rd BH15 . . . 119 E4
Braishfield Gdns BH8 . . . . 90 D2
Brakes Hill DT2 . . . . 184 A2
Bramar Ct 33 BH4 . . . . 121 C2
Bramble Cl SP6 . . . . 42 C5
BRAMBLECOMBE DT2 . . . 209 C4
Bramble Dr DT6 . . . . 100 D2
Bramble Dro DT2 . . . . . . 136 A2
Bramble Edge DT2 . . . . . 136 A2
Bramble La
Haselbury Plucknett
TA18 . . . . 192 C5
Walkford BH23 . . . . 94 B1
Brambles The DT9 . . . . . . 17 D3
Brambling Cl DT3 . . . . . . 152 C4
Bramdon Cl 5 DT3 . . . . 150 A8
Bramdon La DT3 . . . . . . 150 C6
Bramley Cl 13 TA18 . . . 191 F5
Bramley Ct BH22 . . . . 61 C6
Bramley Hill
Bridport DT6 . . . . 100 E8
Mere BA12 . . . . 2 F5
Bramley Rd
Bournemouth BH10 . . . . . 89 C5
Ferndown BH22 . . . . 61 D6
Bramport Rd BH15 . . . . . 119 D6
Bramshaw Gdns BH8 . . . . 90 D2
Bramshaw Way BH25 . . . 126 D8
Branders Cl BH6 . . . . 124 A4
Branders La BH6 . . . . 124 B5
Brandon Ct 6 BH12 . . . . 121 B4
Brandwood Ct BH4 . . . . . 120 A3
Brandy La 2 DT5 . . . . . . 186 E7
Brandy Row 14 DT5 . . . 186 F7
Branksea Ave BH15 . . . . 118 E1
Branksea Cl BH15 . . . . . . 118 E1
BRANKSOME 120 F5
Branksome Cl BH25 . . . . . 95 B2
Branksome Ct 4 BH13 . . 147 F8
Branksome Dene Chine
Nature Reserve★ BH13 . 120 B1
Branksome Dene Rd
BH4 . . . . 121 B2
Branksome Heath Mid Sch
BH12 . . . . 120 C6
Branksome Hill Rd BH4 . 121 B5
BRANKSOME PARK 120 F1
Branksome Sta BH12 . . . . 120 D7
Branksome Twrs BH13 . . . 147 H8
Branksome Wood Gdns
BH2 . . . . 121 C4
Branksome Wood Rd BH2,
BH4 . . . . 121 C4
Bransbury Rd SP8 . . . . 1 E2
Bransford Rd BH23 . . . . . 193 D3
BRANSGORE 93 B8
Bransgore CE Prim Sch
BH23 . . . . 93 B8
Brantwood Cl DT10 . . . . 204 C4
Branwell Cl BH23 . . . . 92 A1
Brassey Cl BH9 . . . . 90 A1
Brassey Rd BH9 . . . . 90 A1
Brassey Terr BH9 . . . . 89 F1
BRAYTOWN BH20 . . . . . . 140 A1
Breach Cl SP8 . . . . 1 E2
Breaches La BH20 . . . . . . 163 A2
Breach Field 4 BH20 . . . 140 A2
Breach La
Kington Magna SP8 . . . . . . 9 C3
Shaftesbury SP7 . . . . 12 D2
Breamore Cl BH25 . . . . . . 94 E3
Brearley Ct BH23 . . . . . . 126 B8

Brecon Cl
Bournemouth BH10 . . . . . 89 E6
New Milton BH25 . . . . 95 C2
Bredy Cl BH17 . . . . 87 D1
Bredy La DT6 . . . . 101 F1
Bredy Rd DT6 . . . . 128 D7
Bremble Cl BH12 . . . . 88 C2
Bremtmere Cl DT3 . . . . . 152 B1
Breston Cl 2 DT5 . . . . . 186 E1
Brewers Quay Sh Village
DT4 . . . . 167 E1
Brian Cl BH20 . . . . 143 A8
BRIANTSPUDDLE DT2 . . . 112 B7
Briar Cl
Christchurch BH23 . . . . . 124 F6
Gillingham SP8 . . . . 5 E2
Mudford BA21 . . . . 208 A8
Poole BH15 . . . . 119 E5
Briarfield 48 BH4 . . . . . 121 C3
Briars End DT2 . . . . 137 E6
Briars The
Wareham BH20 . . . . 139 E1
2 Yeovil BA20 . . . . 26 F2
Briarswood Rd 7 BH16 . 117 E7
Briar Way BH21 . . . . 60 B5
Brickfields Bsns Pk SP8 . 11 F8
Brickfields Ind Est SP8 . . . 10 F8
Brickyard La
Bourton SP8 . . . . 1 E2
Corfe Mullen BH21 . . . . . 58 A1
1 Crewkerne TA18 . . . . 191 F5
Gillingham SP8 . . . . 5 F1
Silton SP8 . . . . 4 E8
Sturminster Newton DT10 197 A7
Swanage BH19 . . . . 179 A5
Bridewell Ct DT9 . . . . 30 C5
Bridewell La SP7 . . . . 7 A4
BRIDGE TA20 . . . . 202 C8
Bridge App BH15 . . . . . . 119 B1
Bridge Cl SP6 . . . . 6 A1
Bridge Farm Cl TA18 . . . 192 B3
Bridge Inn La BH23 . . . . 153 C3
Bridge Pl BH10 . . . . 89 D7
Bridge Rd DT6 . . . . 97 B8
Bridges Cl BH22 . . . . 53 A5
Bridge St
Bourton SP8 . . . . 1 E2
Christchurch BH23 . . . . . 124 B3
1 Lyme Regis DT7 . . . . . 96 C5
Netherbury DT6 . . . . 204 C2
Sturminster Marshall BH21 . 56 D3
Sturminster Newton DT10 197 D8
Bridges The BH24 . . . . 55 A7
Bridgewater Rd BH12 . . . 120 D6
Bridlebank Way DT3 . . . . 152 B3
Bridle Cl BH16 . . . . 117 F7
Bridle Cres BH7 . . . . 123 D7
Bridle Way
Barwick BA22 . . . . 193 E8
Wimborne Minster BH21 . . 60 C6
Bridleways BH31 . . . . 45 A6
BRIDPORT DT6 . . . . 100 B6
Bridport Com Hospl DT6 100 B8
Bridport L Ctr DT6 . . . . . . 100 C7
Bridport Mus & Local Hist
Ctr★ DT6 . . . . 100 D7
Bridport Prim Sch DT6 . . 100 C7
Bridport Rd
Beaminster DT8 . . . . 204 D3
Broadwindsor DT8 . . . . . 203 C8
Dorchester DT1 . . . . 107 C1
Poole BH12 . . . . 120 F8
Verwood BH31 . . . . 45 B6
Brierley Ave BH22 . . . . . . 61 E1
Brierley Cl BH10 . . . . 89 E5
Brierley Hay 9 DT9 . . . . 194 C5
Brierley Rd BH10 . . . . 89 E4
Brigadier Cl 1 BA22 . . . . 26 E5
Brighthay La DT6 . . . . 67 A8
Brightlands Ave BH6 . . . 123 F5
Bright Rd BH15 . . . . 119 E6
Brightsmead DT2 . . . . . . 139 E8
Brimble Cotts DT10 . . . . . 32 F2
Brimclose Rd TA17 . . . . . 191 B7
Brimley Rd EX13 . . . . . . 202 A3
Brincombe Valley Prim Sch
DT3 . . . . 152 B2
Brinscombe La 8 SP7 . . . 13 A1
Brinsley Cl DT10 . . . . 35 A1
Brinsons Cl BH23 . . . . . . 92 C3
Brionne Way SP7 . . . . 13 A3
Brisbane Rd
Christchurch BH23 . . . . . 193 E3
Radipole DT3 . . . . 152 E2
Brister End DT9 . . . . 194 C5
Bristol Rd DT9 . . . . 30 B7
Briston Cl 3 DT11 . . . . . 107 C1
Britannia Cl BH22 . . . . . . 61 D7
Britannia Rd BH14 . . . . . 120 A3
Britannia Way
Christchurch BH23 . . . . . 125 B7
Dorchester DT1 . . . . 134 E8
Britmore La SP7 . . . . 13 F8
Brit The 4 DT6 . . . . 204 D4
Brit View Rd DT6 . . . . . . 204 C5
Britwell Dr BH20 . . . . . . 172 C4
Brixey Cl BH12 . . . . 120 C7
Brixey Rd BH12 . . . . 120 C7
Brixey's La BH20 . . . . . . 142 E4
Broadacres
East Coker BA22 . . . . 193 C8
Gillingham SP8 . . . . 5 F3
Broad Ave BH8 . . . . 122 D8
Broad Cl DT11 . . . . 1 A3
Broadcroft Gdns DT5 . . . 187 A4
Broad Hill BA22 . . . . 192 D7
Broadhill La SP6 . . . . 43 F8

Broadhurst Ave BH10 ... 89 E4
Broad La
 Bridport DT6 ... 100 B5
 East Chinnock BA22 ... 192 E7
Broadlands 27 BH4 ... 121 C3
Broadlands Ave BH6 ... 123 F4
Broadlands Cl
 Bournemouth BH8 ... 90 D3
 Walkford BH23 ... 94 B2
Broadlands Rd DT3 ... 152 B2
Broadleaze BA21 ... 26 F6
BROADMAYNE DT2 ... 136 A1
Broadmayne Fst Sch DT2 ... 136 C3
Broadmayne Rd BH12 ... 121 A8
Broadmead DT2 ... 136 B2
Broadmead Ave DT6 ... 100 B7
Broadmead Cl 4 DT8 ... 204 A8
Broadmeadow Rd DT4 ... 180 D7
Broad Mead Rd BH21 ... 45 A1
Broadmoor Rd BH21 ... 85 E7
BROADOAK DT6 ... 67 D5
BROAD OAK DT10 ... 197 D7
Broadoak Ave 2 DT8 ... 204 A7
Broad Oak Orch★ DT10 ... 197 E7
Broadoak Rd DT6 ... 67 E1
Broad Rd BH19 ... 179 C2
Broad Robin SP8 ... 5 E2
BROADSHARD TA18 ... 191 F5
Broadshard La BH24 ... 47 C1
Broadshard Rd TA18 ... 191 F5
Broad St DT7 ... 96 C5
Broads The BH21 ... 58 F6
BROADSTONE ... 87 B3
Broadstone Fst Sch BH18 ... 87 B4
Broadstone Heath Nature Reserve★ BH18 ... 87 B4
Broadstone La
 Hardington Mandeville BA22 ... 193 A6
 West Chinnock TA18 ... 192 C8
Broadstone L Ctr BH18 ... 87 A4
Broadstone Mid Sch BH18 ... 87 C5
Broadstone Way
 Broadstone BH17 ... 86 F1
 Poole BH17 ... 119 B7
Broadwater Ave BH14 ... 120 C2
Broadway
 Merriott TA16 ... 191 E7
 Southbourne BH6 ... 124 B3
Broadway Ct BH12 ... 121 A5
Broadway Gables BH14 ... 120 E4
Broadway Gdns 6 BH21 ... 59 C4
Broadway Ho BH18 ... 87 B4
Broadway La BH8 ... 90 C4
Broadway Mews BH14 ... 119 F3
Broadway Pk 4 BH21 ... 59 C4
Broadway The BH10 ... 89 D6
BROADWEY DT3 ... 152 A4
Broadwey Cl DT3 ... 152 C4
BROADWINDSOR DT8 ... 203 F5
Broadwindsor CE Prim Sch DT8 ... 203 E5
Broadwindsor Craft & Design Ctr★ DT8 ... 203 F5
Broadwindsor Rd DT8 ... 204 B4
Broadwindsor Road Ind Est DT8 ... 204 B4
Brockenhurst Coll BH23 ... 124 D6
Brockenhurst Rd BH9 ... 90 B2
BROCKHAMPTON GREEN DT2 ... 196 C1
Brockhills La BH25 ... 95 C6
Brockington La BH21 ... 201 C5
Brockley Rd BH10 ... 89 E4
Brocks Pine BH24 ... 54 B3
Brockway BH31 ... 45 A7
Brockwood BH24 ... 53 F2
Brodham Way DT11 ... 198 B5
Brog St BH21 ... 57 E1
Broke La DT9 ... 195 D6
Brombys The 11 BH15 ... 119 C2
Bromley Ho BH12 ... 121 B5
Brompton Ct BH2 ... 121 E3
Bronte Ave BH23 ... 92 A1
Brook Ave BH25 ... 95 B4
Brook Avenue N BH25 ... 95 B4
Brook Cl
 Bournemouth BH10 ... 89 C4
 Dorchester DT2 ... 107 D7
Brookdale Cl BH18 ... 87 A4
Brookdale Farm BH18 ... 87 A4
Brook Dr BH31 ... 45 D4
Brook Ho BH25 ... 126 E7
Brookhouse St 8 DT1 ... 107 D1
Brook La
 Bransgore BH23 ... 93 B7
 Henstridge BA8 ... 19 A4
 Poole BH21 ... 85 E6
 Woodlands BH21 ... 44 B7
Brooklands
 Bournemouth BH4 ... 121 B3
 Milborne St Andrew DT11 ... 79 E8
Brooklands Farm Conservation Ctr (Dorset Wildlife Trust HQ)★ DT2 ... 75 B3
Brookland Way 4 BA8 ... 19 A4
Brooklyn Ct BH25 ... 94 F3
Brookmead Cl DT3 ... 153 D4
Brook Rd
 Bournemouth BH10 ... 89 C4
 Poole BH12 ... 120 C5
 Wimborne Minster BH21 ... 59 E4
Brook Road Ind Est BH21 ... 59 E3
Brooks Cl BH24 ... 55 D6
Brookside
 8 Gillingham SP8 ... 5 F3
 Milborne Port DT9 ... 17 D1
 Ringwood SP6 ... 43 E2
 West Coker BA22 ... 193 A8
Brookside Cl DT3 ... 153 C2
Brookside Park Homes BH21 ... 85 D4
Brookside Rd
 Bransgore BH23 ... 93 A8
 Wimborne Minster BH21 ... 59 F4
Brookside Way BH23 ... 93 E1
Brook St
 Milborne Port DT9 ... 17 D1
 Shipton Gorge DT6 ... 101 D4
Brook Terr SP6 ... 43 B8
Brook Way BH23 ... 125 C7
Broomfield Ct BH22 ... 61 E6
Broomfield Dr SP6 ... 42 C5
BROOM HILL BH21 ... 51 D2
Broom Hill DT2 ... 205 F5
Broomhill Way BH15 ... 119 A1
Broom La BH6 ... 123 B4
Broom Rd BH12 ... 88 C1
Broom Road Bsns Pk BH12 ... 88 C1
Broughton Ave BH10 ... 89 E3
Broughton Cl BH10 ... 89 E3
Broughton Cres DT4 ... 180 C7
Broughtons Dr 2 TA18 ... 192 A3
Brownen Rd BH9 ... 122 B8
Brownes Pl DT2 ... 73 F3
Browning Ave BH5 ... 123 A4
Browning Rd BH12 ... 120 D6
Brownlow Ct 33 BH4 ... 121 C3
Brownlow St DT4 ... 167 D4
Brown's Cres DT3 ... 166 E5
Brownsea Ave BH21 ... 85 F6
Brownsea Cl BH25 ... 94 E3
Brownsea Ct BH14 ... 147 B8
Brownsea Island★ BH15 ... 146 D4
Brownsea Island Nature Reserve★ BH13 ... 145 F5
Brownsea Rd BH13 ... 147 B3
Brownsea View Ave BH14 ... 120 C1
Brownsea View Cl BH14 ... 120 C1
Browns La SP6 ... 190 E3
Brown's La SP8 ... 10 F3
Brown St DT9 ... 196 A7
Brudenell Ave BH13 ... 147 D7
Brudenell Rd BH13 ... 147 D6
Brunel Cl BH31 ... 45 E4
Brunel Dr DT3 ... 153 B3
Brune Way BH22 ... 61 D3
Brunsell's Knap DT10 ... 33 A2
Brunstead Pl 1 BH12 ... 121 B4
Brunstead Rd BH12 ... 121 B4
Brunswick St BA20 ... 27 C4
Brushy Bush La SP5 ... 188 F3
Brutus Cl DT1 ... 134 E7
BRYANSTON DT11 ... 212 A3
Bryanstone Rd BH3 ... 121 E7
Bryanston Sch DT11 ... 212 A5
Bryanston St DT11 ... 212 C3
Bryant Rd BH12 ... 121 A8
Bryants La DT4 ... 180 B8
Brymer Rd DT2 ... 110 B8
Brymers Ave 5 DT5 ... 186 F7
Brympton Ave BA22 ... 26 B4
BRYMPTON D'EVERCY BA22 ... 26 B3
Brympton Way BA20 ... 26 E3
Bryn Rd
 Sandford BH20 ... 143 A8
 Weymouth DT4 ... 167 B2
Bryony Cl BH18 ... 86 F3
Bryony Gdns SP8 ... 5 D2
Bub La BH23 ... 124 E6
Buccaneers Cl BH23 ... 124 E6
Buccleuch Rd BH13 ... 121 A1
Bucehayes Cl BH23 ... 126 A8
Buchanan Ave BH7 ... 122 E6
Buckbury Mews 13 DT1 ... 135 B8
Buckhill Cl 5 TA18 ... 191 F3
Buckholme Towers Sch BH14 ... 120 A4
Buckhorn Cl DT6 ... 69 B8
BUCKHORN WESTON SP8 ... 9 B6
Buckingham Ct
 1 Christchurch BH23 ... 126 A7
 Poole BH15 ... 119 D3
Buckingham Mans 5 BH1 ... 122 A3
Buckingham Rd
 Gillingham SP8 ... 5 F1
 Poole BH12 ... 120 D7
Buckingham Way DT1 ... 135 C8
Buckingham Wlk BH25 ... 94 E3
Buckland Gr BH23 ... 93 E2
BUCKLAND NEWTON DT2 ... 208 A7
Buckland Newton Prim Sch DT2 ... 208 A8
Buckland Rd
 Poole BH12 ... 120 C5
 Yeovil BA21 ... 28 A6
BUCKLAND RIPERS DT3 ... 151 D1
Buckland Terr BH12 ... 120 C5
Buckle Pl BA22 ... 26 C6
Bucklers Mead 1 DT9 ... 194 C5
Bucklers Mead Com Sch BA21 ... 27 E8
Bucklers Mead Rd BA21 ... 27 E8
Bucklers Way BH8 ... 90 D3
Buckthorn Cl BH17 ... 86 F1
Buddens La SP7 ... 23 E4
Buddens Mdw BH21 ... 85 E4
Buddle Hill SP6 ... 43 E4
Buddleia Cl DT3 ... 152 F2
Budmouth Ave DT3 ... 168 A6
Budmouth Com Sports Ctr DT4 ... 166 E3
Budmouth Dr 5 SP8 ... 5 E4
Budmouth Tech Coll DT4 ... 166 E3
Buffalo Mews BH15 ... 119 B2
Buffets Cl DT10 ... 35 B2
Buffetts Rd DT10 ... 35 B2
Bugden's Copse Nature Reserve★ BH31 ... 45 B6
Bugdens La BH31 ... 45 C6
Bugle Cotts DT9 ... 17 C7
BUGLEY SP8 ... 10 A6
Bugway La TA20 ... 202 B8
Bulbury La BH16 ... 115 F7
Bull Bridge Mead BA22 ... 193 D3
Bull Cl DT2 ... 106 E8
Buller Ave BA22 ... 26 C6
Buller's Way DT3 ... 148 E6
Bullfinch Cl BH17 ... 86 F1
Bull Garden La DT10 ... 35 C1
Bull La
 Maiden Newton DT2 ... 72 F8
 Puncknowle DT2 ... 129 E6
Bullocks La DT11 ... 197 A1
Bulls La 4 TA18 ... 191 E4
Bumpers La DT5 ... 187 B4
Bunford La BA20, BA22 ... 26 E4
Bungalows The DT9 ... 16 E5
Bunting Rd BH22 ... 61 B8
Burbidge Cl BH16 ... 84 C2
Burbitt La DT6 ... 101 C4
Burbridge Cl BH17 ... 119 E8
Burcombe Rd BH10 ... 89 C5
Burdens 2 DT10 ... 197 A4
Burdock Cl BH23 ... 93 B1
Bure Cl BH23 ... 125 B6
Bure Haven Dr BH23 ... 125 A6
Bure Homage Gdns BH23 ... 125 B6
Bure Homage La BH23 ... 125 B6
Bure La BH23 ... 125 B6
Bure Pk BH23 ... 125 B6
Bure Rd BH23 ... 125 B6
Burford Cl BH23 ... 91 D1
Burford Ct 4 BH1 ... 122 B3
Burges Cl DT10 ... 20 E4
Burgess Cl BH11 ... 88 F4
Burgess Field BH21 ... 44 C6
Burleigh Rd BH6 ... 123 D5
BURLESTON DT2 ... 78 F1
Burleston Dro DT2 ... 78 F2
Burley Cl
 Barton on Sea BH25 ... 126 D8
 Verwood BH31 ... 45 A5
Burley Rd
 Bransgore BH23 ... 93 A8
 Poole BH12 ... 120 C6
 Winkton BH23 ... 92 D6
Burling Terr 1 BH12 ... 121 A4
Burlington Arc 11 BH1 ... 121 F3
Burlington Rd BH19 ... 179 C4
Burnaby Ct BH4 ... 121 C1
Burnaby Rd BH4 ... 121 C1
Burnage Ct 13 BH13 ... 147 F7
Burnbake Rd BH31 ... 45 B5
Burnbrae Rd BH22 ... 61 D1
Burn Cl BH31 ... 45 D4
Burnett Ave BH23 ... 123 E8
Burnett Rd BH23 ... 123 F7
Burngate Rd BH15 ... 118 E2
Burnham Dr BH8 ... 122 C7
Burnham Rd BH23 ... 92 C2
Burnham's La BH19 ... 178 D5
Burnleigh Gdns BH25 ... 95 C4
Burnside
 Christchurch BH23 ... 125 D8
 Winterborne St Martin DT2 ... 133 C6
Burns Rd
 Bournemouth BH6 ... 123 D7
 Northport BH20 ... 142 D6
Burn View DT2 ... 107 F5
Burraton Sq 6 DT1 ... 107 D1
Burroughes Ave BA21 ... 27 A6
Burrows La BH31 ... 45 B8
Burrs Pond Mdw Nature Reserve★ DT10 ... 35 B2
Burrywells DT2 ... 102 D6
Bursledon Ho 4 BH25 ... 95 A2
BURSTOCK DT8 ... 203 D6
Burstock La DT8 ... 203 C7
Burtley Rd BH6 ... 123 F3
BURTON
 Christchurch ... 92 D2
 Dorchester DT2 ... 107 F4
 Mere BA12 ... 3 D5
 Yeovil BA22 ... 193 C8
BURTON BRADSTOCK DT6 ... 128 B8
Burton Bradstock CE Prim Sch DT6 ... 128 C7
Burton CE Prim Sch BH23 ... 92 C3
Burton Cl
 Burton BH23 ... 92 C1
 Shaftesbury SP7 ... 13 A3
 St Leonards BH24 ... 53 F5
 Wool BH20 ... 139 F2
Burtoncroft BH23 ... 92 C3
Burton Cross BH20 ... 139 E1
Burton Hall BH23 ... 92 C3
Burton Hall Pl BH23 ... 92 D3
Burton Ho BH23 ... 92 D1
Burton La BA22 ... 193 C8
Burton Rd
 Abbotsbury DT3 ... 148 D6
 Bothenhampton DT6 ... 100 E2
 Burton Bradstock DT6 ... 128 A8
 Christchurch BH23 ... 124 E7
 Poole BH13 ... 121 A3
 Wool BH20 ... 139 E1
Burton St DT10 ... 20 E3
Burton Wood BH20 ... 139 F1
Burt's Hill BH21 ... 59 D7
Burt's La BH21 ... 52 C8
Burt's Pl 6 BH19 ... 179 C2
Bury Rd BH13 ... 120 F1
Bushell Rd BH15 ... 119 C7
Bushes Hill SP8 ... 5 A7
Bushes Rd DT11 ... 199 A4
BUSHEY BH20 ... 162 D3
Bushey La BH20 ... 162 D3
Bushey Rd BH8 ... 90 C1
Bushfield Rd 1 TA18 ... 191 E3
Bushmead Dr BH24 ... 54 A5
Bush Pk DT11 ... 81 E8
Bute Dr BH23 ... 126 B8
Butlers La BH24 ... 47 E1
Butt Cl DT2 ... 78 B1
Buttercup Cl 2 SP8 ... 5 D2
Buttercup Dr BH23 ... 93 B1
Buttercup La DT11 ... 212 E5
Buttercup Way DT6 ... 100 D2
Butterstake La SP7 ... 7 D3
Butterwick Dro DT9 ... 195 D6
Buttery The BH23 ... 124 D7
Butt Farm Cl DT2 ... 105 D1
Butt La
 Bere Regis BH20 ... 81 B3
 Whitechurch Canonicorum DT6 ... 66 D2
Butt La Hollow BH20 ... 81 B4
Butts Cl
 Marnhull DT10 ... 20 F2
 Winfrith Newburgh DT2 ... 156 F6
Butts La SP8 ... 21 C7
Butts Mead 1 SP7 ... 13 A1
Butts Pond Ind Est DT10 ... 35 B2
Butts Quarry La TA18 ... 192 A4
Butts The
 12 Child Okeford DT11 ... 198 C7
 Shaftesbury SP7 ... 12 C3
Buxton Cl 2 DT4 ... 180 D8
Buxton Rd DT4 ... 180 D8
Byron Ct BH22 ... 61 D5
Byron Ho 10 BH25 ... 95 A2
Byron Rd
 Barton on Sea BH25 ... 126 E8
 Bournemouth BH5 ... 122 F3
 Wimborne Minster BH21 ... 59 C6

C

Cabot Bsns Village BH17 ... 119 A7
Cabot La BH17 ... 119 B8
Cabot Way BH25 ... 94 F3
Cachy Rd BH20 ... 139 E7
Caddy La BA12 ... 2 F5
Cadhay Cl BH25 ... 94 E3
Cadley Cl DT11 ... 212 D5
Cadnam Way BH8 ... 90 D3
Cadogan Rd BH24 ... 55 D7
Caernarvon Cl 4 DT1 ... 135 C8
Caesar Gn 2 DT1 ... 134 E7
Caesar's Way BH18 ... 86 E4
Caird Ave BH25 ... 95 C2
Cairns Cl BH23 ... 123 F8
Caister Cl BH22 ... 61 C6
Calcraft Rd BH20 ... 177 A8
Calder Rd BH17 ... 119 F8
Caledonian Cl
 Christchurch BH23 ... 125 B7
 Radipole DT4 ... 167 D5
Caledon Rd BH14 ... 120 E3
Cale Way SP8 ... 11 B8
Caley Way DT6 ... 69 A1
Calf Close La DT10 ... 197 F8
Calfhay La DT9 ... 194 E1
Calkin Cl BH23 ... 92 A1
Calluna Rd BH12 ... 120 B8
Calves La SP7 ... 12 B4
Calvin Rd BH9 ... 121 F8
Camborne Pl BA21 ... 28 A5
Camborne St BA21 ... 28 A6
Cambridge Cl BA20 ... 26 F5
Cambridge Gdns BH23 ... 91 F2
Cambridge Rd
 Bournemouth BH2 ... 121 D3
 Dorchester DT1 ... 107 D1
 Weymouth DT4 ... 166 E3
Cambridge Wlk 1 DT1 ... 107 D1
Camden Cl BH9 ... 90 B1
Camden Way DT1 ... 134 F7
Came Down Cl DT3 ... 152 C3
CAMEL GREEN SP6 ... 42 D6
Camel Green Rd SP6 ... 42 D6
Camellia Cl BH21 ... 45 A1
Camellia Gdns
 Bournemouth BH10 ... 89 C2
 New Milton BH25 ... 95 B2
Camelot Way SP8 ... 5 D1
Cameron Rd BH23 ... 124 D7
CAMESWORTH DT6 ... 68 F7
Camesworth La DT6 ... 69 A7
Came View Cl DT1 ... 135 D8
Came View Rd DT1 ... 135 C8
Camilla Ct BH13 ... 121 B2
Cammel Rd BH22 ... 61 D2
Campbell Rd
 Bournemouth BH1 ... 122 E5
 Burton BH23 ... 92 C3
Campion Cl
 5 Gillingham SP8 ... 5 D2
 Radipole DT4 ... 167 E7
Campion Dr BA22 ... 26 D5
Campion Gr BH23 ... 124 F6
Campion Wlk 2 BA21 ... 26 F7
Camp Rd
 Chickerell DT4 ... 180 B8
 West Coker BA22 ... 26 C1
Canberra Cl BH23 ... 91 E1
Canberra Cres DT3 ... 152 E3
Canberra Rd
 Christchurch BH23 ... 91 E1
 Radipole DT3 ... 152 E2
Candys Cl BH21 ... 58 E2
Candys La BH21 ... 57 F2
Candy's La 6 DT11 ... 198 B6
Canford Ave BH11 ... 89 A2
Canford Bottom BH21 ... 60 C6
Canford Bottom Rdbt BH21 ... 60 C5
CANFORD CLIFFS ... 147 E8
Canford Cliffs Ave BH14 ... 120 E2
Canford Cliffs Rd BH13 ... 120 E2
Canford Cres BH13 ... 147 E7
Canford Ct BH13 ... 147 E6
Canford Gdns BH11 ... 89 A1
CANFORD HEATH ... 87 E1
Canford Heath Fst & Mid Schs BH17 ... 119 D7
Canford Heath Nature Reserve★ BH11 ... 88 B4
Canford Heath Rd BH17 ... 87 E1
CANFORD MAGNA ... 60 A1
Canford Magna BH21 ... 60 A1
Canford Park Arena★ BH21 ... 88 B7
Canford Pl 2 BH13 ... 147 F7
Canford Rd
 Bournemouth BH11 ... 89 A1
 Poole BH15 ... 119 D4
Canford Sch BH21 ... 60 B2
Canford Summer Sch of Music DT9 ... 30 B6
Canford View Dr BH21 ... 60 B6
Canford Way BH12 ... 88 C2
CANN SP7 ... 24 A7
CANN COMMON SP7 ... 24 D7
Cann Hill SP7 ... 24 A5
Cannings Court La DT2 ... 196 C3
Cannon Cl BH18 ... 87 A1
Cannon Court Mews 1 DT9 ... 17 D1
Cannon Hill Gdns BH21 ... 60 B7
Cannon Hill Rd BH21 ... 60 A7
Canteen Rd DT5 ... 181 D1
Canterbury Cl
 Ferndown BH22 ... 53 A1
 Weymouth DT4 ... 166 F3
Capella Ct BH2 ... 121 F2
Capesthorne BH23 ... 125 B5
Caphays Dro DT9 ... 195 E7
Capitol Cl DT1 ... 134 E8
Capper Road E BH20 ... 139 E6
Capper Road W BH20 ... 139 E6
Capstan Field BH19 ... 178 A2
Capstans The BH14 ... 147 B8
Capstone Pl BH8 ... 122 D6
Capstone Rd BH8 ... 122 B6
Capston Field BH19 ... 178 A2
Captains Cove BH15 ... 118 E3
Caradon Pl BH31 ... 44 F7
Carbery Ave BH6 ... 123 D5
Carbery Gdns BH6 ... 123 E5
Carbery La 3 BH6 ... 123 C4
Carbery Row 2 BH6 ... 123 C4
Cardigan Rd
 Bournemouth BH9 ... 121 F8
 Poole BH12 ... 120 F4
Cards Mill La DT6 ... 66 A7
Carent Cl DT10 ... 21 A2
Carey App BH20 ... 142 D5
Carey Cl BH20 ... 142 D5
Carey Rd
 Bournemouth BH9 ... 89 F3
 Northport BH20 ... 142 D5
Careys Rd BH8 ... 90 D4
Carina Ct BH13 ... 147 C3
Carisbrooke
 Poole BH13 ... 147 E7
 Radipole DT4 ... 167 B6
Carisbrooke Cres BH15 ... 117 F3
Carisbrooke Ct
 1 Christchurch BH23 ... 126 B7
 New Milton BH25 ... 94 F3
Carisbrooke Gdns BA20 ... 27 B5
Carisbrooke Way BH23 ... 93 E1
Carlinford 5 BH5 ... 122 F3
Carlton Ave BH25 ... 126 D8
Carlton Gr BH12 ... 120 D5
Carlton Mount BH2 ... 121 E2
Carlton Rd BH1 ... 122 C4
Carlton Road N DT4 ... 167 D5
Carlton Road S DT4 ... 167 D5
Carlyle Rd BH6 ... 123 D6
Carmel Cl 5 BH15 ... 117 F2
Carnarvon Rd 4 BH1 ... 122 E4
Carnegie Cl BH12 ... 120 D5
Caroline Ave BH23 ... 124 F6
Caroline Pl 5 DT4 ... 167 D3
Caroline Rd BH11 ... 89 B2
Carpenters Cl DT2 ... 106 E8
Carradale BH23 ... 125 B8
Carraway La DT10 ... 20 F1
Carrbridge Cl BH3 ... 121 D7

Carrbridge Gdns BH3 .... 121 D7
Carrbridge Rd BH3 .... 121 D7
Carrick Cl DT1 .... 135 C8
Carrick Way BH25 .... 95 C2
Carrington Cl ▲ DT4 .... 180 D8
Carrion La ▲ BH20 ...... 142 E4
Carroll Ave BH22 .... 61 E5
Carroll Cl BH12 .... 121 A6
Carsworth Way BH17 ...... 88 A2
Carter Cl DT11 .... 212 E5
Carter Com Sports Sch
  BH15 .... 118 F2
Carters Ave BH15 .... 117 F4
Carters La BA22 .... 192 E8
Carter's La
  Chidcock DT6 .... 98 E8
  ⑥ Poole BH15 .... 119 C2
Cartref Cl BH31 .... 45 B6
Cartwright Cl BH10 ...... 89 C4
Carvers Ind Est BH24 .... 55 C7
Carvers La BH24 .... 55 C7
Carysfort Rd BH1 .... 122 D4
Casebery Ct ⑦ DT1 ...... 107 E3
Cashmoor Cl ◆ BH12 .... 120 F7
Caslake Cl BH25 .... 94 F1
Cassel Ave BH13 .... 121 B1
Casseles Ct ⑧ BH25 .... 95 A2
Cassiobury Rd DT4 ...... 167 D4
Casterbridge Cl
  Pimperne DT11 .... 212 F6
  ⑷ Swanage BH19 ...... 178 E2
Casterbridge Ct ⑤ BH1 .. 122 D5
Casterbridge Ind Est
  DT1 .... 108 B2
Casterbridge Rd
  Dorchester DT1 .... 135 D8
  Ferndown BH22 .... 61 C3
Casterbridge Way SP8 .... 5 E4
CASTLE EX13 .... 202 A4
Castle Ave
  Christchurch BH23. .... 125 E8
  ⑥ Okeford Fitzpaine DT11 197 F6
Castle Cl
  Cranborne BH21 .... 40 B7
  Dorchester DT1 .... 107 D1
Castle Court Prep Sch
  BH21 .... 85 D7
Castle Ct ② BH21 ...... 126 A7
Castledene Cres BH14 ... 120 A2
Castle Farm Rd BH16... .. 84 C4
Castle Gate Cl BH8 ...... 90 C2
Castle Hill BH14 ...... 120 B4
Castle Hill Cl SP7 ...... 12 D3
Castle Hill Cres BA12... .. 3 A5
Castle Hill La
  Cranborne BH21 .... 40 B6
  Mere BA12. .... 3 A5
Castle Hill Rd DT4 ...... 180 B8
Castle La E
  Buckland Newton DT2... 208 B8
  Okeford Fitzpaine DT11,
  DT10 .... 197 F6
  Owermoigne DT2. ...... 155 D8
Castle Lane E BH7 ...... 123 C8
Castle Lane W BH9. .... 90 C2
Castleman Ave BH6 .... 123 C5
Castleman Rd DT3 ...... 152 E2
Castleman Gdns BH24 ... 54 B6
  DT11 .... 212 E6
Castleman Way BH24 .... 55 C6
Castlemews BH24 ...... 54 E5
Castle Parade BH7 ...... 123 D7
CASTLE PARK DT1 ...... 134 D7
Castle Rd
  Bournemouth BH9 ...... 90 A1
  Fortuneswell DT5 ...... 181 A1
  Sherborne DT9 .... 30 D7
Castle Sq DT6 .... 100 C5
Castle St
  Christchurch BH23. .... 124 B6
  Cranborne BH21 ...... 40 B7
  Mere BA12. .... 2 F5
  Poole BH15 .... 119 C1
Castleton TA18 .... 192 C5
Castleton Ave BH10 .... 89 D6
Castleton Rd DT9 ...... 30 C6
Castleton Waterwheel Mus★
  DT9 .... 30 D6
CASTLETOWN DT5 ...... 181 C1
Castletown DT5 .... 181 B1
Castle Town Way DT9 .... 30 C8
Castle View Dr BH16 .... 84 C1
Castlewood BH24 ...... 54 F5
Catalina Cl BH23 ...... 125 A6
Catalina Dr BH15. ...... 119 E1
Caters Pl DT1. .... 108 A2
Catherine Wheel Gdns
  BH23 .... 91 E3
CATHERSTON LEWESTON
  DT6 .... 65 C1
Cathole Bridge Rd
  Crewkerne TA18. ...... 191 C3
  Misterton TA18 .... 191 F3
Cat La DT10 .... 33 A2
Catmead DT2 .... 78 B2
Caton Cl BH12 .... 121 B8
Catsley La DT2 .... 205 B6
CATTISTOCK DT2 ...... 206 C2
Cattistock Rd
  Bournemouth BH8 ...... 90 C2
  Maiden Newton DT2 .... 72 F8
Cauldon Ave BH19 ...... 179 B4
Cauldon Barn Rd BH19 .. 179 B4

Cauldron Cres BH19. .... 179 B4
Cauldron Mdws BH19 .... 179 B4
Caundle La
  Stalbridge DT10. .... 33 A6
  Stourton Caundle DT10... 32 E1
Causeway Cl
  Wareham Town BH20 .... 142 D5
  Weymouth DT4 .... 167 A7
Causeway La DT8 ...... 203 A6
CAUSEWAY THE BA12 .... 3 C4
Causeway The
  Hazelbury Bryan DT10... 196 F4
  Milborne St Andrew DT11.. 79 E8
Cavalier Cl BA21. ...... 27 F8
Cavalier Way BA21 ...... 27 F8
Cavan Cres BH17. ...... 87 B1
Cave Hole, Portland★
  DT5 .... 186 F11
Cavendish Cl BH4 ...... 121 C3
Cavendish Hall BH1 .... 122 A5
Cavendish Pl BH1....... 122 A5
Cavendish Rd BH1...... 122 A5
Caversham Cl BH15 .... 118 E3
Cawdor Rd BH3........ 121 D7
Caxton Cl BH23 .... 125 A7
Cecil Ave BH8 .... 122 C8
Cecil Cl BH21.......... 86 E6
Cecil Hill BH8. .... 122 B8
Cecil Pl BH15.......... 122 B8
Cecil Rd BH21.......... 84 D2
Cecil Rd
  Bournemouth BH5...... 122 E4
  Poole BH12 .... 120 D6
  Swanage BH19 .... 179 A2
Cecil St BA20 .... 27 D5
Cedar Ave
  Bournemouth BH10 ...... 89 D6
  Christchurch BH23...... 123 D8
  St Leonards BH24 ...... 53 F3
Cedar Cl
  Upton BH16........... 117 D8
  ① Wool BH20 .... 140 A2
  Wimborne Minster BH21... 60 A5
Cedar Fields ① BA22... 193 A8
Cedar Gdns BH25 ...... 94 F1
Cedar Gr BA21, BA20... 27 A6
Cedar Grange ⑱ BH13 .. 121 A4
Cedar Manor BH4...... 121 C3
Cedar Rd
  Charminster DT2 ...... 75 D2
  Dorchester DT1........ 107 E2
Cedars The BH4 ...... 121 C4
Cedar Trad Pk BH21 .... 60 F6
Cedar Way DT4 .... 61 C8
Celandine Cl
  Christchurch BH23...... 125 B8
  Radipole DT4.......... 167 A6
Celandine Rd ③ BA22... 26 C5
Cellars Farm Rd BH6.... 124 A3
Celtic Cres DT1........ 134 E7
Celtic Crescent DT1 .... 134 F7
Cemetery Ave BH15 .... 119 F6
Cemetery Junc DT1 .... 121 F5
Cemetery Rd
  ② Gillingham SP8...... 5 F2
  Portesham DT3 .... 150 A8
  Wimborne Minster BH21... 59 B5
Centenary Gdns BA8 .... 19 A4
Centenary Ho BH23 .... 124 B7
Centenary Way BH21.... 122 E5
Central Acre ⑲ BA20.... 27 C4
Central Ave
  Bournemouth BH12 .... 120 E6
  Poole BH15............ 85 F7
Central Bsns Pk BH1 ... 122 C5
Central Dr
  Bournemouth BH2...... 121 E5
  West Moors BH24 ...... 62 B8
Central Farm La DT2.... 79 C2
Central Pk DT11 ...... 199 E3
Central Rd BA20 ...... 27 D5
Centre Pl BH24 .... 55 B8
Centurion Rd DT1 ...... 199 E2
Century Pk BA20 ...... 27 A5
Cereleton Pk DT11 ...... 211 C6
CERNE ABBAS DT2 .... 207 E4
Cerne Abbas BH13 .... 121 A1
Cerne Abbas CE Fst Sch
  DT2. .... 207 C4
Cerne Abbas Giant★
  DT2. .... 207 D3
Cerne Abbas Tithe Barn★
  DT2. .... 207 D3
Cerne Abbey★ DT2 .... 207 D4
Cerne Abbas Rd DT3 .... 11 B8
Cerne Cl BH9 .... 90 A4
Chaddenwick Hill BA12... 3 E6
Chaddesley Glen BH13 .. 147 E6
Chaddesley Grange
  BH13 .... 147 F6
Chaddesley Pines BH13 . 147 E6
Chaddesley Wood Rd
  BH13 .... 147 E5
Chafeys Ave DT4....... 167 A5
Chaffey Cl BH24 .... 55 E8
Chaffeymoor Hill SP8, BA9 . 11 B8
Chaffinch Chase SP8..... 11 B8
Chaffinch Cl
  Broadstone BH17....... 86 F2
  New Milton BH25....... 94 F2
  Radipole DT3.......... 152 D3
CHALBURY BH21........ 201 C1

Chalbury Cl
  Overcombe/Preston
    DT3. .... 168 A8
  Poole BH17............ 88 A2
CHALBURY COMMON
  BH21................ 201 D1
Chalbury Ct ② BH21 ... 120 B4
Chalbury (Hill Fort)★
  DT3.................. 153 A4
Chalbury Lodge ⑪ DT3 . 153 B2
Chaldecott Gdns BH10.. 89 C4
CHALDON HERRING OR EAST
  CHALDON DT2........ 156 C3
Chaldon Rd BH17...... 87 F2
Chalfont Ave BH23 ...... 91 D3
Chalice Cl BH14........ 120 A4
Chalk Pit Cl BH20...... 81 B1
Chalk Pit La
  Litton Cheney DT2...... 103 A2
  Wool BH20 .... 139 F1
Chalk The DT2 .... 37 F1
Chalky Rd DT2 .... 136 A4
Challacombe St DT1 .... 107 B2
Challenger Way BA22 ... 26 C6
CHALMINGTON DT2...... 206 C3
Chalwell ⑨ DT1........ 198 C7
Chalwyn Ind Est BH15,
  BH12................ 120 B8
Chamberlaine Rd DT4... 180 C8
Champernhayes La DT6 . 64 C5
Champions ⑪ DT8...... 204 C4
Chancery La DT6....... 100 D6
Chander Cl BH21...... 61 E4
Chandler Cl DT1 ...... 167 D8
Chandlers DT9........ 30 C7
Chandlers Cl BH7 ...... 123 B8
Chandos Ave BH12.... 121 A8
Channel Cl
  Barton on Sea BH25 .... 126 C4
  Bournemouth BH6...... 123 D3
Channel View Rd DT5... 186 F4
Channons Ct ④ DT1.... 108 B2
Chant Cl BH21 .... 124 D7
Chantmarle La DT2 .... 206 B5
Chantry La DT8 .... 93 F1
Chantry St DT6........ 204 C5
Chantry The DT1...... 122 A4
Chantry The★ BA12..... 3 A5
Chantry View DT2...... 193 D8
Chapel Cl
  Dorchester DT2........ 136 B2
  Langton Herring DT3.... 150 C1
  Poole BH15............ 85 E6
Chapel Gate BH23...... 90 C8
Chapel Gdns DT1 ...... 212 E3
Chapel Hill SP8........ 9 D2
Chapel La
  Bransgore BH23........ 93 A8
  Corfe Mullen BH21 .... 85 E5
  Dimington TA17....... 191 B8
  East Parley BH23...... 90 C8
  Henstridge BA8 ...... 18 E7
  Maiden Newton DT2 .... 72 F8
  ⑦ Milborne Port DT9... 17 D2
  Osmington DT3 .... 154 B1
  Pen Selwood BA9 ...... 1 C3
  ② Pimperne DT11 .... 199 D3
  Poole BH15............ 119 C2
  Radipole DT3.......... 152 C5
  Wimborne Minster BH21... 59 B5
  Woodlands BH21....... 52 B3
  ⑦ Yetminster DT9..... 194 C5
  Zennor BA12 .... 1 E5
Chapel Lane E BA12..... 1 F5
Chapel Mdw ⑥ DT9 .... 194 C5
Chapel Rise BA34...... 54 F2
Chapel St
  Milborne St Andrew DT11... 79 E7
  Shipton George DT3.... 101 D4
Chapel View ⑥ DT2 .... 78 B1
Charberry Rise DT6 .... 96 F7
Charborough Cl BH16... 84 C4
Charborough House★
  BH20................. 83 F8
Charborough Pk★ BH20... 83 F8
Charborough Rd BH18.. 87 B3
Charborough Way ⑪
  BH21.................. 56 D4
CHARD JUNCTION TA20 . 202 B7
Chard La
  Broadwindsor DT8...... 203 C7
  Wayford TA18, TA20.... 191 B2
Chard Rd
  Broadwindsor DT8...... 203 C7
  Crewkerne TA18........ 191 F4
Chards Mead Rd DT6.... 100 C7
Chard St TA20 .... 202 E6
Charing Cl ① BH24 .... 55 C6
Charing Cross SP6...... 42 A5
Charing Cross SP6...... 42 B5
Charles Cres BH25...... 95 D3
Charles Garrett Cl ③ SP7 . 12 D3
Charles Gdns BH10..... 89 D2
Charles Keightley Ct
  BH21.................. 59 D4
Charles Rd
  Burton Bradstock DT6... 128 B8
  Christchurch BH23...... 124 F8
  Poole BH15............ 119 D3
  Yeovil BA21 .... 27 F4
Charles's La BH24 ...... 55 E2
CHALBURY BH21........ 201 C1

Charles St
  Blandford Forum DT11... 212 D4
  Dorchester DT1........ 108 A1
  Radipole DT4.......... 167 D4
CHARLESTOWN DT4 .... 166 E2
Charlotte Cl
  Charminster DT2 ...... 107 C5
  Christchurch BH23...... 125 A6
  ⑧ New Milton BH25.... 95 A2
  Poole BH12 .... 120 F7
Charlton Beeches DT11 . 211 C7
Charlton Cl
  Bournemouth BH8 ...... 90 D3
  ⑫ Verwood BH12...... 191 F4
  Hordle SO41 .... 95 F3
CHARLTON DOWN DT2... 75 D3
Charlton La SP7 .... 11 B5
Charlton Manor ① DT11 211 D6
CHARLTON MARSHALL
  DT11................ 211 D6
Charlton Mead ② DT11 . 211 D6
CHARLTON ON THE HILL
  DT11................ 211 C7
Charltons The BH2..... 121 F5
CHARMINSTER
  90 C2
  DT2 .... 107 C5
Charminster Ave BH9 ... 90 B1
Charminster Cl BH8..... 90 B2
Charminster Pl BH8..... 90 C2
Charminster Rd BH8 ... 122 C7
CHARMOUTH DT6....... 97 B7
Charmouth Cl DT7...... 96 C6
Charmouth Gr BH14.... 120 A4
Charmouth Heritage Coast
  Ctr★ DT6. .... 97 A7
Charmouth Prim Sch DT6 97 A7
Charmouth Rd DT7..... 96 C6
CHARNAGE BA12....... 3 F4
Charnock Cl SO41...... 95 F3
Charnwood Ave BH9.... 90 B3
Charnwood Cl BH22.... 53 A2
Chartcombe BH13...... 147 E6
Charter Rd BH11....... 88 D2
Chartwell
  Poole BH13............ 121 B3
  Radipole DT4.......... 167 B6
Chaseborough Sq ④
  DT1 .... 107 D1
Chase Cres SP5........ 188 E4
Chaseside BH7........ 123 A8
Chase The
  St Leonards BH24...... 54 F5
  Verwood BH31......... 45 B5
Chaston La DT2........ 208 C8
Chatsworth Rd
  Bournemouth BH8...... 122 C6
  Poole BH14............ 120 B5
  Yeovil BA21 .... 27 F7
Chatsworth Way DT4.... 94 F3
Chaucer Cl BH21...... 59 C6
Chaucer Rd BH13...... 147 F8
Chaucombe Pl BH25 .... 94 F1
Cheam Rd BH18....... 86 F4
Cheap St DT9.......... 30 B6
Checkridge La EX13.... 202 A2
Cheddington Rd BH9.... 90 A4
Chedington Cl BH17.... 87 E2
Chedington La DT8 .... 204 B8
Cheese La DT3......... 150 E6
Chelmsford Rd BH16... 84 C4
Chelmsford St DT4..... 167 D4
Chelston Ave BA21..... 27 D7
Cheltenham Rd BH12... 120 C5
Chelwood Cl DT3...... 152 E2
Chelwood Gate DT4.... 166 E3
Chene Rd BH21........ 59 D4
Cherford Rd BH11...... 89 B2
Cheriton Cl BH15...... 119 F6
Cheriton Rd BH21...... 121 C2
Cheriton Ave BH7...... 123 C8
Cheriton Way BH21..... 59 C6
Cherrett Cl BH11....... 88 F4
Cherries Dr BH9....... 90 B4
Cherrybrook La ③ DT1.. 107 B1
Cherry Cl
  Poole BH14............ 120 B4
  Sandford BH20......... 143 B8
Cherry Ct BH14........ 120 B5
Cherryfields SP8....... 5 F4
Cherry Gr BH22........ 61 C6
Cherry Hill Gdns BH16.. 117 D6
Cherry Hill Gr BH16.... 117 D6
Cherry Orchard La
  Cann SP7.............. 11 F2
  Gillingham SP8 .... 5 C2
Cherry Tree La DT3..... 100 B8
Cherry Tree Cl BH24 .... 53 F3
Cherry Tree Ct
  ⑤ Crewkerne TA18..... 191 F5
  ④ New Milton BH25.... 95 B1
Cherry Tree Dr
  Beckley BH25.......... 94 E5
  Yeovil BA20 .... 26 F7
Chescombe Cl DT2..... 207 D3
Chescombe La DT11... 210 B3
CHESELBOURNE DT2 ... 209 B2
Cheselbourne Villiage Sch
  DT2................. 209 A3
Cheshire Dr BH8....... 91 A2
Chesil Beach DT4...... 180 B4
Chesil Beach★ DT3 .... 149 C2
Chesil Beach Visitor Ctr★
  DT4................. 180 D4
Chesilbourne Gr BH8... 90 D3
Chesildene Ave BH8.... 90 D3
Chesildene Dr BH8..... 90 D3

Chesil Gdns BH12 ...... 120 B8
Chesil View DT4........ 180 C7
Chesnut Ave ㉑ TA18... 191 F5
Chessel Ave BH5 ...... 122 F4
Chessels CI BA22 ...... 193 B8
Chester Cl DT1 .... 135 C8
Chesterfield Cl BH13 ... 147 F8
Chesterfield Ct BH13... 122 C3
Chester Rd BH13....... 121 C2
Chestnut Ave
  Barton on Sea BH25 .... 127 A8
  Bournemouth BH6...... 123 C4
  Christchurch BH23...... 123 D8
  Holton Heath BH16 .... 116 B3
  Verwood BH24......... 46 D6
Chestnut Gr
  Blandford Forum DT11 .. 212 B4
  Ferndown BH22........ 60 E6
Chestnut Pl DT3....... 167 C7
Chestnut Rd
  Bridport DT6.......... 100 D4
  Charminster DT2 ...... 75 D2
Chestnut Way
  Burton BH23 .... 92 C3
  Dorchester DT1........ 107 D2
  Gillingham SP8 .... 5 D1
Chetcombe Rd BA12 .... 3 B6
CHETNOLE DT9........ 194 D2
Chetnole Cl BH17...... 88 A1
Chetnole Sta DT9...... 194 C2
Chettell Way DT11 .... 212 D2
CHETTLE DT11 .... 200 B8
Chettle House★ DT11... 200 C8
Chetwode Way BH17.... 87 B2
Cheviot Court Flats
  BH23 .... 124 F8
Cheviots The BH4...... 120 C3
Cheviot Way BH31...... 45 B5
Chewton Common Rd
  BH23 .... 126 B8
Chewton Farm Rd BH23 . 94 C1
Chewton Lodge BH23 .. 126 B8
Chewton Mews BH23 .. 94 A2
Chewton Way BH23 .... 94 B1
Cheyne Cl ① DT5...... 186 E1
Cheyne Gdns BH4..... 121 C2
Chichester Rd BH24.... 47 E1
Chichester Way BH23 .. 125 A5
Chichester Wlk BH21... 59 E1
CHICKERELL DT3....... 166 C5
Chickerell Cl BH9...... 90 B3
Chickerell Hill DT3..... 166 B6
Chickerell Prim Sch
  DT3 .... 166 D5
Chickerell Rd DT3..... 166 B6
CHIDEOCK DT6........ 99 A6
Chideock Hill DT6...... 98 E7
Chigwell Rd BH8....... 90 E1
CHILBRIDGE 58 E7
Chilbury Gdns DT2..... 155 C7
CHILCOMBE DT6....... 102 D3
Chilcombe La DT6...... 102 D3
Chilcombe Rd BH6..... 123 B5
Childhay La DT8........ 203 C6
CHILD OKEFORD DT11 .. 198 B7
CHILFROME DT2........ 206 B1
Chilfrome Cl BH17...... 87 C1
Chilfrome La
  Chilfrome DT2 .... 206 B1
  Maiden Newton DT2 .... 72 E8
CHILSON COMMON
  TA20................ 202 A7
Chiltern Cl
  Old Milton BH25....... 94 F1
  Poole BH4............ 121 B5
Chiltern Ct ⑤ BH23 .... 124 F8
Chiltern Dr
  Barton on Sea BH25 .... 126 E8
  Verwood BH31......... 45 B6
CHILTON CANTELO BA22... 14 A8
Chilton Gr BA21........ 27 A6
Chimes The BH4........ 121 B3
China La ⑪ DT11...... 199 F7
Chine Cres BH2........ 121 D2
Chine Crescent Rd BH2 . 121 D2
Chine Wlk BH22....... 61 E1
Chinnock Hollow BA22 . 192 E8
Chippel La DT10....... 20 F1
Chisels La BH23....... 93 B8
Chislehurst ⑯ BH14.... 121 C3
Chiswell DT5.......... 186 E8
Chiswell Rd BH17...... 87 D1
Chitten Hill BH20...... 115 C7
Chivrick Cl DT10....... 35 C3
Chloe Gdns BH12...... 120 D7
Chorley Cl BH15....... 119 E6
Chowins Rd ⑱ TA18.... 191 F4
Chris Cres ④ BH16..... 117 F8
CHRISTCHURCH 124 D5
Christchurch Bay Rd
  BH25 .... 126 F7
Christchurch By-Pass
  BH23 .... 124 D8
Christchurch Castle★
  BH23 .... 124 B6
Christchurch Hospl
  BH23 .... 123 F8
Christchurch Inf Sch
  BH23 .... 124 A7
Christchurch Jun Sch
  BH23 .... 124 A7
Christchurch Priory★
  BH23 .... 124 C6
Christchurch Rd
  Barton on Sea BH25 .... 126 D8

Christchurch Rd continued
Bournemouth, Boscombe BH1, BH7 . . . .**122** D4
Bournemouth, Iford BH7 . .**123** B6
Ferndown BH22 . . . .**61** A3
Hurn BH23 . . . .**91** C5
Ringwood BH24 . . . .**55** C4
Christchurch Sta BH23 . . . .**124** A7
Christmas Cl BH23 . . . .**142** D3
Christopher Cl BA20 . . . .**27** A5
Christopher Cres BH15 . . .**119** C6
Christ the King RC Prim Sch
BH11 . . . .**89** A5
Christy's Gn SP7 . . . .**12** F3
Christy's La SP7 . . . .**12** F3
Chubb Mews BH20 . . . .**120** C5
Church Acre 3 DT1 . . . . . .**108** B2
Church Cl
Beer Hackett DT9 . . . .**194** D6
Bourton SP8 . . . .**1** D1
Bridport DT6 . . . .**69** A1
Chetnole DT9 . . . .**194** D3
Fontmell Magna SP7 . . . . . .**37** E7
Longburton DT9 . . . .**195** B7
Stour Provost SP7 . . . .**22** C7
5 Swanage BH19 . . . .**179** B2
Todber DT10 . . . .**21** D4
Church Farm DT2 . . . .**205** B8
Churchfield BH31 . . . .**45** A5
Churchfield Cres BH15 . .**119** E4
Churchfield Ct 2 BH15 . .**119** E3
Churchfield La DT4 . . . .**43** A1
Churchfield Rd BH15 . . . .**119** E3
Churchfoot La DT10 . . . . . .**196** F3
Church Gn
Bishop's Caundle DT9 . . . .**196** A8
3 Wareham BH20 . . . .**142** E3
Church Hill
Buckhorn Weston SP8 . . . . . .**9** B6
Dinnington TA17 . . . .**191** B7
Iwerne Minster DT11 . . . . .**37** F2
Kington Magna SP8 . . . .**9** D3
Langton Herring DT3 . . . . .**150** C1
Marnhull DT10 . . . .**79** E7
Milborne St Andrew DT11 . .**79** F7
Piddlehinton DT2 . . . .**76** F7
Shaftesbury SP7 . . . .**12** D3
Stalbridge DT10 . . . .**19** C1
2 Swanage BH19 . . . .**179** B2
West Stour SP8 . . . .**10** A3
Woodlands BH21 . . . .**44** D7
Church Hill La DT2 . . . . . .**104** D7
Church Hill View DT2 . . . .**207** A2
Churchill Cl
Alderholt SP6 . . . .**42** A5
Sturminster Marshall BH21 . .**56** D4
4 Weymouth DT4 . . . .**180** C8
Churchill Cres BH25 . . . . .**120** C6
Churchill Ct BH25 . . . .**94** F2
Churchill Dro DT21 . . . .**40** E7
Churchill Gdns BH12 . . . .**120** C5
CHURCH KNOWLE BH20 . .**176** E8
Church Knowle Animal Rescue & Rehoming Ctr ★
BH20 . . . .**176** B7
Church La
Barwick BA22 . . . .**193** E8
Bere Regis BH20 . . . .**81** B2
3 Blandford Forum DT11 .**212** D3
Charlton Marshall DT11 . .**211** C6
Chickerell DT3 . . . .**151** D2
Christchurch BH23 . . . . . .**124** B6
Coombe Keynes BH20 . . .**158** A3
Crewkerne TA18 . . . .**192** A3
Damerham SP6 . . . .**190** F2
Dorchester DT2 . . . .**106** F6
Easton/Weston DT5 . . . . .**186** F1
East Orchard SP7 . . . .**36** F7
Ferndown BH22 . . . .**89** F7
Frampton DT2 . . . .**73** F3
Godmanstone DT2 . . . .**75** B7
Haselbury Plucknett TA18 .**192** C6
Leigh DT9 . . . .**194** E3
Margaret Marsh SP7 . . . . . .**22** C2
Old Milton BH25 . . . .**94** F1
Osmington DT3 . . . .**154** A1
Overcombe/Preston DT3 . .**169** A8
Owermoigne DT2 . . . .**155** D7
Piddletrenthide DT2 . . . . .**208** B3
Portesham DT3 . . . .**150** A8
Rimpton BA22 . . . .**15** B8
Shaftesbury SP7 . . . .**12** E2
Stinsford DT2 . . . .**108** E3
Stour Provost SP8 . . . .**21** C7
2 Sturminster Newton
DT10 . . . .**197** D8
Sutton Waldron DT11 . . . . .**37** E4
Sydling St Nicholas DT2 . .**207** A2
3 Wareham BH20 . . . .**142** F3
Wool BH20 . . . .**140** B2
Churchmoor Rd BH21 . . . . .**60** A5
Church Ope DT5 . . . .**187** B3
Church Ope Rd DT5 . . . . . .**187** B3
Church Path
3 Crewkerne TA18 . . . . . .**191** E4
Litton Cheney DT2 . . . .**103** C2
Yeovil BA20 . . . .**27** D5
Church Rd
Bournemouth BH6 . . . .**123** F3
Bradford Abbas DT9 . . . . . .**28** D1

Church Rd continued
Ferndown DT11 . . . .**198** E3
Ferndown BH22 . . . .**61** C5
Iwerne Minster DT11 . . . . .**37** F1
Maiden Newton DT2 . . . . . .**72** F8
Overcombe/Preston DT3 . .**168** D8
Pimperne DT11 . . . .**199** D4
Poole BH14 . . . .**120** A4
5 Shillingstone DT11 . . . .**198** B6
Silton SP8 . . . .**2** A1
Studland BH19 . . . .**164** D2
Thornford DT9 . . . .**194** D8
Three Legged Cross BH21 . .**45** A1
West Lulworth BH20 . . . . .**172** C6
Church Row DT11 . . . .**209** C6
Church St
Bridport DT6 . . . .**100** D6
Burton Bradstock DT6 . . .**128** A8
Christchurch BH23 . . . . . .**124** B6
Cranborne BH21 . . . .**40** A7
Dewlish DT2 . . . .**209** C1
5 Dorchester DT1 . . . .**108** A2
Fontmell Magna SP7 . . . . . .**37** F7
Fordingbridge SP6 . . . .**43** A8
Halstock BA22 . . . .**193** C3
Henstridge BA8 . . . .**19** A3
Hinton St George TA17 . . .**191** C7
Kington Magna SP8 . . . .**9** C3
Lyme Regis DT7 . . . .**96** C5
Mere BA12 . . . .**3** A5
Merriott TA16 . . . .**191** F7
Milborne Port DT9 . . . .**17** D2
Poole BH15 . . . .**119** B1
Puncknowle DT2 . . . .**129** E6
Shapwick DT11 . . . .**56** B8
Sturminster Marshall BH21 . .**56** E5
Sturminster Newton DT10 . .**35** B1
Upwey DT3 . . . .**152** A7
3 Wareham BH20 . . . .**142** E3
2 West Coker BA22 . . . . . .**193** A8
West Stour SP8 . . . .**10** A2
Weymouth DT3 . . . .**149** B7
6 Wimborne Minster BH21 .**59** B5
Wimborne Kingston DT11 .**81** E8
Yeovil BA20 . . . .**27** D5
Yetminster DT9 . . . .**194** C5
Church View
6 Blandford Forum
DT11 . . . .**198** F4
Dorchester DT2 . . . .**106** D8
Gillingham SP8 . . . .**5** F3
Churchward Ave DT3 . . . .**153** B3
Churchwell Cl 3 DT9 . . . . .**28** D1
Churchwell St DT9 . . . .**28** D1
Church Wlk
Littlebredy DT2 . . . .**131** D7
Motcombe SP7 . . . .**12** D7
Okeford Fitzpaine DT11 . .**197** F4
Chur La BA22 . . . .**193** A8
Churlands Cl BA22 . . . .**193** A8
Chydyok Rd DT2 . . . .**156** C3
Cinnamon La 7 BH15 . . . .**119** B1
Circle The
8 Bournemouth BH9 . . . . . .**90** A4
Poole BH15 . . . .**147** F7
Claire Ct 6 BH23 . . . .**126** A7
Clammer Hill La TA18 . . . .**191** F4
Clanfield DT9 . . . .**29** F4
CLAPGATE BH21 . . . .**50** E2
Clap La SP5 . . . .**188** B4
Clappentail La DT7 . . . .**96** A5
Clappentail Pk DT7 . . . .**96** A5
CLAPTON TA18 . . . .**191** C1
Clapton Rd TA18 . . . .**191** D3
Clare Ave DT3 . . . .**166** E2
Claremont Ave
Bournemouth BH9 . . . .**90** B2
Gillingham SP8 . . . .**5** F3
Claremont Gdns DT6 . . . .**100** D8
Claremont Rd
4 Bridport DT6 . . . .**100** D8
Clarence Cl 2 DT5 . . . . . .**186** F4
Clarence Ct **27** C5
Clarence Gdns BH7 . . . . . .**87** A2
Clarence Park Rd BH7 . . .**123** A6
Clarence Pl BH23 . . . .**123** F8
Clarence Rd
Dorchester DT1 . . . .**134** F8
Easton/Weston DT5 . . . . .**186** F4
3 Poole BH14 . . . .**120** A3
Weymouth DT4 . . . .**166** F1
Clarence St BA20 . . . .**27** C4
Clarence Terr 14 BA20 . . . .**27** D4
Clarendon Ave DT3 . . . . . .**152** C1
Clarendon Cl
Broadstone BH18 . . . .**87** A4
Gillingham SP8 . . . .**5** D2
Clarendon Ct 3 BH21 . . . . .**59** A5
Clarendon Rd
Bournemouth BH4 . . . .**121** D3
Broadstone BH18 . . . .**86** F4
Christchurch BH23 . . . . . .**124** A7
Clarkham Cross BA22 . . .**193** E2
Clarks Cl BA22 . . . .**26** C5
Clark's Cl BH24 . . . .**55** C7
Clark's La 3 TA18 . . . .**191** E4
Clatcombe La DT9 . . . .**15** F3
Claudius Cl DT1 . . . .**134** E7
Clay Castle TA18 . . . .**192** C5
Clay Castle La TA18 . . . . .**192** C5
Claysmore Prep Sch
DT11 . . . .**37** E2
Claysmore Sch DT11 . . . . . .**37** E2
Clayford Ave BH22 . . . .**61** B7
Clayford Cl BH17 . . . .**87** D2

Clay La
Beaminster DT8 . . . .**204** C4
Puncknowle DT2 . . . .**129** F4
Claylake Dr BH31 . . . .**45** C5
Claylands La DT8 . . . .**204** A3
Clay Pigeon Raceway ★
DT2 . . . .**206** E5
Claypits La
Beer Hackett DT9 . . . .**194** D6
Winfrith Newburgh DT2 . .**157** A6
Clayton Cl
Radipole DT3 . . . .**152** D3
Yeovil BA22 . . . .**26** C6
Clearmount Rd DT4 . . . . .**180** B8
Cleasby Grange 2 BH5 . .**122** F3
Cleeve Ho DT5 . . . .**126** F7
Cleeves Cl BH12 . . . .**88** D2
Clematis Cl BH18 . . . .**125** C8
Clement Mews BH4 . . . . .**121** B3
Clements La DT5 . . . .**186** E8
Clement's La BA12 . . . .**3** B4
Clenston Rd DT11 . . . .**210** C7
Cleveland Ave DT4 . . . . . .**167** D7
Cleveland Cl BH25 . . . . . .**126** D7
Cleveland Ct 4 BH4 . . . . .**121** D2
Cleveland Gdns BH1 . . . . .**122** C5
Cleveland Rd BH1 . . . .**122** D5
Cleverlawns DT3 . . . .**168** F7
Cleves Cl DT4 . . . .**180** E7
Cleve The BA21 . . . .**26** E6
Cliff Ave BH19 . . . .**179** C4
Cliff Cres BH25 . . . .**126** F7
Cliff Dr
Christchurch BH23 . . . .**125** C6
Poole BH13 . . . .**147** E6
Cliff Rd BH25 . . . .**126** E7
Clifford Rd BH9 . . . .**90** A1
Cliff Rd DT6 . . . .**128** B7
Cliff Way DT5 . . . .**186** D1
Cliff Wlk 17 BH4 . . . .**121** C2
Clift La DT2 . . . .**205** D1
Clifton Cl
Swanage BH19 . . . .**179** C4
Yeovil BA21 . . . .**28** A6
Clifton Ct 5
1 Bournemouth BH7 . . . . .**122** F4
Hamworthy BH15 . . . .**118** D4
3 New Milton BH25 . . . . . .**95** A1
Clifton Gdns BH22 . . . .**61** C4
Clifton Hill BA22 . . . .**193** F8
CLIFTON MAYBANK
BA22 . . . .**194** A8
Clifton Pl 1 DT4 . . . .**167** D3
Clifton Rd
Bournemouth BH6 . . . .**123** D3
Clifton Maybank BA22 . . .**194** B8
Poole BH14 . . . .**120** E2
Swanage BH19 . . . .**179** B4
Clifton View 3 BA22 . . . . .**193** F8
Clingan Rd BH6 . . . .**123** D4
Clinton Cl DT21 . . . .**94** B2
Clive Ct 23 BH4 . . . .**121** C3
Cliveden DT8 . . . .**61** C7
Clive Rd
Bournemouth BH9 . . . .**89** F1
Christchurch BH23 . . . .**93** E2
Clivia Cl DT3 . . . .**152** E2
Cloisters The
3 Christchurch BH23 . . . . .**124** A4
2 Ringwood BH24 . . . .**55** C6
Close Dr 5 TA18 . . . .**192** A3
Close The
Barton on Sea BH25 . . . . .**127** A8
Blandford Forum DT11 . . .**212** D3
Broadstone BH18 . . . .**86** F3
Charlton Marshall DT11 . .**211** C6
8 Merriott TA16 . . . .**191** F7
12 Pimperne DT11 . . . . . .**199** D4
Ringwood BH24 . . . .**55** B7
St Leonards BH24 . . . .**54** C4
CLOSWORTH BA22 . . . . . .**193** F5
Clouds Hill (Lawrence of Arabia's Cottage) ★
BH20 . . . .**112** C2
Clough's Rd BH24 . . . .**55** D7
Clovens Rd DT5 . . . .**186** F7
Clover Cl BH23 . . . .**125** B8
Clover Cl BH21 . . . .**95** A4
Clover Dr BH7 . . . .**86** F1
Cloverfields SP8 . . . .**5** E4
Clovermead DT4 . . . .**194** B6
Clovers The BH12 . . . .**121** A8
Claves Ave BH6 . . . .**123** E5
Clump Farm Ind Est
DT11 . . . .**212** D6
Clump Hill BH21 . . . .**44** C1
Cluny Cres BH19 . . . .**179** C2
Clyde Rd BH17 . . . .**87** B2
Clyffe View DT2 . . . .**137** D6
Cryppetts 2 DT11 . . . .**81** E8
Coach House Mews BH22 .**61** F7
Coach House Pl BH1 . . . .**122** A5
Coach Rd
1 Stourpaine DT11 . . . . . .**198** F4
Wimborne St Giles BH21 . .**201** D7
Coach Rd The DT7 . . . .**64** A2
Coastguard Cotts BH25 . .**126** D6
Coastguard Rd
5 Fortuneswell DT5 . . . . .**186** F8
Langton Herring DT3 . . . .**150** B1
Coastguard Way DT21 . . .**124** F5
COBB DT7 . . . .**96** B4
Cobb Rd DT7 . . . .**96** B4
Cobbs La BH15 . . . .**119** E6
Cobb's Rd BH21 . . . .**59** E6
Cobham Dr DT4 . . . .**166** F3
Cobham Rd
Blandford Forum DT11 . . .**212** E6

Cobham Rd continued
Bournemouth BH6 . . . .**90** A3
Ferndown BH21 . . . .**61** A8
Wimborne Town BH22 . . . .**52** D1
Cobham Way BH21 . . . .**59** E1
Coblers La BH19 . . . .**179** B1
COBLEY SP5 . . . .**189** D7
Cobley Cl SP5 . . . .**189** D6
Cockerell Cl BH21 . . . .**59** F1
Cocklands DT7 . . . .**107** E6
Cockles La DT4 . . . .**167** A1
COCKNOWLE BH20 . . . . . .**161** A1
Cockpit Hill DT8 . . . .**203** C4
Cockroad La DT8 . . . .**204** C4
Codge La DT2 . . . .**205** C6
Cod La BA22 . . . .**192** D7
Codogan Ct 3 BH11 . . . . .**122** B3
Cogdean Cl BH21 . . . .**86** E8
Cogdean Elms Nature Reserve ★ BH21 . . . .**86** E8
Cogdean Rd BH17 . . . .**87** D2
Cogdean Way BH21 . . . .**86** E8
Cogdean Wlk BH21 . . . .**86** E8
Coker Hill La BA22 . . . .**193** A7
Colber Medieval Village of ★
DT10 . . . .**34** F1
Colborne Ave BH21 . . . .**59** F6
Colborne Cl BH15 . . . .**119** C1
Colbourne Cl BH23 . . . .**93** A8
Cold Harbour SP8 . . . .**5** E2
Cold Harbour
Milborne Port DT9 . . . .**17** D2
Sherborne DT9 . . . .**30** C7
Cold Harbour Bsns Pk
DT9 . . . .**30** D8
Cold Harbour La BA22 . . .**192** F6
COLEHILL **60** B8
Colehill Cres BH9 . . . .**90** B3
Colehill Dro DT2 . . . .**156** D6
Colehill Fst Sch BH21 . . . . .**60** A7
Colehill La
Holt BH21 . . . .**51** C1
Wimborne Minster BH21 . . .**60** A8
Colehill Rd BH20, BH16 . . . .**83** F6
Coleman Rd BH11 . . . .**89** A3
Colemere Gdns BH23 . . . .**125** F8
Colemore Rd BH7 . . . .**123** C7
Coleridge Gn BH23 . . . . . .**124** F8
Coleridge Pl DT4 . . . .**167** D6
Coles Ave BH15 . . . .**118** E2
COLESBOOK SP8 . . . .**5** E4
Coles Cl DT10 . . . .**35** C1
Cole's Cross DT8 . . . .**203** A5
Coles Gdns BH15 . . . .**118** E2
Coles La
Milborne St Andrew
DT11 . . . .**209** F1
Yetminster DT9 . . . .**194** B6
Cole Street La SP8 . . . .**11** B6
Colin Cl BH21 . . . .**85** F5
Collarway La BA22 . . . .**192** F8
College Arms Cl SP7 . . . . . .**22** B7
College Gn BH21 . . . .**27** C6
College Rd
Blandford Camp DT11 . . . .**199** D3
Bournemouth BH5 . . . .**123** A4
Ringwood BH24 . . . .**55** C7
Collett Cl DT3 . . . .**153** B3
Colletts Cl BH20 . . . .**177** E2
Collier's La BH21 . . . .**139** F1
Collingbourne Ave BH6 . .**123** D7
Collingwood Cl 7 DT11 . .**199** D4
Collingwood Rd BH21 . . . . .**53** A6
Collins La
Ringwood BH24 . . . .**55** C7
Weymouth DT4 . . . .**180** C7
Colliton St DT1 . . . .**108** A2
Coll of Air Traffic Control
BH23 . . . .**90** F7
Collwood Cl BH15 . . . .**119** C7
Collyer's Brook Reserve ★
SP7 . . . .**37** F6
Collyer's Rise SP7 . . . .**37** F6
Colman Ct BH1 . . . .**122** C3
Colmer Rd BA21 . . . .**27** D5
Cologne Rd BH20 . . . .**140** A6
Colonnade Rd 8 BH5 . . . .**123** A5
Colonnade Road W 2 BH5 . . . .**123** A5
Colt Cl BH21 . . . .**60** B6
Coltsfoot Way BH23 . . . . . .**93** C1
Columbian Way BH10 . . . . .**89** C2
Columbia Rd BH10 . . . .**89** C2
Columbia Trees La BH10 . .**89** C1
Columbine Cl BH23 . . . .**93** B1
Colville Cl 4 BH5 . . . .**123** A5
Colville Rd 5 BH5 . . . .**123** A5
Colway La DT7 . . . .**96** B7
Colway La DT7 . . . .**96** B6
Colwell Sh Ctr DT4 . . . . . .**167** D3
COMBE ALMER BH21 . . . . .**84** D7
Combe Hill
Milborne Port DT9 . . . .**17** B3
Templecombe BA8 . . . .**18** E8
Combe Pk BA21 . . . .**27** B7
Comber Rd 1 BH9 . . . .**90** A3
Combe Way DT2 . . . .**137** D5
Comet Cl DT4 . . . .**166** F1
Comet Way BH23 . . . .**125** A6
Comley Rd BH9 . . . .**89** F2
Commercial Rd
Bournemouth BH2 . . . .**121** E3

Commercial Rd continued
Christchurch BH23 . . . .**62** D1
Poole BH14 . . . .**120** A4
Radipole DT4 . . . .**167** D2
1 Swanage BH19 . . . .**179** C2
Common Dro
6 Child Okeford DT11 . . .**198** C8
Farnham DT11 . . . .**188** B3
Common Hill DT8 . . . .**203** D5
Common La
4 Blandford Forum
DT11 . . . .**212** D3
Burton Bradstock DT6 . . .**128** C7
East Stour SP8 . . . .**11** A3
Halstock BA22 . . . .**193** C2
Haselbury Plucknett TA18 .**192** D5
Henstridge BA8 . . . .**18** F8
Kington Magna SP8 . . . .**9** C1
Marnhull DT10 . . . .**34** D8
Ryme Intrinseca DT9 . . . . .**194** B5
Sturminster Newton DT10 .**197** D8
Toller Porcorum DT2 . . . . .**205** D2
Common Mead Ave SP8 . . . .**5** E1
Common Mead La SP8 . . . . .**5** D1
Common Rd SP5 . . . .**188** F4
COMMON THE DT11 . . . . .**197** E5
Common The
Eversholt DT2 . . . .**206** A2
Hazelbury Bryan DT10 . . .**196** E5
Moreton DT2 . . . .**138** C3
Common Water La DT8 . . .**203** F5
COMPTON ABBAS SP7 . . . .**24** A2
Compton Abbas Airfield ★
SP5 . . . .**24** E2
Compton Acres DT2 . . . . . .**28** D7
Compton Acres (Gdns) ★
BH13 . . . .**147** E7
Compton Ave BH14 . . . . . .**120** D1
Compton Beeches BA4 . . . .**54** C5
Compton Cl
Verwood BH31 . . . .**45** B6
Yeovil BA21 . . . .**28** A8
Compton Cres BH22 . . . . . .**53** C1
Compton Ct
4 Bournemouth BH6 . . . .**123** F4
Poole BH14 . . . .**120** C2
Compton Dr BH14 . . . .**120** C2
Compton Gdns BH14 . . . .**120** C2
Compton La 5 BH4 . . . . . .**121** C3
Compton Rd
New Milton BH25 . . . .**95** A4
Over Compton DT9 . . . .**28** C5
Compton Valence
DT2 . . . .**104** E7
Conches Ct 8 BH20 . . . . .**142** E4
Concorde Cl DT4 . . . .**166** F1
Condor Cl BH21 . . . .**53** D6
CONEYGAR DT6 . . . .**100** D7
Coneygar Cl DT6 . . . .**100** D8
Coneygar La
Bridport DT6 . . . .**100** D8
Ferndown BH22 . . . .**61** B3
Coneygar Rd DT6 . . . .**100** D8
Conifer Ave BH14 . . . .**120** B2
Conifer Cl
Christchurch BH23 . . . .**91** D3
Ferndown BH22 . . . .**61** F1
St Leonards BH24 . . . .**53** F4
Conifers 8 BH13 . . . .**121** B3
Conifers Prim Sch DT4 . .**167** A3
Coniston Ave BH11 . . . .**88** F6
Coniston Cl BH31 . . . .**45** A5
Coniston Cres BH23 . . . . .**167** C2
Coniston Gdns BA21 . . . . . .**27** B7
Coniston Rd BH24 . . . .**55** D6
Connaught Cl BH25 . . . .**94** E1
Connaught Cres BH12 . . .**120** E6
Connaught Gdns DT4 . . . .**167** B3
Connaught Rd
Bournemouth BH5 . . . .**123** B5
4 Weymouth DT4 . . . .**180** E8
Connell Rd BH15 . . . .**119** C5
Conniger La BH20 . . . .**142** F3
Consort Cl BH12 . . . .**120** C5
Consort Ho BH12 . . . .**61** D6
Constable Cl
Ferndown BH22 . . . .**61** C4
Yeovil BA21 . . . .**28** A8
Constitution Hill Gdns
BH14 . . . .**120** A5
Constitution Hill Rd
BH14 . . . .**120** A5
Convent Meadow Mobile Home Site BH23 . . . . . .**124** C5
Conway Cl BH25 . . . .**95** B3
Conway Ct 10 BH25 . . . .**95** B3
Conway Dr DT2 . . . .**136** B2
Conways Dr BH14 . . . .**120** A4
Conway Wlk 7 DT11 . . . . .**135** C8
Coode Way DT5 . . . .**181** A1
Cook Cl BH24 . . . .**55** E8
Cooke Gdns BH12 . . . .**120** F6
Cooke Rd BH12 . . . .**120** F6
Cook Row BH21 . . . .**59** B4
Cooks La DT9 . . . .**30** B5
Cook's La DT10 . . . .**33** C3
Cooksons Orch BA21 . . . . .**27** B4
Cookswell 1 DT11 . . . .**198** B6
Coolhurst BH14 . . . .**147** C7
COOMBE
Axminster DT6 . . . .**65** B3
Crewkerne TA18 . . . .**191** B4
Shaftesbury SP7 . . . .**13** E4
Coombe DT9 . . . .**30** A7

Coombe Ave
Bournemouth BH10......89 E3
Radipole DT4......167 E6
Coombe Cl BA21......27 C8
Coombe Drain DT6......65 B8
Coombe Gdns BH9......89 E2
Coombe Heath Reserve★
BH20......158 E6
Coombe Hill BH19......178 C2
COOMBE KEYNES BH20......158 A5
Coombe La
Castleton DT9......15 D1
Stoke Abbott DT8......203 E3
Coombe Rd
Dinnington TA17......191 B7
Puddletown DT2......78 B1
Shillingstone DT11......198 B5
Winterborne Steepleton DT2......105 E1
Coombes Cl DT2......103 C2
Coombe St
Lyme Regis DT7......96 C5
Pen Selwood BA9......1 A3
Coombe Street La BA21......27 C8
Coombe Valley Rd DT3......153 B3
Coombe Water La DT8......203 B6
COOMBSES TA20......202 B8
Cooper Dean Dr BH8......90 F1
Cooper Dean Rdbt The BH7, BH8......91 A1
Cooper Gdns DT11......198 B8
Cooper's Cl ☑ BH20......142 E4
Coopers Dr DT6......100 D3
Coopers La BH31......45 B8
Copeland Dr BH14......120 B2
Copper Beech Cl BH13......121 A4
Copper Beeches ☑ BH21......121 F4
Coppercourt Leaze ☑ BH10......59 C4
Coppern Way DT10......33 D8
Coppers Cl SP6......42 C6
Coppice Ave BH22......61 B7
Coppice Cl
New Milton BH25......95 D4
St Leonards BH24......54 B4
West Coker BA22......26 F7
Coppice Ct DT3......152 C3
Coppice St SP7......12 F2
Coppice The
Chickerell DT3......166 E5
Christchurch BH23......125 B6
Coppice View BH10......89 E3
Copse Ave BH25......95 B2
Copse Cl BH14......119 F3
Copse Hill DT10......197 E2
Copse Rd
Brympton BA22......26 D7
New Milton BH25......95 B2
Verwood BH31......45 B6
Copse The BH24......62 C8
Copse Way BH23......125 E8
Copsewood Ave BH8......90 E1
Copythorne Cl BH5......90 D2
Coral Ct ☑ BH13......121 A4
Coram Ave DT7......96 B4
Corbar Rd BH23......123 E8
Corbiere Ave BH12......88 D1
Corbin Ave BH22......62 A6
Corbin Way DT6......68 E2
Cordery Gdns SP8......5 F3
Cordova Gdns DT6......100 D7
Corfe & Barrow Hills Nature Reserve★ BH21......86 F7
CORFE CASTLE BH20......177 B8
Corfe Castle★ BH20......161 F1
Corfe Castle Fst Sch BH20......177 A8
Corfe Castle Model Village & Gdns★ BH20......177 A8
Corfe Castle Mus★ BH20......162 A1
Corfe Castle Sta★ BH20......162 A1
Corfe Halt Cl BH21......58 E1
Corfe Hills Sch BH18......86 F6
Corfe Lodge Rd BH21......85 F4
Corfe Mews BH15......119 C4
CORFE MULLEN BH21......85 E6
Corfe Mullen Meadow Reserve★ BH21......85 D6
Corfe Rd
Arne BH20......160 F8
Radipole DT3......167 B8
Stoborough Green BH20......142 E1
Corfe View Rd
Poole BH14......120 C3
Poole BH21......85 E5
Corfe Way BH18......86 E3
Corfu BH13......147 E6
Corhampton Rd BH6......123 C6
Cornelia Cres BH12......121 A6
Cornelia Rd BH10......89 B1
Corner Cl DT10......21 B3
Corner Cl ☑ BH21......7 C4
Corner The DT11......198 E7
Cornerways Ct ☑ BH25......95 B2
Cornfields The DT2......79 D1
Cornflower Cl DT3......152 F2
Cornflower Dr BH23......125 C8
Cornhill DT9......30 A6
Cornhill Way DT13......36 A4
Cornish Gdns BH10......89 D1
Cornmarket Cl ☑ BH21......59 B5

Cornpits La SP6......190 E2
Cornwall Cl DT11......167 A3
Cornwall Rd
Dorchester DT1......107 F2
☑ Swanage BH19......179 C2
Coronation Ave
Bournemouth BH9......89 F2
☑ Upton BH16......117 D7
Yeovil BA21......27 A7
Coronation Ct BH31......45 B7
Coronation Rd
Bridport DT6......100 C5
☑ Fortuneswell DT5......186 F8
Gillingham SP8......5 E2
Radipole DT4......167 C7
Verwood BH31......45 B7
Corporation Rd
Bournemouth BH1......122 C5
Weymouth DT4......167 A7
Corpus Christi RC Prim Sch ☑ BH5......123 A5
CORSCOMBE DT2......205 A8
Corscombe Cl
Poole BH17......87 E2
Radipole DT4......167 D3
Cortmeron ☑ BH21......121 C2
Corton Cl BA21......28 A8
Cortry Cl BH12......121 A7
CORYATES DT3......150 F7
Cossins La ☑ TA18......191 F4
Cotes Ave BH14......120 A5
Cotewell Cl DT3......129 A6
Cothayes Dro DT2......209 A5
Cotlands Rd BH8......122 B4
Cotswold Cl BH31......45 B6
Cotswold Ct ☑ BH23......123 F4
Cottage Cl ☑ BH20......140 A2
Cottage Gdns DT2......120 C5
Cottage Mews ☑ BH24......55 B7
Cotton Cl BH18......66 E5
Council Hos BH23......63 F2
Counter Cl DT11......212 F5
Countess Cl BH21......87 E8
Countess Gdns BH7......122 E3
Court Ash BA20......27 D5
Courtauld Dr DT4......180 B8
Court Barton
Bridport DT6......68 F1
☑ Christchurch BH23......124 E7
Court Cl
☑ Christchurch BH23......124 E7
Courtenay Cl BH20......142 F6
Courtenay Dr BH21......59 C6
Courtenay Rd BH14......120 A5
Court Gdns BA21......27 A8
Court Hill
Corscombe DT2......205 B8
Damerham SP6......190 F2
Courthill Fst Sch BH14......120 C4
Courthill Rd BH14......120 C4
Courtlands Rd DT5......100 C8
Courtleigh Manor ☑ BH5......122 D4
Court Mill La TA16......191 F7
Courtney Cl DT11......198 E8
Courtney Pl BH21......59 C6
COURT ORCHARD DT6......100 C8
Court Orchard Rd DT6......100 C8
Court Rd
Bournemouth BH9......90 B1
Radipole DT3......152 B2
Swanage BH19......179 A2
Courtyard Craft Ctr The★ BH16......117 A8
Courtyard The BH23......124 D6
Courtyard The BH12......88 C1
Courtyard The BH21......60 A1
Covena Rd BH1......123 E6
Coventry Cl BH21......85 E4
Coventry Cres BH17......87 A1
Cove Rd BH10......89 C3
Cove Row ☑ DT4......167 A6
Cove St DT4......167 E2
Cowards La DT3......149 A7
Cow Down Rd TA20......202 C8
Cowdrey Gdns BH8......90 F2
Cow Dro BH20......27 C4
Cowdrys Field ☑ BH21......59 B6
Cowell Dr BH7......123 B8
Cowen Cl TA18......191 F3
COWGROVE BH21......57 F4
Cowgrove Rd BH21......57 F4
Cow La
Long Bredy DT2......103 C1
Swanage BH19......179 A1
Wareham BH20......142 E3
Cowlease ☑ BH19......179 A2
Cowleaze DT2......133 D6
Cowleaze Rd DT3......136 B1
Cowley Cl BH17......107 E1
Cowley Rd BH17......119 D8
Cowleys Rd BH23......92 C2
Cowper Ave BH25......95 A1
Cowpitts La BH24......47 F2
Cowslip Rd BH18......86 F2
Cox Ave BH9......90 A4
Cox Cl BH9......90 B4
Cox Hill DT10......34 D7
Cox's La
Litton Cheney DT2......103 B1

Cox's La continued
Long Bredy DT2......130 D8
Coxstone La BH24......55 B6
Coy Pond Rd BH12......121 B5
Crabbswood La SO41......95 E8
Crab La BA12......2 B6
CRAB ORCHARD BH21......45 A2
Crab Orchard Way BH21......45 A4
Crabton Close Rd BH5......122 F4
Crabtree Cl BH23......92 C2
Crack La BH19......178 C3
Cracklewood Cl BH22......62 A8
Crackmore DT9......17 C1
Craigmoor Ave BH8......90 F1
Craigmoor Cl BH8......90 F1
Craigmoor Way BH8......90 E2
Craigside Rd BH24......53 F4
Craigwood Dr BH22......61 E3
CRANBORNE BH21......40 B7
Cranborne CE Fst Sch BH21......40 B7
Cranborne Cres BH12......120 E8
Cranborne Ct
☑ Bournemouth, Westbourne BH4......121 C3
☑ Bournemouth BH9......122 B8
Cranborne Dr ☑ SP7......12 F2
Cranborne Manor Gdns★ BH21......40 A7
Cranborne Mid Sch BH21......40 B8
Cranborne Rd
Alderholt SP6......41 C5
Bournemouth BH12......121 E2
Hinton Parva BH21......50 C5
Swanage BH19......179 B3
Wimborne Minster BH21......59 C7
Cranborne Rd
Cranbourne DT6......166 C4
Cranbrook Mews BH12......120 B6
Cranbrook Rd BH12......120 B6
Crane Cl BH31......45 A7
Crane Dr BH31......45 A6
Cranemoor Ave BH23......93 E2
Cranemoor Cl BH23......93 E2
Cranemoor Gdns BH23......93 E2
Cranes Mdw DT2......208 A8
Cranes Mews BH23......119 D3
Cranesmoor Cl BH20......139 C6
Crane St BH31......40 B7
Cranfield Ave BH21......53 D6
Cranford Ave BH21......167 E5
Cranleigh Cl BH6......123 E5
Cranleigh Gdns BH6......123 E5
Cranleigh Rd BH6......123 D5
Cranmer Rd BH9......121 F8
Cransley C
☑ Bournemouth BH4......121 C2
Bournemouth BH4......121 C2
Crantock Gr BH8......90 F2
Cranwell Cl BH11......88 E4
Crate Hill DT10......197 C5
Crate La SP7......7 F5
Crawford Bridge★ DT11......211 E5
Crawford Down Rd ☑ DT11......199 E2
Crawford Pk DT11......211 E4
Crawshaw Rd BH14......120 B2
Creasey Rd BH11......89 A5
CREECH BH20......160 D3
Creech Folly (Grange Arch)★ BH20......175 C8
Creech Grange★ BH20......160 C1
Creech Rd BH12......120 C5
Creech Way DT3......167 B8
Creedy Dr BH23......124 B5
CREEKMOOR......118 F8
Creekmoor La BH17......119 A8
CRENDELL SP6......41 B7
Crescent C
Barton on Sea BH25......126 D8
☑ Bournemouth BH2......121 D2
Crescent Dr BH25......126 F7
Crescent Rd
Bournemouth BH1......121 D3
Poole BH14......120 E4
Verwood BH31......45 C6
Wimborne Minster BH21......59 C4
Crescent St ☑ DT4......167 E4
Crescent The
Barton on Sea BH25......126 D8
☑ Bournemouth BH1......122 E4
West Moors BH24......62 B8
☑ Yeovil BA20......27 C4
Crescent Wlk BH22......61 E2
Cresscombe Cl SP8......5 E3
Cresta Gdns BH21......61 E2
Crest Rd BH12......120 D6
CREWKERNE TA18......191 E5
Crewkerne Aqua Ctr ☑ TA18......191 F4

CRIPPLESTYLE BH21......41 B5
Crispin Cl BH23......125 F8
Criterion Arc ☑ BH1......121 F3
Crockford Cl BH21......95 B5
Crock La DT6......100 E6
Croft Cl BH21......85 F7
Crofton Ave BH21......91 E1
Crofton Cl BH23......91 E1
Crofton Pk BH21......27 D5
Crofton Rd BA21......27 D6
Croft Rd
Bournemouth BH9......89 F2
Bransgore BH23......93 B6
Christchurch BH23......124 B5
Easton/Weston DT5......186 E4
Poole BH12......120 E8
Ringwood BH24......47 E1
Croft The
Wareham BH20......142 F4
☑ Yeovil BA20......26 E2
Cromer Gdns BH12......120 F5
Cromer Rd
Bournemouth BH8......122 D7
Poole BH12......120 F5
Cromwell Pl ☑ BH5......123 A5
Cromwell Rd
Bournemouth BH5......123 B5
Dorchester DT1......135 A8
Poole BH12......120 D5
Weymouth DT4......167 B3
☑ Wimborne Minster BH21......59 D4
Yeovil BA21......27 F6
Crooked La BA9......4 C3
Crooked Oak Hill DT6......204 D1
CROOKED WITHIES BH21......51 F7
Crookhays SP7......12 F4
Crook Hill DT6......204 C2
Crookhill Brickpits Nature Reserve★ DT2......166 C4
Cropmead Trading Est ☑ TA18......191 F4
Crosby Rd BH4......121 C1
Crossfields DT9......28 F8
Cross & Hand Stone★ DT2......207 A6
Cross La SP8......5 E7
CROSS LANES DT2......209 A5
Crossmead Ave BH25......95 A2
Cross Rd
Bradford Abbas DT9......28 D2
☑ Weymouth DT4......180 E8
Cross The
☑ Bradford Abbas DT9......28 D1
☑ Child Okeford DT11......198 C7
☑ Henstridge BA8......19 A4
☑ Okeford Fitzpaine DT11......197 F5
Shillingstone DT11......198 B6
Wool BH20......140 B2
Crosstree Cl DT2......136 B1
Crossway DT11......199 E3
Cross Way
Bradford Abbas DT9......28 D2
Christchurch BH23......91 D1
CROSSWAYS DT2......137 E5
Crossways ☑ TA20......202 A8
Crossways The BH16......117 F7
CROUCH HILL DT9......196 A5
Crouch La DT9......196 A6
CROW BH24......55 E4
Crow Arch La ☑ BH24......55 D6
Crow Arch Lane Ind Est BH24......55 D6
Crowe Hill Ct ☑ BH15......119 E4
Crow La BH24......55 E6
Crown Cl BH12......120 C5
Crown Ct
Milborne St Andrew DT11......79 E8
☑ Wimborne Minster BH21......59 B5
Crown Gdns DT2......79 C1
Crown Hill SP7......37 F6
Crown Mead BH21......59 C4
Crown Rd BH21......21 A2
Crown Yd DT2......156 F6
Crowthorne La DT2......208 A7
Crumpets Dr BH16......84 F5
Crumplers Cl BH16......84 B3
Crusader Ct ☑ BH4......121 B4
Crusader Rd BH11......88 D4
CRUXTON DT2......73 A5
Cruxton Farm Clyd BH21......59 D2
Cruxton La DT2......73 A6
CUCKLINGTON BA9......4 B4
Cucklington Gdns BH9......90 A4
Cuckoo Hill DT9......194 B4
Cuckoo La
Broadwindsor TA20......202 F7
Hilton DT11......209 C7
Stinsford DT2......109 A6
Cuckoo Rd BH12......120 A8
Cudnell Ave BH11......89 A6
Cuffnells Cl BH23......47 D8
Cul-De-Sac BH25......126 C8
Culford Cl BH8......90 F2
Culford Ct ☑ BH8......122 A5
Culil Cl BH12......120 B5
Culliford Cres BH17......87 E2
Culliford Rd DT1......135 B8
Culliford Road N ☑ DT1......108 B1
Culliford Road S ☑ DT1......135 B8
Culliford Way DT3......152 E3
Cull La BH25......95 A5
Cull Peppers Dish (Sink Hole)★ DT2......112 A6
Cullwood La BH25......95 B5
Culverhayes Cl ☑ BH21......59 B6
Culverhayes Pl BH21......59 B6
Culverhayes Rd BH21......59 B6

Culverlake La EX13......202 D3
Culver Rd BH25......94 F2
Culvers Cl DT9......30 A6
Culvers La SP8......5 C1
Cumberland Dr DT4......166 F4
Cumnor Rd BH1......122 A3
Cunnage La BA12......3 F1
Cunningham Cl
Bournemouth BH11......89 A3
Bovington Camp BH20......139 F6
Christchurch BH23......125 A6
☑ Ringwood BH24......55 E8
☑ Weymouth DT4......180 B8
Cunningham Cres BH11......89 B3
Cunningham Ct BH25......94 F3
Cunningham Pl BH11......89 A3
Cunnington Cl DT11......134 E7
Curlew Cl
☑ Chickerell DT3......166 D5
Ferndown BH22......61 B7
Curlew Rd
Bournemouth BH8......90 D2
Christchurch BH23......125 A6
Curlews The BH21......45 C5
Curlieu Rd BH15......119 E6
Curriott Hill TA18......191 E4
Curriott Hill Rd ☑ TA18......191 E4
Curry Hole La DT2......193 D2
Curtis Cl DT4......196 A8
Curtis Rd BH12......120 C5
Curzon Cl BH24......121 C3
Curzon Rd
Bournemouth BH1......122 D6
Poole BH14......120 A3
Curzon Way BH23......125 D8
Custard Hill BH21......201 B5
Custom House Quay DT4......167 D2
Cuthburga Rd BH21......59 C4
Cuthbury Cl BH21......59 A4
Cuthbury Gdns BH21......59 A5
Cutler Cl
New Milton BH25......95 C3
Poole BH21......121 C7
Cutlers Pl BH21......60 A5
Cutsome Ct DT1......135 B8
Cutt Mill La DT10......34 F6
Cynthia Cl BH12......120 B7
Cynthia Ho BH12......120 B7
Cynthia Rd BH12......120 B7
Cypress Dr BA20......27 A2
Cypress Rd DT3......75 D3
Cypress Way ☑ SP8......5 F2
Cyril Rd BH8......122 C6

D

Dacombe Cl BH16......117 E7
Dacombe Dr BH16......117 E7
DAGGONS SP6......41 E5
Daggons Rd SP6......41 F6
Dagmar Rd DT1......107 F1
Dahlia Cl DT3......152 F2
Dahlia Ct BH15......119 E6
Dairy Cl
Christchurch BH23......124 D7
Poole BH21......85 D4
Dairy Field DT11......212 E6
Daisy Cl BH15......119 D6
Dakota Cl BH23......125 B7
Dale Ave DT4......167 D6
Dale Cl BH15......119 F6
Daler Ct BH20......142 E6
Dale Rd BH15......119 F6
Dales Cl BH21......60 B5
Dales Dr BH21......60 B5
Dales La BH23......90 E7
Dale Valley Rd BH15......119 F7
Dalewood Ave BH11......88 E5
Dalkeith Arc ☑ BH1......121 F3
Dalkeith Rd
Poole BH15......121 A1
Poole BH21......85 F4
Dalling Rd BH12......121 A5
Dalmeny Rd BH6......124 A3
Dalwoods DT9......30 B5
DAMERHAM SP6......190 F2
Damerham Rd BH8......90 D3
Damer's Fst Sch DT1......107 F1
Damer's Rd DT1......212 C6
Damory Court St ☑ DT11......212 D11
Damory St DT11......212 D4
Dampier Pl ☑ BA21......27 E5
Dampier St ☑ BA21......27 E5
Danecourt Cl BH14......119 F4
Danecourt Rd BH14......119 F4
Danecrest Rd SO41......95 F3
Dane Ct BH14......120 A4
Dane Dr BH22......121 C3
Danehurst New Rd SO41......95 C4
Danesbury Ave BH6......123 F4
Danesbury Mdws BH21......95 C5
Danes Cl BH21......122 A7
Danestead Ho ☑ BH25......95 A3
Daneswood Rd BH25......95 C3
Daniel Dr BH20......142 D5
Daniel Gdns ☑ BH21......119 C1
Danielsfield Rd BA20......27 B4
Dansie Cl BH14......120 B4
Darby La ☑ BH15......128 B8
Darby's Cl BH15......119 C5
Darby's Cnr BH17......87 C2
Darby's La BH15......119 D6
Darby's Lane N BH17......119 D8
Darkie La BH19......179 A6

Dark La
Fifehead Neville DT10 . . . . 197 C6
Hinton BH23 . . . . 94 A4
Mere BA12. . . . . 3 A5
Sandford Orcas DT9 . . . . 15 D6
Tincleton DT2 . . . . 110 D5
Witchampton BH21 . . . . 200 F1
Darknoll La DT11 . . . . 197 E6
Darley Rd BH22. . . . . 61 C3
Darracott Rd BH5 . . . . 123 B5
Darrian Ct **7** BH16. . . . . 117 D7
Dartmeet Ct **3** DT1 . . . . 107 B2
Darwin Ave BH23 . . . . 91 E1
Darwin Cl DT3 . . . . 152 D3
Darwin Ct **4** BH13. . . . . 121 A4
Dashwood Cl DT10 . . . . 35 C2
Davenant Cl **5** SP8 . . . . 5 E1
Davenport Ct **9** BH17. . . . . . 88 E4
David's La BH24 . . . . 54 E5
David Way BH15 . . . . 117 F2
Davis Ct BH12 . . . . 120 E5
Davis Field BH25. . . . . 94 F2
Davis Gdns DT11 . . . . 212 E6
Davis Rd BH12 . . . . 120 E5
Dawkins Bsns Ctr BH15 . . . . . 118 D3
Dawkins Rd BH15 . . . . 117 F3
Dawkins Rd BH25. . . . . 95 A2
Dawlish Cres DT4 . . . . 180 D7
Dawn Cl BH10 . . . . 89 C2
Daws Ave BH11 . . . . 89 B2
Daylesford Cl BH14 . . . . 120 A2
Day's Ct BH21 . . . . 59 D4
Day's Rd BH19 . . . . 178 E2
Daytona BH14 . . . . 147 C7
Deacon Gdns BH11. . . . . 89 A5
Deacon Rd BH11. . . . . 89 A5
Deacons La BA12 . . . . 14 A4
Deadman's Hill DT9 . . . . 16 E8
DEAN SP5. . . . . 188 E2
Dean Cl BH15. . . . . 118 E3
Dean Court (Bournemouth
   FC) BH21 . . . . 122 F6
Deane Ave SP8 . . . . 5 E1
DEANEND SP5. . . . . 188 E4
Deane Way **5** TA20 . . . . 202 A8
Dean La SP5. . . . . 188 E4
Dean La Dro SP5. . . . . 188 E4
DEAN PARK. 122 A4
Dean Park Cres BH1 . . . . 121 F3
Dean Park Rd BH1 . . . . 121 F4
Dean's Court Gdns★
   BH21. . . . . 59 C4
Deans Court La BH21. . . . . 59 C4
Deanscroft Rd BH10. . . . . 89 E4
Deans Dro BH16 . . . . 84 D2
Deans Gr BH21. . . . . 59 D7
Deansleigh Ct **5** DT3 . . . . . 153 B2
Deansleigh Rd BH7 . . . . 91 B1
Dean's Rd **6** BH5 . . . . 123 B5
Deans The BH1 . . . . 121 F4
Dean Swift Cres BH14 . . . . . . 147 C8
Dear Hay La BH15. . . . . 119 C2
De Briane Cl DT10 . . . . 196 F3
Decies Rd BH14 . . . . 120 A3
De Courtenai Cl BH11. . . . . 88 E5
Deepdene La BH11. . . . . 88 E5
Deep Ford La DT9 . . . . 194 C3
Deep La DT9. . . . . 194 C3
Deer Gdns SP8 . . . . 11 B8
Deerleap Way BH25. . . . . 95 B5
Deer Park Cl BH25 . . . . 94 F4
Deeprose La BH23 . . . . 119 B1
De Haviland Cl BH21 . . . . 59 F2
De Havilland Ho BH23 . . . . . . 125 A6
De Havilland Way BH23 . . . . . 125 A6
Delamere Gdns BH10. . . . . 89 E3
De Lea Gr DT6. . . . . 100 B7
Delft Mews BH23 . . . . 124 C6
Delhi Cl BH14. . . . . 120 D3
Delhi La DT5. . . . . 187 A4
Delhi Rd BH9 . . . . 89 F2
Delilah Rd BH15 . . . . 117 F2
De Lisle Rd BH3. . . . . 121 F7
Delkeith Ct BH22. . . . . 66 E4
Dell Cl BH18 . . . . 86 E4
Dell The BH23 . . . . 126 C8
Delph Rd BH21. . . . . 87 D8
Delph Woods Woodland
   Trail★ BH18, BH21. . . . . . . 87 C7
Delta Cl BH15 . . . . 125 A7
De Mauley Ct BH13. . . . . 147 E8
De Mauley Rd BH13 . . . . 147 E8
De Montfort Rd BH11 . . . . 59 D1
De Moulham Rd BH19 . . . . 179 B4
Denby Rd BH15 . . . . 119 E4
Dene Cl BH24 . . . . 47 C3
Denecote Lodge BH13 . . . . . . 147 H8
Denes Ave BA12 . . . . 3 A6
Dene The BH13 . . . . 121 A4
Deneve Ave BH17 . . . . 87 C1
Dene Wlk BH22. . . . . 61 E1
Denewood Copse BH22. . . . . . 52 F4
Denewood Rd
   Dominion BH4. . . . . 121 B3
   Ferndown BH22. . . . . 52 F4
Denhall Cl DT10. . . . . 35 A2
Denham Cl BH17. . . . . 87 E3
Denham Dr
   Cann SP7 . . . . 23 A5
   Christchurch BH23. . . . . 93 F1
Denhay La DT6 . . . . 67 B5
Denholm Cl BH24 . . . . 47 E1
Denison Rd BH17 . . . . 87 E3
Denmark La BH15. . . . . 119 D3
Denmark Rd
   Bournemouth BH9 . . . . 89 F1
   Poole BH15 . . . . 119 D3

Denmark Terr BH1 . . . . 122 E6
Denmead BH25 . . . . 95 D4
Denmead Rd BH6 . . . . 123 D7
Dennis Rd
   Poole BH21 . . . . 85 F5
   Weymouth DT4 . . . . 167 B2
Dennistoun Ave BH23 . . . . . . 124 F7
Denzil Cl **3** BA22 . . . . 193 A8
Derby Rd BH1 . . . . 122 C4
Derby St DT4 . . . . 167 D4
De Redvers Ct BH23. . . . . 91 D1
De Redvers Rd BH14 . . . . 120 C2
Dereham Way BH12 . . . . 120 F6
Derritt La BH23 . . . . 93 A7
Derrybrian Gdns BH25. . . . . . 95 A2
Derwent Cl
   Bournemouth BH9 . . . . 90 A2
   Ferndown BH22. . . . . 62 A6
Derwent Gdns BA21 . . . . 27 F6
Derwent Rd
   New Milton BH25. . . . . 95 B5
   Weymouth DT4 . . . . 180 D6
Derwentwater Rd BH21 . . . . . 59 C2
Derwent Way **3** BA21. . . . . 26 E6
Devenish Warren DT4 . . . . . . 180 F8
Deverel Cl BH23 . . . . 124 A8
Deverel Rd DT2 . . . . 75 D2
Devonedge La DT6 . . . . 97 B8
Devon Rd
   Christchurch BH23. . . . . . . 123 E8
   Poole BH15 . . . . 119 E5
   Weymouth DT4 . . . . 167 B4
Deweys La **8** BH24 . . . . . . 55 B7
Dewey's Way SP8 . . . . 5 F2
Dewlands Cl BH21 . . . . 59 B4
Dewlands Common Nature
   Reserve★ BH31. . . . . 44 F5
DEWLANDS COMMON
   BH31. . . . . 44 F6
Dewlands Orch DT9 . . . . 194 E3
Dewlands Rd BH31. . . . . 44 F6
Dewlands Way BH31. . . . . 45 A6
DEWLISH DT2 . . . . 209 C1
Dewlish Cl BH17. . . . . 88 A2
Dewsall Pl **13** DT1 . . . . 107 C1
Diamond Cl SP6 . . . . 43 A8
Diana Cl
   Dorchester DT1 . . . . 134 F7
   Ferndown BH22. . . . . 61 D6
Diana Ct **7** BH23. . . . . 126 A2
Diana Way BH21 . . . . 86 E7
Dibbles La BA22 . . . . 193 A8
Dibden CT BH8. . . . . 90 D3
Dickens Rd BH6. . . . . 123 D7
Dick o' Th' Banks Cl DT2 . . . 137 D6
Dick o' Th' Banks Rd
   DT2 . . . . 137 D6
Didcot Rd BH17 . . . . 119 D7
Digby Rd DT9. . . . . 30 B1
Diggory Cres **4** DT1 . . . . . . 135 B8
Dillons Gdns BH16 . . . . 84 C2
Dilly La BH25 . . . . 127 A7
Diments Gdns **2** DT6 . . . . 100 C8
Dinah's Hollow SP7 . . . . 24 C6
Dingle Rd BH5. . . . . 123 B4
Dingley Rd BH15 . . . . 119 D6
Dinham Cl BH25 . . . . 95 D4
Dinham Rd BH25 . . . . 95 D4
Dinhay DT10. . . . . 20 E4
DINNINGTON TA17. . . . . 191 H8
Dinosauriand Fossil Mus★
   DT7. . . . . 96 C5
Diprose Rd BH21. . . . . 86 F7
Discovery Court Bsns Ctr
   BH12. . . . . 88 E2
Discovery (Interactive
   Science Ctr)★ DT4. . . . . . . 167 C1
Disraeli Rd BH23 . . . . 124 D6
Dock Rd DT5 . . . . 181 C2
Doctor Roberts Cl DT6 . . . . . 100 C5
Dodham Cres BA20 . . . . 27 B4
Dodhams Farm Cl DT6 . . . . . . 68 F1
Dodham's La DT6. . . . . 68 E1
Doe Copse Way BH25 . . . . . . 94 E4
Does La BH31. . . . . 44 F6
Dogbury Gate DT2 . . . . 207 C8
Dogdean BH21. . . . . 59 C8
Dogwood Rd BH18 . . . . 86 E2
Dolbery Road N BH12 . . . . . . 88 D2
Dolbery Road S BH12 . . . . . . 88 C1
Dollings The BH20 . . . . 177 A7
Dollin's La **3** BH20 . . . . . . 142 E4
Dolmans Hill BH20 . . . . 84 A1
Dolphin Ave BH10. . . . . 89 E5
Dolphin Cl BH13 . . . . 121 B2
Dolphin La SP8 . . . . 5 E4
Dolphin Mans BH25 . . . . 127 A6
Dolphin Pl BH25 . . . . 127 A6
Dolphin Quays **9** BH15. . . 119 C1
Dolphin Sh Ctr The **3**
   BH15. . . . . 119 C2
Dolphin Sp Ctr BH15. . . . . . . 119 D2
Dominion Rd BH11 . . . . 88 E3
Dominion Rd BH11. . . . . 88 E3
Doncaster Rd BH11 . . . . 180 D6
Donhead Hollow SP7. . . . . . . 25 D7
Donkey La
   Bere Regis BH20 . . . . 113 A6
   5 Burton Bradstock DT6 . 128 B8
   Sturminster Newton DT10 . 197 D8
Donnelly Rd BH6. . . . . 123 F5
Donnington Dr BH23 . . . . 125 B7
Donoughmore Rd **1**
   BH1 . . . . 122 E4
DORCHESTER DT1 . . . . 107 C2
Dorchester Adult Ed Ctr
   DT1 . . . . 108 B1

Dorchester Gdns BH15 . . 119 E5
Dorchester Hill
   Blandford Forum DT11 . . 212 C2
   Milborne St Andrew DT11. . 79 E8
   Winterborne Whitechurch
   DT11. . . . . 210 C2
Dorchester Mans BH11. . . . . 122 D3
Dorchester Mid Sch DT1 134 E8
Dorchester Mkt DT1 . . . . . . 108 A1
Dorchester Rd
   Askerswell DT2 . . . . 103 A4
   Bincombe DT3 . . . . 134 C1
   Cerne Abbas DT2. . . . . . . 207 D4
   Closworth BA22. . . . . 193 F6
   Loders DT6 . . . . 101 C6
   Maiden Newton DT2 . . . . . 73 A7
   Poole BH15 . . . . 119 E6
   Radipole DT3 . . . . 152 B2
   Stratton DT2 . . . . 106 C8
   Sydling St Nicholas DT2. . 207 A2
   Tolpuddle DT2 . . . . 79 B2
   1 Upton BH16. . . . . . . 117 C7
   Wool BH20. . . . . 139 E1
   Yeovil BA20 . . . . 27 C2
Dorchester South Sta
   DT1. . . . . 108 A1
Dorchester West Sta
   DT1. . . . . 107 F1
Dore Cl BA21 . . . . 26 E7
Dormers The BH25. . . . . 94 F1
Dornie Rd BH13. . . . . 147 E7
Dorset Ave BH22. . . . . 61 D3
Dorset Cl DT4. . . . . 167 A3
Dorset County Mus★
   DT1. . . . . 108 A2
Dorset Teddy Bear Mus
   The★ DT1. . . . . 108 B2
Dorset Terr **8** DT4 . . . . . 167 D2
Dorset History Ctr★ DT1 107 F2
Dorset Ho BH11 . . . . 121 A2
Dorset Lake Ave BH14. . . . 147 B8
Dorset Lake Manor
   BH14 . . . . 120 A2
Dorset Rd
   Bournemouth BH4. . . . . . 121 C5
   Christchurch BH23. . . . . . 124 F8
Dorset St DT11. . . . . 212 D4
Dorset Teddy Bear Mus
   The★ DT1. . . . . 108 B2
Dorsets Walk DT11. . . . . . . 134 F7
Druitt Rd BH23. . . . . 124 F8
Drum La DT10 . . . . 196 F3
Drummond Rd
   Bournemouth BH1 . . . . . . 122 D4
   Swanage BH19 . . . . 179 C1
Drury La DT6 . . . . 204 C2
Drury Rd BH4. . . . . 121 B2
Dryden Cl BH24 . . . . 54 A5
Dry La SP9 . . . . 5 C1
Duart Ct BH25. . . . . 95 C3
Duchy Cl DT1. . . . . 135 C8
Ducking Stool La BH23. . . 124 B6
Duck Island La BH24 . . . . . 55 B6
Duck La
   Bournemouth BH11. . . . . . 88 F4
   Stalbridge DT10. . . . . 19 D1
Duckpool La TA18. . . . . . . 192 B8
Duck St
   Bridport DT6 . . . . 100 A4
   Cattistock DT2 . . . . 206 C2
   Cerne Abbas DT2. . . . . . . 207 D4
   Chideock DT6. . . . . 99 A6
   Child Okeford DT11 . . . . . 198 C7
   Hilton DT11 . . . . 209 D5
   Symondsbury DT6 . . . . . . 99 F7
   Winterborne Kingston DT11 81 E7
   Wool BH20. . . . . 140 B1
Dudley Ave SO41. . . . . 95 F3
Dudley Gdns BH10 . . . . . . 89 D5
Dudley Pl **3** BH25 . . . . 95 B1
Dudley Rd BH10. . . . . 89 D5
Dudmoor Farm Rd BH23. . 91 F3
Dudmoor La BH23 . . . . 91 F4
Dudsbury Ave BH22 . . . . . 61 D4
Dudsbury Cres BH22 . . . . 61 E4
Dudsbury Gdns BH22. . . . 89 E8
Dudsbury Rd BH22 . . . . . . 61 D1
Dudsway Ct BH22 . . . . 61 D4
Dugbury Hill DT6. . . . . 70 B6
Dugdell Cl DT2 . . . . 61 F6
Duke's Ave DT1. . . . . 108 B1
Dukes Cl
   Bournemouth BH6 . . . . . . 123 D6
   Martinstown DT2 . . . . . . 133 C6
Dukes Dr BH11 . . . . 88 E5
Dukesfield BH23 . . . . 124 D7
Dullar La
   Lytchett Matravers BH16. . 84 B6
   Sturminster Marshall BH21. . 56 C2
Dulsie Rd BH3 . . . . 121 C7
Dumbarton Rd DT4. . . . . . 180 D6
Dumpton St BH21. . . . . . . 59 D8
Dunbar Cres BH23 . . . . . . 93 F2
Dunbar Rd BH3. . . . . 121 E6
Dunbury Fst Sch DT11 . . . 210 C7
Dunbury La DT11 . . . . 209 F6
Dunbury Sch DT11 . . . . . . 210 C7
Duncan Cres BH20 . . . . . . 139 F6
Duncan Pl BH20 . . . . 139 F6
Duncan Rd BH25. . . . . 95 D4
Dunch La DT2 . . . . 194 D3
Duncliffe Cl DT10 . . . . 33 E8
Duncliffe View SP8 . . . . . . 10 E3
Duncliff Rd BH6 . . . . 124 A4
Duncombe Dr BH24 . . . . . 46 E3
Dundas Rd BH17 . . . . 119 E8
Dundee Rd DT4 . . . . 180 D6
Dune Crest BH13. . . . . 147 C3

Drake Cl
   Christchurch BH23. . . . . 124 F6
   New Milton BH25. . . . . . . 94 F3
   Ringwood BH24 . . . . 47 E1
Drake Cl **4** BH15 . . . . . 119 C1
Drake Rd BH15 . . . . 119 C1
Drakes Cres **6** TA20 . . 202 A8
Drake's La DT2 . . . . 208 F3
Drakes Mdw BA22 . . . . . . 193 C7
Drakes Rd BH22 . . . . 61 F3
Draper Rd
   Bournemouth BH1 . . . . . . 89 A4
   Christchurch BH23. . . . . . 124 F7
Drax Ave BH20 . . . . 142 E5
Draycott Rd BH10. . . . . . . 89 D2
Dreadnought Trad Est
   DT6. . . . . 100 B6
Dreswick Cl BH23 . . . . 91 D4
Drew Cl
   Bridport DT6 . . . . 68 F1
   Poole BH12 . . . . 121 C7
Drew Grange BH15. . . . . . 118 E4
Drewitt Ind Est BH11. . . . 88 E3
Drew's La DT10 . . . . 19 C1
Driffield Rd BH17 . . . . 88 A2
Drift The DT2 . . . . 202 B8
Driftwood Pk BH23. . . . . . 91 E1
DRIMPTON DT8 . . . . 203 D8
DRIVE END DT2. . . . . 194 A2
Drive The
   Poole, Lilliput BH13 . . . . 147 D2
   Poole, Upper Parkstone
   BH13. . . . . 120 D5
Drones La SP7 . . . . 23 D2
DROOP DT11 . . . . 197 A3
Drove Cl DT10 . . . . 32 F3
Drove La SP7 . . . . 36 F6
Drove Rd DT10 . . . . 32 F3
Drovers DT10 . . . . 35 B1
Droves The SP5 . . . . 188 E4
Drove The
   Arne BH20 . . . . 160 F8
   Shapwick DT11 . . . . 56 C7
   Thornford DT9. . . . . 194 D8
Droveway DT11 . . . . 212 B5
Droxford Rd BH6. . . . . 123 B6
Druce La DT2. . . . . 77 F3
Druids Cl BH22 . . . . 61 D2

Dunedin Cl BH22. . . . . 61 B3
Dunedin Dr BH22. . . . . 61 B3
Dunedin Gdns BH22. . . . . 61 B3
Dunford Pl BH19 . . . . 179 B2
Dunford Rd BH12. . . . . . . 120 D5
Dunkeld Rd BH3. . . . . 121 E6
Dunlin Cl BH23 . . . . 125 B5
Dunnabridge Sq **8** DT1 . 107 B2
Dunnabridge St **6** DT1. . 107 B2
Dunnock Cl BH17 . . . . . . 61 B8
Dunn's La
   Iwerne Minster DT11 . . . 37 F2
   Silton DT11 . . . . 2 A1
Dunsham La TA18. . . . . . . 191 C2
Dunspit La DT11 . . . . 188 B1
Dunstans La BH15. . . . . . 120 A6
Dunstan St DT9 . . . . 30 D7
DUNTISH DT2 . . . . 194 C1
Dunyeats Rd BH18 . . . . . 87 B4
Dunyeats Rdbt BH18 . . . . 87 D5
Duplock Ho DT5 . . . . 95 A3
D'Urberville Cl **4** DT1. . 134 F7
D'Urberville Dr BH19. . . . 179 B4
Durdells Ave BH11 . . . . . 89 A5
Durdells Gdns BH11. . . . . 89 A5
Durland Cl BH21 . . . . 95 A1
Durley Chine Ct **12** BH2 . 121 D2
Durley Chine Rd BH2 . . . 121 D2
Durley Chine Road S
   BH2. . . . . 121 D2
Durley Gdns BH2. . . . . . . 121 D2
Durley Rd BH2. . . . . 121 E2
Durley Rdbt BH2 . . . . 121 E2
Durlston Court Sch
   BH25. . . . . 127 A8
Durlston Cres BH23 . . . . 91 D4
Durlston Ctry Pk★ BH19 . 185 B7
Durlston National Nature
   Reserve★ BH19 . . . . . . 185 B7
Durlston Rd
   Poole BH14 . . . . 120 C2
   Swanage BH19 . . . . 179 C1
Durnford Dro BH19 . . . . . 178 B1
Durngate St DT1 . . . . 108 A2
Durnover Ct DT11 . . . . . . 108 B2
Durrant **4** DT10 . . . . . 197 D8
Durrant Cl DT9 . . . . 30 B5
Durrant Rd
   Bournemouth BH2 . . . . . 121 E4
   Poole BH14 . . . . 120 C2
Durrell Way BH15 . . . . . . 119 D2
Durrington Pl BH7 . . . . . 123 B6
Durrington Rd BH7 . . . . . 123 B7
DURWESTON DT11 . . . . . 198 E3
Durweston CE Fst Sch
   DT11. . . . . 198 F3
Durweston Cl BH9 . . . . . 90 B3
Dyke Head DT9. . . . . 195 B6
Dymewood Rd BH21 . . . . 53 A7

Druids Walk DT11 . . . . . . 134 F7
Dukesbury Ho BH6 . . . . . 123 C5
DUIDSBURY. 61 C1

Dar–Eas 221

Dundry Rd BH8 . . . . 90 D4

E

Eadon Cl DT3 . . . . 168 A7
Eagle House Gdns DT11 . 212 C4
Eagle Rd BH13 . . . . 121 A4
Eagle Rise BH8 . . . . 90 D1
Eaglhurst **3** BH13 . . . . 121 A4
Earl Cl **1** DT1 . . . . 108 B1
Earle Rd BH4 . . . . 121 C1
Earles Rd BH21 . . . . 53 A8
Earle St BA20 . . . . 27 E4
Earlham Dr BH14 . . . . 120 C4
Earls Cl DT9 . . . . 30 D7
Earlsdon Way BH23 . . . . 125 F6
Earlswood **8** BH14 . . . 121 C2
Earlswood Pk SP6. . . . . . 42 B5
Earlswood Pk BH25 . . . . 95 C4
Earthpits La SP5 . . . . 189 C4
East Ave
   Barton on Sea BH25 . . . 126 C7
   Bournemouth BH3 . . . . . 121 D6
East Avenue Rdbt BH3 . . 121 D6
EAST BLOXWORTH BH20. . 82 E1
East Borough BH21 . . . . 59 B5
East Brook SP8 . . . . 55 C5
Eastbrook Row BH21 . . . 59 C4
EAST BURTON BH20. . . . 139 E2
East Burton Rd BH20 . . . 139 F2
Eastbury Ct BH23 . . . . . 124 F4
EAST CHELBOROUGH
   DT2 . . . . 205 D8
EAST CHINNOCK BA22 . 192 E8
East Cl BH15. . . . . 126 D8
East Cliff
   8 Bournemouth BH2 . 121 F4
   Lyme Regis DT7 . . . . . . 96 C5
East Cliff Way BH23 . . . 125 C7
EAST COKER BA22 . . . . 193 D7
East Coker Prim Sch
   BA22. . . . . 193 D7
East Coker Rd BA20. . . . 27 B1
EAST COMPTON SP7 . . . 24 A2
Eastcott Cl DT1 . . . . 123 A8
EAST CREECH BH20 . . . 160 F2
East Dorset Trade Pk
   BH21. . . . . 60 F6
Eastdown Ave DT3 . . . . 167 E8
Eastdown Gdns BH14 . . 168 A6
East Dr BH24 . . . . 62 B7
East Dro BH19 . . . . 178 B2

EAST END 58 E1
Easter Rd BH9 .... 90 A2
East Farm La DT2 .... 155 D7
Eastfield 4 DT9 ..... 194 D8
Eastfield Ct BH24 .... 55 E7
Eastfield La
　North Perrott TA18 ... 192 C4
　Ringwood BH24 .... 55 E7
　West Chinnock BA22 .. 192 D8
EAST FLEET DT3 ..... 166 B5
Easthams Rd TA18 ..... 191 F4
Easthay La TA20 .... 202 D4
East Hill
　Charminster DT2 ...... 107 D6
　Evershot DT2 .... 206 A7
EAST HOLME BH20 .. 159 E8
EAST HOLTON BH16 . 117 A3
EAST HOWE 89 C3
East Howe La BH10 ..... 89 C4
EAST KNIGHTON DT2 157 A8
East Knighton La DT2 . 157 A7
East La TA18 .... 192 B8
Eastlake Ave BA22 ...... 120 C6
Eastland Rd BA21 .... 27 E5
Eastlands
　New Milton BH25 .... 95 B1
　10 Yetminster DT9 .... 194 C5
Eastleaze Rd DT11 ...... 212 D6
EAST LULWORTH BH20 173 D8
EAST MARTIN SP6 .... 190 C6
EAST MELBURY SP7 .. 24 C5
East Mill La DT9 .... 30 C6
EAST MORDEN BH20 .. 83 D4
East Morden Dro BH20 83 D6
EASTON DT5 .... 187 B4
Easton Hollow SP7 .... 188 B7
Easton La DT5 .... 187 A5
Easton Sh Ctr DT5 ..... 187 A4
Easton Sq 4 DT5 .... 187 A4
Easton St DT5 .... 187 A4
Eastop La DT10 .... 33 B5
EAST ORCHARD SP7 .. 36 D4
East Overcliff Dr BH1 122 C3
EAST PARLEY 90 B8
EAST PULHAM DT2 ... 196 D4
East Quay 11 BH15 .... 119 C1
East Quay Rd BH15 .... 119 C1
East Rd DT6 .... 100 E6
East Rd Bsns Pk DT6 .. 100 E6
East St
　Beaminster DT8 .... 204 D4
　Blandford Forum DT11 212 D3
　Bourton SP8 .... 1 E2
　Bridport DT6 .... 100 D6
　Chickerell DT3 .... 166 C6
　Corfe Castle BH20 ..... 162 A1
　Crewkerne TA18 ...... 191 F4
　Fortuneswell DT5 ..... 186 F7
　Milborne Port DT9 ...... 17 D2
　North Perrott TA18 ... 192 C4
　Poole BH15 .... 119 C1
　Radipole DT4 .... 167 E2
　Sydling St Nicholas DT2 . 207 A2
　Wareham BH20 .... 142 E3
　West Coker BA22 ...... 193 A8
　Wimborne Minster BH21 . 59 C3
　9 Winterborne Kingston
　　DT11 .... 81 E8
EAST STOKE BH20 ... 140 F1
East Stoke Fen Reserve★
　BH20 .... 140 E2
EAST STOUR 10 E3
EAST STOUR COMMON
　SP8 .... 11 A3
East View BH24 .... 55 D7
East Walls BH20 .... 142 F3
East Way
　Bournemouth BH8 ...... 90 C1
　Poole BH21 .... 85 F5
East Weare Rd DT5 .... 181 B1
Eastwell La DT10 .... 35 A8
Eastwood Ave BH24 .... 61 E6
Eastworth Rd BH31 .... 45 A7
East Wyld Rd DT4 ..... 167 A3
Eaton Rd BH13 .... 121 C1
EBBLAKE BH31 .... 45 F4
Ebblake Cl BH31 .... 45 E3
Ebblake Ind Est BH31 . 45 E4
Ebenezer La 6 BH24 .. 55 B7
Ebor Cl BH22 .... 61 E2
Ebor Rd
　Poole BH12 .... 120 D6
　Weymouth DT4 .... 180 C8
Ebury Ct 7 BH21 ...... 121 C3
Eccles Rd BH15 .... 119 A2
ECCLIFFE SP8 .... 10 D7
Eddison Ave DT11 .... 108 C1
Eddy Green Rd BH16 ... 84 B2
Eden Ct
　5 Bournemouth BH1 . 122 B3
　11 Bournemouth, Westbourne
　　BH4 .... 121 C2
Eden Gr BH21 .... 59 D3
Edenhurst 12 BH4 .... 121 C3
Edgarton Rd BH17 ..... 87 D3
Edgehill Rd
　Bournemouth BH9 ...... 89 F1
　Bridport DT6 .... 100 B5
Edgemoor Rd BH22 .... 53 C1
Edifred Rd BH9 .... 89 F4
Edith Ct 2 SP8 .... 5 E1
EDMONDSHAM BH21 .. 40 C3
Edmondsham Ho 16 BH2 121 E3

Edmondsham House &
　Gdns★ BH21 .... 40 C4
Edmondsham Rd BH31 . 45 A7
Edmunds Cl BH25 ...... 95 A1
Edward Cl BA22 .... 26 D6
Edward Cres BH20 .... 142 E4
Edward May St BH11 ... 89 A4
Edward Rd
　Bournemouth BH11 ..... 89 B3
　Christchurch BH23 .... 124 F8
　Dorchester DT1 .... 107 F1
　Poole BH14 .... 120 C5
Edwards Ct BH23 ...... 126 A8
Edward St
　Blandford Forum DT11 . 212 D4
　4 Radipole DT4 .... 167 D4
Edwina Cl BH24 .... 47 E1
Edwina Dr BH7 .... 87 B2
Egdon Cl
　Bere Regis BH20 .... 81 B2
　Ferndown BH22 .... 61 D4
Egdon Ct 5 BH16 ..... 117 D7
Egdon Dr BH21 .... 87 E8
Egdon Glen DT2 .... 137 E6
Egdon Rd
　Dorchester DT1 .... 135 B7
　Northport BH20 .... 142 D5
Egerton Ct BH8 .... 122 D6
Egerton Gdns BH8 ... 122 D6
Egerton Rd BH8 .... 122 D6
Eggardon Cl 5 DT8 .. 204 C4
Eggardon Hill (Fort)★
　DT6 .... 71 A2
Egmont Cl BH24 .... 54 E2
Egmont Dr BH24 .... 54 F2
Egmont Gdns BH24 ... 54 E2
Egmont Rd BH24 .... 54 F2
Egmont Rd BH16 ..... 117 D4
Eight Acre Wood Nature
　Reserve★ BH20 ... 140 A5
Eight August Rd BH20 . 139 E7
Elbury View SP7 .... 37 E7
Elderberry La BH23 ... 124 F6
Elder Rd BH20 .... 81 A2
Eldon Ave BH25 .... 126 E8
Eldon Cl BH25 .... 126 E8
Eldon Ct 5 BH14 ..... 120 A4
Eldon Pl BH4 .... 121 B3
Eldon St BH13 .... 121 B3
Eldon Terr 5 BH19 ... 179 B2
Eldridge Cl 3 DT1 .... 134 F7
Eleanor Cl BH25 .... 94 F1
Eleanor Dr BH11 .... 88 D5
Eleanor Gdns BH23 .. 123 E8
Elfin Dr BH22 .... 61 C7
Elgar Rd BH10 .... 89 D4
Elgin Rd
　Bournemouth BH4 .... 121 D6
　Poole BH14 .... 120 C2
Elijah Cl BH15 .... 118 E2
Eliot Ho 8 BH25 .... 95 A2
Eliotts Dr BA21 .... 27 A7
Elise Cl BH7 .... 123 B8
Elizabeth Ave
　Bridport DT6 .... 100 C5
　Christchurch BH23 ... 123 F8
Elizabeth Cl 1 DT7 .... 96 C6
Elizabeth Ct
　1 Bournemouth BH1 . 122 B3
　Ferndown BH22 .... 61 D6
　8 New Milton BH25 ... 95 B2
Elizabeth Gdns BH23 125 D7
Elizabeth Pl DT11 .... 107 D1
Elizabeth Rd
　Blandford Forum DT11 . 212 D5
　Poole BH15 .... 119 D3
　3 Upton BH16 .... 117 D7
　Wimborne Minster BH21 . 59 C5
Elizabeth Way DT3 ... 166 B3
Ellerslie Ct DT1 .... 107 E6
Ellesdon DT6 .... 97 B8
Ellesfield Dr BH22 ..... 61 D2
Elles Rd BH20 .... 139 D7
ELLINGHAM BH24 ..... 47 B5
Ellingham Dr BH24 ... 46 E4
Ellingham Dro BH24 .. 47 E5
Ellingham Rd BH15 .. 126 D8
Elliott Rd BH11 .... 88 F3
Elliott's Hill BA22 .... 192 D7
Elm Ave
　Christchurch BH23 .... 91 E1
　Holton Heath BH16 .. 116 B3
　New Milton BH25 ...... 95 A3
Elm Cl
　Motcombe SP7 .... 7 B1
　Overcombe/Preston DT3 . 168 A6
　Sturminster Newton DT10 . 35 C1
Elm Ct 13 BH25 .... 95 A2
Elmes Rd BH9 .... 89 F2
Elmgate Dr BH7 .... 123 A7
Elm Gdns BH4 .... 121 C5
ELM HILL SP7 .... 7 B1
Elmhurst Ave BA21 .... 27 D7
Elmhurst Rd
　Bournemouth BH11 ..... 89 A5
　Ferndown BH22 .... 53 B1
Elmhurst Way BH22 ... 53 B1
Elm La DT2 .... 75 D2
Elmleigh BA21 .... 26 E7
Elmore Dr BH24 .... 54 A6
Elmrise Cty Prim Sch
　BH11 .... 89 A4
Elms Ave BH14 .... 120 A1
Elms Cl BH14 .... 120 A1
Elmstead Rd BH13 ... 147 F8
Elms Way BH24 .... 196 C3
Elm Tree Wlk BH22 ... 89 E8
Elmwood Way BH23 . 126 A7

Elphinstone Rd BH23 .. 94 B1
Elsdon's La DT6 .... 64 B4
Elston Medieval Village of★
　DT2 .... 207 A3
Eltham Cl BH21 .... 123 B8
Elvastone St 1 DT1 .. 107 C1
Elveroakes Way DT4 . 180 C6
Elvin Cl SO41 .... 95 F3
ELWELL DT3 .... 152 B6
Elwell DT6 .... 100 E5
Elwell Manor Gdns DT4 . 167 D1
Elwell St DT3 .... 152 B6
Elwood Cl BH20 .... 142 F8
Elwyn Rd BH1, BH8 .. 122 C5
Elysium St BH22 .... 61 E3
Elziver Cl DT3 .... 152 B6
Embankment Way BH24 . 55 D6
Emberley Cl BH22 ...... 62 A6
Emerald Cl BH24 .... 54 A6
Emerson Cl 12 BH15 . 119 C2
Emerson Rd
　Poole BH15 .... 119 C2
　Weymouth DT4 .... 167 B2
Emily Cl BH23 .... 92 A1
Emily Ct BH14 .... 120 E5
Emley La 1 BH21 ..... 201 C1
Emma Cl BH10 .... 89 C6
Emmadale Rd DT4 ... 167 A3
Emmanuel CE Mid Sch The
　BH31 .... 45 A4
Emminster Cl DT3 ... 168 A8
Empool Ct DT3 .... 137 D5
Ensbury Rd DT10 ...... 33 C3
Encombe Cl BH12 .... 120 F8
Encombe Rd BH20 .. 142 D3
Endeavour Ind Pk BH4 . 55 D6
Endfield Cl BH23 .... 91 F1
Endfield Rd
　Bournemouth BH9 ..... 90 A2
　Christchurch BH23 .... 91 E1
Enfield Ave BH15 ..... 119 E6
Enfield Cres BH15 ... 119 E6
Enfield Rd BH15 ...... 119 E6
Englands Way BH11 .. 88 D4
English Ct 15 BH2 ... 121 D4
Enkworth Rd DT3 .... 168 A7
ENMORE GREEN SP7 .. 12 D3
ENSBURY 89 F6
Ensbury Ave BH10 ..... 89 D1
Ensbury Cl BH10 .... 89 D1
Ensbury Cl BH10 .... 89 E2
ENSBURY PARK 89 C2
Ensbury Park Rd BH9 . 89 E2
Enterprise Way BH23 . 90 C8
Epiphany CE Prim Sch The
　BH9 .... 90 B4
Erica Dr BH21 .... 85 F6
Ericksen Rd BH11 ..... 89 C3
Erinbank Mans BH11 . 122 C3
Erin Rd BH20 .... 139 E7
Ermine St BA21 .... 26 F7
Erpingham Rd DT4 ... 180 A6
Esmonde Way BH17 .. 119 F8
Esplanade
　Bridport DT6 .... 100 B1
　Poole BH13 .... 147 F7
　Portland DT5 .... 186 E8
　Radipole DT4 .... 167 E2
Esplanade The DT4 .. 167 E5
Essex Ave BH23 .... 91 F1
Essex Rd BH14 .... 167 C3
Etches Cl BH10 .... 89 D4
Ethelbert Rd BH21 .... 59 D4
Eton Gdns BH4 .... 121 C4
Eton Mans 2 BH6 ... 123 E3
Ettrick Rd BH13 ...... 121 A1
Eucalyptus Ave BH24 . 54 C2
Euston Gr BH21 .... 55 C6
Evans Cl
　Bournemouth BH11 .... 88 F1
　St Leonards BH24 ..... 54 A4
Evelyn Mews 11 BH9 . 89 F1
Evelyn Rd BH9 .... 90 A1
Evening Glade BH22 .. 61 E4
Eventide Homes BH8 . 90 E2
Everdene Cl BH22 ...... 61 C2
Everdene Dr DT3 ..... 166 E3
Everdene Rd 2 BH21 . 135 B8
Everest Rd
　Christchurch BH23 ... 124 E8
　Weymouth DT4 .... 167 C1
Everetts La 1 DT11 .. 198 B5
Everglades Cl BH22 .. 61 D7
Evergreen Cl BH21 .... 53 A8
Evergreen Path TA16 . 191 F7
Evergreens Rd BH24 .. 54 A6
Evering Ave BH12 ..... 88 D1
Evering Gdns BH12 ... 88 C1
Everon Gdns BH25 .... 95 B1
EVERSHOT DT2 .... 206 A7
Evershot Rd BH8 .... 90 E2
Evershot Wlk 19 DT1 . 107 D1
Eversleigh 16 BH2 ... 121 D2
Everton Rd 2 BA20 .. 27 C4
Evesham Ave BA21 ... 26 E6
Evesham Cl BH7 ...... 123 A8
Evesham Cl BH13 .... 121 A1
Exbourne Manor BH1 . 122 C3
Exbury Dr BH11 .... 88 F5
Excelsior Rd BH14 ... 120 C3
Exeter Cres BH2 ...... 121 F3
Exeter Ct 5 BH23 .... 126 B7
Exeter La BH2 .... 121 F2
Exeter Park Mans BH2 . 121 F2
Exeter Park Rd BH2 . 121 F2
Exeter Rd
　Bournemouth BH2 .... 121 F3
　4 Swanage BH19 .... 179 C2

Exton Rd BH6 .... 123 D7
Eynon Mews BH24 ..... 55 B6
Eype Down Rd DT6 .... 99 E5

F

Factory Hill SP8 .... 1 F3
Factory La
　Buckland Newton DT2 . 207 F8
　Tatworth & Forton TA20 . 202 A8
Factory Rd BH16 .... 117 E6
Fairclose DT4 .... 167 B1
Faircourt 8 BH25 ...... 95 B3
Faircross Ave DT4 ... 167 C1
Fairey Cl SP8 .... 5 F3
Fairey Cres SP8 .... 5 F3
Fairfax DT6 .... 99 A6
Fairfield
　Christchurch BH23 ... 124 B7
　Crewkerne TA18 ...... 191 E4
　Sherborne DT9 .... 30 B7
Fairfield Bglws DT11 . 212 D5
Fairfield Cl
　Christchurch BH23 ... 124 B7
　22 Okeford Fitzpaine DT11 197 F6
　Wimborne Minster BH21 . 59 F5
Fairfield Hts DT9 ...... 30 B7
Fairfield Pk DT7 ...... 96 C6
Fairfield Rd
　Barton on Sea BH25 . 126 E7
　Blandford Forum DT11 . 212 D4
　2 Dorchester DT1 .... 107 F1
　Wimborne Minster BH21 . 59 D4
Fairhaven Ct 9 BH5 .. 122 E4
Fairhouse Rd BA22 .. 193 F8
Fairies Dr BH22 .... 61 F3
Fairlane BH22 .... 61 F3
Fairlawn BH22 .... 62 A5
Fair Lea BH2 .... 121 E2
Fairlie DH24 .... 47 E1
Fairlie Pk BH24 .... 47 D1
Fairlight La SO41 .... 95 D8
Fairmead Rd BA21 .... 27 E8
Fairmead Specl Sch BA21 27 E8
FAIRMILE 91 F1
Fairmile Parade BH23 . 91 F1
Fairmile Rd BH23 ..... 91 F1
Fair Mile Rd DT11 ... 210 F8
Fairoak Way 3 DT8 .. 204 A7
Fairthorn Ct 3 BH2 .. 121 F4
Fairview Cres BH18 ... 87 A5
Fairview Dr BH18 ...... 87 A5
Fairview Pk BH14 ... 120 C3
Fairview Rd
　Broadstone BH18 ...... 87 A5
　Weymouth DT4 .... 180 D7
Fairway Dr
　Christchurch BH23 ... 123 F6
　Wareham Town BH20 . 142 C6
Fairway Rd BH14 .... 147 C8
Fairwood Rd BH31 ..... 45 E5
Fairways BH22 .... 61 F6
Fairway The BH25 .. 127 B7
Fairway View BA21 .... 27 F6
Fairwinds BH13 ...... 147 B3
Fairwood Rd BH31 ..... 45 E5
Fairy Bridge Wlk 1 SP8 . 5 F3
Falcon Dr BH23 .... 125 A5
Falconer Dr BH15 .... 118 E4
Falkland Sq 38 TA18 . 191 F4
Falkland Sq 2 BH15 . 119 C2
Fallows The BH25 ...... 95 B5
Fancy Rd BH12 .... 120 B8
Fancys Ct DT5 .... 187 A4
Fancy's Row BH16 ... 116 B4
Fantley La SP8 .... 2 B1
Farcroft Rd BH12 .... 120 B5
Far Ends 4 BH14 .... 120 B4
Farfrae Cres DT1 .... 135 B8
Farm Cl
　Radipole DT4 .... 167 A5
　Ringwood BH24 .... 55 C8
Farm Ct BH21 .... 60 A4
Farmdene Ct BH23 .. 125 D8
Farmer Palmer's Farm Pk★
　BH16 .... 116 B5
Farmers Wlk 1 BH21 . 59 B6
Farm La
　Christchurch BH23 ... 125 A5
　Corfe Mullen BH21 .... 86 E8
　West Lulworth BH20 . 172 D6
Farm Lane N BH25 ... 127 A8
Farm Lane S BH25 ... 127 A8
Farm Rd
　Bradford Abbas DT9 .. 28 C2
　Ferndown BH22 .... 52 F2
FARNHAM DT11 .... 188 C2
Farnham Rd BH12 ... 121 A7
Farquharson Rd DT1 . 107 F2
Farrington Cl 2 DT1 . 134 F7
FARRINGTON 37 A3
Farrington 2 BH4 .... 121 C2
Farr's Lodge Gdn★ BA21 . 58 D4
Farr's Orch 5 TA18 .. 191 F7
Farthings Ct The 13 BH1 . 122 A3
Farwell Cl BH23 .... 92 C3
Farwell Rd BH12 .... 88 C2
Faversham
　9 Bournemouth BH2 . 121 D2
　Radipole DT4 .... 167 A6
Fawcett Rd BH25 ...... 94 F2
Fawley Gn BH8 .... 90 D3
Fawn Gdns BH25 ...... 94 F4
Fellowsmead DT10 .... 20 F2
Felton Cres BH23 .... 125 F8
Felton Ct BH14 .... 119 F5
Felton Rd BH14 ...... 119 F5

Fenleigh Cl BH25 .... 95 B1
Fennel Rd BA12 .... 3 B6
Fennel Way BA22 ...... 26 C5
Fenton Rd BH6 .... 123 C5
Fenway Ct DT1 .... 108 D1
Fenwick Ct BH8 .... 122 B5
Fern Bank
　5 Bournemouth BH2 . 121 F3
　Three Legged Cross BH21 . 53 A7
Fern Barrow BH12 ... 121 B7
Fern Brook La SP8 ...... 6 B1
Fern Cl
　Alderholt SP6 .... 42 C5
　Burton BH23 .... 92 D5
Ferncroft Gdns BH10 . 89 D5
Ferncroft Rd BH10 .... 89 D5
Ferndale Gdns BA21 .. 27 A6
Ferndale Rd
　New Milton BH25 .... 95 B4
　Radipole DT4 .... 167 D6
FERNDOWN 61 B5
Ferndown Fst Sch BH22 . 61 C5
Ferndown Ind Est BH21 . 60 F7
Ferndown L Ctr BH22 . 61 A8
Ferndown Mid Sch BH22 . 61 C5
Ferndown Rd DT7 ... 96 C5
Ferndown Upper Sch
　BH22 .... 61 B6
Ferne Hollow SP7 .... 188 A3
Fernglade BH25 .... 95 A3
Fernheath Cl BH11 .... 89 A3
Fernheath Rd BH11 ... 89 A3
Fern Hill SP8 .... 11 A3
Fernhill Ave DT4 ..... 167 D6
Fernhill Cl BH17 .... 88 A2
Fernhill Flats BH25 .. 121 F3
Fernhill La BH25 .... 95 A4
Fernhill Rd BH25 ...... 95 A3
Fernlea BH23 .... 124 C6
Fernlea Ave BH22 ..... 61 D4
Fernlea Cl
　Ferndown BH22 .... 61 D4
　St Leonards BH24 ..... 54 A4
Fernlea Gdns BH22 ... 61 D4
Fern Rd DT2 .... 139 B3
Fernside Ave
　Bournemouth BH9 ... 121 E8
　Ferndown BH22 .... 53 A2
　Poole BH15 .... 119 E4
Fernway Cl BH21 ...... 60 B4
Fernwood Cl BH24 .... 54 D5
Ferris Ave BH8 .... 90 D2
Ferris Cl BH8 .... 90 D2
Ferris Pl BH8 .... 90 D2
Ferrymans Way DT4 . 180 D5
Ferry Rd
　Bournemouth BH6 ... 123 F3
　Poole BH19 .... 147 A3
Poole, Lower Hamworthy
　BH15 .... 119 B1
Studland BH19 .... 164 C3
Ferry Way BH13 ..... 147 B3
Feversham Ave BH8 .. 90 E1
FIDDLEFORD DT11 .. 197 F8
Fiddleford Manor★
　DT10 .... 197 F8
Field Barn Dr DT4 ... 167 B5
Field Cl DT10 .... 35 C2
Fieldfare Cl DT3 ..... 152 D3
Fielding Rd BA21 ...... 27 E6
Fieldings The SP8 ..... 10 D3
Field La
　Gillingham SP8 .... 5 A4
　Kington Magna SP8 .... 9 D2
　Pen Selwood BA9 .... 1 A3
Field Pl
　Barton on Sea BH25 . 126 D8
　Verwood BH31 .... 45 A7
Fields Barn DT2 ...... 156 E5
Field's Gdn DT11 .... 210 C3
Fields Oak DT11 ...... 212 D4
Fields The BA12 .... 3 C4
Field View Rd 2 DT11 . 212 D4
Fieldway BH24 .... 55 D8
Field Way
　Christchurch BH23 .... 93 D1
　Corfe Mullen BH21 .... 86 E8
Fifehead Hill SP8 ..... 20 F7
FIFEHEAD MAGDALEN
　SP8 .... 20 F7
FIFEHEAD NEVILLE
　DT10 .... 197 C5
FIFEHEAD ST QUINTIN
　DT10 .... 197 B5
Fifehead Wood★ SP8 . 20 E8
Filbridge Rise DT10 ... 35 C2
FILFORD DT6 .... 67 E7
Filford La DT6 .... 67 E8
Filleul Rd BH20 .... 115 F1
Fillybrook Bsns Pk SP8 . 9 B5
Finches The DT3 ..... 152 C3
Finchfield Ave BH11 .. 88 F6
Findlay PI BH11 .... 178 F3
Fineshade 7 BH13 ... 147 F7
Finger La DT9 .... 30 B5
Fippenny Hollow 3
　DT11 .... 197 F6
Fir Ave
　Holton Heath BH16 .. 116 B3
　New Milton BH25 ...... 95 B2
Firbank Rd BH9 .... 122 B8
Firch La DT6 .... 101 B6
Fir Cl BH22 .... 53 A3

Fir Dr DT3 . . . 153 C3
Firecrest Cl DT11 . . . 152 C4
Firmain Rd BH12 . . . 88 D1
Firs Glen Rd
  Bournemouth BH9 . . . 121 E8
  Ferndown BH22 . . . 53 A2
  Verwood BH31 . . . 45 B5
Firshill BH23 . . . 125 E8
Firs Rd BH21 . . . 85 E4
Firs Marine Ave BH25 . . . 126 F7
Firs The BH1 . . . 100 B2
First Cliff Wlk ▌ DT6 . . . 100 B2
First Marine Ave BH25 . . . 126 F7
Firsway BH16 . . . 118 C7
Fir Tree Cl
  Dorchester DT1 . . . 107 D2
  St Leonards BH24 . . . 53 F2
Firtree Cres SO41 . . . 95 F3
Fir Tree Hill SP6 . . . 42 C6
Fir Tree La BH23 . . . 93 D1
Fir Vale Rd BH1 . . . 121 F3
Fisherbridge Rd DT3 . . . 168 C8
Fisherman's Ave BH6 . . . 123 D4
Fisherman's Bank BH23 . . . 124 E5
Fishermans Cl DT3 . . . 166 D6
Fishermans Rd BH15 . . . 119 C1
Fisherman's Wlk BH5 . . . 123 E4
Fisher's Cl DT12 . . . 212 C1
Fisher's La DT17 . . . 191 A7
Fishers Pl DT2 . . . 170 A7
Fisherway La SP7 . . . 36 E5
Fishpond Bottom Rd
  DT6 . . . 202 D1
Fishweir Fields ▌ DT6 . . . 68 F1
Fishweir La DT6 . . . 68 F1
Fitzharris Ave BH9 . . . 122 A7
Fitzmaurice Rd BH23 . . . 123 E8
Fitzpain Cl BH22 . . . 61 D2
Fitzpain Rd BH22 . . . 61 D2
Fitzwilliam Cl BH11 . . . 88 E5
Fitzworth Ave BH16 . . . 117 E4
Five Acres
  Charmouth DT6 . . . 97 A7
  Yeovil BA22 . . . 193 F8
Fiveways Sch BA21 . . . 27 F6
Flag Farm BH13 . . . 147 D7
Flaghead BH13 . . . 147 E6
Flaghead Chine Rd BH13 147 E6
Flaghead Rd BH13 . . . 147 E7
Flambard Ave BH23 . . . 92 A1
Flambard Rd BH14 . . . 120 C2
Flanders Cl DT10 . . . 21 A2
Flaxfield Dr ▌ SA18 . . . 191 F4
Flax Cl DT9 . . . 28 F7
Flax Way BA21 . . . 26 E6
Flazen Cl BH11 . . . 88 D3
FLEET DT3 . . . 166 A5
Fleet Cl DT3 . . . 166 E3
Fleet Rd DT3 . . . 166 B5
Fleetsbridge Bsns Ctr
  BH17 . . . 119 B7
Fleet's Cnr BH17 . . . 119 B7
Fleet La BH15 . . . 119 B6
Fleets La BH15 . . . 119 B6
Fleetpoint Bsns Ctr
  BH15 . . . 119 B5
Fleet St DT8 . . . 204 D4
Fleet View DT4 . . . 180 C7
Fleetwood Ct BH15 . . . 119 C7
Fletcher Cl BH10 . . . 89 D3
Fletcher Rd BH10 . . . 89 D3
Flood La DT6 . . . 100 D4
Floral Farm BH21 . . . 60 A2
Florence Rd
  Bournemouth BH5 . . . 122 F4
  Dorchester DT1 . . . 134 E8
  Poole BH14 . . . 120 C4
Floriston Gdns BH25 . . . 95 D3
Flower Cl BH21 . . . 59 D3
Flowers Dro BH16 . . . 84 E4
Flushing Mdw BH21 . . . 28 A5
Folke La DT9 . . . 195 D8
FOLLY DT2 . . . 208 D6
Folly Farm La BH24 . . . 54 E6
Folly Fields BA21 . . . 27 D7
Folly La
  Blandford St Mary DT11 . . . 212 C1
  Gillingham SP8 . . . 10 D5
  Kington Magna SP8 . . . 9 B7
  Nether Compton DT9 . . . 28 E8
  Wareham BH20 . . . 142 E4
  Wool BH20 . . . 140 A2
Folly Mill Gdns DT6 . . . 100 D6
Folly Mill La DT6 . . . 100 D6
Folly The DT2 . . . 207 D4
Font La BA22 . . . 193 B7
FONTMELL MAGNA SP7 . . . 37 F7
FONTMELL PARVA DT11 . . . 36 D2
Fontmell Rd BH18 . . . 87 C3
Font Villas BA22 . . . 193 B7
Footners La BH23 . . . 92 C2
Foot's Hill SP7 . . . 24 E2
Ford Cl BH22 . . . 61 F7
Ford Down La DT12 . . . 208 A7
Forde Abbey & Gdns★
  TA20 . . . 202 C8
Forde Pk BA21 . . . 26 E7
Fordhay BA22 . . . 192 E7
FORDINGBRIDGE SP6 . . . 43 B8
Fordingbridge Rd SP6 . . . 42 C7
Fordington Gdns ▌ DT1 108 B1
Fordington Gn ▌ DT1 . . . 108 B2
Ford La BH22 . . . 62 A7

Forehill Cl DT3 . . . 168 B8
Foreland Cl BH23 . . . 91 D4
Foreland Rd BH16 . . . 117 D4
Fore St
  Evershot DT2 . . . 206 A7
  Thorncombe TA20 . . . 202 E6
Forest Cl
  Christchurch BH23 . . . 93 D1
  Verwood BH24 . . . 45 F4
Forest Edge BH24 . . . 55 C4
Forest Edge Dr BH24 . . . 53 F5
Forest Edge Rd BH20 . . . 142 F7
Forest Gate Cl BH24 . . . 55 B7
Forest Hill BA20 . . . 27 A2
Forest Hills Cl ▌ BH24 . . . 55 F6
Forest Ho ▌ BH1 . . . 122 A3
Forest La
  Corfe Castle BH20 . . . 162 F1
  Verwood BH31 . . . 45 A7
Forestlake Ave BH24 . . . 55 F6
Forest Links Rd BH21 . . . 52 D1
Forest Oak Dr BH25 . . . 95 A5
Fore Store St TA20 . . . 202 A8
Forest Pines BH25 . . . 95 A4
Forest Rd
  Ferndown BH22 . . . 53 B3
  Poole BH13 . . . 121 A2
Forest Rise BH23 . . . 93 D2
Forestside Gdns BH24 . . . 47 E1
Forestside The BH31 . . . 45 F5
Forest View
  Beckley BH25 . . . 94 D5
  Crossways DT2 . . . 137 D6
Forest View Dr BH21 . . . 61 A5
Forest View Dr BH9 . . . 90 A3
Forest Way
  Christchurch BH23 . . . 93 D1
  Ferndown BH21 . . . 61 A5
Forest Wlk BH25 . . . 94 D5
Forge End SP8 . . . 10 D2
Forge La
  East Chinnock BA22 . . . 192 E8
  Verwood BH31 . . . 44 F5
  Zeale SP8 . . . 1 F3
Forsters La DT6 . . . 69 A1
Forsyth Gdns BH10 . . . 89 C1
Fort Cumberland Cl ▌
  BH15 . . . 117 F2
Fortescue Rd
  Bournemouth BH3 . . . 122 A6
  Poole BH12 . . . 120 D6
Forton Cl DT10 . . . 69 E4
Fortress Gn ▌ DT1 . . . 134 E7
FORTUNESWELL DT5 . . . 186 E7
Fortuneswell DT5 . . . 186 E8
Forty Foot Way DT6 . . . 100 B7
Forum Cntr The DT11 . . . 108 A2
Forum Gn ▌ DT1 . . . 134 E7
Forum Gn ▌ DT1 . . . 134 E7
Fosse Cl BA21 . . . 26 F7
Fosse Gn ▌ DT1 . . . 134 E7
Fosse Park Rd BA20 . . . 27 B4
Fossett Way ▌ DT4 . . . 180 B8
Fosse Way ▌ DT4 . . . 180 B8
Foss Orch DT5 . . . 99 A6
Foss Way TA17 . . . 191 C8
Fosters Hill DT9 . . . 196 B5
Fosters Mdws ▌ DT11 . . . 210 C3
Fosters Spring BH16 . . . 84 D2
Foundry Cl DT6 . . . 100 A7
Foundry Knapp BH16 . . . 100 A7
Foundry La DT6 . . . 100 A6
Foundry Sq ▌ BH15 . . . 191 F4
Fountain Cl BH13 . . . 121 B2
Fountain Mead ▌ SP7 . . . 12 F4
Fountains Cl BA21 . . . 26 E7
Fountains Way BH24 . . . 124 B6
Fouracre Cl DT10 . . . 100 D8
Four Acres DT5 . . . 186 E3
Forgates Rd ▌ DT1 . . . 107 E1
Fourth Cliff Wlk DT6 . . . 100 B2
Four Wells Rd BH21 . . . 60 A7
Foxbury BH20 . . . 139 C7
Foxbury Rd BH24 . . . 54 B1
Fox Cl DT6 . . . 69 A1
Foxcote ▌ BH21 . . . 26 E2
Foxcote Gdns BH21 . . . 94 F3
Foxcroft Dr BH21 . . . 60 B5
Foxdale BH23 . . . 91 D1
Foxdale Ct ▌ BH21 . . . 121 E3
Foxes Cl BH31 . . . 45 B5
Foxglove Cl
  Christchurch BH23 . . . 125 C8
  Gillingham SP8 . . . 5 E2
Foxglove Pl BH24 . . . 95 D4
Foxgloves ▌ BH21 . . . 117 D7
Foxglove Way
  Bridport DT6 . . . 100 D3
  Radipole DT3 . . . 152 F2
  Yeovil BA22 . . . 26 C5
Foxhill Cl ▌ BH19 . . . 179 A2
Foxhills BH31 . . . 45 D6
Foxhills Cres BH16 . . . 84 D3
Foxhills Dr BH16 . . . 84 D3
Foxhills Rd BH16 . . . 84 D3
FOXHOLES . . . 120 A6
Foxholes ▌ BH6 . . . 123 F4
Foxholes Rd
  Bournemouth BH6 . . . 123 F4
  Poole BH15 . . . 119 F6
Fox La BA Terr DT10 . . . 35 B1
Fox Mdws ▌ TA18 . . . 191 F5
Foxs Cl DT1 . . . 196 B5

Foxwell La TA18 . . . 192 C7
Foxwood Ave BH23 . . . 124 F5
Foyelbank Way DT5 . . . 181 F3
Foyle Hill SP7 . . . 12 C1
Framerville Rd BH20 . . . 139 E7
FRAMPTON DT2 . . . 73 F3
Frampton Cl BH25 . . . 95 C5
Frampton Pl BH24 . . . 55 C7
Frampton Rd
  Bournemouth BH7 . . . 122 F4
  ▌ Pimperne DT11 . . . 199 D4
Francesca Ct ▌ BH23 . . . 124 E7
Francesca Grange ▌
  BH23 . . . 124 E6
Francesca Lo ▌ BH23 . . . 124 E6
Frances Ct ▌ BH23 . . . 126 B7
Frances Rd BH1 . . . 122 C4
Francis Ct ▌ BH1 . . . 167 D2
Francis Ave BH11 . . . 88 D3
Francis Avenue Ind Est
  BH11 . . . 88 D3
Francis Rd
  Poole BH12 . . . 120 E5
  Weymouth DT4 . . . 167 B2
Francis Wlk DT4 . . . 30 C7
Frankland Cres BH14 . . . 120 C3
Franklin Cl DT4 . . . 167 D1
Franklin Rd
  Bournemouth BH9 . . . 90 A3
  New Milton BH25 . . . 95 C4
  Weymouth DT4 . . . 167 B3
Franklyn Cl BH16 . . . 117 D7
Frankston Rd BH6 . . . 123 C4
Fraser Ave BH14 . . . 166 F1
Fraser Cl BH25 . . . 94 F3
Fraser Rd BH12 . . . 120 F8
Freame Way SP8 . . . 5 D1
Freda Rd BH23 . . . 123 F6
Frederica Rd BH9 . . . 121 E8
Freedom Ave BA21 . . . 27 A6
Freemans Cl BH21 . . . 60 B6
Freemans La BH21 . . . 60 B5
Freemantle Rd DT4 . . . 166 F1
Freesia Cl DT3 . . . 152 D3
Fremington Ct ▌ BH25 . . . 95 B3
French Hill La SP7 . . . 23 F4
French Mill La SP7 . . . 23 F7
French Mill Rise SP7 . . . 12 F1
French Rd BH17 . . . 87 B1
French's Farm Rd BH16 . . . 117 E7
Frensham Cl BH10 . . . 89 E3
Freshwater Cl ▌ DT5 . . . 186 E1
Freshwater Dr BH15 . . . 117 F4
Freshwater Rd BH23 . . . 125 C6
Friars Ave BA21 . . . 26 F6
Friars Cl ▌ BH23 . . . 135 C8
Friars Gate BH23 . . . 125 C6
Friars Moor DT10 . . . 35 C1
Friars Rd BH23 . . . 125 B6
Friars Wlk BH25 . . . 127 A8
Friar Waddon Rd DT3 . . . 151 F8
Friary Hill DT1 . . . 108 A2
Friary La DT1 . . . 108 A2
Friday's Heron BH21 . . . 40 B7
Frinton Ct ▌ BH14 . . . 120 A4
Fritham Gdns BH8 . . . 90 D3
Frizzel's Hill DT10 . . . 196 F4
Frobisher Ave BH12 . . . 88 F1
Frobisher Cl
  Christchurch BH23 . . . 124 F6
  Ringwood BH24 . . . 47 E1
FROGHAM SP6 . . . 43 F7
Frogham Hill SP6 . . . 43 F6
Frog La
  Crewkerne TA18 . . . 192 C5
  Dinnington TA17 . . . 191 B8
  Fordingbridge SP6 . . . 43 A7
  Iwerne Courtney or Shroton
    DT11 . . . 198 F7
  Motcombe SP7 . . . 12 C7
Frogmore La DT2 . . . 71 E8
Frog Rd SP8 . . . 11 B8
Frome Ave BH20 . . . 139 F2
Frome La DT2 . . . 72 F7
Frome Rd BH20 . . . 139 E2
FROME ST QUINTIN DT2 . . . 206 D5
Frome Valley Rd DT1 . . . 107 E2
Frome Valley CE Fst Sch
  DT2 . . . 137 D6
Frome Valley Rd DT2 . . . 137 C6
Frome View
  Bradford Peverell DT2 . . . 107 A6
  Maiden Newton DT2 . . . 73 A8
Front La BH21 . . . 56 D5
Front St
  East Stour SP8 . . . 10 F3
  Portesham DT3 . . . 132 A1
Froom's La BH20 . . . 81 C1
Frost Rd BH11 . . . 88 B4
Froud Way BH21 . . . 85 E4
Froxfield Rd DT11 . . . 212 D5
Fryer Cl BH11 . . . 89 B5
Fryers Copse BH21 . . . 60 C6
Fryers Rd BH21 . . . 53 A8
Frys Cl BH16 . . . 84 C4
Fry's Cl DT3 . . . 150 A8
Fry's La DT2 . . . 75 A7
Fudge Hill DT2 . . . 205 A8
Fulbrooks Cl DT6 . . . 100 C7
Fulbrooks La DT6 . . . 100 C7
Fulcrum Ctr The BH12 . . . 88 C2
Fulmar Rd BH23 . . . 125 A5
Fulwood Ave BH11 . . . 88 E5
Furbers Paddock DT2 . . . 106 E8

Furge Gr BA8 . . . 19 A4
Furge La BA8 . . . 19 A3
Furland Rd ▌ TA18 . . . 191 F4
Furlands BH23 . . . 186 F3
Furlong Ct DT9 . . . 17 B3
Furlong Mews ▌ BH24 . . . 55 B7
Furlong Sh Ctr BH24 . . . 55 B7
Furlongs The DT9 . . . 30 B7
Furlong The BH24 . . . 55 B7
Furnell Rd BH15 . . . 119 D1
FURZEBROOK BH20 . . . 161 A4
Furzebrook Cl BH17 . . . 87 E3
Furzebrook Rd BH20 . . . 161 A4
Furze Croft BH25 . . . 95 A2
FURZEHILL BH21 . . . 50 E1
Furzehill
  Colehill BH21 . . . 59 C8
  Holt BH21 . . . 50 F1
Furze Hill Dr BH14 . . . 120 C1
Furze La BH20 . . . 204 D3
Furzelands BH21 . . . 53 A8
Furze The ▌ BA20 . . . 26 E2
Furzey Rd BH16 . . . 117 D6
Furzy Cl DT3 . . . 168 B7

G

Gablehurst BH16 . . . 118 C7
Gabriel Gn ▌ DT1 . . . 135 B8
Gadbridge Ct ▌ BH21 . . . 121 C2
Gainsborough DT9 . . . 17 C2
Gainsborough Ave BH25 . . . 95 B5
Gainsborough Cl ▌ BH25 . . . 95 B5
Gainsborough Dr DT9 . . . 29 E5
Gainsborough Ho BH25 . . . 127 A6
Gainsborough Rd
  Bournemouth BH7 . . . 122 F7
  St Leonards BH24 . . . 54 A5
Galahad Cl ▌ BA21 . . . 26 E6
Gale Cres DT6 . . . 100 C5
Gales Hill DT2 . . . 207 E2
Gallop's La BH20 . . . 83 C2
Gallop Way BH12 . . . 121 C7
Galloway Rd BH15 . . . 117 F6
Gallows Cnr
  Iwerne Courtney or Shroton
    DT11 . . . 36 F1
  Milton Abbas DT11 . . . 209 D3
Gallows Dr BH22 . . . 61 E1
Gallows Hill
  Arne BH20 . . . 161 C4
  Owermoigne DT2 . . . 155 D6
Gallwey Rd DT4 . . . 180 C7
Galton Ave BH23 . . . 123 F6
GANNETTS DT10 . . . 21 C4
Gannetts Pk BH19 . . . 179 B3
Garden Cl
  Bridport DT6 . . . 100 D7
  Litton Cheney DT2 . . . 103 B2
  New Milton BH25 . . . 95 A1
Garden Ct BH1 . . . 122 D6
Garden Ho ▌ BH1 . . . 122 B3
Gardens Cres BH14 . . . 147 B8
Gardens Cl ▌ BH15 . . . 119 E3
Gardenside ▌ DT1 . . . 97 A7
Garden Terr BH14 . . . 147 B8
Garden Wlk BH22 . . . 61 E7
Gardner Ct BH23 . . . 123 E8
Gardner Rd
  Christchurch BH23 . . . 123 E8
  Ringwood BH24 . . . 55 C6
Garfield Ave
  Bournemouth BH1 . . . 122 D5
  Dorchester DT1 . . . 134 E8
Garfield Cl BH19 . . . 178 B2
Garland Cres DT1 . . . 135 B8
Garland Rd BH15 . . . 119 E1
Garlands La ▌ DT11 . . . 197 D4
Garrett Rd BH20 . . . 26 F3
Garsdale Cl BH11 . . . 89 A6
Garston Hill DT3 . . . 166 C6
Garston Wood (RSPB
  Reserve)★ SP5 . . . 189 B6
Gartells ▌ DT10 . . . 197 A4
Garth Cl BH24 . . . 53 F4
Garth Rd BH9 . . . 90 A1
Gascoigne's La SP7 . . . 23 E8
Gascoyne La DT2 . . . 107 B6
Gas House Hill DT9 . . . 30 C5
Gas La TA17 . . . 191 C7
GASPER BA12 . . . 1 C7
Gasper St BA12 . . . 1 C6
Gassons La DT6 . . . 100 C6
Gate Cl EX13 . . . 202 A3
Gatecombe Cl ▌ DT1 . . . 135 C8
Gatemore Rd DT2 . . . 138 E1
Gateway The BH13 . . . 120 F4
GAUNT'S COMMON BH21 . . . 51 B8
Gaydon Rise BH11 . . . 88 E4
Gazelle Rd BA20 . . . 26 C3
Geneva Ave BH6 . . . 123 D5
Geneva Wk BH6 . . . 123 D5
Gent Cl DT11 . . . 212 C5
George La ▌ TA18 . . . 191 F4
George Rdbt The BH15 . . . 119 C3
Georges Cl DT6 . . . 97 B8
Georges Mews BH21 . . . 85 F7
George Smith Way BA22 . . . 26 C6
George St
  Bridport DT6 . . . 100 C2
  Sherborne DT9 . . . 30 B6
Georgian Cl BH24 . . . 55 C8

Georgian Way BH10 . . . 89 F4
Georgina Cl BH12 . . . 120 C5
Georgina Talbot Ho
  BH12 . . . 121 B8
Gerald Rd BH3 . . . 122 A6
Germaine Cl BH23 . . . 125 F8
Gervis Cres BH14 . . . 120 A4
Gervis Pl BH1 . . . 121 F3
Gervis Rd BH1 . . . 122 B3
Giant's Grave★ DT2 . . . 209 A4
Gibbs Ct ▌ TA18 . . . 191 F5
Gibbs Gn BH16 . . . 84 D2
Gibbs La DT6 . . . 66 C1
Gibbs Marsh Trading Est
  DT10 . . . 20 A4
Gibson Rd BH17 . . . 119 E7
GIDDY GREEN DT11 . . . 139 E1
Giddy Green La BH20 . . . 139 E2
Giddy Green Rd DT11 . . . 139 E2
Giddylake DT11 . . . 59 D6
Giffords La TA18 . . . 192 C5
Gifle View ▌ DT9 . . . 194 D8
Gigg La SP8 . . . 8 E4
Gilbert Cl SP6 . . . 42 D6
Gilbert Rd
  Bournemouth BH8 . . . 122 D6
  Swanage BH19 . . . 179 B2
Giles Cl DT2 . . . 107 A6
Giles's La
  Bishop's Caundle DT9 . . . 196 A7
  Morden BH20 . . . 83 D3
Gillam Rd BH10 . . . 89 D5
Gillett Rd BH12 . . . 121 C7
GILLINGHAM SP8 . . . 5 E1
Gillingham Adult Ed Ctr
  SP8 . . . 5 F1
Gillingham Cl BH9 . . . 90 C4
Gillingham L Ctr SP8 . . . 6 A2
Gillingham Mus★ SP8 . . . 5 F1
Gillingham Prim Sch SP8 . . . 5 F2
Gillingham Rd BH12 . . . 122 B3
Gillingham Sta SP8 . . . 5 F1
Gillion Ct ▌ BH23 . . . 124 E6
Gipsy's Dro DT10 . . . 197 D3
Girdlers Coppice Reserve★
  DT10 . . . 197 E8
Girt La DT2 . . . 205 F7
Giscis DT5 . . . 187 A7
Gladdis Rd BH11 . . . 88 F3
Gladelands Cl BH18 . . . 86 E4
Gladelands Pk BH22 . . . 61 F7
Gladelands Way BH18 . . . 86 E4
Glade The
  Christchurch BH23 . . . 91 E1
  St Leonards BH24 . . . 54 A5
Gladiator Gn ▌ DT1 . . . 134 E7
Gladstone Cl
  Bridport DT6 . . . 100 E7
  Christchurch BH23 . . . 124 D6
  ▌ Radipole DT3 . . . 152 E2
Gladstone Rd
  Bournemouth BH7 . . . 122 F5
  Poole BH12 . . . 120 C5
Gladstone Road E BH7 . . . 122 F5
Gladstone Road W BH1 . . . 122 F5
Glamis Ave BH10 . . . 89 E5
GLANVILLES WOOTTON
  DT9 . . . 195 E2
Glastonbury Ct BA21 . . . 26 F6
Gleadowe Ave BH23 . . . 124 A6
Glebe Cl
  Abbotsbury DT3 . . . 149 C7
  Bridport DT6 . . . 100 D5
  Maiden Newton DT2 . . . 72 F8
  Overcombe/Preston DT3 . . . 169 A8
  ▌ Thornford DT9 . . . 194 D8
  Weymouth DT4 . . . 167 C1
Glebe Ct ▌ DT11 . . . 37 F1
Glebefields DT2 . . . 106 F7
Glebeford Ct DT12 . . . 155 E7
Glebe Gdns SP7 . . . 12 B8
Glebeland Cl DT2 . . . 136 A7
Glebeland Ct DT6 . . . 65 F7
Glebelands BH16 . . . 84 C1
Glebe The
  ▌ Durweston DT11 . . . 198 E3
  Iwerne Courtney or Shroton
    DT11 . . . 198 F7
  ▌ Iwerne Minster DT11 . . . 37 F1
Glebe Way DT2 . . . 136 C3
Glenair Ave BH14 . . . 120 A3
Glenair Cres BH14 . . . 120 A3
Glenair Rd BH14 . . . 120 A3
Glenavon BH25 . . . 95 C2
Glenavon Rd BH23 . . . 93 F1
Glen Cl BH25 . . . 126 D8
Glencoe
  Bournemouth BH7 . . . 122 F7
  Poole BH12 . . . 120 D5
Glendale Ave BH22 . . . 61 E6
Glendale Cl
  Christchurch BH23 . . . 91 D3
  Wimborne Minster BH21 . . . 59 C5
Glendale Rd BH6 . . . 123 D3
Glendinning Ave DT4 . . . 167 D5
Glendon Ave BH10 . . . 89 C6
Glendrive BH25 . . . 126 C8
Gleneagles
  Christchurch BH23 . . . 123 F6
  Poole BH12 . . . 121 B2
Gleneagles Ave BH14 . . . 120 D2
Gleneagles Cl BH22 . . . 61 F6

Glenferness Ave BH4 121 D5
Glen Fern Rd BH1 122 A3
Glengariff Rd BH14 120 C2
Glengarry BH25 95 C2
Glengarry Way BH23 125 C6
Glenives Cl BH24 54 B4
Glenmeadows Dr BH10 89 B5
Glenmoor Cl BH10 89 D1
Glenmoor Gdns 2 BH10 89 D1
Glenmoor Rd
Bournemouth BH9 121 E8
Ferndown BH22 61 D3
Glenmoor Sch for Girls BH10 89 D1
Glenmore Rd DT4 167 B4
Glenmount Dr BH14 120 B4
Glennie Way DT3 166 D4
Glen Rd
Bournemouth BH5 122 F4
Poole BH14 120 B4
Glenroyd Gdns BH6 123 E4
Glenside BH23, BH25 126 B7
Glen Spey BH25 95 D2
Glen The
Poole BH12 120 D6
Poole, Canford Cliffs BH13 147 E8
Glenthorne Ave BA21 27 D7
Glenville Cl BH23 94 B2
Glenville Gdns BH10 89 C2
Glenville Rd
Bournemouth BH10 89 C2
Walkford BH23 94 B2
Yeovil BA21 27 F6
Glenwood Cl BH22 53 A2
Glenwood La BH22 53 A2
Glenwood Rd
Ferndown BH22 53 A2
Verwood BH31 45 A5
Glenwood Way BH22 53 A2
Glissons BH22 61 A2
Globe Cl 3 BH19 178 F2
Globe La 16 BH15 119 C2
Globe Orch TA18 192 C6
Gloucester Cl DT3 166 E3
Gloucester Mews DT4 167 D3
Gloucester Rd
Bournemouth BH7 122 F5
3 Dorchester DT1 107 E1
Poole BH12 120 E5
Gloucester St DT4 167 D3
Glovers Cl 2 DT9 17 D2
Glovers Walk Sh Ctr BA20 27 E4
Glovers Wlk 16 BA20 27 D4
Glue Hill DT10 197 C8
Glyde Path Rd DT1 108 A2
Glyn Pl SP7 24 D6
Glynville Cl BH21 60 A7
Glynville Ct BH21 60 A7
Glynville Rd BH21 60 A7
GOATHILL DT9 31 D7
Goathill Rd
Goathill DT9 31 D6
Milborne Port DT9 17 C1
Goathorn Cl BH16 117 F4
Godlingston Manor★ BH19 178 E5
Godmanston Cl BH17 88 A1
GODMANSTONE DT2 75 A7
GOD'S BLESSING GREEN BH21 51 C3
God's Blessing La BH21 51 B3
Godshill Cl BH8 90 D3
GODWINSCROFT 93 C5
Goldcrest Cl DT3 152 C4
Goldcroft BA21 27 D5
Goldcroft Ave DT4 167 C5
Goldcroft Rd DT4 167 C5
Golden Gates BH13 147 B3
Golden Hill DT10 32 F2
Goldenleas Ct BH11 88 D3
Goldenleas Dr BH11 88 D3
Golden Sands BH13 147 B3
Goldenstones Pools & L Ctr BA20 27 C3
Goldfinch Cl BH25 94 F2
Goldfinch Gate SP8 11 B8
Goldfinch Rd BH17 118 E8
GOLD HILL DT11 198 B8
Gold Hill
Child Okeford DT11 198 B8
Shaftesbury SP7 12 E2
Gold Hill Gall★ SP7 12 E2
Golding's La DT9 17 C1
Gold St DT10 33 C8
Golf Links Rd
Broadstone BH18 87 B5
Ferndown BH22 61 E4
Goliath Rd BH15 117 F2
Good Rd BH12 120 C7
Goodwin's La BH20 83 D2
Gooseacre La BA22 26 C1
Gooseberry La 7 BH24 55 B7
Goose Hill DT3 149 F7
Gordon Cres 1 DT4 166 F2
Gordon Ct 7 BH4 121 C4
Gordon Mount BH23 126 B8
Gordon Rd
Bournemouth BH1 122 D4
Christchurch BH23 126 A8
Poole BH12 121 A5
6 Swanage BH19 179 A2
Wimborne Minster BH21 59 E4
Yeovil BA21 27 E6
Gordon Road S BH12 121 A5
Gordon's La DT9 195 A8
Gordon Way BH23 92 D1
GORE DT9 14 E3
Gore Cross DT6 68 F2
Gore Cross Bsns Pk DT6 68 E2
Gore Cross Way 5 DT6 68 F1
Gore Fields La BH16 116 B5
Gore Grange BH25 94 F2
Gore Hill BH20 142 F7
Gore La DT6 68 F2
Gore Rd BH25 94 E2
Gore Road Ind Est BH25 94 F2
Gorey Rd BH12 88 D1
Gorleston Rd BH12 120 F5
Gorley Lynch SP6 43 F4
Gorley Rd BH24 47 E1
Gorse Cl
New Milton BH25 95 D4
St Leonards BH24 53 F4
Gorsecliff Ct 7 BH5 122 D4
Gorsecliff Rd BH10 89 D1
Gorsefield Rd BH25 95 B4
Gorse Hill Cl BH15 119 F5
Gorse Hill Cres BH15 119 E5
Gorse Hill Rd BH15 119 F5
Gorse Knoll Dr BH31 45 A7
Gorse La BH16 117 F7
Gorseland Ct BH22 61 E3
Gorse Rd
Corfe Mullen BH21 86 C5
Poole BH21 85 E5
Gort Rd
Bournemouth BH11 89 B3
Poole BH17 87 A1
Gosling Cl BH17 119 F7
Goss Pl DT4 167 C4
GOTHAM BH21 41 A3
Gough Cl 11 TA16 191 F7
Gough Cres BH17 87 B2
Goughs Cl DT10 35 A1
Gould's Hill
Upwey DT3 152 A7
Winterborne St Martin DT2 133 F3
Goulds Hill Cl
9 Dorchester DT1 134 E7
Upwey DT3 152 A7
Gouzeaucourt Rd BH20 139 D7
Gover Cl BH20 143 B1
Gower Rd SP7 13 A2
Grace Darling Ho BH15 119 D1
Grafton Ave DT4 167 A6
Grafton Cl
Bournemouth BH3 122 A7
Christchurch BH23 124 D6
Grafton Rd BH3 122 A6
Grammar School La BH21 59 B4
Granby Cl DT4 166 F3
Granby Ind Est DT4 166 E4
Granby Rd BH9 90 A4
Granby Way DT4 167 A5
Grand Ave BH6 123 C4
Grand Par 13 BH15 119 B1
GRANGE BH21 50 F2
Grange BH21 50 E1
Grange Comp Sch The BH23 124 E7
Grangecroft Rd 3 DT5 186 E3
Grange Ct 5 BH1 122 B3
GRANGE ESTATE 62 F8
Grange Gdns BH12 120 E8
Grange Hill BH20 160 C1
Grange La DT8 203 D5
Grange Pk 1 DT9 194 D8
Grange Rd
Bournemouth BH6 123 D3
Broadstone BH18 87 A4
Christchurch BH23 125 B7
Church Knowle BH20 160 D4
Radipole DT4 167 E5
St Leonards BH24 53 F2
Grange Road Bsns Ctr BH23 125 A7
Grangewood Hall BH21 59 D5
Grans Barrow (Long Barrow)★ SP6 190 E6
Grantham Rd BH1 122 E5
Grantley Rd 3 BH5 122 F4
Grant's Ave BH1 122 D6
Grants Cl BH1 122 E6
Granville Gdns 2 SP7 12 F3
Granville Pl 9 BH1 121 F3
Granville Rd
Bournemouth BH5 123 A5
Poole BH12 120 B5
Weymouth DT4 167 C2
Granville Way DT9 30 C8
Grasmere Cl BH23 91 D3
Grasmere Gdns BH25 95 B5
Grasmere Rd
Bournemouth BH5 123 A4
Poole BH13 147 B3
Radipole DT3 167 C6
Grass Royal BA21 27 E6
Grass Royal Jun Sch BA21 27 E6
Gravel Hill BH17, BH18, BH21 87 D5
Gravel La
Charlton Marshall DT11 211 C7
Ringwood BH24 55 C8
Gray Cl BH17 119 F8
Graycot Cl BH10 89 C5
Grays DT4 167 B6
Grays Cl SP7 12 B8
Great Corner BA21 26 E6
Great Cranford St 2 DT1 107 B2
Great Down La DT10 21 B4
Great Gd 3 SP7 13 A4
Great George St DT4 167 D3
Great Head La DT2 206 F7
Great Hill BA9 1 B3
Great La SP7 12 F2
Great Owens Dr BH20 142 D6
Great Pit La BA22 15 B5
Great Western Ind Ctr 5 DT1 107 F1
Great Western Rd DT1 108 A1
Great Western Terr
Radipole DT4 167 D6
Yeovil BA21 27 F5
Greaves Cl BH10 89 C3
Grebe Cl
Broadstone BH17 118 E8
2 Chickerell DT3 166 D5
Christchurch BH23 125 A6
Greenacre
Barton on Sea BH25 127 A8
Charminster DT2 107 E6
Greenacre Cl BH16 117 E6
Greenacres
32 Bournemouth BH4 121 C3
Puddletown DT2 78 A1
Green Acres BH23 124 F7
Greenacres Cl BH10 89 E6
Green Acres Cl BH24 54 F5
Green Bottom BH21 60 A7
Green Cl
Bere Regis BH20 81 B1
Bradpole DT6 100 F8
Charlton Marshall DT11 211 D6
Poole BH15 119 D1
Sturminster Newton DT10 35 C2
Greenclose La BH21 59 D4
Green Dr SP6 42 D6
Greenfield Gdns BH25 127 B8
Greenfield Rd
3 Charlton Marshall DT11 211 D6
Poole BH15 119 E7
Greenfields 1 BH12 120 F7
Greenfinch Cl BH17 86 F1
Greenfinch Wlk BH24 55 E5
Greenford CE Prim Sch DT2 72 E8
Greenford La
Compton Valence DT2 104 C8
Maiden Newton DT2 72 D4
Green Gdns BH15 119 D1
GREENHAM DT8 203 C7
Greenham La TA18 203 B7
Greenham Yd TA18 203 B7
Greenhayes
Broadstone BH18 87 C2
Charmouth DT6 96 F7
2 Okeford Fitzpaine DT11 197 F5
Greenhays Rise BH21 59 C5
Greenhill
Blandford Forum DT11 212 D5
Radipole DT4 167 E5
Sherborne DT9 30 B6
Greenhill Cl BH21 59 D6
Greenhill Down Reserve★ DT11 209 E6
Greenhill La BH21 59 D6
Greenhill Rd
Wimborne Minster BH21 59 D6
Yeovil BA21 27 E7
Greenhill Terr 4 DT5 186 F8
Green La
Ashmore SP5 39 C8
Barton on Sea BH25 127 B8
Bournemouth BH10 89 D3
Bridport DT6 100 E5
Chickerell DT3 166 E5
Crossways DT2 137 D6
East Chinnock BA22 192 E8
Ferndown BH22 61 A1
Hooke DT8 205 C2
Kington Magna SP8 9 C3
Ossemsley BH25 94 E8
Ringwood BH24 55 D3
Salisbury SP5 188 E3
Sixpenny Handley SP5 188 E3
Stour Provost SP7 22 D4
Sturminster Marshall BH21 56 B5
Tatworth & Forton TA20 202 A7
West Coker BA22 193 B8
Weymouth DT4 180 E8
Green Loaning BH23 124 F5
Green Mead BA21 26 E6
Green Pit Knapp DT6 65 B2
Green Pk BH1 122 D3
Green Rd
Bournemouth BH9 122 A8
Poole BH15 119 D1
Greens Cross Dr 4 DT8 204 C4
Greenside Ct BH25 127 B6
Greensleeves Ave BH18 87 B6
Greensome Dr BH22 61 F6
Green St TA17 191 D7
Green The
Burton BH23 92 D2
3 Hazelbury Bryan DT10 197 A4
Mappowder DT10 196 E1
Puddletown DT2 78 B1
Sherborne DT9 30 B6
Stratton DT2 106 D8
Greenway
10 Child Okeford DT11 198 C7
Lyme Regis DT7 96 A5
Greenway Cl DT3 167 C8
Greenway Cres 2 BH16 117 C7
Greenway Rd DT3 152 C1
Greenways
Christchurch BH23 125 F8
Greenways continued
Dorchester DT2 209 C1
Easton/Weston DT5 186 F3
Greenways Ave BH8 90 C3
Greenways Ct BH22 61 E3
Greenwood Ave
Ferndown BH22 61 E6
Poole BH14 147 C8
Greenwood Copse BH24 54 B4
Greenwood Rd
Bournemouth BH9 121 E8
Yeovil BA21 26 F7
Greenwoods 6 BH25 95 B1
Greenwood Way BH24 54 B4
Grenfell Rd BH9 89 F3
Grenville Cl BH24 47 E1
Grenville Ct
11 Bournemouth BH4 121 D4
15 Poole BH15 119 C2
Grenville Rd BH21 59 D4
Gresham Rd BH9 90 B1
Grexy Cross DT2 205 E7
Greycot Cl BH21 53 A8
Greyhound Yd DT2 207 A2
Grey Mare & Her Colts The (Long Barrow)★ DT3 131 C3
Greys Rd 7 TA16 191 F7
Greystoke Ave BH11 88 F5
Greystones Cl DT2 137 D6
Gribb View TA20 202 E6
Griffin Ct BH21 59 D3
Griffiths Gdns BH10 89 B5
Grim's Ditch★ SP5 189 D7
Grimsey La SP8 4 F8
GRIMSTONE DT2 74 B1
Grosvenor Cl BH24 53 F5
Grosvenor Cres DT1 135 A8
Grosvenor Ct
8 Bournemouth BH1 122 B3
2 Bournemouth, Springbourne BH1 122 D4
Christchurch BH23 126 B8
Grosvenor Gdns BH1 122 E4
Grosvenor Ho 6 BH4 121 C3
Grosvenor Lo 8 BH4 121 C3
Grosvenor Pines 13 BH4 121 C3
Grosvenor Rd
Bournemouth BH4 121 C3
Dorchester DT1 135 A8
Easton/Weston DT5 186 F4
Radipole DT4 167 D6
Shaftesbury SP7 12 F4
Stalbridge DT10 33 C8
Swanage BH19 179 C1
GROVE DT5 187 B6
Grove Ave
Radipole DT4 167 D6
Yeovil BA20 27 B5
Grove Gdns BH25 127 A7
Grove Inf Sch DT5 187 C6
Grove La
Abbotsbury DT3 149 B6
Bothenhampton DT6 101 B6
Portesham DT3 150 E5
Stalbridge DT10 33 C8
Grove Lane Cl DT10 33 C8
Groveley Bsns Ctr BH23 124 E6
Groveley Rd
Bournemouth BH4 121 B2
Christchurch BH23 124 E6
Grovely Ave BH5 122 F3
Grove Mans 10 BH1 122 B3
Grove Orch 3 DT6 128 B8
Grove Rd
Barton on Sea BH25 127 A7
Bournemouth BH1 122 B3
Burton Bradstock DT6 128 B8
Easton/Weston DT5 187 B5
Poole BH12 120 B6
Wimborne Minster BH21 59 D4
Grove Road E BH23 124 A8
Grove Road W BH23 123 F8
Grove The
Bournemouth BH9 89 F3
Christchurch BH23 91 E1
Dorchester DT1 107 F2
Ferndown BH22 61 C4
Verwood BH31 45 C5
Grove Trading Est DT1 107 F3
Grower Gdns BH11 89 A4
Grugs La BH21 40 A7
Gryphon L Ctr DT9 30 C8
Gryphon Sch The DT9 30 B8
Guard Ave BA22 26 D6
Guernsey Rd BH12 88 D1
Guernsey St 2 DT5 186 F7
Guest Ave BH12 121 A6
Guest Cl BH12 121 A6
Guest Rd BH16 117 D7
Guildford Ct 2 BH4 121 C4
Guildhall Ct BH15 119 B2
Guildhill Rd BH6 123 E4
Guinevere Cl BA21 26 F7
Gulliver Cl BH14 147 C8
Gulliver Ct 1 BH21 59 C5
Gullivers Orch DT6 101 D4
Gulway Mead 7 TA20 202 A8
Gundry La DT6 100 C6
Gundry Moor Trading Est BH21 53 B6
Gundry Rd DT6 100 F7
Gunners La BA22 26 C5
Gunn La 3 DT11 198 B5
Gunville Cres BH9 90 B3
Gunville Down Rd DT11 199 F4
Gunville La
East Coker BA22 193 D8
Hermitage DT2 195 C2
Gunville Rd DT11 199 F4
Gurjun Cl 2 BH16 117 C8
Gurkha Rd DT11 212 E6
Gurney Rd BH21 86 E6
GUSSAGE ALL SAINTS BH21 201 A6
Gussage Rd BH12 120 F8
GUSSAGE ST ANDREW DT11 188 E1
GUSSAGE ST MICHAEL BH21 200 F6
GUY'S MARSH SP7 23 B6
Gwenlyn Rd BH16 117 E6
Gwynne Rd BH12 120 E5
Gyllas Way SP8 5 F4
Gypshayes BH19 178 B2
Gypsy La
Easton/Weston DT5 186 F3
Lytchett Matravers BH16 84 A2
Ringwood BH24 55 D8
2 Weymouth DT4 167 C2

H

Haarlem Mews BH23 124 D7
Hackney DT2 205 A7
Hadden Rd BH8 122 D8
HADDON HILL 90 E1
Haddon La DT10 19 E2
Haddons Dr BH21 52 F7
Hadley Way BH18 86 E3
Hadow Rd BH10 89 C3
Hadrian Cl BH22 61 D2
Hadrian Way BH21 86 E8
Hahnemann Rd BH2 121 E2
Haig Ave BH13 120 E1
Haimes La SP7 12 E3
Hainault Dr BH31 45 C6
Haines La DT8 203 A5
HAINS DT10 20 F4
Hains La DT10 20 E5
Haking Rd BH23 124 D7
Halcyon Ct BH15 119 C6
HALE BA9 4 A3
Hale Ave BH25 95 B2
Hale Gdns BH25 95 B2
Hale La BA9 4 A3
Hales Mdw BA21 14 A3
Halewood Way BH23 123 F8
Half Acres DT9 30 A5
Half Hide Down SP5 188 B3
Half Moon St DT9 30 B5
Halfpenny La SP5 39 C7
Halifax Way BH23 125 B7
Hallet Ct DT7 96 B6
Hallet Gdns BA20 27 C4
Hall Rd BH11 88 F3
Halls Cnr BH16 84 C1
Halls Rd BH16 84 B1
Hall & Woodhouse Brewery Visitor Ctr★ DT11 212 D2
Halsey Gn DT2 196 B3
HALSTOCK BA22 193 C3
Halstock Cl DT3 153 C2
Halstock Cres BH17 87 D2
Halter Path BH15 118 E3
Halter Rise BH21 60 C6
Halton Cl BH23 93 B8
Halves Cotts BH20 177 A7
Halves La BA22 193 B8
Hambledon Cl
Blandford Forum DT11 212 E4
Todber DT10 21 D4
Hambledon Gdns
Blandford Forum DT11 212 E4
Bournemouth BH6 123 C6
Hambledon Hill National Nature Reserve★ DT11 198 D7
Hambledon Rd
Bournemouth BH7 123 B7
Bournemouth, West Southbourne BH6 123 C6
Hambledon View DT10 35 C2
Hamble Rd BH15 120 A6
Hamblin Way BH8 90 E2
Hambro Rd DT5 186 F7
HAM COMMON SP8 6 C1
Ham Common Nature Reserve★ BH15 117 E2
Hamcroft DT5 186 F4
Hamilton Bsns Pk BH25 94 E2
Hamilton Cl
Bournemouth BH1 122 D5
Christchurch BH23 124 F4
Hamworthy BH15 118 E2
Radipole DT3 152 E2
Hamilton Cres BH15 118 E2
Hamilton Ct
1 Bournemouth BH8 122 B5
1 Wimborne Minster BH21 59 B5
Hamilton Mews BH23 93 B8
Hamilton Rd
Bournemouth BH1 122 D4
Corfe Mullen BH21 86 E5
Hamworthy BH15 118 E2
Hamilton Way BH25 94 E2
Ham La
1 Gillingham SP8 6 B1
Hampreston BH21 60 E3
Marnhull DT10 20 D4
Trent DT9 15 A2
Wimborne Minster BH21 60 C5
Hamlands DT2 105 E1
HAMLET DT9 194 D3
Ham Mdw DT10 20 D4
Hammett Cl DT2 79 D1
Hammond Ave DT4 167 A6

Hammonds Mead DT6...... 97 A7
Hammond St DT10 .....196 E1
HAMMOON DT10......... 36 A4
Hampden La BH6....... 123 B5
HAMPRESTON 60 E2
Hampreston CE Fst Sch BH21.................60 E3
Hampshire CI BH23.....91 F2
Hampshire Ct 3 BH21.. 121 F3
Hampshire Hatches La BH24.................55 B4
Hampshire Ho 2 BH2... 121 F3
Hampshire Rd DT4.....166 F4
Hampton DT3.........132 A1
Hampton CI 8 BA22...193 F8
Hampton CI 5 BH2....121 D4
Hampton Dr BH24.......47 D1
HAMWORTHY BH15.......60 F1
Hamworthy Fst Sch BH15................118 F1
Hamworthy Lodge BH15.118 F2
Hamworthy Mid Sch BH15................118 F1
Hamworthy Sta BH15...117 F4
Hanbury Rd 7 BH19 ...179 A2
Handley Ct BH24.......55 B7
Handley Lodge 3 BH12.120 F7
Hands La DT3..........149 B7
HANFORD DT11.........198 D6
Hanford Sch DT11.....198 D6
Hanham Ct BH12.......121 B8
Hanham Rd
 Poole BH21...........85 F5
 Wimborne Minster BH21..59 C5
Hankinson Rd BH9.....122 A8
Hannam CI BH11.......89 A4
Hannam's CI BH16......84 D3
Hannington PI BH7....123 A5
Hannington Rd BH7....123 A5
Hanover CI DT10......35 A2
Hanover Ct DT11......212 C4
Hanover Gn BH17.....119 F7
Hanover Ho BH15.....119 D3
Hanover La SP8.........5 D1
Hanover Rd DT4......167 D5
HAPPY BOTTOM.......58 F1
Happy Island Way DT6.100 F7
Harbeck Rd BH8........90 C3
Harbour CI BH13......147 D6
Harbour Cres BH23...124 E5
Harbour Ct
 Barton on Sea BH25...124 E6
 Christchurch BH23....124 E6
 Poole BH13..........147 E6
Harbour Hill DT3....166 F8
Harbour Hill Cres BH15.119 D3
Harbour Hill Rd BH15..119 D3
Harbour Hospl (Private) The BH15...............119 D3
Harbour Lights BH15..119 D3
Harbour Prospect BH14.147 C8
Harbour Rd
 Bournemouth BH6....124 A3
 Sherborne DT9........30 C3
Harbour View CI BH14..120 A3
Harbour View Ct 3 BH23..124 E5
Harbour View Rd
 Fortuneswell DT5....186 F8
 Poole BH14..........120 A5
Harbour Watch BH14...147 C7
Harbour Way DT9......30 B7
HARBRIDGE BH24.......43 B1
Harbridge Dro BH24....42 A3
HARBRIDGE GREEN BH24..43 A2
HARCOMBE BOTTOM DT7..64 A4
Harcombe Ct BH7.......87 E3
Harcombe Rd DT7.......64 A3
Harcourt Mews 6 BH5...3 A5
Harcourt Rd BH5......123 A5
Hardings House La DT9..29 F8
Harding's La SP8.......6 A1
HARDINGTON MANDEVILLE BA22................193 A6
HARDINGTON MOOR BA22................193 A7
Hardwick St DT4......167 E4
Hardy Ave DT4........167 B2
Hardy CI
 2 Beaminster DT8...204 C4
 Ferndown BH22.......53 B1
 Marnhull DT10.......21 A3
 Martinstown DT2.....133 D6
 New Milton BH25......94 F3
Hardy Cres
 Stalbridge DT10......33 D8
 Wimborne Minster BH21..59 B7
Hardy Ct 2 TA18.....191 F4
Hardy Monument* DT2..132 C4
Hardy Rd
 Bridport DT6........100 E7
 Ferndown BH22.......53 B1
 Poole BH14..........120 D4
 Wareham BH20.......142 D2
Hardy's Cottage* DT2..109 B5
Hardy's La DT8.......203 D6
Hare La
 Cranborne BH21......40 F5
 New Milton BH25, SO41..95 E3
Hares Gn BH7........123 A8
Harewood Ave BH7....123 A6
Harewood Cres BH7...122 F6
Harewood Gdns BH7...122 F7
Harewood PI BH7.....123 B6
Harewood Rd DT1....107 C3
Harford Rd BH12.....120 C8
Hargrove La DT10......33 F4
Harkwood Dr BH15....118 E4

Harland Rd BH6......124 A3
Harleston Villas 5 BH21..59 D4
Harley Gap BH21....201 B8
Harley La BH21......201 A5
HARMAN'S CROSS BH20..177 F6
Harman's Cross Sta* BH19...............177 E5
Harness Rd BH21......60 B6
Harper Rd 2 TA18...191 F4
Harpitts La SP8........9 E4
Harpway La BH23......92 C6
Harraby Gn BH18.......87 A3
Harrier Dr BH21.......59 D2
Harriers CI BH23.....125 D8
Harrington Ct BH23..125 F7
Harrison Ave BH1.....122 D6
Harrison CI BH23.....125 D8
Harrison Way BH22....53 A3
Harris Way BH25.......95 B6
Harrow CI BH23........93 B7
Harrow Rd BH23.......93 B6
Harry Barrow CI 1 BH24..55 C6
Harry Lodge's La SP8...5 A1
Harry Paye Ct BH14...119 E4
Hart CI BH21..........59 D2
Hartfoot CI DT2......209 B5
Hartfoot La DT2......209 B5
HARTGROVE SP7.........22 F1
Hartland Rd BH6.....123 D7
Hartland Moor National Nature Reserve* BH20.161 E2
Hartlebury Terr 2 DT4.167 D2
Hartley St DT2.......195 B1
Hartmoor Gdns BH10...89 D1
Hartmoor Hill SP8....175 D5
Hartnell Ct BH21......85 F5
Hartsbourne Dr BH7..123 B8
Hart's La DT2.........51 C3
Harvey Rd
 Bournemouth BH5...123 A5
 Oakley BH21..........87 E8
Harveys CI DT2.......193 A8
Harwell Rd BH17.....119 D7
Harwood CI BH25......94 F3
HASELBURY PLUCKNETT TA18...............192 C6
Haselbury Plucknett CE Fst Sch TA18............192 C5
Haskells Rd BH12....120 B7
Haslemere Ave BH23..126 A8
Haslemere PI BH23...126 A8
Hasler Rd BH17........87 D2
Haslop Rd BH7.........60 A7
Hastings Rd
 Bournemouth BH8.....90 F2
 Poole BH17...........87 B2
Hatch Pond Nature Reserve* BH17......119 C8
Hatch Pond Rd BH17..119 C8
Hatfield Ct BH21......94 E3
Hatfield Gdns BH7...123 B8
Hathaway Rd BH1.....123 D4
Hatherden Ave BH14..119 F5
Hathermead Gdns BA21..247 F7
Havelins DT11.......198 E4
Havelock Rd BH1......90 A1
Havelock Way BH23....93 D2
Haven Cotts BH23....125 A4
Haven Ct BH13.......147 B3
Haven Gdns BH25......95 B2
Havenhurst BH13.....147 E6
Haven Rd
 Poole BH13..........147 E7
 Poole BH15...........85 E6
Haverstock Rd BH9.....90 B2
Haviland Mews BH7...122 F5
Haviland Rd
 Bournemouth BH7....122 F5
 Ferndown BH22.......61 A7
Haviland Road E BH1..122 F5
Haviland Road W BH1..122 F5
Hawden Rd BH11.....202 B3
HAWKCHURCH EX13....202 B3
Hawkchurch CE Prim Sch EX13...............202 A3
Hawkchurch Gdns BH17..87 C2
Hawkchurch Rd EX13..202 B3
Hawk CI BH21.........60 A7
Hawkcombe La SP7.....23 E1
Hawker's La SP7......59 F8
Hawkesdene SP7.......12 F1
Hawkesdene La SP7....12 F1
Hawkesworth CI DT3..153 B3
Hawkins Rd BH24......47 E1
Hawkins Rd BH11.....88 F1
Hawkins Way BA21.....26 E6
Hawkmoor Hill EX13..202 E2
Hawkwood Rd BH1, BH5..122 F4
Haworth CI BH23......92 A1
Hawthorn Ave SP8.....5 E2
Hawthorn CI
 5 Dorchester DT1...107 E2
 New Milton BH25......95 C4
 Radipole DT4........167 A6
 1 Shaftesbury SP7...13 A4
Hawthorn Dr BH17.....86 F1
Hawthorne CI 18 TA18.191 F5
Hawthorne Rd DT1....107 E2
Hawthorn Rd
 Bournemouth BH9....121 D8
 Burton BH23.........92 E4
 Charminster DT2.....75 D2
 Yeovil BA21..........27 F7
Hawthorns The
 Christchurch BH23...124 F6
 Stalbridge DT10......33 E7
Haxen La TA17.......191 A8

Haycock Way 2 BH21...56 D4
Haycombe 4 DT11.....198 E3
Haycrafts La BH19....177 E3
HAYDON DT9...........31 C4
Haydon Hill CI DT2...107 D7
Haydon La
 Frome St Quintin DT2..206 D7
 Lydlinch DT10.......197 A6
Haydon Rd BH13......121 B1
Haye CI DT7...........96 A6
Haye Gdns DT7........96 A6
Haye La DT7...........96 A6
Hayes Ave BH7.......122 E6
Hayes CI BH21........60 A4
Hayes La BH21.........60 B5
Hayes The DT8.......203 E5
Hayeswood Fst Sch BH21..60 B6
Hayeswood Rd BH21....60 A6
Haylands DT5........186 F3
Haymoor Ave BH7....167 F8
HAYMOOR BOTTOM......87 F1
Haymoor Mid Sch BH17..87 E1
Haymoor Rd BH11.....120 A7
Haynes Ave BH15.....119 D3
Haysoms CI BH5.......95 B1
Hayters Way SP6......42 C6
HAYTHORNE.........201 F2
Hayward Cres BH31....45 A5
Hayward La DT11.....198 B7
Haywards Ave DT3....167 D7
Haywards Farm CI BH31..45 A5
Haywards La
 Child Okeford DT11..198 C7
 Corfe Mullen BH21....85 E7
Hayward Way BH31.....44 F5
HAZELBURY BRYAN.....196 F3
Hazelbury Bryan Com Prim Sch DT10............197 A3
Hazel CI
 Alderholt SP6........42 C5
 Christchurch BH23....93 C1
Hazel Ct
 Bournemouth BH9.....90 C4
 1 New Milton BH25...95 B1
Hazeldown Ave DT3...167 A8
Hazel Dr
 Ferndown BH22.......61 D8
 2 Overcombe/Preston DT3...............153 B2
Hazel La DT2........129 E3
Hazell Ave BH10.......89 B2
Hazelton CI BH21....123 A8
Hazel View 11 TA18...191 F5
Hazelwood Dr BH31....45 D4
Hazlebury Rd BH17...119 A7
Hazlemere Dr BH24....54 A3
Hazzard's Hill BA12....3 B5
Headinglea 8 BH13...121 B3
Head La SP8...........10 D3
Headland CI 3 DT5...186 F1
Headlands Bsns Pk BH24..47 C2
Headless Cross BH10...89 D5
Heads Farm CI BH10...89 E5
Head's La BH10........89 E4
Headstock Rd TA20...202 F2
Headswell Ave BH10...89 E4
Headswell Cres BH10..89 E4
Headswell Gdns BH10..89 E4
Heanor CI BH10.......89 E5
Heath Ave BH15......119 D6
Heath CI
 Bovington Camp BH20..139 C7
 Wimborne Minster BH21..60 B7
Heathcote CI DT10...108 B1
Heathcote Ct 2 BH7..122 F4
Heathcote Rd BH5, BH7..122 F4
Heatherbank Rd BH4..121 C3
Heatherbrae La BH16..117 E6
Heather CI
 Bournemouth BH8.....90 D4
 Corfe Mullen BH21....86 E6
 St Leonards BH24.....54 A3
 Walkford BH23........94 A3
Heatherdell BH16.....117 D6
Heatherdown Rd BH22..53 C1
Heatherdown Way BH22..53 C1
Heather Dr BH21.......61 D7
Heather Fields 2 SP8...5 F4
Heatherlands Fst Sch BH12...............120 E5
Heatherlands Rise BH12..120 D5
Heatherlea Rd BH6...123 D4
Heather Lo 1 BH25....95 A3
Heather Rd
 Bournemouth BH10...89 D3
 Yeovil BA21..........27 E7
Heatherside BH19....164 C1
Heather View Rd BH12..120 D7
Heather Way
 Ferndown BH22.......61 D7
 Poole BH16...........26 C5
Heath Farm CI BH22...61 C3
Heath Farm La BH22...61 C3
Heath Farm Way BH22..61 C3
Heathfield Ave BH12..121 A8
Heathfield Pk DT5...137 D5
Heathfield Rd BH22...53 C1
Heathfields Way SP7..128 F7
Heath Gate BH21......53 B1
Heath Green Rd BH19..164 B1
Heathland CI DT7....137 D5
Heathlands Ave BH22..61 D2

Heathlands CI
 Burton BH23.........92 C3
 Verwood BH31........45 C6
Heathlands Prim Sch BH11...............89 A3
Heath Rd
 Hordle SO41.........95 F3
 St Leonards BH24.....53 F4
 Walkford BH23.......94 B1
Heathwood Ave BH25..126 E8
Heathwood Rd
 Bournemouth BH9....121 E8
 Weymouth DT4.......167 B4
Heaton CI BH25......126 F8
Heaton Rd BH10.......89 B2
Heavens DOOR.......15 B7
Heavytree Rd BH14..120 B4
Heber's La TA17.....191 A5
Heckford Rd
 Poole BH15..........119 D4
 Poole BH15...........85 E5
Hectors Way DT11...212 C1
Hector's Way DT11...212 C1
Heddington Dr DT11..212 C2
Hedgerley BH21.......127 B8
Heights App BH16....117 E7
Heights Rd BH16.....117 E8
Helena Rd BA20.......26 F1
Helena Rd 2 DT4.....167 E2
Helic Ho BH2..........59 C5
Hell Cnr DT2.........194 D1
Hell La DT6..........199 D7
Hell Stone (Long Barrow)* DT3...............132 A2
Helston CI DT3.......132 A1
Helyar Rd BH8........90 F2
Hembury Rd DT2......102 C7
Hemlet's CI DT6.......68 F1
Hemsbach Ct 1 BH20..142 E3
HEMSWORTH BH21......49 C8
Henbest CI BH21.......60 C5
HENBURY BH21.........56 E1
Henbury CI
 Corfe Mullen BH21....86 D6
 Poole BH17...........88 A2
Henbury Rise BH21....85 E6
Henbury View Fst Sch BH21...............85 E6
Henbury View Rd BH21..85 F6
Henchard CI BH22.....61 C2
Hendford BA20........27 D4
Hendford Gdns BH10...89 D2
Hendford Gr BA20.....27 C4
Hendford Hill BA20...27 B3
Hendford Rd BH10.....89 D2
Hendover Coppice Reserve* DT2...............206 F7
Hendrie CI BH19.....178 F2
Hengistbury Head Nature Reserve* BH6......124 E2
Hengistbury Head Nature Reserve* BH6......124 E2
Hengistbury Rd
 Barton on Sea BH25..126 E8
 Bournemouth BH6....124 A3
Hengist Rd BH1......122 D4
Henhayes La 3 TA18..191 F4
HENLEY
 Buckland Newton DT2..208 A7
 Crewkerne TA18.....191 E2
Henley Gdns BH7.....123 A7
Henley Hillbillies DT2..208 A7
Henley's Park Rd BH15..119 E3
Henning Way DT9.....17 D3
Henry CI DT4........180 E7
Henry's Way DT7.......96 C6
HENSTRIDGE BA8......19 A4
HENSTRIDGE ASH BA8...19 A5
HENSTRIDGE BOWDEN BA8................18 A6
HENSTRIDGE MARSH BA8..19 A5
Henstridge Trad Est BA8..20 A5
Henville Rd BH8......122 C5
Herbert Ave BH12....120 D7
Herbert Ct BH12.....120 D7
Herbert Hospl BH4...121 B2
Herberton Rd BH6...123 C5
Herbert Rd
 New Milton BH25......95 B3
 Poole BH4...........121 B2
Herblay CI BA21.......28 A6
Herbury La DT9......194 D4
Hercules Rd BH15....117 F3
Hereford Cres DT4...167 A3
Hereford Rd DT4....167 A3
Heritage CH BH13....147 F7
HERMITAGE DT2......195 B2
Hermitage Ct 8 DT1..107 C1
Hermitage Rd BH14..120 A5
Hermitage St TA18...191 F4
Hermitage The BH1...122 B3
Herm La SP6..........43 D6
Herm Rd BH11.........88 D1
Heron CI
 8 Chickerell DT3...166 D5
 Overcombe/Preston DT3..168 A4
Heron Court Rd BH3, BH9...............122 A7
Heron Dr BH21........60 A8
Herrington Rd DT1...135 A7
Herrison Rd DT2.......75 E2
HERSTON DT1........178 F3
Herstone CI BH17......87 F1
Herston Halt Sta* BH19..178 E3
Hertford CI 6 BH23..126 B7
Hertford Rd BA21.....28 A8

Hesketh CI BH24.......54 C5
Hessary St 9 DT1.....107 C1
Hestan CI BH23........91 D4
Heston Way BH22......52 F3
Hetherly Rd DT3.....167 C7
HEWISH TA18.........191 D3
Hewish La TA18......191 D3
Hewitt Rd BH15......118 E4
Hewlett's Dro DT10..197 C2
HEWOOD TA20........202 C6
Hexworthy Ct 5 DT1..107 B2
Heysham Rd BH18.....87 A3
Heytesbury Rd BH6..123 D5
Hibbard Ct BH10......89 D1
Hibberds Field BH21..40 B7
Hibberd Way BH10.....89 D1
Hibbs CI
 Northport BH20......142 E5
 Upton BH16..........118 C7
Hickes CI BH11.......88 F4
Hickory CI 1 BH16...117 C8
Highacres DT6........69 D1
Highbridge Rd BH14..120 C3
Highbury CI BH25.....95 B2
High CI BH25..........56 D4
HIGHCLIFFE.........125 E8
Highcliffe Castle* BH23..125 E7
Highcliffe Jun Sch BH23..126 B8
Highcliffe Rd
 Christchurch BH23...125 C7
 Swanage BH19......179 C4
Highcliffe St Mark Prim Sch BH23...............93 F1
Highcliffe Sch BH23..93 D1
Highcliff Rd DT7......96 A5
Highdown DT3........167 F8
Highdown Ave DT1...107 D1
HIGHER ANSTY DT2...209 B6
Higher Barn CI SP7...24 C6
Higher Beadon TA16..191 E7
Higher Blandford Rd
 Corfe Mullen BH18, BH21..86 F6
 Shaftesbury SP7......13 A1
HIGHER BOCKHAMPTON DT2...............109 A5
Higher Bullen BA22..193 F8
Higher Burton BA22..193 G8
HIGHER CHALMINGTON DT2...............206 C4
Higher Charminster DT2..107 D7
Higher Cheap St DT9...30 B6
Higher Coombes TA20..202 A8
Higher Day's Rd BH19..178 E2
Higher Dro DT2......205 F2
HIGHER EASTHAMS La TA18...............192 A5
Higher End DT3......166 C5
HIGHER EYPE DT6......99 F5
Higher Eype Rd DT6...99 F5
Higher Filbank BH20..177 A7
Higher Gdns BH20....177 A8
Higher Gunville 5 DT9..17 C2
HIGHER HALSTOCK LEIGH BA22...............193 A2
Higher Hyde Heath Reserve* BH20...............113 C1
HIGHER KINGCOMBE DT2...............205 E3
Higher Kingsbury DT9..17 D3
Higher Kingsbury CI DT9..17 C3
Higher Kingston BA21..27 C5
HIGHER MELCOMBE DT2..208 F5
Higher Merley La BH21..86 E8
HIGHER NYLAND SP8......8 E1
Higher Ream BA21.....26 E6
HIGHER ROW BH21.....51 F5
HIGHER SANDFORD DT9..15 F5
Higher Sea La DT6.....97 A8
Higher Shaftesbury Rd DT1...............212 D8
Higher St
 Bridport DT6.........69 A1
 Iwerne Minster DT11...37 F2
 Lillington DT9......194 F7
 Merriott TA16.......191 F8
 Morden BH20.........83 D4
 Okeford Fitzpaine DT11..197 F5
 West Chinnock TA18...192 B8
Higher Street La DT8..203 C3
HIGHER TOTNELL DT9..194 F4
Higher Westbury DT9..28 D1
HIGHER WHATCOMBE DT11...............210 C5
HIGHER WOODSFORD DT2...............137 D2
HIGHER WRAXALL DT2..205 F4
High E St DT1.........108 A2
Highfield Ave BH24....55 C8
Highfield CI
 Charminster DT2....107 D7
 Corfe Mullen BH21....86 E5
Highfield Dr BH24.....47 C1
Highfield Gdns DT6...204 C2
Highfield Ho 3 BH14..120 B4
Highfield Rd
 Bournemouth BH9....89 E2
 Corfe Mullen BH21....86 E5
 Ferndown BH22.......53 A4
 Ringwood BH24.......55 C8
 Yeovil BA21..........27 E6
Highfields
 Blandford Forum DT11..212 C6
 West Chinnock TA18...192 B8
Highgate La DT2......136 D6

Highgrove SP8............5 F4
Highgrove Cl DT1 [5] ... 135 B8
High Howe Cl BH11 .... 88 E4
High Howe Gdns BH11 ... 88 E4
High Howe La BH11 .... 88 E4
Highland Ave BH23.... 94 B1
Highland Rd
  Poole BH14 .... 120 B5
  Weymouth DT4 .... 167 C3
  Wimborne Minster BH21 .. 59 D6
HIGHLANDS DT6 .... 100 A4
Highlands Cres BH10.... 89 C4
Highlands Rd BH25..... 127 A8
Highland View Cl BH21 ... 59 D5
High Lea BA21 .... 27 D8
High Marryats BH25 .... 127 A7
High Mead BH22 .... 61 A2
High Mead La BA22 .... 61 A1
Highmere BA22 .... 26 D5
Highmoor Cl
  Poole BH14 .... 120 B3
  Poole BH21 .... 85 F5
Highmoor Rd
  Bournemouth BH11..... 89 A1
  Poole BH14 .... 120 B3
  Poole BH21 .... 85 F5
Highmore Rd DT9....... 30 A7
High Oaks Gdns BH11 ... 88 E4
High Park Rd BH18 ..... 86 E4
High Pines BH23 .... 125 D7
High Ridge Cres BH25 ... 95 C2
High St Fordington DT1 . 108 B2
High St
  Ashmore SP5 .... 39 C8
  Broadwindsor DT8.... 203 E6
  Burton Bradstock DT6 . 128 B7
  Child Okeford DT11 ... 198 C7
  Christchurch BH23 .... 124 B6
  Corscombe DT2 ...... 205 A8
  Cranborne BH21 .... 40 A7
  Damerham SP6 .... 190 F3
  East Chinnock BA22... 192 E8
  [3] Easton/Weston DT5. 186 F1
  Fortuneswell DT5 ..... 186 E7
  Gillingham SP8.......... 5 F2
  Hardington Mandeville
    BA22............... 193 A6
  Henstridge BA8 .... 19 A4
  Hinton St George TA17 . 191 C7
  Lytchett Matravers BH16.. 84 C3
  Milborne Port DT9 ..... 17 D2
  Piddlehinton DT2 ...... 76 E8
  Poole BH15 .... 119 C2
  Puddletown DT2 .... 78 B1
  Rimpton BA22 .... 28 F5
  Ringwood BH24 .... 55 B7
  Shaftesbury SP7 .... 12 E2
  Shapwick DT11 .... 48 C1
  Sixpenny Handley SP5.. 189 A4
  Spetisbury DT11 ...... 211 E5
  Stalbridge DT10......... 33 C8
  St Leonards BH24 ..... 54 A6
  Stourton with Gasper BA12.. 1 E8
  Sturminster Marshall BH21. 56 D4
  Swanage BH19 .... 178 B2
  Sydling St Nicholas DT2 .. 207 A2
  Tarrant Monkton DT11 .. 200 B3
  Thorncombe TA20 .... 202 E5
  Toller Porcorum DT2 .... 71 D8
  Weymouth DT4 .... 180 C7
  Wimborne Minster BH21.. 59 B4
  Winfrith Newburgh DT2.. 156 F5
  Wool BH20 .... 140 B2
  Yeovil BA20 .... 27 D4
  Yetminster DT9 ...... 194 C5
  Zeale SP8.............. 1 F3
High Street Cl BH20.... 140 A2
High Street N BH15 .... 119 D3
HIGHTOWN BH24 .... 55 F6
Hightown Gdns BH24 .... 55 D6
Hightown Ind Est BH24 .. 55 D6
Hightown Rd BH24 ..... 55 C6
High Trees
  Broadmayne DT2 ..... 136 C1
  Poole BH13 .... 147 G8
Hightrees Ave BH8 ...... 90 F1
High Trees Wlk BH22... 61 D7
Highview Cl BH23 .... 93 E3
Highview Gdns BH12 ... 120 C7
High Way BH18 .... 86 F3
High West St
  Dorchester DT1........ 108 A2
  Weymouth DT4 .... 167 D2
HIGHWOOD BH20 ...... 158 F8
Highwood Cl BH16 ...... 47 C6
Highwood La BH16 ...... 47 E4
Highwood Rd BH14 .... 120 E4
Hilary Rd BH17 .... 87 C1
Hilcot Way DT11 ...... 212 D5
Hilda Rd BH12 .... 120 E7
Hiley Rd BH15 .... 119 C6
HILFIELD DT2 .... 207 A7
Hilfield Hill Nature Reserve★
  DT2................ 207 A7
Hilfield La DT2 .... 194 F1
Hillard Ct [7] BH20 .... 142 E3
Hilary Rd BH23 .... 124 E8
Hillborne Gdns [1] BA21.. 26 E5
HILLBOURNE........... 87 A2
Hillbourne Rd
  Poole BH17 .... 87 A2
  [1] Weymouth DT4 .... 180 D7
Hillbourne Sch BH17.... 87 B2
Hill Brow DT9.......... 29 F4
Hillbrow Rd BH6 ...... 123 B6

Hillbury Rd SP6......... 42 D6
HILLBUTTS 58 F6
Hill Cl
  Bransgore BH23 .... 93 A8
  [5] Bridport DT6...... 100 B2
Hillcrest Ave BH22 ..... 61 C8
Hillcrest Cl
  Bournemouth BH9 ..... 90 A3
  Sturminster Newton DT10 197 C8
Hillcrest Rd
  Bournemouth BH9 ..... 90 A3
  Poole BH12 .... 120 A5
  Poole BH21 .... 85 E5
  Weymouth DT4 .... 180 E7
Hill Crest Rd BA21 ...... 27 E6
HILL END BA22 .... 192 F6
Hillfield Cl DT3 .... 152 B4
Hillfort Cl DT1........ 134 E7
Hillfort Mews [6] DT1.. 134 E7
Hillgrove Ave BA20..... 27 B2
Hill House Cl DT9 ...... 30 C7
Hillingdon DT6 .... 100 E8
Hillingdon Ct BA21..... 26 E6
Hilling La DT2 .... 208 A7
Hill La BH23 .... 93 A8
Hillmead Rd BH14.... 120 D5
Hillmeadow BH21 ...... 45 B5
Hill Rd
  Blandford Forum DT11 . 212 E6
  Lyme Regis DT7 .... 96 B5
  Swanage BH19 ...... 179 B5
Hill Rise DT6 .... 100 B2
Hill Rise Rd DT7 .... 96 B5
Hillsea Rd BH19 .... 179 A2
Hillside BA22.......... 26 E5
Hillside Cl BA12.......... 2 E5
Hillside Dr BH23 .... 91 D3
Hillside Gdns BH21 ..... 85 E4
Hillside Mews BH21 .... 85 E4
Hillside Rd
  Blandford Camp DT11 . 199 E3
  Poole BH12 .... 88 F1
  Poole BH21 .... 85 E4
  Verwood BH31 .... 45 C7
  Woodlands BH21....... 44 C6
  [3] Wool BH20 .... 140 A1
Hillside Terr [4] BA21 ... 27 E5
Hillside View [5] BA22.. 193 F8
Hill St BH15 .... 119 C2
Hill Terr BH21 .... 60 A2
Hilltop Cl BH22 .... 61 B7
Hilltop Rd
  Corfe Mullen BH21 ..... 86 E5
  Ferndown BH22 .... 61 B7
HILL VIEW BH21 .... 86 E5
Hillview BH16 .... 68 F1
Hill View
  Bishop's Caundle DT9 .. 196 A7
  Charminster DT2 ...... 107 C6
  [5] Hazelbury Bryan DT10 197 A4
  Maiden Newton DT2 .... 73 A7
  Mudford BA21 .... 14 A3
  Overcombe/Preston DT3. 169 A8
  Yeovil BA21 .... 27 E5
Hill View Cl TA18 ..... 192 B7
Hillview Est Fst Sch BH31. 45 B7
Hillview Rd
  Bournemouth BH10..... 89 D3
  Swanage BH19 ...... 179 A2
Hill View Rd BH22...... 61 C7
Hill Way BH24 .... 54 A5
Hilmar Dr SP8 .... 5 E2
Hiltom Rd BH24 .... 55 D7
HILTON DT11 .... 209 D6
Hilton Cl BH15 .... 120 A6
Hilton Rd BH25 .... 95 B4
Hinchliffe Cl BH18 .... 118 F2
Hinchliffe Rd BH15.... 118 F2
HINCKNOWLE DT6 ...... 69 B8
Hine Cl SP8.............. 11 B8
Hine's Mead La BH22 .. 103 C1
Hine Town La DT11 ... 198 B6
Hingsdon La DT6 ...... 204 B2
Hintock St DT1 .... 107 D1
HINTON
  94 A3
Hinton Admiral Gdns★
  BH23................. 93 F4
Hinton Admiral Mews
  BH23................. 93 E2
Hinton Admiral Sta BH23. 93 F4
Hinton Cl
  Blandford Forum DT11 . 212 D5
  Hinton St George TA17 . 191 C7
Hinton Cross BA22 ..... 14 B5
Hinton La DT10 .... 35 A2
HINTON MARTELL BH21 . 201 B1
HINTON PARVA BH21... 50 B5
Hinton Rd
  Bournemouth BH1..... 121 F3
  West Crewkerne TA18.. 191 E5
HINTON ST GEORGE
  TA17................ 191 D7
Hinton St George CE Sch
  TA17................ 191 C7
HINTON ST MARY DT10... 35 B4
Hinton St Mary Roman Villa
  (site of)★ DT10....... 35 B4
Hinton View DT10....... 35 B2
Hinton Wood BH22 .... 122 A2
Hinton Wood Ave BH23.. 93 E1
Hintonwood La BH23 ... 93 E2
Hitchen [8] TA16 ...... 191 F7
Hive Cl DT6............ 128 C2
Hive Gdns BH13...... 147 D6

Hobart Rd BH25........ 94 F2
Hobbs Pk
  Ringwood BH24 .... 54 B2
  St Leonards BH24 ..... 54 B4
Hobbs Rd BH12 .... 120 C8
Hobgoblin DT11 .... 37 F1
Hoburne Ct BH23 .... 93 C1
Hoburne Gdns BH23.... 93 C1
Hoburne La BH23 .... 125 C8
Hoburne Rd BH19 ..... 179 A2
Hodder's La DT7 .... 64 A2
Hodges Ct BH17....... 119 E7
Hod Hill (Hill Fort & Roman
  Fort)★ DT11 .... 198 E5
Hod View [2] DT11 .... 198 F4
Hodway La DT11 ...... 198 D5
Hogarth Way BH8....... 91 A2
Hog Cliff National Nature
  Reserve★ DT2........ 72 C3
Hogshill St DT8 .... 204 C4
HOGSTOCK DT11 ...... 200 B1
Hogue Ave BH10 .... 89 D5
Holbaek Cl DT1 .... 135 B7
Holburne Naish BH25 . 126 D8
Holbury Cl BH8 .... 90 E3
Holcombe Cl DT3 ..... 168 D8
Holcombe Mead DT2 .. 208 A6
Holcombe Rd BH16 ... 117 D6
Holcombe Valley Rd
  BH8................... 91 A3
HOLDITCH TA20 ...... 202 B5
Holditch Court La TA20.. 202 A5
Holditch La TA20...... 202 A5
Holdscroft La DT6 .... 202 E1
Holebrook La DT10.... 196 F7
Hole House La DT10... 197 D8
Holes Bay North Rdbt
  BH17................ 119 A6
Holes Bay Pk BH15.... 119 B4
Holes Bay Rd BH15.... 119 B4
Holes Bay Rdbt BH15... 119 B5
Holes Cl SO41......... 95 F4
Holland Rd DT4 .... 167 C3
Hollands Rd BH20 .... 176 F8
Hollands Mead Ave DT2 155 C7
Hollands Wood Dr BH25.. 95 B5
Holland Way
  Blandford Forum DT11 . 212 D5
  Corfe Mullen BH21 ..... 86 F5
Holland Way Ind Pk
  DT11................ 212 E6
Hollenden [9] BH13.... 121 A4
Holleys Cl [10] TA20... 202 A8
Hollies The
  [3] Crewkerne TA18... 191 E3
  Yeovil BA21 .... 27 E7
Hollis Way BA22 ...... 193 D3
Holloway Ave BH11 ..... 88 F5
Holloway La DT11 .... 198 C5
Holloway Rd DT1 ..... 108 B2
Hollow Hill DT2 .... 108 F4
Hollow La TA17 .... 191 B7
HOLLOW OAK BH20 ... 113 B8
Hollow Oak BH20 .... 113 B8
Hollow Rd BH20 ..... 142 E1
Hollow The
  Affpuddle DT2 .... 112 B6
  Child Okeford DT11 ... 198 C8
  Sixpenny Handley SP5.. 189 A4
Hollow Way DT10 ..... 100 D4
Holly Cl
  [3] Dorchester DT1 ... 107 E2
  Ferndown BH22......... 52 F2
  [2] Sandford BH20.... 116 A1
  [1] St Leonards BH24 .. 53 F4
  Upton BH16 .... 117 C7
Holly Ct BH15.......... 119 D4
Hollyfields Sch SP8 ..... 4 D7
Holly Gdns BH23 .... 92 D1
Holly Gr
  Merriott TA18......... 191 F5
  Verwood BH31......... 45 A5
Holly Green Rise BH11 .. 88 E4
Holly Hedge La BH17.. 119 C8
Holly La
  Broadwindsor DT8.... 203 D8
  New Milton BH25...... 95 C4
  Walkford BH23 .... 94 F2
Holly Lo [6] BH21 .... 121 A4
Hollymoor Cl [3] BH11. 204 D4
Hollymoor Common La
  DT8................. 204 D4
Hollymoor Gdns [7] BH11 204 D4
Hollymoor La DT8....... 204 D4
Holly Rd DT4 .... 167 C3
Holm Cl DT2............ 107 C8
Holmead Wlk DT1...... 107 D1
HOLMEBRIDGE BH20... 141 E2
Holme La DT1 .... 167 B8
Holme La
  East Holme BH20 ..... 160 B7
  East Stoke BH20 ..... 141 A1
Holme Rd BH23 .... 126 B8
Holmes Rd BH19 ..... 178 E5
Holmfield Ave BH7 .... 123 C7
Holm Hill La BH25..... 94 B7
Holmhurst Ave BH23 ... 93 F1
Holmlea [1] DT11 .... 212 E5
Holm Oak Cl BH31 ..... 45 A8
Holm Pk Quarry National
  Nature Reserve★ DT8.. 204 B5
Holmwood Garth [3] DT1 .. 107 D1
Holnest DT9 .... 195 C4
Holnest Rd BH17....... 87 D1

HOLT BH21............ 51 B4
Holten's La BA22..... 192 E6
HOLT HEATH BH21..... 52 C6
Holt Heath National Nature
  Reserve★ BH21...... 51 E8
Holt Hill DT9............ 31 F1
Holt Ho BH8 .... 122 D5
Holt La
  Bishop's Caundle DT9 .. 196 A8
  Holt BH21 .... 51 B4
  Melbury Osmond DT2 . 194 A3
  South Perrott DT8 .... 192 D1
  Stourton Caundle DT10, DT9 32 B2
HOLTON HEATH BH16 . 116 B3
Holton Heath Ind Est
  BH16................ 116 D2
Holton Heath Sta BH16. 116 D1
Holton Rd BH16....... 116 D2
Holt Pl BH21 .... 61 F7
Holt Rd
  Holt BH21 .... 51 D5
  Horton BH21 .... 52 F8
  Poole BH12 .... 120 F6
  Wool BH20 .... 139 D6
HOLT WOOD BH21 ..... 51 C8
HOLWAY
  Chard TA20 .... 202 E6
  Sherborne DT9 .... 16 A5
Holway TA20 .... 202 A8
Holway La DT2 .... 206 A5
Holway Woods Reserve★
  DT9................. 16 A5
HOLWELL
  Mere BA12............. 3 C5
  Sturminster Newton DT10 196 B5
Holwell Dro DT9 ...... 195 F5
Holwell Rd DT10 ...... 196 C5
Holworth DT2 .... 88 E3
Holyrood Cl BH17 .... 119 A8
Holy Trinity CE Prim Sch [1]
  DT4................ 167 C1
Holy Trintiy CE Prim Sch
  BA20................ 27 A3
HOLYWELL
  Dorchester DT2....... 206 C7
  Yeovil BA22 .... 193 C8
Holywell Cl BH17 ...... 87 D3
Holywell Dro DT9 ..... 195 F5
Holzwiecbeb DT3 ..... 152 F2
Homecliffe Ho DT3 ... 126 B8
Homecorfe Ho BH18 ... 87 B5
Homedale Ho BH2 ... 121 F5
Homedene Ho BH15 ... 119 C4
Home Dr BA21, BA20 ... 27 A6
Home Farm Cl DT6 .... 101 E8
Home Farm La BA22 ... 15 A8
Home Farm Rd BH31 ... 45 A7
Home Farm Way
  Shipton Gorge DT6 ... 101 D3
  Verwood BH31......... 45 A7
Homefield
  [6] Child Okeford DT11 . 198 C7
  Mere BA12............. 2 F5
  Milborne St Andrew DT11. 79 F7
  Shaftesbury SP7 ...... 12 F4
Homefield Ho [7] BH25. 95 A2
Homelake Ho BH14 ... 120 B3
Homelands Est BH21 . 123 B6
Homelands Ho BH22 ... 61 D5
Homeleigh Ho [5] BH8. 122 A5
Homelife Ho [2] BH8.. 122 B4
Homemead DT10 ..... 196 F4
Homemill Ho [5] BH25 .. 95 A3
Homeoaks Ho BH2 ... 121 F5
Home Rd BH11......... 89 B6
Homeside Rd BH9 ...... 90 A2
Homestour Ho [4] BH23. 124 A4
Homeview Ho BH15 ... 119 D3
Homewood Cl BH25.... 95 C3
Honeybourne Cres BH6. 124 A4
Honeybrook Victorian Farm
  & Ctry Pk★ BH21..... 50 D2
Honey Bun Mdw DT10. 196 F4
Honeycombe Rise DT9 . 29 F4
Honeyfields [3] SP8 ..... 5 F4
Honeymead La DT10 ... 35 B2
Honeysuckle Cl DT3 .. 152 F2
Honeysuckle Gdns [2]
  DT11................ 198 B5
Honeysuckle La BH17 .. 86 F1
Honeysuckle Way BH23. 128 B6
Honeysuckle Wlk BH14. 147 C7
Hood Cl BH10........... 89 B1
Hood Cres BH10 .... 89 B1
HOOKE DT8 .... 205 C2
Hooke Cl BH17......... 88 A2
Hooke Ct Sch DT8 .... 205 B3
Hooper's La
  Barwick BA22 .... 193 F7
  Puncknowle DT2 ..... 129 F6
Hop Cl BH16 .... 117 B7
Hope Bottom DT6 .... 204 C2
Hope Cl DT27......... 137 D5
Hope Cross SP8.......... 9 A6
Hopegood Cl [4] DT11 . 211 D6
Hope Sq [9] DT4 ...... 167 E2
Hope Terr DT21 ...... 133 D6
Hopkins Cl BH8......... 91 A2
Hopmans Cl BH16 ..... 84 B4
Hopsfield DT11......... 79 E8
Horace Rd [7] BH5.... 122 E4
HORDLE............... 95 F3
Hordle Mews SO41..... 95 F4
HORN ASH TA18 ...... 203 A7
Hornbeam Cl DT4 .... 167 B6
Hornbeam Rd DT2 ..... 75 D3
Hornbeam Sq BH21 .. 119 D2
Hornbeam Way BH21 ... 59 E5

Horncastles La DT9 .... 29 F6
Horning Rd BH21 ..... 122 D5
Hornpark Quarry Ind Est
  DT8................. 204 A5
Horsa Cl BH23 .... 123 E4
Horsa Ct BH23 .... 123 E4
Horsa Rd BH23........ 123 E4
Horsecastles DT9 ...... 30 A5
Horsecliffe La BH23 ... 179 C3
Horsefields SP8.......... 5 E3
Horsehill La DT8 ...... 204 A3
Horseponds SP7........ 12 D3
Horseshoe Cl BH21.... 60 B6
Horseshoe Common Rdbt
  BH1................. 121 F3
Horseshoe Ct [5] BH1.. 121 F4
Horseshoe Rd TA20 ... 202 D7
Horseshoe The BH11... 147 C4
Horsey Knap DT2 ..... 205 E7
Horsey La
  East Chelborough DT2.. 205 E7
  Yeovil BA20 .... 27 C4
Horsford St DT4 ...... 167 E1
Horsham Ave BH10..... 89 C6
HORTON BH21.......... 201 E2
Horton Cl
  Bournemouth BH9...... 90 C3
  Horton BH21 .... 26 F6
HORTON COMMON BH21... 44 F2
HORTON HEATH BH21 .. 44 E3
Horton Ho BH22 .... 61 F7
Horton Rd
  Horton BH21 .... 44 D1
  St Leonards BH24 ..... 54 D6
  St Leonards & St Ives BH24 53 E6
  Woodlands BH21....... 44 D4
Horton Tower (Folly)★
  BH21................ 201 E1
Horton Way BH31...... 44 F5
Hosey Rd DT10......... 35 C3
Hosker Rd BH5 .... 123 B5
Hospital La
  Allington DT6 .... 100 B8
  Sherborne DT9 .... 30 B8
Hotton Heath National
  Nature Reserve★ BH16. 116 F3
Houlton Rd BH15 ..... 119 E4
HOUND HILL 58 E7
Houndsell Way DT6 ... 100 B7
Hound St DT9........... 30 B6
HOUNDSTONE BA22.... 26 C6
HOUNDSTONE CT BA22 .. 26 E5
Houndstone Ct BA22 .. 26 C5
Hounds Way BH21 ..... 60 B5
Hounslow Cl BH15 .... 118 F1
Howard Cl
  Bothenhampton DT6 .. 101 A4
  Christchurch BH23.... 124 F6
  Weymouth DT4 .... 180 E7
Howard Rd
  Bournemouth BH8..... 122 C8
  Bridport DT6 .... 100 F6
  [5] Swanage BH19 ... 179 A2
  Verwood BH31......... 45 B6
  Yeovil BA21 .... 28 A6
Howard's La BH20 .... 142 E3
Howarth Cl [1] DT6 .. 128 B8
Howe Cl
  Christchurch BH23.... 124 F5
  New Milton BH25...... 94 F3
Howe La BH31 .... 45 A5
Howell Ho BH11 .... 59 F7
Howe's Eype La DT6 ... 99 E5
Howeth Cl BH10 .... 89 D3
Howeth Rd BH10 ...... 89 D3
Howgare Rd SP6...... 189 F8
Howton Cl BH10 .... 89 C5
Howton Rd BH10 ...... 89 C5
Hoxley Rd BH10 .... 89 D4
Hoyal Rd BH15........ 117 F3
Hudson Cl
  Poole BH12 .... 88 C3
  Ringwood BH24 .... 55 E8
Hughes Bsns Ctr BH23 . 125 A7
Huish BA20 .... 27 C4
Huish La DT9 .... 31 E4
Huish Pk (Yeovil Town FC)
  BA22................. 26 D6
Huish Prim Sch BA20 .. 27 C5
Hull Cres BH11 .... 88 D4
Hull Rd BH11 .... 88 E4
Hull Way BH11......... 88 E4
Humber Chase BH20 .. 142 C5
Humber Rd BH22 ...... 62 A6
HUMMER DT9 .... 14 D4
Humpy La DT9.......... 31 B1
Hundredstone Cl BA21.. 27 D8
Hungerford Hill SP6 ... 43 E5
Hungerford Rd BH8 .... 90 D3
Hunger Hill BH15 ..... 119 C2
Hunter Cl
  Christchurch BH23.... 125 A7
  Wimborne Minster BH21. 60 B6
Hunters Cl BH31 .... 45 E5
Hunters Mead SP7 ...... 7 B1
Huntfield Rd BH9 .... 90 B2
Huntick Est BH16 ...... 84 D3
Huntick Rd BH16 ...... 84 A1
Huntingdon Dr BH21 ... 59 E1
Huntingdon Gdns BH23. 92 A2
HUNTINGFORD SP8...... 6 A8
Huntley Down DT11... 209 F1
Huntly Rd BH3 .... 121 D7
Hunt Rd
  Blandford Forum DT11 . 212 E5
  Christchurch BH23.... 124 F8

Hunt Rd continued
Poole BH15 . . . . 119 E4
Hunt's Hill DT10 . . . . . . 21 E5
Hunts Mead DT9 . . . . . . 29 F4
Huntvale Rd BH9 . . . . . . 90 B3
Hurdles The BH23 . . . . . 123 E8
HURN 91 B7
Hurn Court La
Christchurch BH23 . . . . 91 D7
Hurn BH23 . . . . 90 F6
Hurn Ct BH8 . . . . 91 A4
Hurn La BH24 . . . . 54 F6
Hurn Rd
Christchurch BH23 . . . . 91 D3
St Leonards & St Ives BH24 54 F4
Hurn Way BH23 . . . . 91 D1
Hurricane CI DT2 . . . . . 137 D6
HURSEY DT8 . . . . 203 E5
Hursley CI BH7 . . . . 123 C8
HURST DT2 . . . . 111 C1
Hurstbourne Ave BH23 . . 93 E1
Hurst CI
Burton-on-Sea BH25 . . 126 D8
Walkford BH23 . . . . 94 C2
Hurst Ct 4 BH21 . . . . . . 56 D2
Hurstdene Rd BH8 . . . . . 90 C2
Hurst Hill BH14 . . . . . . 147 C8
Hurst Rd
Moreton DT2 . . . . 111 C1
Ringwood BH24 . . . . . . 47 C1
Hussar CI DT3 . . . . 123 F7
Hussey's DT10 . . . . 20 E1
Hutchins CI DT1 . . . . . . 134 E7
Hut Gate TA18 . . . . 192 A8
Hyacinth CI BH17 . . . . . 86 F1
Hybris Bsns Pk DT2 . . . 137 D4
HYDE
Bridport DT6 . . . . 100 F5
Fordingbridge SP6 . . . . 43 F6
Hyde CE Prim Sch SP6 . . 43 F5
Hyde Ct BA21 . . . . 26 E6
Hyde Gdns 6 DT11 . . . . 199 D4
Hyde La SP6 . . . . 43 E6
Hyde Rd
Bournemouth BH10 . . . 89 C5
Gillingham SP8 . . . . 5 E3
Wool BH20 . . . . 140 A2
Hydes La DT10 . . . . 196 D7
Hyde The
New Milton BH25 . . . . . 94 E4
Swanage BH19 . . . . . . 178 C2
Hynesbury Rd BH23 . . . 125 C6
Hythe CI BH15 . . . . 120 A7
Hythe The DT3 . . . . 166 D5

I

IBBERTON DT11 . . . . . . 197 D2
Ibberton CI BH8 . . . . . . 90 F2
Ibberton Rd BH8 . . . . . . 90 F2
Ibberton Way BH8 . . . . . 90 F2
Ibbett Rd BH10 . . . . 89 C3
IBSLEY BH24 . . . . 47 C7
Ibsley CI BH8 . . . . 122 C6
Ibsley Dro BH24 . . . . . . 43 D1
Icen La
Bincombe DT3 . . . . . . 152 C4
Shipton Gorge DT6 . . . 101 E4
Icen Rd DT3 . . . . 167 C7
Icen Way DT1 . . . . 108 A2
Iddesleigh Rd BH3 . . . . 122 A6
IFORD 123 D7
Iford Bridge Home Pk
BH6 . . . . 123 D7
Iford Gdns BH7 . . . . . . 123 C7
Iford La BH6 . . . . 123 E6
Iford Mdws Nature Reserve*
BH6 . . . . 123 C7
Ilchester Rd
Weymouth DT4 . . . . . . 167 C3
Yeovil BA21 . . . . 27 B7
Ilford CI BH23 . . . . 123 F5
Ilminster Rd DT4 . . . . . 179 B2
Ilsington Dr DT2 . . . . . . 78 C1
Ilsington Rd DT2 . . . . . 109 F4
Imber Dr BH23 . . . . . . 125 F8
Imber Rd SP7 . . . . 13 A3
Imbrecourt BH13 . . . . . 147 F7
Imperial Ct 4 BH13 . . . 147 F7
Incline N DT5 . . . . 187 B6
Ingarth 7 BH6 . . . . . . 123 E3
Inglegreen CI BH9 . . . . . 94 F1
Inglewood Ave BH8 . . . . 90 F1
Inglewood Dr BH25 . . . . 95 B2
Ingram Wlk 8 BH21 . . . 59 D4
Ingworth Rd BH12 . . . . 121 A5
Inmosthay DT5 . . . . . . 187 A5
Inner Breakwater Rd
DT5 . . . . 181 B1
Innovation CI DT1 . . . . 120 A8
Insley Cres BH18 . . . . . . 86 E5
Institute Rd BH13 . . . . . 179 C2
International Coll Sherborne
Sch The DT9 . . . . 30 A6
Inverayon BH13 . . . . . . 120 B4
Inverclyde Ho BH14 . . . 120 B4
Inverclyde Rd BH14 . . . 120 C4
Inverleigh Rd BH6 . . . . 123 C6
Inverness Rd BH13 . . . 147 E7
Ipswich Rd BH12 . . . . . 121 B4
Iris Gdns 5 SP8 . . . . 5 E1
Iris Rd BH9 . . . . 89 F1
Irvine Way BH23 . . . . . 124 E8
Irving La BH6 . . . . 123 D5
Irving Rd BH6 . . . . 123 D5

Isaacs CI BH12 . . . . 121 B7
Island View Ave BH23 . . 125 B5
Island View Rd BH25 . . 126 C7
Isle of Wight Rd BH19 . 185 C8
Isle Rd DT5 . . . . 186 E3
Isles La BA22 . . . . 193 D6
Ivamy PI BH11 . . . . 88 F2
Ivel CI DT1 . . . . 135 B8
Ivel Ct BA21 . . . . 27 E4
Ivelway 14 TA18 . . . . . 191 F4
Ivor Rd
Poole BH15 . . . . 119 A1
Poole BH21 . . . . 85 F4
Ivy CI
4 Gillingham SP8 . . . . . 5 D2
St Leonards BH24 . . . . 53 F4
IVY CROSS SP7 . . . . . . 13 A4
Ivy La BH21 . . . . 47 D4
Ivy Mead BA12 . . . . 3 B5
Ivy Rd BH21 . . . . 87 D8
Iwerne CI BH9 . . . . 90 B4
IWERNE COURTNEY OR
SHROTON DT11 . . . . . 198 E7
IWERNE MINSTER DT11 . 37 F1

J

Jacey Ho 6 BH1 . . . . . . 122 A3
Jacklin Ct BH18 . . . . 87 B5
Jack Paul CI BA12 . . . . . . 1 A6
Jack's Hedge Cnr BH21 189 F2
Jackson Gdns DT2 . . . . 120 C6
Jackson Rd BH12 . . . . . 120 C6
Jack the Treacle Eater
(Folly)★ BA22 . . . . 27 E1
Jacmar Ct 4 BH25 . . . . . 95 B2
Jacobean CI BH23 . . . . . 94 B1
Jacobs Ladder 2 DT11 . 198 F7
Jacobs Rd BH15 . . . . . 118 E2
Jacqueline Rd BH12 . . . 120 C7
James CI
Blandford Forum DT11 . 212 F5
Poole BH12 . . . . 134 E8
James Cross La BH21 . . 201 A6
James Day Mead BH19 . 179 B5
Jameson Rd BH9 . . . . . . 89 F1
James Rd
Dorchester DT1 . . . . . 134 E8
Poole BH12 . . . . 121 A5
James St DT4 . . . . 167 D2
Janred Ct BH25 . . . . . . 126 E7
Jarvis CI DT10 . . . . 33 D7
Jarvis Way DT10 . . . . . . 33 D8
Jasmine CI
24 Crewkerne TA18 . . 191 F5
Yeovil BA22 . . . . 26 C5
Jasmine Way 2 DT4 . . 180 B8
Jaundrells CI BH25 . . . . 95 C3
Jay's Ct BH23 . . . . 126 B8
Jay Wlk SP8 . . . . 11 B8
Jeanneau CI 4 SP7 . . . 12 F3
Jefferson Ave BH1 . . . . 122 D6
Jellicoe CI BH14 . . . . . 119 F5
Jellicoe Dr BH23 . . . . . 124 F6
Jellyfields Nature Reserve★
DT6 . . . . 100 F6
Jenner CI BH23 . . . . . . 152 D3
Jenner Way DT3 . . . . . 152 D3
Jenni CI BH11 . . . . 89 A6
Jennings Rd BH14 . . . . 120 C2
Jennys La BH16 . . . . . . 148 F6
Jephcote Rd BH11 . . . . . 88 F4
Jeremy CI BH20 . . . . . . 140 B2
Jersey CI BH12 . . . . 88 D1
Jersey Rd BH12 . . . . . . 88 D1
Jesmond Ave BH23 . . . 125 F8
Jessop CI 1 SP8 . . . . 5 E1
Jessica Ave BH31 . . . . . 44 F7
Jessopp CI DT6 . . . . . . 100 F7
Jessopp Rd BH21 . . . . . 60 B6
Jessopp Ho 6 BH21 . . . 59 C5
Jessopp Rd BH21 . . . . . 60 B6
Jesty's Ave BH12 . . . . . 152 C4
Jewell Rd BH8 . . . . 91 A2
Jimmy Brown Ave BH21 . 53 A5
Jock's Hill DT2 . . . . 78 E6
Johnson Rd BH21 . . . . . 61 A8
Johnson's Ctyd DT9 . . . 30 C5
Johns Rd BH20 . . . . . . 142 D5
Johnstone Rd BH23 . . . 124 E6
Johnston Rd BH15 . . . . 119 D7
Jolliffe Ave BH15 . . . . . 119 D5
Jolliffe Rd BH15 . . . . . 119 D5
Jonson Trading Pk 3
DT1 . . . . 108 C1
Jopps Cnr BH23 . . . . . . 92 C4
Jordan Hill Roman Temple★
DT3 . . . . 168 B7
Jordan Way 5 DT3 . . . 152 C4
Joshua CI BH15 . . . . . . 118 E2
Journeys End DT6 . . . . 100 B6
Jowitt Dr BH25 . . . . 94 F2
Joyce Dickson CI 2
BH24 . . . . 55 D6
Joys Rd BH21 . . . . 53 A8
Juan's La SP8 . . . . 9 D2
Jubilee Bsns Pk DT4 . . 167 D5
Jubilee CI
Corfe Mullen BH21 . . . 86 E7
1 Radipole DT4 . . . . . 167 D4
Ringwood BH24 . . . . . . 55 A4
Jubilee Cres BH16 . . . . 118 D5
Jubilee Cross BH16 . . . 85 A4
Jubilee Ent Ctr DT4 . . . 167 D4
Jubilee Gdns
Bournemouth BH10 . . . 89 D2
Corfe Castle BH20 . . . 177 A7

Jubilee Rd
Corfe Mullen BH21 . . . 86 E7
Poole BH12 . . . . 120 D5
Swanage BH19 . . . . . . 178 F2
Jubilee Trail DT2 . . . . . 135 C4
Jubilee Way DT11 . . . . 212 C5
Julia CI DT3 . . . . 167 D3
Julian's Rd BH21 . . . . . 59 A4
Julyan Ave BH12 . . . . . 121 A8
Jumpers Ave BH23 . . . 123 E8
Jumpers Rd BH23 . . . . 123 F8
Junction Rd
Bournemouth BH9 . . . 121 F8
Upton BH16 . . . . 117 F4
Juniper CI
Ferndown BH22 . . . . . . 61 C8
Three Legged Cross BH21 . 53 A8
Yeovil BA21 . . . . 27 B3
Juniper Dr BH23 . . . . . . 93 C1
Juniper Flats BH23 . . . 123 E8
Juniper Gdns 7 SP8 . . . . 5 E1
Jupiter Way BH21 . . . . . 86 E8
Justin Bsns Pk BH20 . . 142 F5
Justin Gdns BH10 . . . . . 89 E4

K

Kamptee Copse BH25 . . 95 B6
Kangaw PI 3 BH15 . . . . 117 F2
Katherine Chance CI
BH23 . . . . 92 C3
Katie CI BH14 . . . . 120 C4
Katterns CI BH23 . . . . . . 91 E2
Kay CI BH23 . . . . 124 E6
Kayes CI DT4 . . . . 180 C8
K&B Est BH17 . . . . 119 B8
Keats Rd BH23 . . . . 95 A1
Keble CI BH18 . . . . 89 D6
Keble Cres BH18 . . . . . . 89 D6
Keeble Rd BH10 . . . . . . 89 D6
Keepers La BH21 . . . . . . 60 F4
Keep Military Mus The★
DT1 . . . . 107 F2
Keighley Ave BH18 . . . . 86 F1
Keith Rd BH3 . . . . 121 D7
Kellaway Ct 10 DT4 . . . 167 E2
Kellaway Rd BH17 . . . . 119 F8
Kellaway Terr DT4 . . . . 167 C3
Kelly CI BH17 . . . . 119 F8
Kelsall Gdns BH25 . . . . . 95 A3
Kemp Rd BH9 . . . . 121 F8
Kempston Rd DT11 . . . 167 D1
Kemp Welch CI BH12 . . 121 B8
Kendalls La SP8 . . . . 5 E5
Kenelm CI DT9 . . . . 29 F5
Kenilworth Ct DT4 . . . . 167 B4
Kenilworth CI BH25 . . . . 95 B3
Kenilworth Ct
2 Christchurch BH23 . 124 F6
1 Poole BH13 . . . . . . 147 F8
Kenmoor CI DT3 . . . . . 167 F8
Kenmore Rd BA21 . . . . . 27 D6
Kennard Ct BH25 . . . . . . 94 F3
Kennard Rd BH25 . . . . . 94 F3
Kennart Rd BH17 . . . . . 119 B7
Kennel La DT2 . . . . 206 C2
Kennels La DT3 . . . . . . 195 E2
Kennington CI BH23 . . 126 B7
Kennington Sq 5 BH20 . 142 E4
Ken Rd BH6 . . . . 123 E4
Kensington CI 14 BH13 . 121 B3
Kensington Dr 1 BH21 . 121 D4
Kensington Wlk 8 BH15 . 135 C8
Kent CI DT4 . . . . 166 F3
Kent Ho 12 BH4 . . . . . 121 C3
Kentisworth Rd DT10 . . . 20 F1
Kent La BH24 . . . . 43 A1
Kent Rd
Poole BH12 . . . . 120 E6
10 Tatworth DT4 . . . . 202 A8
Kents La 8 TA20 . . . . . 202 A8
Kenwyn Rd DT6 . . . . . 100 E7
Kenyon CI BH15 . . . . . . 119 E7
Kenyon Rd BH15 . . . . . 119 E7
Keppel CI BH24 . . . . 55 D7
Kerley Rd BH2 . . . . 121 E2
Kernells Ct 2 BH4 . . . . 121 C3
Kestrel CI
Ferndown BH22 . . . . . . 61 B7
3 Upton BH16 . . . . . . 117 D8
Kestrel Ct BH24 . . . . 55 C8
Kestrel Dr BH23 . . . . . . 125 A6
Kestrel View DT3 . . . . . 152 C3
Kestrel Way SP6 . . . . . . 42 D5
Keswick Ct BH25 . . . . . . 95 B5
Keswick Rd
Bournemouth BH5 . . . 122 F4
New Milton BH25 . . . . . 95 B5
Keverel Rd BH31 . . . . . . 45 A5
Keverstone Ct BH13 . . . 122 D3
Keyes CI
Christchurch BH23 . . . 124 F6
Poole BH11 . . . . 88 F1
Key Hill BA22 . . . . 193 E6
Keynston Down Rd 7
DT11 . . . . 199 E2
Keysworth BH20 . . . . . 143 B7
Keysworth Dr BH20 . . . 126 F8
Keysworth Dr BH20 . . . 143 A8
Keysworth Rd BH16 . . . 117 E4
Khartoum Rd BH8 . . . . 180 E8
Khyber Rd BH12 . . . . . 120 D5
Kiddles BA21 . . . . 27 E5

Kidmore CI 2 DT6 . . . . . 97 A7
Killicks Hill DT5 . . . . . . 186 F7
Killock CI BH13 . . . . . . 147 F7
Kilmarnock Rd
1 Bournemouth BH11 . 122 B4
Bournemouth BH9 . . . . 89 F1
Kilmington Way BH23 . 125 F8
Kiln CI BH21 . . . . 85 E4
Kiln Way BH31 . . . . 45 E4
Kilwood Reserve★ BH20 . 161 B2
Kimberley CI
Christchurch BH23 . . . 123 F8
1 Radipole DT3 . . . . . 152 E2
Kimberley Rd
Bournemouth BH6 . . . 123 C5
Poole BH14 . . . . 120 B3
Kimber Rd BH11 . . . . . . 88 F3
KIMMERIDGE BH20 . . . 175 D4
Kimmeridge Ave BH12 . 120 E8
Kimmeridge CI DT3 . . . 167 B8
Kingfisher CI
Bournemouth BH6 . . . 123 E6
Ferndown BH22 . . . . . . 53 B2
Weymouth DT4 . . . . . . 180 D6
Kingfisher Ct BH8 . . . . 122 C6
Kingfisher CI BH23 . . . 124 A5
Kingfisher Park Homes 3
BH10 . . . . 89 E1
Kingfishers 4 BH23 . . . 124 A5
Kingfishers The BH23 . . 124 A5
Kingfisher Way
Christchurch BH23 . . . 125 A5
Ringwood BH24 . . . . . . 47 D1
King George Ave BH9 . . 89 F2
King George Mobile Home
Pk BH25 . . . . 94 F1
King George Sh Ctr The BH
TA18 . . . . 191 F5
King George V Rd BH20 . 139 E7
King John Ave BH11 . . . 88 D5
King John CI BH11 . . . . 88 D6
Kinjohn Rd SP8 . . . . 6 A1
King John's Rd BH24 . . . 55 B7
Kings Arms La BH24 . . . 55 B7
Kings Arms Row BH24 . . 55 B7
Kings Ave BH14 . . . . . . 120 D2
King's Ave BH23 . . . . . 123 F6
Kingsbere Ave BH10 . . . 89 B2
Kingsbere Cres DT1 . . . 135 A7
Kingsbere Gdns BH23 . 126 A8
Kingsbere La SP7 . . . . . 13 A4
Kingsbere Rd
Overcombe/Preston
DT3 . . . . 168 A7
Poole BH15 . . . . 119 C5
Kingsbridge Rd BH14 . . 120 C3
Kings Brook 2 SO41 . . . 95 F3
Kingsbury CI BH23 . . . . 55 B7
Kingsbury's La BH24 . . . 55 B7
Kings Chase SP8 . . . . . . 6 B1
Kings CI
Ferndown BH22 . . . . . . 53 A1
Longburton BH19 . . . . 195 B8
Poole BH15 . . . . 119 D5
Kingscourt CI 2 SP8 . . . 6 B1
King's Court Palace★ SP8 . 6 B1
Kingscourt Rd SP8 . . . . . 6 B1
Kings Cres DT9 . . . . 30 B7
Kings Cres BH14 . . . . . 120 E2
Kings Ct Bsns Ctr BH19 . 179 B2
Kingsfield BH24 . . . . . . 55 C7
Kingsgate 10 BH13 . . . 121 B3
Kings Grange 11 BH4 . . 121 D2
Kings High Sch BH10 . . . 89 C3
Kings La BH21 . . . . 201 F4
King's La DT6 . . . . 70 D5
KINGSLAND
Kingsland Ct BH13 . . . . 147 F7
Kingsland Grange 4 . . . 26 E6
Kingsleigh Prim Sch
BH10 . . . . 89 C3
Kingsley Ave BH6 . . . . 124 A4
Kingsley CI BH6 . . . . . 124 A4
Kingsley House 3 BH9 . . 89 F1
Kingsley Paddock DT2 . 72 F7
Kingsman La SP7 . . . . . 12 E2
Kings Mead DT2 . . . . . . 78 B1
Kingsmead Ct 5 BH23 . . 59 B5
Kingsmill Rd BH17 . . . . 119 E7
King's Mill Rd DT10 . . . 34 B6
Kingsmill CI DT6 . . . . . 100 E7
King's Park Athletics Ctr
BH7 . . . . 122 F6
King's Park BH7, BH1 . . 122 E6
King's Park Hospl BH7 . 122 F5
King's Park Prim Sch
BH1 . . . . 122 E5

King's Park Rd BH7 . . . 122 E6
King's Pitt 3 DT1 . . . . . 107 C1
Kings Rd
Dorchester DT1 . . . . . 108 B1
New Milton BH25 . . . . . 95 C3
Radipole DT3 . . . . 167 C3
Sherborne DT9 . . . . 30 B7
King's Rd
Blandford Forum DT11 . 212 E5
Bournemouth BH3 . . . 122 A7
Thornford DT9 . . . . . . 194 D7
Kings Road E BH19 . . . 179 B2
Kings Road W BH19 . . . 179 A2
King's St DT11 . . . . 56 D5
KING'S STAG DT10 . . . . 196 D5
King St
Bridport DT6 . . . . 100 D6
Fortuneswell DT5 . . . . 186 F7
Radipole DT4 . . . . 167 D4
Wimborne Minster BH21 . 59 B4
Yeovil BA21 . . . . 27 D6
Kingsthorn Rd DT1 . . . 107 C2
KINGSTON
Corfe Castle BH20 . . . 176 F3
Ringwood BH24 . . . . . . 55 B1
Sturminster Newton DT10 197 A4
Kingston CI DT2 . . . . . . 22 C5
Kingston Barnyard DT11 . 81 D8
Kingston CI DT11 . . . . . 212 C5
Kingston Hill BH20 . . . 176 F4
Kingston Lacy House★
BH21 . . . . 58 B7
KINGSTON MAURWARD
DT2 . . . . 108 F2
Kingston Maurward Coll
DT2 . . . . 108 F3
Kingston Maurward Park &
Gdns★ DT2 . . . . 108 E3
Kingston Rd BH15 . . . . 119 D4
KINGSTON RUSSELL
DT2 . . . . 104 C3
Kingston View BA21 . . . 27 D6
Kingsway
Ferndown BH22 . . . . . . 61 B8
Lyme Regis DT7 . . . . . . 96 C6
Kingsway CI BH23 . . . . . 91 F1
Kingswell CI BH10 . . . . . 89 D2
Kingswell Gdns BH10 . . 89 B2
Kingswell Gr BH10 . . . . 89 B2
Kingswell Rd BH10 . . . . 89 C2
Kings Williams Head DS
TA18 . . . . 68 F1
Kingswood 2 BH1 . . . . 121 C2
Kingswood CI 2 BH19 . 178 E2
Kingswood Rd 6 TA18 . 191 F3
Kinross Rd BH3 . . . . . . 121 E6
Kinsbourne Ave BH10 . . 89 D2
KINSON 89 B5
Kinson Ave BH15 . . . . . 120 A7
Kinson Comm Nature
Reserve★ BH11 . . . . . . 89 B5
Kinson Gr BH10 . . . . . . 89 C6
Kinson Park Rd BH10 . . 89 C6
Kinson Pottery Ind Est
BH14 . . . . 120 A6
Kinson Prim Sch BH11 . . 89 B5
Kinson Rd BH10 . . . . . . 89 C3
Kiosks The BH15 . . . . . 119 C1
Kipling Rd BH14 . . . . . 120 B5
Kirby CI BH15 . . . . 119 F6
Kirby Way BH6 . . . . . . 123 D4
Kirkham Ave BH23 . . . . 92 C3
Kirkleton Ave DT4 . . . . 167 D5
Kirkway BH18 . . . . 87 B4
Kitchener Cres BH17 . . 87 B2
Kitchener Rd DT4 . . . . 167 B3
Kite's Nest La SP8 . . . . . 1 E2
KITFORD DT11 . . . . . . 197 C3
Kitford La DT11 . . . . . . 197 C3
KIT HILL SP7 . . . . 23 A4
Kithill TA18 . . . . 191 F3
Kit La DT2 . . . . 109 C5
Kitscroft Rd BH10 . . . . . 89 C5
Kitt Hill DT9 . . . . 30 A6
Kittiwake CI BH6 . . . . . 123 D6
Kitton La DT9 . . . . 29 A8
Kiwi CI BH15 . . . . 119 E3
KNACKERS HOLE DT11 . 197 D6
Knap Barrow (Long
Barrow)★ SP6 . . . . . . 190 D6
Knapp CI BH23 . . . . . . 124 A8
KNAPP HILL SP7 . . . . . . 7 C2
Knapp Mill Ave BH23 . . 124 A8
Knapps DT11 . . . . 198 B6
Knapp The
Chickerell DT3 . . . . . . 166 C6
Fontmell Magna SP7 . . . 37 F6
Hilton DT11 . . . . 209 D6
Shaftesbury SP7 . . . . . . 12 D3
Knapwater Wlk 12 DT11 . 135 B8
KNIGHTON
Bournemouth 88 D8
Yetminster 194 E6
Knighton Heath CI BH11 . 88 E4
Knighton Heath Ind Est
BH11 . . . . 88 E4
Knighton Heath Rd BH11 . 88 E4
Knighton House Sch
DT11 . . . . 198 E3
Knighton La
Bournemouth BH21 . . . 88 D7
Broadmayne DT2 . . . . 136 C2
Knighton Pk BH25 . . . . 126 E8

Knightsbridge Ct BH2.... 121 E2
Knights Cl ❶ DT11.... 212 D2
Knightsdale Rd DT4.... 167 B2
Knights Rd BH11.... 88 D5
Knightstone Ct BH20.... 142 F3
Knightstone Gr BH22.... 52 F2
Knightstone Rise DT6.... 68 F1
Knightwood Cl BH23.... 125 D8
Knobcrook Rd ❸ BH21.... 59 B6
KNOB'S CROOK BH21.... 64 B1
Knole Ct ❻ BH1.... 122 D4
Knole Gdns BH1.... 122 D4
Knole Rd BH1.... 122 D4
Knoll Gdns★ BH21.... 60 F4
Knoll Gdns BH24.... 54 B4
Knoll La BH21.... 85 D7
Knoll Manor BH21.... 121 F5
Knoll Pl SP8.... 5 E3
Knoll Rd BH21.... 85 D8
Knoll Rise DT3.... 152 E2
Knollsea Cl ❶ BH19.... 179 C1
Knotts Cl ❼ DT11.... 198 C7
Knotts Paddock DT9.... 30 C6
Knowle Cross DT8.... 203 D6
Knowle Hill BH20.... 140 A1
Knowle La TA18, DT8.... 191 F1
Knowles Cl BH23.... 124 E7
Knowle Wood Knap ❶
  BH20.... 140 A1
Knowl La DT6.... 101 D7
KNOWLTON BH21.... 201 D4
Knowlton Church (remains
  of)★ BH21.... 201 D5
Knowlton Circles★
  BH21.... 201 D5
Knowlton Gdns BH1.... 90 B3
Knowlton Rd BH17.... 87 F2
Knyveton Ho BH1.... 122 B4
Knyveton Rd BH1.... 122 C4
Kyrchil La BH21.... 59 F6
Kyrchil Way BH21.... 59 F7

L

Labrador Dr BH15.... 119 C1
Laburnam Way SP8.... 5 D1
Laburnum Cl
  Ferndown BH22.... 61 B6
  Radipole DT4.... 167 B6
  ❶ Sandford BH20.... 116 A1
  Verwood BH31.... 45 E5
Laburnum Cres ❶ TA18.... 191 F5
Laburnum Ho BH10.... 89 C4
Laburnum Rd DT2.... 75 D3
Laburnum Way BA20.... 26 F2
Lacey Cres BH15.... 120 A6
Lackington Dro DT2.... 208 B1
Lacy Cl ❶ BH21.... 59 C6
Lacy Dr BH21.... 59 C6
Lady Baden Powell Way
  DT11.... 212 E6
Lady Caroline's Dr DT11 210 D7
Lady Mead Cl ❸ BH5.... 187 A4
Lady St Mary CE Fst Sch The
  BH20.... 142 D3
Ladysmith Cl BH23.... 124 F7
Lagado Cl BH14.... 47 C8
Lagland Ct ❶₄ BH15.... 119 C2
Lagland St BH15.... 119 C2
Lagoon Cl BH14.... 147 B8
Lagoon Rd BH14.... 147 B8
Laidlaw Cl BH12.... 121 B8
LAKE BH15.... 117 F1
Lake Ave BH15.... 117 F1
Lake Cres BH15.... 118 E3
Lake Dr
  Poole BH15.... 118 D2
  Upton BH15.... 117 F1
Lake Farm Cl BH22.... 89 B8
Lakefields BH23.... 193 B7
Lakegate La DT9.... 194 A5
Lake Grove Rd BH25.... 95 A4
Lake La DT9.... 100 D4
Lake Rd
  Bournemouth BH11.... 89 C6
  Upton BH15.... 117 F1
Lakeside BH14.... 55 E6
Lakeside Gdns DT3.... 167 B7
Lakeside Pines BH25.... 95 A4
Lakeside Rd BH13.... 121 A1
Lakeview Dr BH24.... 55 E6
Lake View Manor BH25.... 95 A3
Lakewood Rd BH23.... 93 F1
Lambert Cl ❹ DT4.... 17 C2
Lambert's Castle (Fort)★
  DT6.... 202 E2
Lambourne Cl TA18.... 191 F5
Lamb Plot DT9.... 194 D2
LAMBROOK DT6.... 68 E5
Lambs Cl BH17.... 87 C1
Lambsfield DT9.... 30 C7
LAMBS' GREEN.... 58 F2
Lambsgreen La BH21.... 58 F2
Lambs La BH21.... 56 D3
Lammas Cl SP8.... 5 F3
Lampton Cl BH20.... 139 F2
Lampton Gdns ❺ BH9.... 89 F1
Lanark Cl BH15.... 118 E2
Lancaster Cl
  Christchurch BH23.... 125 C7
  Corfe Mullen BH18.... 86 F5
Lancaster Dr
  Corfe Mullen BH18.... 86 F5

Lancaster Dr continued
  Verwood BH31.... 45 A5
Lancaster Rd
  Dorchester DT1.... 108 B1
  Ferndown BH21.... 61 A8
  Radipole DT3.... 152 B1
Lancelot Cl ❸ BA21.... 26 F7
Lancer Cl BH23.... 123 F7
Lanchards ❹ DT11.... 198 B6
Lanchards La DT11.... 198 B5
Lander Cl BH15.... 119 D1
Landers Reach BH16.... 84 D2
Landford Gdns BH8.... 90 D2
Landford Way BH8.... 90 D2
Landscombe Vale DT2.... 208 A8
Landseer Rd ❶ BH4.... 121 C3
Landshire La
  Fifehead Magdalen SP8.... 20 C5
  Stalbridge BA8.... 19 D3
Lane Cl DT11.... 212 F6
LANE END BH20.... 113 C6
Lane End DT11.... 79 F7
LANEHOUSE DT4.... 166 C8
Lanehouse Rocks Rd ❶
  DT4.... 180 C8
Lane Lowther Gdns The ❹
  BH8.... 122 C5
Lane-side SP7.... 12 F4
Lanes The BH25.... 95 A5
Lane The BH20.... 176 F4
Langdon Cl BH14.... 120 D4
Langdon La
  Beaminster DT8.... 204 E4
  Chideock DT6.... 98 E7
Langdon Rd BH14.... 120 D4
Langdons DT9.... 30 C7
Langdons Way ❶ TA20.... 202 A8
Langfords La SP8.... 4 F1
LANGHAM SP8.... 9 E8
Langham Ct BH23.... 91 F1
Langham La SP8.... 4 F1
Langley Chase BH24.... 54 B5
Langley Rd
  Christchurch BH23.... 93 E1
  Poole BH14.... 120 F4
Langmead Pl ❷ TA18.... 191 F3
Langmead Rd TA18.... 191 F3
Langmead Sq ❶ TA18.... 191 F3
Langmoor La EX13.... 202 A2
Lang Rd TA18.... 191 E3
Langside Ave BH11.... 121 A8
Langside Sch BH12.... 121 A8
Langton Ave DT4.... 180 C6
Langton Cl BH25.... 122 D8
Langton Cres DT11.... 212 E3
LANGTON HERRING DT3.... 150 C2
LANGTON LONG BLANDFORD
  DT11.... 212 F3
LANGTON MATRAVERS
  BH19.... 178 A3
Langton Matravers Mus★
  BH19.... 178 B3
Langton Rd
  Blandford Forum DT11.... 212 D3
  Bournemouth BH7.... 122 F5
Lansdell Ct ❹ BH15.... 119 E3
Lansdowne Cres BH1.... 122 B3
Lansdowne Gdns BH1.... 122 A4
Lansdowne Mews ❸
  BH1.... 122 B4
Lansdowne Rd
  Bournemouth BH1.... 122 B3
  Bridport DT6.... 100 D4
Lansdowne Rdbt The
  BH1.... 122 A3
Lansdowne Sq DT4.... 167 C1
Lapwing Rd BH17.... 60 A7
Lara Cl BH8.... 90 D3
Larch Cl
  Broadstone BH17.... 86 E1
  Hordle SO41.... 95 F3
  Sandford BH20.... 143 B8
  St Leonards BH24.... 54 C4
Larch Way BH22.... 61 C7
Larcombe La DT6.... 69 D5
Larkhill Rd BA21.... 27 A6
Lark Rise BH23.... 125 A6
Larks Cl BH22.... 61 B7
Larksfield Ave BH9.... 90 C3
Larkshill Cl BH25.... 95 B4
Larks Mdw DT10.... 33 E8
Larksmead DT11.... 212 E5
Larkspur Cl DT4.... 167 E6
Larkspur Cres DT4.... 167 E6
Larks Rise BH22.... 61 B7
Larmer Tree Gdns★ SP5.... 188 B4
Lascelles Ct ❶ BH7.... 123 B6
Lascelles Rd BH7.... 123 B6
Latch Farm Ave BH23.... 124 A8
Latimer Rd BH9.... 121 F8
Latimers Cl BH23.... 93 F1
Launches The BH23.... 172 C6
Laundry La SP7.... 12 D2
Laurel Ave BH16.... 116 B2
Laurel Cl
  ❶ Bridport DT6.... 100 B8
  Christchurch BH23.... 93 D1
  Hordle SO41.... 95 E4
  St Leonards BH24.... 54 A4
  West Coker BA22.... 193 B8
Laurel Dr BH13.... 87 C4
Laurel Gdns BH18.... 87 C4
Laurel La BH24.... 54 A3
Laurels The
  Broadstone BH18.... 87 B4
  ❼ Crewkerne TA18.... 191 F5
  Ferndown BH22.... 61 C7

Laurels The continued
  ❽ Gillingham SP8.... 5 E1
  Iwerne Courtney or Shroton
    DT11.... 198 E7
Laurel Way DT2.... 75 D2
Lavender Cl BH31.... 45 E5
Lavender Dr
  Bournemouth BH8.... 90 D4
  Hordle SO41.... 95 E3
Lavender Villas BH21.... 126 A8
Lavender Way BH8.... 85 F3
Lavender Wlk BH8.... 90 D4
Laver's La TA20.... 202 C6
Laverstock ❸ BH5.... 122 F3
Lavinia Rd BH12.... 120 C7
Lawford Rd BH9.... 90 A4
Lawn Ct ❶₃ BH2.... 121 D4
Lawns Cl BH21.... 60 C6
Lawns Rd BH21.... 60 C6
Lawns The
  Charmouth DT6.... 97 B7
  Christchurch BH23.... 126 B8
  Lane View BH25.... 94 D5
Lawrence Cl BH10.... 122 C6
Lawrence Dr
  Crossways DT2.... 137 D5
  Poole BH13.... 120 E1
Lawrence La
  Hyde SP6.... 43 D4
  Witchampton BH21.... 201 A2
Lawrence of Arabia's Cottage
  (Cloud Hill)★ BH20.... 112 C2
Lawrence of Arabia's Grave★
  DT2.... 138 E7
Lawrence Rd BH24.... 47 E2
Lawson Rd BH12.... 120 B6
Layard Dr BH21.... 59 D1
Laycock Hill DT9.... 17 C7
Laymoor La BH21.... 60 D5
LAYMORE TA20.... 202 F7
Layton Cl BH12.... 120 D5
Layton La SP7.... 12 E2
Layton Rd BH12.... 120 D5
Lea Cl BA21.... 27 D8
Leamington Rd
  Bournemouth BH9.... 122 A7
  Weymouth DT4.... 166 F2
Leanne Bsns Pk BH20.... 142 E5
Leaphill Rd BH7.... 123 B6
Lea Rd DT4.... 180 B8
Learoyd Rd BH17.... 119 E7
Lea The BH31.... 45 C5
Lea Way BH11.... 88 E6
Leaze La BA21.... 28 A4
Lecher La DT8.... 192 B1
Lechlade Gdns BH7.... 123 B8
Ledbury Rd BH23.... 124 F5
Leddington Way SP8.... 5 E4
Ledgard Cl BH14.... 120 D8
Lee Ct BH22.... 61 D4
Leedam Rd BH10.... 89 D4
Leeds Cres DT4.... 166 F2
Lee La DT6.... 101 A7
Lee Lane BH23.... 91 D4
Leeson Cl ❷ BH7.... 178 F2
Leeson Dr BH22.... 61 B8
Legg La BH21.... 59 D4
Legion Cl
  Dorchester DT1.... 134 E7
  Hamworthy BH15.... 118 E2
Legion Rd
  Hamworthy BH15.... 118 E2
  Yeovil BA21.... 27 B6
Leicester Rd BH13.... 120 F3
LEIGH
  Sherborne.... 194 E3
  Sturminster Newton.... 197 D3
  Wimborne Minster.... 59 E5
Leigham Vale Rd BH6.... 123 D4
Leigh Cl BH21.... 59 E4
Leigh Comm BH21.... 59 E5
Leigh Comm Nature
  Reserve★ BH21.... 59 E5
Leigh Gdns BH21.... 59 D4
Leigh La
  Halstock BA22.... 193 C3
  Ibberton DT11.... 197 D3
  Wimborne Minster BH21.... 59 F5
LEIGH PARK.... 59 E4
Leigh Rd
  New Milton BH25.... 95 A3
  Wimborne Minster BH21.... 59 E5
Leighton Lo ❸ BH2.... 121 D4
Le Neubourg Way SP8.... 5 F1
Lennox St DT4.... 167 D4
Lentham Cl BH17.... 87 D1
Lenthay Cl DT9.... 29 F4
Lenthay Rd DT9.... 29 F4
Le Patourel Cl BH23.... 124 D7
Lerret Rd DT5.... 181 A1
Lerrett Cl DT3.... 166 D6
Leslie Rd
  Bournemouth BH9.... 121 F7
  Poole BH14.... 120 A3
Lessingham Ave DT4.... 180 C6
Letton Cl DT11.... 212 F6
Leven Ave BH4.... 121 C4
Leven Cl BH4.... 121 D4
Levet's La ❹ BH15.... 119 B1
LEWCOMBE DT2.... 193 E2
Lewell Way DT2.... 136 C3
Lewens Cl BH21.... 59 C4
Lewens La BH21.... 59 C4

Lewesdon Cl ❻ DT8.... 204 C4
Lewesdon Dr BH18.... 86 F4
Lewesdon Hill★ DT8.... 203 E4
Lewesdon Prep Sch DT7 195 A7
Lewis Gdns BH10.... 89 C2
Leybourne Ave BH10.... 89 D4
Leybourne Cl BH10.... 89 C5
Leydene Ave BH8.... 90 F1
Leydene Cl BH8.... 90 F1
Leyland Rd BH12.... 88 E2
Leyside BH23.... 124 F6
Leyton Conyers ❶₁ BH13.... 147 F7
Liberty Cl BH21.... 53 D6
Liberty Ct BH23.... 126 A1
Liberty Rd DT5.... 181 A1
Liberty's Raptor & Reptile
  Ctr★ BH24.... 55 E5
Liberty Way BH15.... 119 D2
Library Mews BH12.... 120 D5
Library Rd
  Bournemouth BH9.... 89 F1
  Ferndown BH22.... 61 D5
  Poole BH12.... 120 E5
Lichfield Rd DT4.... 167 A2
Liddington Cres DT11.... 212 D5
Liddon Hill TA18.... 191 C5
Liederbach Dr BH31.... 45 E3
Lifeboat Coll The BH15.... 119 B3
Lighthouse (Arts Ctr)★
  BH15.... 119 D3
Lighthouse Rd BH19.... 185 C7
Lights Cl BH23.... 124 B7
Lilac Cl BH14.... 55 D8
LILLINGTON DT9.... 194 F7
LILLIPUT.... 147 C8
Lilliput CE Fst Sch BH14 147 C8
Lilliput Ct BH14.... 120 B3
Lilliput La DT6.... 100 C6
Lilliput Rd BH14.... 147 D8
Limber Rd BA22.... 26 C6
Lime Cl
  Dorchester DT1.... 134 F8
  Poole BH15.... 119 F6
Lime Hill DT6.... 70 B7
Lime Kiln BA21.... 26 E5
Limekiln Cl DT5.... 186 E2
Lime Kiln La 8A8.... 19 A3
Lime Kiln Rd BH14.... 120 A2
Limerick Cl ❾ DT9.... 17 D2
Limes The SP7.... 12 B8
Lime Tree Ave BH20.... 27 A2
Lime Tree Cl SP6.... 42 B6
Limited Rd BH9.... 90 A1
LIMPERS HILL BA12.... 3 D4
Lin Brook Dr BH24.... 47 E2
Linchild Rd ❸ BH20.... 140 A2
Lincoln Ave
  Bournemouth BH1.... 122 D5
  Christchurch BH23.... 91 F2
Lincoln Farm Animal Rescue
  & Rehoming Ctr★ BH1 .81 D6
Lincoln Rd
  Poole BH12.... 120 D7
  Weymouth DT4.... 166 F2
Lindbergh Rd BH21.... 61 A8
Linden Ave DT1.... 108 A1
Linden Cl BH22.... 61 D1
Linden Gdns ❶ BH24.... 55 B8
Linden Pk SP7.... 13 A2
Linden Rd
  Bournemouth BH9.... 90 A3
  Ferndown BH22.... 61 D1
  Poole BH12.... 120 C6
  Swanage BH19.... 179 A2
  Yeovil BA20.... 27 B5
Lindens Cl DT4.... 167 D6
Lindens The BH23.... 92 D3
Lindford Rd BH24.... 47 F1
Lindlar Cl SP7.... 12 F4
Lindsay Ct ❶₃ BH13.... 121 A1
Lindsay Manor ❶ BH13.... 121 A4
Lindsay Pk ❶₈ BH13.... 121 A4
Lindsay Rd BH13.... 120 F4
Lindum Ct ❸ BH21.... 121 A4
Linen Yard The ❷₇ TA18.191 F4
Lineside BH23.... 124 C8
Linford Cl BH25.... 95 B4
Linford Rd BH24.... 47 F1
Lingdale Rd BH6.... 123 E4
Lingfield Ave BA21.... 27 F7
Lingfield Grange ❶₁
  BH13.... 121 B3
Ling Rd BH12.... 88 B1
Lington Cl DT2.... 137 D6
Lingwood Ave BH23.... 124 F6
Linhay DT2.... 205 A8
Linhorns La BH25.... 95 A5
Linhkay ❶₂ TA20.... 202 A8
Linhkay Cl ❶₁ TA20.... 202 A8
Link Rd BH24.... 47 E1
Link Rise BH21.... 86 E6
Linkside Ave BH7.... 122 F8
Links Rd
  Poole BH14.... 120 D2
  Weymouth DT4.... 167 B4
Links View Ave BH14.... 120 E2
Linmead Dr BH11.... 89 A6
Linnet Cl
  Radipole DT3.... 152 C4
  Ringwood BH24.... 55 E6
Linnet Ct BH25.... 94 F3
Linnet La DT2.... 205 D5
Linnet Rd BH17.... 118 F8
Linsay Rd BH20.... 139 E5
Lintern La SP8.... 11 A5
Linthorpe Rd BH15.... 119 E4
Linton Lawns BH22.... 61 E3

Linwood Rd BH9.... 122 B7
Linwood Sch BH9.... 122 A7
Lionheart Cl BH11.... 88 D5
Lions Hill Way BH24.... 53 E4
Lions La BH24.... 53 F4
Lions Wood BH24.... 54 A4
Liscombe Cl DT1.... 107 D2
Lissenden ❶ BH13.... 121 B3
Litchford Rd BH25.... 95 C3
Little Barrs Dr BH25.... 95 B4
LITTLEBREDY DT2.... 131 E7
Little Britain DT1.... 108 C1
LITTLE CANFORD.... 60 D4
Little Content La SP7.... 12 F3
Littlecroft Ave BH9.... 90 B3
Little Croft Rd BH12.... 120 B6
Little Ct
  Poole.... 147 C2
  Poole, Canford Cliffs BH13 147 F8
Little Dewlands BH31.... 45 A4
LITTLEDOWN.... 123 A7
Littledown SP7.... 12 F5
Littledown Ave BH7.... 122 F7
Littledown Ctr BH7.... 123 A8
Littledown Dr BH7.... 122 F7
Little England DT11.... 79 F7
Littlefield DT9.... 29 F4
Littlefield La SP5.... 189 A4
Little Forest Mans ❶₂
  BH1.... 122 A3
Little Forest Rd BH4.... 121 E5
Little Fosters BH13.... 147 E6
Little Lane DT11.... 198 A6
Little Lonnen
  Colehill BH21.... 59 F8
  Wimborne Minster.... 60 A8
Littlemead
  Broadmayne DT2.... 136 B3
  Radipole DT3.... 152 B3
Littlemead Cl BH17.... 119 A7
Littlemill La SP6.... 190 F3
LITTLEMOOR DT3.... 152 F1
Littlemoor Ave BH11.... 88 D4
Littlemoor Rd
  Overcombe/Preston
    DT3.... 168 A8
  Radipole DT3.... 152 C4
Littlemoor Sh Ctr DT3.... 152 D3
LITTLE PAMPHILL.... 58 F5
Little Tarrat La BA20.... 27 C2
LITTLETON DT1.... 211 C7
Littleton Dro DT11.... 211 B6
Littletowns DT11.... 212 D6
Littleview Rd DT4.... 166 F2
LITTLEWINDSOR DT8.... 203 F7
LITTLE WOOLGARSTON
  BH20.... 177 D8
LITTON CHENEY DT2.... 103 C1
Litton Hill DT2.... 103 B2
Litton La
  Askerswell DT2.... 102 E5
  Litton Cheney DT2.... 103 B1
  Puncknowle DT2.... 129 E7
Liverpool Rd ❹ DT4.... 167 C1
Livingstone Rd
  Bournemouth BH5.... 123 B5
  Christchurch BH23.... 124 D7
  Poole BH12.... 120 C6
  Wimborne Minster BH21... 59 E4
Llewellin Cl BH16.... 117 E8
Llewellin Ct ❻ BH16.... 117 E7
Llewelyn Cl BH16.... 118 C7
Loaders Cl BH9.... 122 A8
Load La DT9.... 194 F1
Local History Ctr★ ❶₅
  BH15.... 119 B1
Locarno Rd BH9.... 179 B2
Loch Rd BH14.... 120 A3
Lockeridge Cl DT11.... 212 C5
Lockett's La DT2.... 207 F7
Locks La
  Glanvilles Wootton DT9.. 195 E3
  Loders DT6.... 101 F6
  Stratton DT2.... 106 B8
Locksley Dr BH22.... 61 C3
Locks Piece ❺ BH20.... 140 A2
Lockwood Terr SP8.... 11 B8
Lockyer Dro BH21.... 61 F6
Lockyers Mid Sch BH21.. 85 F8
Lockyers Rd BH21.... 86 E8
Lockyer's Way BH16.... 84 D3
Lodbourne Gdns ❻ SP8.. 5 F3
Lodbourne Gn ❼ SP8.... 5 F3
Lodbourne Terr ❺ SP8.... 5 F3
Lodden View SP8.... 11 A8
Loders CE Prim Sch DT6. 69 C1
Loders Cl BH17.... 87 D1
LODERS DT6.... 101 E4
Loders La DT6.... 101 E4
Lodge Cl BH14.... 120 E4
Lodge Ct BH14.... 120 E4
Lodge La DT6.... 100 B7
Lodge Rd
  Christchurch BH23.... 123 E8
  Holt BH21.... 51 B6
Lodge The BH2.... 121 E4
Lodge Way DT4.... 180 D8
LODMOOR DT4.... 167 D7
Lodmoor Ave DT3.... 167 D7
Lodmoor Ctry Pk★ DT4.. 167 E7
Lodmoor RSPB Reserve★
  DT4.... 167 D7
Loewy Cres BH12.... 88 D2
Lombard Ave BH6.... 123 D5
Lombardy Cl BH31.... 45 C5
Lomer La SP6, BH24.... 42 E4
Lomond Dr DT4.... 167 C1

London Cl
1 Dorchester DT1 . . . . 108 B2
Piddlehinton DT2 . . . . 76 F7
London La BH23 . . . . 63 F2
London Rd
Dorchester DT1 . . . . 108 B2
Milborne Port DT9 . . . . 17 E1
London Row DT2 . . . . 76 F7
Lone Pine Dr BH22 . . . . . . 61 E3
Lone Pine Pk BH22 . . . . . . 61 F3
Lone Pine Way BH22 . . . . . 61 F2
Long Acre DT5 . . . . 187 A4
Longacre Dr BH22 . . . . . . 61 C4
Long Ash La
Frampton DT2 . . . . 74 A3
Frome St Quintin DT2 . . . 206 D6
Longbarrow Cl BH8 . . . . . . 91 A1
Long Barrow La DT8 . . . . 204 B3
LONG BREDY DT2 . . . . . . 103 F1
Long Bredy Hut La DT2 . . 103 F2
LONGBURTON DT9 . . . . . . 195 C7
Longbury Hill La SP8 . . . . 5 B4
Long Cl
Sturminster Newton DT10 . . 35 C2
Yeovil BA21 . . . . 26 E5
Long Cowleaze DT2 . . . . . . 79 E1
LONG CRICHEL BH21 . . . . 200 E5
Longcroft Rd
Weymouth DT4 . . . . 167 B3
Yeovil BA21 . . . . 27 D6
LONG CROSS BA12 . . . . 2 B5
Long Cross SP7 . . . . 12 E3
Longdown Rd DT9 . . . . . . 194 D7
Long Entry DT2 . . . . 96 C5
Longespee Rd BH21 . . . . . . 87 E8
Longfield Dr
Bournemouth BH11 . . . . . . 89 A6
Ferndown BH22 . . . . 89 E8
Longfield Rd DT1 . . . . . . 167 D1
LONGFLEET 119 D4
Longfleet CE Comb Sch
BH15 . . . . 119 D4
Longfleet Rd BH15 . . . . . . 119 E4
Longford Rd DT9 . . . . . . 194 C7
Longforward Hill TA17 . . . 191 A8
Longforward La TA17 . . . . 191 B8
Long Furlong La BA22 . . . 193 C8
LONGHAM 61 A1
Longham Bsns Ctr BH22 . . 61 B2
Longham Farm Cl BH22 . . 61 B1
Longhayes Ave DT6 . . . . . 100 B8
Long Hill BA12 . . . . 2 F5
Long La
Bothenhampton DT6 . . . . 100 F4
Bourton SP8, BA9 . . . . . . 1 B1
Cann SP7 . . . . 24 A7
Colehill BH21 . . . . 51 B1
Colehill BH21 . . . . 59 E8
Cucklington BA9 . . . . 4 A1
Puddletown DT2 . . . . 78 B2
Ringwood BH24 . . . . 55 D4
Whitechurch Canonicorum
DT6 . . . . 65 C7
Longlands La BA22 . . . . . 193 C8
Longland's La
Littlebredy DT2 . . . . 131 F7
Winterbourne Abbas DT2 . 131 F7
Longleat Gdns BH25 . . . . . 94 E3
Longman's Rd BA21 . . . . 201 A3
Long Mdw DT9 . . . . 195 A2
Longmead SP7 . . . . 12 F3
Long Mead BA21 . . . . 26 E5
Longmead Ind Est SP7 . . . 12 F3
Longmeadow La BH17 . . . 118 B8
Long Rd BH10 . . . . 89 C5
Long's La DT3 . . . . 102 E7
Longspee Sch BH17 . . . . . 119 D7
Long St
Cerne Abbas DT2 . . . . . . 207 D4
Sherborne DT9 . . . . 30 C6
Longstone Cl DT5 . . . . . . 186 E1
Lonnen Rd BH21 . . . . 51 D1
Lonnen Wood Cl BH21 . . . 60 A8
Lonsdale Rd BH3 . . . . . . 121 F6
Looke La DT2 . . . . 129 F6
Lopen Rd TA17, TA13 . . . . 191 D8
Loraine Ave BH23 . . . . . . 126 C8
Lord Cl BH17 . . . . 119 F7
Lordsmead Rd BA12 . . . . . . 3 B4
Loring Rd BH23 . . . . 123 F8
Lorne Park Rd BH1 . . . . . 122 A3
Lorne Rd DT1 . . . . 107 E1
Lornton Wlk 10 DT1 . . . . 135 B8
Lorton La DT3 . . . . 152 E8
Lorton Meadows Reserve &
Wildlife Ctr★ DT3 . . . . . 152 D2
LOSCOMBE DT6 . . . . 69 E8
Loscombe Reserve★
DT6 . . . . 204 F1
Lotmoor Hill SP8 . . . . 10 C2
Louise Rd DT1 . . . . 107 E1
Louse La DT11 . . . . 211 E4
Louviers Rd DT3 . . . . 152 E2
Lovage Way BA12 . . . . 3 B6
Love La
Marnhull DT10 . . . . 21 A4
Shaftesbury SP7 . . . . 12 D2
Lovelands DT2 . . . . 193 A1
Lovells Croft 6 DT6 . . . . 187 A4
Lovells Mead DT10 . . . . . . 20 E3
Loveridge La 18 TA20 . . . 202 A8
Loverley La BH21 . . . . . . 201 B3
Love's La DT6 . . . . 66 C1
Lower Acreman St DT9 . . . 30 B5
LOWER ANSTY DT2 . . . . . 77 E4
Lower Ashley Rd BH25 . . . 95 D2
Lower Beadon TA16 . . . . . 191 E7

Lower Blakemere Rd 12
DT1 . . . . 107 C1
Lower Blandford Rd
Broadstone BH18 . . . . . . 87 B3
Cann SP7 . . . . 24 A7
2 Shaftesbury SP7 . . . . . 12 F2
LOWER BLANDFORD ST
MARY DT11 . . . . 212 E1
LOWER BOCKHAMPTON
DT2 . . . . 109 A2
Lower Boyston La DT9 . . . 16 E3
Lower Catherston Rd DT6 . 65 B1
Lower Comm La BH21 . . . . 53 C7
Lower Comm Rd DT11 . . . 36 D1
Lower Coombses La DT6 . . 65 B1
Lower Coombses Rd DT11 . 202 A8
Lower East Coker Rd
BA20 . . . . 27 B1
LOWER EYPE DT6 . . . . . . 99 F3
Lower Fairmead Rd BA21 . 27 E8
Lower Golf Links Rd BH18 . 87 B5
Lower Gunville 4 DT9 . . . 17 D2
LOWER HALSTOCK LEIGH
BA22 . . . . 193 B2
LOWER HAMWORTHY
BH15 . . . . 119 A1
Lower Hillside Rd DT10 . . 140 A1
LOWER HOLWELL BH21 . . . 40 F6
LOWER KINGCOMBE
DT2 . . . . 205 E1
LOWER MANNINGTON
BH21 . . . . 52 C7
LOWER MARSH BA8 . . . . . 19 F6
LOWER NYLAND SP8 . . . . 19 F8
LOWER ODCOMBE BA22 . . 192 A8
Lower Odcombe BA22 . . . 26 A4
LOWER PARKSTONE 120 B3
Lower Putton La DT3 . . . 166 D6
Lower Rd
Stalbridge DT10 . . . . 33 E7
Toller Porcorum DT2 . . . . 71 E8
LOWER ROW BH21 . . . . . 41 B8
Lower St Alban St 4
DT4 . . . . 167 D2
Lower St Edmund St 8
DT4 . . . . 167 D2
Lower Sch La 2 DT11 . . . . 212 C1
Lower Sea La DT6 . . . . . . 97 A7
Lower South Rd SP5 . . . . 188 C4
Lower St
Lillington DT9 . . . . 194 F7
Merriott TA16 . . . . 191 F7
Morden DT2 . . . . 83 C2
Okeford Fitzpaine DT11 . . 197 F8
West Chinnock TA18 . . . . 192 B8
Witchampton BH21 . . . . . 200 F1
Lower Steppes BH19 . . . . 178 C2
LOWER STRODE DT6 . . . . 204 A2
Lower Townsend DT6 . . . 128 B8
LOWER TURNER BH24 . . . 46 F7
Lower Turners Barn La
BA20 . . . . 27 B1
Lower Walditch La DT6 . . 100 F6
Lower Way DT3 . . . . 166 D6
LOWER WHATCOMBE
DT11 . . . . 210 D4
LOWER WRAXALL DT2 . . . 206 A3
Lower Wraxhill Rd BA20 . . 27 A1
LOWER ZEALS BA12 . . . . . 2 D5
Lowesmore Ct BH14 . . . . 120 C4
Low's Hill La DT9 . . . . 29 C5
Lowther Gdns 8 BH8 . . . 122 C5
Lowther Rd
Bournemouth BH8 . . . . . 122 B6
Yeovil BA21 . . . . 28 A7
Lox La SP7 . . . . 11 E4
Lubbecke Way DT1 . . . . . 108 C1
Lucas Rd
Poole BH15 . . . . 119 B1
Poole, Upper Parkstone
BH12 . . . . 120 C6
Lucerne Ave BH6 . . . . . . 123 D5
Lucetta La DT1 . . . . 135 B8
Luckham Cl BH9 . . . . 90 B2
Luckham Gdns BH9 . . . . . 90 C2
Luckham Pl BH9 . . . . 90 B2
Luckham Rd BH9 . . . . 90 B2
Luckham Road E BH9 . . . . 90 B2
Ludbourne Rd DT9 . . . . . . 30 C5
Ludlow Rd DT4 . . . . 166 F2
Ludney La TA17 . . . . 191 A7
Luff Cl 4 BH22 . . . . 121 C8
LUFTON BA22 . . . . 26 B6
Lufton Coll of FE BA22 . . 26 B7
Lufton Trad Est BA22 . . . . 26 C7
Lugger Cl DT2 . . . . 166 C6
Luke St SP7 . . . . 188 B8
Lulworth Ave BH15 . . . . . 118 C1
LULWORTH CAMP BH20 . . 173 A7
Lulworth Castle★ BH20 . . 158 C1
Lulworth Cl BH15 . . . . . . 118 C1
Lulworth Cres BH15 . . . . . 118 C1
Lulworth Ct BH15 . . . . . . 118 C1
Lulworth Her Ctr★ BH20 . 172 C5
Lulworth Rd BH20 . . . . . . 140 B1
Lulworth & Winfrith CE Fst
Sch BH20 . . . . 172 E6
Lumber La BH21 . . . . 201 C5
Lumby Dr BH24 . . . . 55 D8
Lumby Drive Mobile Home
Pk 4 BH24 . . . . 55 D8
Lumby Drive Pk BH24 . . . . 55 D8
Lupin Way BA22 . . . . 26 D5
Lurmer St SP7 . . . . 37 F6
Luscombe BH14 . . . . 120 C2

Luscombe Valley Nature
Reserve★ BH14 . . . . . . 147 D7
Luther Rd BH9 . . . . 121 F8
Luton Down Rd 3 DT11 . . 199 E2
Luton Dro DT11 . . . . 200 A2
LYATTS BA22 . . . . 193 B6
Lyatts Hill BA22 . . . . 193 A6
Lych Gate St BH24 . . . . . . 55 E6
Lyde La BA21 . . . . 28 B6
Lyde Rd BA21 . . . . 27 F5
Lydford Gdns BH11 . . . . . 89 A2
Lydford Rd BH11 . . . . 89 A2
Lydfords La SP8 . . . . 5 D2
Lydgate St 8 DT1 . . . . . 107 C1
LYDLINCH DT10 . . . . . . 196 F8
Lydlinch Cl BH22 . . . . 61 D1
Lydwell Cl
Bournemouth BH11 . . . . . 88 F5
Weymouth DT4 . . . . 180 E8
Lyell Rd BH12 . . . . 120 C6
Lyewater TA18 . . . . 191 E4
Lym Cl DT7 . . . . 96 C5
Lyme Cres BH23 . . . . 125 F8
Lyme Rd
Crewkerne TA18 . . . . . . 191 E3
Lyme Regis DT7 . . . . 96 A7
LYME REGIS 96 D5
Lyme Regis Marine
Aquarium★ 3 DT7 . . . . . 96 C4
Lyme St DT4 . . . . 180 C8
Lyme Way
Christchurch BH23 . . . . . 125 F7
New Milton BH25 . . . . . . 95 C1
Lynch Cl
Mere SP8 . . . . 3 B5
Milborne St Andrew DT11 . 79 D8
Lynch La
Hardington Mandeville
BA22 . . . . 193 A6
Weymouth DT4 . . . . 166 F2
Lynch Lane Ind Est DT4 . . 166 F2
Lynch Rd DT4 . . . . 166 F2
Lynch The BA12 . . . . 3 B5
Lyndale Rd DT4 . . . . 180 D6
Lyndhurst Rd
Bransgore BH23 . . . . 93 D6
Christchurch BH23 . . . . . . 93 D2
Weymouth DT4 . . . . 167 D5
Lyndon St DT5 . . . . 91 F1
Lynes La BH24 . . . . 55 B7
Lynmoor Rd DT4 . . . . . . 167 E6
Lynn Rd BH17 . . . . 87 F1
Lyniric Cl BH21 . . . . 127 A7
Lynton Cres BH23 . . . . . . 91 D3
Lynwood Cl DT2 . . . . 61 D7
Lynwood Dr BH21 . . . . . . 87 E8
Lynx Trad Est BA20 . . . . . 26 F3
Lynx West Trading Est
BA20 . . . . 26 E3
Lyon Ave BH25 . . . . 95 B3
Lyon Rd BH12 . . . . 88 C2
LYON'S GATE DT2 . . . . . 207 D8
Lysander Cl BH23 . . . . . . 125 C7
Lysander Rd BA20 . . . . . . 26 F3
Lystra Rd BH9 . . . . 90 A3
Lytchett Dr BH18 . . . . 86 F2
Lytchett La BH20 . . . . . . 140 A4
LYTCHETT MATRAVERS
BH16 . . . . 84 D4
Lytchett Matravers Prim Sch
BH16 . . . . 84 C2
LYTCHETT MINSTER
BH16 . . . . 116 F7
Lytchett Minster Sch
BH16 . . . . 116 F8
Lytchett Way BH16 . . . . . 117 D6
Lytham Rd BH18 . . . . 87 A3
Lytton Cl DT2 . . . . 129 F6
Lytton Rd BH1, BH8 . . . . 122 C5

M

Mabey Ave BH10 . . . . 89 D2
MacAndrew Rd BH13 . . . . 147 F7
MacAulay Rd BH18 . . . . . . 87 A4
McCreery Rd DT9 . . . . 30 B7
McIntyre Rd BH23 . . . . . . 91 A3
McKay Way DT4 . . . . 166 E2
McKinley Rd BH4 . . . . . . 121 C2
MacLaren Rd BH9 . . . . . . 89 F3
Maclean Rd BH11 . . . . . . 88 F3
Macville Ave BH6 . . . . . . 124 B3
McWilliam Cl BH12 . . . . . 121 C8
McWilliam Rd 3 BH9 . . . . 90 B3
Madeira Rd
Bournemouth BH1 . . . . . 122 A4
Poole BH14 . . . . 120 D5
Madeline Cl BH12 . . . . . . 120 B7
Madeline Cres BH12 . . . . 120 B7
Madison Ave BH1 . . . . . . 122 C4
MADJESTON SP8 . . . . 10 F7
Maen Gdns DT1 . . . . 108 B1
Magdalen La
Bridport DT6 . . . . 100 B6
Christchurch BH23 . . . . . 124 A4
Magiston St DT2 . . . . . . 106 D8
Magna Cl
Bournemouth BH11 . . . . . 88 F6
Yeovil BA21 . . . . 27 F8
Magna Gdns BH11 . . . . . . 88 F6
Magna Rd BH21 . . . . 88 C7
Magnolia Cl
Bournemouth BH6 . . . . . 124 A5
3 Radipole DT3 . . . . . . 152 E2
Verwood BH31 . . . . 45 E4
Magnolia Dr DT2 . . . . . . 75 E3

Magnolia Ho 8 BH10 . . . . 89 F4
Magpie Cl BH10 . . . . 90 C3
Magpie Gr BH25 . . . . 94 F2
Mag's Barrow BH22 . . . . . 61 E2
Maiden Beech Sch TA18 . 191 E3
Maiden Castle (Hill Fort)★
DT2 . . . . 134 B6
Maiden Castle Rd DT2 . . . 134 C7
MAIDEN NEWTON DT2 . . . 73 A8
Maiden Newton Sta DT2 . . 73 A8
Maiden St DT4 . . . . 167 E2
Maidment Cl BH11 . . . . . . 88 E4
Maincombe Cl 2 TA18 . . . 191 E3
Main Rd
Fortuneswell DT5 . . . . . 181 C1
Tolpuddle DT2 . . . . 79 D1
West Lulworth BH20 . . . . 172 C4
Main St
Bridport DT6 . . . . 100 E4
Broadmayne DT2 . . . . . . 136 B2
Chideock DT6 . . . . 99 A6
Iwerne Courtney or Shroton
DT11 . . . . 198 F7
Maitlands The 2 BH22 . . . 121 D2
Majorca Mans 4 BH2 . . . 121 E3
Major's Comm DT2 . . . . 208 A7
Malan Cl BH17 . . . . 119 E8
Malcomb Cl BH6 . . . . 124 A3
Mallams DT5 . . . . 186 E7
Mallard Bldgs 6 BH25 . . . 95 A3
Mallard Cl
Bournemouth BH8 . . . . . 90 C1
Christchurch BH23 . . . . . 125 A6
Mallard Rd
Bournemouth BH8 . . . . . 90 C1
Wimborne Minster BH21 . . 60 A7
Mallards Gn DT2 . . . . . . 133 F7
Mallory Cl BH23 . . . . 124 F8
Mallow Cl
Broadstone BH18 . . . . . . 86 E3
Christchurch BH23 . . . . . 125 C8
Mallows The BH25 . . . . . . 95 D4
Malmesbury Cl BH8 . . . . 122 C6
Malmesbury Park Cty Prim
Sch BH8 . . . . 122 B5
Malmesbury Park Pl 7
BH8 . . . . 122 C5
Malmesbury Park Rd
BH8 . . . . 122 B6
Malmesbury Rd BH24 . . . . 54 A3
Malmesbury Way BA21 . . 26 E6
Malmsbury Cl 6 BH23 . . . 124 A5
Malorem Way BH22 . . . . . 53 C1
Malta Cl 8 DT1 . . . . 107 E2
Malthouse 8 BH15 . . . . . 119 C2
Malthouse La DT9 . . . . . . 14 F2
Malthouse Mdw DT3 . . . . 149 F8
Maltings The
Blandford Forum DT11 . . 212 C2
Bournemouth BH11 . . . . . 88 F7
Cerne Abbas DT2 . . . . . . 207 D4
8 Poole BH15 . . . . 119 E3
Weymouth DT4 . . . . 167 D1
Malvern Cl
4 Bournemouth BH9 . . . . 90 A2
2 Christchurch BH23 . . . 124 F8
2 Yeovil BA21 . . . . 26 F6
Malvern Ct BH9 . . . . 90 A2
Malvern Terr DT4 . . . . . . 167 E6
Mampitts La SP7 . . . . 13 A2
Mampitts Rd SP7 . . . . . . 13 A2
Mandalay The BH31 . . . . . 45 A5
Mandale Cl BH11 . . . . 89 A4
Mandale Rd BH11 . . . . . . 88 F3
Mandeville Cl DT4 . . . . . 180 B8
Mandeville Rd DT4 . . . . . 180 B8
Mandeville Stoke La DT6 . . 66 B7
MANGERTON DT6 . . . . . . 69 B4
Mangerton La DT6 . . . . . . 69 A3
Mangerton Water Mill★
DT6 . . . . 69 C4
Manington Hall 5 BH4 . . 121 C2
Manning Ave BH23 . . . . . 93 C1
Manningford Rd DT11 . . . 212 D5
Mannings Heath Rd BH12 . 88 B1
Mannings Heath Rdbt
BH12 . . . . 88 B2
Manor Ave
Lyme Regis DT7 . . . . 96 B6
Poole BH12 . . . . 88 C1
Manor Cl
Bradford Abbas DT9 . . . . 28 C2
Dewlish DT2 . . . . 209 C1
Ferndown BH22 . . . . 61 E5
1 Portesham DT3 . . . . . 150 A8
South Perrott DT8 . . . . . 192 F7
Stratton DT2 . . . . 106 E8
Templecombe BA8 . . . . . 18 D8
Manor Ct
Ringwood BH24 . . . . 55 C8
Verwood BH31 . . . . 45 B6
Manor Dr
9 Merriott TA16 . . . . . . 191 F7
West Coker BA22 . . . . . . 193 B8
Manor Farm Cl
Blandford Forum DT11 . . 199 D4
Dorchester DT2 . . . . 72 F8
Litton Cheney DT2 . . . . 103 C2
Old Milton BH25 . . . . . . 94 F1
Manor Farm Ct DT2 . . . . 133 D6
Manor Farm Rd
Bere Regis BH20 . . . . . . 81 B2

Manor Farm Rd *continued*
Bournemouth BH10 . . . . . 89 C7
Manor Farm Wlk DT3 . . . 150 A8
Manor Farmyard BH8 . . . . 91 B3
Manor Fields DT6 . . . . . 100 E6
Manor Gdns
12 Beaminster DT8 . . . . 204 D4
New Milton BH25 . . . . . . 95 B3
2 Ringwood BH24 . . . . . 55 B8
Verwood BH31 . . . . 45 B6
Manor Gr DT2 . . . . 133 D6
Manor Ho BH18 . . . . 87 A4
Manor La
Bradford Peverell DT2 . . 106 F5
Verwood BH31 . . . . 45 B5
Manor Park CE Fst Sch
DT1 . . . . 135 B8
Manor Park Rd BH15 . . . . 119 B5
Manor Rd
Bournemouth BH1 . . . . . 122 C3
Christchurch BH23 . . . . . 124 A6
Dorchester DT1 . . . . . . 135 A8
Gussage St Michael BH21 . 200 F6
Mere BA12 . . . . 2 F7
Milborne Port DT9 . . . . . 17 C3
New Milton BH25 . . . . . . 95 B3
Radipole DT3 . . . . 167 B8
Ringwood BH24 . . . . 55 C7
Stourpaine DT11 . . . . . . 198 F4
Studland BH19 . . . . 164 D2
Swanage BH19 . . . . 179 B2
Verwood BH31 . . . . 45 B6
Yeovil BA20 . . . . 27 C4
Manorside Comb Sch
BH12 . . . . 88 D1
Manor St BA22 . . . . 193 B8
Manor Vale 3 DT8 . . . . . 204 A8
Manor View DT6 . . . . . . 191 E3
Manor Way BH31 . . . . . . 45 B7
Mansard Ct DT3 . . . . . . 147 B3
Manscombe Abbey DT6 . . 66 B2
Mansel Cl BH12 . . . . 121 C7
Mansfield Ave BH14 . . . . 120 C4
Mansfield Cl
Ferndown BH22 . . . . 61 D2
Poole BH14 . . . . 120 C4
Mansfield Rd
Bournemouth BH9 . . . . . 89 E1
Poole BH14 . . . . 120 C4
Ringwood BH24 . . . . 55 B7
Manshay La DT6 . . . . . . 203 A1
MANSTON DT10 . . . . 35 C2
MANSWOOD BH21 . . . . . 200 E3
Manton Cl BH15 . . . . 118 E3
Manton Rd BH15 . . . . . . 118 E3
Manwell Dr BH19 . . . . . . 179 A1
Manwell Rd BH19 . . . . . . 179 B1
Manwell's La BH19 . . . . . 179 B2
Maple Bsns Pk BH21 . . . . 60 F7
Maple Cl
Barton on Sea BH25 . . . . 127 B7
Christchurch BH23 . . . . . 125 C7
4 Overcombe/Preston
DT3 . . . . 153 B2
Sandford BH20 . . . . 143 A8
Shaftesbury SP7 . . . . . . 12 F4
Maple Dr
12 Crewkerne TA18 . . . . 191 F5
Ferndown BH22 . . . . 61 D2
Yeovil BA20 . . . . 27 B3
Maple Gdns DT6 . . . . . . 100 D5
Maple Lo 5 BH16 . . . . . . 117 E7
Maple Rd
Bournemouth BH9 . . . . . 121 F8
Poole BH15 . . . . 119 D3
Maple Way SP8 . . . . 5 D1
MAPPERTON
Beaminster DT8 . . . . . . 204 F2
Spetisbury DT11 . . . . . . 211 D1
Mapperton Cl BH17 . . . . . 87 F2
Mapperton Hill DT8, BA22 . . 2 E1
Mapperton House & Gdns★
DT8 . . . . 69 B8
Mapperton La DT6 . . . . . . 69 B8
MAPPOWDER DT10 . . . . 196 F1
Mappowder Ct★ DT10 . . 208 F8
Marabout Cl BH23 . . . . . 124 D7
Marabout Ind Est DT1 . . . 107 F2
Marchwood Rd BH10 . . . . 89 C3
Margards La BH31 . . . . . . 45 A5
MARGARET MARSH SP7 . . 22 C2
Margaret Pl DT1 . . . . . . 107 E1
Marian Cl BH21 . . . . 85 E4
Marian Pl BH21 . . . . 85 E4
Marie Cl BH12 . . . . 120 D7
Marie Rd DT1 . . . . 107 E1
Marina Ct
2 Bournemouth BH5 . . . 122 C4
Christchurch BH23 . . . . . 126 A7
Marina Dr BH14 . . . . 120 B1
Marina Gdns DT5 . . . . . . 187 B5
Marina The BH5 . . . . 122 E3
Marina Twrs 5 BH5 . . . . 122 E3
Marina View 8 BH23 . . . . 126 A5
Marine Cl BH25 . . . . 126 D7
Marine Dr BH25 . . . . 126 C6
Marine Drive E BH25 . . . . 127 A6
Marine Drive W BH25 . . . 126 C7
Marine Parade DT7 . . . . . 96 B4
Marine Point BH25 . . . . . 126 F7
Marine Prospect BH25 . . . 126 F7

Marine Rd BH6 .... 123 D3
Mariners Ct BH23 .... 125 A6
Mariners Dr BH19 .... 179 A2
Mariners Reach BH25 ..... 127 A6
Mariners Way DT3 .... 166 D6
Market Cl BH15 .... 119 C2
Market Pl
  Blandford Forum DT11 ... 212 D3
  Ringwood BH24 .... 55 B7
  Sturminster Newton DT10 .. 35 B1
Markets La DT6 .... 101 E3
Market St
  Abbotsbury DT3 .... 149 B7
  Poole BH15 .... 119 B2
  Radipole DT4 .... 167 D2
  Yeovil BA20 .... 27 D5
Market Way BH21 .... 59 D4
Markham Ave
  Bournemouth BH10 ...... 89 D7
  Weymouth DT4 .... 167 B2
Markham Cl BH10 .... 89 D6
Mark's La BH25 .... 95 A6
Marksmead DT8 .... 203 C8
Marks Rd BH9 .... 122 A8
Mark View Bsns Pk BA21 .. 28 B7
Marlborough Ave DT4 ..... 180 C7
Marlborough Ct
  30 Bournemouth BH4 .... 121 C3
  3 Wimborne Minster BH21 .. 59 C4
Marlborough Mans 2
  BH7 .... 123 B6
Marlborough Pines 25
  BH4 .... 121 C3
Marlborough Pl BH21 ..... 59 D5
Marlborough Rd
  Bournemouth BH4 .... 121 C3
  Poole BH14 .... 120 C4
  Yeovil BA21 .... 28 A6
Marl Cl BA21 .... 27 A7
Marler Ho 9 BH4 .... 121 B4
Marley Ave BH25 .... 94 F3
Marley Ct
  New Milton BH25 .... 94 F3
  Overcombe/Preston DT3 .. 153 C3
Marline Rd BH12 .... 120 D6
Marl La DT9 .... 28 D6
Marlott Rd
  Gillingham SP8 .... 5 E4
  Poole BH15 .... 119 C5
Marlow Dr BH23 .... 91 E3
Marlow Rd DT4 .... 167 D1
Marlpit Dr BH23 .... 94 A2
Marlpit La BH25 .... 95 A8
Marmion Gdns BH23 ...... 124 F7
MARNHULL DT10 .... 20 F2
Marnhull Rd
  Hinton St Mary DT10 ... 35 A5
  Poole BH15 .... 119 D4
Marpet Cl BH11 .... 88 F6
Marquis Cl DT4 .... 166 F2
Marquis Way BH11 .... 88 D5
Marriage La DT10 .... 35 A6
Marrowbone La DT6 ...... 100 E4
Marryat Ct
  Christchurch BH23 ..... 126 B7
  New Milton BH25 ...... 94 F3
Marryat Rd BH25 .... 94 F3
Marshall Row 5 BH19 .... 179 C2
Marshallsay Rd DT3 ...... 166 D6
Marshal Rd BH17 .... 87 B1
MARSHALSEA DT6 .... 202 F3
Marsh Athletics Ctr The
  DT4 .... 167 B2
Marshfield BH21 .... 59 F7
Marsh Gate DT6 .... 100 D3
Marsh La
  Christchurch BH23 ..... 91 F2
  Hazelbury Bryan DT10,
  DT11 .... 196 F2
  Henstridge BA8 .... 19 D5
  Ibberton DT11 .... 197 D3
  Pen Selwood BA9 ...... 1 A4
  Upton BH16 .... 117 C7
  Wincanton BA9 .... 2 A8
  Winterborne Kingston DT11 .. 81 F7
  Yeovil BA21 .... 27 B7
Marshlands Cl BH23 ...... 124 D6
Marsh Rd DT4 .... 167 C2
MARSH THE 118 A7
Marsh The DT9 .... 194 E3
Marsh Way
  18 Pimperne DT11 ..... 199 D4
  Swanage BH19 .... 178 F2
MARSHWOOD DT6 .... 202 F2
Marshwood Ave BH17 .... 87 F3
Marshwood CE Prim Sch
Marston Cl
  Blandford Forum DT11 .. 212 D5
  New Milton BH25 ...... 95 B5
Marston Gr BH23 .... 93 E1
Marston Rd
  New Milton BH25 ...... 95 B5
  Poole BH15 .... 119 B2
  Stanbridge DT9 .... 30 A7
  Trent DT9 .... 15 D1
Martel Cl DT2 .... 136 A1
Martello Ho 5 BH13 ...... 147 F8
Martello Pk BH13 .... 147 F7
Martello Rd BH13 .... 120 F1
Martello Road S BH13 .... 147 F7
Martello Towers BH13 .... 147 F7
Martells The BH25 .... 127 B7

MARTIN SP6 .... 190 B6
Martin Cl BH17 .... 118 F8
Martindale Ave BH21 ..... 60 B5
Martin Down National Nature
  Reserve★ SP5 .... 189 F6
MARTIN DROVE END
  SP6 .... 190 A8
Martin Drove End 5 ...... 190 A7
Martingale Cl 3 BH16 ..... 117 F7
Martins Cl BH22 .... 61 E7
Martins Dr BH22 .... 61 E7
Martins Hill Cl BH23 ..... 92 C1
Martins Hill La BH23 ..... 92 C1
Martin's La 5 .... 5 C8
MARTINSTOWN OR
  WINTERBOURNE ST
  MARTIN DT2 .... 133 D6
Martins Way DT2 .... 61 E7
Martleaves Cl 6 DT4 ..... 180 C8
Martyr Cl DT11 .... 134 E7
Marwell Cl BH7 .... 123 A7
Mary Cossins Cl DT11 .... 212 C5
Mary Gdns 4 DT11 .... 197 F6
Mary La SP7 .... 52 F2
Maryland Rd BH16 .... 117 E4
Mary St BA21 .... 27 D5
Maskew Cl DT3 .... 166 D5
Mason's La DT8 .... 204 A4
Masters Ct BH4 .... 121 D3
Masterson Cl BH23 ...... 124 D7
Matcham's Karting Ctr★
  BH24 .... 63 B6
Matchams La BH24,BH23 .. 63 B6
Matlock Rd BH22 .... 61 C3
Matthews Pl SP8 .... 5 E3
Matthews Rd BA21 .... 27 E5
MAUDLIN TA20 .... 202 F8
Maudlin Cross TA20 ...... 202 E8
Maudlin La TA20 .... 202 F8
Maud Rd DT1 .... 107 F1
Maumbury Rd DT1 .... 107 F1
Maumbury Rings★ DT1 ... 135 A8
Maumbury Sq DT1 .... 135 A8
Maundeville Cres BH23 ... 123 E8
Maundeville Rd BH23 .... 123 E8
Maunsell Ave DT3 .... 153 B3
Maureen Cl BH12 .... 120 B8
Maurice Rd BH8 .... 122 D8
Mavis Rd BH9 .... 90 B1
Max Gate★ DT1 .... 135 D8
Maxwell Rd
  Bournemouth BH9 ..... 122 A7
  Corfe Mullen BH18 .... 85 F3
  Poole BH13 .... 147 F7
Maycrete Rd BH23 .... 62 D1
Maycroft Rd DT1 .... 167 D1
Mayfair BH4 .... 121 C2
Mayfair Ct BH13 .... 121 B2
Mayfair Gdns BH11 ...... 89 A4
Mayfield DT3 .... 133 E7
Mayfield Ave BH14 ...... 120 E3
Mayfield Cl
  Ferndown BH22 .... 61 C6
  Radipole DT4 .... 167 A6
Mayfield Dr BH22 .... 61 C6
Mayfield Rd
  Bournemouth BH9 ..... 90 A2
  Yeovil BA21 .... 27 F6
Mayfield Way BH22 ...... 61 C6
Mayford Rd BH12 .... 121 B6
May Gdns
  Bournemouth BH11 .... 88 E4
  Walkford BH23 .... 94 B2
May Gr DT11 .... 211 D6
May La DT11 .... 199 F7
Maylyn Rd BH16 .... 85 B2
May Terrace Gdns DT3 ... 166 D6
Mead Ave BA22 .... 26 D6
Mead Bower DT5 .... 186 E1
Mead Cl BH18 .... 87 A1
Mead Fields DT6 .... 100 B8
Mead La
  Allington DT6 .... 100 A8
  Gussage All Saints BH21 .. 201 A5
Meadowbank BH16 ...... 118 C8
Meadow Bank 4 BH16 ... 117 E8
Meadow Bottom DT6 .... 106 D8
Meadow Court Cl BH9 ... 90 A3
Meadowcroft SP8 .... 11 A8
Meadow Ct
  2 Bournemouth BH9 ... 90 A3
  3 Wimborne Minster BH21 .. 59 D4
Meadow Farm La BH21 .. 85 F8
Meadow Gr BH31 .... 45 D5
Meadow La
  Burton BH23 .... 92 C2
  Wool BH20 .... 140 A2
Meadowlands
  Bridport DT6 .... 100 D2
  Ringwood BH24 .... 55 C4
Meadow Rd
  5 Charlton Marshall
  DT11 .... 211 D6
  Langton Long Blandford
  DT11 .... 212 E3

Meadow Rd *continued*
  New Milton BH25 ...... 95 B4
  Ringwood BH24 .... 55 D8
  Yeovil BA21 .... 27 F7
Meadow Rise BH18 ...... 86 F5
Meadows Cl 3 BH16 ..... 117 F8
Meadows Dr 8 BH16 ..... 117 E7
Meadowside 4 DT8 ...... 204 A7
Meadows The
  Bourton SP8 .... 1 F2
  Gillingham SP8 .... 11 A8
Meadowsweet Rd BH17 .. 118 E8
Meadow Vale DT2 .... 196 B3
Meadow View
  5 Blandford Forum
  DT11 .... 212 D3
  Bradford Peverell DT2 .. 107 A6
  Cattistock DT2 .... 206 B2
  Charminster DT2 ..... 107 D6
  East Coker BA22 ..... 193 C8
  7 Stofold BA22 ...... 193 F8
Meadow View 6 BH20 .... 142 F3
Meadow View Rd
  Bournemouth BH11 .... 88 E4
  Radipole DT3 .... 152 C4
Meadow Way
  Barton on Sea BH25 ... 127 A7
  Charmouth DT6 .... 97 B7
  Verwood BH31 .... 45 C4
Mead Rd
  Corfe Castle BH20 .... 177 A7
  Radipole DT4 .... 167 A6
Meads Cl DT2 .... 194 A2
Meads The DT9 .... 17 D2
Mead The
  Henstridge BA8 .... 19 E3
  Shaftesbury SP7 ...... 13 F6
Meadu's La DT20 .... 162 D3
Meadway 4 DT6 .... 100 B2
Meadway DT3 .... 93 D2
Medbourne Cl DT11 ..... 212 C5
Medina Way BH23 ...... 125 C6
Medlar Cl BH23 .... 92 D1
Medway Dr DT3 .... 168 B8
Medway Rd BH22 .... 62 A6
Meech Cl DT6 .... 100 D4
Meech Way DT2 .... 75 E2
MEERHAY DT6 .... 204 D5
Meerhay La DT6 .... 65 A4
Meerhay Manor★ DT6 ... 204 D5
Meeting House La BH24 .. 55 C7
Meeting House Sh Ctr
  BH24 .... 55 C7
Melancholy La BH20 .... 142 E1
Melbourne Rd
  Bournemouth BH8 ..... 122 C6
  Christchurch BH23 .... 91 E1
Melbourne St DT4 ...... 167 B3
MELBURY ABBAS SP7 .... 24 C7
Melbury Abbas Mill★ SP7 .. 24 B6
Melbury Ave BH12 ...... 120 C7
MELBURY BUBB DT2 .... 194 C1
Melbury DT2 .... 61 D4
Melbury House★ DT2 ... 194 A1
MELBURY OSMOND DT2 .. 194 A2
Melbury Pk★ DT2 .... 194 A1
Melbury Rd
  Bournemouth BH9 ..... 90 A2
  Yetminster DT9 .... 194 C5
MELBURY SAMPFORD
  DT2 .... 206 A8
Melbury St SP7 .... 24 C4
Melbury Way SP7 .... 13 A3
Melchester Cl 2 SP8 .... 5 F4
Melcombe Ave DT4 ..... 167 E5
MELCOMBE BINGHAM
  DT2 .... 209 A5
Melcombe Pl DT14 ...... 167 E4
MELCOMBE REGIS DT4 .. 167 E6
Melford St BH21 .... 122 A3
Melgate Ct 7 BH9 .... 89 F1
Mellstock Ave DT3 ...... 167 E4
Mellstock Cres BH17 .... 135 A7
Mellstock Rd BH15 ...... 119 D5
MELPLASH DT6 .... 204 D1
Melplash Ct★ DT6 .... 204 D1
Melrose St DT6 .... 95 C3
Melrose Rd BH21 .... 27 D6
Melstock Ave DT3 ...... 168 A7
Melstock Rd SP8 .... 5 E4
Melton Ct BH13 .... 120 D7
Melville Rd BH9 .... 121 E8
Melverley Gdns BH21 ... 59 D5
Melway Cl DT11 .... 198 C7
Melway La DT11 .... 198 C7
Memorial Ave 19 TA18 .. 191 F4
Memorial Rd BA22 ...... 26 D6
Mendip Cl
  New Milton BH25 ...... 95 B2
Mendip Rd BH25 .... 95 B2
Mendip Cl 4 BH23 ...... 124 F8
Mendip Rd BH31 .... 45 B6
Menin Rd BH20 .... 139 C6
Mentone Rd 2 BH14 .... 120 A3
Meon Rd BH7 .... 123 B7
Mercery Rd DT3 .... 167 C7
MERE BA12 .... 3 B5
Mere By-pass BA12 ..... 2 F6
Mere Castle (site of)★
  BA12 .... 2 F6
Meredith Cl
  Christchurch BH23 .... 124 D7
  Halstock BA22 .... 193 C3
Mere Prim Sch BA12 .... 3 B5
Merevale Way BA21 ..... 26 E7
Meriden SP7 .... 13 A3

Meridians The BH23 .... 123 F6
Merino Way BH22 ...... 53 B1
Merlewood Cl DT2 ...... 107 A4
Merlewood Ct 9 BH25 ... 95 B3
MERLEY 59 D1
Merley Dr BH23 .... 126 A8
Merley Fst Sch BH21 .... 59 D1
Merley Gdns BH21 ...... 59 B1
Merley Ho BH21 .... 59 B1
Merley House La BH21 ... 59 E1
Merley La BH21 .... 59 E1
Merley Park Rd
  Ashington BH21 ...... 87 B8
  Corfe Mullen BH21 ... 86 F8
Merley Rd BH21 .... 59 C1
Merley Rd DT4 .... 180 D6
Merley Ways BH21 ..... 59 D2
Merlin Avenue N DT3 ... 152 B3
Merlin Avenue S DT3 ... 152 B3
Merlin Cl
  6 Bournemouth BH4 ... 55 E6
  8 Yeovil BA21 .... 26 F7
Merlin Rd BA20 .... 26 F3
Merlin Way BH23 ...... 125 A5
Mermaid Ct 3 BH5 ..... 122 E3
Mermond Pl BH19 ...... 179 C2
Merredin Ct DT3 .... 152 D3
Merriefield Ave BH8 .... 87 B5
Merriefield Cl BH18 .... 87 B6
Merriefield Dr BH18 .... 87 B6
Merrifield BH21 .... 59 E8
MERRIOTT
  Beaminster DT6 ...... 70 A4
  Crewkerne TA16 ..... 191 E7
Merriott Fst Sch TA16 .. 191 F7
Merriott Rd
  Ringwood BH24 ...... 55 C7
  Merriott TA18, TA16 .. 191 F6
MERRIOTTSFORD DT6 ... 191 E6
MERRITOWN 90 E7
Merritown La BH23 .... 90 D7
Merrivale 14 DT1 ...... 107 C1
Merrivale Ave BH23 .... 123 E5
Merrow Ave BH12 ...... 121 B7
Merrow Chase 1 BH13 ... 147 F7
Merryfield Cl
  Bransgore BH23 ...... 93 A8
  Verwood BH31 .... 45 B7
Merryfield Ct BH10 ..... 89 C4
Merryfield La BH10 ..... 89 C4
Merryweather Est 5
  BH24 .... 55 E8
Merton Ct
  2 Christchurch BH23 .. 126 B7
  3 Poole BH15 .... 119 E4
Merville Gdns BH9 ..... 121 F8
Methuen Cl 2 BH8 ..... 122 C5
Methuen Rd
  Bournemouth BH8 .... 122 B5
  Poole BH17 .... 87 B2
Mews The
  Bournemouth BH2 ..... 121 D3
  Verwood BH31 .... 45 C4
Meyrick Cl BH23 .... 93 A7
Meyrick Park Cres BH1 .. 121 F6
Meyrick Park Mans 7
  BH2 .... 121 F4
Meyrick Rd BH1 .... 122 B3
Michelgrove Rd BH5 .... 122 E3
Michelmersh Gn BH8 ... 90 D2
Mickleham Cl BH21 .... 121 B8
Middle Bere Dr BH20 ... 142 D6
Middlebere Cres BH16 .. 117 E4
Middlebere Dr BH20 .... 142 D6
MIDDLE BOCKHAMPTON .. 92 F6
MIDDLE CHINNOCK
  TA18 .... 192 C8
Middle Farm Way DT1 .. 107 D1
Middlefield DT20 .... 141 B3
Middle Field La DT9 .... 15 D5
Middle Gn 1 DT8 .... 204 D4
Middlehill Dr BH21 ..... 60 B6
Middlehill Rd BH21 ..... 60 B6
Middle La
  Martin SP6 .... 190 A7
  Ringwood BH24 ...... 55 C7
MIDDLEMARSH DT9 ..... 195 D1
Middlemarsh St DT1 .... 107 D1
Middle Path TA18 ...... 191 E4
Middle Rd
  Bournemouth BH10 ... 89 C5
  Lytchett Matravers BH16 .. 84 B2
  Poole BH15 .... 119 E6
  Sturminster Marshall BH21 .. 56 E3
  Tiptoe SO41 .... 95 E8
Middle St
  Bridport DT6 .... 69 A1
  Burton Bradstock DT6 .. 128 B8
  Crewkerne TA18 ..... 192 A3
  Dewlish DT2 .... 209 C1
  Misterton TA18 ...... 191 E4
  Rimpton BA22 .... 15 B8
  Shapwick DT11 ...... 56 E6
Middleton Mews DT1 ... 107 D1
Middleton Rd
  Bournemouth BH9 .... 89 E2
  Ringwood BH24 ...... 55 C8
Midland Rd BH9 .... 89 F1
Midleaze DT9 .... 29 E5
Midney La SP9 .... 4 B8
Midway Path BH13 .... 147 F5
Midwood Ave BH8 ..... 90 F1
Milborne Cres BH12 .... 120 E8
Milborne Fst Sch DT11 .. 79 E8
MILBORNE PORT 17 C2
Milborne Port Prim Sch
  DT9 .... 17 D2
MILBORNE ST ANDREW
  DT11 .... 79 E7

MILBORNE WICK DT9 .... 17 B6
Milbourne Rd BH22 ..... 61 C6
Milburn Cl 3 BH4 ...... 121 C4
Milburn La DT9 .... 196 A7
Milburn Rd BH4 .... 121 B4
Mildenhall 8 BH2 ...... 121 D2
Miles Ave BH20 .... 142 F8
MILES CROSS DT6 ...... 99 E7
Miles Field DT1 .... 38 A2
Miles Gdns DT3 .... 152 B5
Milestone Rd BH15 ..... 119 D5
Milestone Way SP8 ..... 5 B2
Milford Cl BH22 .... 53 B2
Milford Ct SP8 .... 5 C2
Milford Dr BH11 .... 88 F5
Milford Inf Sch BA21 ... 27 D7
Milford Jun Sch BA21 ... 27 D7
Milford Rd
  Barton on Sea BH25 ... 127 C7
  Dorchester DT1 ...... 107 E1
Military La DT10 .... 197 A4
Milky Down Back La BH24 .. 55 F7
Millbank Ho 5 BH20 .... 59 C5
Millbrook 1 DT2 .... 107 D1
Millbrook Cl 2 DT11 .... 198 C8
Millbrook Cl 3 DT11 .... 198 C8
Mill Cl BA22 .... 193 C8
Milldown CE Prim Sch
  DT11 .... 212 C5
Milldown Rd DT11 ..... 212 C5
Mill End SP6 .... 190 F2
Miller Cl BH25 .... 95 C4
Miller Rd BH23 .... 124 D7
Millers Cl
  Gillingham SP8 ...... 1 F2
  Overcombe/Preston DT3 .. 153 C3
Miller's Cl DT11 ...... 107 E3
Miller's Hill DT9 ...... 17 A5
Miller's La
  Farnham DT11 .... 200 D3
  Sixpenny Handley DT11 .. 188 D1
Miller Way DT9 .... 30 C7
Millfield BH25 .... 94 E3
Millfield BH17 .... 119 A7
Mill Foot DT2 .... 98 C7
Mill Ham Island Reserve★
  DT11 .... 198 B7
Millhams Cl BH10 ..... 89 B6
Millhams Dr BH10 ..... 89 B6
Millhams Mead Nature
  Reserve★ BH11 ...... 89 A6
Millhams Rd BH10 ..... 89 B6
Millhams St BH23 ..... 124 B6
Millhams Street N 2
  BH23 .... 124 B6
Mill Hill Cl BH23 ..... 120 B3
Mill Hollow La SP7 .... 24 B6
Mill House Cider Mus &
  Nurseries★ DT2 .... 137 E3
Mill La
  Bourton SP8 .... 1 E2
  Bradford Abbas DT9 .. 28 D1
  Cann SP7 .... 24 C4
  Cattistock DT2 ...... 206 B2
  Cerne Abbas DT2 .... 207 D4
  Charminster DT2 .... 107 D7
  Chetnole DT9 .... 194 D2
  Chideock DT6 .... 99 A4
  Christchurch BH23 ... 126 B8
  Cranborne BH21 ..... 40 C6
  Durweston DT11 ..... 198 E3
  East Coker BA22 .... 193 C7
  Halstock BA22 ...... 193 C3
  Hawkchurch EX13 ... 202 C3
  Hurn BH23 .... 91 B6
  Ibberton DT11 ...... 197 D3
  Kingstone TA17 ..... 191 B8
  Lyme Regis DT7 ..... 96 A7
  Marnhull DT10 ...... 20 E4
  Mere BA12 .... 3 B5
  Misterton TA18 ..... 192 B3
  Poole BH14 .... 120 C4
  Shapwick DT11 ..... 56 E6
  Silton SP8 .... 1 F2
  Stour Provost SP8 ... 21 C7
  Stratton DT2 .... 106 E8
  Symondsbury DT6 ... 99 F8
  Trent DT9 .... 14 E1
  Wareham BH20 ..... 142 E4
  West Coker BA22 ... 193 B8
  Weymouth DT3 ...... 153 C3
  Wimborne Minster BH21 .. 59 C5
  Wimborne Minster BH21 .. 132 F8
  Wootton Fitzpaine DT6 .. 64 D4
  Yeovil BA20 .... 27 D4
  Yetminster DT9 ..... 194 C5
Mill Race SP8 .... 5 F2
Mill Rd BH23 .... 124 A8
Mill Rise SP8 .... 1 E2
Mill Road N BH8 ..... 90 E3
Mill Road S BH8 ..... 90 D2
Mills Rd DT3 .... 166 C4
Millstream Cl
  Poole BH17 .... 119 A7
  Wimborne Minster BH21 .. 59 C4
Millstream Trad Est BH24 .. 55 C3
Millyford Cl BH25 ..... 126 D8
Milne Rd BH17 .... 87 B1

Milner Rd BH4 ... 121 C1
Milom La DT2 ... 110 C7
MILTON ABBAS DT11 ... 209 F6
Milton Abbey Sch DT11 ... 209 E6
Milton Bsns Ctr BH25 ... 94 E2
Milton Cl
  Poole BH14 ... 120 D3
  Radipole DT4 ... 167 D6
  Yeovil BA21 ... 26 E6
Milton Cres DT3 ... 167 C6
Milton Ct BH22 ... 61 D5
Milton Gr BH25 ... 95 B2
Milton House BA21 ... 14 B3
Milton La DT11 ... 198 D2
Milton Mead ... 94 F2
MILTON ON STOUR SP8 ... 5 D5
Milton on Stour CE Prim Sch
SP8 ... 5 E6
Milton Rd
  Bournemouth BH8 ... 122 A6
  Milborne St Andrew DT11 ... 79 E8
  Poole BH14 ... 120 D3
  Weymouth DT4 ... 167 C3
  Wimborne Minster BH21 ... 59 C6
Milton Road DT2 ... 167 C3
Milton Terr DT1 ... 167 D6
Milton Villas BH8 ... 122 A5
Milvers La DT5 ... 101 B3
Milverton Cl BH23 ... 93 E1
Mimosa Ave BH1 ... 87 E8
MINCHINGTON DT11 ... 188 D1
Minerva Cl DT1 ... 134 F8
Minstead Rd BH10 ... 89 C3
Minster View BH21 ... 59 C5
Minster Way BH16 ... 117 D7
Minterne Grange BH14 ... 147 C2
Minterne House & Gdns*
DT2 ... 207 D6
MINTERNE MAGNA DT2 ... 207 C7
MINTERNE PARVA DT2 ... 207 D6
Minton Cl
  3 Bournemouth BH9 ... 90 A2
  Christchurch BH23 ... 124 E5
  Poole BH14 ... 147 C7
Minton Mews BH2 ... 121 F5
Minton Pl DT14 ... 167 C4
Mission Hall La DT3 ... 153 D4
Mission La BH1 ... 87 A2
Mission Rd BH18 ... 87 A2
MISTERTON La DT13 ... 192 A2
Misterton CE Fst Sch
  TA18 ... 192 A2
Mistover Cl DT1 ... 135 A7
Mistover Rd BH20 ... 142 D5
Mitchell Cl BH25 ... 127 A7
Mitchell Rd
  Ferndown BH21 ... 61 C7
  Poole BH17 ... 119 F8
Mitchell St 1 DT4 ... 167 E2
Mitchelmore Rd BA21 ... 28 E7
Mithras Cl DT1 ... 134 E8
Mitre Ct 5 BH23 ... 124 A7
Mixen La 15 DT1 ... 135 B8
Miz Maze (remains)*
DT9 ... 194 F3
MLS Coll 11 BH1 ... 121 F3
Moat Ct BH4 ... 121 C5
Moat La BH25 ... 126 F8
Moats Cotts DT2 ... 209 C1
MOCKBEGGAR BH24 ... 47 E7
Mockbeggar La BH24 ... 47 C7
Moffat Rd BH23 ... 124 D7
Mohune Way DT3 ... 166 D5
Molyneux Rd BH25 ... 95 D3
Monaco Cl BH9 ... 122 B8
Monarch Ct 22 BH4 ... 121 C3
Monastery La BA20 ... 173 D8
Moneyfly Rd BH31 ... 45 D5
Monk Barton Cl BA21 ... 26 E7
Monkey World Ape Rescue
  Ctr* BH20 ... 140 B6
Monks Cl BH22 ... 62 A8
Monks Dale BA21 ... 26 F7
Monkshood Cl BH23 ... 93 B1
Monks Way BH11 ... 88 D5
Monkswell Gn BH23 ... 124 D6
Monkton Cl BH22 ... 61 D6
Monkton Cres BH12 ... 120 E8
Monkton Down Rd 5
DT11 ... 199 E2
Monkton Dro BH21 ... 189 D1
Monkton Hill DT2 ... 134 E5
MONKTON UP WIMBORNE
  BH21 ... 201 C8
MONKTON WYLD DT6 ... 64 B5
Monkton Wyld Cross DT6 ... 64 A7
Monkton Wyld La DT6 ... 64 C5
Monkwood La DT6 ... 203 E2
Monkworthy Cl BH24 ... 54 B5
Monkworthy Dr BH24 ... 54 B5
Monmouth Ave DT3 ... 167 D7
Monmouth Cl
  Ringwood BH24 ... 55 C6
  Verwood BH31 ... 45 D4
Monmouth Dr BH31 ... 45 C4
Monmouth Rd
  Dorchester DT1 ... 108 B1
  Wareham BH20 ... 142 D3
  Yeovil BA21 ... 27 F7
Monmouth St 5 DT7 ... 96 C5
Monnington La DT11 ... 107 C2
Monsal Ave DT1 ... 167 C3
Montacute Specl Sch
BH17 ... 87 C2
Montacute Way BH21 ... 87 E8
Montague Rd BH5 ... 123 B4
Montagu Pk BH23 ... 126 A7
Montagu Rd BH23 ... 126 B8

Monteray Dr SO41 ... 95 F4
Monterey Ave DT2 ... 139 B2
Montgomery Ave BH11 ... 89 B3
Montrose Cl
  1 Easton/Weston DT5 ... 186 F4
  Verwood BH31 ... 45 B6
Montrose Dr BH10 ... 89 B2
Montrose Rd BA21 ... 28 A7
Moonrakers Way BH23 ... 93 E1
Moorbath DT6 ... 67 C3
Moorcombe Dr DT3 ... 53 B3
MOOR CRICHEL BH21 ... 201 A3
Moorcroft Ave BH23 ... 92 C2
MOORDOWN ... 90 A2
Moordown Ave DT3 ... 167 F8
Moordown Cl BH9 ... 90 A4
Moore Ave BH11 ... 89 A4
Moore Cl BH25 ... 94 F1
Moorfield Gr BH9 ... 89 F2
Moorfield Rd DT5 ... 187 A4
Moorfields Rd BH13 ... 147 F8
Moorhaven BH22 ... 61 D6
Moorhills 3 BH21 ... 59 D4
Moorings Cl BH15 ... 118 F1
Moorings The 2 BH23 ... 124 A5
Moor La
  Buckhorn Weston SP8 ... 4 D1
  East Coker BA22 ... 193 D7
  Hardington Mandeville
    BA22 ... 193 A4
  Sturminster Marshall BH21 ... 56 E3
Moorland Ave BH25 ... 126 F8
Moorland Cres BH16 ... 117 D7
Moorland Gate BH24 ... 55 C5
Moorland Par BH16 ... 118 B7
Moor Land Pk 8 BH16 ... 117 D7
Moorland Rd BH11 ... 122 D4
Moorlands Coll BH23 ... 92 B6
Moorlands S
  Ferndown BH22 ... 53 A3
  Merriott TA18, TA16 ... 191 F6
  Verwood BH31 ... 45 B7
Moorlands Rise BH22 ... 53 B3
Moorland Way BH16 ... 117 D7
Moorlea 2 BH8 ... 122 B5
Moorside
  Broadstone BH18 ... 87 B5
  Swanage BH19 ... 179 B5
Moors Cl BH23 ... 91 B7
MOORSIDE DT10 ... 21 D3
Moorside Ave DT4,DT3 ... 167 E7
Moorside Cl BH11 ... 89 B3
Moorside Gdns BH11 ... 89 B3
Moorside Rd
  Bournemouth BH11 ... 89 B3
  Corfe Mullen BH21 ... 86 D5
  Poole BH21 ... 85 F5
Moors Valley Ctry Pk*
BH24 ... 46 B1
Moor The DT2 ... 78 B2
MOORTOWN BH24 ... 55 C5
Moortown Dr
  Bournemouth BH11 ... 88 B8
  Wimborne Minster BH21 ... 60 B1
Moortown Farm BH21 ... 88 B8
Moortown House BH24 ... 55 C5
Moortown La BH24 ... 55 C4
Moorvale Rd BH9 ... 90 A2
Moor View Rd BH15 ... 119 E6
Moorway La DT5 ... 15 E4
Morant Cl BH24 ... 95 B3
Morant Rd BH24 ... 47 D1
Moraston St 1 DT1 ... 107 C2
Moray Ct 1 BH1 ... 59 B5
Mordaunt Rd BH8 ... 90 E2
Mordae Gr DT6 ... 68 D2
Morden Ave DT1 ... 61 C4
Morden Bog National Nature
  Reserve* BH20 ... 115 D2
Morden La BH20 ... 82 D3
Morden Park Cnr BH20 ... 115 C8
Morden Rd
  Wareham St Martin BH20 ... 115 B3
MORETON DT2 ... 138 E7
Moreton Dr
  Turners Puddle DT2 ... 112 B2
Moreton Gdns* DT2 ... 138 F7
Moreton Rd
  Crossways DT2 ... 137 E5
Moreton's La 1 BH20 ... 142 E3
Moreton Sta DT2 ... 137 F7
Morgan's La SP5 ... 189 E5
Moriconium Quay BH15 ... 118 D1
Morington Ct 8 BH8 ... 122 A5
Morley Cl
  Bournemouth BH5 ... 123 A5
  Burton BH23 ... 92 C3
Morley Rd BH5 ... 123 A5
Mornish Rd BH13 ... 120 F2
Morrison Ave BH12 ... 120 F6
Morrison Rd BH19 ... 179 A2
Morris Rd
  Poole BH17 ... 119 D8
  Wool BH20 ... 139 F6
Morston Rd DT9 ... 194 D8
Mortain Cl DT11 ... 212 D5
Mortimer Cl BH23 ... 125 A6
Mortimer Rd BH8 ... 90 B1
Mossley Ave
  Poole BH12 ... 89 A1
  Swanage BH19 ... 121 A8
MOSTERTON DT8 ... 204 B8
Mosterton Down La DT8 ... 192 A1
MOTCOMBE SP7 ... 12 B8

Motcombe CE Prim Sch
SP7 ... 12 B7
Motcombe Park Sports Ctr
SP7 ... 12 B6
Motcombe Rd
  Poole BH13 ... 121 A2
  Shaftesbury SP7 ... 12 E3
Mountain Ash Rd 4 DT1 ... 107 E2
Mount Ave BH25 ... 95 A1
Mountbatten Cl
  Christchurch BH23 ... 125 A5
  Weymouth DT4 ... 180 B8
Mountbatten Ct DT5 ... 94 F3
Mountbatten Dr BH22 ... 61 C5
Mountbatten Gdns BH15 ... 93 A1
Mountbatten Rd BH13 ... 121 B1
Mount Cl BH25 ... 95 A1
MOUNTERS DT10 ... 20 E1
Mounters Cl DT10 ... 20 E1
Mount Grace BH14 ... 147 D7
Mount Heatherbank 7
BH1 ... 121 F3
Mount Joy DT6 ... 100 D3
Mountjoy Cl BH21 ... 59 F2
Mountjoy Sch
DT6 ... 100 D4
Mount La DT6 ... 99 F3
MOUNT PLEASANT ... 86 E7
Mount Pleasant
  Bridport DT6 ... 100 C7
  Christchurch BH23 ... 125 A5
  East Lulworth BH20 ... 158 E1
  Ringwood BH24 ... 55 C7
  Wareham Town BH20 ... 142 E4
  Yeovil BA21 ... 27 C5
Mount Pleasant Avenue N
DT3 ... 167 B8
Mount Pleasant Avenue S
DT3 ... 167 C7
Mount Pleasant Bsns Pk
DT3 ... 167 C8
Mount Pleasant Dr BH8 ... 90 F1
Mount Pleasant La
  Swanage BH19 ... 178 B2
  Swanage BH19 ... 179 C2
Mount Pleasant Rd
  3 Swanage BH19 ... 179 B3
  BH15 ... 119 D3
Mount Rd
  Bournemouth BH11 ... 89 A4
  Poole BH14 ... 120 B5
Mount Scar BH19 ... 179 B1
Mount Skippet Way DT2 ... 137 D5
MOUNT THE DT6 ... 69 A6
Mount The
  6 Blandford Forum
    DT11 ... 212 D3
  Ringwood BH24 ... 55 B8
Mower La SP7 ... 37 A5
Mowes La DT10 ... 34 F8
Mowleaze 1 BA22 ... 193 F3
Mowlem Theatre* BH19 ... 179 C2
Moyles Court Sch BH24 ... 47 E6
Moynton Cl DT2 ... 137 D6
Moynton Rd 1 DT1 ... 135 B8
Muccleby Way BH21 ... 26 E7
MUCKLEFORD DT2 ... 106 B7
Muckleford Reserve*
DT2 ... 106 C2
Muddyford La DT6 ... 98 D7
MUDEFORD ... 125 A5
Mudeford BH23 ... 207 F5
Mudeford Green Cl
BH23 ... 124 F5
Mudeford Inf Sch 4
BH23 ... 124 F6
Mudeford Jun Sch BH23 ... 124 F6
Mudeford La BH23 ... 124 C7
Mude Gdns BH23 ... 125 A5
MUDFORD BA21 ... 27 D7
Mudford Rd BA21 ... 27 D7
Mudros Rd DT1 ... 199 E3
Mulberry Ave DT5 ... 181 A1
Mulberry Cl SP8 ... 5 F2
Mulberry Ct
  4 Christchurch BH23 ... 124 A7
  Sixpenny Handley SP5 ... 189 B4
Mulberry Gdns
  2 Crewkerne TA18 ... 191 F4
  Fordingbridge SP6 ... 43 A8
Mulberry Mews BH6 ... 123 D5
Mullins Cl BH12 ... 121 C8
Mummies Exhibition The*
  9 DT1 ... 108 A2
Munden's La DT9 ... 31 B1
Munster Rd BH14 ... 120 D3
Murley Rd BH9 ... 122 A8
Murray-Smith Dr BA22 ... 26 C6
Musbury Cl DT10 ... 20 E4
Musbury La DT10 ... 20 E4
MUSCLIFFE ... 90 C4
Muscliffe La BH9 ... 89 F1
Muscliffe Rd BH9 ... 89 F1
Muscliff Prim Sch BH9 ... 90 C4
Musgrave Pl DT4 ... 167 E4
Mus of Electricity*
BH23 ... 124 B7
Muston La DT11 ... 82 A8
Mustons La 4 SP7 ... 12 E3
Mutton St DT6 ... 203 A1
Myrtle Cl
  10 Beaminster DT8 ... 204 C4
  Hordle SO41 ... 95 F4
Myrtle Rd BH8 ... 122 C6

N

Nada Rd BH23 ... 93 D1
Nag's La BH18 ... 191 B1
Nairn Ct BH3 ... 121 E7
Nairn Rd
  Bournemouth BH3 ... 121 E6
  Poole BH13 ... 147 E7
Nash Rd BH25 ... 126 E7
Namu Rd BH9 ... 89 E1
Nansen Ave BH15 ... 119 D5
Nantillo St 1 DT1 ... 107 D1
Napier Ct DT9 ... 29 F4
Napier Rd BH15 ... 117 D3
Napiers Way DT11 ... 37 E4
Napier Way BH20 ... 139 D8
Narrow La BH24 ... 47 F1
Naseby Rd BH9 ... 90 A2
NASH BA22 ... 193 C8
Nash La
  Chillington TA17, TA19 ... 191 A6
  Marnhull DT10 ... 21 A3
  Marshwood DT6 ... 202 E2
  Yeovil BA20 ... 26 F1
Natasha Gdns BH12 ... 120 C7
Nathan Cl BA20 ... 26 F2
Nathan Gdns BH15 ... 117 F3
Nations Rd SP8 ... 10 B6
Navarac Ct BH14 ... 120 C3
NEACROFT ... 93 B6
Neacroft Cl BH23 ... 126 D8
Nea Ct DT8 ... 204 A6
Neal's La DT9 ... 194 D2
Nea Meadows Nature
  Reserve* BH23 ... 125 E8
Nea Rd BH23 ... 125 E8
Neathem Rd BA21 ... 27 E7
Neighbourhood Ctr BH17 ... 87 E2
Neils View DT2 ... 73 A7
Nelson Cl BH25 ... 94 F3
Nelson Ct 13 BH15 ... 119 C2
Nelson Dr BH23 ... 124 F6
Nelson Rd
  Poole BH4, BH12 ... 121 B4
  Tarrant Monkton DT11 ... 199 F3
NETHERBURY DT6 ... 204 C2
Netherby La DT8 ... 204 A3
NETHER CERNE DT2 ... 207 E1
NETHER COMPTON DT9 ... 28 F7
Nethercombe La DT9 ... 30 A7
Nethercote La DT8 ... 204 A3
NETHERHALL GDNS BH1 ... 121 C3
NETHERHAY TA18 ... 203 C8
Netherhay La DT8 ... 203 C8
Nether Mead 1 DT11 ... 197 F6
NETHERSTOKE BA22 ... 193 D3
Netherstoke La BA22 ... 193 C3
NETHERTON BA22 ... 193 E6
Netherton La BA22 ... 193 F6
Netley 3 BH2 ... 26 E6
Netley Cl BH15 ... 120 A7
Netmead La DT11 ... 198 B8
Nettlebed Nursery SP7 ... 12 E3
NETTLECOMBE SP7 ... 13 A3
Nettlecombe DT6 ... 70 B3
Nettleton Cl BH17 ... 119 E7
New Barn Rd DT3 ... 149 D4
Newbery Gdns 8 DT4 ... 167 E2
Newbery Rd DT4 ... 167 D2
Newbery La TA18 ... 192 A3
New Bond St DT4 ... 167 E2
New Borough Rd BH21 ... 59 D3
Newbury SP8 ... 6 A1
Newbury Dr BH10 ... 89 C1
Newchester Cross TA16 ... 191 E7
New Church Cl DT5 ... 187 A4
New Cl
  Bourton SP8 ... 1 E2
  Haselbury Plucknett TA18 ... 192 B5
New Close Gdns DT4 ... 167 D1
Newcombe La DT2 ... 108 E3
Newcombe Rd
  Bournemouth BH6 ... 123 C5
  Ferndown BH22 ... 53 A3
New Cotts BA21 ... 60 E2
Newcroft Gdns BH23 ... 124 A8
Newcross DT9 ... 194 C7
New Cross Gate DT11 ... 198 A2
New Cut BA12 ... 3 A6
Newell DT9 ... 30 A6
New Field La DT11 ... 198 D8
Newfoundland Cl BH15 ... 119 D2
Newfoundland Dr BH15 ... 119 D2
Newfoundland Drive Rdbt
BH15 ... 119 D1
New Gd DT5 ... 187 A7
New Harbour Rd
  Poole BH15 ... 119 B1
  Upton BH16 ... 145 E8
New Harbour Road S
BH15 ... 145 D8
New Harbour Road W
BH15 ... 119 A1
Newhaven DT2 ... 105 C1
New Horizons Coll BH6 ... 124 A3
New Inn St DT6 ... 204 C2

New La
  Bashley BH25 ... 94 F6
  Cann SP7 ... 13 B1
  Caundle Marsh DT9 ... 195 E8
  Haselbury Plucknett TA18 ... 192 C6
  Morden BH20 ... 83 C3
  Motcombe SP7 ... 12 B8
  Stour Provost SP8 ... 11 B2
Newland DT9 ... 30 C6
Newland Gdn DT9 ... 30 C6
Newland La DT9 ... 195 F3
Newlands Rd
  Bournemouth BH7 ... 123 A6
  Christchurch BH23 ... 124 F7
  New Milton BH25 ... 95 B1
Newlands Way BH18 ... 85 F3
Newlyn Way BH12 ... 120 E7
Newman Cl 3 DT11 ... 212 E5
Newmans Cl
  West Moors BH22 ... 53 A5
  Wimborne Minster BH21 ... 59 D3
Newmans Dro DT11 ... 198 B7
Newman's La BH22 ... 52 E4
New Merrifield BH27 ... 95 F5
NEW MILTON ... 94 E5
New Milton Inf Sch BH25 ... 95 A1
New Milton Sta BH25 ... 95 A1
Newmorton Rd BH9 ... 90 A4
New Orchard BH15 ... 119 B2
New Parade BH10 ... 89 E3
New Park Rd BH6 ... 123 C4
NEWPORT BH20 ... 82 C2
Newport La BH20 ... 82 C2
New Quay Rd BH15 ... 119 B1
New Rd
  Arne BH20 ... 143 A1
  Bournemouth BH10 ... 89 E7
  Bourton SP8 ... 1 D7
  Bovington Camp DT2 ... 139 D7
  Brympton BA22 ... 26 C5
  Castleton DT9 ... 30 B4
  Corfe Castle BH20 ... 162 E1
  Ferndown BH22 ... 61 E3
  Gillingham SP8 ... 6 A1
  Haselbury Plucknett TA18 ... 192 D5
  Hinton St George TA17 ... 191 E7
  Loders DT6 ... 101 E7
  Lytchett Minster & Upton
    BH16 ... 116 F7
  Poole BH12 ... 120 D6
  Portesham DT3 ... 150 A8
  Portland DT5 ... 186 F6
  Radipole DT4 ... 167 D4
  Ringwood BH24 ... 55 C4
  Shaftesbury SP7 ... 12 D3
  Shapwick DT11 ... 48 D1
  Stalbridge DT10 ... 33 D8
  Stoborough Green BH20 ... 160 F8
  Stofold BA22 ... 193 F8
  Sturminster Newton DT10 ... 197 D3
  West Crewkerne TA18 ... 191 B4
  Weymouth DT4 ... 167 D2
  Winsham TA20 ... 202 C8
  Winterborne Stickland
    DT11 ... 198 B1
  Woodlands BH21 ... 44 C7
  Wool BH20 ... 139 F1
  Zeale BB, BA12 ... 2 A3
New St
  2 Dorchester DT1 ... 108 A1
  Easton/Weston DT5 ... 187 A4
  Marnhull DT10 ... 20 F2
  North Perrott TA18 ... 192 C4
  5 Poole BH15 ... 119 B1
  Puddletown DT2 ... 78 B1
  Radipole DT4 ... 167 E2
  Ringwood BH24 ... 55 C6
  Wareham BH20 ... 142 E3
Newstead Rd
  Bournemouth BH6 ... 123 D4
  Weymouth DT4 ... 167 C2
New Street La
  Loders DT6 ... 69 C1
  Symondsbury DT6 ... 199 F6
NEW SWANAGE BH19 ... 179 B6
NEWTON DT10 ... 197 D8
Newton Cl
  Gillingham SP8 ... 5 E1
  Sturminster Newton DT10 ... 197 D8
Newton Hill DT10 ... 197 D8
Newton Manor Cl 2
BH19 ... 179 A2
Newton Morrell BH14 ... 120 D3
NEWTON PEVERIL BH21 ... 56 B4
Newton Rd
  Barton on Sea BH25 ... 127 B8
  Maiden Newton DT2 ... 73 A8
  Poole BH15 ... 147 F8
  Stofold BA22 ... 193 F8
  Sturminster Marshall BH21 ... 56 C4
  Swanage BH19 ... 179 C1
  1 Yeovil BA20 ... 27 E3
Newton Rise 4 BH19 ... 179 A2
Newton's Rd DT14 ... 167 C1
NEWTOWN
  Beaminster DT8 ... 204 D5
  Corfe Mullen BH21 ... 85 F7
  Poole ... 120 B7
NEW TOWN
  Gillingham SP8 ... 9 C2
  Milborne Port DT9 ... 17 B2
  Pimperne DT11 ... 188 C2

NEW TOWN continued
Sixpenny Handley SP5.... **188** F6
Verwood BH21........... **201** A2
Yeovil BA21............. **27** E6
Newtown DT8 .... **204** C4
Newtown Bsns Ctr BH12 **122** A7
Newtown Hill BH20 .... **157** F4
Newtown La
Poole BH21............. **85** F7
Ringwood BH24, SP6.... **43** E1
Verwood BH31........... **45** C5
Newtown Rd BH31....... **45** C5
Nichola Cl BH12 .... **120** B7
Nicholas Cl BH24 .... **94** B2
Nicholas Gdns BH10..... **89** C2
Nicholson Cl BH17...... **119** E8
Nightingale Cl BH31..... **45** C5
Nightingale Dr DT3 ..... **152** C4
Nightjar Cl BH17....... **118** F8
Nimrod Way BH21 ...... **60** F6
Nine Springs Ctry Pk
BA20................... **27** D3
Ninesprings Leisure Ctr
BA20................... **27** D3
Nine Stones (Stone Circle)*
DT2................... **105** C1
Noade St SP5........... **25** C1
Noah Henville Cnr 4
DT11.................. **81** E8
Noake Rd DT9 .... **29** F5
Noble Cl DT11 .... **88** F1
Noel Rd BH10........... **89** B2
Noel The BH25.......... **95** C3
Nonesuch Cl 3 BH31..... **135** B8
Noon Gdns BH31........ **45** D6
Noon Hill Dr BH31....... **45** D6
Noon Hill Rd BH31...... **45** D6
Norburton DT6......... **128** B8
Norcliffe Cl BH11 ...... **89** B3
NORDEN BH20.......... **161** C3
Norden Dr BH20 .... **142** C6
Norden La DT2.......... **72** F8
Norden Sta* BH20 ..... **161** F2
Nordon Rd DT11....... **212** D5
Nordons DT6........... **100** E5
Norfolk Ave BH23 ...... **91** F2
Norfolk Rd DT4 .... **167** A4
Norleywood BH23....... **125** F8
Norman Ave BH12 ...... **121** A6
Norman Cl DT6......... **100** F7
Normandy Dr BH23 .... **124** D7
Normandy Way
Bridport DT6........... **100** D5
Dorchester DT1........ **107** E2
Upton BH17............ **117** F2
Norman Gdns BH12 .... **121** A6
Normanhurst Ave BH8 .. **90** E1
Normanton Cl BH23..... **91** F1
Norris Cl BH24......... **54** A4
Norris Gdns BH25...... **95** A1
North Allington DT6.... **100** C7
North Ave
Bournemouth BH10..... **89** D6
Lyme Regis DT7 .... **96** B6
NORTHAY EX13......... **202** D3
Northay La EX13....... **202** C3
North Bestwall Rd BH20 **142** F4
NORTH BOCKHAMPTON
DT7................... **89** E4
NORTHBOURNE **89** C4
Northbourne Ave BH10. **89** C5
Northbourne Gdns BH10. **89** C5
Northbourne Pl 3 BH10. **89** C5
Northbourne Rdbt BH10. **89** C5
NORTH BOWOOD DT6... **203** F2
North Bowood La DT6... **203** F2
NORTHBROOK DT2...... **78** B2
Northbrook Rd
Broadstone BH18....... **87** A2
Swanage BH19 .... **179** A5
Yeovil BA21 .... **27** E7
NORTH CHIDEOCK DT6... **99** A8
Northcote Rd BH1...... **122** C4
North Cres DT9 .... **17** C4
North Cswy BH20 ...... **142** E5
North Dorset Bsns Pk 5
DT10.................. **197** C8
North Dr
Ossemsley BH25........ **94** E8
West Moors BH24 ...... **62** B8
NORTH END
Fordingbridge SP6...... **190** F3
Gillingham SP7......... **7** A3
North End DT9.......... **194** F3
North End La SP6....... **42** F4
Northernhay 1 DT1..... **108** A2
Northey Rd BH6........ **123** E6
Northfield DT11........ **200** A6
Northfield Rd BH24 .... **47** D1
North Fields DT10...... **35** C3
NORTH GORLEY SP6.... **188** D7
North Gr DT1........... **199** E3
North Hill Cl DT6....... **128** B8
North Hill Way DT6.... **100** D4
North Instow BH19..... **177** F5
NORTH KINGSTON BH24. **55** E2
North La
Hardington Mandeville
BA22................. **193** A7
Yeovil BA20............ **27** D5
Northleigh La BH21..... **59** E6
North Lodge Rd BH14 .. **120** E4
Northmead Dr BH17.... **118** F8
Northmere Dr BH12.... **120** F7

Northmere Rd BH12.... **120** F7
North Mills Industrial Est
DT6................... **100** D8
North Mills Rd DT6..... **100** D7
Northmoor Way BH20 . **142** D6
Northover BH3.......... **121** F6
Northover Cl
Burton Bradstock DT6.. **128** C8
Piddletrenthide DT2.... **208** B2
Northover La SO41..... **95** E7
North Pk BH20.......... **142** F8
North Perrott Rd TA18. **192** C5
North Perrott Rd TA18. **192** C5
North Pk DT2........... **73** F3
North Pl DT11.......... **212** D4
North Plumley Dro BA22 **84** A6
NORTH POORTON DT6... **205** B1
NORTHPORT BH20...... **142** E5
Northport BH20........ **142** E5
Northport Dr BH20..... **142** E6
NORTH POULNER BH24.. **47** F2
North Poulner Rd BH24. **47** D2
North Quay DT4........ **167** D2
North Rd
Ashmore SP5........... **25** C1
Bournemouth BH7...... **122** E5
Chideock DT6........... **99** A7
Mere BA12.............. **3** A6
Sherborne DT9 .... **30** C7
Weymouth DT4 .... **180** B8
North Rew La DT2...... **106** B1
Northshore BH13....... **147** C4
North Sq
Chickerell DT3......... **166** C6
2 Dorchester DT1..... **108** A2
North St
Beaminster DT8........ **204** D4
Bere Regis BH20........ **81** B2
Bradford Abbas DT9 ... **28** D2
Bridport DT6........... **100** D7
Charminster DT2....... **75** D1
Crewkerne TA18........ **191** F5
Fontmell Magna SP7.... **37** F7
Haselbury Plucknett TA18 **192** C6
Langton Matravers BH19 **178** A2
Mere BA12............. **3** A5
Milborne Port DT9..... **17** D2
Poole BH15............ **119** C2
Wareham BH20......... **142** E4
Winterborne Kingston BH21 **81** E8
Winterborne Stickland
DT11................. **210** C7
North Terr BA21........ **27** E6
North Walls BH20 ...... **142** D4
NORTH WOOTTON DT9 .. **30** F2
Nortoft Rd BH8........ **122** B6
Norton Cl BH23......... **124** C7
Norton Gdns BH9 ...... **89** E1
Norton La DT11........ **198** D3
Norton Rd BH9......... **121** E8
Norton Way BH15...... **119** A1
Norway Cl 3 BH9....... **89** F1
Norway La BH20........ **203** F4
Norwich Ave BH2...... **121** D3
Norwich Avenue W BH2 **121** D3
Norwich Ct 3 BH2 ..... **121** D3
Norwich Mans BH2..... **121** D3
Norwich Rd
Bournemouth BH2...... **121** D3
Weymouth DT4 .... **167** D1
NORWOOD DT2......... **205** B8
Norwood Pl 2 BH5..... **123** B5
Nothe Fort* DT4 ...... **167** F2
Nothe Par DT4......... **167** E2
NOTTINGTON DT3...... **152** A2
Nottington La
Chickerell DT3......... **151** C2
Radipole DT3.......... **152** A2
NOTTON DT2........... **73** B4
Nouale La BA24........ **55** F7
Noyce Gdns BH8........ **91** B2
Nuffield Health
Bournemouth Hospl
(Private) BH1......... **122** A5
Nuffield Ind Est BH17... **119** D8
Nugent Rd BH16....... **124** A4
Nundico BH20......... **142** E4
Numeray Mead Reserve*
DT2................... **73** D3
Nursery Gdns
Bridport DT6........... **100** E7
Mere BA12............. **3** A5
Wimborne BH21........ **56** D3
Nursery Rd
Blandford Forum DT11. **212** D4
Bournemouth BH9...... **90** A3
Ringwood BH24........ **55** C6
Yeovil BA20............ **27** C3
Nursling Gn BH8....... **90** D2
Nutcombe Cl DT11..... **197** A8
Nutcrack La BH20..... **142** F1
Nutgrove Ave DT4 .... **166** F1
Nuthatch Cl
Broadstone BH17...... **118** F8
Ferndown BH22........ **61** D6
Radipole DT3.......... **152** D3
Nutley Cl BH11........ **88** F4
Nutley Way BH11...... **88** F4
Nutmead Cl 4 DT11 ... **198** C8
Nyland La SP8.......... **8** D1

O

Oak Ave
Christchurch BH23...... **123** D8
Holton Heath BH16..... **116** A3
Oakbury Dr DT3........ **168** A7
Oak Cl
Ferndown BH22........ **61** C1
Poole BH21............. **85** E5
Oak Ct BH20........... **142** F8
OAKDALE.............. **119** D6
Oakdale Rd BH15...... **119** E6
Oakdale South Road Mid Sch
BH15................. **119** C5
Oakdene Cl BH21....... **59** D5
Oakdene Rd BH20...... **139** F1
Oak Dr
20 Crewkerne TA18.... **191** F5
Poole BH15............ **119** D2
Oakery Ct 7 BH21..... **107** B2
Oakfield Rd BH15...... **119** C6
Oakfield St DT11....... **212** D4
Oakford Cl BH8........ **90** D3
Oak Gdns BH11......... **89** B1
Oakham Grange BA22.. **61** E5
Oakhurst BH23......... **124** F7
Oakhurst Cl BA22 ..... **53** B2
Oakhurst La BH21..... **53** B2
Oakhurst Rd BH22..... **53** B2
Oak La
Corscombe DT2........ **205** C6
Mere BA12............. **3** B4
Ringwood BH24........ **55** D8
Oaklands Cl
Verwood BH31......... **45** A6
Wareham BH20......... **160** F8
Oaklands Rd BA21 ..... **27** F7
Oakland Wlk BH20 .... **61** F1
Oakleigh 4 BH20...... **26** F2
Oakleigh Way BH23 ... **125** F7
OAKLEY............... **59** E2
Oakley Gdns 3 BH16... **117** C7
Oakley Hill DT11....... **59** D2
Oakley La
Farnham DT11......... **188** C2
Merley BH21........... **59** E2
Salisbury SP5......... **189** F8
Wimborne Minster BH21. **60** A2
Oakley Pl DT4......... **167** D2
Oakley Rd BH21........ **59** E1
Oakley Sh Ctr BH21... **59** E1
Oakley Straight BH21.. **59** E1
Oakmeade Coll of Tech
BH11................. **88** F4
Oakmead Gdns BH11... **88** F4
Oakmead Rd BH17..... **118** F7
Oak Mews BH11....... **120** C5
Oak Rd
Alderholt SP6.......... **42** B5
Bournemouth BH8..... **122** C6
Charminster DT2....... **75** D2
Dorchester DT2....... **139** B2
New Milton BH25...... **95** A4
Upton BH16............ **117** C6
Oaks Dr BH24.......... **53** F3
Oaks Mead BH16...... **45** B6
Oaks The
Ferndown BH22........ **61** A6
Gillingham SP8......... **5** E1
Verwood BH31.......... **45** A7
Oaktree Cl BH20....... **142** E1
Oak Vale La BA8....... **19** B4
Oak Way BA22.......... **26** C7
Oakwood
Bournemouth BH3...... **121** E7
West Knighton DT2.... **136** C3
Oakwood Ave BH25.... **95** C4
Oakwood Cl BH9....... **90** B2
Oakwood Dr BH25..... **95** B3
Oakwood Dr 9 DT11... **37** F1
Oakwood Rd
Bournemouth BH9...... **90** B2
Christchurch BH23..... **93** E1
Oak Woods SP8........ **5** F1
Oasis Mews 6 BH13.... **147** C7
Oasis The 2 BH13..... **121** A4
Oates Rd BH9.......... **89** E1
OATHILL TA18......... **203** B8
Oathill La
Broadwindsor TA18.... **203** A7
West Crewkerne TA18.. **191** B1
Oban Rd BH3........... **121** F7
OBORNE............... **16** E2
Oborne Rd DT9........ **30** D7
Oceanarium* BH2..... **121** F2
Ocean Hts 13 BH5..... **123** A4
Octagon Theatre* BA20. **27** C4
Odcombe Hollow BA22. **192** E8
OKEFORD FITZPAINE
DT11................. **197** F5
Okeford Fitzpaine CE Prim
Sch DT11.............. **197** F5
Okeford Rd BH18 ...... **87** B2
OK Mobile Home Pk
BH23................. **125** B8
Old Bakery Cl BH11.... **199** D3
Old Bakery The DT8.... **203** E5
Old Barn Cl
Christchurch BH23..... **91** D2
Ringwood BH24........ **55** D8
Old Barn Farm Rd BH21. **53** C5
Old Barn Rd
Bere Regis BH20....... **81** A2
Christchurch BH23..... **91** D2
Old Barn Way BH20... **27** A2
Old Bincombe La DT3.. **153** C4

Old Boundary Rd SP7... **12** F2
Old Bound Rd 4 BH16.. **117** F6
Old Bowden Way DT9 .. **17** C4
Old Brewery The 10
BH15................. **119** C2
Old Brickfields DT2.... **136** C3
Old Bridge Rd BH6..... **123** D7
Old Castle Rd DT4..... **180** E7
Old Chalk Pit BH20.... **81** B1
Old Chapel Dr BH16.... **84** C4
Old Christchurch La 12
BH1................... **121** F3
Old Christchurch Rd
BH1................... **121** F3
Old Church Rd DT6..... **100** E4
Old Coach Mews BH14. **120** A4
Old Coastguard Rd BH13 **147** B4
Old Dairy Farm The
DT10................. **196** F3
Old Depot Rd DT5...... **181** C1
Old Farm Cl BH24 ..... **47** E2
Old Farm Ct DT11..... **212** D6
Old Farm Gdns DT11... **212** D5
Old Farm Rd BH15 .... **119** E6
Old Farm Way DT7.... **137** D5
Old Forge Cl BH16 .... **116** F6
Old Forge Rd BH21..... **60** A6
Old Furzebrook Rd BH20 **160** F8
Old Generator Ho The
BH12................. **121** A5
Old Granary Cl DT3 ... **153** C3
Old Ham La BH21 ...... **60** D4
Old Highway Mews DT1. **59** D4
Old Hitchen 4 TA16 ... **191** F7
Old Hollow 1 BA12....**3** B6
Old Kiln Rd
Ridge BH20 .... **143** B1
Upton BH16............ **117** F6
Old Lifeboat House (Mus)*
BH15................. **119** C1
Old Lyme Hill DT6..... **96** F8
Old Lyme Rd DT6...... **96** F8
Old Malthouse La BH19. **178** B2
Old Manor Cl DT11.... **59** D4
Old Market Rd BH21 .. **84** F6
Old Mill La
17 Crewkerne TA18... **191** F5
Marnhull DT10......... **21** A4
Old Mills DT11......... **211** A3
Old Milton Gn BH25... **94** F1
Old Milton Rd BH25... **95** A2
Old Mkt Rd BH21...... **85** B7
Old Mulberry Cl BH10.. **89** A1
Old Oak Way DT11.... **210** C3
Old Orchard BH15..... **119** C1
Old Orchard Ct DT10.. **196** F8
Old Parish La DT7..... **167** B3
Old Pines Cl BH22..... **61** E4
Old Pound Cl BH16.... **84** C3
Old Pound Ct SP8...... **1** D1
Old Priory Rd BH6 .... **123** F4
Old Rd
Corscombe BA22 ...... **26** A3
Wimborne Minster BH21. **59** B5
Old Rd The DT9........ **18** B2
Old Rectory Cl
4 Charmouth DT6..... **97** A7
1 Poole BH15.......... **85** F8
Old Rectory La DT9.... **195** E3
Old Rectory Mews BH15 **118** F2
Old Ropewalk BH15.... **119** A1
Old Rope Wlk The BH15 **118** F1
Old St John's Mews BH9. **89** F3
Old Sandpit La BH16... **85** C2
Old Sawmill DT31..... **45** A7
Old Sch Cl DT9........ **31** B1
Old Sch La
Dorchester DT2....... **155** D7
Hinton St Mary DT10... **35** A5
Iwerne Minster DT11... **37** F1
Old School Cl
Ferndown BH22........ **61** C5
Old Sch Pl DT19....... **30** A5
Old Stacks Gdns 1 BH24. **55** E3
Old Station Gdns BA8 .. **19** B5
Old Station Rd
Radipole DT3.......... **152** B4
4 Yeovil BA20.......... **27** E4
Old Station Way BA20. **27** E4
OLD TOWN............ **119** C2
Old Town Fst Sch 17
BH15................. **119** C2
Old Town Mews 8
BH15................. **119** C2
Old Vicarage Cl
Bournemouth BH10.... **89** E6
Dorchester DT2....... **107** E6
Old Vicarage Gdn DT7.. **96** B5
Old Wareham Rd
Lytchett Minster & Upton
BH21................. **85** C2
Poole BH12............ **120** A7
Old Watery La BH16... **117** A6
Olga Rd DT1........... **107** F1
Oliver Cl BH16......... **118** C5
Olivers Mead 1 DT11.. **198** C8
Olivers Rd BH21....... **60** A6
Olivers Way BH21..... **60** A6
Olivia Cl BH16......... **117** F5
Onslow Gdns BH21.... **59** D6
Onslow Rd BH21....... **59** D6
Ophir Gdns 1 BH8..... **122** C5
Ophir Rd BH8.......... **122** B5

Oratory Gdns BH13.... **147** F8
Orchard Ave
Bridport DT6........... **100** C8
Poole BH14............. **119** F2
Orchard Chase 2 DT11. **199** C7
Orchard Cl
3 Charmouth DT6..... **97** A7
Cheselbourne DT2..... **209** A3
Christchurch BH23..... **124** A6
East Chinnock BA22.... **192** E8
Fernham BH22.......... **61** E5
Fontmell Magna SP7 ... **37** E6
Lytchett Minster & Upton
BH16................. **116** F6
3 Okeford Fitzpaine DT11 **197** F6
Poole BH21............. **85** F7
Ringwood BH24........ **55** C8
Sherborne DT9 .... **195** B8
4 Stourpaine DT11... **198** F4
Sturminster Newton DT10 **197** C8
Sydling St Nicholas DT2. **207** A3
4 West Coker BA22.... **193** A8
Orchard Cres DT6..... **100** C8
Orchard Ct BH31...... **45** C5
Orchard Dr DT11..... **108** A2
Orchard Gdns 5 DT10. **197** C8
Orchard Gr BH25...... **95** A1
Orchard La
2 Crewkerne TA18.... **191** F4
Poole BH21............. **85** F7
Thorncombe TA20 .... **202** E6
7 Winterborne Kingston
DT11................. **81** E8
Orchard Leigh 3 BH25. **95** B2
Orchard Mead
Broadwindsor DT8..... **203** E5
3 Ringwood BH24.... **55** B8
Orchard Mews
2 Christchurch BH23.. **124** A6
7 Gillingham SP8..... **5** D2
Orchard Rd
Gillingham SP8......... **5** E1
Milborne Port DT9..... **17** C2
Orchard Rise
7 Crewkerne TA18.... **191** F4
Milborne St Andrew DT11. **79** E7
Orchard St
Blandford Forum DT11. **212** C4
Bournemouth BH2..... **121** E3
Dorchester DT1....... **108** A2
Yeovil BA20............ **27** B4
Orchard The
Blandford Forum DT11. **212** C5
Bournemouth BH11.... **88** D6
Bransgore BH23 .... **93** C8
Hazelbury Bryan DT10. **196** F3
Radipole DT3.......... **152** D3
Sixpenny Handley SP5.. **189** B4
Winterborne Whitechurch DT2. **156** F6
Orchard Way
Misterton TA18........ **192** A2
2 Monkton DT8....... **204** A8
Orchard Wlk
15 Bournemouth BH21. **121** E3
Milborne Port DT9..... **17** C2
Orcheston Rd BH8..... **122** C6
Orchid Rd DT2......... **139** B2
Orchid Way BH23..... **124** C7
Orestes Gate BH23 ... **125** A5
Orford Cl BH23........ **91** D4
Orford St DT6.......... **78** B1
ORGANFORD BH16.... **116** B6
Organford Rd BH16... **116** C4
Orion Rd DT4.......... **167** D1
Ormonde Rd BH13.... **121** A2
Osborne Cl BH21...... **135** C8
Osborne Pl TA16...... **191** F7
Osborne Rd
Bournemouth BH9..... **121** E8
New Milton BH25...... **95** B3
Poole BH14............. **120** B3
Swanage BH19 .... **179** B2
Wimborne Minster BH21. **59** C5
Osbourne Ho 4 BH25.. **95** A3
OSEHILL GREEN DT9... **195** E4
Osmay Rd BH19....... **185** D8
OSMINGTON DT3...... **154** A3
Osmington Dro DT2... **136** B1
OSMINGTON MILLS..... **154** C2
Osmington White Horse*
DT3................... **153** F3
Osprey Cl BH23........ **125** A5
Osprey Quay Bsns
Development DT5...... **180** F1
Osprey Rd DT4........ **180** D5
OSSEMSLEY **94** D8
Ossemsley Manor Ho
BH25................. **94** D8
Ossemsley South Dr BH25 **94** F8
Osterley Ct BH23...... **124** A8
Oswald Cl BH9......... **89** E2
Oswald Rd BH9........ **89** F2
Otterbourne 14 BH22. **121** D4
Otter Cl
Lytchett Minster & Upton
BH16................. **117** D6
Verwood BH31......... **45** C5
Otter Rd BH15......... **119** F6
Otter Springs SP8..... **11** B8
Otters Wlk BH25...... **95** C5
Ottery La DT9.......... **30** A5
Oval Gdns BH20....... **160** F8
Oval The BH20......... **172** F8
Overbury Cl DT14..... **166** F2
Overbury Manor BH12. **121** B5
Overbury Rd BH14.... **120** C3

Overcliffe Mans BH1 . . . . 122 C3
OVERCOMBE DT3 . . . . 168 A7
Overcombe BA8 . . . . 18 D8
Overcombe Cl BH17 . . . . . . 87 E2
Overcombe Dr DT3 . . . . . . 168 B7
OVER COMPTON DT9 . . . . . 28 E7
Overlands Rd DT4 . . . . . . 180 B8
Over Links Dr BH14 . . . . . 120 D2
Overton Cl DT7 . . . . 96 C7
Ovington Ave BH7 . . . . . . 123 C3
Ovington Gdns BH7 . . . . . 123 C7
OWERMOIGNE DT2 . . . . . . 155 E7
Owlswlots BH13 . . . . 147 F7
Owls Rd
  Bournemouth BH5 . . . . . 122 E3
  Verwood BH31 . . . . 45 C5
OXBRIDGE DT6 . . . . 68 F8
Ox Drove SP5 . . . . 188 B7
Oxencroft 4 SP7 . . . . 12 F4
Oxen Rd 5 TA18 . . . . 191 F4
Oxey Cl BH25 . . . . 95 A1
Oxford Ave BH6 . . . . 123 B5
Oxford La BH1 . . . . 89 B6

Oxhayes DT8 . . . . 203 C8
Oxley Sports Ctr DT9 . . . . . 30 A4
Ozone Terr DT7 . . . . 96 B4

P

Paceycombe Way DT1 . . 107 C2
PACKERS HILL DT9 . . . . . . 196 C5
Packers' Way 1 TA18 . . . 192 B3
Paddington Cl BH11 . . . . . . 88 D4
Paddington Gr BH11 . . . . . . 88 D4
Paddock Cl
  Ferndown BH21 . . . . 61 A5
  Lytchett Matravers BH16 . . 84 D4
  Poole BH12 . . . . 120 B7
  Shaftesbury SP7 . . . . 13 A1
  Sixpenny Handley SP5 . . 189 A3
  St Leonards BH24 . . . . 54 B4
Paddock Gr BH31 . . . . 45 C5
Paddock's Cross DT6 . . . . . 67 B8
Paddock's La DT6 . . . . 67 B8
Paddocks The
  Bournemouth BH10 . . . . . 89 D4
  Bridport DT6 . . . . 100 E4
  1 Iwerne Minster DT11 . . 37 F1
  Mere BA12 . . . . 3 A5
  5 Mosterton DT8 . . . . . . 204 A8
  Thornford DT9 . . . . 194 D8
Paddock The
  Dorchester DT1 . . . . 105 D2
  West Moors BH24 . . . . 62 D3
  West Stafford DT2 . . . . . 136 B8
Paddock Wlk DT7 . . . . 17 C2
Padfield Cl BH6 . . . . 123 E6
Padget Rd BH24 . . . . 47 E1
Padstow Pl DT7 . . . . 43 A8
Pageant Dr 1 DT5 . . . . . . 186 F1
Page Dr 1 DT5 . . . . 186 F1
Paget Rd BH11 . . . . 89 A4
Paisley Rd BH6 . . . . 123 C5
Palace Rd SP8 . . . . 6 A1
Palfrey Rd BH10 . . . . 89 D5
PALLINGTON DT2 . . . . 111 C3
Palma Ct BH23 . . . . 126 A7
Palmer Rd BH15 . . . . 95 A4
Palmer Rd BH15 . . . . 119 F4
Palmers Brewery * DT6 . 100 C5
Palmers Orch BH16 . . . . . . 84 C3
Palmerston Ave BH23 . . . 124 D6
Palmerston Cl 1 BH16 . . 117 F7
Palmerston Rd
  Bournemouth BH1 . . . . . 122 E4
  Poole BH14 . . . . 120 D4
  Upton BH16 . . . . 117 E7
PAMPHILL 58 E6
Pamphill CE Fst Sch BH21 58 E5
Panorama Rd
  Poole BH13 . . . . 147 B3
  Swanage BH19 . . . . 179 A2
Pans Cnr BH22 . . . . 61 F3
Parade The
  4 Bournemouth BH6 . . 123 B4
  New Milton BH25 . . . . 95 D3
  Old Milton BH25 . . . . 94 F1
  Poole BH17 . . . . 87 B1
Paradise Rd BH21 . . . . 51 F7
Paradise St 14 BH15 . . . . 119 B1
Parcroft Gdns BA20 . . . . . . 27 B5
Parcroft Jun Sch BA20 . . . 27 B5
Pardys Hill BH21 . . . . 85 E8
Parfields BA20 . . . . 27 B5
Parham Ct BH23 . . . . 94 E3
Parham Rd BH10 . . . . 89 C2
Paris Ct SP8 . . . . 5 F1
Parish Mews 3 BA21 . . . . 26 E5
Parish Rd BH15 . . . . 119 E3
Park Ave BH10 . . . . 89 C6
Park Cl
  Burton BH23 . . . . 92 C3
  New Milton BH25 . . . . 95 A4
  8 Stourpaine BH21 . . . . 198 F4
Park Ct 1 DT11 . . . . 121 B3
Park Dr
  Holton Heath BH16 . . . . . 116 B3
  Verwood BH31 . . . . 45 A7
Parkelea 3 BH21 . . . . 56 D4
Parker Rd BH9 . . . . 121 F7
Parkers Cl BH24 . . . . 47 E1

Park Est Rd DT5 . . . . 186 F4
Park Farm Cl DT21 . . . . . . 133 E6
PARK GATE DT11 . . . . . . 196 F2
Park Gate BA7 . . . . 35 A2
Park Gate Mews 7 BA21 121 E3
Park Gdns
  Christchurch BH23 . . . . . 124 E7
  Yeovil BA20 . . . . 27 C5
Park Gr DT10 . . . . 33 C8
Park Hill DT11 . . . . 211 C6
Park Homer Dr BH21 . . . . . 60 A6
Park Homer Rd BH21 . . . . . 59 F6
Park La
  Alderholt SP6 . . . . 42 B6
  Bournemouth BH10 . . . . . 89 F4
  Evershot DT2 . . . . 206 A7
  Glanvilles Wootton DT9 . 195 F2
  Henstridge BA8 . . . . 19 B7
  Radipole DT4 . . . . 167 D3
  Shapwick DT11 . . . . 48 C1
  Thorncombe TA20 . . . . . 202 D7
  Wayford TA18 . . . . 191 B1
  Wimborne Minster BH21 . 59 C4
  Wimborne St Giles BH21 . 201 E7
  Woodlands BH21 . . . . 44 B6
Park Lake Rd BH15 . . . . . 119 E2
Parkland BH31 . . . . 45 F4
Parkland Dr BH25 . . . . . . 126 F8
Parkland Pl BH25 . . . . 95 A2
Parklands 11 BH4 . . . . . . 121 C3
Park Lands 11 . . . . 212 C4
Park Mead Rd DT4 . . . . . 180 C7
Park Rd
  Blandford Forum DT11 . . 212 C4
  Bournemouth BH8 . . . . . 122 A5
  Bridport DT6 . . . . 100 C7
  Easton/Weston DT5 . . . . 187 A4
  Henstridge BA8 . . . . 19 A4
  New Milton BH25 . . . . 95 C5
  Old Milton BH25 . . . . 94 F1
  Poole BH15, BH14 . . . . . 119 F3
  Stalbridge DT10 . . . . 33 C8
  Swanage BH19 . . . . 179 C2
  Yeovil BA20 . . . . 27 D5
Park Sch The
  Bournemouth BH8 . . . . . 122 D7
  Yeovil BA20 . . . . 27 C5
Parkside
  Christchurch BH23 . . . . . . 93 D1
  Ringwood BH24 . . . . 55 B6
Parkside Gdns BH10 . . . . . 89 E2
Parkside Ind Est BH24 . . . . 55 C5
Parkside Rd BH14 . . . . . . 120 C4
Park's La DT2 . . . . 130 D7
Park St
  Radipole DT4 . . . . 167 D3
  Yeovil BA20 . . . . 27 D3
  7 Yeovil BA20 . . . . 27 D4
Parkstone Ave BH14 . . . . 120 D4
Parkstone Gram Sch
  BH17 . . . . 87 B1
Parkstone Hts BH14 . . . . 120 A5
Parkstone Rd BH15 . . . . . 119 E3
Parkstone Sta BH14 . . . . 120 B3
Park The
  Barton on Sea BH25 . . . 126 C7
  Wimborne Minster BH21 . 60 A1
  Yeovil BA20 . . . . 27 C5
Parkview BH2 . . . . 121 E4
Park View
  Crewkerne TA18 . . . . 191 F3
  New Milton BH25 . . . . 95 A2
  7 Poole BH15 . . . . 119 E3
Park View CH BH8 . . . . . . 122 C7
Park View Mews BH25 . . . . 95 A2
Park View Point SP5 . . . . 188 B3
Park Water La DT8 . . . . . 203 C5
PARKWAY BA22 . . . . 14 F7
Parkway DT6 . . . . 97 B7
Park Way BH22 . . . . 53 A2
Parkway Dr BH8 . . . . 122 E8
Parkwood La 7 BH25 . . . 123 B5
Parkwood Rd
  Bournemouth BH5 . . . . . 123 A4
  Wimborne Minster BH21 . 59 C4
Parley Cl BH21 . . . . 61 F1
Parley Cross BH22 . . . . . . 89 E8
Parley Fst Sch BH22 . . . . . 61 D3
PARLEY GREEN 90 C7
Parley Green La BH23 . . . . 90 B7
Parley La BH23 . . . . 90 D7
Parley Green Ln BH9 . . . . . 90 A2
Parmiter Dr BH21 . . . . 59 E4
Parmiter Rd BH21 . . . . 59 E4
Parnham's La BH21 . . . . . . 59 E4
Parr & Axe CE Prim Sch
  DT8 . . . . 204 A7
Parrett Mead DT8 . . . . . . 192 C1
Parr Gr 5 DT11 . . . . 199 D4
Parr Ho 9 BH14 . . . . 120 A4
Parricks La EX13 . . . . 202 A3
Parr St BH14 . . . . 120 A4
Parsonage Barn La 55 C7
Parsonage Ct 9 BH8 . . . . 122 A5
Parsonage Hill BH21 . . . . 200 F6
Parsonage La BH21 . . . . . 201 E7
Parsonage Rd
  Bournemouth BH1 . . . . . 122 A3
  Bridport DT6 . . . . 100 C8
Parsonage St SP7 . . . . 37 F6
Parsonage The SP5 . . . . . 189 B4
Parsons Dr BH19 . . . . 179 B5
Parsons La DT2 . . . . 102 E6
Parsons Pool 3 SP7 . . . . . 12 E3
Partridge Cl BH23 . . . . . . 125 A5
Partridge Dr BH14 . . . . . . 120 C1
Partridge Gn BH25 . . . . . . 95 B6

Partridge Wlk BH14 . . . . 120 B1
Partway DT10 . . . . 35 B1
Partway La
  Hardington Mandeville
    BA22 . . . . 192 F7
  Hazelbury Bryan DT10 . . 196 F3
  Thorncombe TA20 . . . . . 202 C6
Pascoe Cl BH14 . . . . 120 A4
Pasture Way DT6 . . . . 100 D5
Patchins Rd BH16 . . . . . . 117 D4
Patchins The BH14 . . . . . 147 C8
Patson Hill La DT9 . . . . . . 15 C2
Pattinson Cl BA21 . . . . 27 F6
Paul's Mead DT1 . . . . 186 F7
Pauls Way DT2 . . . . 137 D6
Pauncefote Rd BH5 . . . . . 123 B3
Pauntley Rd BH23 . . . . . . 124 E5
Pavan Gdns BH10 . . . . 89 C2
Pavilion Ct BH14 . . . . 121 C2
Pavilion The * BH4 . . . . . 121 F2
Pavilion Theatre * DT4 . 167 E3
Pavyotts La DT2 . . . . 193 E8
Payne Cl BH21 . . . . 53 A5
Paynes Cl DT2 . . . . 76 E7
Peace Cl BH23 . . . . 93 A8
Peaceful La DT10 . . . . . . 196 C6
PEACEMARSH SP8 . . . . 5 E4
Peacemarsh Farm Cl 3
  SP8 . . . . 5 E4
PEAR ASH BA9 . . . . 1 C4
Pear Ash La BA9 . . . . 1 C4
Pearce Ave BH14 . . . . . . 120 A1
Pearce Gdns BH14 . . . . . 120 A1
Pearce Rd BH14 . . . . 120 A1
Pearce-Smith Ct BH25 . . 126 E7
Pear Cl BH12 . . . . 121 B4
Pearl Gdns BH10 . . . . 89 C4
Pearl Rd BH10 . . . . 89 C4
Pearson Ave BH14 . . . . . 120 B5
Pearson Gdns BH10 . . . . . 89 D6
Pear Tree Cl
  Alderholt SP6 . . . . 42 B5
  Bransgore BH23 . . . . 85 F5
Peartree La DT4 . . . . 167 B2
Peascombe Reserve *
  DT6 . . . . 69 E1
Peatons La BH16 . . . . 84 B4
Pebble La DT5 . . . . 186 E8
Peckham Ave BH25 . . . . . . 95 A8
Peddlars Wlk 4 BH24 . . . 55 B7
Peeks Mews DT7 . . . . 123 F5
Peel Cl
  Blandford Forum DT11 . . 212 D5
  Poole BH12 . . . . 120 C5
Peelers Ct DT6 . . . . 100 D7
Pegasus Ct
  Bournemouth BH1 . . . . . 122 A5
  8 New Milton BH25 . . . . 95 A3
Pegasus Lodge BH22 . . . . 61 D5
Peggy's La TA18 . . . . 192 C5
Pelham 3 BH14 . . . . 121 A4
Pelham Cl BH23 . . . . 124 B7
Pelhams Park L Ctr BH10 . 89 C6
Pelican Mead BH24 . . . . . . 55 E5
Pemberton Cl BH23 . . . . . 152 D3
Pembroke Cl BA21 . . . . . . 28 A7
Pembroke Ct 4 BH23 . . . 126 B7
Pembroke Rd
  Bournemouth BH4 . . . . . 121 B2
  Poole BH12 . . . . 120 A1
Penbugle Yd 10 DT1 . . . 107 D1
Pen Craig 2 BH13 . . . . . 147 D1
PENDOMER BA22 . . . . 193 B5
Pendomer Rd BA22 . . . . . 193 B5
Pendruffle La 12 DT1 . . . 107 D1
Penelope Ct 12 BH21 . . . 120 D7
Penfield BA21 . . . . 27 E5
Pengelly Ave BH10 . . . . . . 89 E5
Penhale Wlk 17 DT1 . . . 107 D1
PEN MILL BA21 . . . . 28 A6
Pen Mill Hill BA12 . . . . 1 E3
Pen Mill Inf Sch BA21 . . . . 27 F6
Pen Mill Trading Est
  BA21 . . . . 28 B6
Penmore Rd DT9 . . . . 15 C3
Pennant Way BH11 . . . . . 124 F7
Penn Cl BH21 . . . . 94 E1
Penn Cross DT6 . . . . 64 D1
Penn Hill BA20 . . . . 27 D4
Penn Hill Ave BH14 . . . . . 120 A2
Penn Hill Pk BA20 . . . . . . 27 D4
Penn Hill View DT2 . . . . . 106 D8
Pennine Ct 8 BA21 . . . . . 124 F8
Pennine Way BH31 . . . . . . 45 B5
Pennington Cl BH22 . . . . . 52 F1
Pennington Cres BH22 . . . 52 F2
Pennington Ho 6 BH4 . . 121 C2
Pennington Rd BH22 . . . . . 52 F2
Pennsylvania Rd DT5 . . . 187 B3
Penny Hedge BH25 . . . . . 127 B8
Penny Plot DT7 . . . . 96 A6
Penny's Cnr SO41 . . . . 95 F4
Penny's Ct BH21 . . . . 40 B7
Penny's La BH21 . . . . 40 B7
Penny's Mead BH21 . . . . . 40 B7
Penny's Wlk BH22 . . . . . . 61 D5
Penny Way BH25 . . . . 125 C6
Pennywell Gdns BH25 . . . . 95 D4
Penrith Cl BH31 . . . . 45 A6
Penrith Rd BH5 . . . . 123 A4
Penrose Cl BH16 . . . . 84 C2
Penrose Rd BH22 . . . . 61 D6
PENSELWOOD BA9 . . . . 1 B4

Pentons Hill SP6 . . . . 43 F6
PENTRIDGE SP5 . . . . 189 E4
Pentridge La SP5 . . . . . . 189 E4
Peppercorn Cl BH23 . . . . 124 E8
Pepper Hill DT11 . . . . . . 198 B5
Percivale Rd 6 BA21 . . . . 26 F7
Percy Rd
  Bournemouth BH5 . . . . . 122 F4
  Yeovil BA21 . . . . 27 F6
Peregrine Rd BH23 . . . . . 125 A5
Pergin Cres BH17 . . . . . . 119 B7
Pergin Way BH17 . . . . . . 119 B7
Perrott Hill Sch TA18 . . . 192 B4
Perryfield Gdns BH7 . . . . 123 B8
Perry Gdns BH15 . . . . 119 C1
Perry St TA20 . . . . 202 A7
PERRY STREET TA20 . . . . 202 B8
Persley Rd BH10 . . . . 89 D3
Perth Cl BH23 . . . . 91 E1
Perth St DT4 . . . . 167 B3
Peter Grant Way BA21 . . . 61 C5
Peters Cl BH16 . . . . 117 E6
Petersfield Pl BH7 . . . . . . 123 B7
Petersfield Rd BH7 . . . . . 123 B7
Petersham La BH21 . . . . . 51 A4
Petersham Rd BH17 . . . . 119 A8
Peters Rd BH22 . . . . 61 F3
Peter St 3 BA20 . . . . 27 D4
Petter's Way BA20 . . . . . . 27 D4
Pettitts Cl DT9 . . . . 28 C2
Petwyn Cl BH22 . . . . 61 D5
Peverell Avenue E DT1 . 107 C2
Peverell Avenue W DT1 . 107 B2
Peverell Rd BH17 . . . . . . 117 D4
Peveril Cl BH24 . . . . 55 E4
Peveril Point Rd BH19 . . 179 D2
Peveril Rd BH19 . . . . 179 C1
Pheasant Way SP8 . . . . . . 11 B8
Phelips Rd 2 BH23 . . . . . 85 F6
Philip Green Meml Sch
  BH21 . . . . 190 C1
Philip Rd DT11 . . . . 212 E4
Phillips Rd 3 BH21 . . . . . 21 A2
Philpot Mus The * DT7 . . 96 C5
Phippard Way BH15 . . . . 119 D2
Phyldon Cl BH12 . . . . 120 B5
Phyldon Rd BH12 . . . . . . 120 B6
Piccadilly La DT11 . . . . . . 56 C8
Pickard Rd BH22 . . . . 61 F7
Pickering Cl BH18 . . . . 87 A2
Picket La DT8 . . . . 192 C1
Pickett La BA21 . . . . 27 C7
Picketts Cross DT2 . . . . . . 74 A4
Pickford Rd BH9 . . . . 89 F1
PIDDLEHINTON DT2 . . . . . 76 F7
Piddlehinton Ent DT2 . . . 77 A6
Piddle La DT2 . . . . 207 D3
Piddles Wood Reserve *
  DT10 . . . . 197 E7
PIDDLETRENTHIDE DT2 . . 208 A3
Piddle Valley CE Fst Sch
  DT2 . . . . 208 A3
PIDNEY DT10 . . . . 196 F4
Pidney Hill DT10 . . . . . . 196 F3
Piece Rd DT9 . . . . 17 C3
Piece The 2 TA16 . . . . . 191 F7
Pierston Fields SP8 . . . . . . 5 C6
Pigeon Cl
  Blandford Forum DT11 . . 212 D2
  Winfrith Newburgh DT2 . 156 F5
Pig Hill BA22 . . . . 193 A7
PIG OAK BH21 . . . . 51 A3
Pig Shoot La BH23 . . . . . . 90 F5
Pikes La BH19 . . . . 183 C7
Pile La DT10 . . . . 32 F5
Pilford Cl BH23 . . . . 125 A5
Pilford Heath Rd BH21 . . . 60 B7
Pilford La BH21 . . . . 51 D2
Pilgrim Pk BH24 . . . . 55 E8
Pilgrim's Cl BH25 . . . . 95 C3
Pilgrims Way
  Poole BH17 . . . . 119 A7
Pilley Rd BH22 . . . . 61 F7
Pill Mdw SP8 . . . . 9 C3
PILLWELL DT10 . . . . 21 A3
Pilot Hight Rd BH11 . . . . . 89 A4
PILSDON DT6 . . . . 203 C2
Pilsdon Cl 7 DT8 . . . . . . 204 C4
Pilsdon Dr BH17 . . . . 87 E3
Pilsdon La DT6 . . . . 203 C3
Pilsdon Pen * DT6 . . . . . 203 C4
Pilwell DT10 . . . . 21 A3
Pimperleaze Rd
  Mere BA12 . . . . 3 F1
  Warminster BA12 . . . . 3 E4
Pimpern Cl BH17 . . . . 87 F2
PIMPERNE
  Blandford Forum DT11 . . 199 D4
  Yeovil DT2 . . . . 194 A3
Pimpernel Ct 6 SP8 . . . . . 5 C2
Pimperne Long Barrow *
  DT11 . . . . 199 E5
Pimperne Prim Sch
  DT11 . . . . 199 D4
Pineapple Bsns Pk DT6 . . 68 B6
Pineapple La DT6 . . . . 68 C6
Pine Ave
  Bournemouth BH6 . . . . . 123 C4
  Poole BH12 . . . . 120 F6
Pinebeach Ct BH13 . . . . . 147 G8
Pine Cl
  Barton on Sea BH25 . . . 126 E8
  Ferndown BH22 . . . . 61 C7
Pinecliffe Ave BH6 . . . . . 123 C4

Pinecliffe Rd BH25 . . . . . 126 C7
Pinecliff Rd BH13 . . . . . . 147 G8
Pine Cres
  Christchurch BH23 . . . . . 125 E8
  Holton Heath BH16 . . . . . 116 B3
Pine Dr
  Poole BH13 . . . . 120 F3
  St Leonards BH24 . . . . . . 54 B4
Pine End BH22 . . . . 61 F3
Pine Glen Ave BH22 . . . . . 61 C8
Pine Grange 4 BH1 . . . . 122 A3
Pine Ho BH25 . . . . 95 A3
Pineholt Cl BH24 . . . . 54 C5
Pinehurst Ave BH23 . . . . 124 F5
PINEHURST PARK BH22 . . 53 A1
Pinehurst Rd BH22 . . . . . . 61 F8
Pinehurst Rd BH22 . . . . . . 53 A1
Pine Lodge 10 BH13 . . . . 147 F7
Pine Manor Rd BH24 . . . . 53 F5
Pine Mans 3 BH1 . . . . . . 122 D4
Pinemoor Cl DT3 . . . . 167 F8
Pine Park Mans 16 BH3 . 121 F3
Pine Rd
  Alderholt SP6 . . . . 42 B5
  Bournemouth BH9 . . . . . 122 A8
  East End BH21 . . . . 58 F1
Pine Ridge DT7 . . . . 96 C7
Pine Ridge Cl BH16 . . . . . 98 F5
Pineside BH9 . . . . 122 A8
Pines Mews DT7 . . . . 204 D4
Pine Springs Nature
  Reserve * BH18 . . . . 86 E2
Pines The BH13 . . . . 121 A2
Pine Tree Ave BA20 . . . . . 27 B3
Pine Tree Cl BH21 . . . . . . 59 D5
Pine Tree Glen BH4 . . . . 121 C3
Pinetree Wlk BH17 . . . . . 118 F8
Pine Vale Cres BH10 . . . . . 89 F3
Pine View DT6 . . . . 100 B6
Pine View Cl
  Upton BH16 . . . . 117 E6
  Verwood BH31 . . . . 44 F7
Pine View Gdns BH10 . . . . 89 F4
Pine View Rd BH31 . . . . . . 44 F7
Pine Wlk
  Lyme Regis DT7 . . . . 96 B4
  Verwood BH31 . . . . 45 D5
Pinewood Ave BH10 . . . . . 89 D5
Pinewood Cl
  Bournemouth BH5 . . . . . 89 D5
  5 Upton BH16 . . . . 117 C7
  Walkford BH23 . . . . 94 A2
Pinewood Gdns BH22 . . . . 61 D7
Pinewood Rd
  Christchurch BH23 . . . . . . 93 F1
  Ferndown BH22 . . . . 61 C7
  Hordle SO41 . . . . 95 F3
  Poole BH13 . . . . 121 B1
  St Leonards BH24 . . . . . . 54 B4
  Upton BH16 . . . . 117 C7
Pinford La DT9 . . . . 30 E6
Pink Knoll Hollow DT9 . . . 15 E8
Pinnacle The 7 BH1 . . . . 122 A3
Pipers Ash 2 BH25 . . . . . 55 E8
Pipers Dr BH23 . . . . 125 A7
Pipit Cl DT3 . . . . 152 D3
Pippin Cl BH23 . . . . 91 E2
Pippin Equestrian * BH18 . 10 D7
Pipplepen La DT8 . . . . . . 192 C2
Pirates La DT4 . . . . 180 B7
Pitcher Cl 3 BH22 . . . . . . 61 E6
Pitchers DT6 . . . . 68 B6
Pitcote La 8 DT1 . . . . . . 107 D1
Pitfield Cnr BA22 . . . . 15 A6
Pitt Hill TA17 . . . . 191 B7
Pitman's La DT6 . . . . 66 B1
Pit Rd TA17 . . . . 191 B7
Pitt Cl DT11 . . . . 212 C2
Pitthouse La BH23 . . . . . . 91 D8
Pitt La DT6 . . . . 66 B3
Pittmore Rd BH23 . . . . 92 C2
Pitt's Dro BH21 . . . . 49 E1
Pitts La
  Melbury Abbas SP7 . . . . . 23 F5
  Sedgehill & Semley SP7 . . 7 C5
Pitts Orchard DT10 . . . . . . 35 B1
Pitts Pl BH25 . . . . 95 D2
Pitwines Cl BH15 . . . . . . 119 D2
Pix Mead Gdns SP7 . . . . . 13 A2
Place Mill * BH23 . . . . . . 124 C5
Placket La BA20 . . . . 27 A1
Plain The DT2 . . . . 109 A6
Plaisters La DT3 . . . . 153 C5
Plantagenet Chase BA20 . 27 A2
Plantagenet Cres BH11 . . 88 D5
Plantagenet Pk BA22 . . . . 27 A3
Plantagenet Way 8 SP7 . . 7 D3
Plantation Cl BH17 . . . . . . 87 C1
Plantation Dr BH23 . . . . . 94 A2
Plantation Rd
  Christchurch BH23 . . . . . . 63 B4
  Poole BH17 . . . . 87 C1
Plant Park Rd BH24 . . . . . 54 E2
Plassey Cl DT1 . . . . 107 E2
Plassey Cres BH10 . . . . . . 89 C5
Platts DT10 . . . . 196 F8
Playfield Cl 2 BA8 . . . . . . 19 A4
Playfields Dr BH12 . . . . . 120 E6
Pleasance Way BH25 . . . . 94 F3
PLECK
  Marnhull DT10 . . . . 34 E8
  Sturminster Newton DT9 . 196 B6
Pleck Hill DT10 . . . . 196 E3
Pleck La DT2 . . . . 209 B7

PLECK OR LITTLE ANSTY
DT2 .... 209 C7
Plecy Cl BH22............... 61 D2
Plemont Cl DT11........... 88 E1
Plocks The DT11.......... 212 C3
Plot La DT9................... 14 F1
Plot La BA8................. 19 C5
Plough Est DT11.......... 212 D6
Plover Cl **2** DT9.......... 17 C2
Plover Ct BA21.............. 26 F6
Plover Dr DT3.............. 166 D5
Plover Rd DT9............... 17 C2
Plover Wlk DT4............ 180 D6
Plowman Cl DT10.......... 21 A3
Plucknett Row BA20..... 26 E5
Plumbley Mdws **6** DT11.. 81 E8
Plumbtree Gdns DT6.... 100 E5
Plumer Rd BH17............ 87 A1
Plum Orch DT9.............. 28 F7
Plumptree Gdns DT6.... 100 E5
PLUSH DT2............... 208 C5
Podington Mdws DT3.. 166 D5
Point The BH5............. 122 E3
POKESDOWN ....
 BH5........................ 123 B5
Pokesdown Sta BH7..... 123 A5
Polans DT9................. 194 D2
Policemans La BH16.... 117 B7
Pollards La DT2........... 155 D7
Polly's Cl DT2............. 137 D6
Pomona Cl DT2............. 61 D6
Pompey's Cnr BH21...... 61 A4
Pompey's La BH22........ 61 B2
Pond Cl
 Henstridge BA8........... 19 A4
 New Milton BH25.......... 95 A3
Pond End DT6.............. 68 D2
Pond Head BH21.......... 51 C6
Pond Wlk DT10............. 33 C8
Ponsonby Rd BH14...... 120 D4
Pony Dr BH16.............. 117 F7
POOLE 119 B3
Poole Commerce Ctr
 BH12...................... 120 A6
Poole Gram Sch BH17... 87 D2
Poole High Sch BH15.. 119 C4
Poole Hill BH2............ 122 C3
Poole Hospl BH15....... 119 D3
Poole La BH11.............. 89 B5
Poole Mus **★** BH15..... 119 B1
Poole Rd
 Bournemouth BH4....... 121 C3
 Lytchett Matravers BH16.. 84 F5
 Poole BH13............... 120 B8
 Sturminster Marshall BH21.. 56 D2
 Upton BH16................ 117 E7
 Wimborne Minster BH21.. 59 C4
Poole's Ct **4** DT7........ 96 C5
Poole Sta BH15........... 119 C3
POOLESTOWN DT10..... 33 E5
Pool Lane Rdbt BH11.... 88 E4
Poop Hill TA18............ 192 C8
Poop Hill La TA18........ 192 C8
Poorhouse La DT6........ 66 C8
Pope's La DT9.............. 17 D2
Popes Rd BH15............ 119 D6
Poplar Cl
 Bransgore BH23.......... 93 C8
 Christchurch BH23....... 126 B8
 3 Poole BH15............ 119 B1
 Radipole DT4.............. 167 A6
 Wimborne Minster BH21.. 59 D5
Poplar Cres BH24......... 55 D7
Poplar Dr
 Brympton BA21........... 26 E7
 Dorchester DT2........... 75 D2
Poplar Hill **3** DT11.... 198 B6
Poplar La DT3.............. 93 C8
Poplar Rd BH25........... 95 D4
Poplar Way BH24......... 55 D7
Pople's Well TA18....... 191 E4
Poppies The BH20....... 139 E1
Poppy Cl
 Christchurch BH23...... 125 C8
 Upton BH16............... 117 B7
 Yeovil BA22............... 26 D5
Poppyfields SP8........... 5 F4
Poppy Way DT6........... 100 D2
Portadene **1** DT4....... 121 D2
Portarlington Cl BH14.. 121 D2
Portarlington Ct **44** BH4.. 121 C3
Portarlington Rd BH4... 121 C2
Portchester Ct **3** BH8.. 122 B5
Portchester Pl BH8..... 122 B5
Portchester Rd BH8.... 122 B5
Portchester Sch BH7... 123 A7
Portelet Cl BH12.......... 88 D2
Porter Rd BH17........... 119 B7
Porters La BH21........... 60 C6
Portesham CE Prim Sch
 DT3....................... 150 A8
Portesham Gdns BH9.... 90 B4
Portesham Hill DT3.... 132 A1
Portesham Way BH17... 87 E3
Portfield Cl BH23........ 124 A7
Portfield Rd BH23....... 124 A7
Portfield Sch BH23...... 90 B8
Portiere Ho BH11........ 89 A4
Port La DT9................ 101 D3
Portland Beach Rd DT4.. 180 E3
Portland Bill Lighthouse **★**
 DT5...................... 186 D9
Portland Bird Obsy & Field
 Ctr **★** DT5............. 186 E10

Portland Castle **★** DT5.. 181 A1
Portland Com Hospl
 DT5...................... 181 B1
Portland Cres DT4...... 167 B2
Portland Ct DT7........... 96 A5
Portland Mus **★** DT5... 187 B3
Portland Pl BH21......... 121 F4
Portland Port DT5...... 181 C2
Portland Port Bsns Ctr
 DT5...................... 181 C1
Portland Rd
 Bournemouth BH9....... 122 C4
 Weymouth DT4........... 180 C7
Portman Cres BH5....... 123 B4
Portman Ct BA22........ 192 E8
Portman Dr **5** DT11... 198 C8
Portman Pl DT11......... 212 C4
Portman Rd
 Bournemouth BH7....... 122 F5
 1 Pimperne DT11..... 199 D4
Portman Terr BH5....... 123 B4
Portmore Cl BH18......... 87 C6
Portmore Gdns DT4... 167 C1
Portnell's La BA12......... 1 F4
Portreeve Dr **2** BH10.. 90 A4
Port Regis Sch SP7...... 12 B5
Portswood Dr **2** BH10.. 90 A4
PORTWAY DT2........... 156 F7
Portway DT2............... 102 C6
Portwey Cl DT4........... 167 C1
Possessions Cnr SP5.... 25 B3
POST GREEN BH16..... 116 F7
Post Green Rd BH16.... 116 F7
Post Office Bldgs BH9.. 121 F8
Post Office La BH24..... 54 C5
Post Office Rd
 18 Bournemouth BH1.. 121 F3
 Gillingham SP8............. 5 D6
**Potterne Hill Nature
 Reserve ★** BH31........ 45 C4
Potterne Way
 Verwood BH21............ 45 D4
 Wimborne BH21.......... 45 D4
Potterne Wood Cl BH31.. 45 E4
Potters Way BH14...... 120 C2
Pottery Junc BH14..... 120 E5
Pottery La DT4............ 167 C4
Pottery Lines BH20.... 142 F7
Pottery Rd BH14........ 120 B2
POULNER BH24.......... 55 F8
Poulner Hill BH24........ 55 F8
Poulner Jun & Inf Schs
 BH24...................... 47 E2
Poulner Pk BH24.......... 47 E1
Poundbury Camp ★ DT1.. 107 E3
Poundbury Cres DT1... 107 E2
Poundbury Rd DT1..... 107 E3
Poundbury West Ind Est
 DT1...................... 107 E2
Pound Cl
 Charminster DT2........ 107 D6
 Poole BH15.............. 119 F5
 Ringwood BH24........... 55 C8
 Stalbridge DT10.......... 33 C8
 Yeovil BA21............... 26 E5
Pound Cottage Riding Ctr **★**
 DT2...................... 205 E2
Pound Hill
 Corscombe DT2......... 205 B7
 Witchampton BH21.... 200 F1
Pound La
 Bishop's Caundle DT9.. 196 A7
 Burstock DT8............ 203 D5
 1 Christchurch BH23.. 124 B6
 Damerham SP6.......... 190 E3
 Dewlish DT2............. 209 C1
 2 Dorchester DT1.... 108 B2
 Gillingham SP8............. 5 D2
 5 Okeford Fitzpaine DT11.. 197 F5
 Okeford Fitzpaine DT11.. 198 A5
 Poole BH15.............. 119 F5
 Shaftesbury SP7......... 13 A3
 Wareham BH20.......... 142 E3
 Wootton Fitzpaine DT6.. 202 E7
Pound Piece
 Easton/Weston DT5.... 186 F4
 Maiden Newton DT2.... 72 F8
Pound Rd
 Hawkchurch EX13...... 202 C2
 Lyme Regis DT7.......... 96 B5
 Sherborne DT9............ 30 B3
 Thornford DT9.......... 194 D8
Pound St DT7.............. 96 B5
Pound The BA12............ 3 B5
Powell Rd BH14.......... 120 B3
Powell Theatre **★** DT9.. 30 B6
Powerscourt Rd BH25.. 126 E7
POWERSTOCK DT6..... 70 B5
Powerstock CE Prim Sch
 DT6...................... 70 A5
Powerstock Comm Reserve **★**
 DT6...................... 70 F6
Powis Cl BH21.............. 95 B3
Powys Cl DT1............. 134 C8
Powys Gn DT9.............. 30 A6
Powys La DT9.............. 30 B6
POXWELL DT2........... 154 E5
Poxwell Cairn Circle **★**
 DT2...................... 154 E4
Poxwell Dro DT2......... 154 B4
POYNTINGTON DT9..... 16 D4
Prankerds Rd **3** DT9.. 17 C2
Preetz Way DT11........ 212 F6
PRESTON DT3........... 168 B8
Preston CE Prim Sch
 BA21...................... 26 E7
Preston Cl **11** BH20..... 117 E7

Preston Ct
 Northport BH20.......... 142 E5
 Yeovil BA20................ 27 B4
Preston Gr BA20........... 27 A5
Preston La BH23.......... 92 D3
PRESTON PLUCKNETT
 BA20....................... 26 F4
Preston Rd
 Overcombe/Preston
 DT3....................... 153 C3
 Poole BH15.............. 119 C6
 Weymouth DT3......... 167 F6
 Yeovil BA22............... 26 C5
Preston Sch BA21........ 26 F5
Preston Way BH23..... 125 D8
Prestwood Cl DT4....... 94 F1
Pretoria Terr DT4....... 167 C2
Prideaux Dr SP7........... 7 B1
Pride Cl DT2............... 137 B2
Priest La BH23............. 92 B7
Priestlands DT9............ 30 B7
Priestlands La DT9........ 30 B7
Priestley Rd BH21....... 60 E1
Priest's House Mus The ★ **12**
 BH21...................... 59 B5
Priest's Rd BH19......... 179 A2
Priest's Way BH19...... 178 F2
Prime La DT6.............. 65 F7
Primrose Cl **3** SP8....... 5 D2
Primrose Gdns DT7..... 86 F1
Primrose Hill BA22..... 193 B7
Primrose La BA21........ 14 A1
Primrose Way
 Christchurch BH23..... 125 C8
 Corfe Mullen BH21...... 86 E7
Primula Cl DT3........... 152 F2
Prince of Wales Rd
 Bournemouth BH4...... 121 C4
 Dorchester DT1.......... 108 A1
 3 Weymouth DT4..... 167 C2
Prince of Wales Sch The
 DT1....................... 134 D8
Princes Cl **8** BH13..... 121 A4
Prince's Cl BH22........... 61 D5
Prince's Dr DT4.......... 167 D6
Prince's Pl BH25............ 95 C3
Prince's Rd BH22......... 61 D5
Princess Ave BH23...... 124 B6
Princess Rd
 Bournemouth BH4...... 121 B4
 Bridport DT6............. 100 C5
 Poole BH13.............. 121 A4
 Swanage BH19.......... 179 A2
Princes St BA20............ 27 D4
Prince's St DT11......... 108 A2
Pringles Cl BH22........... 61 E5
Pringles Dr BH22.......... 61 E5
Prior Cl BH7............... 122 F5
Priors Cl BH23............ 125 C7
Priors Cnr **2** BH21...... 201 D1
Prior's Rd BH17......... 119 A8
Priors Wlk **3** BH21..... 59 B5
Priory CE Prim Sch The **6**
 BH23...................... 124 B6
Priory Cl BA20.............. 26 F1
Priory Gdns
 3 Pimperne DT11..... 199 D3
 3 Spetisbury DT11.... 211 E5
 West Moors BH22........ 62 A8
Priory Glade BH23....... 26 E6
Priory Ho BH23.......... 124 C5
Priory Ind Pk BH23..... 125 B7
Priory Quay BH23...... 124 C5
Priory Rd
 Bournemouth BH2...... 121 E2
 Portland DT5............. 186 F6
 West Moors BH22........ 62 A8
Priory View Cl **3** BH21.. 59 B3
Priory View Pl **3** BH9.. 90 A3
Priory View Rd
 Bournemouth BH9........ 90 A3
 Burton BH23.............. 92 C2
Privet Rd BH9............ 121 F8
Promenade BH23....... 125 B5
Prospect Cl **2** SP8........ 6 A1
Prospect Cres BH19... 179 A3
Prospect Pl
 Mere BA12.................. 2 F5
 9 Weymouth DT4..... 167 D2
Prospect Rd
 Dorchester DT1.......... 107 E2
 Lytchett Matravers BH16.. 84 D2
Prosperous St **8** BH15.. 119 C1
Prout Hill **9** DT8...... 204 D4
Prunus Cl BH22............ 61 B7
Prunus Dr BH22........... 61 B7
Pryors Wlk BH16.......... 84 D2
Pud Brook **2** DT9...... 17 D1
Puddledock La DT3.... 153 C3
PUDDLETOWN DT2..... 78 A1
PUDDLE TOWN 143 DT2.. 192 B5
Puddletown CE Fst Sch
 DT2........................ 78 B1
Puddletown Cres DT7.. 87 F2
Puddletown Rd
 Arne BH20................ 142 A3
 Bere Regis BH20........ 140 E7
 East Stoke BH20......... 113 B1
Pugmill La DT1............ 134 C8
Pugs Hole Nature Reserve ★
 BH4....................... 121 C5
PULHAM DT2............. 196 B3
Pullman Way BH24....... 55 C6
Pulmans La **4** TA18.... 191 F4
PUNCKNOWLE DT2..... 129 F6
Purbeck Ave BH15..... 118 E1
Purbeck Cl
 Loders DT6............... 101 F8

Purbeck Cl *continued*
 Lytchett Matravers BH16.. 84 D3
 Upton BH16............... 117 D7
 Weymouth DT4.......... 167 B1
Purbeck Ct
 Bournemouth BH5..... 123 B3
 3 Christchurch BH23.. 124 F8
Purbeck Dr BH31......... 45 B5
Purbeck Gdns BH14.... 119 F5
Purbeck Hts BH14..... 120 B5
**Purbeck Marine Wildlife
 Reserve ★** BH20...... 175 B2
Purbeck Rd
 Barton on Sea BH25... 126 D7
 Bournemouth BH2...... 121 E2
 Lytchett Matravers BH16.. 84 D4
Purbeck Sch The BH20.. 142 C2
**Purbeck Sports Ctr &
 Swimming Pool** BH20.. 142 C2
Purbeck Terr Rd BH19.. 179 C1
Purbeck View **9** BH19.. 178 F2
Purbeck View Pk BH20.. 142 E4
Purbeck View Sch BH19.. 179 B3
Purchase Rd BH12..... 121 C7
Purdy Ho BH11............ 89 A4
PUREWELL BH23....... 124 D7
Purewell BH23........... 124 D6
Purewell Cl BH23....... 124 E6
Purewell Cross BH23... 124 E6
Purewell Cross Rd BH23.. 124 D7
Purewell Cl **2** BH23.... 124 E7
**Purewell Mdws Nature
 Reserve ★** BH23..... 124 D7
Purewell Robb BH23... 124 E6
Purns Mill La SP8.......... 5 F5
PURSE CAUNDLE DT9... 32 B8
PURTINGTON TA20..... 191 A4
Pussex La BH23.......... 91 A7
Putlake Adventure Farm ★
 BH19...................... 178 C2
PUTTON DT3............. 166 E5
Putton La DT3........... 166 D5
Putt's La DT9............... 16 B8
Putton Wood ★ BH17.. 197 B7
Puxey La
 Shillingstone DT11.... 198 B5
 Sturminster Newton DT10.. 197 B3
Pye Cl BH21.................. 86 E7
Pye Cnr BH21............. 59 B4
Pye La
 Cranborne BH21.......... 41 A6
 Tatworth & Forton TA20.. 202 B8
 Wimborne Minster BH21.. 59 B4
PYMORE DT6.............. 68 D1
Pymore La DT6............. 68 C3
Pymore Rd DT6............ 68 E1

Q

Quadrant Ctr The BH1... 121 F3
Quantock Cl **7** BH23... 124 F8
Quar Cl DT10............. 196 E1
Quarr Dr DT9............... 30 B8
Quarr Hill
 Morden BH20.............. 83 C1
 Wool BH20................ 140 B1
Quarr La
 Lytchett Matravers BH16.. 84 A1
 Sherborne DT9............ 30 B8
 Symondsbury DT6....... 99 D8
Quarr Nature Reserve The ★
 DT9......................... 30 B7
Quarry Chase 4 BH4... 121 C3
Quarry Cl
 Shipton Gorge DT6..... 101 D4
 Stour Provost SP8....... 21 D8
 Sturminster Newton DT10.. 35 B2
 8 Swanage BH19..... 178 F2
 Wimborne Minster BH21.. 60 B7
Quarry Dr BH20............ 60 B7
Quarry Fields Ind Est BA12.. 2 E5
Quarry La
 Bothenhampton DT6... 100 C8
 Bradford Abbas DT9.... 28 C3
 Longburton DT9......... 195 B8
 Melbury Abbas SP7...... 24 B5
Quarry Rd BH21........... 60 B7
Quarterjack Mews 1
 BH21...................... 59 C4
Quayle Rd BH11......... 119 C5
Quay Point 7 BH15.... 119 C1
Quay Rd BH23............ 124 B6
Quayside DT6............ 100 C1
Quay The
 Poole BH15.............. 119 C1
 3 Wareham Town BH20.. 142 E3
Quebec Pl **7** DT4....... 167 D3
Queen Anne Dr
 Oakley BH21................ 87 E8
 Wimborne Minster BH21.. 60 A1
Queen Eleanor Rd SP8.... 6 A1
Queen Elizabeth Ct BH21.. 59 B4
Queen Elizabeth L Ctr
 BH21...................... 59 B4
Queen Elizabeth's Sch
 BH21...................... 58 F6
Queen Mary Ave BH9.. 89 F2
QUEEN OAK SP8.......... 2 A3
Queen's Ave
 Christchurch BH23.... 124 B5
 Dorchester DT1......... 134 E8
Queensbury Mans 9
 BH1....................... 122 A3
Queens Cl BH22........... 52 F1
Queen's Copse La BH21.. 51 C8
Queens Ct
 16 Bournemouth BH4.. 121 D4

Queens Ct *continued*
 Bournemouth, Charminster
 BH8....................... 122 B8
 New Milton BH25......... 95 D3
Queens Dr DT2........... 137 F7
Queens Gdns BH20.... 121 D4
Queens Gr
 New Milton BH25......... 95 C4
 Pen Selwood BA9......... 1 C3
Queensland Rd
 Bournemouth BH5..... 123 A5
 Weymouth DT4.......... 167 B3
Queensmead
 Burton BH23.............. 92 A1
 4 Wimborne Minster BH21.. 59 C5
Queens Mead **8** BH19.. 179 B2
Queen's Park Ave BH8.. 122 D8
Queen's Park Gdns BH8.. 122 D8
Queen's Park Inf Sch BH8.. 90 C1
Queen's Park Jun Sch
 BH8....................... 122 D7
Queen's Park Rd BH8.. 122 D7
Queen's Park South Dr
 BH8....................... 122 D7
Queen's Park West Dr
 BH8....................... 122 D7
Queens Rd
 Bradford Abbas DT9..... 28 D2
 Bridport DT6............. 100 C6
 Ferndown BH22.......... 61 D7
 Fortuneswell DT5...... 186 E8
 Mere BA12................... 3 B6
 Radipole DT3............ 167 C7
Queen's Rd
 Blandford Forum DT11.. 212 E4
 Christchurch BH23..... 124 D4
 Christchurch BH23..... 124 C6
 Poole BH14.............. 120 D4
 Poole BH21................ 85 F5
 Swanage BH19.......... 179 B1
Queen St
 Gillingham SP8............. 5 F2
 Radipole DT4............ 167 E4
 4 Yetminster DT9..... 194 C5
Queensway
 New Milton BH25......... 94 E3
 Ringwood BH24........... 55 D7
 Yeovil BA20................ 27 C5
Queensway Pl BA20..... 27 C4
Queens Wlk
 Charmouth DT6.......... 97 B7
 New Milton BH25......... 96 B6
Queenswood Ave BH8.. 90 E1
Queenswood Dr BH22.. 61 E7
Queenwell DT6............ 68 C8
Quibo La DT4............. 167 A3
Quince La BH21............ 59 E6
Quintin Cl BH23.......... 125 F8
Quomp BH24................ 55 C7

R

Rabin Hill DT10............ 35 B2
Rabling La BH19......... 179 B3
Rabling Rd BH19......... 179 B3
Racedown Rd DT11.... 199 E3
Rachel Cl BH12.......... 120 C7
RADIPOLE DT3........... 167 A4
**Radipole Com Woodland
 Nature Reserve ★** DT3.. 167 B8
Radipole La DT4........ 167 A5
**Radipole Lake RSPB
 Reserve ★** DT4........ 167 C4
Radipole Lake Visitor Ctr **★**
 DT4....................... 167 C4
Radipole Park Dr DT4.. 167 C5
Radipole Prim Sch DT3.. 167 B8
Radipole Rd BH17........ 88 A2
Raglan Gdns BH11....... 89 A2
Raglan Terr BA21......... 27 A7
Railway Dr BH21.......... 59 C4
Railway Terr 4 SP8....... 6 A1
Railway Triangle Ind Est
 DT1....................... 107 C2
Raleigh Cl
 Christchurch BH23..... 124 F5
 New Milton BH25......... 94 F3
 3 Ringwood BH24.... 55 E8
Raleigh Rd
 Poole BH12................ 88 E1
 Stalbridge DT10.......... 33 E8
Ralph Jessop Ct BH12.. 120 D7
Ralph Rd BH21............. 94 F1
Ram La DT11................ 48 C1
Rampart Wlk **4** DT1... 134 E7
RAMPISHAM DT2........ 205 F5
Rampisham Hill DT8... 205 C3
Ramsbury DT10......... 196 D5
Ramsbury Ct DT11..... 212 D5
Ramsbury Ct DT11..... 212 C3
Ramsey Ct BH25.......... 94 F3
Ram's Hill DT10........... 21 F2
Randall Cl DT3........... 166 D5
Randalls Hill BH16....... 85 B1
Randolph Rd
 2 Bournemouth BH1.. 122 E4
 Poole BH14.............. 120 C5
Ranelagh Rd
 Christchurch BH23..... 125 F7
 Radipole DT4............ 167 D4
Rashley Rd DT3......... 166 D5
Raspberry La SP7......... 12 D2
Ratcliff's Gdn SP7....... 12 D2
Ratleigh La DT9............ 29 B6
Ravana Ct **8** BH4....... 122 A5
Ravenscourt Rd BH6.. 123 C5
Ravensdale Cl BH12... 120 C6

Ravenshall **7** BH2 . . . . . . 121 D2
Raven Way BH23 . . . . 125 A5
Ravine Ct BH13 . . . . 147 F7
Ravine Gdns **5** BH13 . . . 147 F7
Ravine Rd
 Bournemouth BH5 . . . . 123 B4
 Poole BH13 . . . . 147 F8
Rawles Way DT6 . . . . 100 D7
Rawston Down Rd **6**
 DT11 . . . . 199 E2
Rax La DT6 . . . . 100 D7
Raymond Cl BH31 . . . . . . 45 D6
Raymond Dr DT4 . . . . . . 166 F2
Rayners Dr BH21 . . . . . . 120 D6
Rayscliff **8** BH4 . . . . . . 121 C2
Reap La DT5 . . . . 186 E2
Redbeck Rd BH7 . . . . . . 123 A6
Reckleford BA20 . . . . . . 27 D5
Reckleford Com Sch
 BA21 . . . . 27 E5
Recreation Rd BH12 . . . 120 E6
Rectory Ave BH21 . . . . . 57 F1
Rectory Cl DT2 . . . . 136 B1
Rectory Gdns DT11 . . . . 198 F7
Rectory La
 Child Okeford DT11 . . . 198 C7
 Hardington Mandeville
  BA22 . . . . 193 A7
 Puncknowle DT2 . . . . 129 E6
 Studland BH19 . . . . . 164 C2
 West Stafford DT2 . . . 136 A8
Rectory Rd
 Broadmayne DT2 . . . . 136 B2
 Piddlehinton DT2 . . . . 76 E7
 Poole BH15 . . . . 119 C6
Rectory Way DT4 . . . . . . 167 C1
Redan Cl BH23 . . . . 125 F7
Redbreast Rd BH9 . . . . . 90 A3
Redbreast Road N BH9 . . 90 A3
REDBRIDGE DT2 . . . . . . 138 B5
Redbridge La DT2 . . . . . 137 F5
Redbridge Rd DT2 . . . . . 137 F6
Redcliffe Ct BH23 . . . . . 92 C3
Redcliffe Rd BH19 . . . . . 179 B5
Redcliff View DT4 . . . . . . 167 C1
Redcotts La BH21 . . . . . 59 B5
Redcotts Rd BH21 . . . . . 59 B5
REDFORD DT2 . . . . 206 D8
Redgate Pk TA18 . . . . . . 191 E5
RED HILL 89 F5
Redhill Ave BH9 . . . . 89 F3
Redhill Cl BH10 . . . . 89 E3
Redhill Comm Nature
 Reserve ★ BH9 . . . . . 89 F3
Redhill Cres BH9 . . . . . . 89 F3
Redhill Ct **11** BH10 . . . . . 90 A4
Redhill Dr BH10 . . . . 89 E3
Redhill Park Homes **1**
 BH10 . . . . 89 F4
Redhill Rdbt BH10 . . . . . 89 F4
Redhole La DT9 . . . . 16 B2
Redhorn Cl BH16 . . . . . . 117 E4
Red Horn Cl BH16 . . . . . 118 C4
Red House Cl SP7 . . . . . . 7 B1
Red House Mus & Gdns ★
 BH23 . . . . 124 B6
Red La
 Corfe Mullen BH21 . . . 85 C8
 Seaborough DT8 . . . . 191 B3
 Sixpenny Handley SP5 . 189 A3
 Todber DT10 . . . . . . 21 D4
 Weymouth DT3 . . . . . 149 B7
REDLANDS DT3 . . . . . . 152 B1
Redlands
 Christchurch BH23 . . . 125 A4
 Poole BH12 . . . . 120 F5
Redlands La BH23 . . . . . 143 B3
Red Lion Cl **3** DT10 . . . 197 D8
Red Lion Yd DT11 . . . . . 212 C3
Redmans La SP7 . . . . . . 24 B6
Redmans View BH31 . . . 45 A6
Red Oaks Cl BH21 . . . . . 61 B7
Redpoll Cl **1** DT3 . . . . . 152 C1
Red Post
 Bloxworth DT11 . . . . . 82 C7
 Poyntington DT9 . . . . 16 C4
Redsails BH13 . . . . 147 B3
Redshank Cl BH17 . . . . . 86 F1
Redvers Rd BH23 . . . . . 124 E7
Red Wing Rd DT9 . . . . . 17 C2
Redwood Cl BH24 . . . . . 55 D7
Redwood Dr BH22 . . . . . 61 C8
Redwood Rd
 Upton BH16 . . . . 117 C8
 Yeovil BA21 . . . . 28 A8
Reedling Cl DT3 . . . . . . 152 C3
Reed View Cl DT4 . . . . . 167 A5
Reeves Orchard BH21 . . . 56 D5
Reforne DT5 . . . . 186 F4
Reforne Cl **1** DT5 . . . . . 187 A4
Regency Cres BH23 . . . . 123 F8
Regency Ct **9** SP8 . . . . . 5 D2
Regency Dr **1** DT3 . . . . 152 C4
Regent Cte★ BH23 . . . . 124 B6
Regent Dr BH7 . . . . 122 F8
Regents The **2** BA21 . . . 26 E6
Regent Way BH23 . . . . . 124 B6
Reid St BH23 . . . . 124 A8
Rempstone Rd
 Oakley BH21 . . . . 87 D8
 Swanage BH19 . . . . . 179 B2
Rempstone Sh Arc **8**
 BH20 . . . . 142 E3
Remus Cl DT1 . . . . 134 E7
Renault Dr BH18 . . . . . . 87 A1
Rendalls Wlk DT6 . . . . . 100 B6
Renfrew Cl DT1 . . . . . . 135 C8

Renscombe Rd BH19 . . . . 183 B8
Restharrow BH1 . . . . 122 A4
Retreat Rd BH21 . . . . 59 D4
Reuben Dr BH15 . . . . 117 F2
Revels Hill DT2 . . . . 207 E7
REW DT2 . . . . 208 B8
Rew La DT2 . . . . 208 A8
Rex La DT3 . . . . 166 D5
Rex's La BA22 . . . . 27 F1
Reynard Ct BH15 . . . . . . 119 F3
Reynards Way DT3 . . . . . 153 C3
Rhine Rd BH20 . . . . 139 E6
Rhode La DT7 . . . . 64 A1
Rhosewood Dr BH12 . . . . 120 F6
Rhydderch Way **9** TA18 . 191 F4
Ribble Cl BH18 . . . . 87 A2
Ribbonwood Hts BH14 . . 120 B4
Ricardo Cres BH23 . . . . 125 A6
Rice Gdns BH16 . . . . . . 117 F4
Rice Terr BH16 . . . . 118 D4
Richard Cl **1** BH16 . . . . 117 D8
Richmond Cl DT9 . . . . . . 30 A5
Richmond Ct **7** BH25 . . . 95 A3
Richmond Gdns BH11 . . . 121 F3
Richmond Hill DT9 . . . . . 30 A6
Richmond Hill BH2 . . . . 121 F3
Richmond Hill Dr BH2 . . . 121 F3
Richmond Park Ave BH8 . 122 C7
Richmond Park Cl BH8 . . 122 D6
Richmond Park Cres
 BH8 . . . . 122 C7
Richmond Park Rd BH8 . . 122 C7
Richmond Rd
 4 Blandford Forum
  DT11 . . . . 212 E5
 Poole BH14 . . . . 120 C4
 Sherborne DT9 . . . . . 30 A5
 Swanage BH19 . . . . . 179 B2
 Wimborne Minster BH21 . 59 C4
 Yeovil BA20 . . . . 27 C4
Richmond Rise BH8 . . . . 122 D6
Richmond Way BA21 . . . . 26 E6
Richmond Wood Rd
 BH8 . . . . 122 C7
Ricketts Cl DT4 . . . . 167 E5
Ricketts La DT10 . . . . . . 35 B1
Rickhay Rise TA18 . . . . . 192 B8
RIDGE DT2 . . . . 143 B1
Ridgeback La DT6 . . . . . 69 E8
Ridge Cl SP8 . . . . 10 E3
Ridge Dro DT10 . . . . . . 196 F4
Ridgefield Gdns BH23 . . . 125 D8
Ridge La
 Hazelbury Bryan DT10 . 196 D5
 West Coker BA22 . . . . 193 A8
Ridgemead **5** BA20 . . . . 26 F2
Ridgemount Gdns BH15 . 118 E3
Ridge The DT9 . . . . 16 E5
Ridge View DT10 . . . . . . 196 F8
Ridgeway
 Bradpole DT6 . . . . 68 F1
 Broadstone BH18 . . . . 87 B4
 Corfe Mullen BH21 . . . 86 D8
 Ferndown BH22 . . . . . 89 E8
 Poole BH15 . . . . 85 F8
 Sherborne DT9 . . . . . 29 F5
Ridge Way
 Puddletown DT2 . . . . . 76 F1
 Shaftesbury SP7 . . . . 12 F4
Ridgeway La
 Child Okeford DT11 . . . 198 C8
 Hinton St Mary DT10 . . 35 B4
Ridgeway Rd SP8 . . . . . . 5 E3
Ridgeway The DT3 . . . . . 152 B7
Ridgway TA18 . . . . 192 B8
Ridley Rd BH21 . . . . . . 121 F8
Ridout Cl BH10 . . . . 89 B1
Ridouts DT11 . . . . 197 F6
Ridwood DT6 . . . . 99 B6
Rigg La DT9 . . . . 14 F2
Riggs Gdns BH11 . . . . . 88 F2
Rigler Rd BH15 . . . . . . 119 A2
Rimbrow Cl DT3 . . . . . . 153 C3
Rimbury Way BH23 . . . . 124 A8
RIMPTON BA22 . . . . . . 15 C8
Rimpton Hill BA22 . . . . . 15 B8
Ring St DT10 . . . . 33 D8
Ringstead Cres DT3 . . . . 168 B6
Rings The DT11 . . . . . . 79 F8
RINGWOOD BH24 . . . . . 47 D1
Ringwood CE Inf Sch
 BH24 . . . . 55 C6
Ringwood Cty Jun Sch
 BH24 . . . . 55 C6
Ringwood L Ctr BH24 . . . 55 C7
Ringwood Rd
 Alderholt SP6 . . . . . . 42 C5
 Bournemouth BH11 . . . 88 E4
 Bransgore BH23 . . . . 93 D5
 Ferndown BH22 . . . . 61 C4
 Fordingbridge SP6 . . . 43 C5
 Hyde SP6 . . . . 63 B2
 Poole BH12 . . . . 120 B7
 Sopley BH23 . . . . . . 92 A7
 St Leonards BH24 . . . 53 F7
 Three Legged Cross BH21 . 52 F8
 Verwood BH31 . . . . . 45 D6
 Walkford BH23 . . . . . 94 B1
 West Moors BH22 . . . 62 A8
Ringwood Road Ret Pk
 BH11 . . . . 88 E3
Ringwood Sch BH24 . . . . 55 C6
Ringwood Trad Est BH24 . 55 C6
Ringwood Waldorf Sch
 BH24 . . . . 54 F6
Rip Croft DT5 . . . . 186 E2
Ripley Ct BH22 . . . . 61 F7
Ripon Rd BH9 . . . . 90 A1

Ripp's La DT2 . . . . 208 A5
Rise The
 Radipole DT4 . . . . . . 167 A5
 Stratton DT2 . . . . . . 106 D8
Ritchie Pl DT2 . . . . 52 F3
Ritchie Rd
 Bournemouth BH11 . . . 89 B4
 Yeovil BA22 . . . . 26 C5
River Cl BH21 . . . . 59 C6
Riverdale La BH23 . . . . . 124 A6
River La **2** DT11 . . . . . . 211 D6
Riverland Ct **4** BH23 . . . 124 A6
Riverlea Rd BH23 . . . . . 124 A6
Rivermead Gdns BH23 . . . 91 E2
Rivermead St BH23 . . . . 124 A6
River Mews DT11 . . . . . 212 C3
River Pk BH6 . . . . 123 F6
RIVERS' CORNER DT10 . . 197 C7
Riverside **8** BH23 . . . . . 59 C4
Riverside Rd BH6 . . . . . 124 A4
Riverscene DT11 . . . . . . 48 A6
Riverside
 3 Beaminster DT8 . . . 204 D4
 8 Bournemouth BH10 . . 89 F4
 Ringwood BH24 . . . . . 55 B6
Riverside Ave BH7 . . . . . 91 C1
Riverside Cl DT2 . . . . . . 207 D4
Riverside Ct **7** BH4 . . . . 121 D4
Riverside La BH6 . . . . . . 123 F5
Riverside Park Ind Est
 DT2 . . . . 59 D3
Riverside Pk BH23 . . . . . 124 A5
Riverside Rd
 Blandford Forum DT11 . 212 E3
 Bournemouth BH23 . . . 123 F5
 Ferndown BH22 . . . . . 52 F2
Riverslea Mews BH23 . . . 124 D6
Rivers Mead DT11 . . . . . 198 F6
Riversmeet Ct BH23 . . . . 124 D6
Rivers Rd BA21 . . . . 27 F8
Rivervale DT6 . . . . 100 D8
River View SP8 . . . . 5 E2
River Way
 Charmouth DT6 . . . . . 97 B7
 Christchurch BH23 . . . 91 D2
Riviera **11** BH1 . . . . 122 B3
Riviera Ct
 Bournemouth BH2 . . . 121 D3
 3 Poole BH13 . . . . . 147 F7
RIXON DT10 . . . . 35 C2
Rixon Cl DT10 . . . . 35 C1
Rixon Hill DT10 . . . . . . 35 C1
R L Stevenson Ave BH4 . . 121 B3
RNLI HQ & Mus★ BH15 . 119 C2
Roberts La BH17 . . . . . . 118 F7
Robertson Rd BH20 . . . . 139 D7
Roberts Pl DT1 . . . . 107 E1
Roberts Rd
 Bournemouth BH7 . . . 123 A6
 Poole BH17 . . . . 87 B1
Robin Cl **2** DT3 . . . . . . 152 C4
Robin Cres BH25 . . . . . . 94 D5
Robin Gdns BH23 . . . . . 125 B8
Robin Gr BH25 . . . . 94 F2
Robins Ct **9** BH21 . . . . . 59 C4
Robins Garth DT1 . . . . . 108 B1
Robins Hts DT10 . . . . . . 33 D8
Robinswood Dr BH22 . . . 61 D7
Robsall Cl BH12 . . . . . . 120 E7
Robville Ct **8** BH7 . . . . . 123 B6
Roche Cl BA21 . . . . 26 F7
Rochester Rd BH11 . . . . 89 B4
Rockbourne Gdns BH25 . 126 D8
Rockbourne La SP6 . . . . 190 F3
ROCKFORD BH24 . . . . . 47 E4
Rockford Cl BH6 . . . . . . 123 F3
Rockhampton Cl DT3 . . . 152 D3
Rockley Mews BH15 . . . . 118 E2
Rockley Pk Cvn Est BH15,
 BH16 . . . . 118 B3
Rockley Rd BH15 . . . . . . 118 E1
Rocks La DT2 . . . . 206 A7
Rockway DT6 . . . . 101 C4
Rocky Knap DT3 . . . . . . 150 C5
RODDEN DT3 . . . . 150 C8
Rodden Cl DT4 . . . . 180 C8
Rodden La DT3 . . . . . . 150 C5
Rodden Row DT3 . . . . . 149 B7
Rodgett Cres BH20 . . . . 142 F8
RODGROVE BA9 . . . . . . 8 E6
Rod Hill La DT2 . . . . 78 B1
Rodney Cl BH12 . . . . . . 121 A8
Rodney Ct
 Christchurch BH23 . . . 125 A4
 3 Poole BH15 . . . . . 119 C1
Rodney Dr BH23 . . . . . . 124 F6
Rodway DT4 . . . . 167 D1
RODWELL DT4 . . . . 167 D1
Rodwell Ave DT4 . . . . . . 167 D1
Rodwell Cl BH10 . . . . . . 89 C6
Rodwell Rd DT4 . . . . . . 167 D1
Rodwell St DT4 . . . . 167 D1
Roe Ave BA22 . . . . 26 C5
Roebuck Cl BH25 . . . . . 95 B3
Roe La BA20 . . . . 15 B8
Roeshot Cres BH23 . . . . 93 E1
Roeshot Hill BH23 . . . . . 93 C2
Roi-mar Home Pk BH9 . . 90 A4
Rolfe Cres DT3 . . . . . . 166 D6
Rolls Bridge La SP8 . . . . 5 E2
Rolls Bridge Way SP8 . . . 5 D2
Rolls Dr BH6 . . . . 124 B3
ROLLS MILL DT10 . . . . . 197 C8
Rolls Mill Way DT10 . . . . 197 C8
Roman Cl DT3 . . . . 167 C7

Roman Hill Trading Est
 DT2 . . . . 154 D6
Roman Hts BH21 . . . . . . 86 E8
Roman Rd
 Corfe Mullen BH18 . . . 86 E5
 Dorchester DT1 . . . . . 134 F8
 Lyme Regis DT7 . . . . . 96 A6
 Osmington DT3 . . . . . 154 A1
 Radipole DT3 . . . . . . 167 C7
Roman Way
 Blandford Forum DT11 . 198 B5
 Pamphill BH21 . . . . . . 57 E5
ROMFORD BH31 . . . . . . 44 F7
Romney Cl BH10 . . . . . . 89 E3
Romney Ct **51** BH4 . . . . 121 C3
Romney Rd BH10 . . . . . 89 E4
Romsey Rd BA21 . . . . . . 28 A7
Romulus Cl DT1 . . . . . . 134 E7
Rookery Cl SP8 . . . . 11 B8
Rookery La
 Burstock DT8 . . . . . . 203 C6
 Uplyme DT7 . . . . 64 A2
Rookery The DT2 . . . . . 130 F8
Rook Hill Rd BH23 . . . . . 125 B6
Rook La DT11 . . . . 210 C2
Rook St BA12 . . . . 3 A4
ROOK STREET BA12 . . . . 3 A4
Roosevelt Cres BH3 . . . . 89 B6
Ropers La BH16 . . . . . . 117 F7
Roper's La BH20 . . . . . . 142 E4
Rope Walks DT6 . . . . . . 100 C6
Roping Rd BA21 . . . . . . 27 C6
Ropley Rd BH7 . . . . 123 C7
Rosamond Ave DT6 . . . . 101 D4
Rosamund Ave BH21 . . . 59 E1
Roscrea Cl BH6 . . . . . . 124 B4
Roscrea Dr BH6 . . . . . . 124 B4
Rosebank La BH21 . . . . 212 F6
Rosebery Gdns **3** SP8 . . 5 C1
Rosebery Ave BH31 . . . . 27 F6
Rosebery Rd BH5 . . . . . 123 A5
Rosebud Ave **1** BH9 . . . 90 A2
Rosecrae Cl BH25 . . . . . 94 F4
Rose Cres BH15 . . . . . . 119 F6
Rosecroft Rd DT4 . . . . . 166 F1
Rose Ct
 3 Gillingham SP8 . . . 5 C1
 Poole BH15 . . . . 119 E3
Rosedale Cl **3** BH23 . . . 124 E6
Rose Farm Cl BH22 . . . . 61 B3
Rosefields **2** DT11 . . . . 212 D2
Rose Gdns **1** BH9 . . . . . 90 A3
Rose Gdn The BH23 . . . . 91 D1
Rose La
 1 Crewkerne TA18 . . . 191 E4
 Winsham TA20 . . . . . 191 A4
Roselyn Cres DT9 . . . . . 31 B1
Rosemary Cl BH23 . . . . 126 B7
Rosemary Gdns BH12 . . . 120 B7
Rosemary La DT3 . . . . . 149 B7
Rosemary La DT11 . . . . 212 C2
Rosemary St DT9 . . . . . 17 C2
Rosemount Rd BH4 . . . . 121 B2
Rose's La DT3 . . . . 150 D2
Rosewood Gdns BH25 . . 94 F4
Roslin Gdns BH3 . . . . . . 121 D7
Roslin Rd BH3 . . . . 121 D7
Roslin Road S BH3 . . . . 121 C7
Ross Cl BH20 . . . . 139 F6
Ross Gdns BH11 . . . . . . 88 C5
Ross Glades BH3 . . . . . 121 E6
Rossiters Quay BH23 . . . 124 C6
Rossley Cl BH23 . . . . . . 93 E2
ROSSMORE 120 E7
Rossmore Com Coll
 BH12 . . . . 120 D8
Rossmore L Ctr BH12 . . . 120 D8
Rossmore Par BH12 . . . . 120 D7
Rossmore Rd BH12 . . . . 120 D7
Ross Rd BH24 . . . . 47 E1
Rotary Cl BH21 . . . . 59 F7
Rothbury Pk BH25 . . . . . 95 B2
Rotherfield Rd
 Bournemouth BH5 . . . 123 B3
 Walkford BH23 . . . . . 94 A1
Rotherham Rd DT5 . . . . 181 C1
Rothesay Dr BH23 . . . . . 125 E7
Rothesay Rd
 Bournemouth BH4 . . . 121 C5
 Dorchester DT1 . . . . . 135 A8
Rotterdam Dr BH23 . . . . 124 D7
Rough Down La DT6 . . . . 65 B2
Rough Height DT9 . . . . . 179 B1
Roumelia La BH1, BH5 . . 122 E4
ROUNDHAM TA18 . . . . . 191 D4
Roundham Gdns
 Bridport DT6 . . . . 100 D3
 Weymouth DT4 . . . . . 167 A2
Roundhaye Gdns BH11 . . 88 F6
Roundhaye Rd BH11 . . . 88 F6
Roundhayes Cl DT4 . . . . 167 A2
Roundways BH11 . . . . . 88 F6
Rowan Cl
 Christchurch BH23 . . . 125 D8
 Radipole DT3 . . . . . . 167 A6
 Sandford BH20 . . . . . 143 A4
 St Leonards & St Ives BH24 . 53 F4
Rowan Dr
 Broadstone BH17 . . . . 86 E1
 Christchurch BH23 . . . 125 D8
 Verwood BH31 . . . . . 45 D4
Rowan Way BA20 . . . . . 27 A3
Rowbarrow Cl BH17 . . . . 87 C2
Rowbarrow Hill DT9 . . . . 14 F4
Rowbarrow La BH21 . . . . 200 F2
Rowden Mill La DT10 . . . 32 E1
Rowe Gdns **6** BH12 . . . . 121 A7

Rowena Rd BH6 . . . . 123 F5
Rowland Ave BH15 . . . . . 119 E6
ROWLANDS 59 C5
Rowlands Hill BH21 . . . . . 59 D6
Rowlands Rd **5** DT11 . . . 198 F4
Rowls La BA9 . . . . 4 B3
Rownhams Rd BH8 . . . . . 90 D3
Row The DT10 . . . . 35 A1
Roxborough **11** BH4 . . . . 121 C2
Royal Arc **3** BH1 . . . . . . 122 E4
Royal Bournemouth Hospl
 The BH7 . . . . 91 B1
Royal Cl BA21 . . . . 27 E6
Royal Manor Sch The
 DT5 . . . . 186 F4
Royal Oak Rd BH10 . . . . . 89 C5
Royal Signals Mus★
 DT11 . . . . 199 E3
Royal Victoria Mews
 BH4 . . . . 121 D3
Royster Cl BH17 . . . . . . 87 C1
Royston Dr BH21 . . . . . . 59 D5
Royston Pl BH25 . . . . . . 127 A8
Rozelle Rd BH14 . . . . . . 120 C4
Rozel Manor BH13 . . . . . 121 B2
Ruben Dr BH15 . . . . 118 D2
Rubens Cl BH25 . . . . . . 95 B3
Ruddock Cl BA22 . . . . . 193 B8
Ruddock Way BA22 . . . . 193 A8
Rue La DT9 . . . . 31 F4
Rufford Gdns BH6 . . . . . 123 E5
Rufus Castle★ DT5 . . . . 187 B3
Rufus Way DT5 . . . . 187 B5
Rugby Rd BH17 . . . . . . 87 A1
Ruins La DT6 . . . . 99 A6
Rundlestone Ct **9** DT1 . . 107 B2
Runnymede Ave BH11 . . . 88 E6
Runnymede Rd BA21 . . . 27 F8
Runton Rd BH22 . . . . . . 120 F5
Runway The BH23 . . . . . 125 B7
Rural La DT2 . . . . 73 F3
Ruscombe La DT6 . . . . . 69 E6
Rushall La BH21 . . . . . . 85 C5
Rushcombe Fst Sch BH21 . 85 F6
Rushcombe Way **3** BH21 . 85 F6
Rushetts Cl **4** DT5 . . . . . 186 F1
Rushford Warren BH23 . . 124 F5
Rushmere Rd BH6 . . . . . 123 D7
RUSHTON BH20 . . . . . . 141 B2
Rushton Cres BH3 . . . . . 121 F6
Ruskin Ave BH9 . . . . 90 B3
Russell Ave
 Swanage BH19 . . . . . 179 B1
 Weymouth DT4 . . . . . 167 B1
Russell Cotes Art Gall &
 Mus★ BH1 . . . . 122 A2
Russell Cotes Rd BH1 . . 122 A2
Russell Ct **2** BH25 . . . . . 95 A3
Russell Dr
 Christchurch BH23 . . . 124 D6
 Swanage BH19 . . . . . 179 B1
Russell Gdns
 St Leonards BH24 . . . 54 D5
 Upton BH16 . . . . 117 E4
Russel Pl DT9 . . . . 17 C2
Russet Rd BH10 . . . . . . 89 C6
Russet Cl BH22 . . . . 61 D6
Russet Gdns DT6 . . . . . 100 F8
Russet Way BA20 . . . . . 26 F2
Rutland Manor **10** BH13 . 121 A4
Rutland Rd
 Bournemouth BH9 . . . 122 B8
 Christchurch BH23 . . . 91 F1
 Weymouth DT4 . . . . . 167 B4
RYALL DT6 . . . . 66 D2
Ryall Rd
 Poole BH17 . . . . 87 D1
 Whitchurch Canonicorum
  DT6 . . . . 66 D2
Ryall's La DT9 . . . . 196 A7
Ryan Cl
 Ferndown BH22 . . . . . 61 C7
 Northport BH20 . . . . . 142 E5
Ryan Gdns
 Bournemouth BH11 . . . 89 B6
 Ferndown BH22 . . . . . 61 C7
Rydal Cl BH23 . . . . 91 D4
Rydal Mews BH21 . . . . . 59 D5
Rycroft Ave BH11 . . . . . 88 E5
Ryefields Cl BA22 . . . . . 193 B8
Rye Gdns BH20 . . . . . . 26 F2
Rye Hill BH20 . . . . 81 B1
Rye Hill Cl BH20 . . . . . . 81 B1
Ryemead La DT4 . . . . . 180 C6
Rye Wr La BA22 . . . . . . 193 A1
Ryland's La DT4 . . . . . . 180 D8
Rymbury DT3 . . . . 153 C3
RYME INTRINSECA DT9 . 194 B6
Ryme Rd DT9 . . . . 194 B5

S

Sackmore Gn DT10 . . . . . 20 F3
Sackmore La DT10 . . . . . 20 F3
Sackville St DT11 . . . . . . 81 E8
Sadborow La TA20 . . . . 202 E5
Saddle Cl DT2 . . . . 60 C6
Safety Dr BH17 . . . . . . 119 A7
Saffron Ct BH11 . . . . . . 88 D3
Saffron Dr BH23 . . . . . . 125 B8
Saffron Way BH11 . . . . . 88 D3
St Alban's Ave BH8 . . . . 122 C7
St Alban's Cres BH8 . . . . 122 B8

St Alban's Rd BH8....122 B7
St Alban St DT4....167 D2
St Aldhelm's ⁴ 120 F4
St Aldhelm's CE Comb Sch
  BH12....121 A6
St Aldhelm's Cl BH13....120 F3
St Aldhelm's Rd BH13....120 F4
St Aldhelm's Rd
  Poole BH13....120 F4
  Sherborne DT9....88 D3
St Andrews 3 BH23....124 A6
St Andrews Ave DT3....167 D7
St Andrews CE Prim Sch
  Overcombe/Preston
  DT3....153 A2
  Shaftesbury SP7....37 F6
  Yetminster DT9....194 C6
St Andrew's Cl DT9....194 F4
St Andrews Dr DT6....97 A8
St Andrews Mdw DT7....96 B6
St Andrews Rd
  Broadstone BH18....87 A5
  Yeovil BA21....27 A5
St Andrew's Rd DT6....68 F1
St Andrews Trad Est
  DT6....100 F8
St Andrews View SP7....37 F7
ST ANDREW'S WELL
  DT6....100 E8
St Anne's Ave BH6....123 E5
St Annes Cl SP7....23 B6
St Anne's Gdns BA21....27 A6
St Anne's Rd
  Upton BH16....117 D7
  Weymouth DT4....180 E7
St Ann's Cl 1 BH1....122 C5
St Ann's Hospl BH13....147 E6
St Anthony's Rd BH2....121 F5
St Antony's 6 BH4....121 D2
St Aubyns Cl BH15....119 B2
St Augustine's RC Prim Sch
  DT4....167 B1
St Augustin's Rd BH2....121 F5
St Bartholomew's CE Fst Sch
  8 TA18....191 F4
St Brelades Ave BH12....88 D1
St Catharines BH19....185 C7
St Catherines BH21....59 C4
St Catherines Chapel★
  DT3....149 A6
St Catherine's Cres 2
  DT9....30 A5
St Catherines Par BH21....91 F1
St Catherines RC Prim Sch
  DT6....100 D8
St Catherine's RC Prim Sch
  BH21....60 B6
St Catherine's Rd BH6....123 F3
St Catherine's Way BH23....91 D3
St Cecilia's Gdns DT6....100 D8
St Clair Rd BH13....147 F7
St Cleeve Way BH22....61 C3
St Clement's Gdns BH1....122 C5
St Clements Rd BH15....120 A7
St Clement's Rd BH1....122 C5
St Clement's & St John's CE
  Inf Sch BH1....122 D5
St Davids Cl 9 DT1....135 B8
St David's Cres BA21....27 D7
St David's Ct 3 BH1....122 E5
St David's Rd
  Upton BH16....117 D7
  Weymouth DT4....180 D7
St Denys 8 BH25....95 B1
St Edmund St 2 DT4....167 D2
St Edwards Cl
  Corfe Castle BH20....177 A8
  1 Shaftesbury SP7....12 F3
St Edwards Comp Sch
  BH15....119 F7
St Gabriel's Cl DT6....98 C8
St George's Almshos 2
  BH15....119 B1
St George's Ave
  Bournemouth BH8....122 C8
  Poole BH12....120 B8
  Radipole DT4....167 E6
  Yeovil BA21....27 D7
St Georges CE Fst Sch
  BH19....178 B3
St Georges Cl DT1....108 D1
St George's Cl
  Bournemouth BH8....122 C8
  Christchurch BH23....125 D8
  Swanage BH19....178 B2
St Georges Ct BH22....61 E5
St George's Ct 2 BH1....122 E5
St George's Dr 2 BH12....120 B8
St Georges Dr
  Bournemouth BH11....88 D3
  Bransgore BH23....93 B8
St George's Dr BH22....61 C4
St Georges Est Rd DT5....186 F4
St Georges Hill DT7....96 A6
St Georges Mans 8 BH5....122 F4
St Georges Prim Sch
  DT5....186 F3
St Georges Rd BH1....108 C1
St George's Rd
  Portland DT5....186 F4
  Shaftesbury SP7....12 F2
St George's Sch SP8....1 D1
St Gildas RC Prim Sch
  BA21....27 D5
St Giles Cl DT6....99 A7

St Giles's House★ BH21....201 E6
St Gregory CE Prim Sch
  DT10....20 F2
St Helen's La DT2....206 B2
St Helen's Rd
  Dorchester DT1....107 F2
  Sandford BH20....143 A8
  Weymouth DT4....166 F2
St Helier Ave DT3....152 B4
St Helier Rd BH12....88 D1
St IVES BH24....54 C5
St Ives End La BH24....54 C4
St Ives Fst Sch BH24....54 C5
St Ives Gdns BH24....54 C5
St Ives Pk BH24....54 C5
St Ives Wood BH24....54 D5
ST JAMES SP7....12 E1
St James Ct BH6....42 C6
St James Cl 2 BH15....119 B1
St James Pk DT6....69 A1
St James Rd BH22....61 A6
St James's BH15....122 E3
St James's Cl BA21,BA20....26 E5
St James's Sq BH15....123 A5
St James St SP7....12 E2
ST JOHNS....59 C4
St John's CE Fst Sch 3
  BH21....59 D4
St Johns CE Prim Sch
  DT4....67 D2
St John's CE Prim Sch
  BH9....89 F1
St John's Cl BH21....59 D4
St John's Ct 4 BH1....122 E5
St John's Gdns 2 BH1....89 F1
St John's Hill
  Shaftesbury SP7....12 D2
  Wareham BH20....142 E4
  Wimborne Minster BH21....59 D5
St John's Rd
  Bournemouth BH5....122 E4
  Christchurch BH23....124 A6
  Poole BH15....119 D4
  Yeovil BA21....27 E7
St John Way DT1....107 D2
St Joseph's Prim Sch
  BH23....125 A8
St Joseph's RC Comb Sch
  BH12....120 E7
St Julien Cres DT1....152 B3
St Julien Rd BH20....139 D7
St Just Cl BH21....61 C3
St Juthware Cl BA22....193 C3
St Katharine's CE Prim Sch
  BH6....124 B4
St Katharine's Ave DT6....106 F2
St Katherine's Dr DT6....106 E8
St Lawrence 4 DT6....128 B8
St Lawrence Cres SP7....12 F4
St Lawrence Rd DT3....152 C5
St Ledger's Pl BH8....122 D6
St Ledger's Rd BH8....122 D6
ST LEONARDS BH24....54 A2
St Leonard's Ave DT11....212 E4
St Leonard's Com Hospl
  BH24....53 E1
St Leonards Farm Pk
  BH22....62 A8
St Leonards Rd
  Bournemouth BH8....122 B6
  Weymouth DT4....167 B1
St Leonards Way BH24....53 F5
St Luke's CE Prim Sch
  BH9....121 B8
St Luke's Cl 2 DT6....100 B8
St Luke's Rd BH3....121 C7
St Maradox La BH9....89 F2
St Margarets BH2....121 F5
St Margarets Almshouses
  BH21....59 A5
St Margaret's Ave BH23....124 B5
St Margarets Cl BH21....59 A5
St Margarets Hill BH21....59 A5
St Margaret's Rd
  Bournemouth BH10....89 C2
  Poole BH15....119 D4
St Marks CE Fst Sch
  BH19....178 F2
St Mark's CE VA Prim Sch
  BH10....89 C1
St Mark's Rd BH11....89 B3
St Martins DT2....136 B2
St Martin's Cl 1 BH21....142 E4
St Martins Field DT2....133 D7
St Martin's La BH20....142 E4
St Martins Pl BH20....143 A8
St Martins Rd BH11....117 C7
St Martin's Rd
  3 Fortuneswell DT5....186 F7
  Sandford BH20....143 A8
  Shaftesbury SP7....12 F2
  Weymouth DT4....180 E8
St Martin's Sq SP8....5 F2
St Martins Way BA20....26 F2
St Mary CE Prim Sch DT9 28 D1
St Mary RC Prim Sch
  DT10....21 A5
St Marys CE Fst Sch
  Charminster DT2....107 D6
  Ferndown BH22....52 F3

St Mary's CE Mid Sch
  DT2....110 A8
St Marys CE Prim Sch
  TA20....202 E6
St Mary's CE Prim Sch
  DT8....204 C4
St Marys Cl DT23....93 C8
St Mary's Cl
  Northport BH20....142 C5
  Sixpenny Handley SP5....189 A4
  3 Winterborne Whitechurch
  DT11....210 C3
St Marys Gdns BA21....27 E8
St Mary's Ct BH6....123 E3
St Mary's Gdns 3 DT8....206 C2
St Mary's Maternity Hospl
  BH15....119 C8
St Marys Mews BH22....61 D4
St Mary's Prim Sch DT6....100 C5
St Mary's RC Comb Sch
  BH15....119 C5
St Marys RC Fst Sch
  Dorchester DT1....135 B8
  Swanage BH19....179 B2
  Wool BH20....140 A2
St Mary's Rd
  Bournemouth BH1....122 D6
  Ferndown BH22....61 D5
  Poole BH15....119 E4
  Sherborne DT9....29 F5
St Marys Sch SP7....13 D3
St Mary St 7 DT4....167 D2
St Mary's View
  Bridport DT6....100 C5
  Yeovil BA21....27 E8
St Mary the Virgin CE Prim
  Sch SP8....11 B8
St Mary Well St 8 BH10....89 C4
St Merrin's Cl BH10....89 C4
St Michaels DT7....96 C6
St Michael's DT2....121 D3
St Michael's Ave BA21....27 E7
St Michael's CE Mid Sch
  BH21....59 E7
St Michael's CE Prim Sch
  BH21....121 D3
St Michaels Cl
  Hamworthy BH15....118 E3
  Over Compton DT9....28 E7
  Verwood BH31....45 B5
St Michaels Ct
  1 Bournemouth BH6....123 C4
  BH23....124 A6
St Michael's La DT6....100 C6
St Michael's Mews 9
  BH2....121 D3
St Michael's Pl 11 BH2....121 D3
St Michaels Prim Sch
  DT7....96 C6
St Michael's Rd
  Bournemouth BH2....121 D3
  6 Wareham BH20....142 E3
  Yeovil BA21....27 F6
St Michael's Rdbt BH2....121 D3
St Michaels Trading Est
  DT6....100 C6
St Michaels View BA12....3 A8
St Neots Cl 7 BH16....117 C7
St Nicholas CE Prim Sch
  Child Okeford DT11....198 C7
  Templecombe BA8....19 A5
St Nicholas Cl
  3 Henstridge BA8....19 A4
  11 Yeovil BA20....27 D4
St Nicholas Cl 5 DT11....198 C7
St Nicholas Gdns 2
  DT11....198 E3
St Nicholas Pk 8 BA20....27 D4
St Nicholas & St Lawrence
  CE Prim Sch DT3....152 C2
St Nicholas St DT4....167 D2
St Osmund Cl DT3....194 C5
St Osmund's CE Mid Sch
  DT1....135 A8
St Osmund's Rd BH14....120 D3
St Patricks Ave DT4....166 F1
St Patricks Ind Est DT11....198 E6
St Patrick's Rd BA21....26 F7
St Paul's Cl DT9....30 C7
St Paul's Gn DT9....30 C8
St Paul's La 8 BH8....122 B4
St Paul's Pl 8 BH8....122 B4
St Paul's Rd
  Bournemouth BH8....122 B4
  4 Fortuneswell DT5....186 F7
St Peter's Cl 1 DT11....199 D4
St Peters Ct 3 BH1....122 A3
St Peter's Gate 13 BH1....121 F3
St Peter's RC Sch
  Bournemouth BH6....123 F4
  Bournemouth BH1....123 B8
St Peter's Rd
  Poole BH14....120 A4
St Peter's Rdbt BH1....122 A3
St Peter's Wlk 15 BH1....121 F3
St Rayn Hill TA17....191 A4
St Richards Cl DT11....211 F7
St Rumbold's Rd SP7....12 F2
St Saviours Cl BH17....123 C7
St Stephen's Cl BH1....121 E4
St Stephens La BH31....45 C6
St Stephen's Rd BH2....121 E3

St Stephen's Way 4
  BH2....121 F3
St Swithins Cl BH6....100 C7
St Swithins Cl DT9....30 C6
St Swithins Rd BH6....100 C7
St Swithin's Rd DT9....30 C6
St Swithun's La BH1....122 B3
St Swithun's Rd BH1....122 B3
St Swithun's Rd S BH1....122 B4
St Thomas Cl BH1....89 D2
St Thomas Cross 1 BA21....27 E5
St Thomas Garnet's Sch 8
  BH5....123 A5
St Thomas Rd DT1....107 F2
St Thomas St DT4....167 D2
St Valerie Rd BH2....121 F5
St Vast's Rd BH19....179 C1
St Walburga's RC Prim Sch
  1 BH9....90 B1
St Winifred's Rd BH2....121 F5
Salerno Pl 4 BH15....117 F2
Salisbury Cres DT11....212 D5
Salisbury Rd
  Blandford Forum DT11....212 D4
  Bournemouth BH1....122 E4
  Burton BH23....92 D2
  Donhead St Mary SP7....13 D1
  Pimperne DT11....199 E4
  Poole BH14....120 C5
  Ringwood BH24....47 B7
  Ringwood SP6,BH24....43 C1
  Shaftesbury SP7....12 F2
  Sopley,Winkton BH23....92 B5
  2 Swanage BH19....179 C1
  Weymouth DT4....167 C3
Salisbury St
  Blandford Forum DT11....212 C3
  Cranborne BH21....40 A8
  Dorchester DT1....108 B2
  Marnhull DT10....21 B2
  Mere BA12....3 B5
  Shaftesbury SP7....12 F2
Sally King's La SP7....12 D3
Sally Lovell's La BA8....18 E7
Salterns St BH14....147 B8
Salterns Point BH14....147 B8
Salterns Quay BH14....147 B8
Salterns Rd BH14....120 A3
Salterns Way BH14....147 B8
Salter Rd BH13....147 C3
Salthouse La BA20....27 C4
Saltings Rd BH16....117 D6
SALWAYASH DT6....68 B6
Salway Ash CE Prim Sch
  DT6....68 B8
Salway Dr DT6....68 B8
Samantha Cl BH20....89 E3
Samarate Way BA20....26 E5
Sammy Miller Motorcycle
  Mus★ BH25....94 E5
Samphire Cl DT4....167 D6
Samples Way BH17....119 F8
Samson Rd BH15....117 F3
Samways Cl BH20....126 C3
Sancreed Rd BH12....120 E7
Sancroft Ho BH21....60 A1
SANDBANKS....147 C3
Sandbanks Bsns Ctr
  BH13....147 B3
Sandbanks Rd BH14,
  ....147 B3
Sandbourne Ave DT11....212 E6
Sandbourne Rd
  Bournemouth BH4....121 C6
  Overcombe/Preston DT3....168 B7
  Poole BH15....119 D4
Sandecotes Rd BH14....120 C3
Sanderling Cl 6 DT3....152 C4
Sanderlings 3 DT4....167 D6
Sanders Gn BH20....126 C3
SANDFORD BH20....142 F8
Sandford Cl BH9....90 C3
Sandford Dr BH20....116 B2
Sandford La BH20....142 E5
Sandford Lane Ind Est
  BH20....142 F6
Sandford Mid Sch BH20 116 A1
SANDFORD ORCAS DT9....15 E5
Sandford Orcas Manor★
  DT9....15 E6
Sandford Orcas Rd DT9 15 F4
Sandford Rd
  Northport BH20....142 C5
  Sandford BH20....142 F7
  Wareham St Martin BH20....143 A8
Sandford Way BH18....86 F2
SANDHILLS
  Cattistock DT2....206 B3
  Sherborne DT9....195 F5
Sandhills Cl BH17....89 D2
Sandhills Cres BH20....139 E2
Sandholes Cl DT5....186 E1
Sandhurst Dr BH21....53 C7
Sandhurst Rd BA20....27 B2
Sandilands 7 SP8....10 E3
Sandleheath Rd SP6....42 B7
Sandlewood Cl BA21....28 A8
Sandmartin BH25....126 F7
Sandon Cl BH20....27 C5
Sandown Rd BH23....124 E6
Sandpiper Cl BH17....86 F1
Sandpiper Way DT4....180 D6
SANDPIT DT8....203 D7
Sandringham Cl BH9....90 B4

Sandringham Ct
  Bournemouth BH8....122 C6
  2 Dorchester DT1....108 B2
Sandringham Gdns BH9....90 B4
Sandringham Rd
  Poole BH14....120 C3
  Yeovil BA21....28 A6
Sandringham Sports Ctr
  DT1....108 B1
Sandroyd Sch SP5....188 C5
Sandsfoot Castle★ DT4....180 E7
Sandy Cl
  Poole BH15....117 E5
  Wimborne Minster BH21....60 A8
Sandy Hill La BH20....177 C8
Sandy Hole TA16....191 F8
Sandyhurst Cl BH17....87 C1
Sandy La
  Bournemouth BH6....123 B5
  Christchurch BH23....91 C2
  Hilfield DT2....195 A1
  Lytchett Matravers BH16....34 C6
  Minterne Magna DT2....207 C7
  Pamphill BH21....57 D5
  St Leonards BH24....54 C5
  Upton BH16....117 D6
  Verwood BH31....45 A2
  Verwood BH31....45 C6
  Whitchurch Canonicorum
  DT6....65 A8
  Wimborne Minster BH21....60 A8
Sandy Mead Rd BH8....90 F1
Sandy Plot BH23....124 C8
Sandy Way BH10....89 E4
San Remo Twrs 4 BH5....122 F3
Sansome's Hl 6 DT9....17 D2
Santoy BH13....147 D5
Sarah Cl BH7....123 B8
Sarah Sands Cl BH23....124 D8
Sark Rd BH12....120 D8
Sarum Ave BH22....53 A4
Sarum Ct BH14....120 C4
Sarum St BH15....119 B1
Saulfland Dr BH23....125 D8
Saulfland Ho BH23....125 D8
Saulfland Pl BH23....125 D8
Saville Ct BH17....59 D3
Sawmills La DT1....134 F7
Sawyers La DT2....106 E8
Saxonbury Rd BH6....123 E5
Saxonford Rd BH23....125 C7
Saxon Hts BH6....123 D5
Saxonhurst Cl BH10....89 C5
Saxonhurst Gdns BH10....89 C4
Saxonhurst Rd BH10....89 C4
Saxon King Gdns BH6....124 B4
Saxon Mead Cl SP5....189 A5
Saxon Rise DT11....210 C2
Saxon Spur SP7....12 F4
Saxon Square Sh Ctr
  BH23....124 B6
Saxon Way SP6....42 C5
Scadden's Cnr DT6....66 B8
Scaplen's Court Mus★
  BH15....119 B1
Scarf Rd BH17....119 F7
Schelin Way 6 BH23....198 B5
School Cl
  Chickerell DT3....166 B3
  4 Tarrant Gunville DT11....199 F7
  Verwood BH31....45 C7
School Dr
  Dorchester DT1....137 D7
  Sherborne DT9....30 C6
School Hill
  Chickerell DT3....166 B6
  Cucklington BA9....4 A3
  Powerstock DT6....70 B5
  South Perrott DT8....204 C4
SCHOOL HOUSE TA20....202 D5
School House Cl 9 DT8....204 C4
Schoolhouse La DT10....21 F2
School House La DT2....103 B1
School La
  Askerswell DT2....102 D7
  Bournemouth BH11....89 B6
  Broadwindsor DT8....203 B6
  Chetnole DT9....194 D3
  Dorchester DT1....107 D2
  Dorchester DT2....209 C2
  Gillingham SP8....6 A2
  4 Pimperne DT11....199 D4
  Poole BH15....119 C5
  Ringwood BH24....55 C7
  Shaftesbury SP7....24 C5
  St Leonards BH24....54 C5
  Studland BH19....164 C1
  3 Tarrant Gunville DT11....199 F7
  Toller Porcorum DT2....71 E8
  Verwood BH31....53 B7
  West Lulworth BH20....172 D6
  Wimborne Minster BH21....59 B6
  Winfrith Newburgh DT2....156 F6
  Woodsford DT2....110 C1
School Rd BH12....88 E1
School St DT4....167 D3
School View Cl DT9....30 B7
Scimitar Rd BA22....26 D6
Scotchey Hill SP8....10 D1
Scotchey La SP8....10 F1
Scott Cl
  Poole BH12....88 F1
  Stoborough Green BH20....160 E8
Scotter Rd BH7....123 B6
Scotton Way The DT2....137 D5
Scott Rd BH12....88 F1
Scott's Gn BH23....124 F8

Scotts Hill BH23 . . . . 124 D7
Scott's La DT6 . . . . 64 A5
Scotts Way TA18 . . . . 192 A8
Scouse La EX13 . . . . 202 B2
Scutts Cl BH15 . . . . 84 C4
Seabank Cl 4 BH16 . . . . . 117 C7
SEABOROUGH DT8 . . . . . 191 E1
Seaborough View TA18 . . 191 E3
Seabourne Pl 5 BH5 . . . . 123 B5
Seabourne Rd BH5 . . . . . . 123 B5
Seacliff Ct BH6 . . . . 123 D3
Seacombe Rd BH13 . . . . . 147 B3
Seacroft Ave BH25 . . . . . 126 E8
Seafield Cl DT4 . . . . 167 F6
Seafield Dr BH6 . . . . 123 E5
Seafield Rd
  Barton on Sea BH25 . . . . 126 E8
  Bournemouth BH6 . . . . . . 123 D4
  Christchurch BH23 . . . . . 125 C7
Seager Way BH15 . . . . . . 119 D2
Seagrim Rd BH8 . . . . 90 C3
Seagull Rd DT6 . . . . 90 C1
Sea Hill La DT6 . . . . 99 A5
Sea King Rd BA20 . . . . 26 F3
SEA LIFE, Weymouth★
  DT4 . . . . 167 F6
Seamoor Cl DT4 . . . . 167 F8
Seamoor La BH4 . . . . 121 B3
Seamoor Rd BH4 . . . . 121 B3
Sea Point 8 BH13 . . . . . . 147 F7
Sea Rd
  Barton on Sea BH25 . . . . 126 E8
  Bournemouth BH5 . . . . . . 122 E4
  Bournemouth, Southbourne
    BH6 . . . . 123 F3
Sea Road N DT6 . . . . 100 E7
Sea Road S DT6 . . . . 100 D5
Seaton BH23 . . . . 126 B8
Seaton Rd
  Christchurch BH23 . . . . . . 126 B8
  Yeovil BA20 . . . . 27 B4
SEATOWN DT6 . . . . 99 A4
Seatown Cl BH17 . . . . 88 A1
Sea View 5 DT5 . . . . 186 F8
Sea View Rd
  Barton on Sea BH25 . . . . 126 E7
  Walkford BH23 . . . . 94 C1
Sea View Rd
  Upton BH16 . . . . 120 A6
  Upton BH16 . . . . 117 C7
Sea Vixen Ind Est BH23 . . 125 A8
Seaward Ave
  Barton on Sea BH25 . . . . 126 F7
  Bournemouth BH6 . . . . . . 123 D4
Seaward Gdns DT6 . . . . . 100 D2
Seaward Rd BH19 . . . . . . 179 B4
Seaway BH25 . . . . 127 B8
Seaway Ave BH23 . . . . . . 125 C7
Second Cliff Wlk 2 DT6 . . 100 E7
Second Marine Ave
  BH25 . . . . 127 A8
Seddon Cl BH25 . . . . 127 B8
Sedgefield Cl DT4 . . . . . . 167 C3
SEDGEHILL SP7 . . . . 7 F5
Sedgemoor Cl BA21 . . . . . 27 F6
Sedgley Rd BH9 . . . . 121 F3
Seed Warehouse The 3
  BH15 . . . . 119 C1
Selby Cl BH18 . . . . 87 A3
Seldown BH15 . . . . 119 D3
Seldown Bridge BH15 . . . 119 D2
Seldown La BH15 . . . . 119 D3
Seldown Rd BH15 . . . . . . 119 A2
Self Rd BH15 . . . . 119 A2
Selfridge Ave BH23 . . . . . 124 B3
Selfridge Cl BH6 . . . . 124 B3
Seliot Cl BH15 . . . . 119 D5
Selkirk Cl BH21 . . . . 59 E1
Sellwood Way BH25 . . . . 126 D8
Selwood Cl DT10 . . . . 35 C2
Selwood Pk BH10 . . . . 89 C7
Selworthy Cl BH14 . . . . . 120 A2
Selwyn Cl DT3 . . . . 152 D3
Sentinal Ct BH15 . . . . 119 E3
Sentry Rd BH19 . . . . 179 C2
Serpentine La BH15 . . . . . 119 C3
Serrells Mead BH14 . . . . . 178 C2
Setley Gdns BH8 . . . . 90 E3
Seven Acres 5 DT5 . . . . . 186 E1
Seven Acres Ct DT3 . . . . . 153 C3
Seven Ash Comm Rd
  DT9 . . . . 195 B4
Seven Barrows Rd BH20 . 142 D6
Sevenoaks Dr BH7 . . . . . . 123 A8
Seventh St BH20 . . . . 162 C6
Severalls Park Ave 17
  TA18 . . . . 191 F4
Sewell Rd BH22 . . . . 62 A5
Sewell Rd BH20 . . . . 139 D7
Seymer Cl DT11 . . . . 198 B6
Seymer Rd BH19 . . . . 179 C2
Seymour Rd BH24 . . . . 47 D1
Shadrack Cl DT6 . . . . 128 B8
Shadrack St 2 DT8 . . . . . 204 C4
SHAFTESBURY SP7 . . . . . . 12 E4
Shaftesbury Abbey Mus &
  Gdn★ SP7 . . . . 12 D2
Shaftesbury CE Prim Sch
  SP7 . . . . 13 A4
Shaftesbury Cl BH22 . . . . . 53 B1
Shaftesbury Dr BH3 . . . . . 121 F6
Shaftesbury La DT11 . . . . 212 E6
Shaftesbury L Ctr SP7 . . . 12 F2
Shaftesbury L Pool SP7 . . . 12 F2
Shaftesbury Rd
  Bournemouth BH8 . . . . . . 122 C6
  Child Okeford DT11 . . . . . 198 C8
  Ferndown BH22 . . . . 53 A1

Shaftesbury Rd continued
  Gillingham SP8 . . . . 11 C7
  Henstridge BA8 . . . . 19 D6
  Kington Magna SP8 . . . . . 20 A7
  Mere BA12 . . . . 3 B4
  Poole BH15 . . . . 119 D3
Shaftesbury Sch
  Shaftesbury SP7 . . . . 12 F1
  Shaftesbury SP7 . . . . 12 F3
Shaftesbury Theatre & Gall★
  SP7 . . . . 12 F2
SHAGGS BH20 . . . . 158 C3
Shakespeare Rd
  Bournemouth BH6 . . . . . . 123 D7
  Wimborne Minster BH21 . . 59 C6
Shamrock Ct 2 BH21 . . . . 59 C4
Shapland Ave BH15 . . . . . 88 E5
Shapley Ct 2 DT1 . . . . . . 107 B1
SHAPWICK DT11 . . . . 56 C8
Shapwick Rd BH15 . . . . . 119 A1
Shard Cl DT1 . . . . 45 C6
Sharlands Cl BH18 . . . . . . 87 B3
SHARNHILL GREEN DT2 . . 208 C8
Sharp Rd BH12 . . . . 121 A7
Shaston Cl 4 BH10 . . . . . 178 F2
Shaston Cres DT1 . . . . . . 135 B7
Shaston Rd DT11 . . . . 198 F4
Shatcombe La DT2 . . . . . . 71 D3
Shatter's Hill BH20 . . . . . 142 E4
Shave Cross DT6 . . . . 203 C1
Shave Hill SP8 . . . . 9 B7
Shave La
  Todber DT10 . . . . 21 D5
  West Crewkerne TA18 . . . 191 E3
Shaves La BH25 . . . . 95 A5
Shaw Cl DT11 . . . . 212 D5
Shaw Dr BH20 . . . . 142 F8
Shawford Gdns BH8 . . . . . 90 D2
Shawford Rd BH8 . . . . 90 D3
Shear La BH24 . . . . 47 E2
Shear Plot DT6 . . . . 99 F8
Shears Rd DT4 . . . . 167 D7
Shearstones DT9 . . . . 194 D5
Sheasby Cl SP5 . . . . 189 A3
Shedbush La DT6 . . . . 98 C8
Shedrick Hill TA20 . . . . . . 202 E8
Sheepcroft La BH21 . . . . . 51 D3
Sheepdown Rd DT1 . . . . . 107 C2
Sheepwash Dro BH21 . . . 200 E2
Sheeplands La DT9 . . . . . . 29 F6
Sheeplands The DT9 . . . . . 29 F7
Sheep Market Hill 2
  DT11 . . . . 212 D3
Sheepspine La TA20 . . . . 202 C5
Sheepwashing La DT2 . . . 206 C6
Sheepwash La
  Burstock DT6 . . . . 203 D5
  Tatworth & Forton TA20 . . 202 A6
Sheiling St BH24 . . . . 54 E6
Shelbourne Cl BH8 . . . . . 122 D6
Shelbourne Rd BH8 . . . . . 122 B6
Sheldrake Rd BH23 . . . . . 125 A5
Shell Bay Sailing Ctr★
  BH19 . . . . 147 A1
Shelley Cl
  Bournemouth BH1 . . . . . . 122 E5
  Christchurch BH23 . . . . . 125 C7
  St Leonards BH24 . . . . . . 54 A5
  Yeovil BA21 . . . . 26 F6
Shelley Ct
  10 Bournemouth BH4 . . . . 121 C3
  Ferndown BH22 . . . . 61 D5
Shelley Gdns BH1 . . . . . . 122 E5
Shelley Hamlets BH23 . . . 125 D7
Shelley Hill BH23 . . . . 125 D7
Shelley Ho 2 BH25 . . . . . . 95 A2
Shelley Rd
  Bournemouth BH1 . . . . . . 122 E5
  Poole BH12 . . . . 120 D5
Shelley Road E BH7 . . . . . 122 F5
Shelton Rd BH6 . . . . 123 C6
Shenstone Ct 2 BH25 . . . . 95 A1
Shepherd Cl BH23 . . . . 93 F1
Shepherds Croft DT5 . . . . 187 C5
Shepherds Hill BH24 . . . . 46 E6
Shepherd's Hill SP8 . . . . . . 9 C7
Shepherds La BH24 . . . . . 46 C6
Shepherds Way
  Bournemouth BH7 . . . . . . 123 A7
  West Lulworth BH20 . . . . 172 D6
Sheppards Field 4 BH21 . 59 B6
Sherberton St DT1 . . . . . . 107 B1
Sherborn Cres BH17 . . . . . 88 A2
SHERBORNE DT9 . . . . 30 A8
Sherborne Abbey CE Prim
  Sch DT9 . . . . 30 B6
Sherborne Abbey★ DT9 . . 30 B6
Sherborne Cswy DT9 . . . . 11 E3
Sherborne Dr BH22 . . . . . 61 D4
Sherborne Hill DT9 . . . . . . 30 C3
Sherborne House★ DT9 . . 30 B6
Sherborne La 3 DT7 . . . . . 96 C5
Sherborne New Castle★
  DT9 . . . . 30 D5
Sherborne Old Castle★
  DT9 . . . . 30 D6
Sherborne Prep Sch DT9 . 30 B6
Sherborne Prim Sch DT9 . 30 C7
Sherborne Rd
  Henstridge BA8 . . . . 18 F4
  Milborne Port DT9 . . . . . . 17 C2
  4 Yeovil BA20 . . . . 27 C5
Sherborne Sch DT9 . . . . . 30 B6
Sherborne Sch for Girls
  DT9 . . . . 30 A6
Sherborne Sch Sports Ctr
  DT9 . . . . 30 B6

Sherborne Sta DT9 . . . . . . 30 B5
Sherfield Cl BH8 . . . . 90 D2
SHERFORD BH20 . . . . 115 D8
Sherford Dr BH20 . . . . . . 142 D6
Sherford Dr BH20 . . . . . . 142 E6
Sheridan Cl DT2 . . . . 73 F3
Sheridan Way 5 BH21 . . . 56 D4
Sheringham Rd BH12 . . . . 120 F5
Sherlands 1 TA16 . . . . . . 191 F7
Sherlands Gdns 12 TA16 . 191 F7
Sherren Ave DT2 . . . . 75 E2
Sherrin Cl BH15 . . . . 119 D5
Sherwood Ave
  Ferndown BH22 . . . . 61 C3
  Poole BH14 . . . . 120 A3
Sherwood Cl BH23 . . . . . 123 F7
Sherwood Dr BH31 . . . . . . 45 D6
Shetland View BH31 . . . . . 45 C6
Shiller's La DT9 . . . . 15 B6
SHILLINGSTONE DT11 . . 198 C6
Shillingstone CE Prim Sch
  DT11 . . . . 198 B6
Shillingstone Dr BH9 . . . . . 90 B3
Shillingstone Gdns 3
  BH12 . . . . 120 F7
Shillingstone La DT11 . . . 198 A5
Shillito Rd BH12 . . . . 120 F7
Ship Knapp DT6 . . . . 98 B8
Shipney La DT10 . . . . 19 E2
Shipstal Cl BH16 . . . . 117 C4
Shipstal Nature Trail★
  BH20 . . . . 144 D3
SHIPTON GORGE DT6 . . . 101 C3
Shipton La
  Burton Bradstock DT6 . . . 101 C1
  Loders DT6 . . . . 101 E5
Shipton Rd DT6 . . . . 101 D3
Shirecroft Rd DT4 . . . . . . 167 A3
Shiremoor Hill TA16 . . . . 191 F7
Shires Cl BH24 . . . . 55 C4
Shires Copse BH6 . . . . . . 123 F3
Shires Mead BH31 . . . . . . 45 C6
Shirley Cl
  Ferndown BH22 . . . . 53 A2
  Swanage BH19 . . . . 178 A2
Shirley Rd
  Bournemouth BH9 . . . . . . 90 A1
  Poole BH12 . . . . 120 B6
  1 Upton BH16 . . . . 117 E7
  Wareham BH20 . . . . 142 E7
SHITTERTON BH20 . . . . . . 80 F3
Shoe La DT6 . . . . 100 F8
Shoot Hill TA17 . . . . 191 C8
Shop La DT3 . . . . 150 C1
Shoreacres BH13 . . . . 147 C3
Shore Ave 2 BH16 . . . . . . 117 E6
Shore Cl BH16 . . . . 117 E6
Shoredown La DT7 . . . . . . 17 D6
Shore Gdns BH16 . . . . . . 117 D5
Shore La BH16 . . . . 117 E6
Shore Rd
  Poole BH13 . . . . 147 D6
  Swanage BH19 . . . . 179 C3
Short Cl BH12 . . . . 121 A8
Short Cross DT7 . . . . 206 C6
Shortedge DT10 . . . . 35 C2
Shortlake La DT3 . . . . 169 A8
Shortlands DT5 . . . . 186 A6
Shortlands Rd DT5 . . . . . 152 B5
Shortmarsh La TA18 . . . . 192 F4
Shorts Cl BH23 . . . . 92 C1
Shorts Green La SP7 . . . . . 12 B8
Short's La DT11 . . . . 211 E5
Shottesford Ave DT11 . . . 212 E6
Shottsford Cl 7 BH19 . . . 178 F2
Shottsford Rd BH15 . . . . . 119 C5
Shreen Cl 1 SP8 . . . . 5 F3
Shreen Way SP8 . . . . 5 F3
Shrewsbury Rd
  Brympton BA21 . . . . 26 D7
  Yeovil BA21 . . . . 26 D7
Shrubbery La DT11 . . . . . 212 E6
Shute La BH24 . . . . 54 D8
Shute Lake La 11 TA18 . . 191 F4
Shute's La
  Bridport DT6 . . . . 99 D8
  Buckhorn Weston SP8 . . . . 9 C8
Shyners Terr TA16 . . . . . . 191 F7
Sidings The DT9 . . . . 194 C6
Sidmouth Rd DT7 . . . . 96 A5
Sidney Gdns 2 BH9 . . . . . 90 B4
Sidney Smith Ct BH17 . . . 87 E2
Signals Ave DT11 . . . . . . 212 E6
Silchester Cl BH17 . . . . . 121 F5
SILKHAY DT6 . . . . 204 B1
Silk House Barton DT10 . . 33 C8
Silklake Mews 5 DT5 . . . 187 A4
Sillen La SP6 . . . . 190 B6
SILTON SP8 . . . . 5 A7
Silton Rd SP8 . . . . 121 A4
Silver Birch Cl BH13 . . . . 147 A4
Silver Bsns Pk BH23 . . . . 124 F7
Silverdale BH25 . . . . 127 B7
Silverdale Cl BH14 . . . . . . 86 E4
Silverdale Cres SP6 . . . . . 42 C6
Silverlake Cotts DT9 . . . . . 29 C4
Silver St
  5 Christchurch BH23 . . . 124 B6
  Crewkerne TA18 . . . . 192 B3
  Lyme Regis DT7 . . . . 96 B5
  Overcombe/Preston DT3 . 153 D4
  4 Shaftesbury SP7 . . . . . 12 F1
  Yeovil BA20 . . . . 27 D5
Silver Way DT4 . . . . 167 A4
Silverwood Cl BH21 . . . . . 59 D2
Simmonds Cl BH15 . . . . . 119 D5
Simons Rd DT9 . . . . 30 B7

Simsay Fields DT2 . . . . . . 207 D4
Sinclair Cl 4 BH14 . . . . . 120 A4
Singleton Dr BH14 . . . . . . 89 C2
Sir John Colfox Sch The
  DT6 . . . . 68 E1
Sir Richard Hull Rd
  BH20 . . . . 139 D6
Siskin Cl BH22 . . . . 61 B7
Sitterton Cl BH20 . . . . 81 A3
Sixpenny Cl BH12 . . . . . . 120 F7
SIXPENNY HANDLEY
  SP5 . . . . 189 A3
Sixpenny Handley Fst Sch
  SP5 . . . . 189 A4
Sixth St BH20 . . . . 162 C6
Six Ways Cross BH21 . . . 200 E3
SKILLING DT6 . . . . 100 B5
Skilling Hill Rd DT6 . . . . . 100 C5
Skilling La DT6 . . . . 100 B5
Skinner St BH15 . . . . 119 C1
Skipton Cl BH18 . . . . 87 A2
Slade La BA22 . . . . 15 B6
Slades Farm Rd BH10 . . . . 89 D2
Slades Gn DT6 . . . . 100 E5
Slape Hill DT6 . . . . 68 D8
Sleepbrook Cl BH31 . . . . . 45 A6
Sleight Cl BA21 . . . . 26 E6
Sleight La
  Corfe Mullen BH21 . . . . . 57 E1
  Poole BH21 . . . . 85 E8
SLEPE BH16 . . . . 115 F7
Slepe Cres BH12 . . . . 120 F8
Slepe Mobile Home Pk
  BH16 . . . . 115 F7
Slinn Rd BH23 . . . . 124 E7
Slip Way BH15 . . . . 119 B2
Slodbrook La SP8 . . . . 2 D1
Slop Bog Nature Reserve★
  BH22 . . . . 61 D8
Slopers Mead 2 DT11 . . . 211 E5
Slough Dro BH16 . . . . 205 E7
Slough La
  Horton BH21 . . . . 44 B3
  Lytchett Minster & Upton
    BH16 . . . . 117 B6
Slyer's La
  Puddletown DT2 . . . . 76 F1
  Stinsford DT2 . . . . 108 D6
Smacombe La DT6 . . . . . . 101 D4
Smallmouth Cl DT4 . . . . . 180 D5
Smishops La DT6 . . . . 69 D1
Smithfield Pl BH9 . . . . 89 F1
Smith's Hill BH18 . . . . . . 192 B8
Smith's La DT2 . . . . 208 B3
Smithson Cl BH12 . . . . . . 121 C8
Smith's Terr BA21 . . . . 27 E6
Smithy La BH6 . . . . 94 F6
Smokey Hole La DT1 . . . . 108 C1
Smugglers La BH21 . . . . . 59 E7
Smugglers' La
  Colehill BH21 . . . . 50 F1
  Stourpaine DT11 . . . . 199 D3
Smugglers Lane N BH23 . . 93 E1
Smugglers Lane S BH23 . 125 E8
Smugglers Reach BH23 . . 125 E8
Smugglers Wood Rd
  BH23 . . . . 93 D1
Snag La DT11 . . . . 79 E6
Snail's La BH24 . . . . 47 D3
Snowdon Rd BH4 . . . . . . 121 C4
Snow Down Rd 1 DT11 . . 199 E3
Snowdrop Gdns BH23 . . . . 93 B1
Snow Hill BH20 . . . . 81 B2
Snow Hill La BH20 . . . . . . 81 B2
Snowtrax BH23 . . . . 93 C3
Soberton Rd BH8 . . . . . . 122 D6
SOCKETY DT8 . . . . 192 C1
Sodern La DT1 . . . . 107 C7
Sodom La DT10 . . . . 21 B3
Solar Ct BH13 . . . . 121 A2
Soldiers Rd BH20 . . . . . . 161 C7
Soldier's Ring (Barrow)★
  SP6 . . . . 190 D4
Solent Cl BH25 . . . . 127 A7
Solent Lo 5 BH25 . . . . 95 A1
Solent Rd
  Barton on Sea BH25 . . . . 126 F8
  Bournemouth BH6 . . . . . . 124 A3
  Swanage BH19 . . . . 185 C8
  Walkford BH23 . . . . 94 B2
Solent View BH6 . . . . 124 A3
Solly Cl BH17 . . . . 120 E7
Solomon Way 1 BH15 . . . 117 F2
Somerby Rd BH15 . . . . . . 119 D6
Somerfields DT7 . . . . 96 A5
SOMERFORD 124 E7
Somerford Ave BH23 . . . . 125 B8
Somerford Bsns Pk
  BH23 . . . . 125 E7
Somerford Prim & Com Sch
  BH23 . . . . 124 E7
Somerford Rd BH23 . . . . . 124 F7
Somerford Rdbt BH23 . . . 125 A8
Somerford Way BH23 . . . 124 E6
Somerleigh Rd DT1 . . . . . 108 A1
Somerley Pk★ BH24 . . . . . 46 E5
Somerley Rd BH9 . . . . . . 122 A8
Somerley View BH24 . . . . 55 B8
Somerset Cl SP8 . . . . 5 E3
Somerset Rd
  Bournemouth BH7 . . . . . . 123 A5
  Christchurch BH23 . . . . . 123 B8
  Weymouth DT4 . . . . 167 A4
Somers Rd DT7 . . . . 96 A5

Somerton Cl BH25 . . . . 95 D3
Somerville Ct BH25 . . . . . 94 F3
Somerville Rd
  Bournemouth BH2 . . . . . . 121 D3
  Ringwood BH24 . . . . 55 E8
Sonning Way BH8 . . . . 90 B2
Sopers La
  Christchurch BH23 . . . . . 124 A6
  Poole BH17 . . . . 87 B1
SOPLEY 92 B7
Sopley Cl BH25 . . . . 126 D8
Sopley Common Reserve★
  BH23 . . . . 91 C8
Sopley Farm Bldgs BH23 . 92 B6
Sopwith Cl BH23 . . . . 125 B6
Sopwith Cres BH21 . . . . . 59 E2
Sorrel Cl DT4 . . . . 167 E6
Sorrel Gdns BH18 . . . . 86 F2
Sorrell Cl BH23 . . . . 125 B8
Sorrel Way BH23 . . . . 125 B8
Sorrel Way SP8 . . . . 5 D2
Souter Way DT3 . . . . 167 D8
Southampton Rd BH24 . . . 55 D8
South Annings 2 DT6 . . . 128 B8
South Ave
  Lyme Regis DT7 . . . . 96 B6
  New Milton BH25 . . . . 95 B2
  Sherborne DT9 . . . . 29 F4
SOUTH BOCKHAMPTON . . 92 E4
SOUTHBOURNE 123 F4
Southbourne Coast Rd
  BH6 . . . . 123 F3
Southbourne Cross Roads 6
  BH6 . . . . 123 E3
Southbourne Gr BH6 . . . . 123 C4
Southbourne Lane Central 6
  BH6 . . . . 123 C4
Southbourne Lane E 5
  BH6 . . . . 123 C4
Southbourne Lane W
  BH6 . . . . 123 B4
Southbourne Overcliff Dr
  BH6 . . . . 123 D3
Southbourne Rd BH6 . . . . 123 C4
Southbourne Sands BH6 . 123 D3
SOUTH BOWOOD DT6 . . . 203 F1
SOUTHBROOK BA12 . . . . . 3 B4
Southbrook
  Bere Regis BH20 . . . . 81 B2
  Mere BA12 . . . . 3 C4
Southbrook Cl BH17 . . . . . 88 A2
Southbrook Gdns BA12 . . . 3 B4
SOUTH CHARD TA20 . . . . 202 A7
Southcliffe Rd
  Barton on Sea BH25 . . . . 126 F8
  Christchurch BH23 . . . . . 125 C6
South Cliff Rd
  Bournemouth BH2 . . . . . . 121 F2
  Swanage BH19 . . . . 179 C1
Southcote Rd BH1 . . . . . . 122 C4
South Cres DT11 . . . . 199 E3
Southcroft Rd DT4 . . . . . . 166 F1
South Cswy BH20 . . . . . . 142 E2
South Ct DT9 . . . . 29 F4
South St Ave DT1 . . . . . . 135 C4
Southdown Ave DT1 . . . . 168 A6
Southdown Cl 1 BH23 . . . 124 F8
Southdown Rd DT4 . . . . . 180 E8
Southdown Way BH22 . . . 53 A1
South Dr
  Cattistock DT2 . . . . 206 C2
  West Moors BH24 . . . . . . 62 B7
South Dro DT2 . . . . 135 F1
Southernay BH31 . . . . 45 D6
Southern Ave BH22 . . . . . . 53 C1
Southern Cl BH22 . . . . 53 C1
Southernhay Rd BH31 . . . 45 D6
Southern La
  Barton on Sea BH25 . . . . 126 F8
  Old Milton BH25 . . . . 94 F1
Southern Rd BH6 . . . . 123 C4
Southern Rd BH23 . . . . . . 124 F7
South Farm Cl DT11 . . . . 200 A6
Southfield Ave DT4 . . . . . 167 D6
Southfield Mews 4 BH24 . 55 C6
SOUTH GORLEY SP6 . . . . . 43 E2
South Haven Cl BH16 . . . 118 B3
South Haven Rd BH16 . . . 117 D3
South Holme DT4 . . . . . . 198 E4
SOUTHILL DT4 . . . . 167 A6
South Ave DT4 . . . . 120 C6
South Garden Dr DT4 . . . 167 B6
Southill Gdns BH9 . . . . 90 A1
Southill Prim Sch DT4 . . . 167 A7
Southill Rd
  Bournemouth BH9 . . . . . . 90 A1
  Poole BH12 . . . . 120 D7
South Instow BH19 . . . . . 177 F5
South Kinson Dr BH11 . . . 89 B4
SOUTHLANDS DT4 . . . . . . 180 E8
Southlands Ave
  Bournemouth BH6 . . . . . . 123 F4
  1 Poole BH12 . . . . 85 F6
Southlands Cl BH18 . . . . . 85 F6
Southlands Cl BH18 . . . . . 87 A3
Southlands Rd DT4 . . . . . 180 E8
South Lawns DT6 . . . . . . 100 D5
Southlawns Wlk BH25 . . . 94 F1
Southlea Ave BH6 . . . . . . 123 F4
South Lodge BH23 . . . . . 147 G7
South Mead BH20 . . . . 81 A2
Southmead Cres 20
  TA18 . . . . 191 F4

Southmead La BA8....19 B3
South Mill La DT6....100 D5
SOUTHOVER
Burton Bradstock DT6....128 B7
Dorchester DT2....73 D2
Southover DT6....128 B7
Southover Cl DT11....212 D1
Southover La DT2....79 C1
South Par 3 DT4....167 E2
South Park Rd BH12....121 A8
SOUTH PERROTT DT8....192 C2
SOUTH POORTON DT6....70 C8
South Poorton Reserve★ DT6....70 A8
South Rd
Bournemouth BH1....122 E5
Poole BH15....119 C2
Poole BH21....85 F7
Swanage BH19....179 A2
Weymouth DT4....180 C6
South Somerset Mus of★ BA20....27 C4
South St
Arne BH20....142 E3
Bridport DT6....100 D6
Corfe Castle BH20....176 F3
Crewkerne TA18....191 F4
Dorchester DT1....108 A1
3 Gillingham SP8....5 F2
Hinton St George TA17....191 D7
Kington Magna SP8....9 C2
Leigh DT9....194 E3
Milborne Port DT9....17 D2
Sherborne DT9....30 B5
Yeovil BA20....27 D4
South View
Bournemouth BH2....121 F5
Bradford Abbas DT9....28 D2
Piddletrenthide DT2....208 C1
South View Pl 10 BH2....121 E3
Southview Rd DT4....167 B3
South View Rd
Christchurch BH23....124 A6
Milborne Port DT9....17 C2
Southville BA21....27 E5
Southville Rd BH5....123 B5
South Walks Rd DT1....108 A1
South Way DT5....186 D1
Southway Cl BA21....27 B7
Southway Cres BA21....27 B6
Southway Dr BA21....27 C6
SOUTHWELL DT5....186 F1
Southwell Prim Sch DT5....186 E1
Southwell Rd DT5....187 A2
South Western Bsns Pk DT9....30 B5
South Western Cres BH14....120 B2
Southwick Pl BH6....123 C7
Southwick Rd BH6....123 C6
South Wlk DT6....100 C6
Southwood Ave
Bournemouth BH6....123 C4
Walkford BH23....94 B1
Southwood Cl
Ferndown BH22....61 C6
Walkford BH23....94 A1
Southwoods BA20....27 C3
Sovell Down Reserve★ BH21....201 A5
Sovereign Bsns Ctr BH15....119 B6
Sovereign Cl BH7....122 F8
Sovereign Ctr 6 BH1....122 E4
Spa Ave DT3....167 C7
Spadger La DT2....136 A8
Sparacre Gdns DT6....100 D7
Spa Rd DT3....167 B7
Sparkford Cl BH7....123 B8
Sparrow Croft SP8....11 B8
Sparrow Rd BA21....27 D6
Spearhay La TA20....202 B4
Specket La DT8....203 A5
Speedwell Dr BH23....125 B8
Speke Cl 10 TA16....191 F7
Spence La DT6....64 F5
Spencer Ct 1 BH25....95 B2
Spencer Gdns DT11....198 C5
Spencer Rd
Bournemouth BH1....122 C4
New Milton BH25....95 B2
Poole BH13....147 F8
SPETISBURY DT11....211 D5
Spetisbury Cl BH9....90 B3
Spetisbury Prim Sch DT11....211 D5
Spetisbury Rings (Hill Fort)★ DT11....211 E5
Spicer La BH11....88 E5
Spiller Rd DT3....166 D5
Spinacre BH25....127 B8
Spindle Cl BH18....86 F2
Spindlewood Cl 10 BH25....95 A1
Spingfield Rd BA12....3 B5
Spinners Cl BH22....53 A1
Spinners' La DT6....101 A6
Spinners Way BA12....3 B6
Spinney Cl 2 BH24....53 F4
Spinneys La BH22....61 D5
Spinney The
Broadmayne DT2....136 B1
Lytchett Matravers BH16....84 D2
Radipole DT3....152 B2
St Leonards BH24....54 B6
7 Yeovil BA20....26 F2
Spinney Way BH25....95 B6
Spitfire Cl DT2....137 D5
Spittlefields BH24....55 D7
Spittles La DT7....96 C6
Sprague Cl DT3....152 C5
Spread Eagle Hill SP7....24 C3
Spring Ave DT4....167 D1
Springbank Rd BH7....122 F8
SPRINGBOURNE....122 C5
Springbourne Ct BH1....122 D5
Springbourne Mews BH1....122 C5
Springbrook Cl BH20....177 E6
Spring Cl
4 Bridport DT6....68 F1
Verwood BH31....45 B5
Spring Ct BH12....120 D5
Springdale Ave BH18....86 F5
Springdale Fst Sch BH18....86 E4
Springdale Gr BH21....86 E4
Springdale Rd BH21....85 F4
Springfield
Cerne Abbas DT2....207 D4
Gillingham SP8....6 A8
Puncknowle DT2....129 F6
Springfield Ave
Bournemouth BH6....124 A4
Christchurch BH23....91 D2
Springfield Cl
2 Shaftesbury SP7....13 A4
Verwood BH31....45 B5
Springfield Cres
Poole BH14....120 B4
Radipole DT3....152 B3
5 Sherborne DT9....30 A5
Springfield Gdns BH25....95 D2
Springfield Pl BA21....27 A7
Springfield Rd
Milborne Port DT9....17 D3
Poole BH14....120 A4
Radipole DT3....152 B3
4 Swanage BH19....179 B2
Verwood BH31....45 B5
Yeovil BA21....27 A7
Springfields
East Chinnock BA22....192 E8
Holt BH21....51 B4
Stalbridge DT10....33 E8
Spring Gdns
1 Fortuneswell DT5....186 F7
Poole BH12....120 D5
West Knighton DT2....136 C3
Weymouth DT4....167 D1
Spring Gr DT2....196 A1
Springham Wlk 18 DT1....107 D1
Springhill DT7....96 B6
Springhill Gdns DT7....96 B6
Spring La
Longburton DT9....195 B7
New Milton BH25....95 D2
Sandford Orcas DT9....15 F5
3 Weymouth DT4....167 D2
Spring Rd
Bournemouth BH1....122 D5
Weymouth DT4....167 D1
6 Weymouth DT4....167 E2
Spring St BH20....140 B2
Springvale Ave BH7....122 F8
Springwater Cl BH11....89 A3
Springwater Ct BH23....124 D6
Springwater Dr BH23....124 D6
Springwater Rd BH11....89 A3
Springwell Cl BH20....177 A8
Spruce Cl BH17....86 E1
Spur Cl BH21....60 C6
Spurgeon Rd BH7....123 B6
Spur Hill Ave BH14....120 D3
Spur Rd BH14....120 D3
Spy Cl BH16....84 C3
SPYWAY DT2....102 D7
Spyway Rd DT2....102 C7
Square Cl BH21....60 F3
Square The
Bournemouth BH2....121 F3
Cattistock DT2....206 C2
Corfe Castle BH20....162 A1
Cranborne BH21....40 B7
Dorchester DT2....106 E8
4 Gillingham SP8....5 F2
Langton Herring DT3....150 C1
Mere BA12....3 A5
Milborne St Andrew DT11....79 E8
Powerstock DT6....70 B4
Puddletown DT2....78 B1
6 Wareham BH20....140 A2
West Moors BH24....62 B8
Wimborne Minster BH21....59 B5
Squirrel's Cl BH23....91 D2
Squirrel's Cnr BH21....189 D1
Squirrel Wlk BH31....45 B5
Stables The BH23....123 F7
Stacey Cl BH12....120 C7
Stacey Gdns BH8....90 F2
Stadium Way BH15....119 C3
Stafford Cl DT2....136 C4
Stafford Gdns DT2....136 A8
Stafford Rd
Bournemouth BH1....122 A4
Swanage BH19....179 C2
STAFFORD'S GREEN DT9....16 A7
Stag Bsns Pk BH24....55 C5
Stag Cl BH25....94 E4
Stagswood BH31....44 F6
Stainers Mead SP7....7 B1
Stainforth Cl DT4....166 F3
Stake Ford Cross DT9....194 E4
Staker's Cross TA18, TA20....191 B2
Staker's Cross La TA18....191 B2
Stakes La DT9....195 E6
STALBRIDGE DT10....33 E8
Stalbridge CE Prim Sch DT10....19 D1
Stalbridge Cl DT10....33 D8
Stalbridge Dr BH22....61 D4
Stalbridge La DT10....34 F2
Stalbridge Pk★ DT10....19 B1
Stalbridge Rd
Henstridge BA8....19 B3
Poole BH17....119 A7
Stalbridge DT10....32 F4
Stalbridge Trad Est DT10....33 D8
STALBRIDGE WESTON DT10....33 A6
Stalham Rd BH12....120 F6
Stallards La BH24....55 B7
STALLEN DT9....29 B6
Stalls The DT3....166 D6
Stamford Rd BH6....123 D5
Stammery Hill EX13....202 A1
Stanbarrow Cl BH20....81 A2
STANBRIDGE BH21....50 D4
Standfast Wlk 16 DT1....135 B8
Standpitts La SP8....10 E6
Stanfield Cl BH12....120 D7
Stanfield Rd
Bournemouth BH9....121 E8
Ferndown BH22....61 C6
Poole BH12....120 D7
Stanier Rd DT3....153 B3
Staniforth Ct BH23....124 D6
Stanley Cl BH31....45 C5
Stanley Ct
Bournemouth BH1....122 C5
Poole BH15....119 C6
STANLEY GREEN....119 C6
Stanley Green Cres BH15....119 C5
Stanley Green Crescent Ind Est BH15....119 B5
Stanley Green Fst Sch BH15....119 C6
Stanley Green Rd BH15....119 C5
Stanley Pearce Ho BH17....87 C1
Stanley Rd
Bournemouth BH1....122 C5
Christchurch BH23....126 A8
Poole BH15....119 C1
Stanley St 1 DT4....167 D4
Stannington Cl BH25....95 B2
Stannon St 4 DT1....107 B2
STANPIT....124 F5
Stanpit BH23....124 E5
Stanpit Marsh Nature Reserve★ BH23....124 D5
Stanstead Rd DT2....73 A8
Stanton Cl DT11....212 D5
Stanton Lacy 12 BH13....147 F7
Stanton Rd BH10....89 C2
STAPEHILL....60 E5
Stapehill Cres BH21....60 C5
Stapehill Rd BH21....60 F4
Staple Close La BH15....119 C6
Staple Cross BH23....124 E8
Staplecross La BH23....124 D8
Stapleford Ave BH22....61 F6
Staples Mdw 4 TA20....202 A8
Staples Terr DT7....96 C6
Star La
2 Ringwood BH24....55 B7
Whitechurch Canonicorum DT6....98 D8
Starlight Farm Cl BH31....45 C7
Stars La BA20....27 D4
Station App
Bournemouth BH1....122 E5
Broadstone BH18....87 A4
Dorchester DT1....108 A1
New Milton BH25....95 A3
Station Pl 1 BH19....179 B2
Station Rd
Alderholt SP6....42 B6
Child Okeford DT11....198 C7
Christchurch BH23....124 A7
Christchurch, Highcliffe BH23....93 E2
2 Easton/Weston DT5....187 A4
Ferndown BH22....53 A2
Gillingham SP8....5 F1
Henstridge BA8....19 B5
Holton Heath BH16....116 C3
Maiden Newton DT2....72 F8
Milborne Port DT9....17 D4
Misterton TA18....192 A3
Moreton DT2....138 A7
New Milton BH25....95 A2
Poole, Lower Hamworthy BH15....119 A1
Poole, Lower Parkstone BH14....120 B4
Sherborne DT9....30 B5
2 Shillingstone DT11....198 B6
Stalbridge DT10....19 D1
Sturminster Marshall BH21....56 D3
Sturminster Newton DT10....35 B1
Swanage BH19....179 B2
Tatworth & Forton TA20....202 A8
Verwood BH31....45 A7
Wareham St Martin BH16....116 C1
Wimborne Minster BH21....59 D3
Wool BH20....140 A2
12 Yetminster DT9....194 C5
Station Road Bsns Pk DT10....19 D1
Station Road Ind Est
Gillingham SP8....5 F1
Station Road Ind Est continued
Maiden Newton DT2....72 F8
Station Terr BH21....59 D4
Station Yd SP6....42 A6
Staunton BH2....121 F2
Stavordale Rd DT4....167 C3
Stearts La DT10....35 B5
Stedman Rd BH5....123 B5
Steels La SP6....190 F2
Steel's La BA9....1 A3
Steel Well La BA8....19 B4
Steepdene BH14....120 B3
STEEPLE BH20....175 C6
Steeple Cl
Poole BH17....87 D3
Radipole DT3....167 B8
Steepleton Rd BH18....87 C3
Steep St BA12....3 A6
Steer Rd BH19....178 F2
Stella Ct 13 BH23....126 B7
Stem La BH25....94 E4
Stenhurst Rd BH15....119 E6
Stephen Langton Dr BH11....88 D5
Stephen's Castle Nature Reserve★ BH31....45 C8
Stepnell Reach BH16....117 E5
Steppes BH19....178 C3
Steppes Hill BH19....178 C2
STERTE....119 B3
Sterte Ave BH15....119 B4
Sterte Avenue W BH15....119 B4
Sterte Cl BH15....119 C4
Sterte Ct BH15....119 C4
Sterte Esplanade BH15....119 C3
Sterte Rd BH15....119 C4
Sterte Road Ind Est BH15....119 B4
Stevens Cl 2 DT11....212 E5
Stevenson Cres BH14....120 E3
Stevenson Rd BH6....124 A3
Stevensons Cl 3 BH21....59 C4
Stevens Wlk DT2....208 A8
Steward's La DT11....56 B8
Stewart Cl 5 BH8....122 C5
Stewart Rd BH8....122 B6
Stewarts Way BH22....61 E7
Stibles La DT11....197 D3
Stiby Rd BA21....27 A7
Sticklands Prim Sch DT2....206 A7
Stickway SP5....39 E6
Stileham Bank DT11....79 E8
Stile La DT7....96 B4
Stile Way DT2....206 E6
Stillmore Rd BH11....88 D3
STINSFORD DT2....108 E3
Stinsford Cl BH9....90 B4
Stinsford Hill DT2....108 D3
Stinsford Rd BH17....87 D1
Stinsford View DT1....108 C1
Stirling Bsns Pk BH21....60 F7
Stirling Cl BH25....95 B3
Stirling Ct
3 Bournemouth BH4....121 C2
11 New Milton BH25....95 B3
Stirling Rd
Bournemouth BH3....121 E7
Radipole DT3....167 C8
Stirling Way BH23....125 B6
Stirrup Cl
2 Upton BH16....117 F7
Wimborne Minster BH21....60 C6
STOBOROUGH BH20....142 E1
Stoborough CE Fst Sch BH20....142 E1
Stoborough Cl DT3....167 B8
Stoborough Dr BH18....87 A2
STOBOROUGH GREEN BH20....161 A8
Stoborough Heath National Nature Reserve★ BH20....143 B1
Stoborough Mdw BH20....160 F8
Stockbridge Cl BH17....88 B2
Stock Hill La DT9....195 F4
Stock La SP8....5 A2
Stockley Rd BH20....142 D6
STOCKWOOD DT2....194 C2
STOFORD BA22....193 F8
STOKE ABBOTT DT8....204 A3
STOKEFORD BH20....140 F3
Stokehouse St DT1....107 D1
Stoke La DT10....196 F1
Stoke Mill La DT6....67 A8
Stoke Rd
Beaminster DT8....204 C4
Weymouth DT4....180 D7
Stokes Ave BH15....119 D4
Stokes La DT10....32 F3
STOKE WAKE DT11....197 B1
Stoke Wood Rd BH3....121 F6
Stonage La TA18....192 C5
STONE
Bridport....101 A7
Wimborne Minster....59 A6
Stonebarrow La
Charmouth DT6....97 C7
Hawkchurch EX13....202 D3
Stanton St Gabriel DT6....97 E7
Stonechat Cl
Ferndown BH22....61 B8
3 Radipole DT3....152 C4
Stonechat Ct BH23....124 F7
Stone Cl BH15....119 A1
Stonecrop Cl BH18....86 E2
Stonedene DT9....30 B8
Stone Gdns BH8....91 A2
Stonehill Down Reserve★ BH20....160 E1
Stone La
Wimborne Minster BH21....59 A6
Yeovil BA21....27 C8
Stone Lane Ind Est BH21....59 B6
Stoneleigh 3 BH13....147 F8
Stoneleigh Ave SO41....95 F4
Stoneleigh Mews BA21....26 E7
Stonesfield TA18....192 B5
Stoney La BA22....193 D6
Stoneylawn DT10....21 B2
Stoney Lawn DT11....81 D8
Stonyacres DT9....194 C6
Stony La
Bishop's Caundle DT9....196 A8
Burton BH23....92 C2
Christchurch BH23....124 C7
Damerham SP6....190 E2
Holwell DT10....196 C6
Stony Lane S BH23....124 D6
Stopples La SO41....95 F3
Story La BH18....87 B4
Stottingway St DT3....152 B5
Stourbank Rd BH23....124 A6
Stourcastle Cl 4 SP8....5 E4
Stour Cl
East Stour SP8....10 D2
Ferndown BH21....60 D4
Shillingstone DT11....198 C5
Stourcliffe Ave BH6....123 C4
Stourcroft Dr BH23....91 E1
Stour Ct 6 BH13....121 A4
Stour Dr BH20....142 D6
Stourfield Inf & Jun Schs BH6....123 D6
Stourfield Rd BH5....123 B4
Stour Gdns
Bournemouth BH10....89 E4
Gillingham SP8....5 E1
Stour Hill SP8....9 E1
Stour Hill Pk SP8....9 E1
Stour La SP8....21 E8
Stour Mdws SP8....5 E1
STOURPAINE DT11....198 F4
Stourpaine Rd BH17....87 D2
Stour Park Bsns Ctr DT11....212 D2
Stour Pk
Blandford Forum DT11....212 D2
Bournemouth BH10....89 E6
STOUR PROVOST SP8....21 D8
Stour Rd
Blandford Forum DT11....212 E3
Bournemouth BH8....122 D6
Christchurch BH23....124 A6
Stour Rdbt BH23....123 F5
STOUR ROW SP7....22 C7
STOURTON CAUNDLE DT10....32 E3
Stourton Ct 21 BH4....121 C3
Stourton Way BA21....26 E7
Stourvale Ave BH23....123 D8
Stourvale Pl 3 BH5....123 B5
Stourvale Rd BH6....123 C6
Stour Valley Nature Reserve★ BH10....89 F5
Stour View Cl DT10....35 B2
Stour View Gdns BH21....58 E1
Stour Way BH23....91 D1
Stour Wlk
Bournemouth BH8....90 D4
Wimborne Minster BH21....59 D3
Stourwood Ave BH6....123 D4
Stourwood Mans 4 BH6....123 C4
Stourwood Rd BH6....123 D4
Stowcastle St 9 DT1....107 D1
Stowell Cres BH20....142 D2
Stowell La 15 TA20....202 A8
Stower Provost Prim Sch SP8....21 F8
Stowey St DT1....107 C1
Straight La SP5....188 E3
Straits DT5....187 A4
Strand St BH15....119 C1
Stratfield Pl BH25....94 E3
Stratford Sch BA20....26 F5
Strathmore Dr BH31....45 C6
Strathmore Rd BH9....90 A4
STRATTON DT2....106 E8
Stratton Rd BH9....90 C3
Streche Rd
Swanage BH19....179 C5
Wareham BH20....142 D3
Street La
Longburton DT9....195 C6
Sedgehill & Semley SP7....7 F4
Streets La BH24....55 E4
Street The
Charmouth DT6....97 B8
Moreton DT2....138 E7
Motcombe SP7....7 B1
Sutton Waldron DT11....37 D5
Winterborne Zelston DT11....82 F7
Streetway La DT2....209 B3
Strete Mount 1 BH23....124 E7
Stretton Ct BH14....120 B4
Strides La BH24....55 A7
Strode Gdns BH24....54 D5
Strodes La DT2....75 D2
Strongate La DT6....68 A7
Stroud Cl BH21....60 A6
STROUDEN....90 E1
Strouden Ave BH8....122 C8
Strouden Rd BH9....90 A1
Stroud Gdns BH23....124 E6
Stroud La BH23....124 F6
Stroudley Cres DT3....153 C3

Stroud Park Ave BH23 . . . . 124 E6
Struan Ct BH24 . . . . 54 C6
Struan Dr BH24 . . . . 54 C6
Struan Gdns BH24 . . . . 54 B6
Stuart Cl 3 BH16 . . . . 117 D7
Stuart La SP8 . . . . 5 D2
Stuart Rd BH23 . . . . 126 B8
Stuart Way DT6 . . . . 100 F7
STUBHAMPTON DT11 . . . 199 E8
Stubhampton Bottom
  DT11 . . . . 38 E5
STUCKTON SP6 . . . . 43 E7
Stuckton Rd SP6 . . . . 43 D8
Student Village BH12 . . . . 121 D8
STUDLAND BH19 . . . . 164 D1
Studland Beach & Nature
  Reserve★ BH19 . . . . . 164 C3
Studland Cl BH4 . . . . 121 C3
Studland & Godlingston
  Heath National Nature
  Reserve★ BH19 . . . . . 164 B6
Studland Rd BH4 . . . . 121 C1
Studland Way DT3 . . . . . . 167 B8
Studley Cl BH23 . . . . 126 C8
Studley Ct BH15 . . . . 118 C2
STURMINSTER MARSHALL
  BH21 . . . . 56 E4
Sturminster Marshall Fst Sch
  BH21 . . . . 56 E4
STURMINSTER NEWTON
  DT10 . . . . 35 A1
Sturminster Newton High
  Sch DT10 . . . . 35 B3
Sturminster Newton L Ctr
  DT10 . . . . 35 B3
Sturminster Newton Mill★
  DT10 . . . . 197 D8
Sturminster Newton Mus★
  DT10 . . . . 35 A1
Sturminster Rd 1 BH9 . . . . 90 B4
Styles Cl 3 DT8 . . . . 204 C4
Styles Cl SP7 . . . . 78 B1
Sudan Rd DT4 . . . . 180 E8
Suffolk Ave BH23 . . . . 91 F2
Suffolk Cl BH21 . . . . 60 C5
Suffolk Rd BH2 . . . . 121 E3
Suffolk Rd S BH2 . . . . 121 D3
Sugar Hill BH21 . . . . 114 B6
Summercroft Way BH22 . . . 53 A3
Summerfield Cl BH23 . . . . 124 D2
Summer Field Cl BH21 . . . . 60 A4
Summerfields
  Bournemouth BH7 . . . . . 122 F7
  Henstridge BA8 . . . . 19 B5
Summer Fields BH31 . . . . . 45 A4
Summer Hill TA17 . . . . . . 191 D7
Summerhill Rd DT7 . . . . . . 96 C6
Summer House Terr
  BA20 . . . . 27 D4
Summerhouse View BA21 27 E6
Summer La
  Evershot DT2 . . . . 206 A7
  Hinton St George TA17,
  TA13 . . . . 191 D8
SUMMERLANDS 27 E6
Summerlands
  Ferndown BH22 . . . . 61 D6
  Yeovil BA21, BA20 . . . . . 27 A6
Summerlands Hospl BA21 27 B5
Summerleaze Pk BH20 . . . 27 E5
Summer Oaks SP7 . . . . 7 B1
Summers Ave BH11 . . . . . . 89 B6
Summers La BH23 . . . . 92 D1
Summertrees Ct BH25 . . . . 95 D4
Sunbury Cl BH11 . . . . 89 A6
Sunbury Ct 24 BH4 . . . . . 121 C3
Sunbury Pk 1 BH21 . . . . . 121 E3
Sunderland Dr BH23 . . . . 125 B7
Sundew Cl
  Christchurch BH23 . . . . . . 93 C1
  New Milton BH25 . . . . 95 D4
  Radipole DT4 . . . . 167 E7
Sundew Rd BH18 . . . . 86 E2
Sun La
  Piddletrenthide DT2 . . . . 208 B1
  Whitchurch Canonicorum
  DT6 . . . . 98 D8
Sunningdale
  41 Bournemouth BH4 . . . 121 C3
  Christchurch BH23 . . . . . 123 F6
  6 Poole BH15 . . . . 119 E3
Sunningdale Cres BH10 . . 89 C4
Sunningdale Gdns BH18 . 87 A5
Sunningdale Rd BA21 . . . . 27 E6
Sunningdale Rise DT3 . . . 153 E3
Sunninghill Prep Sch
  DT1 . . . . 108 A1
Sunnybank BH4 . . . . 121 C3
Sunnybank Rd BH21 . . . . . 60 B6
Sunnybank Way BH21 . . . . 60 B6
Sunnyfield Rd BH25 . . . . 127 A8
Sunnyfields DT3 . . . . 153 C3
Sunny Hill Ct BH12 . . . . . 120 D5
Sunnyhill Rd BH6 . . . . . . 123 C5
Sunny Hill Rd BH12 . . . . . 120 D5
Sunnylands Ave BH6 . . . . 123 F4
Sunnymoor Rd BH11 . . . . . 89 A1
Sunnyside
  Ridge BH20 . . . . 143 B1
  West Lulworth BH20 . . . . 172 C6
Sunnyside Rd
  Poole BH12 . . . . 120 D6
  Weymouth DT4 . . . . 180 C7
Sunridge Cl
  Poole BH12 . . . . 121 A6
  Swanage BH19 . . . . 179 B1
Sunrise Bsns Pk DT11 . . . 212 E7
Sunrise Ct BH22 . . . . 61 D5

Sunset Lo BH13 . . . . 121 A2
Surrey Cl
  Christchurch BH23 . . . . . . 91 F2
  Weymouth DT4 . . . . 166 F4
Surrey Gdns BH4 . . . . 121 C4
Surrey Rd BH4, BH12 . . . 121 B4
Surrey Road S BH4 . . . . . 121 C4
Sussex Cl 8 BH9 . . . . 90 B4
Sussex Farm Way 8
  DT9 . . . . 194 C5
Sussex Rd DT4 . . . . 167 B3
Sutcliffe Ave DT4 . . . . . . 167 A6
Sutherland Ave BH18 . . . . 86 E5
Suttil Cres DT6 . . . . 68 E2
SUTTON BINGHAM BA22 193 D6
Sutton Cl
  8 Gillingham SP8 . . . . 5 E1
  Overcombe/Preston DT3 . 153 C4
  Poole BH22 . . . . 88 B2
Sutton Court Lawns DT3 . 153 C4
Sutton Hill BA21 . . . . 26 E6
Sutton Hill BA22 . . . . 193 D6
SUTTON HOLMS 44 B8
Sutton Holms Reserve★
  BH21 . . . . 40 B1
Sutton Pk DT3 . . . . 153 D3
SUTTON POYNTZ DT3 . . . 153 D4
Sutton Rd
  Bournemouth BH9 . . . . . . 90 B1
  Overcombe/Preston DT3 . 153 C4
SUTTON WALDRON DT11 . 37 E5
Swaffield Gdns 5 DT4 . . . 180 C8
Swainson Rd DT11 . . . . . 199 E4
Swallow Cl BH17 . . . . 118 F8
Swallowcliffe Gdns BA20 . 27 C5
Swallowfields 1 SP8 . . . . . 5 F4
Swallow Way BH17 . . . . . . 60 A7
SWANAGE 179 C3
Swanage Com Hospl
  BH19 . . . . 179 C1
Swanage Fst Sch BH19 . . 179 B2
Swanage Mid Sch BH19 . 178 E3
Swanage Mus & Her Ctr★
  BH19 . . . . 179 C2
Swanage Rd BH19 . . . . . . 164 C1
Swanage Rly★ BH19 . . . . 177 D5
Swanage Sta★ BH19 . . . . 179 C2
Swan Gn 8 BH23 . . . . 124 A5
Swan Hill TA18 . . . . 192 B5
Swan La DT2 . . . . 208 B1
Swan Mead BH24 . . . . 55 E6
Swanmore Cl BH7 . . . . . . 123 B7
Swanmore Rd BH7 . . . . . 123 B7
Swan Theatre★ BH7 . . . . . 91 B2
Swan St BH21 . . . . 40 A7
Swan Theatre★ BA20 . . . . 27 D3
Sway Gdns BH8 . . . . 90 E2
Sway Rd BH25, SO41 . . . . 95 C6
Sweep The 1 BH24 . . . . . . 55 B7
Sweet Hill La DT5 . . . . . . 186 E1
Sweet Hill Rd DT5 . . . . . . 186 E1
Sweetmans Rd SP7 . . . . . . 12 F4
Swift Cl BH17 . . . . 118 F8
Swilletts La DT6 . . . . 203 A6
Swinton Ave BH20 . . . . . 139 D7
Swordfish Dr BH23 . . . . . 125 B7
SWYRE DT2 . . . . 129 C3
Swyre Rd DT2 . . . . 129 E3
Sycamore Ave BH16 . . . . 116 B3
Sycamore Cl
  Broadstone BH17 . . . . 86 F1
  Christchurch BH23 . . . . . 123 D8
  Sandford BH20 . . . . 143 B8
  Sixpenny Handley SP5 . . 189 A4
Sycamore Dr
  14 Crewkerne TA18 . . . . 191 F5
  Yeovil BA22 . . . . 27 B2
Sycamore Pl BH21 . . . . . . 60 D5
Sycamore Rd
  Hordle SO41 . . . . 95 F4
  Verwood BH31 . . . . 167 A6
Sycamore Way 4 . . . . 5 D1
Sydenham Cres BH20 . . . 139 F2
Sydenham Rd BH19 . . . . 178 E2
Sydenham Way 4 DT1 . . 108 B1
Sydling Cl BH17 . . . . 88 B2
Sydling Rd
  Cerne Abbas DT2 . . . . . . 207 C3
  Yeovil BA21 . . . . 27 F6
SYDLING ST NICHOLAS
  DT2 . . . . 207 A2
Sydney Pl 3 SP8 . . . . 5 E1
Sydney Rd
  Broadstone BH18 . . . . 87 A3
  Christchurch BH23 . . . . . . 91 E1
Sydney St DT4 . . . . 167 B3
Sydnor Gdns BH9 . . . . 90 A2
Sylvan Cl
  8 Gillingham SP8 . . . . 5 F3
  St Leonards BH24 . . . . . . 53 F4
Sylvan Fst Sch BH12 . . . . 120 B6
Sylvan Rd BH12 . . . . 120 B6
Sylvan Way SP8 . . . . 5 F3
Symes Cl TA18 . . . . 192 C4
Symes Rd BH15 . . . . 118 E4
SYMONDSBURY DT6 . . . . 99 E8
Symondsbury CE Prim Sch
  DT6 . . . . 99 E8
Symonds Cl DT3 . . . . 167 D7
SYNDERFORD TA20 . . . . 202 F6
Syward Cl DT1 . . . . 108 D1
Syward Rd DT1 . . . . 135 C8

T

Tabbit's Hill La BH20 . . . 177 A5
Tabernacle The 7 DT11 . 212 D3
Tadden Cotts BH21 . . . . . . 58 D7
Tadden Wlk BH18 . . . . 86 F2
TADNOLL DT2 . . . . 138 C2
Tadnoll Reserve★ DT2 . . 138 C3
Tail Mill TA16 . . . . 191 F7
Tait Cl BH17 . . . . 119 E7
Talbot Ave BH3 . . . . 121 D8
Talbot Comb Sch BH12 . 121 B8
Talbot Ct BH9 . . . . 89 F1
Talbot Dr
  Christchurch BH23 . . . . . . 93 F2
  Poole BH12 . . . . 121 B8
Talbothays Rd 7 DT11 . . 135 B8
TALBOT HEATH 121 B7
Talbot Heath Sch BH4 . . . 121 C5
Talbot Hill Rd BH9 . . . . . 121 D7
Talbot House Prep Sch
  BH9 . . . . 121 E7
Talbot Manor BH3 . . . . . . 121 D8
Talbot Mdws BH12 . . . . . 121 B8
Talbot Mews BH10 . . . . . . 89 B1
Talbot Rd
  Bournemouth BH9 . . . . . 121 D7
  Lyme Regis DT7 . . . . 96 B7
Talbot Rdbt BH3 . . . . 121 D7
Talbot Rise BH10 . . . . 89 C1
TALBOT VILLAGE 89 C1
TALBOT WOODS 121 E7
Tallidge Cl DT3 . . . . 153 C2
Tamar Cl BH31 . . . . 62 A5
Tamlin St BH20 . . . . 143 A8
Tamlyn's Farm Mews
  BH23 . . . . 124 D6
Tamworth Rd BH7 . . . . . . 122 F5
Tanglewood Ct 8 BH25 . . 95 B3
Tanglewood La DT11 . . . 118 F8
Tangmere Cl BH23 . . . . . 125 B6
Tangmere Pl BH17 . . . . . 119 E7
Tan Howse Cl BH7 . . . . . 123 B7
Tank Mus The★ BH20 . . . 139 D5
Tan La SP8 . . . . 2 A2
Tanner's La 5 BH21 . . . . . 54 E2
Tannery Rd DT6 . . . . 100 C6
Tansee Hill TA20 . . . . 202 E6
Tantinoby La BH20 . . . . . 142 D5
Tanyard DT2 . . . . 206 A7
Tanyard La SP7 . . . . 12 D1
Tanzey La DT10 . . . . 21 B3
Taphouse La DT6 . . . . . . 203 B1
Tapper Ct BH21 . . . . 59 E4
Target Way BH23 . . . . 62 D1
Tark's Hill DT9 . . . . 194 C5
Tarn Dr BH17 . . . . 118 F8
TARRANT CRAWFORD
  DT11 . . . . 211 E6
Tarrant Dr BH20 . . . . 142 D6
TARRANT GUNVILLE
  DT11 . . . . 199 F8
TARRANT HINTON DT11 200 A6
TARRANT KEYNESTON
  DT11 . . . . 48 A5
TARRANT LAUNCESTON
  DT11 . . . . 200 B4
TARRANT MONKTON
  DT11 . . . . 200 B3
Tarrant Rd BH9 . . . . 90 B3
TARRANT RUSHTON DT11 . 48 B8
Tarrants The 17 BH2 . . . . 121 D4
Tarratt Rd BH20 . . . . 27 B1
Tasman Cl BH23 . . . . 123 F8
Tatnam Cres BH15 . . . . . 119 C5
Tatnam Rd BH15 . . . . 119 C4
Tattershall Gdns 4 BH21 . 56 D4
Taunton Rd BH19 . . . . . . 179 C2
Taunustein Way 8 BA20 . 27 D1
Taverner Cl BH15 . . . . . . 119 D2
Taviton Ct BH17 . . . . 107 C1
Taylor Dr BH8 . . . . 90 D4
Taylor's Bldgs 5 BH15 . . 119 C1
Taylor's La
  Mappowder DT10 . . . . . 196 E1
  Whitchurch Canonicorum
  DT6 . . . . 66 B2
Taylor Way BH31 . . . . 45 C4
Teak Cl BH17 . . . . 147 H8
Teal Ave DT11 . . . . 166 D5
Teasel Way BH22 . . . . 53 A1
Tecan Way DT4 . . . . 166 F3
Technology Rd BH17 . . . . 119 A8
Tedder Cl BH11 . . . . 89 B3
Tedder Gdns BH11 . . . . . . 89 B3
Tedder Rd BH11 . . . . 89 B3
Teeling Rd BH17 . . . . 167 D7
Telegraph St DT11 . . . . . 198 E8
Telford Cl DT3 . . . . 153 B2
Telford Rd BH21 . . . . 61 A8
Tellis Cross BH22 . . . . . . 193 D8
Temple Cl BH11 . . . . 134 F8
Templecombe La SP8 . . . . 8 F5
Temple La BA8, BH7 . . . . . 8 B2
TEMPLEMAN'S ASH DT6 . 203 B3
Temple Mews BH1 . . . . . 122 D6
Temple Trees 45 BH4 . . . 121 C3
Temple Trees SP8 . . . . 5 D3
Ten Acres SP8 . . . . 13 A3
Tennyson Rd
  Bournemouth BH9 . . . . . . 89 F2
  1 Poole BH12 . . . . 120 A3
  Weymouth DT4 . . . . 167 C2
  Wimborne Minster BH21 . 59 C6
Tenon Ct BH23 . . . . 124 B7
Tensing Rd BH23 . . . . . . 124 E8

Terence Ave BH17 . . . . 87 C1
Terence Rd BH21 . . . . 85 C3
Termare Ct BA22 . . . . 26 C6
Tern Ct BH6 . . . . 123 D6
Terrace Rd BH2 . . . . 121 E3
Terrace The DT2 . . . . 133 D7
Terracotta Warriors Mus★
  DT1 . . . . 108 B2
Terrington Ave BH23 . . . . 93 E1
Tewkesbury 4 BA21 . . . . . 26 F6
Thames Cl BH22 . . . . 62 A6
Thames Mews 11 BH15 . . 119 B1
Thames St BH15 . . . . 119 B1
Thatcham Cl BA21 . . . . . . 27 B7
Thatcham Park Cl BA21 . . 27 B7
Thatcham Pk BA21 . . . . . . 27 B7
Theobald Rd BH3 . . . . 91 A8
Thessaly Cl 4 BH5 . . . . . 122 F4
Thetchers Cl BH25 . . . . . . 95 B5
Thetford Rd BH12 . . . . . . 120 F5
Thickthorn Cross BH21 . . 200 D7
Thickthorn La DT10 . . . . 197 A2
Third Cliff Wlk 3 DT6 . . . 100 B2
Thistlebarrow Rd BH7 . . 122 E6
Thistle Cl BH23 . . . . 125 C8
Thomas Hardy Dr SP7 . . . 13 A3
Thomas Hardye L Ctr
  DT1 . . . . 134 D8
Thomas Hardye Sch The
  DT1 . . . . 134 E8
Thomas Lockyer Cl BH31 . 45 C5
Thompson Cl
  Allington DT6 . . . . 100 B7
  Puddletown DT2 . . . . 78 A2
Thomson Cl DT6 . . . . 100 B7
Thomson Dr 10 BH20 . . . 191 F4
Thoresby Ct BH25 . . . . 94 E3
Thornbury Rd BH6 . . . . . 123 D6
Thornbury Rd BH6 . . . . . 124 A4
THORNCOMBE TA20 . . . 202 E6
Thorncombe Beacon★
  DT6 . . . . 99 D4
Thorncombe Cl
  Bournemouth BH9 . . . . . . 90 B4
  Poole BH7 . . . . 87 E2
Thorncombe Wood Nature
  Reserve★ DT2 . . . . . . 134 E5
Thorne Cl BH31 . . . . 45 A7
THORNE COFFIN BA22 . . 26 C8
Thorne La BA21 . . . . 26 E7
Thorne La BA21 . . . . 26 E7
Thorners CE Prim Sch
  DT2 . . . . 103 C1
Thorne Way BH21 . . . . 53 D6
Thornfield Dr BH23 . . . . . 62 D1
THORNFORD DT9 . . . . . . 194 D8
Thornford CE Prim Sch
  DT9 . . . . 194 D8
Thornford Rd DT9 . . . . . . 194 C6
Thornford Sta DT9 . . . . . 194 C7
Thornham Rd BH25 . . . . . 95 D3
Thornhill Cl 8 DT1 . . . . . 134 E7
Thornhill Cres DT1 . . . . . 134 E7
Thornhill Rd DT10 . . . . . . 33 D8
Thornicks DT2 . . . . 156 F6
Thorogood Ct 4 BH15 . . 119 E4
Thrasher's La DT1 . . . . . . 162 B3
Thread Mill La
  Allington DT6 . . . . 68 D2
  Bridport DT6 . . . . 68 D2
Three Acre Dr BH25 . . . . 126 F8
Three Acre La BH19 . . . . 178 D2
Three Acres DT2 . . . . 207 A2
Three Corner Mead 2
  BA21 . . . . 26 C5
Three Cross Rd BH21 . . . . 53 A6
Three Lanes Way DT2 . . . 78 A2
THREE LEGGED CROSS
  BH21 . . . . 45 A1
Three Legged Cross Fst Sch
  BH21 . . . . 45 A1
Three Lions Cl 9 BH21 . . 59 B5
Three Yards Cl DT5 . . . . . 186 F7
Thrift Cl DT10 . . . . 33 E8
THROOP
  90 E4
  DT2 . . . . 112 D7
Throop Cl BH11 . . . . 91 A2
Throop Hollow DT2 . . . . . 112 D6
Throop Rd
  Abbas & Templecombe BA8 . 8 A3
  Bournemouth, Holdenhurst
  BH8 . . . . 91 A2
  Bournemouth, Throop BH9 . 90 E4
Thrush Rd BH12 . . . . 88 C1
Thursby Rd BH23 . . . . 93 F1
Thurstin Way SP8 . . . . 5 D3
Thwaite Rd BH12 . . . . . . 121 B5
Tidemill Cl BH12 . . . . 124 A8
TIDPIT SP6 . . . . 42 E1
Tiffany Cl SO41 . . . . 95 F4
Tilburg Rd BH23 . . . . 124 D7
Tilbury Mead BH20 . . . . . 177 A7
TILEY DT9 . . . . 195 E1
Tiley Knap DT2 . . . . 195 E1
Tiller Gdns BH11 . . . . 89 A5

TILLWORTH EX13 . . . . . . 202 A3
Tillycombe Rd DT5 . . . . . 187 A7
Tilly Whim Caves★
  BH19 . . . . 185 C6
Tilly Whim La DT7 . . . . . 106 F3
Timber Rd DT7 . . . . 96 C7
Timewalk★ DT4 . . . . 167 E1
Timothy Cl BH10 . . . . 89 D5
TINCLETON DT2 . . . . 110 D4
Tincleton Cross DT2 . . . . 110 D5
Tincleton Gdns BH9 . . . . . 90 B4
Tinker's La
  Cucklington BA9 . . . . 4 B5
  Wareham BH20 . . . . 142 E4
Tinneys La DT9 . . . . 30 C6
Tin Pot La DT11 . . . . 212 D6
Tintagel Rd BA21 . . . . 26 F7
Tintern BA21 . . . . 26 E6
Tintern La 16 DT11 . . . . . 107 D1
Tintinhull Rd BA21 . . . . . . 27 A8
TIPTOE 95 D8
Tiptoe Prim Sch SO41 . . . 95 D8
Tiverton Ct 34 BH4 . . . . . 121 C3
Tivoli Theatre★ BH21 . . . 59 B5
Tizard's Knap DT6 . . . . . . 66 B1
Toby's Cl DT5 . . . . 186 F3
Tobys Ct SP7 . . . . 12 F5
TODBER DT10 . . . . 21 D4
Todber Cl BH11 . . . . 88 D3
Tollard Cl BH12 . . . . 120 E8
TOLLARD FARNHAM
  DT11 . . . . 188 B2
TOLLARD ROYAL SP5 . . . 188 B4
Tollerdown Rd 4 DT4 . . . 166 F2
TOLLERFORD DT2 . . . . . . 72 E8
Tollerford Rd BH17 . . . . . . 87 D2
TOLLER FRATRUM DT2 . . 72 C7
Toller La DT2 . . . . 206 A1
TOLLER PORCORUM DT2 . 71 E8
TOLLER WHELME DT2 . . 205 B4
Toll Gate BH21 . . . . 139 F1
Tollgate Pk SP7 . . . . 12 F5
TOLPUDDLE DT2 . . . . 79 D2
Tolpuddle Gdns 9 BH9 . . 90 B4
Tolpuddle Martyrs Mus★
  DT2 . . . . 79 B2
Tolstoi Rd BH14 . . . . 120 A6
Tomlins La SP8 . . . . 5 E2
Tomlins Lane Ind Est SP8 . 5 E2
Toms Field Rd BH19 . . . . 178 B2
Tonge Rd BH11 . . . . 89 B6
Toose The BA21 . . . . 26 C6
Topiary The BH14 . . . . . . 119 F5
Top La
  Ringwood BH24 . . . . 55 C7
  Stourton with Gasper BA12 . 1 D7
Torbay Rd BH14 . . . . 120 C3
Torre The BH14 . . . . 26 E6
Torvain Pk BH14 . . . . 120 A5
Totmel Rd BH17 . . . . 88 A2
TOTNELL DT9 . . . . 194 F3
Tourney Rd BH11 . . . . 88 E6
Tout Hill
  East Stoke BH20 . . . . 140 B4
  Shaftesbury SP7 . . . . 12 D3
Tout Hill La DT2 . . . . 104 F7
Tout Quarry Sculpture Pk★
  DT5 . . . . 186 E6
Towans The BH13 . . . . . . 147 C3
Tower Cl 1 BH23 . . . . 201 D1
Tower Ct BH2 . . . . 121 E2
Tower Hill
  Bere Regis BH20 . . . . 81 B2
  Iwerne Minster DT11 . . . . 38 C2
  Netherbury DT6 . . . . 204 B2
Tower Hill Rd 6 TA18 . . . 191 C8
Tower Park Rdbt BH15 . . 119 F7
Tower Rd W BH15 . . . . . . 88 B1
Tower Rd
  Bournemouth BH1 . . . . . 122 E5
  Poole BH13 . . . . 121 B2
  Yeovil BA21 . . . . 27 D8
Tower Road W BH13 . . . . 121 A1
Tower Farm BH21 . . . . 86 D7
Towers Way BH21 . . . . 85 F7
Town Farm SP5 . . . . 189 B4
Town Farm Workshops★
  SP5 . . . . 189 A4
Towngate Bridge BH15 . . 119 C3
Towngate Mews BH24 . . . 55 C6
Towngate Sh Ctr 1
  BH15 . . . . 119 C2
Town Hall La BH19 . . . . . 179 B2
Town Mill★ DT7 . . . . 96 C5
TOWNS END BA8 . . . . 19 B3
TOWN'S END DT20 . . . . . . 81 C3
Townsend
  Blandford Forum DT11 . . 198 C5
  Sturminster Marshall BH21 . 56 D4
Town's End BA22 . . . . 2 F5
Townsend Cl
  Bournemouth BH11 . . . . . 89 B6
  Mere BA12 . . . . 2 F5
Townsend Farm Barton
  BA8 . . . . 19 B3
Townsend Gn BA8 . . . . . . 19 B4
Townsend La SP6 . . . . . . 190 A6
Townsend Mead BH20 . . 177 A7
Townsend Orch TA16 . . . 191 F7
Townsend Rd
  Corfe Castle BH20 . . . . . 177 A7
  Swanage BH19 . . . . 179 B1
Townsend Reserve★
  BH19 . . . . 179 A1

Townsend Way DT6 68 F2
Townsville Rd BH9 90 B2
Tozer Cl BH11 88 F2
Tracey Ct 8 BH23 126 A7
Tradecroft DT5 186 E5
Tradecroft Ind Est DT5 186 F5
Trafalgar Ct BH23 124 F5
Trafalgar Rd BH9 121 F7
Treebys Cl BH23 92 D1
Tree Hamlets BH16 117 E5
Treeside BH23 93 C2
Treetops 9 BH13 147 F7
Trefoil Way BH23 125 C8
Tregonwell Ct 18 BH2 121 E3
Tregonwell Rd BH2 121 E2
Trellech Ct 1 BA22 26 E6
Treloen Ct 3 BH8 122 A5
Trenchard Mdw BH16 84 D3
Trenchard Way DT3 166 D5
Trendle St DT9 30 B5
TRENT DT9 14 E2
Trent Cl
Tolpuddle DT2 79 D1
Yeovil BA21 28 A8
Trent Dr BH20 142 D5
Trentham Ave BH7 123 B8
Trentham Cl BH7 123 B8
Trent Path La DT9 29 E7
Trent Sq SP8 6 B1
Trent Way BH22 62 A6
Tresco Spinney BA21 26 E6
Tresillian Cl BH23 94 B2
Tresillian Way BH23 94 B2
Treves Rd DT1 134 E8
Trevone 5 BH25 95 B3
Triangle The
Bournemouth BH2 121 E3
6 Upton BH16 117 D7
TRICKETT'S CROSS 61 F7
Tricketts La BH22 61 F6
Trigon Rd BH15 119 D7
Trill La DT9 194 B7
Trinidad Cres BH12 120 C8
Trinidad Ho BH12 120 C8
Trinity 2 BH1 122 A3
Trinity CE Fst Sch BH31 45 B8
Trinity Ct 10 DT4 167 D2
Trinity Ind Est BH21 59 E3
Trinity La BH20 142 E3
Trinity Rd
Bournemouth BH1 122 A4
Weymouth DT4 167 D2
Trinity St
Dorchester DT1 108 A2
7 Weymouth DT4 167 E2
Trinity Terr DT4 167 D2
Trinity Way DT6 68 F1
Tristram Cl 7 BA21 26 F7
Troak Cl BH23 124 E8
Troon Rd BH18 87 A5
Trotters La BH21 60 B6
Troublefield Reserve★ BH23 91 A8
Truman Rd BH11 89 B6
Truscott Ave BH9 122 A7
Trusthams DT8 203 E5
Trustin Cl 6 DT6 100 C8
Trystworthy 3 BH2 121 E3
Tuckers La BH15 118 F1
Tuckers Mill Cl BH20 160 F8
Tucks Cl BH23 93 A8
TUCKTON 123 F5
Tuckton Cl BH6 123 D4
Tuckton Gdns BH6 123 E5
Tuckton Rd BH6 123 F5
Tuckton Rdbt BH6 123 F5
Tudor Arc Sh Ctr DT1 108 A2
Tudor Cl SP6 42 C5
Tudor Ct
Bournemouth BH1 122 A5
10 Gillingham SP8 5 D2
Poole BH15 119 E6
Tudor Gdns DT11 212 E5
Tudor Rd BH18 87 B4
Tullon's La DT2 208 B2
Tulse Hill BA12 1 F3
Tuncombe La TA18 191 D4
Tunnel Rd DT8 204 C5
Turbary Cl BH12 120 D8
Turbary Comm Nature Reserve★ BH11 88 F2
Turbary Ct
Bournemouth BH12 89 A1
Ferndown BH22 61 F6
2 Upton BH16 117 E8
Turbary Hts BH11 88 F1
Turbary Park Ave BH11 89 A2
Turbary Rd
Ferndown BH22 61 F6
Poole BH12 120 D8
Turbary Ret Pk BH11 88 E3
Turberville Rd BH20 81 B2
Turbetts Cl BH16 84 C4
Turf Croft Ct BH23 94 B2
Turk's La BH14 120 A1
TURLIN MOOR BH16 117 D4
Turlin Moor Com Sch BH16 117 E4
Turlin Moor Nature Reserve★ BH15 117 D4
Turlin Rd BH16 117 E4
TURMER BH24 46 F8
Turnberry Cl BH23 123 F6
Turner's Barn La BA20 27 B2
Turners La SP8 5 E2
Turner's La
Marshwood DT6 202 E2
Tarrant Monkton DT11 200 B4
TURNERS PUDDLE DT2 112 D8
Turnpike Cl 2 TA18 192 B3
Turnpike Gn 3 TA18 192 B3
Turnpike La DT11 212 C1
Turnstone Cl DT3 152 D4
TURNWORTH DT11 198 B2
Turnworth Cl BH18 87 C3
Turton St 3 DT4 167 D3
Tutankhamun Exhibition The★ 9 DT1 108 A2
Tut Hill DT9 31 E1
Tweedale Rd BH9 90 C3
Twemlow Ave BH14 119 F3
Twin Oak Pk BH23 92 D6
Twin Oaks Cl BH18 87 A3
Twinways La DT6 69 B8
Two Droves DT2 109 F8
Two Elms BA22 14 C8
Two Riversmeet L Ctr BH23 124 C6
Two Tower La BA20, BA22 27 D2
TWYFORD SP7 23 D2
Twyford Cl BH8 90 D2
Twyford Ho BH22 61 F6
Twyford Way BH17 88 A2
Twynham Ave BH23 124 A7
Twynham Rd BH6 123 F4
Twynham Sch BH23 124 A6
Tyberton St DT1 107 C1
Tynedale Cl BH9 90 B4
TYNEHAM BH20 174 C5
Tyneham Ave BH12 120 C8
Tyneham Cl
Radipole DT3 167 B8
Sandford BH20 143 A8
Tyneham Mus★ BH20 174 C5
Tynham Ct BH23 124 C6
Tyrrell Gdns BH8 91 A2
Tytherley Gn BH8 90 D2

U

Ubsdell Cl BH25 95 A3
Uddens Dr
Ferndown Town BH21 51 F1
Wimborne Minster BH21 60 D7
Uddens Rd SP5 188 C4
Uddens Trad Est BH21 60 E6
Ullswater Cres DT3 167 B7
Ullswater Rd BH21 59 C2
ULWELL BH19 179 A6
Ulwell Rd BH19 179 C4
Umbers Hill SP7 12 D2
Undercliff Dr BH1 122 C2
Undercliff Rd BH5 122 E3
Underdown Hollow DT9 28 C3
Underhedge Gdns DT5 186 E1
Underhill
Mere BA12 2 F5
Pen Selwood BA9 1 B2
Underhill Jun Sch DT5 186 E7
Underwater Explorers DT5 181 B2
Underwood Cl BH17 87 B1
Union St 2 BA20 27 D4
Unity La 4 TA18 192 A3
University Rdbt BH10 121 C8
UP CERNE DT2 207 C5
UPHALL DT2 205 E5
Upland Cl DT10 197 D7
Uplands
Bothenhampton DT6 101 A6
2 Yetminster DT9 194 C5
Uplands Ave BH25 127 A8
Uplands Cl BH22 62 A8
Uplands Gdns BH8 90 C2
Uplands Ind Pk DT11 212 D6
Uplands Rd
Bournemouth BH8 90 C2
Ferndown BH22 53 C1
Uplands Sch BH14 120 C3
UPLODERS DT6 101 F8
Uplyme Cl BH17 88 A2
Uplyme Rd DT7 96 A6
UP MUDFORD BA21 14 A2
Upper Fairfield Rd 3 DT1 107 F1
Upper Golf Links Rd BH18 87 B5
Upper Gordon Rd BH23 94 A1
Upper Hinton Rd BH1 121 F3
Upper North Rd SP5 188 C5
Upper Norwich Rd 6 BH2 121 E3
UPPER PARKSTONE 120 B5
Upper Rd BH12 120 C6
Upper School La 1 DT11 212 C1
Upper St 4 DT11 198 C7
Upper Terrace Rd BH2 121 E3
Upper Water St BA12 3 B3
Upper Westhill Rd DT7 96 A5
UPPINGTON BH21 201 D1
Uppington Cl 2 BH21 201 C1
Uppleby Rd BH12 120 C6
UP SYDLING DT2 207 A4
UPTON
Poole BH16 117 F7
Preston DT2 169 E8
Upton Cl BH16 117 D7
Upton Cross Mobile Home Pk 2 BH16 117 E7
Upton Ct BH16 117 E7
Upton Ctry Pk★ BH17 118 F6
Upton Heath Est BH16 117 F7
Upton Heath Nature Reserve★ BH17 117 F8
Upton Heath Reserve★ BH21 85 F2
Upton Ind Est BH16 117 F6
Upton Inf Sch BH16 117 C7
Upton Jun Sch BH16 117 C7
Upton Rd BH17 118 F7
Upton Way BH18 86 F3
Upway St 2 DT4 167 D4
UPWEY DT3 152 A6
Upwey Ave BH15 118 E3
Upwey Sta DT3 152 C3
Utrecht Ct BH23 124 D7

V

Vaggs La SO41 95 E6
Vale Cl
4 Crewkerne TA18 191 F3
Poole BH14 120 E4
Vale Lodge BH1 122 D5
Vale Mans 4 BH1 122 D4
Vale Mead DT10 196 F3
Valencia Cl BH23 91 D4
Vale Pk DT11 212 D2
Vale Rd
Bournemouth BH1 122 D4
Poole BH14 120 E4
Stalbridge DT10 33 D8
West Lulworth BH20 172 E6
Yeovil BA21 28 A6
Vale St BA8 19 A4
Valette Rd BH9 90 A3
Vale View BA8 19 A5
Vale View Pk SO41 95 F7
Valiant Way BH23 125 B7
Valley Cl
Christchurch BH23 91 E3
Overcombe/Preston DT3 153 D3
Yeovil BA21 27 D6
Valley of Stones National Nature Reserve★ DT2 131 F4
Valley Rd
Bournemouth BH8 90 F3
Bridport DT6 100 D4
2 Crewkerne TA18 191 F3
Langton Matravers BH19 178 C3
Worth Matravers BH20 177 D6
Valley View
Bridport DT6 100 F6
Poole BH12 121 B7
Vallis Cl BH15 119 D1
Vanguard Ave DT4 166 F1
Vanguard Rd
Bournemouth BH8 90 E1
6 Poole BH15 119 C2
Vantage Way BH12 88 B2
Veals La DT10 35 A5
Vearse Cl DT6 100 B5
Vecta Cl BH23 125 C6
Vectis Rd BH25 126 D7
Velvet Lawn Rd BH25 94 F4
Venator Pl BH21 59 C6
Venn Hill TA20 202 F6
Venning Ave BH11 88 E5
Venn La
Chideock DT6 66 F2
Stoke Abbott DT6 203 D2
Venn The SP7 12 F3
Ventnor Rd DT5 186 F8
Ventry Cl BH13 120 F4
Ventura Ctr The BH16 118 D6
Ventura Pl BH16 117 F6
Verity Cres BH17 88 A1
Verlands Rd DT3 153 D3
Vermin La BH20, DT11 83 B7
Vernalls Cl BH10 89 D6
Vernalls Ct BH25 95 C5
Vernalls Gdns BH10 89 D5
Vernalls Rd DT9 30 B7
Verne Cl DT4 167 C1
Verne Common Rd DT5 186 F8
Verne Hill Rd DT5 187 A7
Verne Rd
Verwood BH31 45 C5
Weymouth DT4 167 C1
Verne Way DT4 167 C1
Verney Cl BH11 89 B3
Verney Rd BH11 89 A3
Verno La BH23 93 C2
Verona Ave BH6 123 D5
Verriott's La DT6 66 C1
Verulam Pl 8 BH1 121 F3
Verulam Rd BH14 119 F4
VERWOOD BH31 45 B6
Verwood CE Fst Sch BH31 45 A5
Verwood Cres BH6 124 B4
Verwood Heathland Her Str★ BH31 45 B7
Verwood Ind Est BH31 45 D6
Verwood L Ctr BH31 45 B6
Verwood Rd
St Leonards & St Ives BH24 46 C2
Three Legged Cross BH21 45 B1
Verwood BH21 53 A8
Woodlands BH21 44 C7
Verwood Sp Club BH31 45 D6
Vespasian Way DT1 134 E7
Vetch Cl BH23 125 C8
Vian Ct BH25 94 F3
Vicarage Cl 2 BH20 140 A1
Vicarage Cotts BH8 90 F3
Vicarage Ct 4 DT6 100 C8
Vicarage La DT2 107 E6
Vicarage Rd
Bournemouth BH9 89 F1
Poole BH15 119 C6
Verwood BH31 45 B6
Vicarage Way BH23 92 D2
Vickers Cl BH8 91 B2
Vickery Way BH23 124 D8
Victoria Ave
Bournemouth BH9 89 E1
Radipole DT3 152 B5
Swanage BH19 179 A3
Victoria Ave Ind Est BH19 178 F3
Victoria Cl
Poole BH21 85 F4
Wool BH20 139 D6
Yeovil BA21 27 F6
Victoria Cres BH12 120 D6
Victoria Ed Ctr BH13 120 F4
Victoria Gdns
Ferndown BH22 61 D6
Ringwood BH24 55 C6
Victoria Gr DT6 100 D7
Victoria Hospl BH21 59 A5
Victoria Park Pl 4 BH9 89 F1
Victoria Park Rd BH9 89 E1
Victoria Pl
Bournemouth BH1, BH8 122 C5
Easton/Weston DT5 187 A5
Wimborne Minster BH21 59 B5
Victoria Rd
Blandford Forum DT11 212 D4
Bournemouth BH1 122 C5
Christchurch BH23 124 E5
Dorchester DT1 107 F1
Easton/Weston DT5 187 B5
Ferndown BH22 61 D6
Gillingham SP8 6 A1
Poole BH12 120 C6
Swanage BH19 179 C5
Weymouth DT4 180 C7
Wimborne Minster BH21 59 B5
Yeovil BA21 27 F6
Victoria Sq DT5 186 E8
Victoria St
Radipole DT4 167 E4
Shaftesbury SP7 12 E3
Victoria Terr DT9 17 B2
Victor Jackson Ave DT1 107 C1
Victory Cl BH21 53 D6
Victory Rd DT5 186 E8
View Rd DT7 96 B5
Viewside Cl BH21 85 E5
Viking Cl BH6 124 A4
Viking Way
Bournemouth BH6 124 A4
Christchurch BH23 125 A5
Village Rd DT6 68 F1
Village St DT3 154 B3
Villas The BH25 94 E5
Villette Cl BH23 92 A1
Vince Cl BH11 89 B5
Vincent Cl 2 BH25 95 A2
Vincent Pl BA20 27 D5
Vincent Rd 1 BH25 95 A2
Vincents Cl DT9 31 A1
Vine Cl BH7 123 A7
Vine Farm Cl BH12 121 C8
Vine Farm Rd BH12 121 B8
Vine Hill BH21 58 E5
Vineries Cl BH21 59 F6
Vineries The BH21 59 F6
Vinery The BH25 95 B2
Vines Pl DT4 166 F2
Vineyard Cl BH16 84 C3
Vinney Cross DT6 102 A6
Vinneys Cl BH23 92 C2
Violet Farm Cl BH21 86 D8
Violet La BH25 95 A4
Virginia Cl
1 Henstridge BA8 19 A4
Poole BH12 120 C7
Verwood BH31 45 E4
Viscount Cl BH11 88 D5
Viscount Ct BH11 88 D5
Viscount Dr BH23 125 B7
Viscount Rd DT4 166 F1
Viscount Wlk BH11 88 D5
Vista Marina BH13 147 D6
Vivian Pk BH19 179 B4
Vixen Wlk BH25 95 B5
Voss's La DT2 206 B3
Vulcan Cl DT4 166 F1
Vulcan Way BH23 125 B7

W

Waddock Dro DT2 111 E3
Waddon Hill (Roman Fort)★ DT8 203 F4
Waddon Way DT6 69 D2
Wadham Sch TA18 191 F5
Wadmore La BH19 164 C2
Wagtail Dr BH25 94 F2
Wain Rd BH20 139 D7
Wainwright Cl DT3 153 B3
Wakefield Ave BH10 89 E5
Wakeham DT5 187 A4
Wakely Gdns BH11 89 A5
Wakely Rd BH11 89 B5
Walcheren Pl BH15 117 E3
Walcott Ave BH23 91 F1
WALDITCH DT6 101 A6
Walditch Gdns BH17 87 E2
Walditch Rd DT6 100 F6
Waldren Cl BH15 119 E2
Waldrons The 5 DT9 194 D8
Walford Cl BH21 59 C6
Walford Gdns BH21 59 B6
Walford Mill Craft Ctr★ BH21 59 B6
Walker Cres DT4 180 C6
WALKFORD 94 C1
Walkford La BH25 94 D3
Walkford Rd BH23 94 C2
Walkford Way BH23 94 B1
Walking Field La BH15 119 D2
Walkwood Ave BH7 123 B8
Wallace Ct BH18 87 A3
Wallace Rd BH18 87 A3
Walliscott Rd BH11 89 A1
WALLISDOWN 89 A2
Wallisdown Rd BH10 121 C8
Wallisdown Rdbt BH12 89 A1
Wallis Rd BH10 89 B1
Wall La DT8 203 D4
Wallsend Cl 3 DT5 186 E2
Walls View Rd BH20 142 D5
Walnut Ave DT11 198 F1
Walnut Cl BH25 94 F3
Walnut Orch 3 DT3 150 A8
Walnut Rd
Dorchester DT2 139 C2
Mere BA12 3 B4
Walnut Tree Field Nature Reserve★ DT11 56 D5
Walpole Rd BH1 122 E5
Walpole St DT4 167 D4
Walrond Rd BH19 179 B3
Walsford Rd BH4 121 C5
Walsingham Dene BH7 122 F8
Walters Dr 13 DT11 199 D4
Waltham Rd BH7 123 B6
WALTON ELM DT10 34 F8
Walton Elm Hill DT10 35 A8
Walton Rd
Bournemouth BH10 89 C2
Poole BH15 120 A6
Wanchard La DT2 107 C7
Wanderwell DT6 100 D3
Wanderwell Farm La DT6 100 D4
Wanstead Cl BH24 47 D1
Warbler Cl BH16 117 D8
Warburton Rd BH17 119 E8
Wardcliffe Rd DT4 167 C3
Ward's Dro DT11 212 E1
WAREHAM BH20 142 E5
Wareham Com Hospl BH20 142 D4
Wareham Ct
Bournemouth BH7 123 B6
Hamworthy BH15 118 E2
Wareham Mid Sch BH20 142 D3
Wareham Rd
Hawkchurch EX13 202 B2
Lytchett Matravers BH16 84 D3
Lytchett Minster & Upton BH16 116 B6
Owermoigne DT2 155 E7
Poole BH21 85 F5
Wareham St Martin BH16 116 D4
Warmwell DT2 155 B7
Wareham Sta BH20 142 D5
Wareham Town Mus★ BH20 142 E3
Ware La DT7 96 A4
Wares Cl 5 DT11 81 E8
Warland Way BH21 86 E7
WARMWELL DT2 137 A1
Warmwell Cl
Bournemouth BH9 90 B4
Poole BH17 87 F2
Warmwell Leisure Resort DT2 137 C4
Warmwell Rd DT2 137 D5
Warne Hill DT6 100 F7
Warnford Rd BH7 123 B7
WARREN BH20 113 D3
Warren Ave BH23 124 F5
Warren Cl
St Leonards BH24 54 F5
Weymouth DT4 166 F2
Warren Dr BH24 54 F5
Warren Edge Cl BH6 123 F3
Warren Edge Ct BH6 123 F3
Warren Edge Rd BH6 123 F3
Warren Hill DT2 78 C7
Warren La BH24 54 F5
Warren Rd
Bere Regis BH20 113 C4
Bournemouth BH4 121 B2
Poole BH14 120 D4
Puddletown DT2 78 B5
Warren Way BH16 116 D2
Warren Wlk BH22 61 B7
Warrior Ave BA22 26 C6
Warrior Rd BA22 26 D6
Warwick Ave BH25 95 B3
Warwick Pl 1 BH7 123 A5
Warwick Rd
Bournemouth BH7 123 A5
Poole BH14 120 C3
Washington Ave BH1 122 D6
Washpond La BH19 178 F5
Watcombe Rd BH6 123 D5
Watercombe Hts BA20 26 F2
Watercombe La BA20 26 E3
Watercombe Pk BA20 26 F3
WATERDITCH 93 B5
Waterditch Rd BH23 93 A4
Waterford Cl BH14 120 A2
Waterford Gdns BH23 126 A7
Waterford Lodge BH23 125 B6
Waterford Pl BH23 126 B7

Waterford Rd
Christchurch BH23. . . . . . 126 B7
New Milton BH25. . . . . . . 94 F2
Waterfront The★ BH4 . . . 121 F2
Watergardens BH8. . . . . . 122 A5
Watergates La DT2. . . . . 136 C3
Water Knap DT10 . . . . . . 196 F3
Water La
Bournemouth BH6. . . . . . 123 D7
Durweston DT11. . . . . . . 198 E3
Swyre DT6 . . . . 129 C8
Winfrith Newburgh DT2. . 156 F7
Winterborne Stickland
DT11. . . . . 210 B7
WATERLOO 87 B1
Waterloo Ho BH17 . . . . . . 87 B1
Waterloo La
Silton SP8 . . . . 5 B7
Stourton Caundle DT10 . . . 33 A3
Waterloo Rd
Bournemouth BH9 . . . . . . 121 F7
Corfe Mullen BH21 . . . . . . 85 C5
Poole BH17 . . . . 119 C8
Waterloo Way ❸ BH24. . . 55 C6
Watermead
❺ Christchurch BH23. . . . 124 A5
❸ Tatworth TA20. . . . . . . 202 A8
Water Meadow Rd DT10 . 139 E2
Watermill Rd BH23. . . . . . 124 A8
Waterpot Hill DT6. . . . . . 204 C2
Waters Edge BH13 . . . . . 147 D6
Watership Dr BH24. . . . . . 55 F5
Waterside BH24 . . . . 124 F4
Waterside Cl BH24 . . . . . . 47 D1
Watersmeet Ct BH23 . . . . 124 B5
Water St
Berwick St John SP7. . . . . 188 B8
Cranborne BH21 . . . . 40 B7
Mere BA12. . . . . 3 B5
Waterston Cl BH17. . . . . . 87 D1
Waterston La DT2 . . . . . . 77 D3
Water Supply Mus★
DT3 . . . . 153 D4
Water Tower Rd BH18. . . . 87 C4
Watery La
Christchurch BH23. . . . . . 125 A8
Donhead St Mary SP7 . . . 24 F8
Halstock BA22 . . . . 193 D2
Lytchett Minster & Upton
BH16. . . . . 117 B7
Radipole DT3 . . . . 152 B4
Sherborne DT9 . . . . 195 C7
Studland BH19. . . . . 164 D1
Tincleton DT2 . . . . 110 D3
West Crewkerne TA18. . . 191 D2
Watford La DT6 . . . . 153 D4
Watkin Rd ❻ BH5. . . . . . 122 F4
Watling St ❸ BA21. . . . . . 26 F7
WATTON DT6. . . . . 100 B4
Watton Cl BH8 . . . . 91 A2
Watton Cross DT6. . . . . . 100 B5
Watton Gdns DT6 . . . . . . 100 E8
Watton La DT6. . . . . 100 B5
Watton Pk DT6 . . . . 100 C5
Wattons La BH24 . . . . 63 C7
Watton View DT6 . . . . . . 100 B7
Wavell Ave BH17 . . . . 87 A1
Wavell Rd BH11. . . . . 89 B4
Wavendon Ave BH25. . . . 126 E8
Wavering La SP8. . . . . 5 C2
Waverley SP8. . . . . 5 C2
Waverley ❶ BH4. . . . . . . 121 C3
Waverley Cres BH15. . . . 119 D6
Waverley Ho ❸ BH25 . . . 95 B2
Waverley Rd
New Milton BH25. . . . . . . 95 B2
Radipole DT3 . . . . 167 C6
Wayclose La
Buckhorn Weston SP8 . . . . 9 B8
Cucklington SP8. . . . . 4 B2
WAYFORD TA18 . . . . 191 B1
Wayford Hill TA18. . . . . . 191 B1
Wayground Rd BH21 . . . . 58 E1
Wayman Rd BH21 . . . . . . 86 E6
Wayne Rd BH12. . . . . 120 B6
Wayside Rd
Bournemouth BH6. . . . . . 123 E4
St Leonards BH24 . . . . 54 A1
WAYTOWN DT6. . . . . 68 E8
Waytown Cl BH17 . . . . . . 87 D1
Weare Cl DT5. . . . . 186 F7
Weatherby Rd SP8 . . . . . . 5 E3
Weatherbury Way DT1 . . 135 A7
Weatherby Cl ❶ BH4 . . . 121 D4
Weatherbury Castle (Obelisk &
Hill Fort)★ DT11 . . . . . . 79 F5
Weavers Cl
Crewkerne TA18. . . . . . . 191 F4
Ferndown BH22 . . . . 53 A1
Webbers Cl BH20 . . . . . . 176 F8
Webbers Piece DT2 . . . . 206 C1
Webb La DT10 . . . . 196 E8
Webbs Cl BH24 . . . . 53 F6
Webb's Way BH11. . . . . . 88 F1
Webster Rd BH9 . . . . 90 A3
Wedgewood Rd DT4 . . . . 167 E2
Wedgwood Dr BH14. . . . 120 A2
Weiner Cl DT11. . . . . 199 E2
Weir End Rd DT1. . . . . . . 107 C2
Weir The DT3. . . . . 153 C3
Weir View DT2. . . . . 107 C6
Welbeck Rd BA21. . . . . . . 28 A7
Weldon Ave BH11. . . . . . . 88 E5
Welland Cl ❻ DT11. . . . . 107 E1
Welland Rd
Wimborne Minster BH21 . . 59 D4
Yeovil BA21 . . . . 27 F7
WELL BOTTOM SP5 . . . . . 39 D6

Wellbridge Cl DT1 . . . . . . 135 A7
Well Cl BH25 . . . . 94 F2
Wellesley Ave BH23 . . . . 125 C7
Wellfield Hill EX13 . . . . . 202 E2
Wellfields Dr DT6. . . . . . 100 F8
Wellington Ave BH23. . . 125 C7
Wellington Ct
❼ Bournemouth, Dean Park
BH8. . . . . 122 A5
Bournemouth, Westbourne
BH2. . . . . 121 D3
New Milton BH25. . . . . . . 95 C4
Wellingtonia Gdns SO41. . 95 F4
Wellington Rd
Bournemouth BH8. . . . . . 122 A5
Poole BH14 . . . . 120 B4
Well La
Poole BH15 . . . . 119 C4
Powerstock DT6 . . . . 70 B4
Shaftesbury SP7 . . . . 12 D3
Wellmans Cnr DT2 . . . . . 206 A7
Wellow Gdns BH15. . . . . 119 F6
Well Plot DT6. . . . . 101 D8
Wellstead Rd BH20. . . . . 142 D6
Wendover DT3 BH25. . . . . 94 F1
Wendy Cres DT2 . . . . 61 F3
Wenlock Ct ❾ BH23. . . . . 124 F8
Wentwood Gdns BH25. . . 95 D2
Wentworth BH14. . . . . . . 147 C7
Wentworth Ave
Bournemouth BH5. . . . . . 123 B4
Radipole DT3 . . . . 152 E2
Wentworth Dr
Broadstone BH18 . . . . . . 87 B5
Christchurch BH23 . . . . . 123 F6
Wentworth Grange BA22. 61 D7
Wentworth Rd BA21. . . . . 28 A7
Wentworths Yd BH21. . . . 59 E4
Wescott Way BH11. . . . . . 88 E4
Wesley Cl
❷ Bournemouth BH8 . . . 122 C5
Charmouth DT6 . . . . 97 B8
Wesley Gdns ❹❻ BH4 . 121 C3
Wesley Grange ❹❻ BH4 . 121 C3
Wesley Ho BH22 . . . . 61 F6
Wessex Ave
New Milton BH25. . . . . . . 95 A2
❹ Shillingstone DT11. . . 198 B5
Wessex Cl BH23. . . . . 125 C7
Wessex Ct BA8. . . . . 19 A4
Wessex Dr DT9 . . . . 28 D1
Wessex Est BH24. . . . . . . 55 D8
Wessex Gate Ret Pk
BH15. . . . . 119 B6
Wessex Oval BH20 . . . . . 142 C5
Wessex Rd
Dorchester DT1 . . . . 107 D2
Poole BH14 . . . . 120 A3
Ringwood BH24. . . . . 55 D8
Stalbridge DT10. . . . . 33 E8
Weymouth DT4 . . . . 167 B3
Yeovil BA21 . . . . 27 A8
Wessex Ridgeway DT3 . . . 39 C5
Wessex Stadium The
(Weymouth FC) DT4 . . . 166 F5
Wessex Trade Ctr BH12. . 120 A7
Wessex Way
Bournemouth, Springbourne
BH8. . . . . 122 C5
Bournemouth, Westbourne BH2,
BH4. . . . . 121 D3
Dorchester DT1. . . . . 107 D2
Gillingham SP8. . . . . 5 E3
Swanage BH19 . . . . 179 B4
WEST ALLINGTON DT6 . . 100 B7
West Ave BH21. . . . . 53 A8
WEST BAY DT6. . . . . 100 C2
West Bay Cres DT4. . . . . 180 C7
West Bay Rd DT6. . . . . . . 100 C2
WEST BEXINGTON DT2 . 129 E2
West Bexington Reserve★
DT2. . . . . 129 D2
West Borough BH21. . . . . 59 B5
WESTBOURNE. 121 C3
Westbourne Acad BH4 . . 121 B3
Westbourne Cl
Bournemouth BH4. . . . . . 121 C3
Yeovil BA20 . . . . 27 A5
Westbourne Gate ❶❺. . . 121 C3
Westbourne Park Rd
BH4 . . . . 121 B2
Westbourne Rd DT4. . . . . 167 D5
WEST BOURTON SP8 . . . . 4 C7
West Bourton Rd SP8 . . . . 1 D1
Westbridge Pk DT9 . . . . . 29 F4
West Brook BA21 . . . . 26 F6
Westbrook Cl BH10 . . . . . 89 D2
Westbrook Rd SP8. . . . . . 10 A8
Westbury
Bradford Abbas SP8 . . . . . 28 D2
Sherborne DT9 . . . . 30 B4
Westbury Cl
Charminster DT2 . . . . 107 D6
Eversholt DT2. . . . . 206 A7
Milborne Port DT9. . . . . . 17 D2
Westhill Cl DT4 . . . . 180 B8
West Hill Pl ❽ BH2 . . . . . 121 E3
Westhill Rd DT4 . . . . 180 C7
West Hill Rd
Bournemouth BH2. . . . . . 121 E2
Lyme Regis DT7 . . . . 96 B5
WEST HOLME BH20 . . . . 159 D8
WEST HOWE 88 E4
West Howe Cl BH11. . . . . 89 A4
West Howe Ind Est BH11 . 88 E3
WEST HURN 90 F6
WEST KNIGHTON DT2 . . 136 C3
West La
Arne BH20. . . . . 142 E1
Christchurch BH23 . . . . . 93 A8
Hazelbury Bryan DT10. . . 196 F4
Melbury Abbas SP7 . . . . . 24 B6
Mosterton DT8. . . . . 204 A8
North Wootton DT9. . . . . 31 A3
Westlake Cl DT3 . . . . 152 B4
Westland Rd BA20 . . . . . 27 B4
Westlands Ct BH23. . . . . 93 A8
Westlands Dr BH13 . . . . 147 F8
Westleaze DT1 . . . . 107 E5
Westleaze Cl DT2 . . . . . . 107 E5
WEST LULWORTH BH20. . 172 D6
Westmacott Rd DT3. . . . . 152 B1

West Mans ❸ BH4 . . . . . 121 C3
West Mead DT6 . . . . 100 B7
WEST MELBURY SP7 . . . . 24 A5
West Mill Cres BH20 . . . 142 D5
West Mill La
Castleton DT9 . . . . 30 A3
Stalbridge DT10. . . . . 20 A3
West Mills Rd DT1 . . . . . 107 F2
WEST MILTON DT6. . . . . . 69 E6
Westminster Cl BH23 . . . 124 F6
Westminster Cl ❷ SP7 . . 12 F4
Westminster Ct BH25 . . . 126 F7
Westminster Meml Hospl
SP7. . . . . 12 E2
Westminster Rd
Northport BH20. . . . . 142 C5
Poole BH13 . . . . 121 B1
Westminster Road E
BH13. . . . . 121 B1
Westminster Road Ind Est
BH20. . . . . 142 C5
Westminster St ❿ BA20. . 27 C4
WEST MOORS BH22. . . . . 53 B2
West Moors Mid Sch
BH22. . . . . 53 B1
West Moors Rd
Ferndown BH22. . . . . 61 D7
Three Legged Cross BH21. 53 A7
West Moors BH22 . . . . . . 52 F4
WEST MORDEN BH20. . . 83 B4
Westmoreland Ct SO41. . 95 F3
WESTON
Beaminster DT2. . . . . 204 F8
Fortuneswell DT5 . . . . . . 186 E3
Weston Cl BA22. . . . . 192 E8
Weston Dr BH1 . . . . 122 B3
Weston Hill SP8 . . . . 9 B6
Weston La
Closworth BA22. . . . . 193 E5
Corscombe DT2 . . . . 205 A8
Weston Rd
Colehill BH21. . . . . 59 F7
Easton/Weston DT5 . . . . 186 F4
Weymouth DT4 . . . . 167 C2
Worth Matravers BH19. . . 183 C7
Weston St
East Chinnock BA22. . . . . 192 E8
Easton/Weston DT5 . . . . 187 A2
Gillingham SP8. . . . . 9 A6
WEST ORCHARD SP7. . . . 36 D6
West Overcliff Dr BH4. . . 121 D1
Westover Hill DT6 . . . . . . 64 F2
Westover La BH24 . . . . . . 54 F6
Westover Rd
Bournemouth BH1. . . . . . 121 F3
❹ Bournemouth DT1 . . . 107 F1
Westover Retail Pk BH9 . . 90 A4
West Park Dr SP6. . . . . . . 190 F3
West Park La SP6. . . . . . . 190 F3
WEST PARLEY 61 E1
Westport Rd BH20 . . . . . 142 D3
WEST PULHAM DT9 . . . . 196 A3
West Quay Rd BH15 . . . . 119 B2
Westray Hall BH4 . . . . . . 121 C1
West Rd
Bournemouth BH5. . . . . . 123 B4
Bransgore BH23 . . . . 93 A8
Symondsbury DT6 . . . . . . 100 A7
West Lulworth BH20 . . . . 172 C6
Westridge ❻ DT9 . . . . . . 30 A5
West Row BH20 . . . . 59 B4
West Row Mews BH21. . . 59 B4
WEST SOUTHBOURNE. . . 123 D5
West St
Abbas & Templecombe
BA8. . . . . 18 C8
Abbotsbury DT3. . . . . 149 A7
Bere Regis BH20. . . . . 81 A3
Blandford Forum DT11 . . 212 C3
Bridport DT6 . . . . 100 C6
Broadwindsor DT8. . . . . . 203 E5
Chickerell DT3 . . . . 166 C6
Corfe Castle BH20. . . . . . 162 A1
Crewkerne TA18. . . . . . . 191 E4
Fontmell Magna SP7 . . . . 37 E6
Hinton St George TA17 . . 191 C7
Kington Magna SP8. . . . . 9 F2
Poole BH15 . . . . 119 B2
Radipole DT4 . . . . 167 D2
Ringwood BH24. . . . . 55 A7
Shapwick DT11 . . . . 56 B8
Wareham BH20. . . . . 142 E3
Wimborne Minster BH21. 59 B1
Winterborne Kingston DT11 81 D8
Winterborne Stickland
DT11. . . . . 210 C7
Yeovil BA20 . . . . 27 B4
WEST STAFFORD DT2 . . 136 B6
West Station Terr BH4 . . 121 D3
WEST STOUR SP8. . . . . . 10 A2
West Street Ct ❽ BH21. . 59 B5
West Undercliff Prom
Bournemouth BH2. . . . . . 121 D1
Poole BH13 . . . . 147 F7
West View SP7 . . . . 37 E7
West View Rd
Christchurch BH23. . . . . . 124 E6
Poole BH15 . . . . 119 C4
Westville BA21. . . . . 27 E5
West Walks Rd DT1 . . . . . 107 F2
West Walls BH20 . . . . . . 142 D3
West Way
Bournemouth BH9 . . . . . . 90 B2
Broadstone BH18 . . . . . . 86 F3
Easton/Weston DT5 . . . . 186 E1
Winterbourne Abbas DT2. 105 D2
West Way Cl BH9 . . . . 90 B1

West Ways BA22. . . . . . . 192 D8
Westwey Rd DT4. . . . . . . 167 D2
West Wlk DT6 . . . . 100 B2
Westwood Ave BH22 . . . . 61 D6
Westwoods & Glendene Ho
BH25. . . . . 94 D6
West Wools DT5 . . . . 186 A4
Wetherby Cl DT11. . . . . . 212 E6
Wetherby Cl
Broadstone BH18 . . . . . . 87 A2
Milborne St Andrew DT11. 79 F7
Wet La BA12. . . . . 3 D2
Weyman's Ave BH10 . . . . 89 C6
Weymans Dr BH10 . . . . . . 89 C6
WEYMOUTH DT4. . . . . . . 167 E3
Weymouth Ave DT1. . . . . 134 F8
Weymouth Bay Ave DT3 . 167 B7
Weymouth Coll DT4 . . . . 167 E5
Weymouth Coll Com Sports
Ctr DT4 . . . . 167 E6
Weymouth Com Hospl
DT4. . . . . 167 E5
Weymouth Marina★
DT4. . . . . 167 D2
Weymouth Mus★ DT4 . . 167 E1
Weymouth & Portland
National Sailing Acad★
DT4. . . . . 181 A2
Weymouth & Portland
Swimming Pool DT4 . . . 167 B2
Weymouth Rd
Dorchester DT1. . . . . 134 F7
Poole BH14 . . . . 120 C5
Weymouth Road DT2. . . . 133 B8
Weymouth Sports Club
DT3. . . . . 152 B1
Weymouth Sta DT4 . . . . . 167 D6
Weymouth Way DT4 . . . . 167 B6
Wey Valley Sch & Sports Coll
The DT3 . . . . 152 B2
Weyview Cres DT3 . . . . . 153 B4
Wharf Cl BH12 . . . . 120 E6
Wharfdale Rd
Bournemouth BH4 . . . . . . 121 D4
Poole BH12 . . . . 120 E6
Wharncliffe Cl BH23 . . . . 125 F7
Wharncliffe Gdns BH23. . 126 A7
Wharncliffe Rd
Bournemouth BH5. . . . . . 122 D4
Christchurch BH23. . . . . . 126 A7
Whatcombe Rd DT11. . . . 210 D4
Whately Rd SO41. . . . . . . 127 F5
Whatleigh Cl BH15. . . . . 119 C1
Whatley La TA20. . . . . . . 202 C8
Wheat Cl ❹ DT10 . . . . . . 197 A4
Wheatear Cl ❹ BH23 . . . 152 C5
Wheat Farland DT1 . . . . . 166 D6
Wheathill Cl ❶ DT9. . . . . 17 D2
Wheathill La DT9 . . . . 17 E2
Wheathill Way DT9. . . . . 17 D2
Wheatlands DT5 . . . . 186 E1
Wheaton Grange ❹
BH4. . . . . 121 D4
Wheaton Rd BH7. . . . . . . 123 A5
Wheatplot Park Homes ❷
BH10. . . . . 89 F4
Wheelers La BH11 . . . . . . 88 D6
West House La TA20 . . . . 202 E7
Wheelwright's Cl SP5 . . . 189 A4
Whetham Mill La DT8 . . . 203 C6
Whetland's La DT6. . . . . . 69 D1
Whimbrel Ct BH23 . . . . . 125 A6
Whincroft Cl BH22 . . . . . . 61 E7
Whincroft Dr BH22. . . . . . 61 E6
Whitby Ave BH18 . . . . 87 A2
Whitby Cl BH23. . . . . 91 D4
Whitby Cres BH18 . . . . . . 87 A2
WHITCHURCH BA8. . . . . . 19 A6
Whitchurch Ave BH18. . . 87 C3
WHITCHURCH
CANONICORUM DT6. . . 66 A4
Whitchurch La BA8 . . . . . 19 A6
Whitcliff Mill Hill DT11 . . 212 C4
WHITCOMBE DT2 . . . . . . 135 F5
Whitcombe Rd DT8 . . . . . 204 D3
Whitcross ❷ BA22 . . . . . 193 F8
Whitebeam Cl DT2 . . . . . 75 D2
Whitebeam Way BH31. . . 45 D5
White Cl
❸ Bridport DT6 . . . . 68 F1
Poole BH15 . . . . 120 A7
Whitecliff Cres BH14. . . . 120 A2
Whitecliff Gdns DT11. . . . 212 C4
Whitecliff Mill St DT11 . . 212 C4
Whitecliff Rd
Poole BH14 . . . . 119 F2
Swanage BH19 . . . . 179 B5
WHITECROSS BA12. . . . . . 1 E5
White Cross BA12. . . . . . . 1 E5
Whitecross Cl BH17 . . . . . 87 D2
Whitecross Dr DT4. . . . . 180 E8
White Farm Cl BH10. . . . 121 D8
WHITEFIELD BH20 . . . . . . 83 A2
Whitefield Dr SP8. . . . . . . 10 D3
Whitefield Rd
New Milton BH25. . . . . . . 95 A2
Poole BH14 . . . . 120 A7
Whitehall BH13 . . . . 124 B6
Whitehall Cl ❹ TA18 . . . 191 F5
White Hart Cl DT10. . . . . 196 D5
Whitehart Fields ❶ BH24. 55 E8
White Hart La SP7 . . . . . . 12 E2
Whitehayes Cl BH23. . . . 92 D2
Whitehayes Rd BH23. . . . 92 C1
Whitehead Dr DT4 . . . . . 180 D5

WHITE HILL BA12 . . . . 3 C2
White Hill DT2 . . . . 110 A8
White Hill La DT2 . . . . 79 C2
White Horse Dr
Overcombe/Preston
DT3 . . . . 153 D3
Poole BH15 . . . . 119 C5
White Horse La
Hinton St Mary DT10 . . . . 35 B5
Overcombe/Preston DT3 . 153 D4
White Horse Mews DT2 . . 72 F8
White Horses BH25 . . . . . . 126 E7
White House La DT9 . . . . 195 A4
Whitehouse Rd BH21 . . . . 59 F2
White Knights 126 F7
White La DT2 . . . . 205 D7
WHITE LACKINGTON
DT2 . . . . 208 C1
White Lane Cl DT10 . . . . . . 35 B1
Whiteleg Way BH10 . . . . . . 89 F5
White Lovington BH20 . . . . 81 B1
Whitemarsh BA12 . . . . 3 B4
White Mead BA21 . . . . 26 E6
White Mill★ DT11 . . . . 56 F6
White Mill Bridge★ BH21 . 56 F5
White Pit DT11 . . . . 198 B5
White Pit La SP7 . . . . 24 A4
Whitepost Gate DT9 . . . . . . 16 E3
White Rd BA12 . . . . 3 B6
Whites Cl DT2 . . . . 76 E8
Whitesheets Prim Sch
BA12 . . . . 2 A4
Whites Mdw 7 BA21 . . . . 204 A8
White Way
Buckland Newton DT2 . . 208 B6
Litton Cheney DT2 . . . . . 103 C3
Whiteway Hill BH21 . . . . 201 B4
White Way La DT10 . . . . . . 21 E1
Whiteways BH21 . . . . 59 E6
Whitfield Pk BH24 . . . . 54 D5
Whitfield Rd DT11 . . . . . . 107 D1
Whithay La DT6 . . . . 68 B7
Whittingham Ct 8 BH5 . . 123 B5
Whitley Way BH25 . . . . 95 B5
WHITMORE BH21 . . . . 44 B6
Whitmore La BH21 . . . . 44 B7
Whitsbury Cl BH8 . . . . 90 D2
Whittle Rd BH21 . . . . 60 F7
Whittles Way BH15 . . . . . . 119 B2
Whynot Way DT3 . . . . 166 D4
WICK 124 B4
Wick 1 Ind Est BH25 . . . . . . 94 E2
Wick Cl BH25 . . . . 94 E2
Wick Dr BH25 . . . . 94 E2
Wicket Rd BH10 . . . . 89 C5
Wicketsbeer Rd BA22 . . . 193 C6
Wick Farm BH6 . . . . 124 C4
Wickfield Ave BH23 . . . . . 124 B6
Wickfield Cl BH23 . . . . . . 124 B6
Wickford Ho BH23 . . . . . . 124 A6
Wickham Ct BH21 . . . . 61 E6
Wickham Dr BH21 . . . . 85 F4
Wickham Rd BH7 . . . . 123 A5
Wick Hill DT9 . . . . 17 B6
Wick La
Bournemouth BH6 . . . . . . 124 C4
Christchurch BH23 . . . . . 124 A5
Wicklea Rd BH6 . . . . 124 B4
Wickmeads Rd BH6 . . . . . 124 A5
Wick Point Mews BH23 . . 124 B5
Wick Rd DT9 . . . . 17 C4
Widdicombe Ave BH14 . . 120 E2
Wide St DT5 . . . . 186 F5
Widget Cl BH21 . . . . 89 B2
Widworthy Dr BH18 . . . . . . 86 F5
WIGBETH BH21 . . . . 201 F2
Wightman's Orch DT2 . . . 208 B2
Wight Wlk DT2 . . . . 61 E2
Wilderness The DT9 . . . . . . 30 C6
Wilderton Rd BH13 . . . . . . 120 F3
Wilderton Road W BH13 . 121 A4
Wildfell Cl BH23 . . . . 92 A1
Wildown Gdns BH6 . . . . . 124 A3
Wildown Rd BH6 . . . . 124 A3
Wilfred Rd BH5 . . . . 122 F4
Wilkins Gdns BH8 . . . . 122 C6
Wilkinson Dr BH8 . . . . 91 B2
Wilkins Way BH15 . . . . 119 B2
Willett Rd BH21 . . . . 59 A2
William Barnes Prim Sch
DT10 . . . . 197 D8
William Cl BH23 . . . . 94 A2
William Ct 11 BH21 . . . . . 126 B7
William Rd BH7 . . . . 122 F7
Williams Ave DT1 . . . . 107 F2
William's Ind Pk BH25 . . . . 94 E2
William St DT4 . . . . 167 E4
Williams Way DT11 . . . . . 212 E6
Williford La DT2 . . . . 195 C2
Willis's La TA18 . . . . 192 B4
Willis Way BH15 . . . . 119 A4
Willoughby Cl 3 DT2 . . . . 78 B1
Willow Cl
Bournemouth BH4 . . . . . 121 B5
St Leonards BH24 . . . . 53 F4
Upton BH16 . . . . 117 F5
Willow Cres
Holton Heath DT2 . . . . . 116 B3
Overcombe/Preston DT3 . 153 B2
Willow Ct BH7 . . . . 123 C6
Willowdene Cl BH23 . . . . . 95 C3
Willow Dr
Christchurch BH6 . . . . . . 124 A5

Willow Dr continued
Ringwood BH24 . . . . 55 C5
Wimborne Minster BH21 . 60 C6
Willow Farm 11 DT9 . . . . 194 C5
Willow Gr 6 DT8 . . . . 204 D4
Willow La 11 BH1 . . . . 122 D4
Willow Mead BH6 . . . . 90 D4
Willow Pk BH14 . . . . 120 A3
Willow Pl BH23 . . . . 124 C6
Willow Rd
Dorchester DT2 . . . . 139 C2
Yeovil BA21 . . . . 27 B6
Willows The BH25 . . . . . . 127 B8
Willow Tree Rise BH11 . . . 89 E3
Willow View
Charminster DT2 . . . . 75 D3
Hamworthy BH16 . . . . . . 118 C4
Willow Way
Bridport DT6 . . . . 100 F7
Christchurch BH23 . . . . . 124 A5
Crewkerne TA18 . . . . . . 191 F5
Ferndown BH22 . . . . 61 D7
Motcombe SP7 . . . . 12 B8
Northport BH20 . . . . 142 D5
Willow Wlk BH25 . . . . 127 B7
Wills Cl BH21 . . . . 85 F4
Wills La DT2 . . . . 207 D4
Wills Rd
Poole BH12 . . . . 120 F4
Swanage BH19 . . . . 178 F2
Wilmslow Rd DT3 . . . . . . 166 D6
Wilmur Cres BH15 . . . . . . 119 E6
Wilson Pk DT11 . . . . 212 E4
Wilson Rd
Bournemouth BH1 . . . . . 122 E6
Dorchester DT1 . . . . 108 C1
Poole BH1 . . . . 122 C4
Wilton Cl BH23 . . . . 91 D1
Wilton Dr DT4 . . . . 167 B1
Wilton Gdns BH25 . . . . 94 F3
Wilton Pl 10 BH4 . . . . 121 C2
Wilton Rd
Bournemouth BH7 . . . . . 122 F5
Yeovil BA21 . . . . 28 A8
Wiltshire Ave DT4 . . . . . . 167 A3
Wiltshire Cl SP8 . . . . 5 E3
Wiltshire Gdns BH23 . . . . . 92 F8
Wiltshire Rd BH23 . . . . 92 F8
Wilverley Ave BH8 . . . . 90 F2
Wilverley Rd BH23 . . . . . . 125 A2
Wilverly Gdns DT11 . . . . . 212 E4
Wimborne County Fst Sch
BH21 . . . . 59 B5
Wimborne Ho BH22 . . . . . . 61 F7
WIMBORNE MINSTER . . . 59 A6
Wimborne Minster★ 59 B4
Wimborne Minster Model
Town & Gdns★ BH21 . . . 59 B4
Wimborne Rd
Blandford Forum DT11 . 212 E3
Bournemouth, Dean Park
BH9 . . . . 121 F5
Bournemouth, Kinson BH11 . 89 C6
Bournemouth, Moordown
BH9 . . . . 121 F8
East End BH21 . . . . 58 F1
Langton Long Blandford
DT11 . . . . 199 D1
Lytchett Matravers BH16 . . 84 E4
Poole BH21 . . . . 85 F8
Poole, Longfleet BH15 . . 119 D4
Tarrant Rushton DT11 . . . 48 A6
Wimborne Minster BH21 . 59 E6
Wimborne Road E
Ferndown BH22 . . . . 61 B6
Trickett's Cross BH22 . . . 61 E7
Wimborne Road W
Ferndown BH21 . . . . 60 E6
Wimborne Minster BH21 . 60 B4
WIMBORNE ST GILES
BH21 . . . . 201 D7
Wimborne St Giles CE Fst
Sch BH21 . . . . 201 E7
Wimborough La BA22 . . . 192 F7
Wincanton Fold DT2 . . . . 156 F6
Winchelsea Special Sch
BH12 . . . . 88 D1
Winchester Cl DT4 . . . . . . 166 F3
Winchester Gdns BA21 . . . 27 E7
Winchester Pl 5 BH15 . . . 119 C2
Winchester Rd BH25 . . . . . 95 B4
Wincombe Bsns Pk SP7 . . 13 A5
Wincombe Cl BH22 . . . . . . 61 D2
Wincombe Dr BH22 . . . . . . 61 D4
Wincombe La SP7 . . . . 12 F3
Wincombe Pk★ SP7 . . . . . 13 C5
Windermere BA20 . . . . 27 B2
Windermere Cres DT3 . . . 167 B6
Windermere Rd BH3 . . . . 122 A7
Windgreen Est BH21 . . . . . 86 E7
Windham Mews DT1 . . . . 122 D5
Windham Rd BH1 . . . . 122 D5
Windmill Cl
Shaftesbury SP7 . . . . 12 F4
St Leonards BH24 . . . . 54 F4
Windmill La BH24 . . . . 54 F4
Windmill Rd DT11 . . . . . . 212 D3
Windmill Rise 6 TA18 . . . 191 F5
Windslade St 13 DT11 . . . 107 D1
Windsor Cl
Bovington Camp DT2 . . . 139 E6
Hordle SO41 . . . . 95 E4
Mosterton DT8 . . . . 204 A7
St Leonards BH24 . . . . 54 B5

Windsor Ct
3 Christchurch BH23 . . 126 A7
Poole BH21 . . . . 126 B3
Windsor La SP8 . . . . 5 D1
Windsor Mans 1 BH6 . . . 123 E3
Windsor Rd
Bournemouth BH5 . . . . . 122 E4
Christchurch BH23 . . . . . 122 E3
Dorchester DT1 . . . . 107 E1
Poole BH12 . . . . 120 B3
Radipole DT3 . . . . 152 B4
Windsor Way SP6 . . . . 42 C6
Windwhistle Cnr SP7 . . . . 13 E4
Wind Whistle La 11 DT11 . 81 E8
Windy Cnr DT11 . . . . 200 C1
Wine St 13 BA20 . . . . 27 D4
Winfrith Cres BH12 . . . . . 120 E8
Winfrith Dro
West Lulworth BH20 . . . 172 E8
Winfrith Newburgh DT2 . 156 F6
WINFRITH HEATH
DT2 . . . . 138 E2
WINFRITH NEWBURGH
DT2 . . . . 156 F6
Winfrith Tech Ctr DT2 . . . 139 B2
Wingate BA21 . . . . 27 E7
Wingfield Ave
Christchurch BH23 . . . . . . 93 D1
Poole BH15 . . . . 119 D6
Wingfield Cl BH1 . . . . 122 C3
Wingreen Cl 3 DT3 . . . . . 153 B2
Win Green View SP7 . . . . . 13 A3
Winifred Rd BH15 . . . . 119 E5
WINKTON 92 C5
Winkton Cl BH23 . . . . 92 C5
Winkton Gn BH23 . . . . 92 C5
Winkton Ho BH23 . . . . 92 C4
Winnards Cl BH22 . . . . 61 C2
Winniford Cl DT6 . . . . 99 A7
Winsford Cl BH23 . . . . 93 D1
Winsley Ave BH6 . . . . 123 C4
Winslow Rd DT3 . . . . 153 D3
Winspit Cl BH15 . . . . 118 E3
Winspit Rd BH20 . . . . 183 C7
Winstone Ave BH12 . . . . . 121 A6
Winston Cl
3 Christchurch BH23 . . 124 A7
4 Old Milton BH25 . . . . . 95 A1
Winston Dr BA21 . . . . 27 B8
Winston Gdns BH12 . . . . . 121 A6
Winston Par 6 BH12 . . . . . 95 A1
Winston Pk BH12 . . . . 121 A6
Winston Rd BH9 . . . . 90 A3
Winston Way BH24 . . . . 55 D8
WINTERBORNE CAME
DT2 . . . . 135 D5
WINTERBORNE CLENSTON
DT11 . . . . 210 D6
WINTERBORNE
HERRINGTON DT2 . . . . . 134 F5
WINTERBORNE HOUGHTON
DT11 . . . . 210 B7
WINTERBORNE KINGSTON
DT11 . . . . 81 D8
WINTERBORNE MONKTON
DT2 . . . . 134 C4
WINTERBORNE MUSTON
DT11 . . . . 82 A7
WINTERBORNE STICKLAND
DT11 . . . . 210 C7
WINTERBORNE TOMSON
DT11 . . . . 82 D7
WINTERBORNE
WHITECHURCH DT11 . . 210 D3
WINTERBORNE ZELSTON
DT11 . . . . 82 F7
WINTERBOURNE ABBAS
DT2 . . . . 105 C2
Winterbourne CE Fst Sch
BH15 . . . . 118 F3
Winterbourne Copse
DT4 . . . . 180 D8
Winterbourne Hospl
(Private) The DT1 . . . . . 134 F7
Winterbourne Rd BH15 . . 119 D5
WINTERBOURNE
STEEPLETON DT2 . . . . . 132 F8
Winterhayes Cl BH17 . . . . . 87 E3
Winter La DT9 . . . . 15 F6
Winters Cl 6 DT3 . . . . 150 A8
Winter's La DT3 . . . . 150 D8
WINTON 121 F7
Winton Arts & Media Coll
BH10 . . . . 89 E2
Winton Prim Sch BH9 . . . . 89 E2
Winton Way
Bournemouth BH10 . . . . . 89 E1
New Milton BH25 . . . . 95 B5
WINYARD'S GAP DT8 . . . 192 E1
Winyards View TA18 . . . . 191 F3
Wisbech Way SO41 . . . . . . 95 F5
Wishart Gdns BH9 . . . . 90 B5
Wishay St 2 DT1 . . . . 107 D1
Wistaria Ho 1 BH6 . . . . . . 89 F4
Wisteria Cl BA22 . . . . 26 C5
Wisteria Dr BH31 . . . . 45 E4
Witcham La DT2 . . . . 205 F5
WITCHAMPTON BH21 . . . 201 C5
Witchampton CE Fst Sch
BH21 . . . . 200 F1
Witchampton La BH21 . . . 50 B8
Witchampton Rd BH18 . . . 86 F2
Witch Cl SP8 . . . . 10 D3
Witch La SP8 . . . . 10 D3
Withermoor Rd BH9 . . . . . 121 E8
Withies Croft DT5 . . . . 187 C5

Withingham Rd BH13 . . . 120 F3
Withybed La BA9 . . . . 4 C3
Witley BH14 . . . . 147 C7
Witney Rd BH17 . . . . 87 D1
Wittey's La TA20 . . . . 202 E6
Wivenhoe Ho BH22 . . . . . . 61 F6
Woburn Rd BA21 . . . . 28 A7
Woking Rd BH14 . . . . 120 C4
Wolfe Cl BH23 . . . . 124 D7
Wolfeton House★ DT2 . . 107 D5
Wollaston Rd
Bournemouth BH6 . . . . . 123 F3
Dorchester DT1 . . . . 108 A1
Wollaton Cres BH22 . . . . . 61 C3
Wollaton Rd BH22 . . . . 61 C3
Wolstonecraft Rd 1
BH5 . . . . 122 F3
Wolseley Rd BH12 . . . . . . 120 D6
Wolterton Rd BH12 . . . . . 121 A5
Wolverley Ct 12 BH4 . . . . 121 C3
WOLVERTON BA12 . . . . 2 B4
Wolverton Rd BH7 . . . . . . 122 F5
Wonderholm Par BH11 . . . 89 B2
WONSTON DT10 . . . . 19 F6
Woodacre Gdns BH22 . . . . 61 E4
Woodbridge SP7 . . . . 23 B1
Woodbury BH1 . . . . 122 A2
Woodbury Ave BH8 . . . . . . 90 F2
Woodbury Dro DT2 . . . . . . 91 E3
Woodbury Dro DT2 . . . . . 137 C6
Woodbury Hill (Hill Fort)★
BH20 . . . . 81 C2
Wood Cl La TA17 . . . . 191 A8
Woodcocks Cres BH7 . . . 123 A8
Woodcote
Upton BH16 . . . . 117 D6
2 Yeovil BA20 . . . . 26 F2
Woodcote Dr BH16 . . . . . 117 D6
WOODCUTTS SP5 . . . . . . 188 D4
Woodend Rd BH9 . . . . 121 E8
Woodfield Gdns BH23 . . . . 93 D1
Woodfield Rd BH11 . . . . . . 89 A5
Woodford Cl BH24 . . . . 55 D7
Woodford Rd BH1 . . . . 122 C4
Woodgreen Dr BH11 . . . . . 88 D4
Woodhayes BA8 . . . . 19 A3
Wood Ho 6 BH13 . . . . 121 B3
Woodhouse Cross SP8 . . . 4 F3
Woodhouse La EX13 . . . . 202 A1
Woodhouse Rd EX13 . . . . 202 A1
Woodhouse Sch EX13 . . . 202 A1
Wood La
Bournemouth BH11 . . . . . 88 E6
Broadwindsor DT8 . . . . . 203 B7
Crewkerne TA18 . . . . . . 192 D2
Hinton St Mary DT10 . . . . 35 A4
Stalbridge DT10 . . . . 33 C7
Symondsbury DT6 . . . . . . 67 D5
Woodlake Cl BH17 . . . . 87 D1
Woodland Ave BH25 . . . . 123 A4
Woodland Cl BH21 . . . . 45 A7
Woodland Ct BH17 . . . . . . 122 F5
Woodland Gr 12 BA20 . . . 27 D4
Woodland Mans BH14 . . . 120 B5
WOODLANDS BH21 . . . . . . 44 A6
Woodlands
Broadmayne DT2 . . . . . . 136 B1
Hazelbury Bryan DT10 . . 196 F2
1 Lymington SO41 . . . . . 95 F3
20 Poole BH15 . . . . 120 A3
Woodlands Ave BH23 . . . 123 A4
Woodlands Cl BH23 . . . . . . 93 A8
WOODLANDS COMMON
BH21 . . . . 44 C6
Woodlands Cres
Dorchester DT1 . . . . 107 C2
Woodlands Dr BH15 . . . . . 118 F3
Woodlands Ct BH21 . . . . . 121 B5
Woodlands Dr BH20 . . . . . 143 B8
Woodlands Manor★ BA12 . . 20 L4
Woodlands Rd
Barton on Sea BH25 . . . . 126 F7
Mere BA12 . . . . 3 B2
Woodlands Rd Ind Est
BA12 . . . . 3 B4
Woodlands Way
New Milton BH25 . . . . 95 B5
St Leonards BH24 . . . . 54 A1
Woodland Terr 9 BA20 . . . 27 C4
Woodland Way BH23 . . . . 125 D8
Woodland Wlk
Ferndown BH22 . . . . 61 F7
Wood Lawn Cl
Barton on Sea BH25 . . . . 126 F8
New Milton BH25 . . . . 94 F1
Woodleaze Cl BH18 . . . . . . 87 B6
Woodlinken Cl BH31 . . . . . 45 D4
Woodlinken Dr BH31 . . . . . 45 D4
Woodlinken Way BH31 . . . 45 E4
Woodmead Rd DT7 . . . . . . 96 B5
Woodmill Cl DT10 . . . . 19 D1
Woodpecker Cl BH31 . . . . . 45 B5
Woodpecker Dr BH17 . . . 118 F5
Woodpecker Mdw SP8 . . . 11 A8
Woodpeckers The DT3 . . 152 D4
Woodrising BH13 . . . . 147 B3
Woodrisings The 6
BH2 . . . . 121 D4
Woodroffe Mdw DT7 . . . . . 96 A6
Woodroffe Sch The DT7 . . 96 A6
WOODROW DT10 . . . . 196 F4
Wood Row BH9 . . . . 90 E4
Woodruff Cl BH23 . . . . . . 125 C8

Woodsage Dr SP8 . . . . 5 D2
Woods Edge BH18 . . . . 87 A2
WOODSFORD DT2 . . . . . . 110 D2
Woodsford Castle★ DT2 . 110 B1
Woodsford La DT2 . . . . . . 138 A7
Woodsford Rd DT2 . . . . . . 137 D7
Woodside Cl BH22 . . . . 61 E6
Woodside La BH25 . . . . 95 C5
Woodside Rd
Bournemouth BH5 . . . . . 123 B4
Ferndown BH22 . . . . 52 F4
Ferndown BH22 . . . . 61 E6
Poole BH14 . . . . 120 C3
Woodstock Cl BH14 . . . . . 120 B2
Woodstock La BH24 . . . . . . 55 C7
Woodstock Rd
Burton BH23 . . . . 92 C2
Poole BH14 . . . . 120 A2
Yeovil BA21 . . . . 27 E7
Woods View Rd BH9 . . . . 121 D8
Woodswater La 5 DT6 . . 204 D4
Woodvale Gdns BH25 . . . . 95 C4
Wood View BH21 . . . . 60 A8
WOODVILLE SP8 . . . . 21 F8
Woodward Pl DT4 . . . . . . 167 E6
WOODYATES SP5 . . . . . . 189 D6
WOOL BH20 . . . . 140 B2
Wooland Gdns DT4 . . . . . 180 C8
Woolands La SP7 . . . . 12 D4
WOOLBRIDGE HEATH
BH20 . . . . 140 A6
Wool CE Fst Sch BH20 . . 140 B1
Woolcombe Rd DT5 . . . . . 186 E3
Woolcott La SP8 . . . . 1 D1
WOOLFORD'S WATER
DT2 . . . . 208 A8
WOOLGARSTON BH20 . . 177 F8
WOOLLAND DT11 . . . . . . 197 C1
Woolmer La BH24 . . . . 54 A2
WOOLMINSTONE TA18 . . 191 B3
Wool Rd BH12 . . . . 120 B8
WOOLSBRIDGE BH21 . . . . 53 D7
Woolsbridge Ind Est
BH21 . . . . 53 D6
Woolsbridge Rd BH24 . . . . 54 A4
Woolsbridge Small Bsns Ctr
BH21 . . . . 53 D5
Woolslope Cl BH22 . . . . . . 53 A1
Woolslope Gdns BH22 . . . 53 B1
Woolslope Rd BH22 . . . . . 53 A1
Wool Sta BH20 . . . . 140 B2
Woolven Cl BH14 . . . . 120 A5
Wooperton St 4 DT4 . . . . 167 D3
WOOTH DT6 . . . . 68 E3
WOOTTON 95 B8
Wootton Cross DT6 . . . . . . 65 C4
WOOTTON FITZPAINE
DT6 . . . . 65 B4
Wootton Gdns BH1 . . . . . 122 A3
Wootton Gr DT9 . . . . 30 A8
Wootton La DT6 . . . . 65 A8
Wootton Mount BH1 . . . . 122 A3
Wootton Rd BH25 . . . . 95 D7
Wootton Rough BH25 . . . . 95 B8
Worbarrow Gdns BH12 . . 120 C8
Wordsworth Ave BH8 . . . . 90 E1
WORGRET BH20 . . . . 142 B2
Worgret Hill BH20 . . . . . . 141 F2
Worgret Rd
Poole BH15 . . . . 119 D7
Wareham BH20 . . . . 142 C3
Worley Way BH22 . . . . 61 F3
Worrell Dr BH12 . . . . 120 C8
Worthington Cres BH14 . . 120 A3
WORTH MATRAVERS
BH19 . . . . 183 D7
Worthy Rd BH25 . . . . 95 A3
Wortley Rd BH23 . . . . 126 A7
Wrackle Cl DT2 . . . . 106 E8
Wraxall Cl BH17 . . . . 87 D1
Wraxall La
Chilfrome DT2 . . . . 206 B2
Wraxall DT2 . . . . 206 A3
Wraxhill Rd BA20 . . . . 27 A1
Wren Cl
Christchurch BH23 . . . . . 125 B5
New Milton BH25 . . . . 94 F2
Wren Ct BH22 . . . . 55 E6
Wren Cres BH12 . . . . 121 B5
Wren Gdns SP6 . . . . 42 D5
Wren Pl SP8 . . . . 11 B8
Wriggle River La DT2 . . . 194 E1
Writh Rd DT9 . . . . 31 C1
Wroxham Rd BH12 . . . . . . 120 F5
Wyatts Cl BH21 . . . . 85 F6
Wyatts La BH21 . . . . 86 C6
Wyatt's La BH20 . . . . 142 F3
WYCH DT6 . . . . 100 E2
Wych Hill DT6 . . . . 100 D3
Wych Ridge DT6 . . . . 100 D3
Wychside Cl DT6 . . . . 100 D3
Wychwood 88 BH4 . . . . . 121 C3
Wychwood Cl BH2 . . . . . . 121 F4
Wychwood Dr BH2 . . . . . . 121 F4
Wychwood Grange 1
BH2 . . . . 121 F4
Wycliffe Rd BH9 . . . . 121 F8
Wydford Cl DT9 . . . . 29 F5
Wyelands Ave BH21 . . . . . . 60 D5
WYKE SP8 . . . . 5 D2
Wykeham Cl BH17 . . . . . . 119 E8
Wyke Oliver Rd DT3 . . . . . 153 A1
Wyke Prim Sch SP8 . . . . . . 5 D1
Wyke Rd
Gillingham SP8 . . . . 5 E2
Weymouth DT4 . . . . 167 B1
WYKE REGIS DT4 . . . . . . 180 D7

Wyke Regis CE Jun Sch
DT4 . . . . 180 C7
Wyke Regis Com Ctr
DT4 . . . . 180 C6
Wyke Regis Com & Sports
Ctr DT4 . . . . 180 C6
Wyke Regis Inf Sch DT4 . 180 B7
Wyke Sq **7** DT4 . . . . 180 C8
Wynchard Bank **1** DT11. 198 E3
Wyncombe Rd BH5 . . . . . 123 B5
Wyndham Cl BH23 . . . . . . 94 B2
Wyndham Rd
Poole BH14 . . . . 120 B3
Walkford BH23 . . . . 94 B2
Wyndham St **5** BA20. . . . . 27 E5
Wyndham View BA21. . . . . 27 F5
WYNFORD EAGLE DT2. . . . . 72 D4
Wynford Rd
Bournemouth BH9 . . . . . . 90 B4
Poole BH14 . . . . 120 C4
Wynne Cl BH18 . . . . 86 F4
Wynnes Cl **4** DT9. . . . . . . 30 A5
Wynnes Rise DT9 . . . . 30 A5
Wynter Cl BH7. . . . . 122 F7
Wytch Pas BH20 . . . . 162 D8
Wyvern Cl
East Coker BA20 . . . . 26 E1
Poole BH12 . . . . 120 D7
Wyvern Ct **24** TA18. . . . . 191 F4
Wyvern Rd **1** DT1 . . . . . 107 E2

Wyvern Specl Sch DT3 . . 152 C2
Wyvern Way DT11. . . . . . . 212 E6

Y

Yalbury La DT2 . . . . 137 C6
Yalbury Wood SP8 . . . . 5 E3
Yarde Farm **5** DT11. . . . . 199 D3
Yard La DT6 . . . . 203 D2
Yardworthy **4** DT1. . . . . . 107 B1
Yarlands DT4 . . . . 166 E3
Yarmouth Cl BH12 . . . . . 121 A5
Yarmouth Rd BH12. . . . . 120 F6
Yarnbarton DT8. . . . . 203 E5
Yarn Barton
10 Beaminster DT8. . . . . 204 D4
5 Yeovil BA20. . . . . 27 C4
Yarn Mill Cl DT6 . . . . 100 C8
Yarrells Cl **1** BH16. . . . . . 117 E6
Yarrells Dr BH16. . . . . . . 117 D7
Yarrells La BH16 . . . . 117 E6
Yarrells Prep Sch BH16. . 117 D7
Yarrow Cl
Christchurch BH23. . . . . . 125 B8
Poole BH12 . . . . 88 B1
Yarrow Ct **1** SP8 . . . . 5 D2
Yarrow Rd BH12 . . . . 120 A8
Yearlings' Dro BH20 . . . . 113 A7
Yeates Rd DT5. . . . . 186 F6

Yeatman Hospl DT9 . . . . . . 30 B6
Yeatmans Cl SP7. . . . . 12 D3
Yeatmans La SP7 . . . . 12 D3
Yeatmans Old Mill **10**
BH15 . . . . 119 B1
Yeatminster Rd BH17 . . . . 87 F2
Yellowham Hill DT2. . . . . 109 C8
Yellow La DT6 . . . . 69 C2
Yelverton Rd **10** BH1 . . . 121 F3
YENSTON BA8. . . . . 18 E7
Yenston Hill BA8. . . . . 18 E8
Yeolands Rd **5** DT5. . . . . 186 E3
Yeo L Pk BA20 . . . . 27 E4
Yeomans Ind Pk BH8. . . . . 90 F2
Yeomans Lodge **6** BH25 . 95 B2
Yeomans Rd BH8 . . . . 90 E3
Yeomans Way BH8. . . . . . . 90 E2
Yeo Valley BA22 . . . . 27 F1
YEOVIL BA20. . . . . 27 A4
Yeovil Airfield BA20. . . . . 27 A4
Yeovil Coll
Sherborne DT9 . . . . 30 C7
Yeovil BA21 . . . . 27 C6
Yeovil BA21 . . . . 28 A6
Yeovil BA22 . . . . 26 D6
Yeovil Coll IT Ctr BA20 . . 27 E4
Yeovil District Hospl
BA21. . . . . 27 C6
Yeovil Hundred Stone★
BA21. . . . . 27 D8

Yeovil Junction Sta BA22. 28 A1
Yeovil Pen Mill Sta BA21 . 28 A5
Yeovil Railway Ctr★ BA22 28 A1
Yeovil Rd
Crewkerne TA18. . . . . 192 A5
Halstock BA22. . . . . 193 D3
Sherborne DT9 . . . . 30 A6
Yeovil BA20, B22. . . . . 27 B1
Yeovil Small Bsns Ctr
BA22 . . . . 26 D6
Yeovil Sports Club BA21. . 27 A7
Yerville Gdns SO41. . . . . . 95 F3
YETMINSTER DT9. . . . . . . 194 D5
Yetminster Sta DT9 . . . . 194 C5
Yew La BH25 . . . . 95 C4
Yews The BA12 . . . . 3 A6
Yewstock Specl Sch DT10 35 B2
Yew Tree Cl
Weymouth DT3 . . . . 168 B8
Wimborne Minster BH21. . 59 D5
Yeovil BA20 . . . . 27 A2
Yew Tree Ct **5** BH25. . . . 95 B1
Yew Tree Gdns BH24. . . . . 55 C6
Yew Tree La DT2. . . . . . . 106 F6
YONDOVER DT6 . . . . 101 D8
York Ave BH25. . . . . 95 B3
York Cl
Broadstone BH18 . . . . 87 A2
Charminster DT2 . . . . 107 E6
Christchurch BH23. . . . . . 123 F7

York Pl
Bournemouth BH7. . . . . . 123 A5
7 New Milton BH25. . . . . 95 B3
Yeovil BA20 . . . . 27 C5
York Rd
Bournemouth BH1. . . . . . 122 B4
Broadstone BH18 . . . . 87 A2
Dorchester DT1. . . . . 108 B1
York Terr **7** DT1. . . . . . 135 B8
Youngs Endowed Prim Sch
DT9. . . . . 14 E2
Youngs Rd BH11 . . . . 89 A5

Z

Zamek Cl BH11 . . . . 89 A5
ZEALS BA12. . . . . 2 A4
Zeals Green Dr BA12. . . . . . 2 A4
Zeals Rise BA12. . . . . .1 F4
Zetland Ct BH4 . . . . 121 B1
Zig Zag Hill SP7 . . . . 24 E6
Zinnia Cl BH10. . . . . 89 E2
Zoar La DT10 . . . . 197 B4